THE OFFICIAL PRICE GUIDE
BOTTLES

ELEVENTH EDITION

THE OFFICIAL®
PRICE GUIDE
BOTTLES

ELEVENTH EDITION

JIM MEGURA

HOUSE OF COLLECTIBLES • NEW YORK

Important Notice. All of the information, including valuations, in this book has been compiled from the most reliable sources, and every effort has been made to eliminate errors and questionable data. Nevertheless, the possibility of error, in a work of such immense scope, always exists. The publisher will not be held responsible for losses which may occur in the purchase, sale, or other transaction of items because of information contained herein. Readers who feel they have discovered errors are invited to *write* and inform us, so they may be corrected in subsequent editions. Those seeking further information on the topics covered in this book are advised to refer to the complete line of *Official Price Guides* published by the House of Collectibles.

Published by: House of Collectibles
201 East 50th Street
New York, New York 10022

Distributed by Ballantine Books, a division of Random House, Inc., New York, and simultaneously in Canada by Random House of Canada Limited, Toronto.

Text design by Holly Johnson

Manufactured in the United States of America

ISBN: 0-876-37843-2

Eleventh Edition: December 1991

10 9 8 7 6 5 4

To my late mother, Julia Bukoch Megura,
who instilled in me my interest in antiques and glass;
and to Nathanial James Megura,
the coming generation of treasure hunters.

CONTENTS

ACKNOWLEDGMENTS

My sincere thanks are given to those who provided help, expertise, and support in the writing of this book, including, but not limited to (in alphabetical order): Phil Bernard, Debbie Delli Bovi, Neil Grossman, Jim Hagenbach and Glass Works Auctions, Harmer Rooke Galleries, Norman Heckler, Ken Previtali, Gail Quick and Time in a Bottle, David Smith, Skinners, Inc., and Art and Judy Turner of Homestead Collectibles. And special thanks to Pete and Tony for the fun and friendship shared through 20-plus years of bottle digging.

INTRODUCTION

ABOUT THIS BOOK

The intention in writing this book was to develop a good, basic reference guide which could be of value to beginning and advanced collectors, as well as those in the antiques field desirous of a better understanding of early bottles and glass. As this is meant to be merely a general reference source, throughout the book the reader will be referred to recommended reference books and articles which will delve much more deeply into specific areas.

Besides being a reference guide, however, this book is also mainly a price guide to bottles, and determining the value of old and new bottles is a difficult undertaking. The various pricing sources available, such as auction results, dealers' price lists, bottle show prices, and nationally advertised prices, often point to major valuation discrepancies. For example, those of you who attend bottle shows would probably agree that it is not unusual to find both very overpriced, as well as bargain-priced, bottles for sale. Also, factors such as economic conditions, the type of bottles that are currently "hot," and supply and demand all play a major role in the daily fluctuations in price. With this in mind, the reader should know that the majority of valuations listed herein are basically auction results, where available, and dealers' sales lists. These values may or may not be consistent with the fair market value of a bottle today or in the future.

MARKET REVIEW

Flasks continue to be the main area of interest among bottle collectors, as is evidenced by the record prices that continue to be established. Ink bottles continue to do well also, though the more common varieties appear to be stationary. Tea kettles appear to be dropping in price, but unusually colored, blown three-mold examples are doing well. In October 1989, a record $26,400 was set for an ink bottle, a gallon sapphire blue Harrison's Columbian. However, two other gallon Harrison's Columbian inks have sold in the 12-month period after the record was set for $12,100 and $17,600 respectively, which points to the fact that the market may be adjusting to the true value.

Blown three-mold bottles and blown three-mold glass in general are two of the areas which have seen dramatic increases in price for the rarer colored examples, whereas the common colorless examples appear to be stationary. Colored pontiled medicine bottles, for instance, are showing mixed results, generally holding or dropping slightly, whereas pontiled colorless medicines have fallen off dramatically in price since the massive Greer collection was sold several years ago.

Target balls and fire extinguisher bottles are on the rapid increase in value, and bitters bottles also appear to be very hot today, with barrel bitters one of the most popular areas in all bottle collecting. Poison bottles showed an upsurge in interest in recent years, though recent sales results are not as encouraging. Pitkins are dropping in price, whereas barber bottles and sodas seem to be holding their own. Dairy bottles are doing extremely well, with war slogan and baby-faced bottles leading the way.

As I write this, the American economy is not doing well, and the results of this have recently surfaced at major bottle auctions and shows. The economic impact is generally being felt in the antiques field, and the average person is less likely to be as extravagant in his or her bottle buying when concerns over job security and bill payments override the need to purchase another bottle.

What does the future hold for bottle collectors? If one realizes that economic conditions and the whims of collectors continually put certain classes of bottles in and out of vogue, coupled with the theory of supply and demand whereby a large number of bottles of a specific type can hit the market all at once, it is easy to see why the future is anything but certain. What we can do, however, is historically compare prices of specific bottles to show which have appreciated or depreciated.

What follows is a listing that shows how certain bottles have fared over the years, from as far back as 1945. Note that the prices listed are the actual sales prices. The items listed were picked at random, so let's go back in time and have some fun!

Bottle Type	1945	1971	1978	1986	1990
BININGER					
Bininger handled urn		$425		$900	$700–1000
Bininger's Travelers Guide, ½ pt., amber		$140			$200–300
BITTERS					
Drake's Plantation		$45			$65
Fish Bitters, amber		$140		$100	$140–180
Fish Bitters, colorless		$380			$500–700
Greeley's, aqua			$950		$1200–1500
HP Herb Wild Cherry		$140			$250–400
Kelly's Old Cabin		$300			$400–600
Kimball's Jaundice			$210		$250–350
National Bitters		$170			$225–325
Pineapple-shaped, olive yellow			$600		$2000–3000
Pocahontas, aqua		$570			$1000–1200
Simon's Centennial, aqua		$300	$500		$800–1200
Suffolk Pig Bitters			$400		$400–600
BLOWN THREE-MOLD DECANTERS					
GII-6, light green	$85				$4000–6000
GIII-2, olive green	$60				$5000–8000
GIII-5, colorless	$35			$130	$150–225
GIII-16, olive amber			$200	$210	$450–550
GV-8, colorless	$55				$300–450
COLOGNE					
Wickered demijohn figural, aqua		$10			$20–30
Monument, black, 12″		$50			$800–1200
FIGURAL					
Atterbury Duck, milk glass				$220	$300–400
John Bull, amber		$85		$170	$200–250
Kummel Bear, black		$25			$40–60
Eye opener, milk glass		$45			$200–275
Pretzel, ceramic		$7			$40–60

Bottle Type	1945	1971	1978	1986	1990
FIRE GRENADE					
Harden's, cobalt				$160	$200–250
FLASKS					
GI-14, aqua				$150	$125–175
GI-16, aqua		$70			$100–150
GI-17, colorless	$12				$50–75
GI-28, pale blue green				$150	$400–550
GI-34, olive amber				$180	$125–175
GI-35, cobalt				$5100	$4000–5500
GI-109, light green	$50				$1200–1500
GI-117, aqua				$250	$300–500
GII-24, sapphire blue	$90				$1800–2600
GIII-16, deep aqua				$180	$125–150
GV-5, olive green				$135	$150–250
GV-9, olive amber				$130	$150–250
GV-8, olive amber		$190			$150–250
GII-60, light amber		$500			$800–1200
GVIII-2, green		$325			$300–500
GX-25, olive amber	$385				$15,000+
GVII-3, amber		$130			$800–1200
FOOD					
Peppersauce, ridged sides, aqua		$10			$15–25
FRUIT JARS					
Belle, qt., aqua				$500	$400–475
Moore's Patent, qt., aqua		$20			$70–90
INK					
Farley's, olive amber, 1¾″				$235	$300–350
Blown three-mold, green			$70		$125–175
Cabin-shaped, colorless			$110		$350–400
LABEL UNDER GLASS					
Flask, woman's portrait, ½ pt.		$5			$250–400
MEDICINE					
Clemen's Indian Tonic, labeled, pontiled				$310	$250–350
Schenck's Pulmonic Balsam	$15				$10–20
Jelly of Pomegranate, pontiled		$110			$80–120

Bottle Type	1945	1971	1978	1986	1990
MINERAL WATER					
Clark & White, emerald green		$25			$60–90
Syracuse Springs				$40	$100–150
Avon, qt., red amber				$260	$300–400
PICKLE					
Cathedral, aqua, pontiled		$45			$200–300
WHISKEY					
Star Whiskey, handled, amber, pontiled	$210				$200–300
Casper's, cobalt				$230	$250–350

HISTORY OF BOTTLES

It is unclear just when glass was first made and used, but it *is* known that glass has been around for at least the last 5000 years. The earliest known glass vessels were made by the core form method, whereby a molten string of glass was wrapped around and around a clay body which resembled the shape of the vessel which the craftsman meant to make from glass. Once the entire object was coated with glass, it was cooled, or annealed, which is a gradual cooling process taking 12 or more hours. The clay was then chipped out and a glass bottle was born. Early glass-makers also used molds into which they poured molten glass.

Around the 1st century B.C. the blow pipe was invented. The blow pipe is a long hollow metal rod, the tip of which is dipped into molten glass. The glass blower then blows into the rod and is able to manipulate the molten glass into any number of desired forms. Though the basic glass recipe of sand and wood ash will generally result in a greenish-colored glass (though the actual coloring is based on the minerals in the sand used), man discovered early on how to use various substances, mainly metallic oxides, in order to make an endless and varied range of colors.

The first attempt to make glass in America was believed to have been at the Jamestown settlement in Virginia in 1608, and it is interesting to note that the main purpose of the glasshouse was not to supply the early American settlers with bottles, window glass or drinking vessels. Rather, the great majority of any glass produced at the Jamestown settlement was intended to be shipped back to England, where there were virtually no forests left to fuel the glasshouse furnaces and to supply the ash for the glass mixture. As far as is known, the Jamestown glass-blowing venture was a total misadventure, and it is doubtful that any glass was ever made there. Later in the 17th century, several glasshouses were started in America to partially satisfy the colonists' need for bottles and window glass. Glasshouses were erected in Salem, Massachusetts, New Amsterdam, New York, and Philadelphia, Pennsylvania. Although it is unclear what products were produced at these houses, the fact that a few were in existence for several decades points to their prosperity.

The first truly successful American glasshouse was started in 1739 in southern New Jersey by Caspar Wistar, a Philadelphia brass button manufacturer who had emigrated from Germany. It is known that the main commercial output of his glasshouse was window glass and bottles. The next major glass enterprise was formed by Henry William Stiegel, who operated several glasshouses out of the Manheim, Pennsylvania, area from 1763 to 1774. More is known about the Stiegel line of products than of all previous American glass enterprises combined, and two particular pattern flasks, the diamond daisy and the daisy hexagon, can be attributed exclusively to Stiegel. Pattern molds, which were used to a very limited degree in earlier American glasshouses, were widely used in the Stiegel enterprise.

During the late 18th century, American glassmakers attempted to take full advantage of the strong anti-British sentiments prevalent at the time. Advertisements were taken in local newspapers attempting to convince Americans to buy American-made products, and these ads touted the fact that domestic wares were of the same quality and style as imported wares. Because the vast majority of American glasshouses attempted to copy imported bottles and tableware until the 19th century, it is generally very difficult, if not impossible, to specifically attribute any early glasswork as being made in America.

Despite the early attempts to establish glass blowing in America, the output of glass factories at that time was minimal at best, and right up through the first quarter of the 19th century the vast majority of all glass used in America was imported. The early American government was greatly in favor of developing the American glass industry, however, and a lottery system was developed to help finance prospective glass factories. In the lottery, citizens could purchase "lottery tickets," the proceeds of which were used to finance the glassworks. Also, it was common practice in Colonial days for the government to grant a license to a specific glassworks which restricted other enterprising glasshouses from opening and competing in the same geographical area. As a result of this, more and more glassworks began to appear late in the 18th and early 19th centuries.

The locations of the glasshouses were generally based on several factors. These included the presence of a sufficient supply of raw materials such as sand and wood, the possibility of securing competent glass blowers, and close proximity to thoroughfares or navigable rivers to transport raw materials and finished products to the major markets in Boston, Philadelphia, and New York.

The Pitkin Glassworks of East Hartford, Connecticut, was opened in 1783 and has the distinction of probably being the first American glasshouse to have produced figured flasks. Around 1810, Mr. J.P. Foster became manager of the Pitkin Glassworks, and it is believed that the "JPF" initials on several early figured flasks were indeed made at the

Pitkin Glassworks. Pitkin flasks were also named for the Pitkin Glassworks, since for many years it was believed that they were the exclusive products of the Pitkin Glassworks. However, it is now believed that no Pitkin-type flasks were ever produced there. In addition to producing all types of bottles and early glassware, the Pitkin Glassworks also was known to have produced window glass in the early days as well as "clock glasses," which is the glass covering a clock face. The Pitkin Glassworks was quite successful until it closed around 1830 due to the cost of wood for fuel. Pitkin's necessity to discontinue operations due to the lack of wood was not uncommon. Other reasons for early glasshouses shutting down were often the loss of skilled glass blowers, who had a tendency to migrate from one glass factory to another, and accidental fires, which leveled many a glasshouse building.

By the early 19th century, the use of bottle molds was becoming more and more widespread, with ribbed-type molds being the most common. In addition, we have seen where some 18th-century glasshouses such as Stiegel used molds extensively, and we also know that the first molded figured flasks were probably made in Connecticut around 1815. Nothing, however, could compare to the skyrocketing usage of molds that started around 1820. Around that time in America, "blown three-mold" products began to appear, which were intricate geometric-type patterns meant to inexpensively copy the fashionable imported Irish and English blown glass which had real cut designs. Though the major output in blown three-mold was decanters, a few rare flasks were patterned as well as a vast array of pitchers, dishes, bowls, and other tableware. Much of this blown three-mold glass was made at the Sandwich Glassworks in Sandwich, Massachusetts, though factories in Stoddard, New Hampshire, and Ohio also played a major role. Blown three-mold began to lose its appeal around 1840, and the advances in fine lacy and patterned pressed glass helped mark its demise.

Also around 1820, figured flasks exploded in popularity, and dozens of glass factories produced literally thousands of these fine flasks in a wide variety of designs and colors. Though America was still dependent on imported glassware, through the domestic production of blown three-mold, figured flasks and spirits, and medicine bottles, America was soon able to fill its own glass needs with less of a dependence on imported wares.

Throughout the 19th century, glasshouses continued to come and go, opening and closing due to changes in demand and technological improvements. In the early 20th century, the invention of the automatic bottle-making machine marked the end of the handblown bottle.

HOW BOTTLES ARE MADE

Glass is basically a mixture of sand and ash, heated to the desired temperature of approximately 1500°–2500° F. Though these two ingredients would ordinarily result in a greenish-colored glass, the minerals present in the sand and the varying proportion of ash to the mixture might result in a range of coloring from almost colorless to a dark green or black glass. There are also a wide assortment of chemicals and metallic oxides which one could use to make artificial colors, which run the entire color spectrum.

Right up until the late 19th and into the 20th century, the vast majority of collectible bottles were blown. This was accomplished by the glass blower "gathering" glass on the tip of his 3- or 4-foot metal blow pipe, which was done by dipping the pipe end into a molten tank of glass. After insuring that the gather was symmetrical, the glass blower would forcibly blow into the hollow blow pipe to expand the molten glass into a variety of shapes. The making of molded bottles involved the same steps, except the glass blower would insert the molten glass into a mold, usually made of metal, and impress the mold shape onto the molten glass by blowing. Once the bottle had been blown, it needed to be removed from the blow pipe in order to finish the lip. On pre–Civil War bottles, this was accomplished through the use of a 3- or 4-foot metal pontil rod, which was dipped into the tank of molten glass and then applied to the bottom of the bottle. The neck of the bottle was then touched with a wet stick, which separated it from the blow pipe. Now the lip could be evened off, or a lip could be attached. The earliest lip treatments were often uneven, since they resulted from the bottle being pontiled and removed from the blow pipe, and then reheated to melt down the jagged areas only. In later years, shears were used to evenly trim the molten lip. The shears were very similar to tin snips available in hardware stores today. In the second quarter of the 19th century, several lipping techniques were developed which allowed the use of a wide range of lip styles.

Around the mid-19th century, the snap case became popular. This was a springlike metal cage which fit around the base of the bottle and held it while the lip was finished. The snap case was used extensively throughout the 19th century and into the 20th, until the invention of the automatic bottle-making machine virtually eliminated the handmade bottle in America.

For most of the 20th century, the art of handblown glass had all but been forgotten in America, except for a few small factories such as Blenko and Clevenger Brothers. Beginning in the 1960s, a revival in the interest of handblown glassware led to the Studio Movement whereby individual glass artisans were able to establish small glass-blowing studios. Today these studios are flourishing, and thousands of glass blowers, plus numerous universities and craft schools, continue to practice the time-honored art of handblown glass. It is strongly recommended that all serious glass and bottle collectors and dealers have a good working knowledge of how glass and bottles are blown, and every attempt should be made to visit a local glass studio or public facility—such as the Corning Museum of Glass in Corning, New York, or Wheaton Village in Millville, New Jersey—in order to watch firsthand how glass is fashioned. I cannot overemphasize the importance of a good working knowledge of glass techniques, as it can prove to be invaluable when watching for fakes and reproductions. Those interested in watching a local glass blower might find one by contacting a local crafts gallery or by attending one of the many nationwide crafts shows.

STARTING A COLLECTION

If one were to interview each and every bottle collector and inquire as to why they became interested in the hobby, one might be surprised at the wide range of responses. One of the main reasons would be that bottle collecting is such a social hobby, where groups of friends or relatives quite naturally spread their enthusiasm for collecting to everyone around them. Many of us began our pursuit of bottles as teenagers, or perhaps even children, when in our adventures in the woods we stumbled upon an old dump. No matter how we began in the hobby, however, there are many things which continue to attract us throughout the years. Some are drawn to the historic aspect, for example, and wonder what life may have been like 150 years ago when a given bottle may have been made. And how many of us have fantasized over which famous personality may have drank from our bottle in years past? The wide range of beautiful colors and shapes also attracts many, and the economic and investment aspects surely attract some.

The choice of which type of bottles to collect is also influenced by a wide range of factors. Personal finances are an important consideration, since certain areas of bottle collecting, such as figured flasks, can be quite expensive. The amount of space for display and storage can also be an important consideration, as can the amount of free time that an individual has to pursue the hobby. Some pursue a given type of bottle because it relates to their profession, such as a barber collecting hair bottles, whereas others search for the bottles that have their last name on them. No matter how the choices are made, the fact is that most collectors eventually tend to specialize in a given field of bottle collecting. Specialization has its advantages over the general collecting of bottles since the specialist, who may well be an expert in his given area of bottle collecting, is usually more knowledgeable on market trends and pricing in his given area, and is thus more likely to find a bargain. The general bottle collector has a much wider range of knowledge of many different bottle categories, which is advantageous since he may be able to spot a rare or underpriced bottle that a specialist may pass by. The general bottle collector, however, may not know a rarity or its price range in a specialized field.

Regardless of where your interests lie, a good collection in almost any bottle category can be easily started with a minimum investment. Many bottle collectors are avid bottle diggers, and it is quite common for a digger to find a rare bottle which may not be in his area of collecting, which opens up the possibilities of selling the item or trading it to someone who may have something that he wants for his collection.

There are several basic guidelines which any beginning collector should seriously consider. First, join a local bottle club where you will meet others with similar interests and have the opportunity to handle more and more bottles. If you do not know where your local bottle club is, consult Appendix B at the end of this book and contact the nearest one in your area and inquire about local club activities. Next, in order to become familiar with bottle shapes, colors, rarity, and reproductions, all collectors should try to handle as much glass as they possibly can. Though it is of great help to study the reference books mentioned in this guide and to visit museum collections, there is no substitute for the actual handling of both old and new bottles. By handling the items, one will begin to get a feel for the weight and texture of glass, as well as gain a better understanding of what ordinary exterior wear on a bottle is, as opposed to a mint bottle with no exterior wear or a heavily worn bottle. Again, I must emphasize that when going to bottle shows, just walking up and down the aisles and looking at the bottles is not enough; ask the dealers questions and get their permission to handle the glass! Finally, the collector should attempt to learn as much as he possibly can about bottles in general or about his field of specialization. This will usually require studying many of the specialized glass books, many of which are listed in this book, as well as joining one of the speciality clubs operating throughout the country.

DETERMINING VALUES

As previously discussed, there are many factors which determine the value of any given bottle. The laws of supply and demand come fully into play when a highly sought-after bottle is pursued by many collectors, with a corresponding increase in sales price. Factors such as economic conditions, the number of known bottles in a given color or form, and the "what's in and what's out" syndrome, among other things, all have an effect. No matter what the area of bottle specialization, collectors of both old and new bottles must be able to spot the rarities, and there are certain characteristics that the astute collector should note on his mental checklist when looking at a bottle. These characteristics are:

Unusual Color: In the area of old bottles, color is the major ingredient in determining rarity and price. Generally speaking, aqua and colorless bottles are the most common and are thus less pursued and lower in price; however, there are many categories of bottles where aqua and colorless are rarities, and the knowledgeable collector would realize that the National Bitters bottle in the shape of an ear of corn is a $250 bottle in amber, whereas in aqua it is priced at around $1500 to $2000. The serious collector must become familiar with the rare colors by studying the auction catalogs, going to bottle shows, and reading the speciality reference books.

Unusual Size: Bottles come in a wide assortment of sizes, from as small as 1 inch to well over 5 gallons. Generally speaking, the extremities in size, both large and small, are generally rarer than the "normal size" of a given bottle. The collector must become familiar with what is "normal" for a given bottle. Be on the lookout for those rare miniature blown bottles, such as chestnuts, globulars, and early spirits bottles.

Unusual Method of Manufacture: Most bottles made after the Civil War have smooth bases since they were made by the use of a snap case. The snap case fitted over the bottle while the lip was being finished. This is in contrast to a rough pontil, which is a jagged scar on the bottom of a bottle and is generally found on pre–Civil War bottles; it involved the use of a pontil rod with a bit of glass on the end which was attached to the base of the bottle so that the lip could be finished. Be on the lookout for those common bottles which have a rough pontil. For example, the Drake's Plantation, cabin-shaped bitters bottle is quite common with a smooth base; however, a variant with the rough pontil scar is an extreme rarity. The collector should also become familiar with the common lip treatments used for bottles. For example, the average Pitkin-type flask exhibits a straight sheared lip. However, a few very rare examples show a flaring lip. Also, many flasks were made with a wide variety of lip treatments, and collectors should become familiar as to which ones are the rarer variants.

Striations: Striations are strands of color running through a bottle which are a different shading than the bottle itself. For example, an aqua bottle may have stringlike lines of amber or dark green running throughout it, which can often greatly enhance the collectivity and rarity of a given bottle.

Bubbles: In the natural melting process of making glass, the glass goes through what is called a "fining out" process. This is where air bubbles, trapped between the layers of raw materials, slowly rise through the viscous glass mixture to the surface, where they pop. If a tank of glass is given adequate time at the proper temperature, the fining out will result in glass which is relatively free of bubbles. However, some batches were never given the opportunity to fine out, thus resulting in bottles that are full of tiny bubbles or seeds. Sometimes the presence of very seedy glass can either make the bottle more attractive or reduce its desirability.

Labels and Original Contents: Many collectors pursue those bottles which have their original labels, boxes, and contents. Obviously, old bottles such as these are rare and bring a premium. The collector should be on the lookout for labeled bottles which do not have the original label or have reproduction labels.

Historic Import: Bottles which were once part of a famous collection have generally commanded a premium, and for such bottles it is not uncommon for a relatively common item to sell for considerably more than its fair market value. Collections put together by such bottle and glass experts as Charles Gardner and George McKearin, among others, have historically brought strong prices. Usually when bottles from a noted collection are sold, they have some type of identification to help authenticate which collection they came from.

Quantity Known: The quantity of bottles of a given type on the market can dramatically impact the fair market value of a given bottle. For example, the so-called "Dutch Squat" spirits bottle, manufactured in the early 18th century, was at one point considered to be quite rare and was valued at around $200. In the past several years, literally thousands of these bottles have been discovered in the freshwater lakes and bays of South America where they had been imported in the 18th century. The recovery of massive quantities of these bottles by divers has resulted in a flooding of the market, thus driving the average price down on these to $50–100 each. Another example was when a major medicine bottle collection was sold several years ago, which negatively impacted the values of many other pontiled medicines which, up to that point, had been considered very rare.

Fakes and Reproductions: A reproduction is a copy of an earlier style which is sold and advertised as a reproduction. Many museums sell reproduction bottles and glassware, since certain styles, popular in the 18th and 19th centuries, appear to be timeless in their form and beauty. Fakes, on the other hand, are attempts by unscrupulous individuals to fool and deceive. It is recommended that all collectors become familiar with fakes and reproductions, and there are several books on the market that cover this subject such as *American Bottles and Flasks and Their Ancestry* by McKearin and Wilson, *Antique Fakes and Reproductions* by Ruth Webb Lee, and *Fake, Fraud or Genuine* by Kaye, just to mention a few. The experienced collector should have minimal problems in identifying fake- and reproduction-mold blown bottles, but the early pattern-molded pieces and free-blown items can be quite deceiving. The collector should always deal with reputable dealers and auction houses who are willing to stand behind what they sell.

Contents: As mentioned earlier, many collectors seek bottles which contain the original labels and contents. However, all collectors should be *extremely careful* of the contents of early bottles, such as poisons, fire grenades, medicines, chemical bottles, etc., since the contents may still be toxic, perhaps even fatal. It is very important that bottles with contents be kept out of reach of children, and that proper measures be taken to prevent the bottles from falling over, since the contents may leak through the corks.

Wear, Stains, Chips, and Cracks: The closer a bottle is to mint condition—that is, relatively free of wear, chips, cracks or stains—the greater the value. Considerable damage on any piece can have a major impact on its value, and value reductions of 50%–70% or more are not uncommon. Even if a piece is free of chips, cracks or stains, heavy exterior wear is a detriment. Collectors must handle enough glass to know what is ordinary wear and what is heavy wear. The collector should be very careful to look for "potstones"; these are small stones, usually about $1/8$–$1/4$ inch in diameter, that are generally white in color and are frequently found embedded in a bottle. It is not unusual for tiny cracks to radiate from the potstone, which can have a major impact on the collectibility of the bottle.

HOW DO YOU TELL IF YOUR BOTTLE IS OLD?

Determining the age of a bottle, and knowing how to spot a fake or reproduction, is a necessity for those willing to invest time and money on a bottle collection. A bottle or piece of glass that has been used for many years, or one which has been buried in the ground for a long time, develops certain wear patterns on the high points of the bottle. Look for wear on the bottom and on the sides. Legitimate wear will usually appear very fine and feel almost silky smooth when a fingernail is rubbed against it. Artificially induced wear often feels rough, with large uneven scratches often extending beyond those areas which would have actually touched the surface, table, or ground. The most reliable wear indicator is usually the bottom of the bottle. If you are suspicious of the wear pattern, place the standing bottle on a sheet of paper and, with a sharp pencil, trace the outline of the base, and then see where the base touches the surface. If the wear pattern on the base matches the outline that shows where the base actually touches the table, then you are more comfortable as to the bottle being genuine.

Often, scratches on the sides, small chips or flakes on the lip, and a light inner haze may lend support to the bottle's age. But the astute collector realizes that many things can be done to make a bottle look old. As in everything else in life, nothing can compensate for hands-on experience and study. Go to a bottle club or show and *handle* as much glass as possible. Study the books that can tell you which items have been reproduced. Buying from reliable dealers who stand behind their merchandise is also a good idea.

DIGGING FOR BOTTLES

There are many ways to hunt for bottles, and one of the most favorite is through digging. For both the beginning and advanced collector, digging for bottles is both an exciting and economical way to add to any collection. Prospecting for old bottles has become one of the favorite pastimes for collectors, and there is certainly no shortage of bottles waiting to be uncovered by the enterprising explorer. Though the thrill of finding a rare and valuable bottle is paramount in every bottle collector's dreams, exploring for the bottles is half the fun. It's like a treasure hunt! One of the great things about digging for bottles is that it allows the young collector, who may be unable to afford the more valuable bottles, to prospect for his own bottles and build a stock from which he can sell and trade for better bottles. Though some American cities had refuse removal services as far back as the 18th century, most early American families handled their refuse themselves. Oftentimes the garbage was thrown over a stone wall at the back end of the property or dumped into the privy hole in the outhouse. Other times trash was thrown into the ocean or down a river bank. All of these places are potential bonanzas for bottle collectors, and one often has to research to find which areas of which cities were thriving in the 18th and 19th centuries.

Before we go any further in prospecting for bottles, however, it is of paramount importance that we discuss some of the safety hazards associated with bottle digging. Unless you are one of the lucky people who discovers a dump in their own backyard, odds are you will be looking for bottles on someone else's private property. Always get permission to dig for bottles on someone's property. Since you may find yourself prospecting in the woods, be aware of bees, poison ivy, ticks, snakes, barbed wire fences, dogs, etc., and it might not hurt to have a good supply of Band-Aids and hydrogen peroxide on hand. As far as the actual digging goes, it is highly recommended that you never do it alone, since cave-ins are not uncommon. Twenty years ago a cousin of mine returned to an excavated foundation, which we had together explored the day before, to dig for bottles on his own. During his tunneling a large rock fell free and knocked him unconscious. This can happen to you!

WHERE TO DIG

Though taking a leisurely walk in the woods in search of a bottle dump on a summer's day is pleasurable even if nothing is found, there are ways in which the bottle archeologist can improve his chances for success. As mentioned earlier, behind stone walls in back of old houses are often good places to look, and some of the best prospects, if you are able to locate them, are where old outhouses or privys stood.

The problems with outhouse digging are numerous, since they are probably no longer standing and are difficult to locate. The very early privys had stone linings; in the 19th century wood liners were used. The lucky prospector may find the privy lining visible at ground level, though this is doubtful. Occasionally one may be able to find the privy location through an unexpected clump of small trees or brush, since vegetation may be drawn to the well-fertilized grounds. Finding the outhouse location at a rural or country home is very difficult, whereas 19th-century urban home locations may be more accessible. Often in large cities very specific property plans were drawn up which specifically stated where on the property an outhouse must be situated. Once you have a guesti-mate as to where the outhouse may have been, one method of finding it is by the use of a "probe." This is a long narrow metal rod which, when pushed into the earth, will often meet very little resistance when pushed into a privy location, as opposed to being pushed into the rocky soil which surrounds it.

Now that you have found your outhouse, it is probably located in the middle of the lawn of the backyard of the house. Surprisingly, it is not uncommon for homeowners to allow bottle diggers access to their yards, and arrangements can be made with homeowners to split up the bottles found. When digging up the lawn, you can use a garden tool to cut an even perimeter in the lawn area which you expect to excavate, and then gently roll up the grass, removing it in small squares which should be put on a plastic sheet alongside the hole. After the excavation is com-pleted, you will often need to use some type of filler in order to even out the ground. Before you go digging up a stranger's lawn, however, it is recommended that you experiment in your own backyard to learn the methods of grass removal and transplantation.

Looking for bottles behind walls in the woods is often difficult because the bottles you are seeking were thrown there 100 or 200 years ago, and they are ordinarily covered with leaves and years of sediment. Often, however, the same dumping area was used for a long period of time, and it is often possible to discover an early dump through finding early 20th-century cans and bottles on the surface, and then just digging deeper.

Construction excavations are a great place to look for bottles. Once again, getting permission is imperative. Street and sewer excavations are other good sites for bottle hunters, and this year a bottle was found in a Massachusetts street excavation which sold for $9000. Probably one of the largest untapped sources of bottles is in our streams, lakes, and oceans. Obviously, this presents major problems in locating the bottles, but river banks and stream beds continue to be major sources of bottle finds for many prospectors.

Apart from actually digging for bottles, many good finds can be also found in attics, basements, crawl spaces, and barns. Over the years I have heard many stories of people finding bottles and early glass dating to the early 19th century, with original contents, in the corners of attics in old homes. Those of you in the construction business should also be on the lookout for early American bottles and antiques which may have been placed inside walls, which are often uncovered during renovations.

DIGGING TOOLS

There are several tools which the bottle hunter should consider bringing. A shovel will be required, and for all tall bottle collectors out there, such as myself, be sure the shovel has a long handle, which will do wonders for your back. A pitchfork is good in rocky areas, and a thin metal probe, which can be purchased at bottle shows or through bottle magazines, can often come in handy when searching for privys or in swamps. As for small hand tools, small scratchers and shovels are good, and some people prefer trowels, which is a favorite tool of professional archeologists. Extreme caution should be taken, however, to dig a site gently so as not to break any of the precious bottles that may lie underneath. (Many of us have put a pitchfork through a rare medicine or historical flask over the years.) Also, work boots, gloves, and eye protection, along with durable clothing, are recommended. Make sure to bring a heavy-duty canvas or other bag, along with newspaper, to wrap your new-found treasures!

BUYING, SELLING, AND TRADING

Though some bottles are dug up or found, most of the items in any collection are acquired through buying or trading. Since most bottle collectors tend to specialize in a given area, a rare bottle found in a dump site may be of little interest except for its potential monetary or trade value.

There are many places to buy and trade bottles, the largest being bottle shows and clubs. Virtually every weekend of the year, bottle shows and club meetings take place where all sorts of dealings are made. Those actively involved in the bottle business know who collects what, and often the major collector will be given a phone call before a given bottle is made available to the general public. Often at bottle shows some of the best merchandise is not to be found on the tables, but rather under the tables, where dealers and collectors attempt to make their own private sales and trades. Though the bottle shows will display the wares of many dealers to thousands of collectors, it is often difficult to find bargain merchandise. More people are knowledgeable as to bottle rarity and value now than at any other time, and one may have to look for bargains in unusual areas of bottle collecting, where there may be less interest and subsequently less knowledgeable dealers and collectors. Also, it is becoming harder and harder to find top-quality bottles for sale at bottle shows, since the rarer bottles are being sold more and more frequently through the bottle auction houses, where many believe higher prices can be obtained than would be received at a bottle show.

Other sources of buying bottles are antique shops, flea markets, antique shows, pawn shops, Salvation Army thrift shops, and tag sales. In many instances, the astute collector may be able to find an incredible bargain since he is often probably purchasing the bottle from someone who knows nothing about bottle value.

Bottles are also available through nationwide bottle magazines and specialty collectors' newsletters, as well as through local newspapers and antiques publications. Of course, when one deals through the mail it is difficult to be certain of what one is receiving. Care should be taken that the bottles are properly wrapped and insured, and a seven- or ten-day return privilege should always be asked for.

Bottle and early glass auction houses have increased in number over the last ten years and represent probably the major methods of disposing of, and acquiring, major bottles for a collection. Several of the auction houses have on-site auctions whereby prospective buyers can actively bid while the piece is on the block; mail bids and phone bids are also encouraged. Other auction houses are of the absentee type, whereby buyers bid over the phone and through the mail. All of the auction houses publish impressive sale catalogs, which generally cost $10 to $20 each. These are filled with descriptive information, including bottle condition, along with photographs. The catalogs themselves are important reference tools, and serious collectors should obtain them whenever possible. The auction houses charge a commission to sell the bottles, which generally ranges from 10% to 20% of the gross selling price; in addition, a buyer's premium is often added to the sales price, which is usually a 10% charge added onto the purchase price and assessed against the successful bidder.

Should you decide to sell or purchase bottles through one of the major auction houses, you may wish to contact one or all of the following:

Old

Skinners, Inc.
Route 117
Bolton, MA 01740
(508) 779-6241

Norman Heckler
Bradford Corner Road
Woodstock Valley, CT 06282
(203) 974-1634

Glass Works Auctions
P.O. Box 187
East Greenville, PA 18041
(215) 679-5849

Harmer Rooke Galleries
3 East 57th Street
New York, NY 10022
(212) 751-1900

Modern

Homestead Collectibles
P.O. Box 173
Mill Hall, PA 17751-0173
(717) 726-3597

BOTTLE CARE

Compared to many other types of collector items, bottles require very little care and maintenance. Once the hobbiest has learned to keep his bottles properly and safely, he will have few maintenance problems. Storage and display problems are minimal.

When a freshly dug bottle has been brought in from the field, the surface condition is likely to be so miserable that it offers very little encouragement of ever being successfully cleaned. However, most bottles will clean up well with a bit of patience and hard work. The first step is to remove loose surface particles (sand, small stones, etc.) with a brush. Care should be taken not to exert any pressure while removing loose debris as it may scratch the bottle. Surface dirt can be removed by soaking the bottle, but caution should be exercised to avoid any scratching. To soften and break down the tough impacted grime, the bottle must soak in something stronger than plain water. There are several cleaners which are used to successfully remove any dirt and stains. The combination of ammonia and water is a good cleaner, assuming adequate ventilation is present. Some may wish to use dish detergent, while other collectors use a few tablespoons of bleach in a gallon of lukewarm water. The water should never be too hot nor too cold, as this may shock the bottle and result in breakage. Depending on the amount of dirt and stain on a given bottle, it may require soaking for over a week. In addition, some bottles may be cleaned with steel wool or a stiff brush, but be wary of this method since it may result in scratching the surface.

Quite frequently a collector will purchase a bottle which has an interior stain, which is often difficult to clean. Some collectors use an ammonia solution. Another popular way of cleaning interiors is to fill the bottle with approximately 1/2 inch of water and add ordinary beach sand; when shaken vigorously, it may help to loosen much of the staining.

In addition to the above-mentioned ways of cleaning, there are professional bottle cleaners who use a variety of methods to rid even the harshest of stains. One of the methods employed by professionals is called the "tumbler," whereby copper pellets and water are added to the inside of the bottle. The bottle is then put into a tumbling machine which rapidly vibrates the bottle, causing the copper pellets to scrub the inner bottle. The professional also may use cerium oxide, which is a very fine powder used in glass polishing, to help rid the bottle of any scratches or stains. Still others employ strong chemicals and acids, which actually may eat away the surface of the glass. Exterior stains may also be removed by the use of a buffing wheel, which can often obscure the sharpness of the lettering of a bottle or make an impression slightly fuzzy. Others often oil bottles both inside and out, which will often hide any stains and small scratches. Some of these cleaning methods are used to deceive prospective purchasers into believing that a damaged bottle is in perfect condition. Care should be taken to be aware of any acid or oil polishing, or repairs, as such treatments may actually lower the value of the bottle.

Now that your bottles are clean, you will wish to display them. The chief consideration in display is to prevent breakage while allowing the specimens to be viewed and handled. The collector may wish to keep his bottles in a cabinet, on wall shelving, or distributed at random about the house to provide decorative touches. While certainly appealing, this last approach tends to be riskier. When a collection is not grouped together in one place or one part of the house, it becomes more difficult to guard against accident. This is especially true if pets or small children are around. When a collection is within a cabinet or on shelves, it is less likely to be broken. What some collectors do is hang a ⅛-inch sheet of Plexiglas from two hooks along the top of their cabinet, which helps to minimize accidental breakage but still allows easy access to bottles. Almost any type of cabinet is suitable for a bottle collection; the choice will depend on personal taste, room decor, size of the collection, and the cost of the unit. An ordinary bookcase with glass doors or grill work will do if it has adjustable shelves and is not too small, whereas a case with wooden sides will not provide as much visibility or light penetration to the inside. However, with very little expense or trouble a lighting fixture can be installed inside. Cabinets with glass sides are ideal for displaying bottles and can often be picked up at antique shops or from used furniture dealers.

No matter how you decide to display your bottle collection, care should be taken to avoid any rapid changes in temperature which can actually crack a bottle. Many people display their bottles in windows, and I have never heard of any bottles breaking due to the sunlight flowing through a window. Care should be exercised in certain parts of the country which may experience a rapid change in window temperature.

As for the storage of bottles, the collector may wish to obtain empty liquor boxes with cardboard dividers, which, along with each bottle being individually wrapped with newspaper, should provide the necessary protection for long-term storage. Once again, care should be taken to ensure that the bottles are not going to be subject to extreme temperatures, and be careful when moving the boxes, since any floor dampness may weaken the bottoms.

FAKES, REPRODUCTIONS, AND REPAIRS

As bottle values continue to escalate, often into the thousands of dollars, the importance of being able to spot a fake, reproduction or repaired bottle is paramount. There is a major difference between a fake and a reproduction; the reproduction is a legitimately produced item, meant to copy the timeless beauty of items from the past. Generally, reproductions are marked in some way, such as on the blown three-mold decanters made for the Metropolitan Museum of Art which are engraved "MMA" on or around the pontil mark. A fake, on the other hand, is a copy whose main purpose is to deceive the purchaser into believing it is a genuine article.

The purpose of this section is by no means to provide a master listing of fakes and reproductions, but rather to alert the collector and dealer to certain more commonly seen bottles and to suggest ways to help identify copies. The reader is strongly advised to obtain a copy of *American Bottles and Flasks and Their Ancestry* by McKearin and Wilson, which gives the most detailed information on fakes available anywhere. Some of the reproduction flasks tend to have a pebbly or granularlike surface which is the result of using inferior or plaster molds. Note that there are several genuine flasks that also exhibit this grainy type of surface, and the astute collector must memorize which flasks were genuinely made in that fashion. Sometimes the pontil scars on reproductions are unusual, with unusual indentations in the base of the bottle meant to simulate pontil scars. On bitters and medicines, the collector must watch for an unusual mold seam; the mold seam will come to within ¼ inch of the lip and stop, and then continue to the lip, but the mold seams are not aligned. I have seen this on a reproduced Suffolk Pig Bitters. Sometimes a copy is discovered because it simply does not "feel right," such as if the glass is too transparent or too light in weight, or there is simply not enough wear on the item.

As mentioned before, both beginning and advanced bottle enthusiasts should attempt to handle as much glass as possible, rather than relying on pictures in books or pieces behind glass showcases in museums. Visit your local bottle dealer, go to bottle shows or club meets, and physically pick up as many bottles as you possibly can to get a feel for what is right and what is not right. Tell the dealer that you are interested in learning about fakes and reproductions, and he may be able to show you some or alert you to a new copy he has just found. Recently my bottle club, the Southern Connecticut Antique Bottle Collectors Association, devoted one of its monthly meetings to reproductions, and approximately 50 reproduced items were on display for all to see and handle. Why not do it with your club?

COMMON REPRODUCTIONS AND FAKES

Here is a selective listing of certain categories of bottles that have been faked or reproduced.

Bitters Bottles:

   Simons Centennial Bitters: Reproduced in green, blue, and amber. The embossing on the reproduced item is virtually impossible to read, and unlike the original, the copy has a pontil scar.
   Suffolk Pig Bitters: This bottle of greenish amber has an unusual mold seam, which is discussed above.

Blown Bottles: There is a reproduction chestnut flask going around which has a flared lip. Chestnut bottles were never made with a flared lip, and generally have a crude applied string lip. The reproduction is also heavier in weight than the original. The collector should be wary when purchasing any blown bottle, and be aware that it is very easy for a glass blower of today to closely copy an 18th-century bottle form.

Blown Three-Molds: There have been blown three-mold copies on the market since as far back as the 1920s. Usually the copies are of unusual coloration, such as blue, purple or amber. An example of a copied pattern is the GIII-5. One of the telltale signs of this copy is that the diamond pattern does not run straight across, but goes up at an angle. Also, there are several blown three-mold items being reproduced for the Museum of Metropolitan Art, similar to McKearin pattern GV-9, which should have the initials "MMA" engraved on the pontil mark.

Enameled Bottles: Enameled bottles made in the half-post method in the Germany/Switzerland area in the 18th century are popular, and very good reproductions are made today. Oftentimes the enameling on the modern pieces is much brighter and sharper, and the designs may differ from the earlier pieces. Also, look for lack of wear and be suspicious if an item is of especially bubbly glass.

Fruit Jars: There are both free-blown and patterned fruit jars which have been reproduced. The free-blown jars are often difficult to identify, and collectors should check to see if wear on the item is legitimate or induced, and if the form and color are consistent with an early jar. Many of the reproduced molded jars, such as Mason jars, have a number impressed on the base which will help to identify it as a reproduction. Interested parties should refer to the *Red Book of Fruit Jars* by Creswick for more detailed information on reproduced fruit jars.

Ink Bottles: There are several funnel-shaped ink bottles which are free-blown and unpatterned, and these are elaborated on in Covill's book on inks. Be wary of any free-blown ink bottles, and check for legitimate wear.

Medicine Bottles: There are several reproduced medicines on the market, and the collector should watch for unusual mold seams and termination, as mentioned previously for Suffolk Pig Bitters.

Nailsea-Type Bottles: These free-blown bottles, which have multicolored loopings, are easily reproduced. Check for legitimate wear and unusual form or colors.

Pattern-Molded Bottles: I have seen several midwestern-type globular bottles in amber which are reproductions, and these differ from the originals in that they have flaring lips and do not have the grace and fluidity of the originals. There are some straight-sided, cylindrical jarlike pieces on the market, some having swirled ribs and some unribbed, which are reproductions. These items have folded rims and I have seen them in amber and amethyst. The Stiegel diamond and daisy flask has also been copied, with the distinguishing feature on the copy being six diamonds, whereas the original only has five. Be wary of any ribbed flasks and bottles since many continue to be made in Mexico and are easily confused with the original American pieces. Emil Larsen was a prolific glass blower who worked in the New Jersey area in the early part of this century. He made some beautifully patterned flasks, such as those in a 12-diamond pattern, and the pieces can often be confused with Stiegel by the untrained eye. However, once you have had the opportunity to handle the Larsen pieces, you will notice a slight difference in form and uses of color from the 18th-century pieces.

Figured Flasks: Fakes and reproductions among figured flasks are the most numerous and often the most difficult to detect. In the "Figured Flasks" section in this book, I have put an asterisk next to those flasks which are known to be copied. Here I will discuss some of the better copies and how to identify them.

GI-26, Washington—Eagle: This well-reproduced quart flask is similar to the original in most ways except the mold seam goes almost all the way to the top of the lip on the copy.

GI-107A, Jenny Lind—Fislerville: This is a well-made copy and is difficult to distinguish from the original. However, the copy holds exactly one quart of liquid and the skirting at the neck and shoulder differs on the copy from the original.

GIV-1, Masonic—Eagle: This is a fairly good reproduction pint flask, and the main way to distinguish it from the original is by the letters "JP" that are enclosed within the oval, as opposed to "IP" which was on the original bottle.

GV-5, Success to the Railroad: This pint flask is one of the finest reproductions you will ever see, with the main difference being that the mane on the horse's neck stands straight out.

GVIII-2: This is a very well-made reproduction, distinguishable only from the original because it is much lighter in weight.

GVII-4, EG Boozs Old Cabin Bottle: This reproduction is distinguishable from the original since the corner edges extend below the first row of shingles, whereas on the original they do not.

GVII-3, EG Boozs Old Cabin Bottle: This is a well-made reproduction, made in New Jersey beginning in the 1930s. On the originals, a period can be found after the word whiskey. Also, on the reproduction a mold seam is evident on the base, whereas the original does not have a mold seam. If the Boozs bottle does not have a period after whiskey, this does not necessarily make it a fake, as a cold mold may have resulted in the period not being filled in.

GII-76, Concentric Ring—Eagle: This is one of the most difficult reproductions to distinguish from the original, with the reproductions each having a serial number engraved in the base of the bottle.

REPAIRS

There are two major types of bottle repairs that must be watched for: 1) the epoxy type wherein epoxy or some other type of hardener is used to create a new lip or to fill in a chip; and 2) polishing repairs, which ordinarily involve felt or cork belts to remove any traces of a chip or jagged edge. The epoxy-type repairs are often extremely well done, and it is not uncommon for an entire neck to be replaced right down to a bottle's shoulder, for a hole in the side of a piece to be filled, or for a rough area to have a surface coating of resin.

There are several ways to help spot a repair. Sometimes a repair will show an odd color when exposed to black light, and the epoxy will have a different, slippery type of feel than the glass. Some people apply acetone to a suspected repaired area, which will frost the resin. Sometimes the repair just does not look right, and a noticeable line can be seen where the epoxy begins and the bottle ends. However, some repairs are very difficult to spot. This is not to say that epoxy-type repairs are all bad, as major bottles are often repaired to enhance their display quality.

As to polish-type repairs, these are often the most difficult to detect. In fact, if a lip has been properly polished to hide a chip, it is very possible that even the most experienced bottle collector will not be able to tell with certainty that the item has been polished. What can you look for to determine if a bottle has been polished? If the lip is suspected, there may be a "file mark" that runs completely around the lip perimeter. If the file mark suddenly stops and there is a small indentation, with a sheen or luster that is unlike the rest of the lip, then you may have a polishing job. Sometimes polishing may be used to rid scratches from the side of a bottle; look for an unusual indentation on one area of the bottle that may be overly shiny or dull, and look for embossing that may seem dull, both of which may indicate that a light buffing may have been done. As stated before, the best practice is to handle as much glass as possible and to ask other bottle collectors if they can show you any repaired items or suspected repairs.

BOTTLE AGE AND
BOTTLE SHAPES

BOTTLE AGE

Free-Blown Bottles: B.C.–1860; some are still free blown today.

Pontil: 1618–1866; also some modern handblown bottles.

Raised Letters: 1790 to date.

Three-Part Mold: 1806–1889.

Amethyst or Sun-Colored Glass: 1800 to date.

Sheared Lip: 1800–1830 (the top has been sheared off).

Machine-Made Bottles: 1903 to date (mold line runs from base through the top).

Black or Dark Olive Green Glass: 1700–1800 approx.

Blob Top: Thick rounded lip; on most soda and mineral water bottles.

Crown Cap or Top: 1895 to date.

AGE AS DETERMINED BY MOLD LINE

-1800+   *-1880+*   *-1890+*   *-1903+*   *1910 to Date*

BOTTLE SHAPES

Cone Ink

Glue

Eight-sided Conical
or Umbrella

Conical

Cylindrical

Old Beer

New Beer

Old Soda

New Soda

Shoe Polish

Hutchinson-type
Stopper

Tear Drop
or Torpedo

Round Bottom

Old Whiskey

New Whiskey

Broken Pontil

Sheared Lip (1800s)

18 "Seal"

Graphite Pontil

Two-part Mold

Three-part Mold

Side Mold

Lady Leg Neck

*Medicine or
Bitters, label*

Old Medicine

New Medicine

Free Blown

Ten Pin

Fire Extinguisher

Squat or Onion

Wide Mouth Case Bottle

Scroll

HOW TO USE THIS BOOK

This book is divided into old and new bottles. The "Old Bottles" section is categorized by bottle type such as beer, flasks or inks. The listings are organized alphabetically by trade name or subject. The listings include the written material exactly as it appears on each bottle along with a bottle description.

The "New Bottles" section is arranged alphabetically by manufacturer. Some of the most popular modern bottle companies in the collector market are listed including Avon, Jim Beam, Ezra Brooks, Ski Country, and Old Commonwealth. The listings are organized alphabetically by trade name or subject. The bottle's description is given in each listing.

Read the printed descriptions carefully in both sections. The prices given are for the specific bottles listed. A bottle which is similar might have a higher or lower value than the item which appears in this book.

The prices given in both sections range from good to mint condition. A bottle in very poor condition would bring less than the values stated.

The following condition key should be of help in noting the condition of your bottles.

MINT (M): An empty bottle complete with new intact labels. Color bright and clean, no chips, scrapes or wear. Tax stamp like new, but cut. Box in like-new condition. All stoppers, handles, spouts like new.

EXTRA FINE (EF): A bottle complete with labels, stamps, etc. All color clean and clear, slight wear on labels and tax strip, gold or silver embellishments perfect. Stoppers, handles, spouts in fine condition. Box or container missing. *Worth 10% less than listed retail price.*

FINE (F): The bottle shows slight wear, but color is clear and bright overall. Tax stamp complete but worn. Labels can be missing. Gold or silver embellishments perfect. Stoppers, handles, spouts complete and undamaged. No box or container. *Worth 15% less than listed retail price.*

VERY GOOD (VG): The bottle shows some wear; gold or silver slightly worn. Labels missing. Tax stamp missing. Stoppers, handles, spouts complete. No box or container. *Worth 25% less than listed retail price.*

GOOD (G): The bottle shows wear; complete but color faded. Gold or silver shows wear. Labels and tax stamp missing. Stoppers, handles, spouts complete. No box or container. *Worth 40% less than listed retail price.*

FAIR (FR): The bottle color is worn and the gold or silver embellishments are faded. Labels and tax stamp missing. Stoppers, handles, spouts complete but worn. An undesirable category. No box or container. *Worth 50% to 75% less than listed retail price.*

Please note throughout the listings the abbreviations "IP" and "OP." "IP" means an iron pontiled bottle, which is generally from the 1850–1870 period. "OP" means an open pontiled bottle, which is generally pre–Civil War.

OLD BOTTLES

BARBER BOTTLES

An area of bottle collecting which offers one of the widest ranges of colors and bottle styles and decorations is the barber bottle area. As early as the 1860s, and continuing right through until about 1920, barbers used very colorful and highly decorated bottles which they often filled with their own tonics and colognes. Though the usage of barber bottles peaked around the turn of the century, the Pure Food and Drug Act of 1906, which restricted the usage of alcohol-based substances and unlabeled and refillable containers, marked the slow demise of these beautiful and distinctive bottles. During this time period, many of the bottles were made in the United States, with many others being imported from Europe. It is generally difficult to differentiate between an American-made bottle and its European counterpart. The earlier bottles often had rough pontil scars. The popular types of ornamentation included fancy pressed designs, cutting, enameling, painting, and labels under glass. The bottles were generally fit with cork and metal or porcelain-type closures. The reader is referred to *Collecting Barber Bottles* by Richard Holiner, which the letter "H" denotes in the list below.

ADAM WAGNER BAY RUM, with girl's face label under glass, 8", colorless.......
.... $250–300
AF PETERSON BAY RUM, with girl's head label under glass, 9½", colorless.....
.... $300
BARREL-SHAPED, citron with white and orange enamels, 7½", OP.... $120–175
BAY RUM, on label under glass, 10¼", milk glass $250–300
BAY RUM, with enameled grist mill, 8⅛", amethyst, OP............... $300–350
BAY RUM, with floral design, 10", milk glass................................$110–140
BAY RUM, with girl's bust on label under glass, 10⅛", milk glass.....$780–850
BAY RUM, globular body, straight neck with ring, 7½", milk glass, florals, OP
.... $80–110
BAY RUM, painted bottle, 8⅞", milk glass with multicolored design .$225–275
BIRD AND FLORAL DECORATION, 8¾", blue milk glass, OP............$350–450
BULBOUS BODY WITH LONG STRAIGHT NECK, with white enamel decor, cobalt, 8", OP $50–70
CHERUBS WITH FLOWERS, 7¾", milk glass, OP $300–400
COIN SPOT DESIGN, 8½", teal blue.. $100–125
COIN SPOT DESIGN, straight-sided cylinder, 8½", pale blue with opal blue overlay, OP.. $200–300
COIN SPOT, RH-81, 7⅛", opalized cranberry.................................$90–110
COIN SPOT, 6¾", cranberry red shading $80–120

Coin Spot Design, PG 62, 7″, turquoise, OP, edge chip $30–35
Coin Spot Pattern With Enamels, 7¾″, turquoise, OP $80–120
Cologne, with floral decoration, square, 10″, milk glass...............$110–140
CS Fay, on label under glass, 6⅜″, milk glass, OP $125–150
Daisy And Fern Pressed Design, 7½″, opalized canary yellow.....$150–200
Enameled Daisy And Dot Design, H-49, 8″, amber, OP $120–150
Floral Decor, similar in form to H-29, 8⅛″, amethyst, OP..........$100–125
Floral Decoration, handpainted, 8½″, milk glass, OP, 1″ pontil crack......
.... $60–80
Fox Hunt With Flowers, 7½″, milk glass, OP.......................... $200–300
Globular, with white dot and floral design, H-37, 8″, cobalt, OP.... $80–100
Globular Body, with white and yellow dot and florals, H-36, 8″, amethyst,
OP..$125–160
Hair Tonic, label under glass, 10¼″, milk glass $250–300
Hobnail, 7″, yellow amber...$35–45
Hobnail, bright blue with opal hobnails, 6¾″, OP $65–80
Hourglass Shape, multicolored design, H-57, 7½″, cobalt, OP $130–170
John Wagner Bay Rum, with grist mill, 10¼″, milk glass $350–450
John Wagner Tonic, with grist mill, 10¼″, milk glass $400–450
Joseph Booth, with floral decor, 8¾″, milk glass.......................$250–300
JV Rice Tonic, with girl's face label under glass, 8⅛″, colorless.....$450–500
KDX For Dandruff, on label under glass, 7¾″, colorless $110–140
Lady's Leg-Type Form, with ribs, citron with red and white enamels, 8⅛″,
OP...$40–55
Lady's Leg Shape, amethyst with orange, yellow, and blue enameled design,
8⅛″, OP...$70–85
M Snell Bay Rum, with florals, 10¼″, milk glass $300–350
Mary Gregory, boy with florals, H-12, 8″, amethyst, OP $350–400
Mary Gregory, girl and flowers, H-14, 8″, citron, OP................$350–400
Mary Gregory, tennis player, H-15, 8″, cobalt blue, OP...............$300–400
Mary Gregory Type, with resting girl, 7¾″, medium amethyst, OP............
.... $160–190
Mary Gregory Type, with standing boy, 7⅛″, bright green, OP $150–200
Mary Gregory Type, with standing boy, H-12, 7⅞″, green, OP $250–350
Mary Gregory Type, with tennis racket, 8¼″, cobalt blue, OP..... $200–225
Mary Gregory Type, with child playing tennis, 7¾″, cobalt, OP .. $200–300

Barber, two Mary Gregory types.
PHOTO COURTESY OF SKINNER'S, INC.

MARY GREGORY TYPE, with girl and florals, 8″, green, OP $200–250
MULTICOLORED DAISY DESIGN, H-84, 6¾″, amethyst, OP.............. $125–160
OPALIZED BLUE, with vertical white stripes, 6¼″, bulbous body $80–120
OPALIZED BLUE, with white spirals, 8¼″ $110–135
OPALIZED CRANBERRY, with white spots, 7⅛″ $100–150
OPALIZED CRANBERRY, with white spirals, H PG 77, 6⅞″ $150–200
OPAQUE WHITE WITH PINK SWIRLS, lady's leg, 8½″.......................$110–140
ORNATE BODY FORM, with multicolored florals, H-50, 7¾″, amethyst, OP
.... $125–175
R FINCH TONIC, with girl's face label under glass, 8⅛″, colorless ... $250–300
RIBBED, amethyst with white, blue, and yellow enamels, 7″, OP, H PG 85.....
.... $60–90
RIBBED, amethyst with white and orange enamel design, OP, PG 87,
6¾″ $60–85
RIBBED, emerald green with white and orange enamel, 6½″, OP $80–120
RIBBED, turquoise with silver and yellow enameled persian design, 6¾″, OP...
....$40–55
RIBBED BODY, with colorful floral decor, H-50, 7¾″, cobalt blue, OP ....
.... $80–120
RIBBED BODY, with white and brown florals, H-37, 7¾″, emerald green, OP
.... $60–90
RIBBON DECORATION, with florals, amethyst, 8″, ribbed with multicolors, OP
.... $60–80
ROSEWOOD DANDRUFF CURE, with woman's bust on label under glass, 8″,
colorless $200–225
S BRUNNER BAY RUM, with birds, 10″, milk glass........................ $400–500
SEA FOAM, with small birds, cylinder, 9″, milk glass, OP..............$110–140
SHAMPOO, with enameled grist mill, 8″, amethyst, OP................. $300–400
SILVER DESIGN, H PG 72, 7″, cobalt, OP, persian design $50–65
SILVER FLORAL OVERLAY, flared lip, cut glass stopper, 8¼″, turquoise, OP.....
.... $100–140
SLIGHTLY TAPERED BODY, long neck, ring lip, H PG 86, turquoise with red and
white enamels $50–65
SPANISH LACE DESIGN, colorless with white opal overlay, 9½″ $90–120
STARS AND STRIPES, bright blue with opal stars, 7″, OP $200–250
STARS AND STRIPES, colorless with opal stars, 7″, OP................... $160–190
STARS AND STRIPES PRESSED-IN PATTERN, opal blue..................... $300–400
STRAIGHT-SIDED BODY, long neck, H PG 84, 6¾″, amethyst, OP, ribbed,
enameled $60–75
STRIPE PATTERN, opal cranberry, bulbous base, 7⅛″ $80–120
THUMBPRINT PATTERN, with multicolored design, H PG 49, 8″, yellow amber,
OP... $100–130
TOILET WATER, with Mary Gregory-type house, 8″, amethyst, OP....$250–350
TONIC, with floral decoration, square, 10″, milk glass $110–140
VEGEDERMA, with wispy woman's bust, 7⅞″, medium green, OP.... $400–500
VENETIAN STYLE, threaded, H PG 30, 8¾″, colorless with colored strands,
OP...$200–325
WITCH HAZEL, with floral decor, square, 10″, milk glass................$110–140
WITCH HAZEL, globular body, with straight neck, 7″, milk glass, with florals,
OP... $60–90

BEER BOTTLES

Beer has long been a staple of American life, and it is believed that as early as 1587 a brewery was established in Roanoke, Virginia. This early beer was sold and transported in wooden barrels, and it was not until the mid-18th century that advertising references were made to bottled beer. Though it is unclear as to which type of bottle was used in the early days, it is quite possible that free-blown globular and chestnut-type bottles were used, as well as early wine bottles.

As to where these early bottles were made, it must be remembered that up until the first quarter of the 19th century most of the bottles used in the beer and spirits industries were imported. Up until around the mid-19th century the standard beer bottle was the familiar black glass pontiled bottle, often made in a three-piece mold and rarely embossed. Around 1850, embossed bottles began to appear and were usually marked "ale" or "porter." Later in the 1860s, beer and ale bottles began to be embossed with breweries' names, a practice which has continued into the 20th century.

During the late 19th century, there were many different shapes, colors, and closure styles used, including "torpedo"-shaped bottles and beer bottles in shades of cobalt blue and green. Around this time, the lightning stopper was developed, which was a convenient way of sealing and resealing blob top bottles. The reader is referred to *American Bottles and Flasks and Their Ancestry* by McKearin and Wilson, pgs. 229–232.

ADAM BEZ, LOUISVILLE, KY, 9″, amber.......................................$25–35
AUDUBON BOTTLING CO, crown top, colorless..................................$1–2
BAY BOTTLING CO, SAN FRANCISCO, CAL, pt. $40–50
BINDERS, RENOVO, PA, crown top, amber.......................................$1–2
BOARDMAN, sapphire blue, IP...$50–75

Beer, ca. 1860, three-piece mold.
PHOTO COURTESY OF NEIL GROSSMAN.

BRECKENFELDER & JOCHEM, OAKLAND, CAL, pt. $20–25
BUFFALO BREWING CO, SF AGENCY, "BBCo" mono., qt. $200–300
BUFFALO BREWING CO, SF AGENCY, "BBCo" mono., pt. $140–180
BURR & WATERS CELEBRATED ALE, deep yellow amber, IP, large lip chip ......
....$180–250
CAL BOTTLING CO, JOHN WIELAND EXPORT BEER, SF, ½ pt. $70–85
CAL BOTTLING CO, JOHN WIELAND EXPORT BEER, pt. $50–70
CALIFORNIA BOTTLING WORKS, T BLAUTH, qt. $38–48
CASCADE BOTTLING CO, PEREIRA BROS, SANTA CLARA, CAL, pt.........$25–30
CHAMPION P&C SCOTCH ALE, blob top, golden amber $240–280
CJ VATH & CO, SAN JOSE, qt. $9–12
CJ VATH & CO, SAN JOSE, pt. $7–10
COLUSA BOTTLING WORKS, T ROCHE, COLUSA, CAL, qt. ....:........$40–55
COLUSA BOTTLING WORKS, T ROCHE, COLUSA, CAL, pt. $30–37
COOPER & CONGER ST LOUIS ALE BREWERY, 9⅜", yellow olive $300–400
COWLEY CO, FLEMINGTON, NJ, blob top, aqua................................ $8–12
CREAM ALE A TEMPLETON LOUISVILLE, 9", amber $50–75
D DAVIS, 12-sided, 10", cobalt blue, lip repair $900–1200
D MEINKE, SAN FRANCISCO, qt. $30–35
DH EVANS NO 211 MAIN ST ST LOUIS, 9¾", black, three-piece mold, OP ......
.... $75–100
DOTTERWEICH BEER CO, OLEAN, NY, 9½", light amber $4–5
DOTTERWEICH BOTTLING CO, NY, blob top, colorless.........................$5–7
DR. BROWNS LEMON BEER, stoneware, 9¾", gray body with blue letters........
....$110–160
DR CRONK C, stoneware, 9⅜", yellow olive...................................$20–24
DR CRONK GIBBONS & CO SUPERIOR ALE, deep green, IP............. $600–850
DR CRONK GIBBONS & CO SUPERIOR ALE, green, IP $150–200
DR CRONK RMC C, 12-sided, 10", cobalt blue, IP.................. $2400–3400
DR CRONK, stoneware, 7¼", grayish glaze $50–65
DUBOIS, DB (ON BASE), crown top, light green, BIMAL $1–2
DUHME & MEYER, 115 CHRISTOPHER ST, NEW YORK, qt. $50–65
E TOUSLEY CRONKS BEER, 12-sided, 10", cobalt blue, major repair.. $300–400
EM KEANE XXX ALE, 9¹⁄₁₆", deep blue..................................$450–650
ENTERPRISE BREWING CO, SF CAL, "EBCo" mono., qt. $8–11
ENTERPRISE BREWING CO, SF CAL, qt. $7–10
ENTERPRISE BREWING CO, SF, CAL, "EBCo" mono., qt. $25–34
ERIE BOTTLING CO, ERIE, PA, blob top, lady's leg, amber $18–25
EUGENE KLEMT, PHILA, blob top, colorless.....................................$4–6
F WOLF, NEW YORK CITY, blob top, sun-colored amethyst $13–18
FISHKILL WINE & LIQUOR STORE, FISHKILL, NY, blob top, aqua $24–32
FO BRANDT, HEALDSBURG, qt. $18–25
FO BRANDT, HEALDSBURG, CAL, qt. $20–30
FREDERICKSBURG BOTTLING CO, SF, CAL, "FBCo" mono., pt. $75–100
FREDERICKSBURG BREWERY, PROPERTY OF, CAL, 11¼", red amber $10–14
FREDERICKSBURG PROPERTY OF BREWERY SAN JOSE, CAL, miniature... $90–130
G WOBORN, OAK HILL, NY, amber, blob top..................................$4–5
GAMBRINUS BOTTLING CO, SAN FRAN, CAL, with "GBCo" mono., pt. $30–37
GEO BURRILL, squat cylinder, ½ pt., dark golden amber, IP $350–450
GEORGE OTTO, PHILADELPHIA, PA, blob top, aqua $8–12
GOLD EDGE BOTTLING WORKS, JF DEININGER, VALLEJO, pt. $30–35

GOLD EDGE BOTTLING WORKS, JF DEININGER, VALLEJO, qt. $36–42
GOLD MEDAL AGENCY, C MAURER, SAN JOSE, CAL, ½ pt. $75–100
GRACE BROS BREWING CO, SANTA ROSA, CAL, qt. with "GBCo" mono. ....
....$40–50
GRACE BROS BREWING CO, SANTA ROSA, CAL, pt., with "GBCo" mono. ....
....$30–36
H DENHALTER & SON SALT LAKE CITY, aqua, Hutchinson.................$35–45
HANSEN & KAHLER, OAKLAND, CAL, qt. $9–13
HENRY C MEYER, SAN FRANCISCO, CAL, pt. $20–25
HHP, 12-sided, 9¾″, cobalt blue, ¼″ crack $500–750
HONOLULU B&M CO LTD, aqua...$15–20
JBG, 12-sided, 10″, cobalt blue, IP $1500–2000
JF ZIMMER, GLOUCESTER CITY, NJ, blob top, colorless, 9½″, wire bail, ceramic
top $18–22
JL LEAVITT BOSTON, olive green, IP, three-piece mold $100–165
JOHANN HOFF, 7½″, dark amber..$4–5
JOHN DOOLEY GINGER BEER, ½ pt., greenish aqua, IP............. $200–250
JOHN KUHLMANN BREWING CO, ELLENVILLE, NY, blob top, aqua....... $14–18
JOHN RAPP & SON, SF, CAL, pt. $5–7
JOHN RAPP & SON, SF, CAL, qt. $10–12
JOHN RAPP & SON, SF, CAL, pt. $8–10
JOHN RAPP & SONS, SF, CAL, qt. $8–10
JOHN RYAN PHILADA XX PORTER & ALE, cobalt blue, IP................. $75–100
JOHN TONS STOCKTON CAL, with "JT" mono., qt. $50–65
JOHN TONS STOCKTON, CAL, "JT" mono., pt. $5–8
JOHN ULRICH, BROOKLYN, NY, blob top, colorless............................$4–6
JOHN WIELANDS EXPORT BEER, SF, ½ pt. $70–90
JSP, teal blue green $9–12
KIRCHNER & MANTI, OAKLAND, CAL, pt. $7–11
KOCHS, 12 oz., crown top, colorless...$1–2
L BLOCKS BOTTLES ST LOUIS, 9½″, deep olive green, three-piece mold ....
....$40–60
L POTTER & CO COMPOUND, POTTERY, 9¼″, brown glaze $140–200
M KEELEY CHICAGO ILL W MCCULLY, 10⅛″, deep amber.................$50–70
MARUSVILLE BOTTLING WORKS, CAL, pt. $40–50
MCCAFFERY BROS, SLO, qt. $8–11
MCCLURE, PEEKSKILL, NY, blob top, aqua $13–17
MOERLEINS OLD JUG LAGER KRUG BEER, pt., pottery $30–35
MOERLEINS OLD JUG LAGER KRUG BIER, qt., pottery $35–40
MORGANS BREWERY CO LTD, 9½″, green, screw top $3–5
NATIONAL LAGER BEER, "HR" mono., ½ pt., H Rohrbacher agent, Stockton,
Cal $13–18
NORTH STAR BOTTLING WORKS, TRADE MARK (STAR), qt. $35–45
OHIO BOTTLING WORKS, 122 N MAIN ST, LA, qt. $70–90
PACIFIC BOTTLING CO, SF, with "JW" mono., qt. $75–100
PB MILWAUKEE, pt..$22–28
PERKINS, TANNERVILLE, NY, blob top, sun-colored amethyst............. $12–18
PROP OF CHICAGO BREWERY, PINE ST, SF, CAL, qt. $25–34
RIZZUTO BROS, FOREST GLEN, NY, blob top, sun-colored amethyst $9–14
ROBERT PORTNER BREWING CO, medium olive green........................$35–45
ROCCO DI NUBILE, PHILA REGISTERED, paneled, blob top, sun-colored ame-
thyst $8–12

SALINAS BOTTLING CO, SALINAS, CAL, ½ pt. $30–40
SAN JOSE BOTTLING CO, C MAURER, PROP, qt. $30–35
SAN JOSE BOTTLING CO, C MAURER, pt. $18–24
SAN JOSE BOTTLING CO, C MAURER, qt. $18–24
SANTA FE BOTTLING CO, CV & CO, SF, qt. $35–42
SCHEIDT, NORRISTOWN, PA, crown top, aqua..................................$1–2
SCHWARZENBACH BREWING CO, 7¼″, colorless...............................$2–3
SEBASTOPOL BOTTLING WORKS, CAL, pt. $15–20
SH BOUGHTON ROOT PORTER, cobalt blue, IP............................$300–450
SONOMA BREWING CO, SONOMA, CAL, "SBCo" mono., qt. $37–47
ST HELENA BOTTLING & COLD STORAGE, ST HELENA, CAL, qt. $25–33
ST LOUIS BOTTLING CO McC & B, VALLEP, CAL, qt. $30–36
ST LOUIS BOTTLING CO McC & B, VALLEP, CAL, pt. $22–27
STANDARD SF BOTTLING CO, qt. $30–42
STANDARD SF BOTTLING CO, pt. $25–32
SWAN BREWERY CO, ½ pt., yellow olive, base chip.......................$75–100
T BLAKELY, KNAPPS CREEK, NY, aqua, blob top $9–12
T&R BOTTLING CO, CAMDEN, NJ, blob top, sun-colored amethyst.......$16–19
THEO GIER CO OAKLAND & SAN FRANCISCO, picnic flask...............$100–150
UNEMBOSSED, blob top, honey amber...$9–12
US BOTTLING CO, JOHN FAUSER & CO, SF, pt. $30–35
US BOTTLING CO, JOHN FAUSER & CO, SF, qt. $30–35
US BOTTLING CO, JOHN FAUSER & CO, SF, qt. $35–45
UTICA CLUB, UTICA, NY, crown top, greenish aqua $1–2
V & S (ON BASE) LIGHTNING STOPPER, aqua, blob top.......................$5–8
W EAGLE CANAL ST NY PHILADELPHIA PORTER, medium blue green, IP ....
....$100–125
W McCULLY & CO PITTSBURGH PA (ON BASE), 10″, deep olive green, three-
piece mold $40–60
WACHER LITTLE DUTCH LAGER BEER, 7 oz., amber, painted label....... $13–17
WATSONVILLE BOTTLING WORKS, HA PETERSON, PROP, qt. $30–35
WELLSVILLE BOTTLING CO, NY, blob top, honey amber $4–6
WM M DILMORE, CAMDEN, NJ, blob top, sun-colored amethyst $9–12
WM POND & CO . . . PORTER & ALE, emerald green, IP $110–150
WUNDER BOTTLING WORKS, OAKLAND, CAL, pt. $5–8
WUNDER BOTTLING WORKS, OAKLAND, ½ pt. $30–40
YUENGLING, POTTERSVILLE, PA, crown top, colorless $1–2
ZIEGLER, SAUGERTIES, NY, blob top, aqua..................................$14–18
ZIMMER, GLOUCESTER, NJ, blob top, colorless, porcelain top $8–12

BININGER BOTTLES

Bininger and Co. ran a grocery business in New York City prior to 1830, and for over 50 years operated a thriving spirits business. The earliest spirits bottles used by Bininger and Co. were imported from England.

Over the years some of the finest figural whiskey bottles ever made were used by Bininger's, with shapes such as barrels, cannons, and urns. One can often determine the approximate date during which a particular bottle was used by checking the address imprinted on the label or embossed on the bottle. For example, the 329 Greenwich Street address was used for the period from 1852 through 1857; 17 Broad Street was used from 1859 to 1861; and 19 Broad Street was used from 1861 through 1864.

AM BININGER & CO, barrel shape, 7³⁄₄″, deep amber, OP $70–100
AM BININGER & CO, cannon figural, 12⁵⁄₈″, yellow amber, small chip at base $200–275
AM BININGER & CO, cannon shape, 12¹⁄₄″, yellow amber..............$400–450
AM BININGER & CO, cannon figural, 12¹⁄₂″, light amber $300–375
AM BININGER & CO, cannon shape, labeled, 12¹⁄₂″, medium amber.............
.... $800–1200
AM BININGER & CO, handled bottle, 8″, olive green, handle tail broken ....
.... $500–600
AM BININGER & CO, handled urn, 8⁷⁄₈″, golden amber.............. $700–1000
AM BININGER & CO, NEW YORK, gin bottle, 9¹⁄₄″, bright green, IP ....
.... $1500–2000
AM BININGER & CO NY, SUPERIOR LONDON DOCK GIN (ON LABEL), IP, 9¹⁄₄″, emerald green $1200–1600
AM BININGER & CO OLD KENTUCKY BOURBON, 9¹⁄₄″, golden amber, light inner stain $80–110
AM BININGER & CO OLD KENTUCKY RESERVE BOURBON, barrel, 9¹⁄₂″, medium amber, OP $160–200
AM BININGER & CO OLD KENTUCKY RESERVE BOURBON, barrel, 8″, medium amber, potstone crack $90–120
AM BININGER OLD LONDON DRY DOCK GIN, 9⁵⁄₈″, olive green.........$80–110
BININGERS KNICKERBOCKER, 6¹⁄₂″, yellow amber, globular handled body, OP..
.... $800–1200
BININGERS NIGHT CAP, flask, amber, OP....................................$150–200
BININGERS NIGHT CAP, whiskey flask, pt., golden amber............... $200–225
BININGERS NIGHT CAP, No 19 BROAD STREET, flask, yellow amber ...$120–150
BININGERS OLD DOMINION WHEAT TONIC, 10″, olive green, 55% label ....
.... $75–100

Bininger, regulator. PHOTO COURTESY OF NEIL GROSSMAN.

BININGERS OLD DOMINION WHEAT TONIC, olive green......................$60–70
BININGERS OLD KENTUCKY BOURBON, 19 BROAD ST, 9¾″, square, olive green
.... $125–170
BININGERS OLD TIMES FAMILY RYE, 9½″, yellow green $300–400
BININGERS PEEP O' DAY, flask, medium amber............................. $75–100
BININGERS PEEP O' DAY, flask shape, pt., yellow amber $180–220
BININGERS REGULATOR, clock figural, 5¾″, yellow amber, OP, inner lip flake
.... $175–225
BININGERS REGULATOR, clock shape, pt., deep golden amber, OP $280–320
BININGERS REGULATOR, clock shape, 6″, honey amber, OP, inner lip flake.....
.... $175–225
BININGERS REGULATOR, clock shape, 5¾″, aqua, OP $600–800
BININGERS TRAVELERS GUIDE, teardrop shape, 6½″, amber........... $200–300
DISTILLED IN 1848 OLD KENTUCKY 1849 RESERVE BOURBON, barrel, 8″, amber,
OP... $90–120
OLD KENTUCKY RESERVE BOURBON, barrel, 9¾″, yellow amber, OP $125–150
OLD KENTUCKY RESERVE BOURBON, barrel, 7⅞″, medium amber, OP, lip.....
flake.. $90–110

BITTERS BOTTLES

One of the most highly collectible and sought-after types of bottles are the bitters bottles, of which an amazing variety of shapes, sizes, and colors were used. The term "bitters" comes from a type of medicine made from roots and herbs having a bitter and disagreeable taste, and many 17th- and 18th-century books on medicine, cooking, and drugs contain recipes for homemade bitters. In the 18th century, bitters were generally added to spring water, ale or spirits, and were intended to cure a wide assortment of maladies.

Beginning in the 1830s, embossed bitters bottles with brand names began to appear. It was around this time that the medicinal small dosage of bitters began to increase dramatically. With the growing Temperance Movement, most bitters were becoming alcoholic beverages under the guise of medicine through the addition of bitter herbs, roots, and barks. Also around this time a wide variety of figural bitters bottles, in an incredible variety of colors unequalled in any other bottle collecting category, began to appear. Collectors should become familiar with the common and unusual colors of the figural bitters, since an unusual coloration may result in one bottle being worth 50 to 100 times more than its more commonly colored twin. The reader is referred to *For Bitters Only* by Carlyn Ring, which the letters refer to below.

ACORN BITTERS, A-9, 9″, medium amber................................$250–350

African Stomach Bitters, A-15, 9½", amber $35–50
All Laxative Stomach Bitters, A-26, amber, labeled, contents..... $80–100
Allens Congress Bitters, A-29, 10⅛", aqua $150–200
Allens-Congress Bitters, A-29, 10⅛", deep aqua $125–175
Alpine Bitters, handled jug, R PG 49, 6½", bright yellow green.... $80–100
Alpine Herb Bitters, A-37, 10", orange amber.......................... $90–120
American Life Bitters, A-49, 9", deep golden amber..............$1500–2500
American Stomach Bitters, A-54, 8½", amber..........................$90–110
American Stomach Bitters Co, A-55, 10¾", medium amber $125–175
AMS2 1864 Seward & Bentley, C-222, 9⅜", deep amethyst, major repair ...
.... $90–130
AMS2 1864 Seward & Bentley, C-222, 9⅛, amber, 2" shoulder crack........
.... $120–160
AMS2 1864 Seward & Bentley, C-223, 9½", medium amber $400–600
Andrews Vegetable Jaundice, A-57, 8¼", aqua, OP............... $400–500
Angelica Bitters Or Poor Man's Tonic, A-58, aqua.................$250–350
Appetine Bitters, Geo Benz, A-78, 8", amber......................... $140–180
Aromatic Orange Stomach Bitters, A-90, 9", golden amber $350–450
Arps Stomach Bitters, clear, labeled...................................... $80–100
Arrow Orange Bitters, 4½", colorless with labels.....................$25–30
Arthurs Renovating Syrup A & A, A-23, 9⅛", medium blue green, IP .....
.... $900–1200
Atwoods Jaundice Bitters, 5¾", aqua, ABM $3–5
Atwoods-Jaundice-Bitters, A-116, 6⅛", aqua, OP $60–75
Atwoods Quinine Bitters, A-129, aqua, square $55–70
Atwoods-Vegetable/Dyspeptic, A-130, 6⅝", aqua, OP $70–90
Augauer Bitters, A-134, green, labeled $135–150
Augauer Bitters, A-134, green $85–100
Augauer Bitters, label, contents, A-134, 8", bright yellow green..... $60–80
Bakers Orange Grove Bitters, B-9, golden amber, labeled..........$250–350
Bakers Orange Grove Bitters, B-9, red puce, labeled...............$350–450
Bakers Orange Grove Bitters, B-9, 9⅜", amber $140–180
Bakers Orange Grove Bitters, B-9, 9½", apricot.....................$275–350
Bakers Orange Grove Bitters, B-9, 9¼", yellow $650–850
Barrel Shape, unembossed, 9¾", deep sapphire blue, IP........... $700–1000
Bartos Great Gun Bitters, B-32, 11", amber, cannon figural .. $3000–3500
Bavarian Bitters Hoffmeimer, B-34, 9¼", amber.....................$100–150
Bavarian Bitters, square, B-34, 9¼", olive green.......................$450–550
Beggs Dandelion Bitters, B-51, amber, BIMAL.........................$70–90
Bells Cocktail Bitters, lady's leg, B-58, 10½", amber $350–425
Bennetts Celebrated Stomach, B-73, 9", yellow amber $70–90
Bennetts Wild Cherry Bitters, B-74, 9", amber $500–600
Berkshire Bitters, Amann & Co, B-81, 9½", amber, short thin variant......
.... $800–1200
Berkshire Bitters, pig shape, B-81, 9¾", golden amber............$900–1200
Best Bitters In America, B-92, 9¾", amber, square cabin, roped corners....
.... $2000–2500
Big Bill Best Bitters, B-95, 12", amber.................................$140–165
Bismarck Bitters WH Muller, B-107, 6⅛", amber..................... $75–100
Bismarck Stomach Bitters (On Label), 9½", amber..................$125–150
Bitter Witch, 8¼", amber flask...$70–80

BLAKES ANTI-DESPEPTIC BITTERS, B-119, 7¼″, aqua, IP $1200–1500
BLAKES TONIC & DIURETIC BITTER, B-122, 9¾″, aqua.....................$25–35
BOKERS STOMACH BITTERS (ON LABEL), B-138L, 12½″, amber $50–60
BONECAMP MAAGEN (ON LABEL), B-150L, 12¼″, amber..................$35–45
BONECAMP STOMACH BITTERS (ON LABEL), B-141L, 7¾″, colorless.....$40–50
BONNICAMP/ANTEWPEN, B-160, 12¼″, amber, lady's leg $60–80
BOURBON WHISKEY BITTERS, B-171, 9¼″, strawberry amber, lip chips .$50–75
BOURBON WHISKEY BITTERS, barrel, B-171, 9¼″, puce, lip flakes $160–200
BOURBON WHISKEY BITTERS, barrel, B-171, 9″, deep amethyst $225–275
BOURBON WHISKEY BITTERS, barrel, B-171, 9¼″, puce, inner stain .. $150–175
BOURBON WHISKEY BITTERS, barrel, B-171, 9⅜″, deep red puce......$200–275
BOURBON WHISKEY BITTERS, barrel, B-171, 9⅜″, medium strawberry puce....
.... $200–250
BOURBON WHISKEY BITTERS, barrel, B-71, 9¼″, smoky puce......... $300–400
BRADYS FAMILY BITTERS, B-193, 9⅞″, olive amber.....................$200–250
BRADYS FAMILY BITTERS, B-193, 9⅝″, yellow amber....................$500–700
BRADYS FAMILY BITTERS, square, 9⅞″, olive amber $275–350
BRAND BROS CO EIGENTHUMER, B-201L, 10½″, amber....................$45–65
BROWN & DRAKE CATAWBA BITTERS, C-81, 11½″, deep puce, IP................
....$12,000–15,000
BROWN & LYONS BLOOD BITTERS, B-218, 9⅞″, amber................. $200–250
BROWNS CELEBRATED INDIAN HERB, B-223, 12¼″, bright yellow..$1200–1500
BROWNS CELEBRATED INDIAN HERB, B-223, 12″, dark chocolate amber.........
....: $700–1000
BROWNS CELEBRATED INDIAN HERB, B-223, 12″, light amber, potstone crack
.... $125–175
BROWNS CELEBRATED INDIAN HERB, B-225, 12¼″, light yellow green...........
.... $2800–3500
BROWNS CELEBRATED INDIAN HERB, B-225, 12″, yellow green.... $2500–3500
BROWNS CELEBRATED INDIAN HERB, B-226, 12″, colorless with amethyst tint..
.... $2500–3500
BROWNS CELEBRATED INDIAN HERB, B-226, 12⅜″, medium amber . $280–360
BROWNS CELEBRATED INDIAN HERB, B-226, 12⅛″, amber, lip chip .. $210–250
BROWNS CELEBRATED INDIAN HERB, B-226, 12¼″, yellow amber, small lip
chip.. $300–350
BROWNS CELEBRATED INDIAN HERB, B-226, 12⅛″, aqua $8000–12,000
BROWNS GERMAN BITTERS, B-228, amber, labeled............................$75–90
BROWNS IRON BITTERS, B-231, 8½″, yellow..................................$40–48
BROWNS IRON BITTERS, B-231, 8⅝″, amber..................................$25–40
BUHRERS GENTIAN BITTERS, B-252, 9″, medium amber $140–180
BURDOCK BLOOD BITTERS, B-262, colorless, labeled $40–45
BURDOCK BLOOD BITTERS, B-262, 8″, aqua, with labels $60–80
BURGUNDY BITTERS, B-266, 8¼″, medium amber, round............$225–275
C&C BITTERS-PR DELANY & CO, C-1, 10½″, aqua $225–260
CABIN-SHAPED, unembossed, similar to Drake's Bitters, 10⅛″, dark amber.....
....$80–110
CABIN-SHAPED, unembossed, similar to Drake's Bitters, 10″, yellow amber ....
.... $120–140
CALDWELLS HERB BITTERS, C-8, 12¼″, amber, IP.......................$140–180
CALIFORNIA FIG & HERB BITTERS, C-16, 9⅞″, yellow amber.............$25–35
CALIFORNIA FIG & HERB BITTERS, C-16, 9¾″, amber......................$30–40

CALIFORNIA FIG BITTERS, C-15, 9¾", amber..................................$25–40
CANTEEN BITTERS, C-34, 9¾", deep blue green, John Hart & Co.. $800–1000
CANTON BITTERS, C-35, 12¼", medium amber............................$300–375
CANTON BITTERS, lady's leg shape, C-35, 12", golden amber.......... $175–250
CANTON BITTERS, lady's leg, C-35, 12", amber.............................$225–275
CAPUZINER STOMACH BITTERS (ON LABEL), C-41L, 8⅝", amber $275–350
CARL MAMPE BITTERS, M-24, amber, labeled $50–70
CARMELITER BITTERS, BROOKLYN, NY, C-51, amber.................... $90–120
CARMELITER BITTERS, NEW YORK, C-54, amber, "SJ" mono. $140–160
CARONI BITTERS, amber...$4–5
CARONI BITTERS, sample, C-60, light green, BIMAL $55–70
CARPATHIAN BITTERS, C-80, 10", yellow amber $250–350
CARPATHIAN HERB BITTERS, C-62, 8⅛", amber $90–120
CATAWBA WINE BITTERS,, C-85, 9¾", deep olive amber .. $650–800
CATAWBA WINE BITTERS, C-85, 9⅜", deep red amber................... $750–900
CATAWBA WINE BITTERS, C-85, 9½", yellowish emerald green.... $1500–2000
CAVES DE H MOUQUIN ORANGE BITTERS, 4⅝", colorless, with labels and contents $25–30
CELEBRATED CATAWBA BITTERS COMPOUND, on stoneware jug, qt. $40–50
CELEBRATED CROWN BITTERS, C-93, 8⅞", amber........................ $150–180
CHARTREUSE DAMIANA BITTERS, C-132, 9⅜", yellow amber........... $120–140
CHINESE MAN FIGURAL, embossed "DK," man with moustache and pigtail, 10½", aqua, OP $3000–4000
CLARKES SARSAPARILLA BITTERS, C-154, 7⅝", aqua, OP $200–250
CLARKES SHERRY WINE BITTERS, C-162, 9¾", aqua, Rockland, ME....$40–60
CLARKES SHERRY WINE BITTERS, C-165, 8", aqua $60–80
CLARKES SHERRY WINE, ONLY 25C, C-164, 8", aqua, OP $60–80
CLARKES SHERRY WINE, ONLY 42 C, C-161, 9⅞", aqua, OP $110–125
CLARKES VEGETABLE, ONLY, 75 CTS, C-159, 11¼", aqua, OP $150–175
CLARKES VEGETABLE SHERRY WINE, C-155, 14¼", aqua, inner stain. $100–120
CLARKES VEGETABLE SHERRY WINE, C-155, aqua, 14", OP $325–425
CLARKES VEGETABLE SHERRY WINE, C-160, 11¼", aqua, smooth base ....
.... $90–120
CLARKS COMPOUND MANDRAKE, C-151, 7½", aqua $90–120
CLARKS GIANT BITTERS, C-166, 6⅞", pale green............................$50–70
CLOTWORTHYS ORIENTAL TONIC, C-176, 9¾", yellow amber........... $80–100
COGNAC BITTERS, C-187, 11⅛", olive green $750–1000
COLE BROS VEGETABLE BITTERS, C-189, 7⅝", orange amber $70–95
COLE BROS VEGETABLE BITTERS, C-189, 7⅝", pale aqua....................$40–60
COLTONS STOMACH BITTERS, 11¾", dark amber $140–180
COLUMBO PEPTIC BITTERS, C-200, 9", amber..............................$18–22
CONGRESS BITTERS, C-217, 10⅜", light greenish aqua $125–160
CONSTITUTION BITTERS, C-223, 9⅛", deep golden yellow............. $600–800
CONSTITUTION BITTERS, AMS2, C-222, 9¼", dark amethyst $1500–1800
COOLEYS ANTI DISPEPTIC OR JAUNDICE BITTERS, C-228, 6¼", aqua, OP ....
....$325–400
CORN JUICE BITTERS, 8", aqua coffin-shaped flask $450–550
CORWITZ STOMACH BITTERS, C-236, 7¾", medium amber $85–110
COVERTS MODOC STOMACH BITTERS, C-241, 8¾", amber.............. $200–225
CURTIS & PERKINS WILD CHERRY, C-262, 6⅞", aqua, OP $100–125
CURTIS CORDIAL CALISAYA, C-261, 11½", olive yellow.............. $3000–4000

CURTIS CORDIAL CALISAYA BITTERS, C-261, 11¾", yellow amber $550–750
CW ABBOTT BITTERS, amber...$4–5
DAMIANA BITTERS, D-4, 11¾", aqua $15–20
DAMIANA BITTERS, D-5, aqua $60–70
DAVIS' KIDNEY & LIVER BITTERS, D-28, 10⅛", medium amber $125–175
DE WITTS STOMACH BITTERS, D-64, 9⅜", yellow amber, 95% label .. $90–120
DEKYPERS ORANGE BITTERS, NY, D-40, green, labeled $60–70
DEWITTS STOMACH BITTERS, D-66, 7½", dark amber flask................$60–85
DEWITTS STOMACH BITTERS, D-66, 7½", medium amber flask $75–100
DEWITTS STOMACH BITTERS, CHICAGO, D-66, 7¾", amber..............$90–120
DEWITTS STOMACH BITTERS, CHICAGO, D-64, 9¼", amber.............$30–40
DIAMOND STOMACH BITTERS, D-69, 9⅞", medium amber $140–180
DIAMONDS BLOOD BITTERS, D-70, 7½", amber........................ $180–210
DIGESTINE BITTERS, D-73, amber $350–450
DIMMITTS 50 CTS BITTERS, D-75, 6½", amber flask $200–250
DITTMARS STOMACH BITTERS, D-78, 10¼", deep olive green.......... $300–400
DOTY & CO, D-86L, 8½", yellow amber, 75% label $80–100
DOYLES (UPSIDE DOWN) HOP BITTERS, D-95, 9½", amber............ $250–300
DOYLES HOP BITTERS (IN AN ARCH) 1872, D-94, 70% label, 10", amber.......
.... $80–120
DOYLES HOP BITTERS, 1872, D-93, 9¾", bright yellow with olive tone ....
.... $225–300
DOYLES HOP BITTERS, 1872, D-93, 9½", medium amber, original label ....
....$40–60
DOYLES HOP BITTERS, 1872, D-93, 9⅝", amber $18–22
DOYLES HOP BITTERS, 1872, D-94, 9⅞", amber $100–140
DR BALLS VEGETABLE STOMACHIC, B-14, 6¾", aqua, OP............... $90–120
DR BEARDS ALTERNATIVE TONIC, B-41, 8⅞", aqua......................$60–75
DR BELLS BLOOD PURIFYING BITTERS, B-56, 9⅝", amber.............. $90–120
DR BELLS GOLDEN TONIC BITTERS, bell shape, 9¾", deep red amber, IP.......
.... $4000–5000
DR BELLS GREAT ENGLISH REMEDY, B-56, 9⅝", amber.................. $80–100
DR BELLS LIVER & KIDNEY BITTERS, B-61, 9", deep aqua $175–225
DR BISHOPS WAHOO BITTERS, B-103, 10", medium amber $300–400
DR BLAKES AROMATIC BITTERS NEW YORK, B-120, 7⅜", aqua, OP ..$275–300
DR BLAKES AROMATIC BITTERS, B-120, 7⅜", deep aqua, OP $200–300
DR BOYCES TONIC BITTERS, 7½", aqua.....................................$40–50
DR CALDWELLS HERB BITTERS, C-9, 12⅜", amber......................$160–200
DR CAMPBELLS SCOTCH BITTERS, C-31, 6¼", amber $200–250
DR CD WARNER . . . GERMAN HOP BITTERS, 9⅞", honey amber $275–350
DR CDE WARNERS GERMAN HOP BITTERS, W-32, 9⅞", medium amber.........
.... $75–100
DR CW ROBACKS STOMACH BITTERS, barrel, R-74, 9⅜", golden amber, base
bruise $75–85
DR CW ROBACKS STOMACH BITTERS, barrel, R-73, 10", amber........ $150–190
DR CW ROBACKS STOMACH BITTERS, R-73, 10", yellow with amber cast, IP ...
.... $275–350
DR CW ROBACHS STOMACH BITTERS, R-73, 9⅝", deep olive green barrel.......
.... $2000–3000
DR CW ROBACKS STOMACH BITTERS, R-74, 9⅜", yellow, smooth base ....
.... $300–400

DR CW ROBACKS STOMACH BITTERS, R-75, barrel, 9¼″, dark amber $150–175
DR DE CURLYS CELEBRATED HERB BITTERS, D-37, 10″, golden amber..........
....$350–450
DR DUNLAPS ANCHOR BITTERS (ON LABEL), D-122L, 10³⁄₈″, amber $400–500
DR EP EASTMANS YELLOW DOCK BITTERS, E-14, 7⁷⁄₈″, aqua, IP......$750–850
DR F FLESCHHUTS CELEBRATED, F-54, 8¾″, deep aqua $200–300
DR FA SABINES HARVEST BITTERS, S-6, 9″, medium amber $125–175
DR FFW HOGGUERS BITTERS, H-141, 9¼″, amber $300–350
DR FISHS BITTERS, fish shape, F-44, 11¾″, amber $160–190
DR G PIERCES INDIAN RESTORATIVE, P-96, 7⁷⁄₈″, aqua, OP $130–160
DR GEO PIERCE INDIAN RESTORATIVE BITTERS, 8″, deep aqua, OP.....$80–110
DR GEO PIERCES INDIAN RESTOR. BITTERS, P-95, 7⁷⁄₈″, aqua, OP $50–70
DR HARTERS WC BITTERS, H-44, 4¾″, amber $150–180
DR HARTERS WILD CHERRY BITTERS ST LOUIS, H-50, 7⁷⁄₈″, amber......$40–50
DR HARTERS WILD CHERRY BITTERS ST LOUIS, H-47, 7³⁄₈″, amber... $100–125
DR HARTERS WILD CHERRY BITTERS, amber $35–45
DR HARTERS WILD CHERRY BITTERS, amber, miniature....................$25–35
DR HARTERS WILD CHERRY BITTERS, DAYTON, O, H-46, 8″, amber ....
.... $100–150
DR HARTERS WILD CHERRY BITTERS, H-50, 7³⁄₈″, amber................$20–30
DR HARTERS WILD CHERRY BITTERS, H-51, amber, with embossed cherries ....
.... $140–180
DR HARTERS WILD CHERRY, sample, 4″, amber $15–20
DR HENLEYS WILD GRAPE ROOT IXL, H-84, 12″, medium green.... $400–650
DR HENLEYS WILD GRAPE ROOT IXL, H-84, 12″, deep aqua ....$90–$120
DR HENLEYS WILD GRAPE ROOT IXL, H-85, 12½″, greenish aqua .. $600–900
DR HOOFLANDS GERMAN BITTERS, H-168, 7⅛″, aqua, OP $50–60
DR J HOSTETTERS STOMACH BITTERS, "WMCC & Co (on base), H-195, 8⁷⁄₈″,
light olivish green $450–550
DR J HOSTETTERS STOMACH BITTERS, H-195, 9⁵⁄₈″, deep olive green...$80–110
DR J HOSTETTERS STOMACH BITTERS, H-195, 9¼″, olive green........ $120–150
DR J HOSTETTERS STOMACH BITTERS, H-195, 9⅛″, deep amber, small base
bruise $20–30
DR J HOSTETTERS STOMACH BITTERS, H-195, 9⅛″, golden yellow $60–80
DR J HOSTETTERS STOMACH BITTERS, H-195, 9″, olive yellow with 90% label
.... $75–100
DR J HOSTETTERS STOMACH BITTERS, H-195, 8⁷⁄₈″, yellow amber, light inner
stain $40–50
DR JACOBS BITTERS, J-11, aqua, OP...$50–65
DR JOHN BULLS CEDRON BITTERS, square, 10″, dark yellow olive ... $750–900
DR JOHN BULLS COMPOUND CEDRON BITTERS, B-254, 9⁵⁄₈″, red amber, ⅛″ lip
chip...$225–275
DR JOHN BULLS COMPOUND CEDRON BITTERS, B-254, 9½″, olive green........
.... $450–550
DR KAUFMANNS SULPHUR BITTERS, aqua, labeled $30–35
DR LAMOTS BOTANIC BITTERS, L-9, 8⁵⁄₈″, medium amber $130–170
DR LANGLEYS ROOT & HERB, L-22, 6¾″, apple green....................$40–55
DR LANGLEYS ROOT & HERB BITTERS, 76 UNION STREET, L-26, 6⁷⁄₈″, light/
medium green $75–100
DR LANGLEYS ROOT & HERB BITTERS, 76 UNION STREET, L-26, 6¾″, aqua,
OP...$40–55

Dr Langleys Root & Herb Bitters, 76 Union Street, L-25, 8½", blue green $75–90

Dr Langleys Root & Herb Bitters, R-L21, 8½", medium amber .. $90–120

Dr Langleys Root & Herb Bitters, with "99" backwards, L-23, 9", aqua, IP $70–90

Dr Langleys Root & Herb Bitters, L-21, 8¾", light/medium apple green $60–80

Dr Langleys Root & Herb Bitters, L-22, 7¼", aqua $30–40

Dr Langleys Root & Herb Bitters, L-22, 7⅛", yellow amber $80–100

Dr Langleys Root & Herb Bitters, L-22, 6⅞", dark amber $70–90

Dr Langleys Root & Herb Bitters, L-24, 6¾", aqua, OP............ $60–80

Dr LG Bertrams Long Life Aromatic Life, B-91, 9½", amber, base chip $160–190

Dr Loews Celebrated Stomach, L-111, 9¼", bright yellow green $250–300

Dr Lovegoods Family Bitters, L-124, 10¼", deep gold amber .. $1000–1300

Dr Lowes Celebrated Stomach Bitters, bright medium green $200–250

Dr Mampes Herb Stomach Bitters, M-26, 6⅞", aqua $40–60

Dr Manly Hardy Genuine Jaundice Bitters, H-34, 6⅜", aqua, OP ....
....$350–450

Dr Manly Hardy Genuine Jaundice Bitters, H-35, 7¼", aqua, OP ....
....$150–200

Dr Med Kochs Universal Magen-Bitter, 8⅜", olive green $175–225

Dr Owens European Life Bitters, O-98, 7", aqua, OP, highpoint wear .....
....$100–125

Dr Petzolds Genuine German Bitters, P-77, 7", golden amber ... $75–100

Dr Petzolds Genuine German Bitters, P-78, 10½", yellow amber...........
....$90–120

Dr Petzolds German Bitters Patd 1884, P-74, 10⅜", amber $60–80

Dr Petzolds German Bitters, Patented 1884, P-74, 10⅝", medium amber $50–75

Dr Petzolds German Bitters, Patd 1884, P-76, 8", dark amber......$75–90

Dr Petzolds German Bitters, Patd 1884, P-76, 8", medium amber .$70–90

Dr Renzs Herb Bitters, R-38, 9⅞", yellow amber $125–150

Dr Renzs Herb Bitters, R-38, 9⅞", olive amber $100–120

Dr S Griggs Aromatic Bitters, G-117, 11", medium amber $175–225

Dr Sawens Life Invigorating Bitters, S-41, 10⅛", medium amber .. $35–45

Dr Sawens Life Invigorating, yellow $90–110

Dr Shepards Compound Wahoo Bitters, S-99, 7½", aqua..........$175–200

Dr Sims Anti-Constipation, S-108, 7", amber $200–250

Dr Skinners Celebrated Bitters, S-115, 8½", aqua, OP $100–125

Dr Skinners Sherry Wine Bitters, S-116, 8⅝", aqua, OP $135–175

Dr Skinners Sherry Wine Bitters, S-116, 8¾", aqua, OP $200–235

Dr Soule Hop Bitters 1872, S-147, 8¼", topaz $250–325

Dr Soules Hop Bitterine, 9½", yellow with orangish cast........... $125–175

Dr Soules Hop Bitters, S-145, 9⅜", olive amber with striations....$350–425

Dr Soules Hop Bitters, S-145, 9⅞", orange yellow, 95% back label ....
....$100–140

Dr Stephen Jewetts Celebrated, J-37, 7⁵⁄₁₆", yellow amber, OP.............
....$900–1200

Dr Stanleys South American Indian, S-174, 9", aqua, labeled....$250–325

DR STANLEYS SOUTH AMERICAN INDIAN, S-174, 8⅞″, amber $200–250

DR STEPHEN JEWETTS CELEBRATED, J-37, 7⅛″, green aqua, IP $100–150

DR STEPHEN JEWETTS CELEBRATED, J-38, 7½″, deep olive yellow, IP ....
....$1000–1500

DR STEPHEN JEWETTS CELEBRATED, J-38, 7¼″, yellow olive, IP, labeled ....
.... $900–1200

DR STOEVERS BITTERS, S-199, 9¾″, amber $140–180

DR STOUGHTONS NATIONAL BITTERS, HAMBURG, PA, S-208, 10″, medium
amber $1300–1900

DR THOS HALLS CALIFORNIA PEPSIN, H-11, 9″, medium amber $70–100

DR TOMPKINS VEGETABLE BITTERS, T-36, 8⅝″, medium green, full back label
.... $650–800

DR VAN DYKE, V-7L, 10″, colorless, with label $70–90

DR VGB SIEGERT & SONS BITTERS $4–6

DR VON HOPFS CURACO BITTERS, 9″, amber $60–70

DR WALKINSHAWS CURATIVE BITTERS, W-14, 10⅛″, amber with 90% label ....
....$275–350

DR WASHINGTONS AMERICAN LIFE BITTERS, W-53, 9¼″, amber $175–225

DR WHEELERS SHERRY WINE BITTERS, W-86, 8″, aqua $40–60

DR WHEELERS TONIC SHERRY WINE BITTERS (PAINTED ON DECANTER), 8½″,
colorless $90–110

DR WHEELERS TONIC SHERRY WINE, W-87, 9⅜″, aqua, square with roped
edges $1500–2500

DR WM TUTTS GOLDEN EAGLE, T-71, 9½″, golden amber $350–450

DR WONSERS BITTERS, W-145, 9″, deep aqua $550–650

DR WONSERS USA INDIAN ROOT, W-146, 11″, deep amber, round, fluted
shoulders $1500–2500

DR WOODS SARSAPARILLA AND WILD CHERRY BITTERS, W-151, 8¾″, aqua,
OP.. $200–250

DR XX LOVEGOODS FAMILY BITTERS, L-125, 9½″, amber $700–850

DRAKES 1860 PLANTATION X BITTERS, D-105, 9⅞″, medium bluish green ......
.... $3000–4000

DRAKES PLANTATION BITTERS, D-102, 9⅞″, medium puce, arabesque motif....
....$175–225

DRAKES PLANTATION BITTERS, D-103, no "x," 10⅛″, yellow amber, six-log
....$100–125

DRAKES PLANTATION BITTERS, D-104, 10⅛″, medium amber, four label panels
....$150–200

Bitters, Drake's Plantation cabin.
PHOTO COURTESY OF NEIL GROSSMAN.

DRAKES PLANTATION BITTERS, D-105, 9⅞", yellow amber $70–90
DRAKES PLANTATION BITTERS, D-105, 9¾", medium puce, six-log.... $80–100
DRAKES PLANTATION BITTERS, D-105, 10", medium puce, six-log $70–90
DRAKES PLANTATION BITTERS, D-105, 10⅛", amber, light stain, six-log.........
....$40–50
DRAKES PLANTATION BITTERS, D-105, 9⅞", deep yellow olive, six-log ....
....$175–225
DRAKES PLANTATION BITTERS, D-105, 9⅞", greenish yellow $300–400
DRAKES PLANTATION BITTERS, D-105, 10", medium amber, six-log $50–70
DRAKES PLANTATION BITTERS, D-105, 9⅞", medium apricot puce, six-log......
.... $80–100
DRAKES PLANTATION BITTERS, D-105, 10⅛", orange puce at top, red puce at
base $110–150
DRAKES PLANTATION BITTERS, D-105, 10⅛", medium amber, double collar lip
....$80–95
DRAKES PLANTATION BITTERS, D-108, 9⅞", medium strawberry puce, six-log
....$110–140
DRAKES PLANTATION BITTERS, D-108, 9¾", dark red amber, six-log...$80–110
DRAKES PLANTATION BITTERS, D-108, 10", apricot puce, light stain, base flake
....$30–40
DRAKES PLANTATION BITTERS, D-108, 10", bright green with olive tint ....
.... $2000–2500
DRAKES PLANTATION BITTERS, D-108, 9⅞", yellow with olive tone, six-log ,...
.... $200–250
DRAKES PLANTATION BITTERS, D-109, 9¾", medium amber, five-log ....
.... $200–250
DRAKES PLANTATION BITTERS, D-110, 10⅛", amber, four-log.............$40–60
DRAKES PLANTATION BITTERS, D-110, 10¼", medium amber, 90% label ....
.... $125–160
DRAKES PLANTATION BITTERS, D-105, labeled, orange amber $75–90
DRAKES PLANTATION, D-105, 9⅞", puce, six-log...........................$70–90
E DEXTER LOVERIDGE WAHOO BITTERS, L-126, 9⅞", amber, labeled ....
.... $475–575
E DEXTER LOVERIDGE WAHOO BITTERS, L-126, 10⅛", yellow amber, panel
crack, labeled $300–375
E DEXTER LOVERIDGE WAHOO BITTERS, L-126, 9¾", yellow amber, small lip
chip.. $300–400
E DEXTER LOVERIDGE WAHOO BITTERS, L-126, 9⅞", deep amethyst.............
.... $3000–5000
EAGLE ANGOSTURA BARK BITTERS, E-2, 7", amber $60–80
EDGARS ENGLISH LIFE, E-18, 8½", amber $350–400
ELECTRIC BITTERS, amber, labeled, ABM $30–35
ERSO BITTERS, GAINES, PENN, E-49, aqua, labeled........................ $60–80
EXCELSIOR HERB BITTERS, E-65, 10¼", amber................................$275–350
EXCELSIOR HERB BITTERS, E-65, 10¼", medium amber................. $200–300
F BROWN BOSTON SARSAPARILLA, S-36, 9⅛", aqua, OP $90–120
FAVORITE BITTERS, POWELL & STUTEN ROTH, F-6, 9⅛", amber barrel ....
.... $6000–9000
FERRO QUINA STOMACH BITTERS, F-40, 9", amber...................... $100–130
FISCH BITTERS, F-45, 11½", amber, base chip, fish figural $100–125
FISCH BITTERS, F-45, 11½, orange amber, fish figural $140–170

FISCH BITTERS, F-46, 11⅝″, colorless, fish figural $500–700
FISCH BITTERS, F-46, 11¾″, amber, fish figural $125–145
FISH BITTERS, F-46, 11⅝″, bright yellow green....................... $1200–1500
FISH BITTERS, F-46, 11¼″, deep cobalt blue $5000–7000
FISH BITTERS, F-46, 11⅝″, lime green................................ $3500–4500
FISH BITTERS, F-46, 11⅝″, dark chocolate amber $350–550
FITZPATRICKS 50 CENT STOMACH BITTERS, 7¾″, aqua................... $225–275
FOURNIERS COCKTAIL BITTERS, 3¾″, colorless, with labels and contents........
....$20–25
FRANKLIN BITTERS (ON LABEL), F-80L, 9⅝″, amber, OP $300–500
FRANKS PANACEA BITTERS, F-79, 10¼″, golden amber............... $1000–1500
FRANKS PANACEA BITTERS, F-79, 10″, dark amber $1100–1400
FRANKS-PANACEA BITTERS, F-79, 10⅛″, yellow amber $800–1100
FRAZIERS ROOT BITTERS, F-83, aqua $140–180
GATES & CO LIFE OF MAN BITTERS, G-7, 8¼″, medium sapphire blue,
labeled $300–400
GATES BITTERS, G-7, aqua, labeled $80–100
GATES LIFE OF MAN BITTERS, aqua $55–70
GENTIANA ROOT AND HERB BITTERS, G-11, 10″, aqua $200–225
GENUINE BLACK WALNUT BITTERS, G-14, 7¾″, colorless $140–180
GENUINE OLD FASHIONED BITTERS, 5¾″, colorless, with label and contents
....$20–25
GERMAN BALSAM BITTERS, G-18, 8⅞″, opaque white.................. $300–400
GERMAN HOP BITTERS 1872, G-24, 9⅝″, amber, partial label and contents.....
....$50–75
GERMAN HOP BITTERS 1880, G-22, 10″, yellow amber $240–280
GERMAN TONIC BITTERS, G-28, 9¾″, aqua, IP $550–675
GILBERTS SARSAPARILLA BITTERS, G-42, 8⅝″, amber $250–300
GLOBE BITTERS, G-47, 10¾″, yellow amber bell or cannon form..... $500–800
GLOBE TONIC BITTERS, G-49, 9¾″, light amber $70–90
GLOBE TONIC BITTERS, G-49, 9¾″, medium amber...................... $80–110
GOLD LION CELERY BITTERS, 6″, colorless, label $20–25
GOLDEN BITTERS, G-63, 10⅛″, aqua.. $325–400
GOLDEN SEAL BITTERS, G-64, 9″, medium amber, 95% label $500–600
GRAVES & SONS TONIC BITTERS, G-96, 10″, aqua $325–400
GREAT WESTERN TONIC BITTERS, G-100, 9⅛″, amber, 85% front and back
labels.. $250–350

Bitters, Greeley's. PHOTO COURTESY OF NEIL GROSSMAN.

GREELEYS BOURBON BITTERS, G-101, 9″, puce amber, barrel $160–190
GREELEYS BOURBON BITTERS, G-101, 9¼″, puce amber, panel chip, barrel .....
....$120–140
GREELEYS BOURBON BITTERS, G-101, 9¼″, gray copper, lip flake, barrel ....
....$110–140
GREELEYS BOURBON BITTERS, G-101, 9½″, smoky amber, barrel $150–200
GREELEYS BOURBON BITTERS, G-101, 9¼″, medium olive green, barrel ....
....$500–600
GREELEYS BOURBON BITTERS, G-101, 9⅛″, amber, barrel $160–180
GREELEYS BOURBON BITTERS, G-101, 9¼″, medium pinkish puce, barrel ....
....$350–450
GREELEYS BOURBON BITTERS, G-101, 9¼″, olive green, barrel $425–550
GREELEYS BOURBON BITTERS, G-101, 9½″, light smoky amber, rib crack, barrel..$40–55
GREELEYS BOURBON BITTERS, G-101, 9½″, smoky gray, barrel........ $140–180
GREELEYS BOURBON BITTERS, G-102, 9⅜″, medium puce, light stain, barrel
....$250–280
GREELEYS BOURBON WHISKEY, G-102, 9⅜″, aqua, barrel............$1200–1500
GREELEYS BOURBON WHISKEY, G-102, 9⅛″, deep puce, large lip chip, barrel
.... $60–80
GREELEYS BOURBON WHISKEY, G-102, barrel, 9¼″, medium copper, lip flake
.... $140–175
GREELEYS BOURBON WHISKEY, G-102, 9½″, puce, barrel.............. $225–300
GREELEYS BOURBON WHISKEY, G-102, 9¼″, light red puce, barrel .. $350–400
GREEN MOUNTAIN CIDER BITTERS, G-103, aqua $160–200
GREERS ECLIPSE BITTERS, G-110, yellow amber $126–165
GREERS ECLIPSE BITTERS, G-111, amber $60–90
GW DAYS STOMACH BITTERS, 9½″ × 3″ × 3″, aqua.................. $600–850
H KANTOROWICZ BERLIN, square, 9″, amber......................$100–130
H KANTOROWICZ COMPANY, HAMBURG, 8⅞″, milk glass $40–50
H KANTOROWICZ COMPANY, NEW YORK, 9″, milk glass...................$50–70
H&K STOMACH TONIC BITTERS, square, 8¾″, amber $150–200
HAGANS BITTERS, triangular, H-5, 9¾″, amber $250–350
HALLS BITTERS, H-9, 9½″, medium amber with puce tint $1800–2500
HALLS BITTERS, barrel, H-10, 9⅛″, yellow with olive overtones $350–450
HALLS BITTERS, barrel, H-10, 9¼″, light amber, light inner stain..... $100–140
HALLS BITTERS, barrel, H-10, 9¼″, orange amber $140–180
HARTLEYS PERUVIAN BARK BITTERS, H-55, 9⅛″, yellow amber, 85% original label... $200–250
HARTS STAR BITTERS, H-58, 8⅜″, aqua $400–550
HARTS VIRGINIA AROMATIC, 7¾″, olive green, IP.................... $3000–4500
HARTWIG KANTOROWICZ NACHFLO., 9⅜″, milk glass $60–90
HARTWIG KANTOROWICZ NACHFLO, 10″, opaque white...................$50–60
HARTWIG KANTOROWICZ, 3¾″, milk glass............................... $100–135
HARTWIG KANTOROWICZ, L-106L, 9⅜″, milk glass........................$35–50
HARTWIG KANTOROWICZ, POSEN, L-106L, 9½″, milk glass, labeled .. $80–100
HELLMANNS CONGRESS BITTERS, H-79, 12″, amber......................$175–225
HENRY C WEAVER MEXICAN BITTERS, ''ASF5'' on shoulder, rectangular, 9⅜″, gold amber $1200–1600
HENTZS CURATIVE BITTERS, sample, aqua...............................$30–40
HERTRICHS GESUNDHEITS BITTER, H-104, 12″, yellow green........$1500–2500

HIBERNIA BITTERS, H-112, 9¾", amber $90–120
HIERAPICRA BITTERS EXTRACT, H-116, 9⅝", deep aqua $150–200
HIGBY TONIC BITTERS, T-40, 9½", amber $45–55
HIGHLAND BITTERS, barrel shape, H-117, 9¾", deep amber............ $280–320
HOFFELDS LIVER BITTERS, H-132, 9¾", amber $400–500
HOLLOWAYS AROMATIC BITTERS, H-150L, labeled, 11⅜", amber, with label ....
.... $25–35
HOLTZERMANNS BITTERS, H-154, amber, labeled $240–280
HOLTZERMANNS PATENT STOMACH BITTERS, PIQUA, 9¼", dark amber ....
.... $225–300
HOLTZERMANNS PATENT STOMACH, H-155, cabin-shaped, 9½", amber, label
.... $800–1000
HOLTZERMANNS PATENT STOMACH, H-154, 9⅞", medium amber, 100% label
.... $250–300
HOLTZERMANNS PATENT STOMACH, H-155, 9¾", bright golden amber ....
.... $600–750
HOLTZERMANNS PATENT STOMACH, H-155, 9¼", medium amber $600–750
HOLTZERMANNS PATENT STOMACH, H-155, 9¼", golden amber $500–550
HOLTZERMANNS STOMACH BITTERS ESTAB 1836, 4¹/₁₆", amber, labeled...........
.... $300–400
HOLTZERMANNS STOMACH BITTERS, H-154, 9¾", amber................ $150–200
HOLTZERMANNS STOMACH BITTERS, round, ring, PG 246, colorless bar bottle,
11¼" $225–250
HOME RULE, 9⅜", amber $50–75
HOME STOMACH BITTERS, H-162, 8½", golden amber $50–60
HOME FH GRAU BUFFALO NY, H-164L, 9½", amber, labeled........... $60–90
HOP BITTERS CO, G-45, 9½", aqua $225–275
HOP TONIC BITTERS, H-174, 9¼", amber.................................... $80–110
HOPKINS BITTERS, lady's leg, H-177, 12¼", amber...................... $400–550
HOPKINS UNION STOMACH BITTERS, H-178, 9¾", yellow green $250–350
HOPS & MALT BITTERS, H-186, 9¾", medium amber $100–140
HOSTETTERS BITTERS, light olive green, blob top......................... $400–500
HP HERB WILD CHERRY BITTERS, H-93, 10", golden amber, light stain ....
.... $100–125
HP HERB WILD CHERRY BITTERS, H-93, 10⅛", yellow amber........ $350–400
HP HERB WILD CHERRY BITTERS, H-93, 10⅛", medium amber...... $225–300
HP HERB WILD CHERRY BITTERS, H-94, 8¾", bright Seven-Up green, labeled
cabin $3000–4500
HP HERB WILD CHERRY BITTERS, H-94, 8⅞", medium amber $375–475
HURLEYS STOMACH BITTERS, H-214, 10½", medium yellow amber....$500–750
HUTCHINGS DYSPEPSIA BITTERS, H-218, aqua, OP, 2" base crack........$40–50
HUTCHINGS DYSPEPSIA BITTERS, H-218, 8½", aqua, IP, 110X $120–140
HUTCHINGS DYSPEPSIA BITTERS, H-218, 8⅜", aqua, IP $250–300
HVS ASPARAGUS STOMACH BITTERS (ON LABEL), 8⅝", amber, Wait's Wild
Cherry Tonic $350–450
INDIAN VEGETABLE, GEO GOODWIN, I-125, 8½", greenish aqua, OP.$350–450
IRON AND QUININE BITTERS, BURLINGTON, VT, labeled................... $50–60
J&W NICHOLSON & CO ORANGE, 4⅝", colorless, with label $25–30
JACKSONS AROMATIC LIFE BITTERS, J-4, 9", olive green $800–1000
JC & CO, pineapple figural, P-100, 8¾", golden amber, OP........... $275–400
JC & CO, pineapple figural, P-100, 8½", deep amber, OP $300–450

J.C. & Co., pineapple shape, P-100, 8¾", deep amber, OP $300–400

JEWEL BITTERS, A FORTLOUIS & CO, J-35, 9¾", medium amber ... $900–1200

JEWEL BITTERS, JOHN BOWMAN & CO, J-34, 9¾", amber $450–550

JOHN MOFFAT PRICE 1.00, M-112, 5⅜", olive yellow $300–400

JOHN MOFFAT PRICE 1.00, M-112, 5½", aqua, OP $60–70

JOHN P FIXMER STOMACH BITTERS, 8¾", colorless $60–80

JOHN ROOTS BITTERS, R-90, 9½", deep aqua $2500–3500

JOHN ROOTS BITTERS, 1834, R-90.43, 10¼", medium blue green $650–850

JOHN ROOTS BITTERS 1834, R-90.4, 10⅛", medium amber $500–600

JOHN ROOTS BITTERS 1834, R-90.4, 10", yellow amber, base crack .. $125–175

JOHN ROOTS BITTERS 1834, R-90.4, 10¼", emerald green $600–900

JOHN ROOTS BITTERS 1834, R-90.4, 10⅛", blue green $600–900

JOHN ROOTS BITTERS 1834, R-90.4, 10¼", aqua $250–300

JOHN ROOTS BITTERS 1867, R-90.8, 9¾", medium amber $600–850

JOHNSONS CALISAYA BITTERS, J-45, 10⅛", yellow amber $55–75

JOHNSONS INDIAN DYSPEPTIC, J-46, 6¾", aqua, OP $300–400

JONES INDIAN SPECIFIC HERB, J-51, 9⅛", amber $800–1000

JW COLTONS NERVINE STRENGTHENING BITTERS, amber $25–30

KAGYS SUPERIOR STOMACH BITTERS, K-3, 9½", dark amber $140–180

KAISER WILHELM BITTERS, K-5, 10⅛", amber $35–40

KAISER WILHELM BITTERS, K-5, 10⅛", colorless $25–35

KALAMAZOO BITTERS (ON LABEL), K-7L, 9", colorless $40–50

KAPUZINER KLOSTER BITTERS (ON LABEL), K-10, 7⅝", no embossing, amber
.... $80–100

KASKARETA BITTERS, COOKSHIRE, K-13, in box, unopened $80–100

KELLYS OLD CABIN BITTERS, K-21, 9⅛", yellow amber, cabin figural ....
.... $700–1000

KELLYS OLD CABIN BITTERS, K-21, 9⅛", dark olive green, cabin figural ....
.... $3500–5000

KELLYS OLD CABIN BITTERS, K-22, 9⅜", amber $650–775

KELLYS OLD CABIN BITTERS, cabin, K-21, 9⅛", golden amber $500–650

KELLYS OLD CABIN BITTERS, cabin, K-22, 9½", red amber, inner and outer
stain, chip $200–250

KELLYS/OLD CABIN/BITTERS, cabin, K-21, 9⅛", golden amber, ¼" potstone
crack $300–375

KEYSTONE BITTERS, barrel, K-36, 10¼", amber $250–300

KEYSTONE BITTERS, barrel shape, K-36, 9¾", golden amber $200–300

KIMBALLS JAUNDICE BITTERS, K-42, 7", olive amber, IP $250–325

KING SOLOMONS BITTERS, K-49, 8⅜", amber $60–80

KING SOLOMONS BITTERS, K-50, 7½", amber $60–90

KINGS 25 CENT BITTERS, K-56, 6¾", aqua $125–175

KOEHLER & HEINRICHS RED STAR, R-25, 11¼", amber $200–250

KREINBROOKS BITTERS, K-78, 8¼", amber $150–200

LACOURS BITTERS, L-3, 9½", deep gold amber $400–450

LACOURS BITTERS, L-3, 9⅛", amber, inner stain $350–450

LACOURS BITTERS-SARSAPARIPHERE, L-3, 9", amber $400–500

LACOURS BITTERS SARSAPARIPHERE, L-3, 9⅜", yellow amber $650–800

LADY'S LEG, unembossed, 12", olive green $40–55

LANDSBERGS CENTURY BITTERS, L-134, 11¼", medium amber $1600–2200

LANGENBACHS STOMACH BITTERS, 4½", aqua, labels $30–35

LASH KIDNEY & LIVER BITTERS, L-38, 9", red puce $70–90

LASHS BITTERS, L-32, amber, labeled $30–35
LASHS BITTERS, back bar bottle, L-41, honey amber $55–70
LASHS BITTERS CO, amber, cylinder $12–15
LASHS BITTERS NATURAL LAXATIVE, L-33, 4¾″, amber, sample bottle .$35–45
LASHS BITTERS NATURAL TONIC LAXATIVE, amber, miniature $35–45
LASHS BITTERS NATURAL TONIC LAXATIVE, yellow amber, miniature $40–50
LEAKS KIDNEY & LIVER BITTERS, L-53, 9¾″, amber.....................$60–80
LEDIARDS CELEBRATED STOMACH, L-60, 10⅛″, deep blue green $350–450
LEGENDRE ORANGE BITTERS, 5¾″, colorless, with label and contents...$25–30
LEROUX COCKTAIL BITTERS, 4¾″, colorless with labels and contents ...$25–30
LIPPMANS GREAT GERMAN BITTERS, L-99, amber........................ $300–400
LITTHAUER STOMACH BITTERS, L-101, 9½″, colorless $110–140
LITTHAUER STOMACH BITTERS, L-102, 9½″, milk glass, Berlin......... $80–100
LOEWS STOMACH BITTERS, THE HG CHRISTY CO, 9¼″, yellow green, 95%
label... $400–500
LOHENGRIN BITTERS, L-117, 9⅛″, milk glass $150–200
LOVERIDGES WAHOO BITTERS, stoneware jug, 10¾″ $750–900
LUTZS GERMAN STOMACH, L-134L, 7¾″, amber, label under glass.. $800–900
MACKS SARSAPARILLA BITTERS, M-4, 9⅜″, medium amber.............$350–450
MAKEEVERS ARMY BITTERS, M-58, 10½″, amber.....................$1500–2500
MALABAC BITTERS, lady's leg, M-13, 11¾″, yellow amber.............$225–275
MANNS ORIENTAL, PROFESSOR BE, M-29, 10″, amber $375–450
MARKS KIDNEY & LIVER BITTERS, M-39, 9½″, amber $18–23
MARSHALLS BITTERS, M-40, 8¾″, amber, small corner base chip........$30–40
MARSHALLS BITTERS, M-40, 8⅞″, amber $40–60
MCKELVYS STOMACH BITTERS, M-59, 8⅞″, aqua.........................$250–350
MILBURNS KOLA BITTERS, M-81, 9½″, amber...........................$250–350
MISHLERS HERB BITTERS, M-100, 9″, amber, light stain...................$30–35
MISHLERS HERB BITTERS, DR BS HARTMAN, M-101, amber $35–45
MISHLERS HERB BITTERS, M-99, golden yellow $120–150
MISHLERS HERB BITTERS, DR HARTMAN, M-99, 8⅝″, orange yellow ...$50–70
MISHLERS HERB BITTERS, DR HARTMAN, M-99, 8¾″, yellow olive... $170–210
MORNING BITTERS, M-135, 13″, amber.....................................$125–175
MORNING INCEPTUM BITTERS, M-134, 10⅞″, aqua......................$325–400
MORNING STAR, M-135, 12⅝″, yellow amber, IP $150–175
MORNING STAR BITTERS, medium light amber, IP $200–260
MORNING STAR BITTERS, medium light amber, IP, spotty haze $180–235
MOULTONS OLOROSA BITTERS, M-145, 11⅜″, aqua, applied ring lip. $200–250
MOUNTAIN HERB & ROOT BITTERS, M-150, 9½″, deep golden amber $250–300
NAPOLEON BITTERS 1866, 10¼″ × 3⅝″, emerald green.............$1500–2500
NAPOLEON BITTERS 1866, N-2, 10″, deep puce, major cracks..........$250–350
NAPOLEON COCKTAIL, DINGENS, N-3, 10″, yellow amber, IP...... $2300–2800
NAPOLEON COCKTAIL, DINGENS, N-3, 10¼″, yellow amber, IP ... $2500–3500
NAPOLEON COCKTAIL, DINGENS, N-3, 10¼″, yellow green, IP.. $7500–10,000
NATIONAL BITTERS, CC JEROME & CO, N-10, 10⅝″, deep amethyst, rectangular
coffin $8000–12,000
NATIONAL BITTERS, EAR OF CORN, N-8, 12½″, yellow with tint of amber ......
....$325–375
NATIONAL BITTERS, EAR OF CORN, N-8, 12⅜″, deep puce $900–1200
NATIONAL BITTERS, EAR OF CORN, N-7, 12⅛″, amber, with unusual sheared
lip...$300–375

NATIONAL BITTERS, EAR OF CORN, N-8, 12½″, light amber $280–350
NATIONAL BITTERS, EAR OF CORN, N-8, 12½″, medium amber, 1½″ base crack $70–90
NATIONAL BITTERS, EAR OF CORN, N-8, 12¼″, amber................. $200–250
NATIONAL BITTERS, EAR OF CORN, N-8, 12⅜″, yellow with hint of olive $450–575
NATIONAL BITTERS, EAR OF CORN, N-8, 12¼″, medium pinkish puce $1000–1500
NATIONAL BITTERS, EAR OF CORN, N-8, 12½″, golden yellow $250–350
NATIONAL BITTERS, EAR OF CORN, N-8, 12⅜″, amber, base edge chip.......... .... $150–170
NATIONAL BITTERS, MILWAUKEE, WISC, N-5L, 9¾″, square, yellow green, label only $120–150
NATIONAL TONIC BITTERS, N-13, 9½″, aqua............................... $500–700
NECTAR HB BITTERS, N-16, 12½″, light gold amber, neck crack..... $600–750
NEW YORK HOP BITTERS, N-28, 9¾″, aqua.................................. $125–165
NEW YORK HOP BITTERS COMPANY, greenish aqua.......................$235–260
NEWMANS GOLDEN FRUIT BITTERS, round, 10⅞″, amber $325–425
O'LEARYS 20TH CENTURY BITTERS, O-55, 8⅝″, medium amber $60–90
OK 1840 PLANTATION, six-log cabin, O-14, 9⅞″, deep puce....... $2000–3000
OK PLANTATION, O-13, 11⅛″, topaz...................................... $700–1000
OK PLANTATION 1840, cabin-shaped, 11¼″, golden amber, three-sided.......... .... $700–900
OK PLANTATION 1840, cabin-shaped, three-sided, 11¼″, apricot, small spider crack $350–450
OLD ABBEY COCKTAIL BITTERS, 4½″, colorless, with label and contents $20–25
OLD CABIN BITTERS, O-19, 9¼″, amber $750–900
OLD CONTINENTAL BITTERS, O-25, 9⅞″, yellow with amber striations $700–900
OLD DR TOWNSENDS CELEBRATED, T-51, 8½″, amber, handled jug, OP $10,000–12,500
OLD HICKORY CELEBRATED STOMACH, O-31, 9″, golden amber......... $75–100
OLD HOMESTEAD WILD CHERRY, O-37, 9½″, medium amber $200–250
OLD HOMESTEAD WILD CHERRY, O-37, 9½″, medium orange yellow, cabin form.. $2000–3000
OLD HOMESTEAD WILD CHERRY, O-37, 9½″, golden amber, light inner stain $140–180
OLD HOMESTEAD WILD CHERRY, O-37, 9¾″, golden yellow............$275–350
OLD HOMESTEAD WILD CHERRY, O-37, 9½″, deep amber $130–160
OLD SACHEM AND WIGWAM TONIC, O-46, 9¾″, medium golden amber, barrel, OP $600–900
OLD SACHEM BITTERS, barrel, O-46, 9¼″, golden amber.............. $200–240
OLD SACHEM BITTERS, barrel shape, O-46, 9¼″, aqua $1500–1800
OLD SACHEM BITTERS, barrel shape, O-46, 9¼″, yellow with amber tint in lip $325–400
OLD SACHEM BITTERS, barrel shape, O-46, 9⅜″, deep red puce $425–525
OLD SACHEM BITTERS, barrel shape, O-46, 9⅛″, straw yellow $475–600
OLD SACHEM BITTERS, barrel shape, O-46, 9⅜″, yellow with hint of puce...... .... $400–550
OLD SACHEM BITTERS WIGWAM TONIC, O-46, 9½″, deep puce $250–350

OLD SACHEM BITTERS WIGWAM TONIC, O-46, 9½″, aqua with greenish tone
.... $1300–1800
OLD SACHEM BITTERS WIGWAM TONIC, O-46, 9⅜″, amber, OP $650–750
OLD SACHEM BITTERS WIGWAM TONIC,, O-46, 9½″, light gold yellow ....
.... $500–600
OLD SACHEM BITTERS & WIGWAM TONIC, O-45, 10¼″, aqua, OP, barrel-shaped,
large chip.. $500–700
OLD SACHEM BITTERS & WIGWAM TONIC, O-46, 9⅜″, bright lemon yellow,
green tint.. $2000–3500
OLD SACHEM BITTERS & WIGWAM TONIC, O-46, 9⅜″, grayish moss green,
barrel...$1750–2600
ORANGE BITTERS (ON LABEL UNDER GLASS) BAR BOTTLE, 6⅞″, colorless......
....$60–70
ORIGINAL POCAHONTAS BITTERS, O-86, barrel, 9¼″, aqua $1000–1200
ORRURO BITTERS, green, labeled $75–90
OSWEGO BITTERS, O-93, 7″, medium amber..................................$75–90
OSWEGO BITTERS 25 CENTS, O-93, 7⅛″, amber $60–90
PATENTED—DR JOHN BULLS CEDRON BITTERS, square, 10″, medium amber....
.... $500–600
PEPSIN BITTERS, P-44, 8⅛″, medium yellow green, 90% label........ $140–180
PEPSIN BITTERS FRANCIS CROPPER & CO, 11⅛″, colorless.............$150–200
PEPSIN CALISAYA BITTERS, P-50, green... $80–105
PEPSIN CALISAYA BITTERS, R-51, 4⅛″, medium yellow green..........$100–150
PEPSIN WILD CHERRY BITTERS, P-54, 8″, amber $175–200
PERUVIAN BITTERS, P-65, 9¼″, amber $60–75
PERUVIAN BITTERS-KW, P-67, 9⅛″, amber.................................. $60–80
PEYCHAUDS AMERICAN AROMATIC, amber, cylinder......................... $9–12
PEYCHAUDS AROMATIC COCKTAIL, 5⅞″, amber, labels $25–30
PHOENIX BITTERS, M-112, 5⅝″, deep olive green, OP $200–260
PINEAPPLE FIGURAL, unembossed, 9″, amber..................................$55–75
PINEAPPLE FIGURAL, PATD OCTOBER 1ST 1870 BY AL LACRAIX (ON BASE),
P-101, 9″, aqua $700–1000
PINEAPPLE-SHAPED, unembossed, 9¼″, deep golden amber........... $100–130
POOR MAN'S FAMILY BITTERS, P-123, 6½″, aqua $25–35
PRICES AROMATIC STOMACH, P-137, 9″, golden amber, light inner stain ....
....$250–325

Bitters, pineapple shaped. PHOTO COURTESY OF
NEIL GROSSMAN.

PRICKLEY ASH BITTERS, P-142, amber..$30–40
PRICKLY ASH BITTERS, P-140, 9¼″, labeled with box, amber, ABM . $130–160
PRICKLY ASH BITTERS, P-141, 9¾″, olive amber.............................$25–35
PROFESSOR GEO J BYRNE NEW YORK, B-280, medium amber...........$750–950
PRUNE STOMACH AND LIVER BITTERS, P-151, 9⅛″, amber................$65–80
QUININE TONIC BITTERS, Q-6, 8″, colorless...................................$60–85
RB (ON CASE) GIN-SHAPED BOTTLE, full label, 8⅞″, milk glass $110–150
RED JACKET BITTERS, lady's leg, R-28, 12¾″, red amber, light wear, base
chip... $90–120
RED JACKET BITTERS, BENNETT, R-19, square, 9¼″, amber...............$70–85
RED STAR STOMACH BITTERS, R-25, 11½″, amber....................... $200–240
REEDS BITTERS, R-28, 12⅜″, golden amber, light inner stain........... $90–120
REEDS BITTERS, lady's leg, R-28, 12⅜″, amber.......................... $300–400
RENAULT BITTERS, amber, labeled, ABM....................................$25–30
REUTER BITTERS, R-40, 10⅛″, milk glass.................................$325–400
RICHARDSONS BITTERS, R-57, 6⅞″, aqua, OP.............................$120–150
RICHARDSONS BITTERS, R-58, 6⅞″, aqua, OP.............................$190–220
RITMEIRS CALIFORNIA WINE, R-67, 9½″, amber $25–35
ROCKY MOUNTAIN TONIC BITTERS, R-82, 9¾″, yellow amber $250–300
ROSES MAGADOR BITTERS, R-98, 8¾″, amber.............................. $125–175
ROSSWINKLES CROWN BITTERS, R-102, 9⅛″, amber, 50% label.......$150–225
ROYAL ITALIAN BITTERS, R-111, 13½″, amethyst..........................$400–450
ROYAL ITALIAN BITTERS, R-111, 13½″, purple amethyst $325–425
ROYAL PEPSIN STOMACH BITTERS, R-113, 8⅞″, amber.....................$80–110
ROYCES SHERRY WINE BITTERS, R-119, 8″, aqua........................... $60–80
RUSHS BITTERS, R-124, 9″, amber, light stain...............................$30–35
RUSS ST DOMINGO BITTERS NEW YORK, R-125, 10″, square, bright yellow olive
green... $400–550
RUSS'S ST DOMINGO BITTERS, deep puce $350–450
RUSSIAN IMPERIAL TONIC BITTERS, R-133, 9½″, square, roped edges, aqua ....
.... $600–900
S & S BITTERS, S-4, 9½″, colorless with amethyst tint...................$110–140
S&S BITTERS DER DOCTOR ⅕ GAL, S-4, 9½″, colorless $225–275
SAINT JACOBS BITTERS, S-13, 8½″, amber $40–50
SANBORNS KIDNEY & LIVER VEGETABLE LAXATIVE, amber...............$65–90
SANFORD CHAMBERLAIN STOMACH BITTERS, 9½″, amber, 75% label ....
.... $1500–2000
SARRACENIA LIFE BITTERS, S-35, 9¼″, light amber...................... $140–180
SAZARAC AROMATIC BITTERS, S-47, 12¼″, milk glass $300–400
SAZARAC BITTERS, S-48, 10″, milk glass $300–400
SCHOENINGS SWEDISH, S-57, 7″, aqua.....................................$110–130
SCHROEDERS BITTERS, S-64, 11⅝″, golden amber, surface bruise $180–220
SCHROEDERS BITTERS, lady's leg, S-64, 11½″, amber................... $200–250
SCHROEDERS BITTERS, lady's leg, S-69, 5¼″, golden amber...........$275–350
SCHROEDERS BITTERS ESTAB 1845, S-69, 5¼″, amber $400–500
SCHROEDERS GERMAN BITTERS, S-73, 10″, amber $350–450
SEGURS GOLDEN SEAL BITTERS, S-84, 8¼″, aqua, OP, lip edge bruise .$40–50
SHAMROCK BITTERS, colorless, labeled $75–90
SHARPS MOUNTAIN HERB BITTERS, S-95, amber $250–320
SHURTLEFFS BITTERS, S-103, 12⅜″, medium amber $500–600
SIMONS CENTENNIAL BITTERS, S-110, 10″, golden amber $900–1100

SIR EDWARD RIVIERE ORANGE BITTERS, aqua, labels, contents $70–90
SIR ROBERT BURNETT ORANGE BITTERS, 5¾", colorless with full label .$25–30
SMITHS DRUID BITTERS, S-124, 9¼", deep golden amber, barrel shape ....
.... $300–425
SMITHS DRUID BITTERS, S-124, 9½", yellow amber..................... $300–400
SMITHS DRUID BITTERS, S-124, 9½", deep amber, barrel.............. $300–400
SOLOMONS STRENGTHENING BITTERS, S-140, 9⅝", cobalt blue $450–575
ST GOTTHARD HERB BITTERS, S-12, 8⅞", amber............................$40–45
STAR ANCHOR BITTERS, S-176, 9¼", yellow amber with hint of olive ....
.... $160–200
STAR KIDNEY & LIVER BITTERS, S-178, 8⅞", amber....................... $60–90
STEELE NIAGARA BITTERS, S-184, 10", amber............................ $200–300
STEELES NIAGARA BITTERS, S-182, 10", medium amber.................$225–275
STEINFELDS FRENCH COGNAC BITTERS, S-185, 11¼", golden amber ..$200–325
STEKETEES BLOOD PURIFYING, S-188, 9⅝", amber........................ $125–175
STEPHEN JEWETTS CELEBRATED, aqua, OP $125–145
STOMACH BITTERS, enameled on bar bottle, 10¾", colorless $60–90
STOUGHTONS MAGEN BITTER, 7⅛", colorless, OP $60–90
SUFFOLK BITTERS, pig shape, S-217, 10¼", light yellow amber, ½" lip chip ...
.... $180–220
SUFFOLK BITTERS, PHILBROOK TUCKER, S-217, pig, 10", amber, repaired foot,
chip..$25–35
SUFFOLK BITTERS, PHILBROOK TUCKER, S-217, 10", yellowish amber ....
.... $600–700
SUFFOLK PIG BITTERS, S-217, 10½", light gold amber................... $375–475
SUN KIDNEY & LIVER BITTERS, S-222, 9¾", amber, labeled...........$100–150
SUNNY CASTLE STOMACH BITTERS, S-223, 9", amber.......................$50–65
SWISS STOMACH BITTERS, S-243, 9⅜", amber, with label and contents ....
.... $400–500
THAYERS IRON BITTERS, T-15, 7⅛", deep aqua $250–350
TIP TOP BITTERS, 9", light olive green....................................... $300–500
TIP TOP BITTERS, T-31, 9", yellow amber....................................$160–200
TIPPECANOE BITTERS, canoe shape, 9", golden amber..................... $80–120
TIPPECANOE BITTERS, canoe, with full label, 9", golden amber........ $125–150
TO NI TA BITTERS, NEW YORK, T-44, amber, labeled.......................$75–90
TONOLA BITTERS, T-47, 8⅜", aqua, small potstone crack $70–95
TRAVELERS BITTERS, T-54, 10⅜", yellow amber $2500–3500
TURNERS BRAZILIAN BITTERS, Y-69, 8", colorless $40–50
UNDERBERG BITTERS, 4½", amber, labels...................................$15–20
VIGO BITTERS, FG ALTMAIER & CO, CHICAGO, 9", amber $130–180
VINO CASTELLANO/DEBROWN, 12", yellow amber, IP $250–350
VIRGINIA DARE BITTERS, amber, full labels, ABM...........................$25–30
VLARKES COMPOUND MANDRAKE, aqua $15–20
VON HUMBOLDTS STOMACH, V-31, 9½", olive amber................... $400–525
W & CO, pineapple-shaped, P-100, 8½", bright blue green, IP ... $2000–2400
W & CO, pineapple figural, P-100, 8⅜", medium blue green, OP $2000–3000
W & CO, pineapple figural, P-100, 8⅜", deep olive green, IP....... $800–1200
W & CO, pineapple figural, P-100, 8⅜", bright yellow green, IP. $2000–3000
W & CO, pineapple figural, with applied handle, 8⅜", medium amber, OP ....
.... $3000–4000
W & CO, NY, pineapple-shaped, 8¼", olive green, IP $2000–2500

W & Co, NY, pineapple figural, P-100, 8½", golden amber, OP..... $125–165
W & Co, NY, pineapple-shaped, 8½", deep olive yellow, IP..........$550–750
W And Co, NY, pineapple figural, 8½", citron, OP $2000–3000
Wahoo & Calisaya, W-3, 10", golden amber $190–230
Wahoo & Calisaya Bitters, W-3, 9¾", medium amber $200–240
Wahoo & Calisaya Bitters, W-3, 9¾", amber $250–300
Waits Kidney & Liver Bitters, W-6, 8⅞", amber........................$35–45
Waits Kidney & Liver Bitters, W-6, 8¾", medium amber, with label........
.... $80–120
Walkers Cocktail Bitters, W-12, 10⅞", amber $500–600
Walkers Tonic Bitters, W-13, 11½", medium yellow amber, lady's leg.......
.... $700–900
Wallaces Tonic Stomach Bitters, W-16, 9", golden amber......... $150–175
Wampoo Bitters, W-24, 10", light citron................................$225–260
Warners Safe Bitters, W-34, 9½", deep golden amber $300–400
Warners Safe Bitters, W-34, 9½", amber $500–700
Warners Safe Tonic Bitters, W-39, 7⅜", medium amber, 70% original
label.. $400–500
Warrens Quaker Bitters, W-48, 9⅝", aqua, labels $200–300
WC Bitters, W-57, 10½", amber.. $500–625
Webbs Improved Stomach Bitters, W-57, 9", medium amber $110–140
Webbs Old Rye Bitters, W-61, 9⅛", dark amber $200–300
Weis Bros Knickerbocker Stomach, W-68, 12", amber............. $600–750
West India Stomach Bitters, amber, square $40–60
WH Ware Patented 1866, The Fish Bitters, 11½", colorless, fish figural ...
.... $400–600
Whites Stomach Bitters, W-101, 9⅝", medium amber..............$150–200
Whitwells Temperance Bitters, W-105, 7¾", aqua, OP..............$80–95
Wilder & Co Stomach Bitters, W-116, colorless........................ $125–175
Wilders Stomach Bitters, W-116, 10½", colorless, building-shaped...........
....$110–135
Willards Golden Seal Bitters, W-119, 7⅝", aqua......................$40–55
William Allens Congress Bitters, A-29, 10¼", emerald bluish green.......
.... $500–650
William Allens Congress Bitters, A-29, 10¼", puce amethyst ....
.... $4000–5500
Winters Stomach Bitters, W-141, 9½", amber $60–80
Woodburys Bitters, W-156, 8½", amber $60–90
Wooden Box, "Toneco Stomach Bitters", 10 ¼" H × 13" L $90–110
Woods Tonic Wine Bitter, W-153, 9½", aqua $125–175
Wryghtes Bitters, London, W-165, 6", deep olive green $300–400
Yerba Buena Bitters, amber, full labels................................... $80–100
Yerba Buena Bitters, Y-3, 9⅝", amber $50–65
Yochim Bros Stomach Bitters, Y-5, 8¾", amber, with full labels . $125–175
Zingari Bitters, Z-4, 12", pinkish puce $350–400
Zingari Bitters, Z-4, 12", amber $190–240
Zingari Bitters, Z-4, 11⅝", medium pinkish puce, lady's leg.... $5000–7000
Zu Zu Bitters, Z-9, 8⅞", amber... $140–180

BLOWN BOTTLES, INCLUDING BLACK GLASS AND CHESTNUT BOTTLES

Blown bottles, or free-blown bottles, are those which are made without the use of any molds and are totally shaped by the glass blower during formation. Blown bottles are the earliest types of bottles made, and it is often difficult to know the origin or date of a given blown bottle, since the forms were made overseas as well as in the United States for a long period of time. The novice and experienced collector alike should be wary when purchasing free-blown types of bottles, since it is fairly easy to reproduce such bottles. Become familiar with how the bottles were made and what forms and colors were originally used, and then watch for indicators such as wear and methods of manufacture. The reader is referred to *American Bottles and Flasks and Their Ancestry* by McKearin and Wilson, which the letter "H" refers to below, with plate number.

APOTHECARY BOTTLE, straight-sided sloping shoulder, narrow lip, with label, 13″, green, OP $150–200
APOTHECARY JAR FORM, with two bands on sides, 11″, colorless, OP, with cover $50–75
BLACKING BOTTLE, square, 4⅞″, olive amber, OP........................ $70–100
BLUEBERRY BOTTLE, cylinder with a tapering shoulder, wide mouth, OP, 9¼″, olive amber $175–200
BULBOUS HANDLED WHISKEY JUG, 6⅜″, smoky puce, OP, handle crack, chip..$50–70
BULBOUS HANDLED WHISKEY JUG, 7¾″, deep puce, IP................. $100–150
CHESTNUT BOTTLE, 4½″, yellow amber, OP............................ $200–250

Blown, Chestnut, with flattened sides. PHOTO COURTESY OF NEIL GROSSMAN.

CHESTNUT BOTTLE, 6¼″, olive amber, OP, ½″ neck crack $90–110
CHESTNUT BOTTLE, 6⅛″, olive yellow, OP................................$100–125
CHESTNUT BOTTLE, 5⅝″, light olive green, OP $90–150
CHESTNUT BOTTLE, 7″, yellow green, OP, few scratches, stain $60–80
CHESTNUT BOTTLE, 10″, deep olive green, OP $180–220
CHESTNUT BOTTLE, very bubbly, 6″, deep green, OP $175–250
CRIMPED-FOOT HANDLED JUG, 6½″, aqua, OP $500–600
CUT OVERLAY DECANTERS, opaque white over colorless cut with grape pattern, 15″, pair $300–500
CYLINDRICAL, similar in form to H45-6, 11¾″, olive amber, OP..... $200–250
CYLINDRICAL BOTTLE, 6¼″, olive amber, OP, heavy collared lip........$70–90
CYLINDRICAL WIDE-MOUTH JAR, with slight taper on sides, 6⅝″, olive green, OP..$450–550
CYLINDRICAL WIDE-MOUTH JAR, 11⅝″, 4″ mouth, olive amber, OP, flared lip $200–250
CYLINDRICAL WIDE-MOUTH JAR, 10″, 4⅛″, mouth, olive amber, OP, flared lip.. $200–240
DECANTER, two bands of chainlike decoration around body, qt., colorless, OP $375–450
DECANTER, with broken chain-type decoration, two rings on body and neck, qt., ring stopper $400–550
DEMIJOHN, bulbous form, 16¾″, golden amber, OP..................... $100–175
DEMIJOHN, pear-shaped, 17½″, olive green................................. $75–100
DEMIJOHN, kidney-shaped, 18¾″, light golden amber $45–75
DEMIJOHN, kidney-shaped, 18½″, olive amber, OP $125–225
DEMIJOHN, straight-sided cylinder, 11¼″, olive amber, OP $25–40
DUTCH ONION, H52-17, olive amber, OP, light wear $75–90
DUTCH ONION, H52-17, 7⅝″, olive amber, OP, mint condition....... $125–175
ETCHED GLOBULAR BOTTLE, with Masonic emblems and names, 10½″, olive amber, OP $500–750
FLASK, 5¼″, light yellow amber, OP $75–100
FLASK, chestnut form, ½ pt., amethyst, OP $500–600
FLATTENED EGG SHAPE, M222-16a, 7″, olive amber, OP.............. $300–350
FLYTRAP, bulbous body, 7½″, colorless $70–90
GLOBULAR BOTTLE, 5¼″, medium olive yellow, rolled lip, OP........ $110–150
GLOBULAR BOTTLE, 9⅜″ × 6¼″, olive amber, OP $125–150
GLOBULAR BOTTLE, large, 11″ × 9″, olive amber, OP $250–300

Left, blown, Dutch squat. Right, blown, globular form. PHOTOS COURTESY OF NEIL GROSSMAN.

GLOBULAR-SHAPED BOTTLE, 12¼", applied string ring below lip, OP ....
.... $175–250
HANDLED CHESTNUT, 8½", golden amber, OP $45–60
HANDLED ENGLISH ONION BOTTLE, 5½" × 4¼", olive green, OP, lip chip
.... $3500–4000
HANDLED JUG, cylindrical with long conical shoulder, 8⅛", aqua, OP...........
.... $100–120
HANDLED ONION BOTTLE, 4⅞" × 2½", medium olive green, OP ....
.... $1600–2000
HANDLED WHISKEY, bulbous body, 6¼", puce, OP $100–120
INVERTED CONE-SHAPED WHISKEY, 10¼", deep red amber, IP $150–175
JAR, cylinder with flaring lip, 8½" × 5⅞", milk glass, OP........... $400–550
JAR FORM, cylindrical, flaring lip, 8" × 4¾", greenish aqua, OP $125–175
JAR FORM, straight-sided and flared lip, 11½", olive amber, OP....... $175–225
JAR FORM, straight-sided body with shoulder and straight neck, 14½", olive
amber $300–400
JAR FORM, straight-sided cylinder with flaring lip, 11½", amber....... $125–150
LONG-NECKED ONION, 8⅞" × 5", olive green, OP $500–600
LOOPED CHESTNUT FLASK, black with white loopings, 4⅞", OP..... $350–400
MALLET-SHAPED BOTTLE, H52-8, 8" × 4½", olive amber, OP.......$150–220
MALLET-SHAPED BOTTLE, H52-7, 6" × 3⅞", olive amber, OP...... $200–250
MALLET-SHAPED WINE, H52-8, 7½" × 5⅛", olive, amber, OP......$200–275
MALLET WINE BOTTLE, H52-7, 7¾" × 4⅞", olive amber, OP.......$200–275
MEDICINE BOTTLE, rectangular with beveled edges, 7¼", olive green, OP......
.... $200–250
MINIATURE BOTTLE, straight neck and tapering bottom, 2¾", olive amber,
OP...$175–210
MINIATURE CHESTNUT BOTTLE, 3¼", medium olive green, OP.... $500–600
MINIATURE DECANTER, with applied threading around neck, 3½", colorless,
OP, stopper $125–225
MINIATURE GLOBULAR BOTTLE, 2⅞", medium olive yellow, OP, crude ....
.... $500–600
MINIATURE GLOBULAR BOTTLE, 3⅞", light olive green, OP $200–250
OCTAGONAL, rounded shoulders, H52-18, 10", olive amber, OP $400–550
OCTAGONAL, rounded shoulders, 10" × 3⅝", olive green, OP, applied collared
lip...$550–650
OCTAGONAL, squared shoulders, H52-18, 7¾", olive amber, OP $350–450

Blown, mallet-shaped wine, ca. 1720. PHOTO
COURTESY OF NEIL GROSSMAN.

OCTAGONAL, squared shoulders, H52-18, 10″, olive amber, OP, large base chip.. $450–600

OCTAGONAL WIDE-MOUTH JAR, 13⅜″ × 4¾″, olive green, OP...... $500–700

ONION, H52-4, 5⅜″ × 4⅞″, olive green, OP............................. $400–500

ONION, H52-4, 7⅞″ × 4¾″, olive green, OP............................. $400–500

ONION, wide and squat, 5¼″ × 5″, olive green, OP.....................$550–650

ONION BOTTLE, H52-5, 6¾″ × 5⅛″, olive green, OP $200–250

PINCH BOTTLE, three depressed sides, 9⅛″, yellow milk glass, with stopper ...
....$40–60

POCKET FLASK, probably Midwestern, 4¾″, golden amber, OP $90–120

PRESERVE JAR, cylinder, flaring lip, 4⅝″ × 3¹/₁₆″, olive green, OP .. $175–250

RECTANGULAR UTILITY BOTTLE, with beveled edges, H72-2, 7″, olive amber, OP, light wear.. $200–250

ROLLING PIN WHIMSEY, 14½″, greenish aqua, OP $50–65

SCENT BOTTLE, hourglass shape in cobalt with colorless rigaree, 3″, OP........
.... $500–600

SHAFT AND GLOBE BOTTLE, TYPE 2, H52-3, 7⅛″ × 3¼″, olive green, OP ...
.... $800–1000

SHAFT AND GLOBE BOTTLE, TYPE 1, 4¾″ × 2″, medium blue green, OP, light stain, rare color $1500–2000

SHAFT AND GLOBE BOTTLE, TYPE 1A, 5½″ × 1⅞″, olive green, OP, two small cracks... $1500–2000

SHAFT AND GLOBE BOTTLE, TYPE 2, 5⅞″ × 2¾″, olive green, OP.............
....$800–1100

SHAFT AND GLOBE BOTTLE, TYPE 2, 6¾″ × 3¼″, olive green, OP, repairs, cleaned $300–400

SHAFT AND GLOBE FORM, TYPE 2, 7⅜″ × 3⅞″, olive green, OP, ¾″ lip chip.. $700–900

SHAFT AND GLOBE FORM, TYPE 1, H52-1, 8⅝″ × 2¾″, olive green, OP, lip repair.. $1500–2000

SHAFT AND GLOBE FORM, TYPE 1A, H52-2, 8¹/₁₆″ × 2½″, deep olive green, OP, mint $3500–4000

SNUFF, rectangular with beveled edges, 6¼″, olive green, lip chip, wear........
....$30–40

SQUARE MALLET FORM, 7¼″ × 3½″, OP................................ $700–800

SQUARE-SIDED BOTTLE, 7⅞″ × 3⅜″, olive green, OP, sheared lip . $300–400

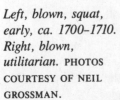

Left, blown, squat, early, ca. 1700–1710. Right, blown, utilitarian. PHOTOS COURTESY OF NEIL GROSSMAN.

Blown, utilitarian. PHOTO COURTESY OF
NEIL GROSSMAN.

SQUARE WITH TAPERING SIDES RUM JAR, H47-13, 11″, deep olive green, OP,
flaring lip.. $750–900
TOILET WATER BOTTLE, unpatterned, 6½″, cobalt blue, OP, with stopper.......
.... $175–250
UTILITARIAN BOTTLE, crudely made, 15½″, olive green, OP, crude lip..........
....$550–650
UTILITARIAN BOTTLE, straight-sided cylinder, applied lip, 9″, deep green, OP
.... $600–900
UTILITY BOTTLE, cylindrical, 5⅛″, dark olive green, OP, crude $200–300
UTILITY BOTTLE, squatty cylinder with flaring lip, 3″, pale green, OP...........
....$180–220
WHISKEY JUG, handled, bulbous with slightly flat sides, 7″, OP, cobalt blue
.... $125–150
WIDE-MOUTH ONION BOTTLE, 6⅞″ H × 6¾″ W, olive amber, OP, with 4″
mouth opening $300–500

BLOWN THREE-MOLD BOTTLES

Blown three-mold is a term given to bottles and glass which is blown
into a three-piece mold. Generally, such glass was produced between
1820 and 1840 in the New England area; however, blown three-mold was
also produced in France, Portugal, and England and is often difficult to
differentiate from American pieces.

It is very important for the collector to differentiate between blown
three-mold glass and pressed three-mold glass. On blown three-mold
glass, since the impression was obtained by the glass blower blowing a
bubble into a mold, the mold impression can always be felt on the inside,
as well as the outside, of the piece. On pressed three-mold pieces, the
impression can only be felt on the outside of the piece.

Blown three-mold glass was made in a wide variety of patterns and colors. The colors vary from amethyst, sapphire blues, and a wide assortment of greens. All blown three-mold pieces should have rough pontil scars. Collectors should become familiar with the patterns listed in *American Glass* by McKearin, as there are many foreign lacy patterns to be contended with, as well as numerous reproductions and outright fakes. The Metropolitan Museum of Art has been selling well-made and realistic blown three-mold reproductions which should have the initials "MMA" roughly engraved on or next to the pontil mark. Collectors should also become familiar with the products of the Clevenger Brothers Glassworks, which began operations in New Jersey in the 1920s, and which made faithful reproductions, but often in unusual colors not characteristic of the originals.

Anyone who is seriously considering pursuing blown three-mold glass collecting is well advised to obtain a copy of the article "Unmasking an American Glass Fraud" by Dwight Lanmon (*Antiques Magazine*, Jan. 1983), which goes into great detail on some extremely well-made blown three-mold fakes. The reader is also referred to *American Glass* by McKearin, which the letter "G" refers to below.

BAR BOTTLE, GII-6, 7½" × 4¾", pale yellow green, OP $3000–4000
BRANDY EMBOSSED DECANTER, GIII-2-2, qt., colorless, chip on stopper bottom $475–600
CASTOR BOTTLE, GI-14, 4⅜", colorless, OP, no stopper $20–25
CASTOR BOTTLE, GI-7, 4¼", colorless, no cap..............................$15–20
CRUET, GII-11, 4⅜", colorless, OP... $90–120
CRUET, GII-37, 4¼", colorless, OP $75–90
DECANTER, GII-3, ½ pt., dark olive green, OP........................$7500–9500
DECANTER, GI-18, 6½", colorless, OP....................................$200–260
DECANTER, GI-29, pt., colorless, OP..$85–110
DECANTER, GI-29, ½ pt., cobalt blue, OP................................$700–900
DECANTER, GI-29, 5¼", purple blue, OP $600–850
DECANTER, GI-29, qt., colorless, OP.......................................$400–550
DECANTER, GI-29, 7", colorless, OP..$100–150

Left, Blown Three-Mold, condiment bottle, GI-24. Right, Blown Three-Mold, decanter, GII-18, sunburst stopper. PHOTOS COURTESY OF NEIL GROSSMAN.

DECANTER, GI-29, qt., blue green, OP...................................... $2000–2500
DECANTER, GI-7-3, qt., colorless, OP, with stopper...................... $225–275
DECANTER, GII-18, 10¼″, colorless, OP, with stopper.................. $100–175
DECANTER, GII-18, qt., colorless, OP $140–180
DECANTER, GII-43, qt., light olive green, OP $4000–5500
DECANTER, GII-6, pt., pale bluish green, OP $3500–5000
DECANTER, GII-7, 6¾″, colorless, OP....................................... $140–180
DECANTER, GIII-16, pt., olive amber, OP $350–450
DECANTER, GIII-16, pt., rich olive green, OP $350–450
DECANTER, GIII-16, pt., olive amber, OP $350–450
DECANTER, GIII-16, pt., pale blue green, OP, flared lip............. $3000–5000
DECANTER, GIII-16, pt., olive amber, OP $350–450
DECANTER, GIII-16, pt., olive amber, OP $300–375
DECANTER, GIII-16, pt., olive amber, OP, with rare flared lip $1500–2500
DECANTER, GIII-16, pt., olive amber, OP $450–550
DECANTER, GIII-16, pt., olive green, OP $375–500
DECANTER, GIII-19, qt., olive amber, OP, ½″ base crack............. $200–275
DECANTER, GIII-19, qt., deep olive amber, OP $500–800
DECANTER, GIII-19, qt., olive amber, OP $700–825
DECANTER, GIII-19, qt., olive green, OP................................... $650–850
DECANTER, GIII-19, qt., olive green, OP, 2″ lip crack................. $200–275
DECANTER, GIII-2, 7″, colorless, OP, no stopper, 2″ crack $20–30
DECANTER, GIII-2-1, pt., olive green, OP, major lip repairs $400–550
DECANTER, GIII-2-1, pt., deep yellowish olive, OP $3000–4000
DECANTER, GIII-2-1, pt., colorless, OP, small lip chip................... $90–120
DECANTER, GIII-2-1, pt., deep yellow olive, OP, ⅛″ lip chip $550–650
DECANTER, GIII-2-2, pt., yellow olive, OP $2000–3000
DECANTER, GIII-24, pt., colorless, OP, lip chip, no stopper $40–60
DECANTER, GIII-5, 10″, colorless, OP, with stopper..................... $125–175
DECANTER, GIII-5, qt., colorless, OP $125–175
DECANTER, GIII-5, qt., colorless, OP, light base stain.................. $200–225
DECANTER, GIII-6, pt., colorless, OP, large lip chip...................... $90–120
DECANTER, GIII-6, pt., colorless, OP $125–175
DECANTER, GIII-6, ½ pt., colorless, OP, lip chip, light stain $90–120
DECANTER, GIV-7, qt., colorless, OP, with stopper...................... $200–250
DECANTER, GV-14, 11¼″, colorless, OP, with stopper.................. $190–250
DECANTER, GV-8, 9″, colorless, OP, light base stain.................... $175–200
DECANTER, GV-8, qt., colorless, OP, light stain $100–125
DECANTER, barrel shape, GII-7, 8¼″, bright yellow olive, OP $2300–2750
DECANTER, barrel shape, GII-7, 8⅜″, light olive green, OP $1800–2200
DECANTER, barrel shape, GII-7, pt., colorless, OP $160–190
DECANTER, globular, GIII-5, qt., colorless, OP, acorn stopper........$250–350
DECANTER, horn of plenty design, GV-17, qt., colorless, OP, original stopper
.... $1000–1500
DECANTER, nontapered sides, GIII-20, qt., colorless, OP, acorn stopper.........
.... $350–450
DECANTER, plume and arch pattern, qt., deep purple blue, OP, chips ....
.... $200–250
DECANTER, square, GII-28, pt., colorless, OP, no stopper.............. $180–225
DECANTER, square, GII-28, pt., emerald green, OP, with stopper. $3000–4000
DECANTER, square, GII-29, 7″, medium lavender, OP, lip bruise... $900–1200

Blown Three-Mold, toilet water bottle, GI-7-4.
PHOTO COURTESY OF NEIL GROSSMAN.

DECANTER, square, beveled edges, GII-28, pt., light yellow green, OP, no stopper $1500–2000
DECANTER, square, beveled edges, GII-28, pt., yellow green, OP, flaring lip $2500–3500
DECANTER, square, chamfered edges, GII-28, pt., yellow green, OP, shoulder bruise $1000–1200
DECANTER, straight-sided, GIII-20, qt., colorless, OP, waffle stopper $250–300
FLASK, chestnut shape, similar to H121-3, GII-24, 5″ × 4¾″, deep sapphire blue, OP $15,000–20,000
GIN EMBOSSED DECANTER, GIII-2-2, qt., colorless, OP $300–400
INK, GII-18, 1½″ × 2¼″, yellow olive, OP $140–180
INKWELL, GII-18, 1½″ × 2¼″, olive amber, OP $100–120
MINIATURE DECANTER, GIII-12, 2¾″, colorless, OP, no stopper $200–300
MINIATURE DECANTER, GIII-12, 2½″, colorless, OP, no stopper $160–190
MUSTARD JAR, GI-10, 3¾″, colorless, OP $40–60
MUSTARD JAR, GIII-23, 5½″, colorless, OP, with cover $150–200
RUM EMBOSSED DECANTER, GIII-2-2, qt., colorless, body bruise and ½″ crack $175–250
TOILET WATER BOTTLE, ribbed, GI-7-2, 6½″, deep blue, OP, with stopper..... .... $175–200
TOILET WATER BOTTLE, GI-3-1, 6½″, cobalt blue, OP, with stopper . $275–350
TOILET WATER BOTTLE, GI-7-2, 6″, purple blue, OP, with stopper ... $180–225
TOILET WATER BOTTLE, GI-7-4, 6¼″, colorless, OP, with stopper $60–90
TOILET WATER BOTTLE, GI-7-4, 5⅜″, colorless, OP, no stopper $60–75
WINE EMBOSSED DECANTER, GIII-2-2, qt., colorless $325–400

CANDY CONTAINERS

Figural glass candy containers are an area of bottle collecting that is becoming more and more popular. The first candy container is believed to be the Liberty Bell which was sold at the 1876 Centennial Exhibition in Philadelphia. From the 1890s up until around 1960, when glass candy containers were all but discontinued, thousands of different figural candy containers in all shapes, sizes, and colors were made. Though some candy containers were sold to merchants already filled with candy, it is uncertain which ones came filled and which ones were filled by the merchants at their stores.

When collecting and buying candy containers, be watchful for original paint and original closures. Try to be certain that all the parts and accessories are present and, if possible, that they are original to the piece. The reader is referred to *The Compleat American Glass Candy Containers Handbook* by George Eikelberner and Serge Agadjanian, which the numbers below refer to.

AIRPLANE, 306, complete with cap and wing $50–75
AIRPLANE, 4A, with contents $40–70
AIRPLANE, LIBERTY MOTORS, BIPLANE, 10, with complete paint .. $2500–4000
AIRPLANE, SPIRIT OF GOODWILL, 8C, complete and painted, contents ....
.... $100–150
AIRPLANE, SPIRIT OF GOODWILL, 8A, complete and painted............ $100–150
AUTO, 43, with tin roof and wheels.. $70–100
AUTOMOBILE, 38, colorless glass, complete, painted $40–55
AUTOMOBILE, 37, colorless glass, complete $30–45
AUTOMOBILE, 35, colorless glass, complete $30–45
AUTOMOBILE, 45, tin wheels $50–80
BABY SWEEPER, 132, complete with contents and handle $400–600
BARNEY GOOGLE, 72A, with closure and some paint $140–190
BILLIKEN, 90, with original paint, closure...................................$100–125
BOAT, THE COLORADO, complete with rigging and tin cover............$200–325
BOAT CANDY CONTAINERS, various shapes and sizes........................$30–70
BOOT, 111, with closure...$20–30
BUILDING, 807, with glass insert and pin $125–175
BUILDING, 324B, closure... $60–90
BUREAU, 112, with original paint, closure...................................$100–150
CANNON, RAPID FIRE, 129, tin, with glass walls, in working order... $200–300
CARS, VARIOUS TYPES, colorless glass $20–90
CHARLIE CHAPLIN, 137, closure and contents.............................. $80–120

Candy Container, Liberty Motor.
PHOTO COURTESY OF NEIL GROSSMAN.

CHICK, 145A, with all paint, contents $75–125
CHICKEN, 147C, with original paint, closure $45–65
CHICKEN, 147A, with original paint, no closure $40–60
CHICKEN, 149B, with closure $40–45
CHICKEN, 148A, with closure $30–50
CLOCK, 162, white, with some paint $100–150
CLOCK, 163, colorless glass, octagonal, no closure $40–60
CLOCK, 164A, paper dial, closure, colorless $40–60
CROWING CHICKEN, 151, painted and with full contents $200–325
DIRIGIBLE, 176A, with closure $125–175
DOG, SEATED BULLDOG, 189A, with black paint, closure $40–65
DOG, SEATED BULLDOG, 189A, with gold paint, closure..................$40–65
DOG-SHAPED, various shapes and sizes, colorless or blue $10–45
DRUM MUG, 543, with some paint $30–45
DUCK, 198, complete and with contents......................................$30–45
DUCK, 197, complete and with some paint $30–40
DUCK WITH LARGE BILL, 199, with most of its paint $100–150
ELEPHANT IN SWALLOW-TAIL SUIT, 207, colorless with tin top........ $200–300
FAT BOY ON DRUM, 208, original paint....................................$125–175
FIRE ENGINE, 213C, with contents $30–50
FIRE ENGINE, 217, with contents and paint $40–55
FIRE ENGINE, 223B, complete, colorless.....................................$30–45
FIRE ENGINE, 221B, complete, colorless.....................................$30–45
FIRE ENGINE, 219, complete with contents and closure $100–150
GAY HEAD LIGHTHOUSE, colorless $60–90
GUN, INDIAN HEAD HANDLE, 285, with cap $40–55
GUN, COLT, 285, with black paint $60–90
GUNS, various shapes and sizes, colorless glass $10–50
HAT, UNCLE SAM'S, milk glass with original paint.........................$50–80
HORN, 313, complete and full $25–40
HOT DOGGIE, 320, blue glass, cap $750–1000
HOUSE, 324A, original paint, closure.......................................$125–175
IRON, 343, with closure $20–30
JACK O' LANTERN, original paint, no cap..................................$90–120
JITNEY BUS, 114, with tin wheels and tin top, paint.....................$250–350
LIBERTY BELL, 87A, blue with closure.......................................$40–60
LIBERTY BELL, 87A, yellow amber, closure.................................$40–60

Candy Container, Colt pistol.
PHOTO COURTESY OF NEIL
GROSSMAN.

Candy Container, Toonerville trolley.
PHOTO COURTESY OF NEIL GROSSMAN.

LOCOMOTIVE, various types, colorless glass $15–55
MAIL BOX, 521-2, milk glass, no closure $70–110
MAIL BOX, 521, complete and painted $60–90
MAIL BOX, 521-1, complete, no closure......................................$50–75
MAN ON MOTORCYCLE, 522A, original paint, closure $500–800
MOON MULLINS, 534, complete with some paint............................$25–35
NEW YORK CENTRAL RAIL CAR SET, 495, all three cars, minor damage..........
.... $400–600
OPERA GLASSES, with closures, milk glass................................. $125–175
OVERLAND LIMITED TRAIN SET, three-piece set, damage to couplers. $600–900
OWL, 566B, complete with closure ....
....$30–42
PIANO, 577, with tin closure... $140–180
RABBIT, 606A, complete with contents, some paint........................$30–45
RABBIT, 609, colorless glass, with no closure...............................$20–25
RABBIT, 617A, with closure, contents, colorless glass $25–35
RABBIT, RUNNING ON A LOG, 603A, with closure $80–120
RABBIT FAMILY, 604, with original paint.................................. $500–800
RABBIT IN EGG SHELL, 608B, with closure, contents $70–95
RABBIT PUSHING CHICK IN SHELL CART, 602A, original paint, closure ....
....$350–550
RABBIT WITH WHEELBARROW, 601B, with some paint.......................$45–75
RADIO, 643B, with closure and some paint $100–135
RADIO, 643, missing closure $50–80
ROCKING HORSE WITH CLOWN, blue-tint glass............................ $90–135
ROCKING HORSE WITH CLOWN, colorless glass $75–100
SANTA, 671, with some paint, closure $50–70
SANTA, 670, with original candy and cotton, closure $150–200
SANTA, LEAVING CHIMNEY, 673B, with paint, closure..................... $60–90
SPARK PLUG, HORSE FIGURAL, colorless $75–100
SPARK PLUG, HORSE-SHAPED, with some original paint, no closure ... $100–140
SPIRIT OF GOODWILL, 8A, complete and painted $100–150
SPIRIT OF GOODWILL, 8C, complete and painted, contents $100–150
SPIRIT OF ST LOUIS, with original paint................................... $400–600
SUITCASE, 707F, with handle and closure, contents...........................$35–55
SUITCASE, 707A, with handle and closure $30–50
SUITCASE, 707, milk glass, original paint $150–200
TANK, assorted shapes and sizes, colorless glass $20–45

TELEPHONE, 746, contents and closure......................................$150–190
TELEPHONE, 742 variant, cork top and cardboard shield, 5⅛″ $300–400
TOP WITH WINDER, 776, complete $90–140
VILLAGE BUILDING, 813, missing glass insert and pin $20–25
VILLAGE BUILDING, 812, missing glass insert and pin $20–25
VILLAGE BUILDING, 815, missing glass insert and pin $20–25
VILLAGE LOG CABIN, 816, complete with glass liner and bracket $350–550
WAGON, 822, complete and full..$30–50
WAGON, 323, colorless glass..$30–50
WAGON, 539D, complete and full $35–55
WAGON, 539A, complete and full...$35–55
WATCH, 823, closure and fob.. $200–300
WINDMILL, 843B, with contents $90–120

COLOGNE BOTTLES

Cologne bottles were used by both ladies and gentlemen, and the shapes
and colors of the bottles were as varied as the colognes that filled them.
Though colognes were popular in 17th- and 18th-century America, most
of the fancy bottles encountered by collectors are from the 1830 to 1880
period. The reader is referred to *American Bottles and Flasks and Their
Ancestry* by McKearin and Wilson, pgs. 378–407, which the letter ''H''
refers to below.

BEADED RIB PATTERN, 5⅛″, opalescent $225–250
BEADED RIB PATTERN, 10⅛″, milk glass $90–120
BEADED RIBBING DESIGN, H114-4, 8″, milk glass $50–70
BEADED RIBBING DESIGN, H114-4, 8″, colorless $15–25
BUNKER HILL MONUMENT, 12″, colorless....................................$30–40
CORSET WAISTED, eight-sided, H114-7, 5⅝″, colorless $100–125
CORSET WAISTED, eight-sided, H114-7, 5⅞″, deep lavender blue $550–650

*Left, Cologne,
fancy, ca. 1840–
1850. Right,
Cologne,
hourglass-
shaped, six-
sided.* PHOTOS
COURTESY OF
SKINNER'S, INC.

CYLINDRICAL, 10¾″, blue milk glass, smooth base $25–35
CYLINDRICAL, 10⅞″, blue milk glass, OP..$75–90
DANCING INDIAN OR POCAHONTAS TYPE, diamond-shaped, 4¾″, fiery opal
white, OP $2500–3500
FLARING PETALED BASE, six-sided, "CB" on base, 4⅛″, OP, cobalt blue ......
.... $80–100
FLOWER-SHAPED, ON PEDESTAL, 4½″, colorless, OP....................$125–150
FOUNTAIN, SQUARE, H113-1, 4¾″, colorless, OP.............................$75–90
HOURGLASS, eight panels, H114-7, 6″, amethyst, OP $500–600
INDIAN, diamond-shaped, H108-10, 4⅞″, aqua, OP......................$110–130
KNIGHT, H392-10, 5⅝″, aqua, OP $50–70
LION, labeled "cologne water," H111-5, 4½″, aqua, OP $150–175
MONUMENT, 12″, milk glass...$100–125
MONUMENT, 11¾″, colorless ,...$30–40
MONUMENT, 12″, deep emerald green $1200–1800
MONUMENT FIGURAL, 6½″, clambroth $150–250
MONUMENT SHAPE, 9⅛″, fiery opalescent...............................$160–180
MONUMENT SHAPE, 6″, deep grayish clambroth......................... $200–240
PANELED, 12-sided, 5″, light teal green, few lower lip chips $60–80
PANELED, 12-sided, 7½″, opal light blue....................................$500–600
PANELED, 12-sided, 7⅝″, bright yellow green, labeled................. $500–625
PANELED, 12-sided, 5″, teal blue.. $200–300
PANELED, 12-sided, 4¾″, deep blue... $100–140
PANELED, 12-sided, 5½″, medium amethyst, two lip chips $40–55
PANELED, 12-sided, 5½″,.teal green...$140–180
PANELED, 12-sided, 6⅜″, medium teal green............................$100–130
PANELED, 12-sided, 5⅝″, medium amethyst $80–100
PANELED, 12-sided, 7⅜″, deep amethyst $250–350
PANELED, 12-sided, 7⅜″, medium sapphire blue $125–175
PANELED, 12-sided, 8⅝″, medium amethyst $110–150
PANELED, 12-sided, 8⅞″, aqua, OP...$50–75
PANELED, 12-sided, sloping shoulders, 4⅝″, medium green, lip chip ...$40–60
PANELED, 12-sided, sloping shoulders, 6¼″, medium pink amethyst . $125–175
PANELED, 12-sided, sloping shoulders, 4⅞″, amethyst..................... $80–100
PANELED, 12-sided, sloping shoulders, 4¾″, teal blue.................... $140–180
PANELED, 12-sided, sloping shoulders, 6¼″, cobalt blue, OP $650–750
PANELED, 12-sided, sloping shoulders, 4⅝″, medium pink amethyst . $110–150
PANELED, 12-sided, sloping shoulders, 4⅞″, teal blue.................. $200–225
PANELED, 12-sided, 7¼″, teal blue, OP, two small lip chips...........$180–220
PEDESTAL FOOTED-VASE SHAPE, H112-7, 5⅛″, aqua, OP $55–75
PLUME AND COLUMN, H109-15, 4⅛″, aqua, OP, lip chips................. $8–10
PLUME-PATTERNED, H11-8, 8″, colorless, OP $70–90
PRESSED BOTTLE, hexagonal star and punty pattern, 7″, canary $150–200
RECTANGULAR WITH BEVELED EDGES, urn and floral decor on three panels,
7⅛″, olive amber, OP..$1000–1500
ROMAN COLUMN, H112-14, 8⅛″, colorless, OP.............................$55–65
SHIP EMBOSSED ON SIDE, H110-5, 4¾″, colorless, OP.....................$65–80
SIX ALTERNATING DIAMOND AND PLAIN PANELS, 11⅛″, cobalt blue $400–550
SQUARE WITH CENTRAL RIB, 5½″, amethyst, two small lip chips.... $200–225
SQUARE WITH CENTRAL RIB, 5⅝″, amethyst $300–375

SQUARE WITH STAR PATTERN AND ROPED EDGES, 8⅛″, milk glass $70–90
SQUARE WITH THUMBPRINT PATTERN, 5¾″, medium amethyst $450–550
SQUARE WITH UPWARDLY POINTING DIAMONDLIKE POINTS ON EDGES, 6⅜″,
amethyst $500–700

COSMETIC BOTTLES

The category of cosmetic bottles covers mainly hair treatment and restorer bottles, as well as products for the teeth, skin, and scalp. Hair
bottles are a popular collecting field because of the unusual colors of the
bottles, such as amethyst and dark blues, which were often used because
it was felt that light would not be able to neutralize some of the alcohol
properties of the medications through the darker bottles.

ALTENHEIM MEDICAL DISPENSARY, FOR HAIR, SCALP, 8″, colorless $6–9
ARNOLDS VEGETABLE HAIR BALSAM, 6⅛″, colorless $18–24
AYERS HAIR VIGOR, 7¼″, peacock blue, stopper $30–40
BALCHELORS LIQUID HAIR DYE # 1, 3″, aqua $10–15
BARRYS PEARL CREAM, 4¾″, milk glass $7–9
BOGLES HYPERION FLUID FOR THE HAIR, aqua.................................$9–12
BOSWELL & WARNERS COLORIFIC, 5⅝″, cobalt blue $135–175
BOSWELL WARNERS COLORIFIC, 5⅝″, deep amethyst.....................$100–140
BUCKINGHAM WHISKER DYE, 3¾″, amber $3–4
BUSHS ARGENTINE HAIR DYE #2, aqua, OP...................................$34–42
CARPENTER MORTON CO COLORITE, 4¼″, colorless $6–9
CATALAN HAIR RENEWER, six-sided, 6⅛″, cobalt blue $80–100
CIRCASSIAN HAIR RESTORATIVE, CINCINNATI, 7″, deep amber $190–235
CLIREHUGHS TRICOPHEROUS FOR THE HAIR & SKIN, 7″, aqua............$50–65
DAMSCHINSKY LIQUID HAIR DYE, NY, 4¼″, aqua $5–6
DAMSCHINSKY LIQUID HAIR DYE, NY, 3½″, aqua, stain $3–4
DODGE BROTHERS MELENINE HAIR TONIC, 7½″, puce $400–500
DR D JAYNES HAIR TONIC PHILADA, aqua, OP $15–18
DR GORHAMS GRAY HAIR RESTORER, 5⅝″, light amber....................$20–35
DR HAYS HAIR HEALTH, 6⅝″, light amber...................................$25–35
DR LEONS ELECTRIC HAIR RENEWER, 7¼″, amethyst.................... $300–400
DR TEBBETTS PHYSIOLOGICAL HAIR REGENERATOR, 7½″, medium amethyst ....
....$150–200
DR TEBBETTS PHYSIOLOGICAL HAIR RE-GENER, reddish amethyst $110–140
DR TEBBETTS PHYSIOLOGICAL HAIR REGENERATOR, 7⅝″, medium puce.........
.... $300–400
DR TIBBETTS PHYSIOLOGICAL HAIR RESTORER, 7½″, light amber.........$20–26
DR WM KORONG HAIR COLORING MFG CHEMIST, 4½″, colorless $8–11
EUREKA HAIR RESTORATIVE, 7″, aqua $10–15
FARRS GRAY HAIR RESTORER, 5½″, amber....................................$20–32

Cosmetic, an early hair bottle.
PHOTO COURTESY OF NEIL GROSSMAN.

FITCH'S QUINOILS FOR THE HAIR (ON LABEL), 6″, emerald green, metal cap $6–9
FLORIDA WATER DRUGGISTS, NY, 9¼″, colorless............................ $9–11
FONTAINES CREAM OF WILD FLOWERS, 4⅞″, aqua, OP $400–550
FRIXIE HAIR OIL, HOWARD DRUGS & MEDICINE Co, 2¼″, colorless........$3–4
GRANITONIC HAIR & SCALP FOOD, 8½″, colorless $3–5
HAGONS CLEANSER FOR CHILDRENS HAIR, aqua $25–32
HAIR RESTORER E & R QUINN, 6″, colorless..................................$20–25
HAYS HAIR HEALTH, amber, label and box $9–12
HOODS TOOTH POWDER, CI HOOD & CO, 3½″, colorless $5–7
HUMPHREYS MARVEL WITCHHAZEL, 5½″, colorless, ABM $3–4
IDEAL DANDRUFF REMOVER, FW FITCH, 6″, colorless $5–6
IMPERIAL HAIR REGENERATOR, NEW YORK, 4½″, light green $6–9
J MYERS BAVARIAN HAIR TONIC, 7″, aqua......................................$25–30
JEROMES HAIR COLOR RESTORER, 6⅜″, cobalt blue $250–350
JL GIOFRAY & CO HAIR RENOVATOR, 8¼, red amber $400–475
JOHN FITCH CO, YOUNGSTOWN, OHIO, 5¾″, colorless $7–10
KLINKERS HAIR TONIC, CLEVELAND, 6″, colorless $7–10
LARKIN CO, BUFFALO, cylinder, 3¾″, colorless $3–4
LARKIN CO, BUFFALO, cylinder, 6″, colorless $4–5
LARKIN CO, BUFFALO, oblong, 5″, colorless $4–5
LEVARNS GOLDEN WASH SHAMPOO, label under glass, 7¾″, colorless ..$40–50
LONDON HAIR RESTORER, 7¼″, aqua $24–30
LORRIMERS EXCELSIOR HAIR FORCER, 6⅜″, light amber....................$20–25
LUCKY HEART, MEMPHIS, TENN (ON BASE), jar, 2″, colorless, metal cap.$6–9
LUCKY TIGER FOR SCALP & HAIR, 7½″, colorless, metal cap $7–10
LUFKIN ECZEMA REMEDY, 7″, colorless, label $5–8
LYONS KATHAIRON FOR THE HAIR, aqua, OP.................................$20–30
LYONS POWDER, 4⅜″, deep amethyst, OP.................................. $90–120
LYONS POWDER, lime green...$20–30
MARY GOLDMAN, ST PAUL, MINN (WITH 100% LABEL) HAIR, COLOR RESTORER, amber $8–12
MELANINE HAIR TONIC DODGE BROTHERS, 7½″, puce amethyst $250–300
MELANINE HAIR TONIC DODGE BROS, 7¼″, amethyst $300–350
MEXICAN HAIR RESTORER, 7″, cobalt $20–30
MORLEYS HAIR RESTORER, amber, flask-shaped $40–50
MRS ALLENS WORLDS HAIR RESTORER, 7¼″, violet....................$150–200

Mrs Allens Worlds Hair Restorer, 7″, amber $7–9
Mrs S Allens World Hair Restorer, deep olive green.............. $300–350
Mrs SA Allens Worlds Hair Balsam, 6¾″, aqua, OP.................$50–70
Mrs SA Allens Worlds Hair Restorer, 7⅛″, yellow amber $30–40
Mrs SA Allens Worlds Hair Restorer, 7⅜″, deep purple amethyst/violet..
.... $500–700
Mrs SA Allens Worlds Hair Restorer, 7¼″, deep amethyst $150–180
Nathan Jarvis Orris Tooth Wash, N-332, 4⅞″, aqua, OP $90–150
Nattans Crystal Discovery For The Hair, 7½″, cobalt.............$150–225
Natures Hair Restorative, 7″, aqua $20–30
Newbros Herpicide For The Scalp, 7″, colorless.......................... $8–10
Newbros Herpicide For The Scalp, 4 oz., 6½″, colorless $5–7
Newbros Herpicide Kills Dandruff Germ, 7″, colorless............... $10–15
Newbros Herpicide (In Script) Kills The Dandruff Germ, 7″, colorless...
.... $15–18
Newhalls Magic Hair Restorer, 7½″, cobalt blue, base crack/bruise........
....$60–75
Noonans Hair Petrole, 7″, aqua...$20–30
Noonans Hair Petroleum, Boston, 6½″, aqua............................$20–30
Oldridge Balm Of Columbia For Restoring Hair, 6¼″, aqua.......$40–55
Palmolive Shampoo, BJ Johnson, 7¼″, colorless, ABM, rectangular ...$4–6
Palmolive Shampoo, BJ Johnson, ten panels, 4″, aqua, ABM............$5–7
Parisian Sage & Hair Tonic, 7¼″, aqua $6–8
Parkers Hair Balsam, 6⅝″, yellow green.................................$30–40
Parkers Hair Balsam, New York, 6½″, amber, rectangular $6–9
Parkers Hair Balsam, New York, emerald green.......................... $9–12
Parkers Hair Balsam, NY, 6¾″, amber....................................$3–4
Paul Westphal Auxiliator For The Hair, 6¾″, colorless.................$6–9
Paul Westphal Auxiliator For The Hair, 8″, colorless $22–26
Paul Westphal Auxiliator For The Hair, 6½″, colorless..............$20–24
Perrys Hungarian Balm For The Hair, 5¾″, aqua, OP, rectangular ....
....$35–50
Ponds Extract, 5½″, sun-colored amethyst.................................$15–20
Ponds Extract, 5½″, colorless $8–10
Prof Jr Tilton The Great Hair Producer, 6⅞″, medium cobalt.. $175–225
Rauchfuss Eureka, 7½″, teal blue, IP $170–200
Rhodes Hair Rejuvenator, 6½″, light amber..............................$20–25
Rose Hair Tonic & Dandruff Cure, label under glass, 7¾″, colorless........
....$40–50
Royal Foot Wash, Eaton Drug Co, Altanta, Ga $8–12
RP Halls Improved Preparation Of The Hair, 7½″, cobalt blue. $200–300
Rubifoam For The Teeth, Put Up By EW Hoyt & Co, 4″, colorless...$6–9
Sanitol For The Teeth, 4½″, colorless.......................................$6–8
Scheffler Hair Colorine, 4″, colorless....................................$5–8
Sutherland 7 Sisters Hair Grower, 6⅛″, colorless.................. $10–15
Sutherland Sisters Hair Grower, New York, 5¼″, colorless, ABM..$5–8
Sutherland Sisters Hair Grower, New York, 5¼″, aqua.............. $7–10
Teaberry For The Teeth & Breath, 3½″, colorless $6–9
W Fitch Co, This Bottle Loaned by, 7¾″, colorless, OP, lady's leg ....
....$25–35
Wagners For The Hair Sapajo, 6⅛″, deep cobalt $75–100

WALNUT LEAF HAIR RESTORER, 7⅝", yellow amber.........................$60–75
WC MONTGOMERYS HAIR RESTORER, 7½", medium amethyst, labeled...........
....$300–450
WC MONTGOMERYS HAIR RESTORER, deep amethyst.....................$150–200
WC MONTGOMERYS HAIR RESTORER, 7¼", light amber...................$20–27
WH HARRIS HAIR RESTORATIVE, 7¼", aqua................................ $60–90
WILDROOT COMPANY, BUFFALO, NY, 6", amber...............................$6–8
ZEMO ANTISEPTIC LOTION FOR SKIN & SCALP, 6", colorless.................$7–9

ENAMELED BOTTLES

Bottles with enameled decoration have been popular in Europe since the Middle Ages. The process of enameling involves the painting on of the enamels, with subsequent heating of the glass which fuses the enamel to the body of the piece. Most, if not all, of the enameled pieces found in this country were imported from the Germany/Switzerland area in the mid to late 18th century. Ordinarily, the designs are of florals, birds, and people, and occasionally German inscriptions. Most of the bottles are fitted with pewter screw caps, and most of the glass is clear and bubbly. Collectors should be watchful for the occasional sapphire blue pieces. The pewter screw caps are ordinarily not found with the bottles, and finding a matching cap adds to the value. Collectors should be aware that enameled glass continues to be made and it is often difficult to distinguish from the original 18th-century pieces. For background and beautiful examples of enameled glass, the reader is referred to *European Glass from 1500–1800*, of the Ernest Wolf Collection by Brigitte Klesse and Hans Mayr.

COLOGNE, enameled with bird and florals, 4", deep blue, OP $500–750

Enameled, with pewter cap, late 18th century.
PHOTO COURTESY OF SKINNER'S, INC.

CORDIAL BOTTLE, rectangular with beveled edges, 5″, colorless, OP, with pewter cap $200–250
CORDIAL BOTTLE, rectangular with beveled edges, with multicolored design, colorless, OP $150–200
CORDIAL BOTTLE, rectangular with beveled edges, 4¾″, fiery opal white ....
....$200–275
CORDIAL BOTTLE, with multicolored woman and flowers, colorless, 5¾″, OP
.... $150–180
FLASK, colorless with multicolored enamel design of swords, flowers, 5″, OP..
.... $200–225
FLASK, with multicolored bird on heart, ½ pt., colorless, OP $250–350

FIGURAL BOTTLES

These bottles cover a wide area and include figures of people, animals, and objects, all in a wide variety of colors and sizes. Many of the sought after figural bottles were made in the late 19th century, but 20th-century bottles are also popular. The reader is referred to *Collectible Character Bottles* by Umberger.

ACORN, 2¾″, colorless..$20–25
BANJO BOTTLE, 9¾″, light apple green.......................................$15–20
BARREL, 9¾″, deep sapphire blue $700–1000
BARREL, LAM A & F (ON BASE), 9¾″, emerald green $75–90
BARREL-SHAPED, unembossed, 9¾″, deep sapphire blue, IP $700–1000
BARREL WATER COOLER, 17″, cobalt blue $300–400
BEAR FIGURAL, black $40–50
BEAR FIGURAL, with applied face, aqua, base crack $30–40
BEAR POMADE JAR, 3¾″, milk glass..$300–375
BEAR POMADE JAR, removable head, 3¾″, deep amethyst.............. $125–175

Figural, kummel bear. PHOTO COURTESY OF NEIL GROSSMAN.

BEAR POMADE JAR, BA PHILA (ON BASE), 4½″, black, paws are folded between legs $800–1200
BEAR POMADE JAR, FB STROUSE NY (ON BASE), 3¾″, black $350–450
BEAR POMADE JAR, R & CA WRIGHT (ON BASE), 5¼″, white body and black head $800–1200
BENJAMIN HARRISON BUST, 16″, frosted bust on black base $400–600
BOB FITZSIMMONS, PRIZEFIGHTER, lower torso only, colorless frosted glass $70–90
BOB FITZSIMMONS, PRIZEFIGHTER, upper body is flesh-colored, lower is frosted, 14½″ $1000–1200
BOOK, POTTERY, "Departed Spirits," 5¾″, brown and orange glazes $250–350
BOOK, POTTERY, "Coming Thro the Rye," 5″, blue glaze $90–120
BOOK, POTTERY, "History of Holland" (on edge), 5½″, blue glaze . $200–250
BOOK, POTTERY, "Bennington Battle," 10½″, brown, tan, cream, and green glazes $800–1200
BOOK, POTTERY, unembossed, 10¾″, brown and cream glazes........ $300–350
BOOK, POTTERY, unembossed, 5¾″, brown, cream, and yellow glazes............ .... $300–400
BOOT, LADY'S, 3¾″, colorless.. $10–18
BOOT, NAILSEA TYPE, colorless with white loopings, 8¾″, OP $100–130
BOOT, SARATOGA DRESSING, 4¼″, aqua $30–45
BOOT, "SARATOGA DRESSING," 4½″, aqua $30–40
BUGLE, 8¼″, colorless with metal screw cap $200–275
BUNKER HILL MONUMENT, 12″, colorless..................................... $30–45
CAMEL, ceramic with mother-of-pearl glaze, 4″, with stopper $30–40
CANNON, PHALON & SON, 7⅛″, colorless $40–45
CAT, 8″, colorless.. $8–12
CHERUB HOLDING CLOCK, 14¼″, colorless $10–20
CHILDREN CLIMBING TREE, 14¾″, colorless................................... $25–25
CHINAMAN WITH PONYTAIL, 5¼, colorless...................................... $20–25
CIGAR, 5⅜″, light amber $20–25
CIGARS, BUNCH OF, 5¼″, light amber, screw cap.............................. $25–35
CLAM SHELL, 5⅛″, with all its paint, screw cap $35–45
CLAM SHELL, colorless with metal cap, original paint $28–40
CLAM SHELL, screw top, 3⅞″, colorless $30–40
CLASSIC BUST ON PEDESTAL, 15½″, black $175–225
CLEVELAND FIGURAL, U-140, 9½″, colorless, OP, frosted $80–120
CLOCK FLASK, 6½″, colorless $15–25
CLOCK, GRANDFATHER, 7¾″, colorless, with label........................... $15–20
COACHMAN, POTTERY, 10½″, tan and brown glaze, boot chip.......... $225–275
COACHMAN, VAN DUNCKS, 8½″, black glass $50–80
COACHMAN, VAN DUNCKS GENEVER, dark amber $100–150
COAL CHUNK, screw cap, 3¼″, amethyst $125–175
COLUMBUS, square milk glass with metal figure stopper, 18¼″ $275–350
COLUMBUS COLUMN, milk glass base with metal statue of Columbus, 18″ $250–350
COLUMBUS METAL FIGURE, on milk glass column, 18⅜″ $500–650
CRYING BABY, 6″, colorless $40–60
CRYING BABY, 5¾″, opaque white $600–900
CRYING BABY, "TPS&CO" (ON BASE), 6⅛″, colorless.................... $20–30

CRYING BABY, head only, colorless $70–90
CZAR, 10⅛", milk glass $400–600
CZARINA ALEXANDRA, 10½", milk glass $400–600
DICE BOTTLE, square, 1¹/₁₆", colorless......................................$35–45
DOG, 9½", green $7–9
DOG, ATTERBURY (ON BASE), JLD DAWES, 11½", milk glass.......$1200–1800
DOG JAR, 5", colorless, screw cap..$12–15
DUCK, 12⅝", opaque white, OP $700–1000
DUCK, ATTERBURY (ON BASE), 11⅝", milk glass........................ $300–500
DUCK, PATD APRIL 11TH 1871 (ON BASE), 11⅝", opaque white....... $450–600
EAR OF CORN, 5½", colorless...$12–15
EIFFEL TOWER, 13⅞", colorless..$12–15
ELEPHANT, 10½", amber $8–11
ELEPHANT AND TREE, 3⅞", colorless $12–15
ELEPHANT WITH UPLIFTED TRUNK, 18", colorless frosted $125–160
ELEPHANT WITH UPTURNED TRUNK, 12", colorless...................... $10–15
ELKS BUST WITH CLOCK, 11¾", colorless with original paint...........$75–150
ELKS TOOTH FLASK, 4", opaque white $80–110
ELKS TOOTH, white porcelain with clock face, 4½" $40–50
EYE OPENER, EYEBALL FIGURAL, 5¼", opaque white $200–275
FIDDLE, 6½", light amber, thick glass, early bottle $40–60
FIREMAN OR POLICEMAN, 11¼", colorless, ¼" shoulder crack $60–80
FISH, 11", aqua...$10–15
FISH, 7", colorless $10–15
FISH, colorless, 4" $8–12
FISH, with original paint, 8¾", colorless, with screw cap $50–65
FOX READING BOOK, ceramic, beige with brown mottling..................$30–48
GIRL WITH HANDS AT WAIST, 7", colorless, early bottle.................. $60–90
GLOBE-SHAPED JAR, pt., colorless, with screw cap $4–5
GOAT, 11½", colorless.. $8–12
GOLD NUGGET, 6", milk glass with metal cap...............................$45–55
GOLD NUGGET, colorless with paint, screw cap..............................$40–60
GOLF BAG, 3¼", colorless with original paint........................$25–40
GRANTS TOMB, 10", opaque white with metal Grant bust cover $450–600
GRANTS TOMB, milk glass base with metal bust of Grant, 11⅛" $200–275
GROVER CLEVELAND, 9½", colorless and frosted $80–100
HAM, colorless with paint, screw cap.......................................$20–30
HAND, 5¼", colorless...$30–40
HAND HOLDING BOTTLE, 11⅛", colorless with frosted hand, pontil $40–55
HAND HOLDING BOTTLE, 13⅞", colorless....................................$20–30
HAND HOLDING BOTTLE, colorless with frosted hand......................$40–60
HEART, JOHN HART & CO, 7¼", golden amber............................ $90–120
HENRY CLAY, 11", colorless, OP...$250–350
HESSIAN SOLDIER, 7", colorless...$30–50
JOHN BULL FIGURAL, 11⅜", golden amber $200–250
LANCASTER GLASS WORKS LANCASTER NY (ON BASE), barrel, orange amber
....$160–230
LANCASTER GLASS WORKS LANCASTER NY (ON BASE), barrel, olive yellow .....
....$250–350
LIGHTHOUSE, 5½", colorless, tin cap $50–60
LITTLE GIRL READING BOOK, 4¼", milk glass............................. $125–175

Figural, Moses spring water. PHOTO COURTESY OF
NEIL GROSSMAN.

MAN IN THE MOON, decanter set, 13″, yellow amber moon $1400–1800
MAN ON BARREL, 11½″, colorless with paint $15–25
MAN SITTING ON BARREL, 13½″, light olive yellow, with shot glass top ....
.... $90–120
MAN WITH SHOES UNDER ARM, 13¾″, colorless $10–14
MARCHAND BUST, 13″, milk glass $800–1000
MARIE ANTOINETTE, 11¾″, colorless $150–200
MATADOR, 12″, colorless $9–12
MAXIMILLIAN, 11″, colorless, OP $250–350
MERMAID BOTTLE, ceramic, 7¾″, brown glaze $70–90
MONKEY, pottery, 5½″, olive green glaze $60–80
MONKEY JAR, 5″, colorless $12–15
MONUMENT, 12″, deep emerald green $1200–1800
MONUMENT, 5⅛″, colorless with slight purple tint $15–20
MOSES BOTTLE, POLAND SPRING WATER, qt., amber, cork top $450–550
MOSES BOTTLE, POLAND SPRING WATER, qt., aqua, cork top $50–70
MOSES IN THE BULRUSHES, 4¾″, colorless $50–60
MOSES, POLAND SPRING WATER, 11¼″, aqua $50–65
MOSES, POLAND SPRING WATER, 11″, colorless, pontil scar $60–80
MOSES, POLAND SPRING WATER, 11″, honey amber $400–550
MOSES, POLAND SPRING WATER, 11″, green with flaring lip $150–200
MOSES, POLAND SPRING WATER, with flared lip, 10⅞″, green, ABM. $175–250
MOSES, POLAND SPRING WATER, 10¾″, amber........................: $425–550
NAPOLEON OR STANDING SOLDIER, 7¼″, colorless $40–60
NEGRO WAITER, U-14, 14½″, colorless with black head $150–200
NIGHT STICK, 10½″, amber, with screw cap $15–25
NUGGET, with traces of gold paint, screw cap, 5⅞″, opaque white $50–60
OWL JAR, 5″, colorless, screw cap $12–15
OYSTER, colorless, with metal screw cap $25–35
OYSTER SHELL, 5⅛″, colorless, screw cap $20–30
PARROT, 8″, opaque white, cracked neck $50–65
PICKLE, 4½″, medium green $90–120
PIG, ceramic, unembossed, 6½″, tan glaze with blue eyes $175–250
PIG, pottery, Anna Railroad pig with map of railroad lines, 7″, dated 1882.....
.... $4000–6000
PIG, BIELERS RONNY CLUB, pottery, 9½″, brown and tan glaze $350–450

PIG, DRINK WHILE IT LASTS FROM THE HOGS . . . , 6¾″, colorless .$150–200
PINEAPPLE, 4¾″, colorless $10–15
PINEAPPLE, 7½″, colorless $10–15
PINEAPPLE, unembossed, 9″, amber..$45–65
PINEAPPLE, W & Co, NY, 8½″, deep olive yellow, IP $550–750
PISTOL, DUELING, pottery, 11½″, brown glaze........................... $200–240
POINGARE BUST, 13¼″, milk glass...$750–1150
POMADE JAR, BEAR FIGURAL, R & CA WRIGHT, 5¼″, white body and black
head $800–1200
POTATO, 4¼″, aqua $25–35
POTATO, colorless with brown paint, screw cap............................$20–30
POWDER HORN, 5″, colorless, with metal cap $20–25
PRETZEL, ceramic $50–60
RABBIT JAR, 5″, colorless, screw cap $12–15
SAD HOUND DOG, 10¾″, citron, some original paint $30–45
SANTA CLAUS, colorless $80–120
SANTA CLAUS, "MG Husted" on side, 12½″, colorless.................. $60–90
SANTA CLAUS, U-41, 12¼″, colorless $90–120
SANTA CLAUS, MC HUSTED, 12″, colorless.............................. $200–240
SCALLOP SHELL, 5″, aqua, screw cap $25–35
SCALLOP SHELL, colorless, with metal screw cap.........................$25–35
SEATED BEAR, 11″, deep red amethyst $30–40
SEATED BEAR, 11″, milk glass $60–80
SEATED WOLF WITH BOOK, GERMANY (ON BASE), 4⅞″, brown/beige glaze,
ceramic $40–60
SEEING EYE, "EYE OPENER" (ON REVERSE), 5″, milk glass........... $130–160
SENORITA, 13½″, colorless...$25–30
SHIELD SHAPE, with American flag and Texas flag, 5⅜″, white, screw cap .....
.... $125–175
SHOE, 3½″, black amethyst $40–60
SHOE, fancy, 5½″, colorless, with applied lip..............................$30–45
SHOE, with floral buckle, 3½″, colorless $15–20
SITTING MONKEY, 4½″, milk glass $110–150
SOLDIER'S BUST, 10½″, colorless $15–25
SPANISH SENORITA, 12″, colorless $8–12
STANDING DUCK, 9¾″, colorless, with shot glass stopper................. $60–90
STANDING KUMMEL BEAR, 10½″, olive green............................$40–60

Figural, Santa. PHOTO COURTESY OF NEIL GROSSMAN.

STANDING KUMMEL BEAR, 11¼″, milk glass...............................$60–90
STANDING KUMMEL BEAR, 11¼″, black...$55–65
SWEET POTATO, 7″, ceramic $50–75
TALL CLOCK, 12″, light purple $8–12
TURTLE "MERRY XMAS" (ON BOTTOM), colorless, 5¼″, with tin cap ..$25–40
TURTLE, "MERRY XMAS" (ON BASE), colorless with metal screw cap...$25–35
UNCLE SAM, colorless...$40–60
UNCLE SAM BOTTLE, 9½″, colorless, missing screw cap.................$90–120
VAN DUNCKS, COACHMAN BOTTLE, 8½″, deep amber.....................$70–90
VAN DUNCKS GENEVER, COACHMAN, 8⅝″, deep amber, ¼″ lip chip .. $60–80
VICTOR HUGO, 11¾″, painted bust of man with lyre $300–400
VIOLIN, 9¾″, electric blue $15–20
WAITRESS, Negro, frosted glass body with painted black head, 14″ .$800–1200
WHISK BROOM, "DUST REMOVER," 6¼″, white, blue, and brown glaze.........
....$40–60
WICKERED DEMIJOHN, 3″, aqua, pontil..$25–30
WINDMILL, ceramic, 9½″, blue-decorated $12–15
WOMAN FIGURAL, full body, 10½″, milk glass $300–400
WOMAN POTTERY BOTTLE, Rockingham glaze, 8¾″ $110–130
WOMAN WITH CROSSED ARMS, 14¾″, colorless $10–15
WOMAN'S BUST, ceramic, with angels on lower half, 8¼″ $40–60
WOMAN'S TORSO, colorless, 6½″, screw cap................................$20–25
WOMAN'S TORSO, screw top, 6⅝″, colorless $35–45

FIGURED FLASKS

Among the most highly prized and sought after of all bottles are the figured flasks, which make up the group of decorative, Masonic, historical, and pictorial flasks. No other area of bottles comes close to equaling the wide variety of design and colors used, as is evidenced by the record prices set for these types of bottles.

Figured flasks first appeared in the United States about 1815 in Connecticut, and then spread to glasshouses across the country, which produced these items into the 20th century. Generally speaking, the earlier the flasks, the more skillfully and elaborately made was the design. Around the mid-19th century, the flasks began to become thinner in shape with less attention given to design detail and eye appeal. Among the earliest flasks made were those which pictured American heroes such as George Washington, Jackson, and Taylor, as well as eagles, Masonics, cornucopias and urns, and sunburst flasks. These types of flasks continued to be made into the mid to late 19th century, when other types such as scroll flasks, Pike's Peak varieties, and those with the glasshouse name embossed became more common.

Nowhere in the field of bottle collecting does color have such an effect on the rarity and value of a given bottle than it does in the area of figured flasks. For example, a Columbia-Eagle flask in aqua can be purchased for approximately $300 to $400, whereas the same flask in cobalt blue will be well in excess of $30,000. In the area of flasks, many collectors attempt to specialize in a given area, such as sunbursts or eagle flasks, whereas others attempt to obtain every color known for a given type of flask.

Because of the immense interest in figured flasks, the collector should also be aware of the wide range of both legitimate reproductions and outright fakes available on the market. While most of the reproductions and fakes are easily distinguished from the originals, there are several which are very difficult to identify as 20th century. It is strongly recommended that interested parties become familiar with the reproductions and fakes by reading the previous chapter on "Fakes, Reproductions, and Repairs," and by studying the well-written chapters in *American Bottles and Flasks and Their Ancestry* by McKearin and Wilson, from which all references in this chapter are drawn.

Note: An asterisk (*) following an entry title means that the item has been reproduced. Also, all entries are arranged numerically according to reference number.

WASHINGTON-EAGLE, GI-1, pt., deep aqua, OP, strong impression ...$275–350
WASHINGTON-EAGLE, GI-1, pt., light blue green, OP, small lip chip .$425–525
WASHINGTON-EAGLE, GI-1, pt., bright green, OP......................... $400–550
WASHINGTON-EAGLE, GI-1, pt., light blue green, OP $500–750
WASHINGTON-EAGLE, GI-2, pt., deep greenish aqua, OP............... $250–300
WASHINGTON-EAGLE, GI-2, pt., pale green, OP........................... $200–240
WASHINGTON-EAGLE, GI-2, pt., light greenish, aqua, OP $225–275
WASHINGTON-EAGLE, GI-2, pt., greenish aqua, OP.......................$250–325
WASHINGTON-EAGLE, GI-2, pt., greenish aqua, OP, lip flake........... $140–180
WASHINGTON-EAGLE, GI-3, pt., aqua, OP................................. $600–800
WASHINGTON-EAGLE, GI-3, pt., deep aqua, OP $800–1000
WASHINGTON-EAGLE, GI-3, pt., aqua, OP, 1″ medial rib crack $100–140
WASHINGTON-EAGLE, GI-6, pt., aqua, OP................................. $300–400
WASHINGTON-EAGLE, GI-6, pt., colorless with amethyst tint, OP...$1200–1500
WASHINGTON-EAGLE, GI-7, pt., greenish aqua, OP, base crack........ $175–225
WASHINGTON-EAGLE, GI-8, pt., pale green, OP.....................$9000–12,000
WASHINGTON-EAGLE, GI-9, pt., pale yellow green, OP................. $400–600
WASHINGTON-EAGLE, GI-9, pt., deep greenish aqua, OP............... $450–600
WASHINGTON-EAGLE, GI-9, pt., greenish aqua, OP...................... $700–900
WASHINGTON-EAGLE, GI-10, pt., pale blue green, OP $90–120
WASHINGTON-EAGLE, GI-10, pt., greenish aqua, OP, base chip....... $200–250
WASHINGTON-EAGLE, GI-10, pt., aqua, OP................................$500–750
WASHINGTON-EAGLE, GI-10, pt., aqua, OP, light stain $180–240
WASHINGTON-EAGLE, GI-11, pt., aqua......................................$400–500
WASHINGTON-EAGLE, GI-11, pt., deep aqua, OP, lip ground down... $300–400
WASHINGTON-EAGLE, GI-11, pt., aqua, OP, lip bruise $175–225

WASHINGTON-EAGLE, GI-11, pt., aqua, OP, ³/₈″ lip chip $250–325
WASHINGTON-EAGLE, GI-11, pt., greenish aqua, OP $450–600
WASHINGTON-EAGLE, GI-12, pt., pale blue green, OP $1500–2500
WASHINGTON-EAGLE, GI-13, pt., pale yellow green, OP............. $4500–6500
WASHINGTON-EAGLE, GI-14, pt., greenish aqua, OP $175–225
WASHINGTON-EAGLE, GI-14, pt., aqua, OP, polished lip chip $100–125
WASHINGTON-EAGLE, GI-14, pt., aqua, OP, stain in neck................ $80–120
WASHINGTON-EAGLE, GI-14, pt., aqua, OP, lip chip $80–100
WASHINGTON-EAGLE, GI-14, pt., aqua, OP.................................... $125–175
WASHINGTON-EAGLE, GI-14, pt., aqua, OP, light stain $110–150
WASHINGTON-EAGLE, GI-14, pt., colorless with amethyst tint, OP... $900–1200
WASHINGTON-EAGLE, GI-14, pt., bright medium green, OP, light wear ....
....$1800–2300
WASHINGTON-EAGLE, GI-14, pt., pale aqua, OP........................... $120–140
WASHINGTON-EAGLE, GI-15, pt., aqua, OP $110–150
WASHINGTON-EAGLE, GI-16, pt., aqua, lip bruise........................... $60–90
WASHINGTON-EAGLE, GI-16, pt., aqua, OP................................... $100–150
WASHINGTON-EAGLE, GI-16, pt., aqua, OP, lip flake, stain $50–70
WASHINGTON-TAYLOR, GI-17, pt., pale yellow green, OP $200–250
WASHINGTON-TAYLOR, GI-17, pt., greenish aqua, OP $55–65
WASHINGTON-TAYLOR, GI-17, pt., light pinkish amethyst, OP $500–650
WASHINGTON-BALTIMORE GLASS WORKS, GI-18, pt., light gray blue, OP.........
.... $1100–1400
WASHINGTON-BALTIMORE GLASS WORKS, GI-18, pt., bright aqua, OP.$150–200
WASHINGTON-BALTIMORE GLASS WORKS, GI-18, pt., yellow green, OP...........
.... $2800–3500
WASHINGTON-MONUMENT, GI-19, pt., aqua, OP $300–500
WASHINGTON-MONUMENT, GI-19, pt., puce, OP $2500–4000
WASHINGTON-MONUMENT, GI-20, pt., bright yellow green, OP...... $700–1000
WASHINGTON-MONUMENT, GI-20, light greenish aqua, OP $200–250
WASHINGTON-MONUMENT, GI-20, pt., aqua, OP............................ $80–120
WASHINGTON-MONUMENT, GI-20, pt., colorless with blue tint, OP $90–130
WASHINGTON-MONUMENT, GI-20, pt., cobalt blue, OP $3000–5000
WASHINGTON-MONUMENT, GI-21, qt., aqua, OP, stain $40–50
WASHINGTON-MONUMENT, GI-21, qt., aqua, OP $80–120
WASHINGTON-MONUMENT, GI-21, qt., medium topaz yellow green, OP..........
.... $1500–2000
WASHINGTON-MONUMENT, GI-21, qt., colorless, OP, lip roughness......$70–85
WASHINGTON-CLASSICAL BUST, GI-22, qt., greenish aqua, OP $200–230
WASHINGTON-CLASSICAL BUST, GI-22, qt., pale yellow green, OP $240–280
WASHINGTON-CLASSICAL BUST, GI-23, qt., strawberry puce, OP .. $2500–3500
WASHINGTON-TAYLOR, GI-24, pt., blue green, OP, potstone crack $250–350
WASHINGTON-TAYLOR, GI-24, pt., golden amber, OP $350–500
WASHINGTON-TAYLOR, GI-24, pt., aqua, OP $120–150
WASHINGTON-CLASSICAL BUST, GI-25, qt., aqua, OP, inner stain.........$35–45
WASHINGTON-CLASSICAL BUST, GI-25, qt., light cornflower blue, OP.$275–350
WASHINGTON-CLASSICAL BUST, GI-25, qt., aqua, OP $160–220
WASHINGTON-EAGLE,* GI-26, qt., aqua, OP................................. $140–180
WASHINGTON-EAGLE,* GI-26, qt., medium emerald green, OP $900–1200
WASHINGTON-EAGLE,* GI-26, qt., citron, OP $600–800
WASHINGTON-EAGLE,* GI-26, qt., blue green, OP....................... $400–600

Washington-Eagle,* GI-26, qt., aqua with milky striations, OP...... $75–120
Washington-Eagle,* GI-26, qt., aqua, OP, light inner stain $80–110
Washington-Eagle, GI-27, qt., deep olive yellow, OP............. $2000–3000
Washington-Eagle, GI-27, qt., medium blue green, OP $900–1000
Washington-Sailing Ship,* GI-28, pt., bluish green, OP $500–650
Washington-Sailing Ship,* GI-28, pt., aqua, OP, pontil chip $60–80
Washington-Sailing Ship,* GI-28, pt., light sapphire blue, OP . $2500–3000
Washington-Sailing Ship,* GI-28, pt., golden yellow, IP $750–1000
Washington-Sailing Ship,* GI-28, pt., aqua, OP $110–140
Washington-Sailing Ship,* GI-28, pt., golden amber, IP $700–900
Washington-Sailing Ship,* GI-28, pt., deep golden amber, IP, edge hole ....
.... $90–120
Washington-Sailing Ship,* GI-28, pt., pale green with amber striations, IP
.... $500–650
Washington-Sailing Ship,* GI-29, pt., electric blue, OP $30–50
Washington-Albany Glass Works, GI-30, ½ pt., aqua, OP........ $125–160
Washington-Albany Glass Works, GI-30, ½ pt., greenish aqua, OP ....
.... $125–150
Washington-Albany Glass Works, GI-30, ½ pt., bright green, OP ....
.... $250–400
Washington-Jackson, GI-31, pt., yellow olive $125–175
Washington-Jackson, GI-31, pt., olive amber, OP...................... $100–150
Washington-Jackson, GI-31, pt., light yellow amber, OP $100–130
Washington-Jackson, GI-31, pt., deep golden yellow, OP $275–350
Washington-Jackson, GI-31, pt., olive amber, OP...................... $100–130
Washington-Jackson, GI-32, pt., aqua, OP $200–300
Washington-Jackson, GI-32, pt., yellow olive, OP, ground lip chip .. $60–90
Washington-Jackson, GI-32, pt., yellow olive, OP $90–120
Washington-Jackson, GI-33, pt., olive amber, OP $90–120
Washington-Jackson, GI-34, ½ pt., olive amber, OP $125–175
Washington-Jackson, GI-34, ½ pt., deep olive amber, OP $100–125
Washington-Jackson, GI-34, ½ pt., yellow olive, OP $125–160
Washington-Tree, GI-35, calabash, sapphire blue, OP............. $4000–5000
Washington-Tree, GI-35, calabash, aqua, OP, light inner stain.........$40–60
Washington-Tree, GI-35, calabash, aqua, OP $70–85
Washington-Tree, GI-36, calabash, aqua, OP $60–90
Washington-Taylor,* GI-37, qt., olive yellow $325–425
Washington-Taylor,* GI-37, qt., bright medium green $160–210

Figured Flask, Washington–Taylor, GI-38. PHOTO
COURTESY OF NEIL GROSSMAN.

WASHINGTON-TAYLOR,* GI-37, qt., medium blue green, OP............$250–350
WASHINGTON-TAYLOR,* GI-37, qt., sapphire blue, OP $900–1100
WASHINGTON-TAYLOR,* GI-37, qt., amethyst, lip flakes $1000–1400
WASHINGTON-TAYLOR,* GI-37, qt., copperish amber.....................$300–500
WASHINGTON-TAYLOR, GI-38, pt., strawberry puce, OP $800–975
WASHINGTON-TAYLOR, GI-38, pt., aqua, OP, lip and pontil chip $50–70
WASHINGTON-TAYLOR, GI-38, pt., aqua, OP $60–90
WASHINGTON-TAYLOR, GI-38, pt., emerald green $250–300
WASHINGTON-TAYLOR, GI-38, pt., emerald green, OP, lip chip/bruise$150–200
WASHINGTON-TAYLOR, GI-38, pt., dark olive green, OP $500–700
WASHINGTON-TAYLOR, GI-38, pt., medium green, OP $150–200
WASHINGTON-TAYLOR, GI-38, pt., puce $750–850
WASHINGTON-TAYLOR, GI-38, pt., deep yellow olive, OP $325–500
WASHINGTON-TAYLOR, GI-39, qt., medium pinkish amethyst, OP . $2000–3000
WASHINGTON-TAYLOR, GI-39, qt., blue green, OP.........................$225–250
WASHINGTON-TAYLOR, GI-39, qt., colorless, OP $200–225
WASHINGTON-TAYLOR, GI-39, qt., medium blue green, OP, stain $140–175
WASHINGTON-TAYLOR, GI-39, qt., aqua, OP, lip chip, stain $35–50
WASHINGTON-TAYLOR, GI-39, qt., medium blue green, OP $175–200
WASHINGTON-TAYLOR, GI-39, qt., deep blue green, OP $250–325
WASHINGTON-TAYLOR, GI-39, qt., medium emerald green, OP $400–500
WASHINGTON-TAYLOR, GI-39a, qt., light yellow green $175–225
WASHINGTON-TAYLOR, GI-39b, qt., dark yellow olive, OP $350–450
WASHINGTON-TAYLOR, GI-40, pt., deep olive yellow/green, OP...... $700–1000
WASHINGTON-TAYLOR, GI-40, pt., opal aqua, OP...........................$75–90
WASHINGTON-TAYLOR, GI-40a, pt., deep golden yellow, OP $550–650
WASHINGTON-TAYLOR, GI-40b, pt., cobalt blue, OP..................$1200–1500
WASHINGTON-TAYLOR, GI-40c, pt., aqua, OP, stain $20–35
WASHINGTON-TAYLOR, GI-41, ½ pt., olive green, OP $2000–3000
WASHINGTON-TAYLOR, GI-41, ½ pt., deep greenish aqua..................$75–95
WASHINGTON-TAYLOR, GI-42, qt., aqua, OP, slight inner stain............$40–50
WASHINGTON-TAYLOR, GI-42, qt., cobalt blue, OP $800–1100
WASHINGTON-TAYLOR, GI-42, qt., aqua, OP, double-collared lip $75–90
WASHINGTON-TAYLOR, GI-42, qt., cobalt blue, OP $1500–2500
WASHINGTON-TAYLOR, GI-42, qt., milky aqua, OP $175–250
WASHINGTON-TAYLOR, GI-43, aqua, OP $75–90
WASHINGTON-TAYLOR, GI-43, qt., medium blue green, OP $250–350
WASHINGTON-TAYLOR, GI-43, qt., smoky mauve, OP $1000–1200
WASHINGTON-TAYLOR, GI-43, qt., medium smoky amethyst, OP $900–1200
WASHINGTON-TAYLOR, GI-43, qt., gray puce, OP $700–900
WASHINGTON-TAYLOR, GI-43, qt., smoky puce, OP $1500–1800
WASHINGTON-TAYLOR, GI-44, pt., citron, OP.............................$750–1000
WASHINGTON-TAYLOR, GI-44, pt., golden yellow, OP....................$500–750
WASHINGTON-TAYLOR, GI-44, pt., cobalt blue, OP $1000–1500
WASHINGTON-TAYLOR, GI-44, pt., dark golden amber, OP.............$500–750
WASHINGTON-TAYLOR, GI-45, qt., pale yellow green....................$180–220
WASHINGTON-TAYLOR, GI-45, citron...$150–200
WASHINGTON-TAYLOR, GI-46, qt., light blue green, OP $80–120
WASHINGTON-REVERSE PLAIN, GI-47, qt., medium blue green, OP ...$120–150
WASHINGTON-REVERSE PLAIN, GI-47, medium teal green, OP $200–250
WASHINGTON-REVERSE PLAIN, GI-48, pt., aqua $60–90
WASHINGTON-REVERSE PLAIN, GI-48, pt., bright medium green, OP .$150–225

WASHINGTON-REVERSE PLAIN, GI-48, pt., brilliant citron, OP $600–900
WASHINGTON-REVERSE PLAIN, GI-48, pt., bright bluish green, OP.... $175–250
WASHINGTON-TAYLOR, GI-49, pt., aqua, OP, light inner stain.............$40–50
WASHINGTON-TAYLOR,* GI-50, pt., emerald green, OP................. $400–550
WASHINGTON-TAYLOR,* GI-50, pt., light gray blue, OP $600–750
WASHINGTON-TAYLOR,* GI-50, pt., deep forest green, OP $500–600
WASHINGTON-TAYLOR, GI-51, qt., yellow green, IP $250–350
WASHINGTON-TAYLOR, GI-51, qt., blue green, OP $80–100
WASHINGTON-TAYLOR, GI-51, qt., golden amber, IP $250–350
WASHINGTON-TAYLOR, GI-51, qt., medium amethyst, OP $1200–1800
WASHINGTON-TAYLOR, GI-51, qt., medium blue green, IP, nice impression .....
....$180–250
WASHINGTON-TAYLOR, GI-52, pt., yellow green, IP $450–700
WASHINGTON-TAYLOR, GI-52, pt., apple green, OP...................... $250–400
WASHINGTON-TAYLOR, GI-52, pt., sage green, OP.........................$350–550
WASHINGTON-TAYLOR, GI-53, ½ pt., greenish aqua, OP $50–60
WASHINGTON-TAYLOR, GI-54, qt., emerald green, OP, ground-down lip ....
....$75–100
WASHINGTON-TAYLOR, GI-54, qt., copper $550–700
WASHINGTON-TAYLOR, GI-54, qt., yellow olive, OP $400–500
WASHINGTON-TAYLOR, GI-54, qt., citron, tiny lip chip..................$160–200
WASHINGTON-TAYLOR, GI-54, qt., light apple green, OP $75–100
WASHINGTON-TAYLOR, GI-54, qt., bright green............................ $180–210
WASHINGTON-TAYLOR, GI-54, qt., sapphire blue, medial crack........ $200–250
WASHINGTON-TAYLOR, GI-54, qt., aqua, OP $40–50
WASHINGTON-TAYLOR, GI-54, qt., bright medium green, OP $290–230
WASHINGTON-TAYLOR, GI-54, qt., shaded emerald green, OP, medial bruise ...
....$150–250
WASHINGTON-TAYLOR, GI-54, qt., deep aqua, OP, stain, two base chips.........
....$20–25
WASHINGTON-TAYLOR, GI-54, qt., light/medium teal, OP $190–230
WASHINGTON-TAYLOR, GI-54, qt., light blue green, OP $90–120
WASHINGTON-TAYLOR, GI-55, pt., deep golden amber, OP $200–300
WASHINGTON-TAYLOR, GI-55, pt., light green, OP.........................$40–50
WASHINGTON-TAYLOR, GI-55, pt., olive yellow, OP $300–425
WASHINGTON-TAYLOR, GI-55, pt., medium emerald green, OP $300–450
WASHINGTON-TAYLOR, GI-56, ½ pt., light blue green, OP $300–500
WASHINGTON-TAYLOR, GI-56, ½ pt., yellow, OP......................$1000–1500
WASHINGTON-SHEAF OF WHEAT, GI-57, qt., aqua, OP, light haze........$45–60
WASHINGTON-SHEAF OF WHEAT, GI-57, qt., aqua, OP.................... $90–120
WASHINGTON-TAYLOR, GI-58, pt., aqua, OP $60–90
WASHINGTON-SHEAF OF RYE, GI-59, ½ pt., bluish aqua, OP..............$45–55
WASHINGTON-LOCKPORT, GI-60, qt., deep blue aqua, IP............... $400–600
WASHINGTON-WASHINGTON, GI-61, qt., deep blue green, OP $700–900
WASHINGTON-WASHINGTON, GI-61, qt., aqua, OP, inner stain $75–90
ADAMS-EAGLE, GI-62, pt., greenish aqua, OP $7000–10,000
HARRISON-CABIN, GI-63, pt., aqua, OP, ⅛″ medial hole repair... $5000–6500
JACKSON-EAGLE, GI-64, pt., greenish aqua, OP $400–600
JACKSON-EAGLE, J.T. & Co, GI-65, pt., greenish aqua, OP, ½″ lip crack......
....$60–90
JACKSON-EAGLE, J.T. & Co, GI-65, pt., light blue green, OP..........$500–750

JACKSON-EAGLE, GI-66, pt., colorless, OP $1200–1800
JACKSON-B & M EAGLE, GI-67, pt., colorless, OP....................$6000–9000
JACKSON-FLORAL MEDALLION, GI-68, pt., light blue green, OP, 1″ potstone crack $600–725
JACKSON-FLORAL MEDALLION, GI-68, pt., aqua, OP $800–1100
JACKSON-EAGLE, GI-69, pt., aqua, OP $25,000–30,000
JACKSON-MASONIC, GI-70, pt., aqua, OP $25,000–35,000
TAYLOR-RINGGOLD, GI-71, pt., colorless with grayish cast, OP $150–200
TAYLOR-RINGGOLD, GI-71, pt., aqua, OP, two big medial rib flakes $75–90
TAYLOR-RINGGOLD, GI-71, pt., aqua, OP................................ $100–130
TAYLOR-RINGGOLD, GI-71, pt., colorless with amethyst streak, OP... $200–260
TAYLOR-RINGGOLD, GI-71, pt., aqua, OP....................................$80–110
TAYLOR-RINGGOLD, GI-72, pt., aqua, OP................................. $80–100
TAYLOR-MONUMENT, GI-73, pt., amethyst, OP......................... $2500–3500
TAYLOR-MONUMENT, GI-73, pt., bright green, OP.....................$1300–1800
TAYLOR-MONUMENT, GI-73, pt., deep amethyst, OP $2000–2500
TAYLOR-MONUMENT, GI-73, pt., deep grass green, OP $1750–2250
TAYLOR-MONUMENT, GI-73, pt., aqua, OP $80–120
TAYLOR-CORN FOR THE WORLD, GI-74, pt., apricot puce, OP, neck broken off $125–175
TAYLOR-CORN FOR THE WORLD, GI-74, pt., apricot, OP $5000–7500
TAYLOR-CORN FOR THE WORLD, GI-74, pt., brilliant olive yellow/green, OP ...
.... $4000–6000
TAYLOR-CORN FOR THE WORLD, GI-74, pt., aqua, OP, shoulder crack..... $350–400
TAYLOR-CORN FOR THE WORLD, GI-74, pt., aqua, OP, base flake, light wear...
.... $75–100
TAYLOR-CORN FOR THE WORLD, GI-74, pt., aqua, OP...................$350–450
TAYLOR-CORN FOR THE WORLD, GI-75, pt., aqua, OP.................. $225–300
TAYLOR-EAGLE, GI-76, pt., deep greenish aqua, OP, neck crack $250–400
TAYLOR-MASTERSON EAGLE, GI-77, qt., deep aqua, lip chip............$300–450
TAYLOR-MASTERSON EAGLE, GI-77, qt., pale blue green, OP.......... $600–800
TAYLOR-MASTERSON EAGLE, GI-77, qt., deep aqua, OP $1100–1400
TAYLOR-MASTERSON EAGLE, GI-77, qt., pale greenish blue, OP $750–1000
TAYLOR-RAMSAY, GI-78, pt., aqua, OP $1000–1200
GRANT-EAGLE, GI-79, pt., aqua, tiny bottom hole...........................$30–60
GRANT-EAGLE, GI-79, pt., aqua $90–120
GRANT-EAGLE, GI-79, pt., amber $225–300
LAFAYETTE-DEWITT CLINTON GI-80, pt., medium olive green, neck repair......
.... $60–90
LAFAYETTE-DEWITT CLINTON, GI-80, pt., yellow olive, OP, rib chip.$250–350
LAFAYETTE-DEWITT CLINTON, GI-80, pt., deep olive yellow, OP..... $550–700
LAFAYETTE-DEWITT CLINTON, GI-80, pt., olive amber, OP............$450–550
LAFAYETTE-DEWITT CLINTON, GI-80, pt., light olive amber, OP $400–475
LAFAYETTE-DEWITT CLINTON, GI-80, pt., olive green, OP $350–500
LAFAYETTE-DEWITT CLINTON, GI-80, pt., yellow olive, OP $425–525
LAFAYETTE-DEWITT CLINTON, GI-80, pt., olive green, OP, lip chip ..$180–220
LAFAYETTE-DEWITT CLINTON, GI-81, ½ pt., yellow olive, OP $650–800
LAFAYETTE-DEWITT CLINTON, GI-81, ½ pt., yellow olive, OP, lip chips ....
.... $400–500
LAFAYETTE-DEWITT CLINTON, GI-81, ½ pt., yellow olive, OP, base flake.......
.... $475–575

LAFAYETTE-DEWITT CLINTON, GI-82, ½ pt., yellow amber, OP... $2500–4500
MASONIC-EAGLE, GI-83, pt., yellow olive, OP $2000–3000
LAFAYETTE-MASONIC, GI-83, pt., olive green, OP, medial rib crack. $500–600
LAFAYETTE-MASONIC, GI-84, ½ pt., olive green, OP $1800–2200
LAFAYETTE-LIBERTY CAP, GI-85, pt., olive amber, OP, spider crack . $125–150
LAFAYETTE-LIBERTY CAP, GI-85, pt., olive amber, OP $300–400
LAFAYETTE-LIBERTY CAP, GI-85, pt., olive amber, OP $350–450
LAFAYETTE-LIBERTY CAP, GI-85, pt., greenish aqua, OP............ $2000–3000
LAFAYETTE-LIBERTY CAP, GI-85, pt., olive yellow, OP $350–450
LAFAYETTE-LIBERTY CAP, GI-86, ½ pt., yellow amber $300–450
LAFAYETTE-LIBERTY CAP, GI-86, ½ pt., olive amber, OP............. $250–350
LAFAYETTE-LIBERTY CAP, GI-86, ½ pt., olive green, OP............... $350–450
LAFAYETTE-LIBERTY CAP, GI-86, ½ pt., olive amber, OP, two lip flakes ....
.... $300–375
LAFAYETTE-LIBERTY CAP, GI-86, ½ pt., olive amber, OP, light stain $250–300
LAFAYETTE-LIBERTY CAP, GI-86, ½ pt., olive amber, OP.............. $400–500
LAFAYETTE-LIBERTY CAP, GI-86, ½ pt., olive amber, OP, lip and pontil chips
.... $90–120
LAFAYETTE-LIBERTY CAP, GI-87, ½ pt., light yellow olive, OP $3000–5000
LAFAYETTE-MASONIC, GI-88, pt., olive green, OP..................... $1300–1900
LAFAYETTE-MASONIC, GI-89, ½ pt., deep olive amber, OP $1100–1400
LAFAYETTE-MASONIC, GI-89, ½ pt., olive amber, OP, weak impression ....
.... $350–475
LAFAYETTE-EAGLE, GI-90, pt., aqua, OP, stain $125–165
LAFAYETTE-EAGLE, GI-90, pt., aqua, OP, large lip chip................... $50–60
LAFAYETTE-EAGLE, GI-90, pt., aqua, OP, lip flake $90–120
LAFAYETTE-EAGLE, GI-90, pt., pale aqua, OP $140–180
LAFAYETTE-EAGLE, GI-90, pt., aqua, OP $150–225
LAFAYETTE-EAGLE, GI-91, pt., aqua, OP $180–220
LAFAYETTE-EAGLE, GI-92, pt., medium green, OP, mid-edge crack .. $550–750
LAFAYETTE-EAGLE, GI-92, pt., greenish aqua, OP.................... $2000–2500
LAFAYETTE-EAGLE, GI-93, pt., deep greenish aqua, OP $1200–1500
LAFAYETTE-EAGLE, GI-93, pt., light blue green, OP $1000–1300
FRANKLIN-TW DYOTT, GI-94, pt., aqua, OP $200–300
FRANKLIN-TW DYOTT, GI-94, pt., pale aqua, OP......................... $125–175
FRANKLIN-TW DYOTT, GI-94, pt., aqua, OP, base flake $100–150
FRANKLIN-TW DYOTT, GI-94, pt., colorless with blue/gray tint, OP.. $200–275
FRANKLIN-TW DYOTT, GI-94, pt., aqua, OP, small corner base chip. $125–175
FRANKLIN-TW DYOTT, GI-95, pt., aqua, OP $250–350
FRANKLIN-TW DYOTT, GI-96, pt., aqua, light inner stain $75–100
FRANKLIN-TW DYOTT, GI-96, qt., pale grayish blue, OP $400–550
FRANKLIN-TW DYOTT, GI-96, qt., amethystine tint, OP................. $250–325
FRANKLIN-TW DYOTT, GI-96, pt., aqua, OP $125–175
FRANKLIN-FRANKLIN, GI-97, qt., aqua....................................... $110–150
FRANKLIN-FRANKLIN, GI-97, qt., grayish blue aqua, OP $110–140
FRANKLIN-FRANKLIN, GI-97, qt., aqua, OP, lip bruise $50–75
FRANKLIN-FRANKLIN, GI-97, qt., greenish aqua, OP..................... $100–130
FRANKLIN-DYOTT, GI-98, pt., yellow amber, OP $7500–10,000
JENNY LIND-HUFFSEY GLASSWORKS, GI-99, calabash, aqua, iron pontil $75–100
JENNY LIND-HUFFSEY GLASSWORKS, GI-99, calabash, emerald green, OP.............
.... $450–550

JENNY LIND-HUFFSEY GLASSWORKS, GI-99, qt., bright yellow, OP $1500-2000
JENNY LIND-HUFFSEY GLASSWORKS, GI-99, calabash, canary, OP. $1500-2000
JENNY LIND-HUFFSEY GLASSWORKS, GI-99, calabash, light blue green, OP, collar ring chips $100-130
JENNY LIND-HUFFSEY GLASSWORKS, GI-99, calabash, deep emerald green, OP $800-1000
JENNY LIND-HUFFSEY GLASSWORKS, GI-99, calabash, medium lime green, OP $250-350
JENNY LIND-HUFFSEY GLASSWORKS, GI-99, calabash, emerald green, OP, ½″ lip crack..$375-450
JENNY LIND-HUFFSEY GLASSWORKS, GI-99, qt., aqua, OP $60-80
JENNY LIND-HUFFSEY GLASSWORKS, GI-99, calabash, emerald green, OP $575-700
JENNY LIND-KOSSUTH, GI-100, calabash, aqua, OP $80-110
JENNY LIND-GLASSWORKS, GI-101, calabash, aqua, OP $70-120
JENNY LIND-GLASSWORKS, GI-101, qt., aqua, OP, lip chip................$70-80
JENNY LIND-GLASS FACTORY, GI-102, calabash, aqua, OP $80-120
JENNY LIND-GLASS FACTORY, GI-102, calabash, aqua, OP $60-90
JENNY LIND-GLASS FACTORY, GI-102, qt., aqua, OP $100-150
JENNY LIND-GLASS FACTORY, GI-103, calabash, aqua, open pontil, light haze $40-60
JENNY LIND-GLASS FACTORY, GI-103, calabash, aqua, OP $70-100
JENNY LIND-GLASS FACTORY, GI-103, calabash, aqua, OP $70-90
JENNY LIND-GLASS FACTORY, GI-104, calabash, cornflower blue, OP $250-300
JENNY LIND-GLASS FACTORY, GI-104, calabash, cornflower blue, IP. $300-500
JENNY LIND-GLASS FACTORY, GI-104, calabash, sapphire blue, OP.$1800-2500
JENNY LIND-GLASS FACTORY, GI-104, calabash, sapphire blue, IP, weak impression... $1500-2000
JENNY LIND-GLASS FACTORY, GI-104, calabash, aqua, IP $70-110
JENNY LIND-GLASS FACTORY, GI-104, calabash, light sapphire blue, IP $900-1100
JENNY LIND-GLASS FACTORY, GI-104, calabash, deep aqua, IP......... $100-150
JENNY LIND-GLASS FACTORY, GI-104, calabash, blue green, IP $350-450
JENNY LIND-GLASS FACTORY, GI-104, calabash, blue aqua, IP $90-120
JENNY LIND-GLASS FACTORY, GI-104, calabash, deep aqua, IP, light inner stain $90-110
JENNY LIND-GLASS FACTORY, GI-105, calabash, deep aqua, IP.........$250-325
JENNY LIND-GLASS FACTORY, GI-105, calabash, deep aqua, IP, round collared lip.. $140-180
JENNY LIND-TREE, GI-106, calabash, aqua, OP $7000-10,000
JENNY LIND-GLASS FACTORY,* GI-107, calabash, pale green, OP...... $100-175
JENNY LIND-GLASS FACTORY,* GI-107, calabash, deep green, OP $400-700
JENNY LIND-GLASS FACTORY, GI-107a, calabash, emerald green, OP, ... reproduction $10-15
JENNY LIND-GLASS FACTORY, GI-107a, calabash, aqua, OP, reproduction........ .... $10-15
JENNY LIND-GLASS FACTORY, GI-107a, calabash, golden amber, OP, reproduction... $10-15
JENNY LIND-GLASS FACTORY, GI-107a, calabash, purple, OP, reproduction...... ....$25-35
JENNY LIND LYRE, GI-108, pt., aqua $500-700

JENNY LIND LYRE, GI-108, pt., deep aqua, OP $800–1200
JENNY LIND LYRE, GI-109, qt., deep aqua, OP $1200–1500
JENNY LIND LYRE, GI-110, qt., aqua, OP.................................. $900–1200
JENNY LIND LYRE, GI-110, qt., pale blue green, OP $750–1000
KOSSUTH-SLOOP, GI-111, pt., light green, OP............................ $400–500
KOSSUTH-SLOOP, GI-111, pt., aqua, OP $150–200
KOSSUTH-FRIGATE, GI-112, calabash, aqua, OP, lip flake................ $125–160
KOSSUTH-FRIGATE, GI-112, calabash, golden amber, IP.............. $1500–2000
KOSSUTH-FRIGATE, GI-112, qt., aqua, OP................................. $160–210
KOSSUTH-FRIGATE, GI-112, calabash, deep golden amber, OP, lip chip...........
.... $750–1000
KOSSUTH-FRIGATE, GI-112, calabash, medium emerald green, IP .. $1500–2000
KOSSUTH-FRIGATE, GI-112a, qt., aqua, OP $250–275
KOSSUTH-TREE, GI-113, calabash, olive yellow, OP.....................$350–450
KOSSUTH-TREE, GI-113, calabash, bright yellow green, OP $175–240
KOSSUTH-TREE, GI-113, calabash, olive yellow, OP, stain $250–350
KOSSUTH-TREE, GI-113, calabash, pale green, IP........................... $60–80
KOSSUTH-TREE, GI-113, calabash, pale green, IP, small lip flakes $60–80
KOSSUTH-TREE, GI-113, qt., light olive yellow, OP, base chip.......... $250–350
KOSSUTH-TREE, GI-113, calabash, copper yellow, OP $350–475
ADAMS-JEFFERSON, GI-114, ½ pt., light yellow olive, OP $125–175
ADAMS-JEFFERSON, GI-114, ½ pt., golden amber, OP $120–160
ADAMS-JEFFERSON, GI-114, ½ pt., light olive amber, OP............... $140–180
ADAMS-JEFFERSON, GI-114, ½ pt., copper amber, OP...................... $90–110
SHORT-HAIRED BUST-FAIRVIEW WORKS, GI-115, pt., pale blue green, OP........
....$1500–2500
SHORT-HAIRED BUST-FAIRVIEW WORKS, GI-115, pt., blue green, OP..............
.... $2500–3500
LONG-HAIRED BUST-FAIRVIEW WORKS, GI-116, pt., blue green, OP ....
.... $5000–7000
LONG-HAIRED BUST-FAIRVIEW WORKS, GI-116, pt., light blue green, OP.........
....$1750–2000
LONG-HAIRED BUST-FAIRVIEW WORKS, GI-116, pt., deep aqua, OP...............
.... $3000–4000
COLUMBIA-EAGLE, GI-117, pt., aqua, OP, small hole on medial rib......$50–70
COLUMBIA-EAGLE, GI-117, pt., aqua, OP, lip chip, 1″ spider crack .. $140–180
COLUMBIA-EAGLE, GI-117, pt., aqua, OP $450–600
COLUMBIA-EAGLE, GI-117, pt., aqua, OP, light inner stain............. $400–500
COLUMBIA-EAGLE, GI-117, pt., pale aqua, OP $700–850
COLUMBIA-EAGLE, GI-118, ½ pt., aqua, small lip chip.................. $200–250
COLUMBIA-EAGLE, GI-118, ½ pt., pale aqua, OP.......................... $600–900
COLUMBIA-EAGLE, GI-118, pt., deep sapphire blue, OP........ $30,000–40,000
COLUMBIA-EAGLE, GI-118, ½ pt., citron, OP $2000–2300
COLUMBIA-EAGLE, GI-118, ½ pt., cobalt blue, OP.......................$35,000+
COLUMBIA-EAGLE, GI-118, ½ pt., pale yellow green, OP............ $1500–2500
COLUMBIA-EAGLE, GI-118, ½ pt., pale yellowish green, OP $3000–5000
COLUMBIA-EAGLE, GI-119, pt., cobalt blue, OP $20,000–30,000
COLUMBIA-EAGLE, GI-121, pt., aqua, OP....................................$250–350
COLUMBIA-EAGLE, GI-121, pt., light blue green, OP $2500–3500
COLUMBIA-EAGLE, GI-121, pt., medium greenish yellow, OP, large base crack
.... $350–450

Figured Flask, Columbia–eagle, GI-121. PHOTO
COURTESY OF NEIL GROSSMAN.

COLUMBIA-EAGLE, GI-121, pt., greenish aqua, OP $300–400
COLUMBIA-EAGLE, GI-122, pt., colorless, OP $4500–5500
GROVER CLEVELAND-REVERSE PLAIN, GI-123, pt., aqua $200–235
CLEVE & STEVE-CROWING COCK, GI-124, ½ pt., yellow amber........$325–400
CLEVE & STEVE-CROWING COCK, GI-124, ½ pt., gold amber, half-barrel form
....$325–375
McKINLEY-BEE, GI-125, pt., colorless................................... $500–600
BRYAN-EAGLE, GI-126, ½ pt., colorless, coin-shaped $500–750
BRYAN-EAGLE, GI-126, ½ pt., yellow amber, coin-shaped $400–550
BRYAN-EAGLE, GI-126, ½ pt., amber, coin-shaped $650–800
COLUMBUS-REVERSE PLAIN, GI-127, ½ pt., colorless, no metal cap...$150–200
CLEVELAND-HENDRICKS, GI-128, pt., colorless........................... $500–700
ROOSEVELT-TVA, GI-129, calabash, aqua $80–110
DOUBLE EAGLE, GII-1, pt., deep aqua, ¼″ base crack $60–90
DOUBLE EAGLE, GII-1, pt., aqua $175–250
DOUBLE EAGLE, GII-1, pt., aqua, OP, small shoulder star crack..........$50–65
DOUBLE EAGLE, GII-1, pt., deep aqua, OP $175–225
DOUBLE EAGLE, GII-1, pt., aqua, OP, light stain $175–200
DOUBLE EAGLE, GII-1a, pt., aqua..$225–300
DOUBLE EAGLE, GII-3, pt., aqua $150–250
DOUBLE EAGLE, GII-4, pt., greenish aqua, OP............................ $200–250
DOUBLE EAGLE, GII-4a, pt., greenish aqua, OP, lip chips $80–120
DOUBLE EAGLE, GII-4a, pt., pale yellow green, OP, lip chip...........$275–350
DOUBLE EAGLE, GII-4a, pt., greenish aqua, OP...........................$250–350
EAGLE-CORNUCOPIA, GII-6, pt., pale green, highpoints wear........... $125–175
EAGLE-CORNUCOPIA, GII-6, pt., aqua, OP $275–300
EAGLE-CORNUCOPIA, GII-6, pt., greenish aqua, OP $250–350
EAGLE-CORNUCOPIA, GII-6, pt., light green, OP...........................$175–225
EAGLE-SUNBURST, GII-7, pt., bright blue green, OP $2500–3500
EAGLE-SCROLLED MEDALLION, GII-8, pt., deep red amber, OP...................
....$20,000–30,000
EAGLE-SCROLLED MEDALLION, GII-8, pt., yellow olive, OP $8000–12,000
EAGLE-EAGLE AND SNAKE, GII-9, pt., colorless, OP $3000–3500
EAGLE-AGRICULTURE, GII-10, pt., deep greenish aqua, OP $450–600
EAGLE-AGRICULTURE, GII-10, pt., deep greenish aqua, OP $500–700
EAGLE-CORNUCOPIA, GII-11, ½ pt., aqua, OP, lip bruise $200–275
EAGLE-CORNUCOPIA, GII-11, ½ pt., greenish aqua, OP, slight haze .. $125–160
EAGLE-CORNUCOPIA, GII-11, ½ pt., deep aqua, OP $150–175
EAGLE-CORNUCOPIA, GII-11, ½ pt., aqua, OP, slight bubble stain $100–140
EAGLE-CORNUCOPIA, GII-11, ½ pt., colorless, OP.......................$600–900

EAGLE-CORNUCOPIA, GII-11, ½ pt., greenish aqua, OP................ $300–400
EAGLE-CORNUCOPIA, GII-11, ½ pt., aqua, OP........................... $200–250
EAGLE-CORNUCOPIA, GII-11, ½ pt., aqua, OP, slight interior haze.... $125–175
EAGLE-CORNUCOPIA, GII-11a, ½ pt., pale blue green, OP $200–275
EAGLE-CORNUCOPIA, GII-11a, ½ pt., aqua, OP, lip bruise.............. $175–225
EAGLE-CORNUCOPIA, GII-11a, ½ pt., light yellow green, OP.......... $700–850
EAGLE-CORNUCOPIA, GII-11a, ½ pt., yellow green, OP $2000–2500
EAGLE-CORNUCOPIA, GII-12, ½ pt., greenish aqua, OP, ¼″ medial crack ......
....$110–160
EAGLE-CORNUCOPIA, GII-12, ½ pt., aqua, OP........................... $300–500
EAGLE-CORNUCOPIA, GII-12, ½ pt., greenish aqua, OP $900–1200
EAGLE-CORNUCOPIA, GII-13, ½ pt., aqua, light exterior wear..........$250–350
EAGLE-CORNUCOPIA, GII-13, ½ pt., aqua, OP...........................$375–450
EAGLE-CORNUCOPIA, GII-14, ½ pt., olive yellow, OP, large crack $110–130
EAGLE-CORNUCOPIA, GII-15, ½ pt., deep aqua, OP..................... $400–500
EAGLE-CORNUCOPIA, GII-15a, ½ pt., aqua, OP $350–450
EAGLE-CORNUCOPIA, GII-15a, ½ pt., deep aqua, OP....................$350–450
EAGLE CORNUCOPIA, GII-16, ½ pt., deep aqua........................... $200–300
EAGLE-CORNUCOPIA, GII-16, ½ pt., aqua, OP........................... $140–180
EAGLE-CORNUCOPIA, GII-17, ½ pt., aqua, OP...........................$180–200
EAGLE-CORNUCOPIA, GII-17a, ½ pt., pale blue green, OP $125–175
EAGLE-CORNUCOPIA, GII-18, ½ pt., deep aqua, OP, small crack $150–200
EAGLE-CORNUCOPIA, GII-18, ½ pt., bright golden amber, OP...... $2200–2600
EAGLE-CORNUCOPIA, GII-18, ½ pt., deep red amber, OP $1400–2000
EAGLE-MORNING GLORY, GII-19, pt., aqua................................ $350–500
EAGLE-MORNING GLORY, GII-19, pt., greenish aqua, OP................$275–375
EAGLE-MORNING GLORY, POTTERY, GII-19, pt., brown and tan $150–250
EAGLE-PIKES PEAK PROSPECTOR, GII-21, pt., deep blue aqua...........$150–200
EAGLE-PIKES PEAK PROSPECTOR, GII-21, pt., aqua $70–85
EAGLE-PIKES PEAK PROSPECTOR, GII-21, pt., bluish aqua $70–90
EAGLE-LYRE, GII-22, pt., aqua $400–500
EAGLE-FLORAL MEDALLION, GII-23, pt., deep aqua, lip chip........... $175–250
EAGLE-FLORAL MEDALLION, GII-23, pt., deep aqua, pontil chip...... $600–750
EAGLE-FLORAL MEDALLION, GII-23, pt., aqua, OP...................... $400–500
EAGLE-FLORAL MEDALLION, GII-23, pt., aqua, OP...................... $400–500
DOUBLE EAGLE, GII-24, pt., aqua, small inner lip chip $60–90
DOUBLE EAGLE, GII-24, pt., deep amber, OP $750–950
DOUBLE EAGLE, GII-24, pt., deep aqua, OP $125–160
DOUBLE EAGLE, GII-24, pt., aqua, OP.....................................$100–150
DOUBLE EAGLE, GII-24, pt., deep aqua, OP $175–225
DOUBLE EAGLE, GII-24, pt., pale blue, OP $260–320
DOUBLE EAGLE, GII-24, pt., yellow green, OP............................$450–575
DOUBLE EAGLE, GII-24, pt., aqua, OP, lip chips $70–90
DOUBLE EAGLE, GII-24, pt., deep sapphire blue, OP, pontil chip ..$1800–2200
DOUBLE EAGLE, GII-24, pt., bright lemon yellow, OP...............$1500–2200
DOUBLE EAGLE, GII-24, pt., sapphire blue, OP.......................$1800–2600
DOUBLE EAGLE, GII-24, pt., cornflower blue, OP $225–260
DOUBLE EAGLE, GII-24, pt., ice blue, OP.................................. $200–225
DOUBLE EAGLE, GII-24, pt., golden amber, IP............................$550–750
DOUBLE EAGLE, GII-24, pt., aqua, OP, pontil chip $100–125
DOUBLE EAGLE, GII-24, pt., bright medium green, OP, base chip .. $750–1000

DOUBLE EAGLE, GII-24, pt., aqua, OP, pontil chip, light haze $90-120
DOUBLE EAGLE, GII-24, pt., aqua, OP...$50-70
DOUBLE EAGLE, GII-24, pt., yellow green, OP, ½" shoulder crack . $200-250
DOUBLE EAGLE, GII-24, pt., light green, OP, small lip chips $300-400
DOUBLE EAGLE, GII-24, pt., blue green, OP $2000-3000
DOUBLE EAGLE, GII-25, pt., pale blue green, OP, lip rough $150-175
DOUBLE EAGLE, GII-26, qt., aqua, OP......................................$100-130
DOUBLE EAGLE, GII-26, qt., amber, OP................................$1000-1400
DOUBLE EAGLE, GII-26, qt., yellow olive, IP.............................$900-1200
DOUBLE EAGLE, GII-26, qt., pale yellow green, IP, lip chip $140-180
DOUBLE EAGLE, GII-26, qt., deep golden amber, OP.................$1000-1300
DOUBLE-EAGLE, GII-26, qt., yellow olive, OP, ¼" lip chip............$425-480
DOUBLE EAGLE, GII-26, qt., deep green, IP...............................$650-900
DOUBLE EAGLE, GII-26, qt., blue green, IP.................................$650-850
DOUBLE EAGLE, GII-26, qt., light yellow green, IP $500-650
DOUBLE EAGLE, GII-26, qt., medium emerald green, IP................ $700-800
DOUBLE EAGLE, GII-26, qt., pale grayish blue, OP, lip chips $200-260
DOUBLE EAGLE, GII-26, qt., moonstone, OP $400-500
DOUBLE EAGLE, GII-26, qt., yellow green, OP.........................$800-1200
DOUBLE EAGLE, GII-26, qt., ice blue, IP..................................$300-400
DOUBLE EAGLE, GII-26, qt., clambroth with grayish tint, OP $500-700
DOUBLE EAGLE, GII-26, qt., medium green, OP, chips, stone crack. $200-250
DOUBLE EAGLE, GII-26, qt., deep aqua, IP $180-240
EAGLE-FARLEY & TAYLOR, GII-27, 2½ qts., deep golden amber, OP ....
.... $20,000-30,000
EAGLE-FARLEY & TAYLOR, GII-27, 2½ qts., greenish aqua, OP.... $3000-5000
EAGLE-REVERSE PLAIN, GII-28, 2½ qts., aqua, OP $1000-1500
DOUBLE EAGLE, GII-29, pt., aqua, OP, ¼" burst bubble $300-400
DOUBLE EAGLE, GII-30, ½ pt., pale green, OP, light stain.............$150-200
DOUBLE EAGLE, GII-30, ½ pt., aqua, OP $250-350
DOUBLE EAGLE, GII-30, ½ pt., aqua, OP, inner lip chip...................$40-60
DOUBLE EAGLE, GII-31, qt., aqua, small lip chip....................... $200-300
DOUBLE EAGLE, GII-31, qt., aqua..$250-350
DOUBLE EAGLE, GII-31, qt., emerald green, OP $1400-1600
DOUBLE EAGLE, GII-31, qt., emerald green, OP, chips, stain $750-1000
DOUBLE EAGLE, GII-32, pt., pale green, tiny lip chip....................$150-250
DOUBLE EAGLE, GII-32, pt., deep aqua, OP, few lip flakes............$125-150
DOUBLE EAGLE, GII-32, pt., aqua, OP, lip flake...........................$150-200
DOUBLE EAGLE, GII-32, pt., pale aqua, OP...............................$175-225
DOUBLE EAGLE, GII-32a, pt., aqua, ⅜" shoulder crack....................$40-60
DOUBLE EAGLE, GII-32a, pt., aqua, OP $150-200
DOUBLE EAGLE, GII-32a, pt., pale green, OP, inner stain $80-120
DOUBLE EAGLE, GII-32a, pt., deep aqua, OP.............................$200-300
EAGLE-LOUISVILLE, GII-33, ½ pt., amber, OP, 2" crack $60-80
EAGLE-LOUISVILLE, GII-33, ½ pt., deep yellow green $1100-1400
EAGLE-LOUISVILLE, GII-33, ½ pt., aqua $120-150
EAGLE-LOUISVILLE, GII-33, ½ pt., deep golden amber $800-1100
EAGLE-LOUISVILLE GLASSWORKS, GII-34, pt., greenish aqua, IP $500-700
EAGLE & LOUISVILLE GLASSWORKS, GII-35, qt., grass green $700-1000
EAGLE LOUISVILLE GLASS WORKS, GII-36, pt., light blue aqua, lip flake.........
....$160-200

EAGLE LOUISVILLE GLASS WORKS, GII-36, pt., deep aqua................ $90–120
EAGLE-RAVENNA GLASS COMPANY, GII-37, pt., deep olive green, IP .$500–750
EAGLE-RAVENNA GLASS COMPANY, GII-37, pt., yellow amber..........$300–450
EAGLE-RAVENNA GLASS COMPANY, GII-37, pt., olive yellow.......... $800–1200
EAGLE-RAVENNA GLASS COMPANY, GII-37, pt., deep blue green, IP ....
.... $1000–1400
EAGLE-RAVENNA GLASS COMPANY, GII-37, pt., deep aqua, lip bruise ...$40–60
EAGLE-DYOTTSVILLE GLASS WORKS, GII-38, pt., aqua, OP $80–140
EAGLE-REVERSE PLAIN, GII-39, pt., aqua $45–65
DOUBLE EAGLE, GII-40, pt., bright medium green, OP $350–450
DOUBLE EAGLE, GII-40, pt., emerald green, OP, double collar....... $750–900
DOUBLE EAGLE, GII-40, pt., aqua, OP..$70–90
DOUBLE EAGLE, GII-40, pt., deep greenish aqua, OP.................... $125–150
EAGLE-TREE, GII-41, pt., aqua, OP, lip bruise $90–110
EAGLE-TREE, GII-41, pt., aqua, OP..$100–150
EAGLE-TREE, GII-41, pt., aqua, OP, lip flake.................................$75–90
EAGLE-FRIGATE, GII-42, pt., aqua, OP.. $130–175
EAGLE-FRIGATE, GII-42, pt., aqua, OP, ³/₄" medial rib crack $40–60
EAGLE-CORNUCOPIA, GII-43, ¹/₂ pt., aqua, OP $80–110
EAGLE-CORNUCOPIA, GII-44, ¹/₂ pt., pale aqua, OP $150–250
EAGLE CORNUCOPIA, GII-45, ¹/₂ pt., aqua, OP $120–140
EAGLE-CORNUCOPIA, GII-45, ¹/₂ pt., pale blue green, OP, lip flake $60–80
EAGLE-CORNUCOPIA,* GII-46, ¹/₂ pt., aqua, OP $100–150
EAGLE-TREE, GII-47, qt., aqua, OP..$325–425
EAGLE-FLASK, GII-48, qt., medium emerald green, OP $1500–2500
EAGLE-FLAG, GII-48, qt., pale green, OP, lip chip....................$125–150
EAGLE-FLAG, GII-48, qt., light green, OP, crack $50–60
EAGLE-FLAG, GII-48, qt., aqua, OP, stain, lip flake........................ $80–100
EAGLE-FLAG, GII-48, qt., aqua, OP $125–150
EAGLE-FLAG, GII-48, qt., aqua, OP, small lip flake.........................$70–90
EAGLE-STAG, GII-49, pt., aqua, OP, inner lip chip $160–190
EAGLE-STAG, GII-50, ¹/₂ pt., aqua, OP $160–190
EAGLE-COFFIN & HAY HAMMONTON, GII-51, ¹/₂ pt., light green, OP $600–900
EAGLE-FLAG, GII-52, pt., aqua, OP $110–140
EAGLE-FLAG, GII-52, pt., aqua, OP, inner stain $50–70
EAGLE-FLAG, GII-52, pt., aqua, OP, lip flake $70–90
EAGLE-FLAG, GII-53, pt., aqua, OP $110–150
EAGLE-FLAG,* GII-54, pt., aqua, OP..$90–125
EAGLE-FLAG,* GII-54, pt., deep olive amber, OP $1800–2500
EAGLE-GRAPES,* GII-55, qt., dark amber, OP.......................... $800–1200
EAGLE-GRAPES,* GII-55, qt., deep aqua, OP, lip flake $40–60
EAGLE-GRAPES,* GII-55, qt., aqua, OP......................................$90–110
EAGLE-GRAPES,* GII-55, qt., medium yellow green, OP $800–1200
EAGLE-GRAPES, GII-56, ¹/₂ pt., aqua.. $175–225
EAGLE-GRAPES, GII-56, ¹/₂ pt., aqua, OP, lip chip....................... $150–180
EAGLE-GRAPES, GII-56, ¹/₂ pt., medium yellow green, OP $800–1000
EAGLE JPF-CORNUCOPIA, GII-57, pt., olive yellow, OP $15,000–25,000
EAGLE-CORNUCOPIA, GII-58, ¹/₂ pt., medium yellow, OP, few flakes on lip .....
.... $3500–4500
EAGLE-OAK TREE, GII-60, ¹/₂ pt., aqua, OP.................................$350–450
EAGLE-OAK TREE, GII-60, ¹/₂ pt., light-cornflower blue, OP........ $2000–3000

EAGLE-OAK TREE, GII-60, ½ pt., amber, OP............................ $900–1200
EAGLE-OAK TREE, GII-60, ½ pt., pale yellow green, OP.............. $500–800
EAGLE-OAK TREE, GII-60, ½ pt., OP, pale aqua........................ $300–350
EAGLE-OAK TREE, GII-60, ½ pt., deep greenish aqua, OP.............$350–450
EAGLE-OAK TREE, GII-60, ½ pt., deep golden amber, OP........... $1300–1700
EAGLE-OAK TREE, GII-60, ½ pt., amber, OP, lip flake, pontil crack $350–400
EAGLE-OAK TREE, GII-60, pt., aqua, OP, base and pontil chips....... $140–180
EAGLE-WILLINGTON, GII-61, qt., red amber $150–250
EAGLE-WILLINGTON, GII-61, qt., deep green $150–200
EAGLE-WILLINGTON, GII-61, qt., deep yellow olive $150–180
EAGLE-WILLINGTON, GII-61, qt., deep olive green, OP, lip chip $125–150
EAGLE-WILLINGTON, GII-61, qt., olive green $175–250
EAGLE-WILLINGTON, GII-62, pt., dark forest green...................... $150–175
EAGLE-WILLINGTON, GII-62, pt., yellowish olive green $125–160
EAGLE-WILLINGTON, GII-63, ½ pt., yellow olive, double-collared lip $140–165
EAGLE-WILLINGTON, GII-63, ½ pt., emerald green $75–90
EAGLE-WILLINGTON, GII-63, ½ pt., olive green, OP, sheared lip $200–250
EAGLE-WILLINGTON, GII-63, ½ pt., olive amber.......................... $90–120
EAGLE-WILLINGTON, GII-63, ½ pt., olive green $110–150
EAGLE-WILLINGTON, GII-63, ½ pt., deep yellow olive $90–120
EAGLE-WILLINGTON, GII-63a, ½ pt., yellow olive, base flake.......... $120–150
EAGLE-WILLINGTON, GII-64, pt., olive green, double-collared lip..... $140–180
EAGLE-WILLINGTON, GII-64, pt., red amber, neck crack, base chip $50–60
EAGLE-WILLINGTON, GII-64, pt., golden amber........................... $80–120
EAGLE-WESTFORD, GII-65, ½ pt., olive amber $110–175
EAGLE-WESTFORD, GII-65, ½ pt., reddish olive amber $150–175
EAGLE-NEW LONDON GLASS WORKS, GII-66, qt., yellow.............. $750–900
EAGLE-NEW LONDON GLASS WORKS, GII-67, ½ pt., bright green, OP ....
.... $600–750
EAGLE-NEW LONDON GLASS WORKS, GII-67, ½ pt., light yellow green ....
....$275–350
EAGLE-NEW LONDON GLASSWORKS, GII-68, pt., light blue green, OP, potstone
crack $180–220
EAGLE-NEW LONDON GLASSWORKS, GII-68, pt., bright green, OP ... $400–600
EAGLE-NEW LONDON GLASSWORKS, GII-68, pt., golden amber $450–575
EAGLE-CORNUCOPIA, GII-69, ½ pt., moonstone, OP.................... $350–400
EAGLE-CORNUCOPIA, GII-69, ½ pt., blue green, OP $600–900

Figured Flask, eagle–Willington, GII-64. PHOTO
COURTESY OF NEIL GROSSMAN.

EAGLE-CORNUCOPIA, GII-69, ½ pt., colorless, OP $350–450
DOUBLE EAGLE, GII-70, pt., yellow olive, OP, medial rib bruise $90–120
DOUBLE EAGLE, GII-70, pt., olive green, OP................................ $160–190
DOUBLE EAGLE, GII-70, pt., olive amber, OP, base potstone bruise .. $100–150
DOUBLE EAGLE, GII-70, pt., olive amber, OP $160–250
DOUBLE EAGLE, GII-70, pt., deep olive green, OP $175–250
DOUBLE EAGLE, GII-71, ½ pt., olive amber, OP, base bruise........... $90–120
DOUBLE EAGLE, GII-71, ½ pt., olive amber, OP........................... $110–150
DOUBLE EAGLE, GII-71, ½ pt., olive amber, OP, lip flake............... $90–120
DOUBLE EAGLE, GII-71, ½ pt., olive amber, OP, 1″ potstone crack $50–70
EAGLE-CORNUCOPIA, GII-72, pt., light olive amber, OP.................$60–70
EAGLE-CORNUCOPIA, GII-72, pt., deep olive green, OP, lip flake $70–85
EAGLE-CORNUCOPIA, GII-72, pt., olive amber, OP, pontil chip...........$60–70
EAGLE-CORNUCOPIA, GII-72, pt., light yellow olive, OP, lip flake $70–90
EAGLE-CORNUCOPIA, GII-73, pt., amber, OP................................. $60–90
EAGLE-CORNUCOPIA, GII-73, pt., medium olive green..................... $60–90
EAGLE-CORNUCOPIA, GII-73, pt., deep forest green, OP $140–180
EAGLE-CORNUCOPIA, GII-73, pt., olive amber, OP, light stain............$65–85
EAGLE-CORNUCOPIA, GII-73, pt., greenish aqua, OP.......................$70–90
EAGLE-CORNUCOPIA, GII-73, pt., yellow amber, OP $60–90
EAGLE-CORNUCOPIA, GII-73, pt., olive amber, OP $60–80
EAGLE-CORNUCOPIA, GII-73a, pt., forest green, OP...................... $180–210
EAGLE CORNUCOPIA, GII-74, pt., aqua, OP................................. $60–90
EAGLE-CORNUCOPIA, GII-74, pt., pale blue green, OP.....................$80–110
EAGLE PANTALOON-CORNUCOPIA, GII-75, pt., deep olive amber, OP ....
....$1800–2200
EAGLE PANTALOON-CORNUCOPIA, GII-75, pt., dark olive green, OP, sloping
collar lip... $2000–3000
EAGLE, CONCENTRIC RING,* GII-76, qt., yellow green, OP, major neck repair
.... $500–700
EAGLE, CONCENTRIC RING, GII-77, qt., yellow green, OP, lip chip...............
.... $20,000–30,000
DOUBLE EAGLE, GII-78, qt., yellow amber, OP, potstone crack..........$40–60
DOUBLE EAGLE, GII-79, qt., olive amber, OP $140–180
DOUBLE EAGLE, GII-80, qt., yellow olive, OP $450–550
DOUBLE EAGLE, GII-80, qt., golden amber, OP............................$350–425
DOUBLE EAGLE, GII-80, qt., olive amber, OP............................. $400–500
DOUBLE EAGLE, GII-81, qt., deep golden amber, OP $90–120
DOUBLE EAGLE, GII-81, qt., olive amber, OP $80–120
DOUBLE EAGLE, GII-82, pt., olive amber, OP................................$80–110
DOUBLE EAGLE, GII-83, pt., olive amber, OP................................$70–80
DOUBLE EAGLE, GII-83, pt., golden amber, OP..............................$70–90
DOUBLE EAGLE, GII-83, pt., deep yellowish olive, OP $80–120
DOUBLE EAGLE, GII-83, pt., olive amber, OP, base bruise $55–70
DOUBLE EAGLE, GII-84, pt., yellow amber, IP............................. $140–180
DOUBLE EAGLE, GII-84, pt., olive amber, OP................................$70–90
DOUBLE EAGLE, GII-85, pt., yellow amber, OP, tiny base flake $40–60
DOUBLE EAGLE, GII-85, pt., yellow amber, OP $100–150
DOUBLE EAGLE, GII-86, ½ pt., yellow amber, OP $60–85
DOUBLE EAGLE, GII-86, ½ pt., olive amber, OP $65–90
DOUBLE EAGLE, GII-86a, ½ pt., golden amber, OP........................$80–110

Figured Flask, concentric ring eagle, GII-76a. PHOTO
COURTESY OF SKINNER'S, INC.

DOUBLE EAGLE, GII-87, ½ pt., olive amber, OP $70–90
DOUBLE EAGLE, GII-88, ½ pt., yellow amber, OP $75–100
DOUBLE EAGLE, GII-88, ½ pt., olive green, OP, lip flake $75–95
DOUBLE EAGLE, GII-88, ½ pt., olive amber, OP $75–90
DOUBLE EAGLE, GII-89, pt., yellow amber, IP.............................. $75–100
DOUBLE EAGLE, GII-91, qt., yellow olive....................................$125–200
DOUBLE EAGLE, GII-91, qt., golden amber.................................$100–180
DOUBLE EAGLE, GII-92, pt., yellow green $200–250
DOUBLE EAGLE, GII-92, pt., aqua, IP...$80–110
DOUBLE EAGLE, GII-92, pt., yellow olive, OP...............................$160–200
DOUBLE EAGLE, GII-93, pt., light emerald green $200–250
DOUBLE EAGLE, GII-93, pt., aqua, lip flake...............................$25–35
DOUBLE EAGLE, GII-93, pt., sapphire blue, IP $900–1200
DOUBLE EAGLE, GII-95, ½ pt., deep golden amber $100–150
DOUBLE EAGLE, GII-95, ½ pt., light blue green $100–150
DOUBLE EAGLE, GII-98, qt., aqua $50–75
DOUBLE EAGLE, GII-98a, pt., bluish aqua $110–140
DOUBLE EAGLE, GII-101, qt., emerald green, smooth base $350–450
DOUBLE EAGLE, GII-102, qt., olive green $100–150
DOUBLE EAGLE, GII-102, qt., cornflower blue............................. $600–900
DOUBLE EAGLE, GII-103, pt., yellowish aqua, smooth base............. $100–125
DOUBLE EAGLE, GII-103, qt., cobalt blue, major repair to base........$250–350
DOUBLE EAGLE, GII-103, qt., deep golden amber......................... $200–250
DOUBLE EAGLE, GII-104, qt., deep olive green, OP...................... $180–230
DOUBLE EAGLE, GII-105, pt., light yellow green, bad shoulder stain.....$50–60
DOUBLE EAGLE, GII-105, pt., golden amber $125–160
DOUBLE EAGLE, GII-105, pt., deep sage green $100–130
DOUBLE EAGLE, GII-106, pt., aqua $40–60
DOUBLE EAGLE, GII-106, pt., deep golden amber..........................$70–90
DOUBLE EAGLE, GII-106, pt., olive amber $125–175
DOUBLE EAGLE, GII-108, pt., deep aqua, light stain $50–60
DOUBLE EAGLE, GII-108, pt., olive green $110–150
DOUBLE EAGLE, GII-108, pt., deep olive green, lip flake.................. $60–80
DOUBLE EAGLE, GII-108, pt., deep forest green.......................... $140–180
DOUBLE EAGLE, GII-108, pt., dark olive green $125–175
DOUBLE EAGLE, GII-109, ½ pt., emerald green $200–275
DOUBLE EAGLE, GII-110, qt., citron $350–450
DOUBLE EAGLE, GII-111, pt., aqua...$40–50
DOUBLE EAGLE, GII-113, pt., yellow $125–185
DOUBLE EAGLE, GII-113, pt., aqua...$50–60
DOUBLE EAGLE, GII-114, qt., medium yellow green..................... $400–600

DOUBLE EAGLE, GII-114, qt., deep greenish aqua.........................$225–300
DOUBLE EAGLE, GII-115, pt., aqua...$50–75
DOUBLE EAGLE, GII-116, qt., aqua..$90–120
DOUBLE EAGLE, GII-117, pt., blue green.......................................$250–350
DOUBLE EAGLE, GII-118, pt., medium sapphire blue $700–800
DOUBLE EAGLE, GII-118, pt., yellow $350–500
DOUBLE EAGLE, GII-118, pt., sapphire blue $550–650
DOUBLE EAGLE, GII-118, pt., aqua...$30–40
DOUBLE EAGLE, GII-118, pt., deep golden amber $120–140
DOUBLE EAGLE, GII-119, ½ pt., aqua $35–45
DOUBLE EAGLE, GII-125, ½ pt., greenish aqua $30–45
DOUBLE EAGLE, GII-125, ½ pt., aqua, interior stain $20–30
DOUBLE EAGLE, GII-126, ½ pt., golden amber, base chip $80–100
DOUBLE EAGLE, GII-126, ½ pt., reddish amber...........................$200–250
DOUBLE EAGLE, GII-126, ½ pt., golden amber............................$120–150
DOUBLE EAGLE, GII-127, ½ pt., aqua..$45–60
DOUBLE EAGLE, GII-128, ½ pt., aqua..$25–35
DOUBLE EAGLE, GII-129, pt., aqua, stain.....................................$30–45
DOUBLE EAGLE, GII-130, pt., aqua $50–70
EAGLE-EAGLE, GII-131, qt., aqua $50–75
EAGLE KIRKPATRICK-REVERSE PLAIN, GII-134, qt., green aqua........$500–700
EAGLE AND D KIRKPATRICK & CO, GII-134a, pt., aqua $300–400
EAGLE-REVERSE PLAIN, GII-135, qt., pale yellowish aqua.................$25–35
EAGLE-REVERSE PLAIN, GII-138, ½ pt., yellow amber.....................$40–50
EAGLE-REVERSE PLAIN, GII-138, ½ pt., reddish amber....................$40–50
EAGLE-REVERSE PLAIN, GII-139, ½ pt., yellow amber.....................$40–50
EAGLE-DRAFTED MAN, GII-140, pt., deep aqua $300–500
EAGLE-INDIAN, GII-141, qt., light bluish aqua $150–225
EAGLE-INDIAN, GII-141, qt., aqua...$125–175
EAGLE-INDIAN, GII-142, qt., cornflower blue $50–75
EAGLE-INDIAN, GII-142, qt., aqua, potstone crack..........................$40–60
EAGLE-INDIAN, GII-142, qt., aqua $100–125
EAGLE-INDIAN, GII-142, qt., aqua, light stain $50–70
EAGLE-REVERSE PLAIN, GII-143, qt., bright grass green, IP $100–140
EAGLE-REVERSE PLAIN, GII-143, calabash, bright green, IP, inner base stain ...
....$90–110
EAGLE-REVERSE PLAIN, GII-143, calabash, bright green, IP $100–125
CORNUCOPIA-MEDALLION, GIII-1, ½ pt., deep greenish aqua, OP $1500–2000
CORNUCOPIA-MEDALLION, GIII-1, ½ pt., pale yellow green, OP, 1″ crack ......
....$400–475
CORNUCOPIA-CORNUCOPIA, GIII-2, ½ pt., aqua, OP $60–90
CORNUCOPIA-CORNUCOPIA, GIII-2, ½ pt., aqua, OP, pontil chip.........$40–60
CORNUCOPIA-CORNUCOPIA, GIII-3, 1½ pt., pale green, OP $4500–6500
CORNUCOPIA-URN,* GIII-4, pt., olive green, OP $60–90
CORNUCOPIA-URN,* GIII-4, pt., greenish aqua, OP $110–150
CORNUCOPIA-URN,* GIII-4, pt., olive amber,OP, potstone crack.........$20–30
CORNUCOPIA-URN,* GIII-4, pt., olive amber, OP...........................$60–75
CORNUCOPIA-URN,* GIII-4, pt., deep olive amber, OP $60–70
CORNUCOPIA-URN,* GIII-4, pt., olive green, OP $50–75
CORNUCOPIA-URN,* GIII-4, pt., teal green, OP............................$175–250
CORNUCOPIA-URN,* GIII-4, pt., yellow olive, OP $60–75

Figured Flask, cornucopia–urn, GIII-4. PHOTO
COURTESY OF SKINNER'S, INC.

CORNUCOPIA-URN,* GIII-4, pt., olive amber, OP, rough lip $60–70
CORNUCOPIA-URN,* GIII-4, pt., bright green, OP $175–250
CORNUCOPIA-URN,* GIII-4, pt., deep olive green, OP.....................$50–60
CORNUCOPIA-URN, GIII-5, pt., olive amber, OP $60–90
CORNUCOPIA-URN, GIII-6, pt., golden amber.................................$25–35
CORNUCOPIA-URN, GIII-7, ½ pt., olive yellow, OP $60–90
CORNUCOPIA-URN, GIII-7, ½ pt., deep golden yellow, OP..............$90–100
CORNUCOPIA-URN, GIII-7, ½ pt., bright green, OP $90–120
CORNUCOPIA-URN, GIII-7, ½ pt., yellow olive, OP, lip flake $50–65
CORNUCOPIA-URN, GIII-7, ½ pt., olive amber, OP.........................$75–85
CORNUCOPIA-URN, GIII-7, ½ pt., olive green, OP $75–100
CORNUCOPIA-URN, GIII-7, ½ pt., medium emerald green, OP......... $125–175
CORNUCOPIA-URN, GIII-7, ½ pt., olive green, OP $75–100
CORNUCOPIA-URN, GIII-7, ½ pt., light olive yellow, OP $75–100
CORNUCOPIA-URN, GIII-7, ½ pt., olive amber, OP, exterior wear........$50–60
CORNUCOPIA-URN, GIII-7, ½ pt., olive green, OP, large pontil chip $55–65
CORNUCOPIA-URN, GIII-8, ½ pt., aqua, OP $75–90
CORNUCOPIA-URN, GIII-8, ½ pt., olive yellow, OP $60–90
CORNUCOPIA-URN, GIII-9, ½ pt., aqua, OP $80–100
CORNUCOPIA-URN, GIII-10, ½ pt., yellow amber, OP $60–90
CORNUCOPIA-URN, GIII-10, ½ pt., yellow olive, OP $70–90
CORNUCOPIA-URN, GIII-10, ½ pt., deep forest green, OP...............$100–150
CORNUCOPIA-URN, GIII-11, ½ pt., olive green, OP, lip bruise............$40–55
CORNUCOPIA-URN, GIII-11, ½ pt., yellow amber, OP $60–85
CORNUCOPIA-URN, GIII-12, ½ pt., yellow amber, OP $60–90
CORNUCOPIA-URN, GIII-12, ½ pt., olive yellow, OP $60–85
CORNUCOPIA-URN, GIII-12, ½ pt., golden amber, OP $80–120
CORNUCOPIA-URN, GIII-13, ½ pt., aqua, OP $90–120
CORNUCOPIA-URN, GIII-14, ½ pt., emerald green, OP $180–240
CORNUCOPIA-URN, GIII-14, ½ pt., emerald green, OP $250–325
CORNUCOPIA-URN, GIII-14a, ½ pt., aqua, OP.............................$125–175
CORNUCOPIA-URN, GIII-14a, ½ pt., emerald green, OP.................$250–350
CORNUCOPIA-URN, GIII-14a, ½ pt., medium blue green, OP...........$175–245
CORNUCOPIA-URN, GIII-15, ½ pt., aqua, OP $90–140
CORNUCOPIA-URN, GIII-15, ½ pt., colorless, OP $400–550
CORNUCOPIA-URN, GIII-16, pt., medium teal blue, OP, medial rib chip ....
....$250–300

CORNUCOPIA-URN, GIII-16, pt., deep aqua, OP $125–150
CORNUCOPIA-URN, GIII-16, pt., ice blue, IP............................$900–1300
CORNUCOPIA-URN, GIII-16, pt., aqua, OP.................................. $90–150
CORNUCOPIA-URN, GIII-16, pt., golden amber, OP.................. $2500–3200
CORNUCOPIA-URN, GIII-16, pt., deep amber, IP $600–800
CORNUCOPIA-URN, GIII-17, pt., deep blue green, OP................... $250–400
CORNUCOPIA-URN, GIII-17, pt., deep aqua, OP $125–160
CORNUCOPIA-URN, GIII-17, pt., aqua, OP, lip chip $80–110
CORNUCOPIA-URN, GIII-17, pt., deep olive yellow, OP $300–400
CORNUCOPIA-URN, GIII-17, pt., emerald green, olive striations, OP . $500–650
CORNUCOPIA-URN, GIII-17, pt., grass green, OP $375–450
CORNUCOPIA-URN, GIII-17, pt., teal blue, OP............................$200–275
CORNUCOPIA-URN, GIII-17, pt., blue green, OP $160–210
CORNUCOPIA-URN, GIII-18, pt., olive green with yellow tone, OP ... $600–900
MASONIC-EAGLE,* GIV-1, pt., light green, OP.............................$175–225
MASONIC-EAGLE,* GIV-1, pt.., aqua, OP, inner and outer haze $90–120
MASONIC-EAGLE,* GIV-1, pt., greenish aqua, OP $200–225
MASONIC-EAGLE,* GIV-1, pt., blue green, OP, base chips $140–180
MASONIC-EAGLE,* GIV-1, pt., light blue green, OP, base chips.......$125–160
MASONIC-EAGLE, GIV-1a, pt., medium blue green, OP $175–225
MASONIC-EAGLE, GIV-1a, pt., blue green, OP $175–225
MASONIC-EAGLE, GIV-1a, pt., blue green, OP $170–210
MASONIC-EAGLE, GIV-1a, pt., colorless with moonstone cast, OP $275–300
MASONIC-EAGLE, GIV-2, pt., pale greenish aqua, OP................... $350–500
MASONIC-EAGLE, GIV-2, pt., medium green, OP........................$300–375
MASONIC-EAGLE, GIV-2, pt., deep yellow olive, OP $1000–1200
MASONIC-EAGLE, GIV-2, pt., light green, OP $450–500
MASONIC EAGLE, GIV-2, pt., light yellow green, OP $400–425
MASONIC-EAGLE, GIV-3, pt., greenish aqua, OP, light wear $200–250
MASONIC-EAGLE, GIV-3, pt., bright medium green, OP............... $750–1000
MASONIC-EAGLE, GIV-3, pt., medium emerald green, OP $600–800
MASONIC-EAGLE, GIV-3, pt., smoky aqua, OP............................ $500–700
MASONIC-EAGLE, GIV-4, pt., yellow green, OP, light stain, base chip ....
....$450–575
MASONIC-EAGLE, GIV-4, pt., light green, OP $425–525
MASONIC-EAGLE, GIV-4, pt., aqua shading to dark green, OP $750–900
MASONIC-EAGLE, GIV-5, pt., light green, OP $300–450
MASONIC-EAGLE, GIV-5, pt., yellow green, OP, lip chips $180–220
MASONIC-EAGLE, GIV-6, pt., bright green, OP $500–750
MASONIC-EAGLE, GIV-7, qt., medium yellow green, OP............... $500–700
MASONIC-EAGLE, GIV-7, pt., medium green aqua, OP, heavy applied lip ....
.... $400–550
MASONIC-EAGLE, GIV-7, pt., colorless with amethyst streaks, OP ... $400–600
MASONIC-EAGLE, GIV-7, pt., blue green, OP, 1″ base crack, bruise.. $90–120
MASONIC-EAGLE, GIV-7, pt., bright emerald green, OP $4500–5500
MASONIC-EAGLE, GIV-7, pt., colorless, OP, light haze................. $400–500
MASONIC-EAGLE, GIV-7, pt., medium olive green, OP $450–600
MASONIC-EAGLE, GIV-7a, pt., light blue green, OP...................... $500–650
MASONIC-EAGLE, GIV-8, pt., yellow green, OP........................... $500–650
MASONIC-EAGLE, GIV-8a, pt., medium yellow green, OP, inner stain...........
.... $300–400

MASONIC-EAGLE, GIV-8a, pt., colorless, OP, 1/4″ medial rib chip ... $300–500
MASONIC-EAGLE, GIV-10b, pt., bright yellow green, OP, cracked $90–120
MASONIC-EAGLE, GIV-11, pt., colorless, OP, lip and pontil chip $300–375
MASONIC-EAGLE, GIV-11, pt., colorless, OP $450–550
MASONIC-EAGLE, GIV-11, pt., deep yellow green, OP $500–700
MASONIC-EAGLE, GIV-12, pt., blue green, OP $750–1000
MASONIC-EAGLE, GIV-13, 1/2 pt., colorless, OP $900–1400
MASONIC-EAGLE, GIV-14, 1/2 pt., light yellow green, OP $325–425
MASONIC-EAGLE, GIV-14, 1/2 pt., greenish aqua, OP $300–400
MASONIC-EAGLE, GIV-14, 1/2 pt., light blue green, OP, neck crack $110–140
MASONIC-EAGLE, GIV-14, 1/2 pt., aqua, OP $450–600
MASONIC-EAGLE, GIV-14, 1/2 pt., light green, OP $400–500
MASONIC-EAGLE, GIV-15, pt., pale green, OP $3000–5000
MASONIC-EAGLE, GIV-16, pt., olive green, OP $1500–2000
MASONIC-EAGLE, GIV-16, pt., pale green, OP $1000–1500
MASONIC-EAGLE, GIV-17, pt., yellowish amber, OP $125–175
MASONIC-EAGLE, GIV-17, pt., olive amber, OP $100–125
MASONIC-EAGLE, GIV-17, pt., deep amber, OP $100–140
MASONIC-EAGLE, GIV-18, pt., olive amber, OP $150–175
MASONIC-EAGLE, GIV-18, pt., light olive amber, OP, large lip chip $70–90
MASONIC-EAGLE, GIV-18, pt., olive amber, OP, lip flake $75–95
MASONIC-EAGLE, GIV-19, pt., yellow amber, OP, 1/4″ lip chip $60–90
MASONIC-EAGLE, GIV-19, pt., olive amber, OP $160–185
MASONIC-EAGLE, GIV-19, pt., olive amber, OP, base and rib flakes ... $80–100
MASONIC-EAGLE, GIV-19, pt., olive amber, OP, lip roughness $90–120
MASONIC-EAGLE, GIV-19, pt., yellow amber, OP $150–175
MASONIC-EAGLE, GIV-20, pt., olive amber, OP, base flake $120–150
MASONIC-EAGLE, GIV-20, pt., olive amber, OP $130–160
MASONIC-EAGLE, GIV-20a, pt., olive amber, OP $140–180
MASONIC-EAGLE, GIV-21, pt., olive amber, OP, light inner stain $90–120
MASONIC-EAGLE, GIV-22, pt., colorless, OP $5000–8000
MASONIC-EAGLE, GIV-24, 1/2 pt., olive amber, OP $150–200
MASONIC-EAGLE, GIV-24, 1/2 pt., olive amber, OP, exterior wear $110–140
MASONIC-EAGLE, GIV-24, pt., olive green, OP, pontil chip $110–150
MASONIC-EAGLE, GIV-24, 1/2 pt., greenish aqua, OP $400–500
MASONIC-EAGLE, GIV-24, 1/2 pt., olive amber, OP $130–160
MASONIC-EAGLE, REDWARE, GIV-24, 1/2 pt., tan and brown $450–650
MASONIC-EAGLE, GIV-25, 1/2 pt., olive amber, OP $600–800
MASONIC-EAGLE, GIV-26, 1/2 pt., pale green, OP, potstone crack $90–120
MASONIC-EAGLE, GIV-26, 1/2 pt., olive amber, OP, highpoint wear. $800–1200
MASONIC-EAGLE, GIV-27, pt., pale yellow green, OP, weak impression ....
.... $90–120
MASONIC-EAGLE, GIV-27, pt., ice blue, OP $400–600
MASONIC-EAGLE, GIV-27, pt., pale blue, OP $500–600
MASONIC-EAGLE, GIV-27, pt., blue green, OP $250–350
MASONIC-EAGLE, GIV-27, pt., light green, OP, weak impression $200–250
MASONIC-EAGLE, GIV-27, pt., greenish aqua, OP $125–150
MASONIC-MASONIC, GIV-28, 1/2 pt., deep aqua, OP $175–225
MASONIC-MASONIC, GIV-28, 1/2 pt., blue green, OP, light exterior haze ....
.... $250–300
MASONIC-MASONIC, GIV-28, 1/2 pt., light green, OP $200–300

Figured Flask, Masonic–eagle, GIV-32. PHOTO
COURTESY OF NEIL GROSSMAN.

MASONIC-MASONIC, GIV-28, ½ pt., pale blue green, OP, lip bruise...$110–140
MASONIC-MASONIC, GIV-28, ½ pt., medium blue green, OP $250–300
MASONIC-MASONIC, GIV-28, ½ pt., blue green, OP, tiny lip chip $180–250
MASONIC-MASONIC, GIV-28, ½ pt., olive green, OP..................$1000–1200
MASONIC-MASONIC, GIV-28, ½ pt., blue green, OP $250–300
MASONIC HOURGLASS, GIV-29, ½ pt., olive green, OP.............. $3500–4000
MASONIC CROSSED KEYS, GIV-30, ½ pt., golden yellow, OP....... $4000–6000
MASONIC-EAGLE, GIV-31, pt., greenish aqua, OP $1500–2500
MASONIC-EAGLE, GIV-32, pt., yellow amber, OP, burst side bubble. $200–300
MASONIC-EAGLE, GIV-32, pt., deep aqua, OP............................ $175–225
MASONIC-EAGLE, GIV-32, pt., red amber, OP, bold impression $375–450
MASONIC-EAGLE, GIV-32, pt., golden amber, OP $225–300
MASONIC-EAGLE, GIV-32, pt., amber, OP $350–425
MASONIC-EAGLE, GIV-32, pt., red amber, OP, lip repair $150–180
MASONIC-EAGLE, GIV-32, pt., deep golden amber, OP................. $300–350
MASONIC-EAGLE, GIV-32, pt., light blue green, OP, light inner haze ....
.... $250–300
MASONIC-EAGLE, GIV-32, pt., golden amber, OP $250–300
MASONIC-EAGLE, GIV-32, pt., medium yellow green, OP, inwardly folded lip
....$900–1150
MASONIC-EAGLE, GIV-32, pt., pale blue green, OP, exterior wear $120–150
MASONIC-EAGLE, GIV-32, pt., pale greenish blue, OP.................. $300–400
MASONIC-EAGLE, GIV-32, pt., yellow, OP $750–1000
MASONIC-EAGLE, GIV-32, pt., red amber, OP, light inner stain $300–400
MASONIC-EAGLE, GIV-32, pt., light blue green, OP..................... $500–700
MASONIC-EAGLE, GIV-32, pt., dark red amber, OP $350–425
MASONIC-EAGLE, GIV-32, pt., bright yellow with olive tone, OP..... $600–700
MASONIC-EAGLE, GIV-32, pt., yellow green, OP $650–800
MASONIC-EAGLE, GIV-32, pt., greenish aqua, OP $190–220
MASONIC-EAGLE, GIV-32, pt., light blue green, OP.....................$225–325
MASONIC-EAGLE, GIV-32, pt., orange amber, OP, base crack $400–500
MASONIC-EAGLE, GIV-32, pt., light golden amber, OP................. $500–700
MASONIC-EAGLE, GIV-32, pt., dark red amber, OP, two lip flakes... $200–250
MASONIC-EAGLE, GIV-33, pt., deep blue green, OP $2500–3000
MASONIC-FRIGATE, GIV-34, pt., emerald green, OP $5000–6000
MASONIC-FRIGATE, GIV-34, pt., aqua, OP, sharp impression $200–250
MASONIC-FRIGATE, GIV-34, pt., aqua, OP, light highpoint wear $125–150

MASONIC-FRIGATE, GIV-36, pt., pale yellow green, OP $375–450
MASONIC-FRIGATE, GIV-36, pt., greenish aqua, OP $400–500
MASONIC-EAGLE, GIV-37, pt., aqua, OP $125–175
MASONIC-EAGLE, GIV-37, pt., aqua, OP, light spotty stain..............$80–120
MASONIC-EAGLE, GIV-37, pt., deep aqua, OP..............................$90–120
MASONIC-EAGLE, GIV-37, pt., aqua, OP, faint inner stain $60–90
MASONIC-EAGLE, GIV-38, qt., golden amber $100–150
MASONIC-EAGLE, GIV-39, qt., aqua, light haze $40–50
MASONIC-EAGLE, GIV-40, pt., golden amber $275–150
MASONIC EAGLE-CLASPED HANDS, GIV-41, ½ pt., aqua, OP...........$90–150
MASONIC-EAGLE,* GIV-42, calabash, aqua, OP...........................$60–80
MASONIC-EAGLE,* GIV-42, calabash, aqua, OP...........................$60–80
MASONIC-EAGLE,* GIV-42, qt., aqua, light stain $20–35
MASONIC-EAGLE,* GIV-42, qt., aqua, OP.................................$55–65
MASONIC, SEEING EYE, GIV-43, pt., deep olive amber, OP $125–150
MASONIC, SEEING EYE, GIV-43, pt., olive amber, OP...................$125–150
SUCCESS TO THE RAILROAD, GV-1, pt., light ice blue, OP...........$250–350
SUCCESS TO THE RAILROAD, GV-1, pt., golden amber, OP $1200–1500
SUCCESS TO THE RAILROAD, GV-1, pt., aqua, OP, lip and neck imperfections..
....$75–90
SUCCESS TO THE RAILROAD, GV-1, pt., apricot yellow, OP.........$1200–1800
SUCCESS TO THE RAILROAD, GV-1, pt., golden amber, OP.........$1500–1800
SUCCESS TO THE RAILROAD, GV-1, pt., olive green, OP $1500–2000
SUCCESS TO THE RAILROAD, GV-1, pt., light citron, OP, ¼″ rib crack ....
....$375–450
SUCCESS TO THE RAILROAD, GV-1, pt., deep aqua, OP, small lip chip...........
....$125–150
SUCCESS TO THE RAILROAD, GV-1, pt., aqua, OP, stain on inner bubble ....
....$160–180
LOWELL RAILROAD-EAGLE, GV-10, ½ pt., olive green, OP, ½″ shoulder crack
....$50–75
LOWELL RAILROAD-EAGLE, GV-10, ½ pt., yellow olive, OP............$180–240
LOWELL RAILROAD-EAGLE, GV-10, ½ pt., olive amber, OP, minor stain ....
....$125–150
LOWELL RAILROAD-EAGLE, GV-10, ½ pt., yellow olive, OP...........$250–300
LOWELL RAILROAD-EAGLE, GV-10, ½ pt., olive amber, OP $200–300
SUCCESS TO THE RAILROAD, GV-1a, pt., deep aqua, OP $175–200
SUCCESS TO THE RAILROAD, GV-1a, pt., sapphire blue, OP $2000–2600
SUCCESS TO THE RAILROAD, GV-1b, pt., bright apricot, OP........$2000–2500
SUCCESS TO THE RAILROAD, GV-1b, pt., olive amber, OP $1200–1500
SUCCESS TO THE RAILROAD, GV-1b, pt., blue green, lip is double-collared .....
....$600–900
SUCCESS TO THE RAILROAD, GV-3, pt., dark olive green, OP $125–150
SUCCESS TO THE RAILROAD, GV-3, pt., dark olive amber, OP $145–190
SUCCESS TO THE RAILROAD, GV-3, pt., olive amber, OP................$160–190
SUCCESS TO THE RAILROAD, GV-3, pt., golden amber, potstone crack $80–120
SUCCESS TO THE RAILROAD, GV-3, pt., yellow olive, OP $145–190
SUCCESS TO THE RAILROAD, GV-3, pt., deep forest green, OP........ $200–240
SUCCESS TO THE RAILROAD, GV-3, pt., honey amber, OP $180–225
SUCCESS TO THE RAILROAD, GV-3, pt., yellow olive, OP $160–190
SUCCESS TO THE RAILROAD, GV-3a, pt., olive amber, OP $175–210

Figured Flask, Success to the Railroad, GV-5. PHOTO
COURTESY OF NEIL GROSSMAN.

SUCCESS TO THE RAILROAD,* GV-4, pt., deep yellowish olive, OP... $200–300
SUCCESS TO THE RAILROAD,* GV-4, pt., light olive amber, OP........$275–350
SUCCESS TO THE RAILROAD,* GV-5, pt., deep yellow amber, ¼" lip crack .....
.... $60–80
SUCCESS TO THE RAILROAD,* GV-5, pt., olive green, OP, very bubbly glass....
.... $200–225
SUCCESS TO THE RAILROAD,* GV-5, pt., olive amber, OP $160–200
SUCCESS TO THE RAILROAD,* GV-5, pt., amber, OP.....................$150–170
SUCCESS TO THE RAILORAD,* GV-5, pt., emerald green, OP...........$240–280
SUCCESS TO THE RAILROAD,* GV-5, pt., deep olive yellow, OP $150–200
SUCCESS TO THE RAILROAD,* GV-5, pt., deep forest green, OP, bubbly ....
.... $300–400
SUCCESS TO THE RAILROAD, GV-6, pt., olive amber, OP................ $140–165
SUCCESS TO THE RAILROAD, GV-6, pt., olive amber, OP, two base chips........
....$70–90
SUCCESS TO THE RAILROAD, GV-6, pt., olive amber, OP, lip flake.... $130–165
RAILROAD HORSE AND CART, GV-7, pt., deep olive amber, OP........$350–425
RAILROAD HORSE AND CART, GV-7, pt., deep olive green, OP $450–600
RAILROAD HORSE AND CART, GV-7, pt., olive green, OP, base chips ....
.... $250–300
HORSE & CART-EAGLE, GV-7a, pt., olive green, OP $225–300
SUCCESS TO THE RAILROAD-EAGLE, GV-8, pt., deep yellow amber, OP..........
.... $125–150
SUCCESS TO THE RAILROAD-EAGLE, GV-8, pt., olive amber, OP, small lip chip
.... $100–130
SUCCESS TO THE RAILROAD-EAGLE, GV-8, pt., olive green, OP $200–300
SUCCESS TO THE RAILROAD-EAGLE, GV-8, pt., olive amber, OP.......$160–200
RAILROAD HORSE & CART-EAGLE, GV-9, pt., olive amber, OP $130–200
RAILROAD HORSE & CART-EAGLE, GV-9, pt., yellow olive, OP........$150–225
BALTIMORE MONUMENT-SLOOP, GVI-2, ½ pt., citron, OP, two body cracks ....
.... $250–300
BALTIMORE MONUMENT-SLOOP, GVI-2, ½ pt., light olive green, OP, lip crack
....$275–325
BALTIMORE MONUMENT-SLOOP, GVI-2, ½ pt., amethyst, OP....... $1500–2000
BALTIMORE MONUMENT-SLOOP, GVI-2, ½ pt., light aqua, OP $250–300
BALTIMORE MONUMENT-SLOOP, GVI-2, ½ pt., rich olive green, OP ....
.... $2600–3200

BALTIMORE MONUMENT-LIBERTY & UNION, GVI-3, ½ pt., greenish aqua, OP
.... $80–120

BALTIMORE MONUMENT-LIBERTY & UNION, GVI-3, pt., aqua, OP....$275–350

MONUMENT-CORN FOR THE WORLD, GVI-4, qt., aqua, smooth base, 1″ neck
crack $20–40

MONUMENT-CORN FOR THE WORLD, GVI-4, qt., olive yellow, IP, lip chips ....
.... $160–190

MONUMENT-CORN FOR THE WORLD, GVI-4, qt., light yellow amber, IP, small
lip chip $175–225

MONUMENT-CORN FOR THE WORLD, GVI-4, qt., aqua, IP.............. $100–125

MONUMENT-CORN FOR THE WORLD, GVI-4, qt., golden amber....... $350–400

MONUMENT-CORN FOR THE WORLD, GVI-4, qt., apricot, lip flake....$450–550

MONUMENT-CORN FOR THE WORLD, GVI-4, qt., aqua, OP, lip rough.. $60–80

MONUMENT-CORN FOR THE WORLD, GVI-4, qt., yellow olive $900–1200

MONUMENT-CORN FOR THE WORLD, GVI-4, qt., golden amber........$260–320

MONUMENT-CORN FOR THE WORLD, GVI-4, qt., medium green, OP.............
.... $800–1000

MONUMENT-CORN FOR THE WORLD, GVI-4, qt., cornflower blue, lip chip......
.... $400–600

MONUMENT-CORN FOR THE WORLD, GVI-4, qt., yellow amber, OP, lip bruise
....$250–350

MONUMENT-CORN FOR THE WORLD, GVI-4, qt., ice blue.............. $125–175

MONUMENT-CORN FOR THE WORLD, GVI-5, qt., aqua, smooth base .. $80–100

MONUMENT-CORN FOR THE WORLD, GVI-5, qt., aqua, OP...............$80–110

MONUMENT-CORN FOR THE WORLD, GVI-6, pt., aqua, OP................$70–90

MONUMENT-CORN FOR THE WORLD, GVI-7, ½ pt., yellow olive, OP ....
.... $800–1000

MONUMENT-CORN FOR THE WORLD, GVI-7, ½ pt., aqua, OP $75–125

NORTH BEND-TIPPECANOE, GVII-1, pt., deep green, OP ....$30,000+

TIPPECANOE, GVII-2, pt., deep green, OP ....$30,000+

EG BOOZS OLD CABIN WHISKEY,* GVII-3, qt., honey amber $900–1200

EG BOOZS OLD CABIN WHISKEY,* GVII-3, qt., amber................. $900–1300

EG BOOZS OLD CABIN WHISKEY,* GVII-4, qt., amber................. $900–1300

EG BOOZS OLD CABIN WHISKEY, GVII-5, qt., greenish aqua....... $1500–2000

JACOB'S CABIN TONIC BITTERS,* GVII-6, qt., colorless, OP ... $15,000–20,000

SUNBURST, GVIII-1, pt., yellow green, OP................................ $800–1000

SUNBURST, GVIII-1, pt., deep green shading to burgundy, OP $2500–3500

Figured Flask, EG Booz cabin, GVII-3. PHOTO
COURTESY OF SKINNER'S, INC.

SUNBURST, GVIII-1, pt., medium yellow green, OP.................... $400–550
SUNBURST, GVIII-1, pt., deep emerald green, OP $2500–3500
SUNBURST, GVIII-1, pt., emerald green, OP, large lip chip............ $250–300
SUNBURST, GVIII-1, pt., pale aqua, OP, ¾″ base ring chip........... $300–400
SUNBURST, GVIII-1, pt., colorless, OP...................................... $500–650
SUNBURST,* GVIII-2, pt., clear green, OP, mold imperfection........ $300–350
SUNBURST,* GVIII-2, pt., light yellow green, OP...................... $500–700
SUNBURST,* GVIII-2, pt., medium green, OP $400–600
SUNBURST,* GVIII-2, pt., aqua, OP, bruise on shoulder $250–300
SUNBURST,* GVIII-2, pt., medium green, OP $300–400
SUNBURST,* GVIII-2, pt., colorless, OP $400–600
SUNBURST, GVIII-3, pt., medium olive yellow, OP...................... $300–400
SUNBURST, GVIII-3, pt., olive green, OP.................................. $250–300
SUNBURST, GVIII-3, pt., medium olive amber, OP $300–450
SUNBURST, GVIII-3, pt., medium olive green, OP $400–550
SUNBURST, GVIII-3, pt., yellow olive, OP.................................. $300–500
SUNBURST, GVIII-3, pt., light yellow amber, OP $350–450
SUNBURST, GVIII-3, pt., light olive amber, OP $400–500
SUNBURST, GVIII-3, pt., olive amber, OP.................................$375–450
SUNBURST, GVIII-3a, pt., yellow amber, OP $250–375
SUNBURST, GVIII-4, pt., blue green, OP $10,000–14,000
SUNBURST, GVIII-5, pt., medium olive green, OP........................ $400–550
SUNBURST, GVIII-5a, pt., yellow amber, OP, ⅛″ potstone bruise $350–450
SUNBURST, GVIII-5a, pt., light olive amber, OP $800–1200
SUNBURST, GVIII-5a, pt., deep olive yellow, OP.......................... $650–750
SUNBURST, GVIII-5a, pt., yellow olive, OP $1200–1800
SUNBURST, GVIII-6, pt., yellow olive, OP................................ $2000–3000
SUNBURST, GVIII-7, pt., yellow olive, OP, shoulder bruise.............$250–350
SUNBURST, GVIII-7, pt., light olive amber, OP $700–950
SUNBURST, GVIII-8, pt., yellow amber, highpoints wear................$240–280
SUNBURST, GVIII-8, pt., yellow amber.................................... $250–300
SUNBURST, GVIII-8, pt., olive green, OP.................................. $450–600
SUNBURST, GVIII-8, pt., dark olive green, OP, weak impression......$160–200
SUNBURST, GVIII-8, pt., olive amber, OP..................................$350–450
SUNBURST, GVIII-8, pt., deep olive green, OP $400–450
SUNBURST, GVIII-8, pt., olive amber, OP, lower lip edge chip $275–325
SUNBURST, GVIII-8a, pt., olive amber, OP................................$250–350
SUNBURST, GVIII-9, ½ pt., yellow amber, OP $250–300
SUNBURST, GVIII-9, ½ pt., light olive amber, OP, lip rough...........$180–220
SUNBURST, GVIII-9, ½ pt., olive amber, OP, weak impression $150–180
SUNBURST, GVIII-9, ½ pt., amber, OP $220–250
SUNBURST, GVIII-9, pt., olive green, OP.................................. $300–400
SUNBURST, GVIII-9, ½ pt., olive green, OP, medial rib cracks..........$40–60
SUNBURST, GVIII-9, ½ pt., aqua, OP $700–900
SUNBURST, GVIII-10, ½ pt., medium olive green, OP $250–300
SUNBURST, GVIII-10, ½ pt., medium amber, OP, highpoints wear... $250–300
SUNBURST, GVIII-10, ½ pt., olive green, OP $200–325
SUNBURST, GVIII-10, ½ pt., olive amber, OP $250–300
SUNBURST, GVIII-11, ½ pt., olive amber, OP $1200–1800
SUNBURST, GVIII-11, ½ pt., deep yellow olive, OP $2800–3500
SUNBURST, GVIII-11, ½ pt., medium green, OP, ⅛″ crack $1000–1400

Figured Flask, sunburst, GVIII-16. PHOTO
COURTESY OF NEIL GROSSMAN.

SUNBURST, GVIII-12, pt., deep olive green, OP, lip chip $4000–6000
SUNBURST, GVIII-12, pt., greenish aqua, OP $600–900
SUNBURST, GVIII-13, ½ pt., colorless, OP $2500–3500
SUNBURST, GVIII-14, ½ pt., yellow green, OP $800–1100
SUNBURST, GVIII-14, ½ pt., bright clear green, OP...................$1000–1500
SUNBURST, GVIII-14, yellow, OP, base chip, two ¼" potstone cracks ....
.... $300–400
SUNBURST, GVIII-14a, ½ pt., emerald green, OP.....................$1400–1800
SUNBURST, GVIII-15, ½ pt., light green, OP $800–1200
SUNBURST, GVIII-16, ½ pt., medium olive green, OP $250–300
SUNBURST, GVIII-16, ½ pt., deep emerald green, OP $550–650
SUNBURST, WOODEN REPLICA, GVIII-16, 6" $30–45
SUNBURST, GVIII-16, ½ pt., yellow olive, OP, base edge chip.........$190–220
SUNBURST, GVIII-16, ½ pt., light olive yellow, OP...................... $200–250
SUNBURST, GVIII-16, ½ pt., deep clear green, OP $650–800
SUNBURST, GVIII-16, ½ pt., olive green, OP $275–325
SUNBURST, GVIII-16, ½ pt., deep green, OP, large burst bubble $200–250
SUNBURST, GVIII-16, ½ pt., light olive green, OP....................... $250–300
SUNBURST, GVIII-16, ½ pt., olive amber, OP, ground base $250–300
SUNBURST, GVIII-17, ½ pt., colorless, OP $2000–3000
SUNBURST, GVIII-18, ½ pt., yellow amber, OP $400–500
SUNBURST, GVIII-18, ½ pt., olive amber, OP $325–400
SUNBURST, GVIII-18, ½ pt., medium olive green, OP $450–550
SUNBURST, GVIII-18, ½ pt., light olive green, OP....................... $350–400
SUNBURST, SNUFF JAR, GVIII-19, pt., olive green, OP, 6" crack ... $700–1000
SUNBURST, SNUFF JAR, GVIII-19, pt., moss green, OP $10,000–15,000
SUNBURST, GVIII-20, pt., aqua, OP, inner stain $50–70
SUNBURST, GVIII-20, pt., aqua, OP, ¾" medial rib crack.................$30–40
SUNBURST, GVIII-20, pt., aqua, OP $100–125
SUNBURST, GVIII-20a, pt., golden amber, OP $180–250
SUNBURST, GVIII-21, pt., aqua, OP $200–350
SUNBURST, GVIII-22, pt., pale canary, OP $150–200
SUNBURST, GVIII-23, pt., colorless with amethyst tint, OP $4000–6000
SUNBURST, GVIII-24, ½ pt., deep chocolate, OP $5000–7000
SUNBURST, GVIII-24, ½ pt., aqua, OP....................................... $175–275
SUNBURST, GVIII-24, ½ pt., black, OP...................................... $750–900
SUNBURST, GVIII-25, ½ pt., pale aqua, OP, lip bruise and chip........ $80–100

SUNBURST, GVIII-25, ½ pt., light pinkish copper, OP............... $4000–6000
SUNBURST, GVIII-25, ½ pt., aqua, OP, small potstone crack $75–100
SUNBURST, GVIII-25, ½ pt., red puce, OP............................. $2500–3500
SUNBURST, GVIII-25, ½ pt., medium green, OP....................... $2500–3500
SUNBURST, GVIII-26, pt., light green aqua, OP $175–225
SUNBURST, GVIII-26, pt., greenish aqua, OP.............................$250–350
SUNBURST, GVIII-26, pt., aqua, OP, sharp impression $250–325
SUNBURST, GVIII-26, pt., bright yellow green, OP, cracked............ $180–230
SUNBURST, GVIII-26, pt., light blue green, OP $400–600
SUNBURST, GVIII-26, pt., deep olive green, OP....................... $900–1300
SUNBURST, GVIII-26, pt., colorless, OP, light stain $200–300
SUNBURST, GVIII-27, ½ pt., light pale green, OP, ³⁄₁₆″ lip chip..........$40–60
SUNBURST, GVIII-27, ½ pt., aqua, OP...................................... $125–175
SUNBURST, GVIII-27, ½ pt., bright medium green, OP.............. $2000–3000
SUNBURST, GVIII-27, ½ pt., emerald green, OP $800–1000
SUNBURST, GVIII-27, ½ pt., pale yellow green, OP..................... $500–700
SUNBURST, GVIII-27, ½ pt., aqua, OP, lip flake........................... $125–160
SUNBURST, GVIII-27, ½ pt., colorless, OP.................................$190–225
SUNBURST, GVIII-27, pt., pale aqua, OP, pontil chip................... $175–225
SUNBURST, GVIII-28, ½ pt., light lavender, IP........................... $400–500
SUNBURST, GVIII-28, ½ pt., aqua, OP..................................... $140–180
SUNBURST, GVIII-28, ½ pt., colorless, OP................................. $125–175
SUNBURST, GVIII-28, ½ pt., light yellow olive, OP $240–320
SUNBURST, GVIII-28, ½ pt., deep aqua, OP $180–240
SUNBURST, GVIII-29, ¾ pt., aqua, OP..................................... $75–125
SUNBURST, GVIII-29, ¾ pt., deep aqua $75–125
SUNBURST, GVIII-29, ½ pt., blue green, OP $150–200
SUNBURST, GVIII-29, ½ pt., blue green, OP, lip flake................... $125–150
SUNBURST, GVIII-29, ¾ pt., medium yellow olive, OP.............. $1500–2000
SUNBURST, GVIII-29, ½ pt., blue green, OP, lip bruised and rough ... $90–120
SUNBURST, GVIII-29, pt., colorless, OP $350–450
SUNBURST, GVIII-29, ½ pt., colorless, OP, lip chip $125–175
SUNBURST, GVIII-29, pt., medium green, OP $250–350
SUNBURST, GVIII-29, ½ pt., greenish aqua, OP $150–175
SUNBURST, GVIII-29, pt., bluish emerald green, OP $150–175
SUNBURST, GVIII-30, ¾ pt., light blue green, OP $700–1000

Figured Flask, scroll, GIX-1. PHOTO COURTESY
OF NEIL GROSSMAN.

SCROLL, GIX-1, qt., bright spruce green, IP.............................$1400–1800
SCROLL, GIX-1, qt., blue aqua, OP... $60–90
SCROLL, GIX-1, qt., medium sapphire blue, IP, stain................... $600–800
SCROLL, GIX-1, qt., cornflower blue, IP, ground lip......................$120–150
SCROLL, GIX-1, qt., olive yellow, IP..$450–550
SCROLL, GIX-1, qt., aqua, OP.. $60–90
SCROLL, GIX-2, qt., aqua, IP.. $60–90
SCROLL, GIX-2, qt., medium green, OP $450–600
SCROLL, GIX-2, qt., spruce green, OP...................................... $600–900
SCROLL, GIX-2, qt., cobalt blue, IP $1500–1850
SCROLL, GIX-2, qt., greenish yellow, OP.................................. $300–500
SCROLL, GIX-2, qt., bright green, OP...$225–325
SCROLL, GIX-2, pt., olive amber, OP $400–550
SCROLL, GIX-2, qt., moonstone with pinkish tint, OP $450–525
SCROLL, GIX-2, qt., moonstone with amethyst tint, OP $500–700
SCROLL, GIX-2, qt., olive yellow, OP...$550–650
SCROLL, GIX-2, qt., deep golden amber, IP, 1″ crack $80–120
SCROLL, GIX-2, qt., pinkish moonstone, lip bruise, OP................ $400–500
SCROLL, GIX-2, qt., aqua, IP.. $60–90
SCROLL, GIX-3, qt., grass green, OP...$250–350
SCROLL, GIX-3, qt., sapphire blue, IP, lip flakes $550–700
SCROLL, GIX-3, qt., sea green, IP $350–500
SCROLL, GIX-3, qt., black, IP $600–700
SCROLL, GIX-3, qt., amber, IP, 3/8″ lip chip $175–250
SCROLL, GIX-3, qt., aqua, large lip chips $20–25
SCROLL, GIX-3, qt., cornflower blue, OP, lip roughness $200–250
SCROLL, GIX-3, qt., sapphire blue, IP ....:$900–1200
SCROLL, GIX-3, qt., light green, OP, lip chips, stain $75–100
SCROLL, GIX-3, qt., olive, OP... $500–700
SCROLL, GIX-3, qt., olive yellow with white flakes, OP $750–1000
SCROLL, GIX-4, qt., bright green, IP...$250–400
SCROLL, GIX-4, qt., blue green, OP... $250–400
SCROLL, GIX-4, qt., light blue green, IP $200–275
SCROLL, GIX-5, qt., light green, OP, IP.....................................$150–200
SCROLL, GIX-5, qt., aqua, OP.. $60–90
SCROLL, LOUISVILLE KY, GIX-6, qt., aqua, IP, lip chip $75–100
SCROLL, LOUISVILLE KY, GIX-6, qt., aqua, IP, ground lip.................$35–45
SCROLL, GIX-7, qt., citron, IP... $500–650
SCROLL, GIX-8, pt., yellow green, IP $650–800
SCROLL, GIX-8, qt., aqua, IP..$70–80
SCROLL, GIX-8, pt., aqua, OP, lip roughness.............................. $60–90
SCROLL, GIX-8, pt., greenish aqua, IP...................................... $110–150
SCROLL, GIX-9, pt., deep aqua, OP $125–175
SCROLL, GIX-9, pt., amber, IP $800–1200
SCROLL,* GIX-10, pt., cobalt blue, OP $1200–1500
SCROLL,* GIX-10, pt., golden amber, OP, lip and pontil chip..........$125–150
SCROLL,* GIX-10, pt., dark olive amber, OP $400–500
SCROLL,* GIX-10, pt., blue green, OP $200–300
SCROLL,* GIX-10, pt., deep golden amber, lip flake $140–170
SCROLL,* GIX-10, pt., cobalt blue, IP $1000–1300
SCROLL,* GIX-10, pt., sapphire blue, IP.................................. $1500–2000

SCROLL,* GIX-10, pt., medium blue, OP.................................. $400–550
SCROLL,* GIX-10, pt., colorless, OP $175–225
SCROLL,* GIX-10, pt., deep olive green, OP.............................. $350–450
SCROLL,* GIX-10, pt., olive yellow, IP, lip flake $350–500
SCROLL,* GIX-10, pt., amber, OP $275–350
SCROLL,* GIX-10, pt., bluish aqua, OP $40–45
SCROLL,* GIX-10, pt., deep sapphire blue, OP, lip bruise $900–1200
SCROLL,* GIX-10, pt., yellow green, OP, light inner stain.............. $300–375
SCROLL,* GIX-10, pt., moonstone, OP, lip chip $150–200
SCROLL,* GIX-10, pt., aqua, OP $50–75
SCROLL,* GIX-10, pt., light yellow green, IP.............................. $150–250
SCROLL,* GIX-10, pt., black amethyst, OP, large crack $70–90
SCROLL,* GIX-10, pt., deep gold amber, IP $250–300
SCROLL, GIX-10a, pt., deep aqua, OP...................................... $60–90
SCROLL, GIX-10a, pt., sapphire blue, IP..................................$1000–1500
SCROLL, GIX-10a, pt., sage green, IP $500–700
SCROLL, GIX-10b, pt., deep olive yellow, IP, tiny lip flake $300–400
SCROLL, GIX-10b, pt., olive yellow, IP $350–450
SCROLL, GIX-10b, pt., bright yellow green, IP $400–500
SCROLL, GIX-10b, pt., medium emerald green, IP........................ $250–400
SCROLL, GIX-10c, pt., medium citron, OP $375–450
SCROLL, GIX-10c, pt., blue green, OP $600–850
SCROLL, GIX-10d, pt., aqua, IP, tiny side bruise $40–60
SCROLL, GIX-10e, pt., aqua, IP, light stain $30–40
SCROLL,* GIX-11, pt., ice blue, IP $150–200
SCROLL,* GIX-11, pt., amber, light highpoint wear...................... $175–225
SCROLL,* GIX-11, pt., aqua $60–80
SCROLL,* GIX-11, pt., golden amber, IP $200–230
SCROLL,* GIX-11, pt., yellow amber, OP, ¼" lip chip.................. $100–150
SCROLL,* GIX-11, pt., deep golden yellow, lip flake and bruise........ $125–160
SCROLL,* GIX-11, pt., yellow green, OP $200–250
SCROLL,* GIX-11, pt., amber, IP... $225–275
SCROLL,* GIX-11, pt., aqua, OP $50–70
SCROLL,* GIX-11, pt., bright olive green, OP $300–400
SCROLL,* GIX-11, pt., golden amber, IP $225–260
SCROLL, GIX-11a, pt., midnight blue, OP $5000–7500
SCROLL, GIX-11a, pt., olive green, OP...................................... $250–350
SCROLL, GIX-11a, pt., medium golden amber, OP, lip flake............ $150–185
SCROLL, GIX-12, pt., deep olive green, OP, lip rough................... $250–300
SCROLL, GIX-12, pt., yellowish olive green, IP $375
SCROLL, GIX-13, pt., yellow olive, IP..$500–750
SCROLL, GIX-13, pt., emerald green, IP, lip chip.........................$400–450
SCROLL, GIX-14, pt., yellow olive, OP......................................$450–650
SCROLL, GIX-14, pt., aqua, OP, lip flakes..................................$50–65
SCROLL, GIX-14, pt., light green, OP.. $80–100
SCROLL, GIX-14, pt., grayish tint, OP....................................... $300–500
SCROLL, GIX-14, pt., deep golden amber, OP $200–250
SCROLL, GIX-14, pt., deep yellow green, OP $600–750
SCROLL, GIX-15, pt., medium citron, OP $500–800
SCROLL, GIX-15, pt., colorless with moonstone cast, OP $200–350
SCROLL, GIX-16, pt., aqua, IP...$50–75

SCROLL, GIX-16, pt., dark olive amber, OP..............................$250–400
SCROLL, GIX-16, pt., colorless, OP......................................$200–250
SCROLL, GIX-16a, pt., aqua, OP $40–60
SCROLL, GIX-17, pt., brown, OP...$250–300
SCROLL, GIX-17, pt., deep aqua, OP, light stain...........................$40–55
SCROLL, GIX-18, pt., aqua, OP $60–90
SCROLL, GIX-18, pt., sapphire blue, OP $800–1200
SCROLL, GIX-18, pt., yellow, OP $500–700
SCROLL, GIX-19, pt., pale yellow green, OP.............................$200–350
SCROLL, GIX-19, pt., deep tobacco amber, OP...........................$400–550
SCROLL, GIX-19, pt., light blue green, OP $200–350
SCROLL, GIX-20, pt., amber, OP...$300–450
SCROLL, GIX-20, pt., aqua, OP $100–150
SCROLL, GIX-20, pt., bright yellow green, OP $450–550
SCROLL, GIX-21, pt., aqua, OP..$70–100
SCROLL, GIX-22, pt., aqua, OP..$80–120
SCROLL, GIX-23, pt., medium yellow green, OP.........................$800–1200
SCROLL, GIX-23, pt., pale blue green, OP, ½″ rib crack $50–70
SCROLL, GIX-24, pt., aqua and yellow green, neck shading $150–200
SCROLL, GIX-24, pt., yellow green, OP $2000–3000
SCROLL, GIX-25, pt., aqua, OP, tiny inner lip chip $40–60
SCROLL, GIX-25, pt., aqua, OP $50–75
SCROLL, GIX-25, pt., aqua, OP, rough lip $40–60
SCROLL, GIX-25, pt., deep aqua, OP, light inner haze....................$50–70
SCROLL, S MCKEE, GIX-26, pt., greenish aqua, OP $600–900
SCROLL, GIX-27, pt., deep aqua with aqua striations, OP...........$5000–7500
SCROLL, ROUGH & READY, GIX-28, pt., deep bluish aqua, OP......$1200–1500
SCROLL, GIX-29, 2 qts., aqua, OP, light haze.............................$125–150
SCROLL, GIX-30, gal., aqua, ground pontil mark $600–900
SCROLL, GIX-30a, gal., 12″, aqua, OP $400–600
SCROLL, GIX-31, ½ pt., aqua, OP $70–100
SCROLL, GIX-31, ½ pt., yellow green, OP, ground lip....................$350–450
SCROLL, GIX-31, ½ pt., aqua, OP, inner haze, lip flake..................$20–30
SCROLL, GIX-31, ½ pt., medium light green, IP $200–250
SCROLL, GIX-31, ½ pt., cornflower blue, IP $500–700
SCROLL, GIX-31, ½ pt., bluish aqua, IP, 1″ lip crack $22–28
SCROLL, GIX-31, ½ pt., amber, OP $450–650
SCROLL, GIX-32, ½ pt., deep aqua, IP $80–100
SCROLL, GIX-33, ½ pt., light sapphire blue, IP $2000–3500
SCROLL, GIX-33, ½ pt., blue green, OP.................................$350–500
SCROLL, GIX-33, ½ pt., light yellow green, OP $250–400
SCROLL, GIX-33, ½ pt., aqua, IP, double-collared lip $70–90
SCROLL, GIX-33a, ½ pt., amber, IP.....................................$300–450
SCROLL, GIX-34, ½ pt., olive yellow, OP $1000–1400
SCROLL, GIX-34, ½ pt., colorless, OP $100–150
SCROLL, GIX-34, ½ pt., deep golden amber, OP $350–450
SCROLL, GIX-34, ½ pt., citron, OP......................................$500–700
SCROLL, GIX-34a, ½ pt., golden amber, OP.............................$350–450
SCROLL, GIX-34a, ½ pt., aqua, OP......................................$90–120
SCROLL, GIX-35, ½ pt., aqua, IP, ⅛″ base chip $40–50
SCROLL, GIX-36, ½ pt., golden amber, IP, lip chip.....................$250–325

SCROLL, GIX-36, ½ pt., aqua, OP, two 1″ cracks............................$15–20
SCROLL, GIX-36, ½ pt., medium emerald green, OP $500–800
SCROLL, GIX-36, ½ pt., light yellow green, OP $450–600
SCROLL, GIX-36, ½ pt., pinkish moonstone, OP......................... $300–500
SCROLL, GIX-36, ½ pt., sapphire blue, OP $2000–3000
SCROLL, GIX-36, ½ pt., light sapphire blue, OP...................... $500–600
SCROLL, GIX-36, ½ pt., aqua, OP, light haze $30–40
SCROLL, GIX-37, ½ pt., sapphire blue, OP $2000–3000
SCROLL, GIX-37, ½ pt., aqua, OP... $80–100
SCROLL, GIX-37, ½ pt., black, OP $800–1000
SCROLL, GIX-37, ½ pt., deep yellowish green, IP.................... $2000–2500
SCROLL, GIX-38, ½ pt., aqua, OP..$180–230
SCROLL, GIX-38a, ½ pt., apple/olive green, OP $1200–1800
SCROLL, BP & B, GIX-39, ½ pt., aqua, OP, inner stain ....:$65–80
SCROLL, BP & B, GIX-39, ½ pt., light green with amber striations, OP.........
.... $800–1200
SCROLL, BP & B, GIX-39, ½ pt., light green, OP...................... $1100–1400
SCROLL, BP & B, GIX-39, ½ pt., moonstone, OP........................$275–325
SCROLL, MINIATURE, GIX-40, mini, 2½″, colorless, OP $500–700
SCROLL, MINIATURE, GIX-40, 1 oz., cobalt blue, OP............... $4000–6000
SCROLL, ANCHOR, GIX-41, ½ pt., deep aqua, OP, lip chip............. $125–150
SCROLL, ANCHOR, GIX-41, ½ pt., light emerald green, OP............. $500–750
SCROLL, ANCHOR, GIX-41, ½ pt., deep aqua, OP $200–275
SCROLL, GIX-42, ½ pt., colorless with amethyst tint, OP $1200–1800
SCROLL, GIX-42, ½ pt., aqua, OP.. $250–400
SCROLL, GIX-42, ½ pt., deep purple, OP, major repair $4000–6000
SCROLL, J R & SON CORSET WAISTED, GIX-43, pt., aqua, OP $400–600
SCROLL, J R & SON CORSET WAISTED, GIX-43, pt., aqua, OP, 1″ vertical rib
crack $180–220
SCROLL, J R & SON CORSET WAISTED, GIX-43, pt., medium amethyst, OP .....
.... $4000–6500
SCROLL, J R & SON WAISTED CORSET, GIX-43, pt., greenish aqua, OP..........
....$400–450
SCROLL, CORSET WAISTED, GIX-44, pt., deep greenish aqua, OP......$300–375
SCROLL, CORSET WAISTED, GIX-45, pt., greenish aqua, OP, inner lip chip......
.... $300–350
SCROLL, CORSET WAISTED, GIX-45, pt., aqua, OP........................$300–400
SCROLL, CORSET WAISTED, GIX-45, pt., light blue green, OP $700–850
SCROLL, CORSET WAISTED, GIX-45, pt., deep aqua, OP................. $400–600
SCROLL, CORSET WAISTED, GIX-45, pt., deep greenish aqua, OP.... $800–1200
SCROLL, CORSET WAISTED, GIX-45, pt., deep aqua, OP................. $400–500
SCROLL, CORSET WAISTED, GIX-46, qt., aqua, OP...................... $800–1000
SCROLL, CORSET WAISTED, GIX-46, qt., emerald green, OP........ $2500–4000
SCROLL, R KNOWLES & CO, GIX-47, pt., pale blue green, OP....... $900–1200
SCROLL, MCCARTY & TORREYSON, GIX-48, pt., deep blue aqua, IP . $450–600
SCROLL, M'CARTY & TORREYSON, GIX-49, qt., blue green, OP $800–1000
SCROLL, M'CARTY & TORREYSON, GIX-49, qt., aqua, OP $1000–1400
SCROLL, M'CARTY & TORREYSON, GIX-50, qt., light blue green, IP..............
.... $1000–1500
SCROLL, M'CARTY & TORREYSON, GIX-50, qt., aqua with amber striations, IP
.... $1000–1400

Scroll, Hearts & Flowers, GIX-51, qt., aqua, OP $1800–2200
Scroll, Hearts & Flowers, GIX-51, qt., pale blue green, OP... $2400–3000
Scroll, Hearts & Flowers, GIX-51, qt., greenish aqua, OP..... $2000–3000
Good Game Stag-Willow Tree, GX-1, pt., aqua, light highpoints wear ....
....$70–90
Good Game Stag-Willow Tree, GX-1, pt., aqua, OP $140–180
Good Game Stag-Willow Tree, GX-2, ½ pt., aqua, OP, light inner stain ....
.... $200–225
Sheaf Of Rye-Grapes, GX-3, ½ pt., light yellow green, OP......... $350–500
Sheaf Of Rye-Grapes, GX-3, ½ pt., aqua, OP $80–110
A Little More Grape Capt Bragg, GX-4, pt., greenish aqua, OP . $175–225
A Little More Grape Capt Bragg, GX-4, pt., apricot yellow, OP.............
....$1500–2500
A Little More Grape Capt Bragg, GX-5, pt., aqua, OP, 3/16″ lip chip.......
....$125–150
A Little More Grape Capt Bragg, GX-5, pt., bright blue green, OP.........
.... $400–550
A Little More Grape Capt Bragg, GX-5, pt., olive green, OP .$1500–1800
A Little More Grape Capt Bragg, GX-5, pt., olive green, OP, shoulder
crack $450–600
A Little More Grape Capt Bragg, GX-6, ½ pt., pale clear green, OP ....
.... $200–240
A Little More Grape Capt Bragg, GX-6, ½ pt., bright green, OP............
.... $175–275
A Little More Grape Capt Bragg, GX-6, ½ pt., deep olive yellow, OP .....
.... $500–700
A Little More Grape Capt Bragg, GX-6, ½ pt., aqua, OP......... $125–175
A Little More Grape Capt Bragg, GX-6, ½ pt., medium green, OP.........
.... $700–850
A Little More Grape Capt Bragg, GX-6, ½ pt., aqua, OP, base flake.......
.... $60–90
Sloop-Bridgetown, GX-7, ½ pt., aqua, OP...............................$150–200
Sloop-Star, GX-8, ½ pt., light yellow green, OP........................$175–225
Sloop-Star, GX-8, ½ pt., aqua, OP $100–130
Sailboat Star, GX-9, ½ pt., citron, OP..................................$300–400
Sailboat-Star, GX-9, ½ pt., medium greenish aqua, OP $250–300
Sheaf Of Rye-Star, GX-11, ½ pt., aqua, OP $400–600
Men Arguing-Grotesque Head, GX-12, ½ pt., cobalt blue, OP $350–450
Men Arguing-Grotesque Head, GX-12, ½ pt., aqua, OP............ $125–175
Murdock & Cassel-Zanesville, GX-14, pt., light blue green, OP .$750–950
Murdock & Cassel-Zanesville, GX-14, pt., light green, OP........$750–950
Murdock & Cassel-Zanesville, GX-14, pt., pale bluish green, OP, lip flake
.... $650–800
Summer Tree-Winter Tree, GX-15, pt., aqua $60–90
Summer Tree-Winter Tree, GX-15, pt., citron, interior stain $350–450
Summer Tree-Winter Tree, GX-15, pt., citron $500–650
Summer Tree-Winter Tree, GX-15, pt., medium olive yellow $275–350
Summer Tree-Winter Tree, GX-15, pt., citron......................... $700–900
Summer Tree-Winter Tree, GX-16, ½ pt., aqua........................ $70–100
Summer Tree-Winter Tree, GX-16, ½ pt., aqua, OP $125–150
Summer Tree-Summer Tree, GX-17, pt., brilliant yellow............ $750–1000

SUMMER TREE-SUMMER TREE, GX-17, pt., deep aqua, OP, base chip....$40–60

SUMMER TREE-SUMMER TREE, GX-17, pt., olive yellow................. $600–800

SUMMER TREE-SUMMER TREE, GX-18, qt., citron, OP $400–500

SUMMER TREE-SUMMER TREE, GX-18, qt., bright green, OP........... $500–600

SUMMER TREE-SUMMER TREE, GX-18, qt., cobalt blue, OP $5000–6000

SUMMER TREE-WINTER TREE, GX-19, qt., orangish yellow, OP...... $800–1000

SUMMER TREE-SUMMER TREE, GX-19, qt., apricot yellow, OP $750–900

SUMMER TREE-WINTER TREE, GX-19, qt., yellow amber, OP $350–500

SUMMER TREE-WINTER TREE, GX-19, qt., citron, light haze............$450–550

AMERICAN SYSTEM STEAMBOAT, GX-20a, pt., aqua, OP, 1″ hole, repaired, crack $2000–3000

AMERICAN SYSTEM STEAMBOAT, GX-21, pt., aqua.................$11,000–15,000

AMERICAN SYSTEM STEAMBOAT, GX-21, pt., aqua, OP, major repair, crack, stain $900–1200

HARD CIDER-CABIN, GX-22, pt., deep aqua, OP, lip chip............. $800–1200

HARD CIDER-CABIN, GX-22, pt., aqua, OP $4000–5500

JARED SPENCER, GX-24, pt., light yellow amber, OP, ⅛″ lip chip...............
.... $9000–12,000

MEDALLIONS AND DIAMONDS, GX-25, pt., olive yellow, OP .. $20,000–30,000

JARED SPENCER BEADS & PEARLS, GX-26, pt., light olive yellow, OP, ½″ crack $8000–10,000

STODDARD-FLAG, GX-27, pt., golden amber, OP...................... $3000–3500

STODDARD FLAG, GX-27, pt., olive amber, OP, major neck repair $350–450

STODDARD-FLAG, GX-27, pt., olive amber, OP $2800–3500

STODDARD FLAG, GX-28, ½ pt., deep olive green, OP............... $3000–5000

GREAT WESTERN TRAPPER-STAG, GX-30, pt., aqua $325–450

PIKES PEAK PROSPECTOR-PLAIN, GXI-1, qt., deep aqua.....................$75–90

PIKES PEAK PROSPECTOR, GXI-2, pt., aqua....................................$30–40

PIKES PEAK PROSPECTOR, GXI-4, pt., aqua...................................$80–110

PIKES PEAK, GXI-6, ½ pt., aqua $50–60

PIKES PEAK PROSPECTOR-EAGLE, GXI-7, qt., aqua..........................$75–90

PIKES PEAK PROSPECTOR-EAGLE, GXI-8, qt., teal green $700–1000

PIKES PEAK PROSPECTOR-EAGLE, GXI-8, qt., aqua, light stain.............$40–50

PIKES PEAK PROSPECTOR-EAGLE, GXI-8, qt., aqua, small lip chip........$25–35

PIKES PEAK PROSPECTOR-EAGLE, GXI-9, pt., greenish aqua, light interior haze
....$40–50

PIKES PEAK PROSPECTOR-EAGLE, GXI-9, pt., pale yellow green........ $140–180

Left, Figured Flask, Jared Spencer, GX-24. PHOTO COURTESY OF DAVID SMITH, NORM HECKLER. *Right, Figured Flask, Pikes Peak, GXI-2.* PHOTO COURTESY OF NEIL GROSSMAN.

PIKES PEAK PROSPECTOR-EAGLE, GXI-9, ½ pt., aqua $90–110
PIKES PEAK PROSPECTOR, GXI-10, ½ pt., aqua $60–90
PIKES PEAK PROSPECTOR-EAGLE, GXI-11, pt., aqua......................... $70–80
PIKES PEAK PROSPECTOR-EAGLE, GXI-14, pt., greenish yellow........ $600–900
PIKES PEAK PROSPECTOR-EAGLE, GXI-15, pt., bright green............ $600–800
PIKES PEAK PROSPECTOR-EAGLE, GXI-16, pt., aqua $200–300
PIKES PEAK PROSPECTOR-EAGLE, GXI-17, pt., aqua, lip flake.............. $40–45
PIKES PEAK PROSPECTOR-EAGLE, GXI-17, pt., deep yellow olive...... $600–700
PIKES PEAK PROSPECTOR-EAGLE, GXI-18, ½ pt., aqua $100–150
PIKES PEAK PROSPECTOR-EAGLE, GXI-20, ½ pt., deep yellow green ....
.... $1000–1400
PIKES PEAK PROSPECTOR-EAGLE, GXI-21, pt., aqua, OP.................... $60–70
PIKES PEAK PROSPECTOR-EAGLE, GXI-21, pt., aqua with yellow/green streak ...
.... $60–80
PIKES PEAK PROSPECTOR-EAGLE, GXI-22, pt., aqua $60–90
PIKES PEAK PROSPECTOR-EAGLE, GXI-23, ½ pt., golden amber....... $500–600
PIKES PEAK PROSPECTOR-EAGLE, GXI-24, qt., deep amber............. $700–900
PIKES PEAK PROSPECTOR-EAGLE, GXI-24, qt., aqua $130–160
PIKES PEAK PROSPECTOR-EAGLE, GXI-25, pt., aqua $75–95
PIKES PEAK PROSPECTOR-EAGLE, GXI-26, ½ pt., aqua, IP.............. $200–230
PIKES PEAK PROSPECTOR-EAGLE, GXI-27, pt., yellow amber $500–700
PIKES PEAK PROSPECTOR-EAGLE, GXI-28, pt., golden amber $700–900
PIKES PEAK PROSPECTOR-EAGLE, GXI-30, qt., olive yellow $600–800
PIKES PEAK PROSPECTOR-EAGLE, GXI-30, qt., deep aqua, light stain $45–60
PIKES PEAK PROSPECTOR-EAGLE, GXI-30, qt., aqua $70–100
PIKES PEAK PROSPECTOR-EAGLE, GXI-32, ½ pt., aqua...................... $55–70
PIKES PEAK PROSPECTOR-EAGLE, GXI-32, ½ pt., aqua, OP, light base stain.....
.... $100–130
PIKES PEAK PROSPECTOR-EAGLE, GXI-34, qt., deep yellow olive, lip bruise.....
.... $500–600
PIKES PEAK PROSPECTOR-EAGLE, GXI-34, qt., green yellow $900–1200
PIKES PEAK PROSPECTOR-EAGLE, GXI-34, qt., citron..................... $400–500
PIKES PEAK PROSPECTOR-EAGLE, GXI-35, pt., aqua, base crack $15–20
PIKES PEAK PROSPECTOR-EAGLE, GXI-36, ½ pt., aqua, small lip chip...$35–45
PIKES PEAK PROSPECTOR-EAGLE, GXI-36, ½ pt., yellow green......... $110–150
PIKES PEAK PROSPECTOR-EAGLE, GXI-37, pt., aqua $60–80
PIKES PEAK PROSPECTOR-EAGLE, GXI-40, qt., deep golden yellow $500–750
PIKES PEAK PROSPECTOR-EAGLE, GXI-41, pt., aqua, light inner stain $40–45
PIKES PEAK PROSPECTOR-EAGLE, GXI-41, pt., aqua $60–90
PIKES PEAK PROSPECTOR-EAGLE, GXI-41, pt., bluish aqua $50–60
PIKES PEAK PROSPECTOR-EAGLE, GXI-42, pt., aqua $75–100
PIKES PEAK PROSPECTOR-EAGLE, GXI-44, pt., aqua, IP $500–750
PIKES PEAK PROSPECTOR-EAGLE, GXI-44, pt., ice blue, IP ...../....... $750–1000
PIKES PEAK PROSPECTOR-EAGLE, GXI-45, pt., deep aqua, IP........... $375–475
PIKES PEAK PROSPECTOR-HUNTER, GXI-46, qt., aqua, interior stain $60–80
PIKES PEAK PROSPECTOR-HUNTER, GXI-47, qt., deep aqua $125–200
PIKES PEAK PROSPECTOR-HUNTER, GXI-47, qt., light greenish blue.. $200–250
PIKES PEAK PROSPECTOR-HUNTER, GXI-47a, 1½ pt., aqua.............. $300–400
PIKES PEAK PROSPECTOR-HUNTER, GXI-48, qt., bright green.......... $400–600
PIKES PEAK PROSPECTOR-E KAUFFELD GXI-49, qt., colorless with pinkish tint .
.... $2000–3000

PIKES PEAK PROSPECTOR-HUNTER, GXI-50, pt., deep golden amber ..$550–750
PIKES PEAK PROSPECTOR-HUNTER, GXI-50, pt., deep yellow olive ... $500–650
PIKES PEAK PROSPECTOR-HUNTER, GXI-50, pt., yellow green..........$500–750
PIKES PEAK PROSPECTOR-HUNTER, GXI-50, pt., light blue green $250–300
PIKES PEAK PROSPECTOR-HUNTER, GXI-50, pt., light yellow olive ..$900–1200
PIKES PEAK PROSPECTOR-HUNTER, GXI-52, ½ pt., light yellow green, IP ....
.... $750–1000
PIKES PEAK PROSPECTOR-HUNTER, GXI-52, ½ pt., deep aqua..........$150–200
PIKES PEAK PROSPECTOR-HUNTER, GXI-52, ½ pt., greenish aqua, IP $125–150
PIKES PEAK PROSPECTOR-HUNTER, GXI-52, ½ pt., deep blue aqua... $250–300
PIKES PEAK PROSPECTOR-HUNTER, GXI-52, ½ pt., aqua.................. $90–120
PIKES PEAK PROSPECTOR-HUNTER, GXI-52, ½ pt., deep aqua, OP, base chip...
.... $170–210
PIKES PEAK PROSPECTOR-HUNTER, GXI-53, pt., ice blue $1200–2000
PIKES PEAK PROSPECTOR-HUNTER, GXI-54, qt., aqua $900–1400
CLASPED HANDS-EAGLE, GXII-1, qt., deep golden amber.............. $100–150
CLASPED HANDS-EAGLE, GXII-1, qt., aqua $60–90
CLASPED HANDS-EAGLE, GXII-2, qt., aqua, broad-collared lip........ $200–240
CLASPED HANDS-EAGLE, GXII-6, qt., citron............................$300–375
CLASPED HANDS-EAGLE, GXII-7, qt., greenish aqua $40–45
CLASPED HANDS-EAGLE, GXII-7, qt., yellow olive, lip bruise.......... $100–120
CLASPED HANDS-EAGLE, GXII-8, qt., olive yellow $110–160
CLASPED HANDS-EAGLE, GXII-8, qt., light sapphire blue $400–600
CLASPED HANDS-EAGLE, GXII-9, qt., aqua $70–90
CLASPED HANDS-EAGLE, GXII-13, qt., golden amber $300–400
CLASPED HANDS-EAGLE, GXII-13, qt., yellow........................... $250–300
CLASPED HANDS-EAGLE, GXII-15, qt., olive yellow $400–500
CLASPED HANDS-EAGLE, GXII-17, pt., greenish aqua, medial rib bruise.$25–35
CLASPED HANDS-EAGLE (L & W ON BASE), GXII-18, pt., aqua, small base
chip...$25–35
CLASPED HANDS-EAGLE, GXII-19, pt., golden amber, two lip chips $50–60
CLASPED HANDS-EAGLE, GXII-21, pt., deep golden amber............... $80–100
CLASPED HANDS-EAGLE, GXII-22, pt., golden amber.................... $100–150
CLASPED HANDS-EAGLE, GXII-23, pt., aqua $60–90
CLASPED HANDS-EAGLE, GXII-25, pt., aqua $50–70
CLASPED HANDS-EAGLE, GXII-28, pt., amber $160–200
CLASPED HANDS-EAGLE, GXII-29, ½ pt., deep golden yellow $80–110
CLASPED HANDS-EAGLE, GXII-29, ½ pt., dark golden amber $90–120
CLASPED HANDS-EAGLE, GXII-29, ½ pt., amber........................... $80–120
CLASPED HANDS-EAGLE, GXII-30, ½ pt., golden amber................. $100–135
CLASPED HANDS-EAGLE, GXII-31, ½ pt., golden amber.................. $80–120
CLASPED HANDS-EAGLE, GXII-32, ½ pt., aqua............................ $125–150
CLASPED HANDS-EAGLE, GXII-33, ½ pt., deep amber..................... $80–110
CLASPED HANDS-EAGLE, GXII-33, ½ pt., golden amber................. $120–150
CLASPED HANDS-UNION EAGLE, GXII-34, ½ pt., aqua $40–60
CLASPED HANDS-LAUREL, GXII-36, ½ pt., aqua $30–40
CLASPED HANDS-CLASPED HANDS, GXII-37, qt., aqua.....................$40–50
CLASPED HANDS-CANNON, GXII-38, qt., golden yellow $500–700
CLASPED HANDS-CANNON, GXII-39, pt., aqua $60–80
CLASPED HANDS-CANNON, GXII-40, pt., amber $150–200
CLASPED HANDS-CANNON, GXII-40, pt., aqua, light haze $40–50

CLASPED HANDS-CANNON, GXII-40, pt., aqua $60–90
CLASPED HANDS-CANNON, GXII-40, pt., olive yellow $300–450
CLASPED HANDS-CANNON, GXII-40, pt., deep aqua....................... $90–130
CLASPED HANDS-CANNON, GXII-40, pt., golden amber $150–200
CLASPED HANDS-CANNON, GXII-41, pt., aqua................................$40–50
CLASPED HANDS-CANNON, GXII-41, pt., medium citron $800–1200
CLASPED HANDS-CANNON, GXII-41, pt., amber, light haze...............$80–110
CLASPED HANDS-CANNON, GXII-41, pt., golden amber.................. $175–225
CLASPED HANDS-CANNON, GXII-42, ½ pt., aqua $90–120
CLASPED HANDS-EAGLE, GXII-43, qt., bright citron, OP.............. $250–300
GIRL ON A BICYCLE-REVERSE PLAIN, GXIII-1, pt., deep golden amber..........
.... $700–900
GIRL ON BICYCLE-REVERSE PLAIN, GXIII-2, pt., aqua, lip flake........ $90–120
GIRL ON BICYCLE-REVERSE PLAIN, GXIII-2, pt., aqua.................$180–250
EAGLE-GIRL ON BICYCLE, GXIII-3, pt., aqua.............................$125–150
HUNTER-FISHERMAN, GXIII-4, qt., apricot, IP, ½″ lip crack $75–100
HUNTER-FISHERMAN, GXIII-4, calabash, apricot, IP $220–250
HUNTER-FISHERMAN, GXIII-4, calabash, golden amber, IP.............$150–200
HUNTER-FISHERMAN, GXIII-4, calabash, amber, IP $150–200
HUNTER-FISHERMAN, GXIII-4, calabash, deep red amber, IP $225–260
HUNTER-FISHERMAN, GXIII-4, qt., aqua.....................................$50–60
HUNTER-FISHERMAN, GXIII-4, calabash, blue green $190–225
HUNTER-FISHERMAN, GXIII-4, calabash, red amber, IP $200–250
HUNTER-FISHERMAN, GXIII-5, qt., aqua, OP................................$60–70
HUNTER-FISHERMAN, GXIII-6, calabash, aqua, OP....................... $80–100
HUNTER-HOUNDS, GXIII-7, pt., olive yellow, OP........................ $200–250
SAILOR-BANJO PLAYER, GXIII-8, ½ pt., light golden amber $250–325
SAILOR-BANJO PLAYER, GXIII-8, ½ pt., aqua................................$60–70
SAILOR-BANJO PLAYER, GXIII-10, ½ pt., aqua, OP, shoulder bruise.....$25–35
SAILOR-BANJO PLAYER, GXIII-10, ½ pt., deep greenish aqua, OP...... $75–100
SOLDIER-BALLET DANCER, GXIII-11, pt., pale greenish blue, IP....... $140–180
SOLDIER-BALLET DANCER, GXIII-12, pt., golden amber, base flake, chip........
....$250–350
SOLDIER-BALLET DANCER, GXIII-13, pt., yellow olive...................$300–450
SOLDIER-BALLET DANCER, GXIII-13, pt., golden amber $300–450
ARMY OFFICER-FLOWER, GXIII-15, calabash, light blue green, IP..... $160–190
ARMY OFFICER-FLOWER, GXIII-15, calabash, aqua, IP $80–120
ARMY OFFICER-FLOWER, GXIII-15, calabash, deep aqua, IP.............$110–140
ARMY OFFICER-FLOWER, GXIII-15, calabash, light blue green, IP...... $90–120
ARMY DRAGOON-HOUND, GXIII-16, qt., yellow amber, inner stain ... $150–180
ARMY DRAGOON-HOUND, GXIII-16, qt., golden amber, OP $150–200
HORSEMAN-HOUND, GXIII-17, pt., aqua $40–60
HORSEMAN-HOUND, GXIII-18, ½ pt., pale yellow green $150–175
FLORA TEMPLE-REVERSE PLAIN, GXIII-19, qt., dark red amber........$150–290
FLORA TEMPLE-REVERSE PLAIN, GXIII-19, qt., handled, puce amber, lip flake
and bruise...$175–225
FLORA TEMPLE-REVERSE PLAIN, GXIII-19, qt., handled, puce $300–350
FLORA TEMPLE-REVERSE PLAIN, GXIII-20, qt., bright blue green ..$1500–2500
FLORA TEMPLE-REVERSE PLAIN, GXIII-21, qt., strawberry apricot, handled.....
....$225–350
FLORA TEMPLE, REVERSE PLAIN, GXIII-21, pt., amber, handled...... $200–250

FLORA TEMPLE-REVERSE PLAIN, GXIII-21, qt., puce amber, handled .$250–350
FLORA TEMPLE WITH HORSE, GXIII-23, pt., copper amber, lip rough $180–220
FLORA TEMPLE, GXIII-24, pt., puce.. $175–225
GEO W ROBINSON-WHEELING W VA, GXIII-26, pt., aqua ....:.$250–350
WILL YOU TAKE A DRINK-DUCK SWIM, GXIII-27, qt., pale blue green ....
.... $300–425
WILL YOU TAKE A DRINK-DUCK SWIM, GXIII-27, pt., greenish aqua ....
.... $200–225
WILL YOU TAKE A DRINK, DUCK SWIM, GXIII-27, pt., aqua $200–225
WILL YOU TAKE A DRINK, DUCK SWIM, GXIII-28, pt., deep greenish aqua ....
.... $200–300
WILL YOU TAKE A DRINK, GXIII-29, pt., deep greenish aqua $180–220
WILL YOU TAKE A DRINK, DUCK SWIM, GXIII-29a, ½ pt., aqua......$300–450
WILL YOU TAKE A DRINK-DUCK SWIM, GXIII-30, ½ pt., aqua........ $100–150
SHEAF OF WHEAT-REVERSE PLAIN, GXIII-31, pt., aqua $60–90
DOUBLE SHEAF OF WHEAT, GXIII-32, pt., aqua $60–90
SHEAF OF WHEAT-TIBBY BROS, GXIII-33, pt., colorless.................$150–200
WHEAT SHEAF-MECHANIC GLASS WORKS, GXIII-34, qt., bright green, OP ......
....$350–450
WHEAT SHEAF-MECHANIC GLASS WORKS, GXIII-34, qt., aqua, OP $90–125
WHEAT SHEAF-MECHANIC GLASS WORKS, GXIII-34, qt., deep green, OP........
....$325–400
SHEAF OF WHEAT-WESTFORD, GXIII-35, pt., olive amber $90–120
SHEAF OF WHEAT-WESTFORD, GXIII-35, ½ pt., deep red amber $80–100
SHEAF OF WHEAT-WESTFORD, GXIII-35, pt., amber $75–100
SHEAF OF WHEAT-WESTFORD, GXIII-35, pt., dark olive amber $100–120
WESTFORD GLASS CO-WHEAT, GXIII-36, pt., red amber $100–175
SHEAF OF WHEAT-WESTFORD, GXIII-37, ½ pt., amber, few inner neck bruises
....$50–70
SHEAF OF WHEAT-WESTFORD, GXIII-37, ½ pt., deep olive amber $75–100
SHEAF OF WHEAT-WESTFORD, GXIII-37, ½ pt., red amber.............. $125–175
SHEAF OF WHEAT-WESTFORD, GXIII-37, ½ pt., brown amber $110–140
SHEAF OF WHEAT-STAR, GXIII-38, qt., emerald green, IP............. $300–500
SHEAF OF WHEAT-STAR, GXIII-39, pt., bright green......................$450–550
SHEAF OF WHEAT-STAR, GXIII-39, pt., bright yellow green.............$280–230
SHEAF OF WHEAT-STAR, GXIII-40, ½ pt., deep golden amber $190–230
SHEAF OF WHEAT-STAR, GXIII-40, ½ pt., bright yellow olive, OP.$1000–1500
SHEAF OF WHEAT-STAR, GXIII-41, calabash, aqua, OP................... $80–120
SHEAF OF GRAIN-STAR, GXIII-42, calabash, aqua, OP $50–75
SHEAF OF WHEAT-STAR, GXIII-43, qt., aqua, OP $55–75
SHEAF OF WHEAT-STAR, GXIII-43, qt., light yellow green, OP $140–180
SHEAF OF WHEAT-STAR, GXIII-43, calabash, pale grayish blue, OP ..$350–450
SHEAF OF WHEAT-STAR, GXIII-44, qt., light blue green, IP............$150–225
SHEAF OF WHEAT-STAR, HANDLED, GXIII-45, qt., deep gold amber, IP.........
....$250–350
SHEAF OF WHEAT-STAR, HANDLED, GXIII-45, calabash, amber, IP...$350–425
SHEAF OF WHEAT-STAR, HANDLED, GXIII-45, calabash, golden amber, IP......
.... $300–400
SHEAF OF WHEAT-TREE, GXIII-46, qt., bright green, OP............... $300–350
SHEAF OF WHEAT-TREE, GXIII-46, qt., aqua, OP, light inner stain......$60–75
SHEAF OF WHEAT-TREE, GXIII-47, qt., bright green, OP.............. $200–250

SHEAF OF WHEAT-TREE, GXIII-47, calabash, bright green, IP, 3″ neck crack
....$30–35
BALTIMORE GLASSWORKS-WHEAT, GXIII-48, qt., aqua, IP $100–150
BALTIMORE GLASSWORKS-WHEAT, GXIII-48, qt., golden amber, lip rough.......
.... $300–350
BALTIMORE GLASS WORKS-WHEAT, GXIII-48, qt., aqua....................$55–70
BALTIMORE GLASSWORKS-WHEAT, GXIII-49, ½ pt., deep olive yellow............
.... $300–400
BALTIMORE GLASSWORKS-WHEAT, GXIII-49, ½ pt., olive amber, OP, base
bruise $150–225
BALTIMORE GLASSWORKS-WHEAT, GXIII-49, ½ pt., aqua, lip flake.......$25–35
BALTIMORE GLASS WORKS-WHEAT, GXIII-52, qt., aqua, OP...............$70–85
BALTIMORE GLASS WORKS-RESURGAM, GXIII-53, pt., aqua $50–75
BALTIMORE GLASS WORKS-RESURGAM, GXIII-53, pt., golden amber, exterior
wear... $140–180
BALTIMORE GLASS WORKS-RESURGAM, GXIII-53, pt., golden yellow amber, OP,
lip chip $250–300
BALTIMORE GLASS WORKS-RESURGAM, GXIII-53, pt., light copper yellow, OP,
¼″ lip chip..$175–225
BALTIMORE GLASS WORKS-RESURGAM, GXIII-53, pt., light golden amber, double-
collared lip..$175–200
BALTIMORE GLASSWORKS ANCHOR, GXIII-54, pt., golden amber $250–350
ISABELLA GLASS WORKS-GLASSHOUSE, GXIII-55, qt., aqua, OP, stain...$70–90
ISABELLA GLASS WORKS-GLASSHOUSE, GXIII-55, qt., aqua, OP, potstone crack
.... $60–80
ISABELLA GLASSWORKS ANCHOR-WHEAT, GXIII-56, pt., aqua, OP $90–120
ISABELLA ANCHOR-GLASS FACTORY, GXIII-57, ½ pt., aqua, OP $150–200
SPRING GARDEN GLASS WORKS-CABIN, GXIII-58, pt., light apricot $1200–1800
SPRING GARDEN GLASS WORKS-CABIN, GXIII-58, pt., aqua...............$70–110
SPRING GARDEN GLASS WORKS-CABIN, GXIII-58, pt., deep red amber...........
.... $300–400
SPRING GARDEN GLASS WORKS-CABIN, GXIII-58, pt., deep red amber...........
.... $550–700
SPRING GARDEN GLASS WORKS-CABIN, GXIII-59, pt., yellow olive, OP..........
.... $900–1200
SPRING GARDEN ANCHOR-CABIN, GXIII-60, ½ pt., light golden amber ....
....$250–350
SPRING GARDENS-CABIN, GXIII-61, ½ pt., yellow amber $300–450
ANCHOR-REVERSE PLAIN, GXIII-64, qt., golden amber.....................$20–30
ANCHOR-REVERSE PLAIN, GXIII-65, pt., golden amber.....................$35–50
ANCHOR-REVERSE PLAIN, GXIII-66, ½ pt., golden amber $25–35
KEY-REVERSE PLAIN, GXIII-75, pt., aqua $30–40
SAFE-REVERSE PLAIN, GXIII-80, ½ pt., aqua.................................$25–35
STAR-REVERSE PLAIN, GXIII-82, ½ pt., golden amber......................$20–30
STAR-RAVENNA GLASSWORKS, GXIII-83, pt., deep golden yellow, IP .$300–450
EASLEYS ROUGH & READY-SALOON, GXIII-89, qt., deep aqua, OP, heavy dam-
age.. $500–600
TRAVELERS COMPANION-GRAIN, GXIV-1, qt., olive amber, light exterior stain
....$70–90
TRAVELERS COMPANION-GRAIN, GXIV-1, qt., amber $100–125
TRAVELERS COMPANION-GRAIN, GXIV-1, qt., brown amber $175–200

TRAVELERS COMPANION-GRAIN, GXIV-1, qt., olive amber $130–190
TRAVELERS COMPANION-GRAIN, GXIV-1, qt., deep red amber $75–90
TRAVELERS COMPANION-RAVENNA, GXIV-2, qt., deep golden amber.. $275–375
TRAVELERS COMPANION-RAVENNA, GXIV-2, qt., golden amber, IP... $450–600
TRAVELERS COMPANION-RAVENNA, GXIV-2, qt., deep ice blue, IP ... $250–300
TRAVELERS COMPANION-RAVENNA, GXIV-2, qt., bright yellow green, IP ....
.... $900–1200
TRAVELERS COMPANION-RAVENNA, GXIV-2, qt., bright medium green, IP ......
.... $600–900
TRAVELERS COMPANION-RAVENNA, GXIV-3, pt., deep olive yellow, IP ....
.... $600–800
TRAVELERS COMPANION-RAVENNA, GXIV-3, pt., aqua $70–80
TRAVELERS COMPANION-RAVENNA, GXIV-3, pt., golden amber, IP, double-collared lip...$350–450
TRAVELERS COMPANION-RAVENNA, GXIV-3, pt., golden amber, IP, lip crack and bruise $140–180
TRAVELERS COMPANION-RAVENNA, GXIV-3, pt., amber, IP.............$225–325
TRAVELERS COMPANION-LANCASTER, GXIV-4, pt., aqua................. $175–250
TRAVELERS COMPANION-LANCASTER, GXIV-4, pt., medium yellow green........
.... $1500–2000
TRAVELERS COMPANION-LANCASTER, GXIV-5, pt., green aqua $140–180
TRAVELERS COMPANION-LANCASTER, GXIV-5, pt., aqua, OP $300–425
TRAVELERS COMPANION-LANCASTER, GXIV-5, pt., reddish puce $1500–2200
TRAVELERS COMPANION-LOCKPORT, GXIV-6, pt., blue green, OP $650–800
TRAVELERS COMPANION-LOCKPORT, GXIV-6, pt., deep emerald green, OP ......
.... $2400–3000
TRAVELERS COMPANION-LOCKPORT, GXIV-6, pt., deep blue green, OP ....
....$1000–1500
TRAVELERS COMPANION-STAR, GXIV-7, ½ pt., aqua, IP, lip flake.......$80–110
TRAVELERS COMPANION-STAR, GXIV-7, ½ pt., golden amber, IP..... $350–400
TRAVELERS COMPANION-STAR, GXIV-7, ½ pt., olive yellow, OP..... $800–1000
TRAVELERS COMPANION-STAR, GXIV-7, ½ pt., yellow, IP.............. $600–900
TRAVELERS COMPANION, GXIV-8, ½ pt., aqua............................$150–200
TRAVELERS COMPANION, GXIV-8, ½ pt., pale green $200–275
TRAVELERS COMPANION-GUIDE, GXIV-9, ½ pt., deep olive green, OP ....
.... $2000–3000
TRAVELERS COMPANION-GUIDE, GXIV-9, ½ pt., pale blue green, OP ....
.... $200–300
TRAVELERS COMPANION-WHEAT, GXV-1, qt., olive amber $140–170

FIRE GRENADES

Fire extinguisher bottles are bottles that held a special fluid which, when the fire grenade and contents were smashed into a fire, would put the fire out. Most of the fire grenades were made after 1870 and come in a

wide variety of shapes, sizes, and colors. Since the extinguisher bottles
were made to be destroyed, they are fairly rare. Many can be found with
the original closures, contents, and labels, which enhances their value.

ACME FIRE EXTR PATD JUNE 29TH 1869, 5⅞″, yellow amber $2000-3000
AMERICAN FIRE EXTINGUISHER CO HAND GRENADE, 6″, colorless, light inner
haze $200-225
AMERICAN FIRE EXTINGUISHER CO, 6¼″, colorless $400-450
BABCOCK, AMERICAN LA FRANCE FIRE ENGINE CO, ELMIRA, NY, amber ....
.... $500-700
BARNUMS HAND FIRE EXT DIAMOND, 6″, aqua, patented June 25, 1869 ....
....$250-350
DESCOUTS & CO FIREWATCHER (ON LABEL), 5¼″, colorless $400-500
FIREX GRENADE, with original box, 3¾″, cobalt blue $50-70
FLAGGS FIRE EXTINGUISHER, PATD 1868, 6¼″, orange amber......... $400-500
GRENADE-PREVOYANTE, ribbed, 5⅝″, orange amber $700-900
HAND H GRENADE, with hobnails, 6¼″, cobalt blue................... $600-700
HARDEN STAR GRENADE, set of two with wire holder, one is cobalt, one pale
green.. $400-500
HARDEN STAR HAND GRENADE FIRE EXTINGUISHER STAR, 6½″, cobalt..........
....$90-110
HARDEN STAR HAND GRENADE FIRE EXTINGUISHER STAR, 6½″, light green....
.... $160-190
HARDEN STAR HAND GRENADE FIRE EXTINGUISHER, ribbed, 6½″, cobalt blue
.... $90-120
HARDEN STAR HAND GRENADE FIRE EX, 6½″, cobalt $120-150
HARDEN STAR HAND GRENADE FIRE EX, 6″, colorless $600-750
HARDEN STAR HAND GRENADE, set of two in wire holder, blue and aqua, 6½″
.... $400-500
HARDENS HAND FIRE EXTING, set of three in wire holder, turquoise blue, 6½″
.... $175-250
HARDENS HAND FIRE EXTINGUISHER GRENADE, 6¾″, turquoise blue, original
contents.. $90-120
HARDENS HAND FIRE EXTINGUISHER GRENADE-STAR, 6¾″, turquoise blue......
....$50-70
HARDENS HAND FIRE EXTINGUISHER GRENADE-STAR, qt. size, 8¼″, olive
green.. $600-800
HARDENS HAND FIRE EXTINGUISHER PATD 1871, 6¼″, turquoise blue, original
contents.. $90-120
HARDENS HAND FIRE EXTINGUISHER, 6¾″, turquoise blue $75-90
HARDENS HAND FIRE EXTINGUISHER, 7¾″, bright green $400-600
HARDENS HAND FIRE EXTINGUISHER, PATD 1871, 6½″, turquoise..... $100-140
HARDENS HAND FIRE GRENADE PATD 1871 & 1883, 6½″, turquoise blue ....
.... $60-80
HARDENS HAND FIRE GRENADE PATD 1871, 1883, 6½″, turquoise blue, 50%
label.. $75-100
HARDENS HAND GRENADE, set of two with wire holder, both medium cobalt
blue..$350-450
HARDENS IMPROVED GRENADE, two pieces of glass held together by wire, clear,
5″ $225-275
HARKNESS FIRE DESTROYER, 6″, sapphire blue........................... $400-525

Fire Grenade, Hayward. PHOTO COURTESY OF
SKINNER'S, INC.

HARKNESS FIRE DESTROYER, with horizontal rings, 6″, cobalt $500–600
HAYWARD, diamond paneled, olive green $275–375
HAYWARD HAND GRENADE, "DESIGN H PATD" (ON BASE), 6″, cobalt blue ....
.... $200–240
HAYWARD HAND GRENADE, "DESIGN H PATD" (ON BASE), 5¾″, colorless .....
.... $140–180
HAYWARDS HAND FIRE GRENADE PATD 1871, square, 6¼″, yellow with olive
tone $200–300
HAYWARDS HAND FIRE GRENADE PATD 1871, square, 6¼″, light green, olive
tint... $400–550
HAYWARDS HAND FIRE GRENADE PATD 1871, square, 6⅛″, cobalt blue, with
label... $225–275
HAYWARDS HAND FIRE GRENADE PATD 1871, 6¼″, apple green $200–250
HAYWARDS HAND FIRE GRENADE PATD 1871, square, 6⅛″, cobalt blue ....
.... $200–225
HAYWARDS HAND FIRE GRENADE, PATD 1871, 6¼″, yellow amber $225–275
HAYWARDS HAND GRENADE SET, in wire holder, two are blue, one is colorless,
5¾″ $500–650
HAZELTON HIGH PRESSURE CHEMICAL FIRE KEG, 11″, amber, handled..........
.... $100–135
HAZELTONS HIGH PRESSURE CHEMICAL FIRE KEG, 10¾″, golden amber, two lip
chips $75–95
HSN, with embossed diamonds, 7¼″, yellow amber $160–190
HSN, diamond design, 7″, yellow amber $150–200
HSN, diamond-shaped, 7¼″, yellow amber $110–130
IMPERIAL FIRE EXTINGUISHER CO, 6½″, medium green............... $400–500
IMPERIAL FIRE EXTINGUISHER, 6½″, colorless, with 85% label $500–600
IMPERIAL TRADE MARK VARIANT, colorless................................. $500–700
LONDON FIRE APPLIANCE CO, 9¼″, amber................................. $400–500
LONDON FIRE APPLIANCE CO, 8⅞″, amber................................. $450–600
P.R.R., horizontally ribbed, 7⅛″, colorless $700–850
PRONTO FIRE GRENADE (ON LABEL), 11¼″, amber, ABM, with label ..$40–50
RACK, METAL, with four grenades, lightbulb-shaped, pyro ball on metal label
.... $150–200
SINCLAIR, cobalt blue...$350–450
SINCLAIR FIRE GRENADE, TOOT (ON BASE), 7¼″, cobalt blue $350–450
SINCLAIR FIRE GRENADE, TOOT (ON BASE), 7″, cobalt $225–280

SPONG & COS HAND FIRE EXTING, tubular, 13½", olive yellow.......$350–425
STAR HARDENS GRENADE SPRINKLER, 17⅜", cobalt blue................ $800–950
STAR HARDENS GRENADE SPRINKLER, tubular, 17¼", cobalt.......... $900–1200
SYSTEME LABBE-GRENADE EXTINCTEUR, 5½", yellow shade $900–1200
UNEMBOSSED FIREX GRENADE, 3¾", medium cobalt..................... $125–175
UNEMBOSSED WITH RAISED VERTICAL RIBS, 5¼", green $500–700
UNIC GRANADE EXTINCTRICE, 5½", orange amber....................$1200–1500
UNIC GRANADE EXTINCTRICE, 5⅞", orange amber...................... $900–1200
UNIVERSAL FIRE EXTINGUISHER, 7¼", light sapphire blue, OP $700–900
WD ALLEN, CHICAGO, colorless.. $900–1200

FOOD BOTTLES

Food bottles come in a wide variety of shapes and sizes. Peppersauce
bottles come in a wide range of colors and are very collectible. References preceded with a "Z" are for *Ketchup, Pickles and Sauces* by Betty
Zumwalt, and those prefaced by an "H" are from *American Bottles and
Flasks and Their Ancestry* by McKearin and Wilson.

ACKER MERRALL & CONDIT CAFE DE LUXE, 8¼", amber, screw-top jar........
....$40–60
ACKERS/SELECT/TEA, SQUARE, Z16, 11⅛", bright yellow green $275–350
B & D, barrel shape, wide mouth, Z36, 5¼", aqua, OP................. $125–175
BAKER FLAVORING EXTRACT, 5", colorless, OP $8–12
BERRY BOTTLE, unembossed, small ring at shoulder, 13½", aqua, OP ..$60–75
BERTIN BRAND PURE OLIVE OIL, 7½", dark green.......................... $12–15
BLUEBERRY BOTTLE, cylinder with fluted shoulder and neck, H73-3, 11¼" .....
.... $340–400
BRIDAL BRAND OLIVES, THOS ROBERTS & CO, stoneware...................$45–50
BRYANTS ROOT BEER, four panels, colorless.......................................$1–2
BURNETTS STANDARD FLAVORING EXTRACT, 6¾", light green $5–6
BURNETTS STANDARD FLAVORING EXTRACT, 5½", aqua.........................$3–4
CATHEDRAL PEPPERSAUCE, six panels, 8⅞", light blue green, OP.... $300–400
CATHEDRAL PEPPERSAUCE, Z455-4 top, 9", deep aqua, OP..............$110–140
CAYUGA COUNTY/TOMATO CATSUP, Z74, 10", aqua with yellow green swirls ...
....$50–75
CHAS GULDEN, NY, mustard jar, 4¾", colorless $1–2
CHAS GULDEN/NEW YORK, sauce bottle, Z189, 11⅜", colorless $50–75
CL STICKNEY, peppersauce, Z393, 9", aqua, OP $75–90
CORBYN COOKS & CO LONDON, peppersauce, 7", aqua, OP $25–35
CRISCO (AROUND SHOULDER FOUR TIMES), ½ gal., colorless, screw cap...$3–4
DILLS FAMILY EXTRACTS, 6¼", colorless..$1–2
DR FENNERS CONCENTRATED FLAVORS, 6", aqua $2–3

DR PRICE DELICIOUS FLAVORING EXTRACT, 6¾″, colorless $4–5
DR PRICE DELICIOUS FLAVORING EXTRACT, 5″, colorless.....................$3–4
EAST INDIA PICKLES (ON NECK), qt., aqua $14–18
EC HAZARD & CO/QUEENS/OLIVES, Z198, 6⅞″, bright yellow green...$60–70
EIFFEL TOWER FRUIT JUICES, 4″, aqua...$1–2
ESKAYS ALBUMINIZED FOOD PATD (ON BASE), pt., amber, with vacuum cap ....
....$3–4
FORBES DELICIOUS FLAVORING EXTRACT, 5″, colorless $4–5
G MILLER/N YORK, peppersauce, 20 vertical flutes, 10″, aqua, OP...$120–150
GEO BARRETT/NEW YORK-SPICES, square, Z40, 5″, aqua, OP...........$75–100
GIESSENS UNION MUSTARD, barrel, Z171, 5″, colorless $75–100
GIESSENS/UNION/MUSTARD/NY, barrel-shaped, Z171, 4⅝″, colorless, OP ......
....$75–100
GOLDEN TREE MAPLE SYRUP, 20 oz., colorless, screw top....................$1–2
GOLDEN TREE PURE HONEY, 4 oz., colorless, screw top.......................$1–2
GRAND UNION TEA CO, 5″, colorless...$1–2
GREAT ATLANTIC & PACIFIC TEA CO, 5½″, colorless $1–2
GREAT SEAL, STYRON BEGGS CO, 9″, colorless $1–2
HALLOCKS PURE EXTRACTS, 6″, colorless $1–2
HANFORDS FLAVORING EXTRACTS, 5¼″, colorless $1–2
HARRIS PURE FLAVORS, 5½″, colorless..$1–2
HIRES IMPROVED ROOT BEER, four panels, colorless $1–2
HJ HEINZ PICKLING & PRESERVING, 6¼″ × 5¼″, gray stoneware ...$120–160
HORMEL GOOD FOOD (IN FRAME), oval, colorless, glass lid....................$5–7
J FAU/BORDEAUX, Z143 lower, 6½″, colorless, OP $125–150
J FAU/PRUNES DENTE/BORDEAUX, Z143 top, 8½″, smoky aqua, OP ..$90–120
JOHN ANNEAR & CO, PHILADELPHIA, Z28, 8″, aqua.......................$35–40
JUMBO 10½ OZ PEANUT BUTTER, pt., colorless $3–4
JUMBO BRAND 7 OZ NET PEANUT BUTTER, dated on base, colorless........$4–5
KEMP DAY & CO/NEW YORK, jar form, Z260, 9¼″, aqua $50–60
KINGS FLAVORING EXTRACT, 6¾″, colorless $3–5
LICENSED BY PFP CO, BALT, MD (ON BASE), OLNEYS WAX BEANS (ON LABEL),
pt., colorless...$12–15
M & GM/NY (ON BASE), round ribbed, 10⅛″, aqua, OP $50–65
MAPLE SAP & BOILED CIDER VINEGAR, 11¼″, cobalt...................$600–700
MARCEAU SPANISH OLIVES (LABELED), barrel figural, 7¾″, colorless ...$12–15
MARCELIN/DAVID (ON SEAL), jar form, 9½″, aqua, OP................$200–250
MRS CHAPINS MAYONNAISE, pt., colorless...$3–5
MUSTARD JAR, barrel-shaped, 3⅞″, dark olive amber........................$60–90
NEWMANS PURE COLD EXTRACTS, 5½″, colorless $1–2
NW/OPERMAN-, MUSTARD FACTORY, Z323, 4¾″, aqua, OP............$150–200
OLD RELIABLE TEA BAGS (ON LABEL), 8 oz., 4½″, red glass, tumbler .$15–25
OLD STYLE MUSTARD, pt., colorless, label $5–6
PEPPERSAUCE, cathedral, square, 8½″, pale yellowish green $70–90
PEPPERSAUCE, 20 vertical flutes, Z450, 10″, aqua, OP.....................$40–60
PEPPERSAUCE, 20 vertical flutes, Z450, 9¾″, colorless with gray/purple tint,
OP...$50–65
PEPPERSAUCE, cathedral, 9⅜″, aqua..$60–80
PEPPERSAUCE, roped edges with stars, Z456, 11″, aqua, OP............$120–150
PEPPERSAUCE, six-sided, cathedral, 8¾″, aqua................................$40–55

Food, three peppersauces. PHOTO COURTESY OF
SKINNER'S, INC.

PEPPERSAUCE, square with rib and lattice design, 13″, cobalt $500–750
PEPPERSAUCE, square with roped edges and star design in panels, 8⅞″, aqua,
IP $75–90
PEPPERSAUCE, square with roped corners, H74-5, 8⅝″, light green... $150–175
PIONEER, sauce bottle, six-sided, 9¼″, amber $150–175
PURE HORSE/RADISH/HD GEER, square, Z166-1, 7″, aqua.................$12–15
PURITY OATS, with flower, screw-cap jar, qt., colorless.....................$12–15
REMEMBER THE MAINE, pt., milk glass, with milk glass insert $125–185
RJC, mustard jar, six-sided, Z66, 6¼″, aqua, OP $40–50
S&P PAT APP FOR (ON BASE), peppersauce, spiral ridges, 8″, deep green ......
....$35–45
S&P PAT APP FOR (ON BASE), peppersauce, spiral ridges, 8″, blue green.......
.... $18–24
SAUERS EXTRACTS, 6″, colorless $3–4
SCHMIDT PATENT, tapered cylinder, 6⅛″, cobalt, OP.....................$80–110
SJVC CO (ON MONO.), 9″, aqua $30–35
SKILTON FOOTE & CO, BUNKER HILL PICKLES, 5¼″, colorless...............$4–6
TA BRYAN & COS PERFECTION TOMATO SAUCE, 8¼″, yellow amber..$150–200
TA BRYAN & COS/TOMATO SAUCE, Z61, 8½″, yellow amber.......... $300–400
TEITCHELL CHAMPLIN COS FLAVORING EXTRACT, 4½″, colorless $3–5
THOMPSON & TAYLOR ROOT BEER FLAVORING, 4″, colorless $2–3
TWIN HILLS PICKLES (ON LABEL) ON KERR FRUIT JAR, qt., colorless $5–6
VALENTINES MEAT JUICE, 3″, amber, egg shape................................$4–5
VANILLA ETCHED DISPENSER, cylinder, cobalt blue with metal cap, 10″ ....
.... $90–120
W DIEDZ A CO/MUSTARD/FACTORY, round, Z116, 5″, aqua, OP..........$50–60
W&E, peppersauce, square, Z433, 8⅞″, aqua, OP $150–175
W.M. & P./NY, sauce bottle, round, 9⅜″, aqua, OP.....................$50–75
WARSAW SALT CO CHOICE TABLE SALT, 5¾″, amber $60–90
WELLS-MILLER-& PROVOST, peppersauce, Z429-4 bottom, 8″, aqua, OP ....
....$50–70
WINE CURED PICKLES, MANHATTAN PICKLE CO, qt., colorless..............$4–5
WKL & CO, cathedral, peppersauce, Z277-2, 10⅛″, aqua, OP, light stain .....
.... $400–600

FRUIT JARS

Due to the lack of refrigeration and the spoilage of foods, ways had to
be found to store and preserve foods. The earliest food jars were not
airtight and were made principally to keep the food moist and to prevent
dirt and dust from mixing with the food. In the early 1800s, a Frenchman
discovered a way to preserve food by enclosing it in an airtight container.
The earliest fruit jars were free-blown vessels which were covered with
a wax cloth or with a tightly fitting cork. In the mid-19th century, "wax
sealer" jars led to jars with clamps and then screw threads.

The jars come in a wide variety of sizes, from as small as half pints
to as large as five-gallon jars. Aqua and clear jars are fairly common,
whereas jars made of milk glass, greens, blacks, blues or ambers are
very rare. Jars with their original lids, covers, and metal bails can add
to their price and rarity. It is not uncommon to see replaced wire bails
and other metal parts on jars. The reader is referred to *Red Book #5 on
Fruit Jars* by Alice Creswick.

A KLINE (ON STOPPER), C-1466, ½ gal., aqua $50–75
A KLINE PATD OCT 27 1863, USE A PIN (ON STOPPER), C-1463, pt., aqua......
....$35–40
A KLINE PATD OCT 27 1863, USE PIN (ON STOPPER), C-1467, qt., aqua, two
side lugs $110–135
A STONE & CO PHILADA, pt., aqua $400–500
A STONE & CO PHILADA, C-2874, pt., wax sealer.......................$340–420
A STONE & CO (IN ARCH), PHILA, two inner lugs, qt., aqua.......... $300–400
ABC, C-4, ½ gal., aqua, potstone crack....................................$150–190
ABC, cylindrical, C-44, qt., aqua...$200–325
ABC, large letters, no periods between letters, C-4, pt., aqua........ $300–360
ACKERS HG REGISTERED FINLEY ACKER & CO, stoneware $75–90
ACME, ON SHIELD, STARS & STRIPES, C-14, ½ gal., colorless $7–9
ACME, ON SHIELD, STARS & STRIPES, C-14, qt., colorless $1–1.50
ACME, ON SHIELD, STARS & STRIPES, C-14, pt., colorless $1–1.50
ADLAM PATENT BOSTON, MASS (ON BASE), C-25, ½ gal., colorless, with metal
cap and bail...$30–40
ADLER PROGRESS (ON BASE), qt., colorless, German........................ $10–12
AG SMALLEY & CO, BOSTON (ON BASE), C-2773, qt., amber.............$30–35
AGEE, qt., amber..$25–30
AGEE SPECIAL, no base mark, qt., amber.....................................$25–35
AIR TIGHT FRUIT JAR, qt., aqua, IP... $425–475
AIRTIGHT, C-53, qt., colorless $35–40
AIRTIGHT FRUIT JAR, C-54, qt., deep aqua, IP $400–500
ALLENS PAT JUNE 1871 (ON BASE), C-61, qt., aqua, repro top $100–150
ALLENS PATENT JUNE 1871, qt., aqua $225–275
AMAZON SWIFT SEAL, C-73, qt., colorless $8–10
AMAZON SWIFT SEAL, C-73, pt., colorless $8–10

AMERICAN FRUIT JAR, EAGLE & FLAG, C-77, qt., greenish aqua....... $100–120
AMERICAN MALT CREAM CO, 6″, aqua $7–9
AMERICAN NAG CO, C-79, midget, greenish aqua.........................$100–140
AMERICAN NAG CO, C-79, midget, aqua $100–140
AMERICAN (NAGCO) PORCELAIN-LINED, C-79, midget pt., aqua $100–115
ANCHOR HOCKING (H IN ANCHOR) MASON, C-85, pt., colorless.../......$1–1.50
ANCHOR MASONS PATENT, C-89, qt., colorless $10–14
ARS (FANCY SCRIPT), C-100, qt., aqua $60–75
AT LAS EZ SEAL, C-115, qt., aqua...$4–5
AT LAS EZ SEAL, C-115, ½ gal., aqua..$3–5
AT LAS EZ SEAL, C-115, ½ gal., colorless $1–1.50
ATLAS E-Z SEAL, C-115, qt., cornflower blue..............................$20–25
ATLAS E-Z SEAL, C-115, qt., apple green.....................................$6–8
ATLAS E-Z SEAL, C-115, ½ gal., olive green with amber swirls..........$30–40
ATLAS E-Z SEAL, C-115, ½ gal., cornflower blue $30–38
ATLAS E-Z SEAL, C-120, qt., amber..$20–24
ATLAS E-Z SEAL, C-123, squatty pt., green $7–8
ATLAS E-Z SEAL, C-123, pt., light green $4–6
ATLAS E-Z SEAL, ATLAS TRADEMARK REG (ON BASE), C-126, ½ pt., aqua......
.... $9–12
ATLAS E-Z SEAL, bell-shaped, C-122, pt., aqua, lip flakes.................$3–4
ATLAS EZ SEAL, C-113, qt., aqua $8–12
ATLAS (CLOVER) GOOD LUCK, C-133, qt., colorless $2–3
ATLAS (CLOVER) GOOD LUCK, C-133, pt., colorless $2–3
ATLAS (HA IN CIRCLE) MASON, C-139, ½ gal., colorless $3–5
ATLAS HA E-Z SEAL, C-137, qt., colorless....................................$4–5
ATLAS HA MASON, mini bank, C-140, ½ pt., colorless.......................$6–9
ATLAS MASON (NONSERRIFIED LETTERS), qt., aqua $4–5
ATLAS MASON (SERRIFIED LETTERS), C-145, qt., aqua $4–5
ATLAS MASON PATENT, C-157, pt., aqua.......................................$3–5
ATLAS MASONS PATENT NOV 30TH 1858, C-159, ½ gal., aqua $6–7
ATLAS MASONS PATENT NOV 30TH 1858, C-159, ½ gal., medium green ...$8–9
ATLAS-MASONS PATENT, C-155, qt., aqua $1–2
ATLAS-MASONS PATENT, C-155, pt., aqua $3–4
ATLAS SPECIAL MASON, C-163, qt., greenish aqua...........................$6–8
ATLAS SPECIAL MASON, C-163, ½ gal., aqua $7–9
ATLAS SS MASON, C-169, qt., cornflower blue $30–35
ATLAS SS MASON, C-169, pt., apple green.....................................$5–6
ATLAS STRONG SHOULDER MASON, C-167, pt., colorless .... $.75–1.25
ATLAS STRONG SHOULDER MASON, C-167, pt., aqua $2.50–3.50
ATLAS STRONG SHOULDER MASON, C-169, pt., cornflower blue........... $18–23
ATLAS STRONG SHOULDER MASON, C-169, ½ gal., medium cornflower blue ....
.... $10–13
ATLAS STRONG SHOULDER MASON, mini bank, ½ pt., colorless..............$6–9
ATLAS-STRONG SHOULDER MASON, C-166, qt., aqua .... $.75–1.25
ATLAS WHOLE FRUIT, C-175, pt., colorless...............................$1.50–2.50
ATLAS WHOLE FRUIT, C-175, qt., colorless...............................$1.50–2.50
ATLAS WHOLE FRUIT, C-175, ½ gal., colorless $8–12
AUTOMATIC SEALER, CLAYTON BOTTLE (ON BASE), C-183, ½ gal., aqua ....
.... $120–145
BAKER BROS & CO, BALTIMORE, MD (ON BASE), C-192, ½ gal., aqua ..$30–35

BALL (3-L LOOP), C-197, qt., olive green $65–85
BALL (3-L LOOP UNDERLINED), C-197, ½ gal., aqua $3–5
BALL (3-L LOOP UNDERLINED), C-197, qt., aqua $1.50–2.50
BALL (STIPPLED LETTERS), ribbed, qt., colorless, circa 1979 fruit jar.......$2–3
BALL DELUXE JAR, C-205, qt., colorless..$7–9
BALL ECLIPSE, wide mouth, C-209, pt., colorless......................$.75–1.25
BALL ECLIPSE, wide mouth, C-209, qt., colorless......................$.75–1.25
BALL ECLIPSE, wide mouth, C-210, qt., colorless.............................$3–4
BALL FREEZER JAR, ALLOW ¾″ HEAD SPACE, pt., colorless.................$4–5
BALL HOME CANNING, WILLIAM G HANNAH, qt., teal green, modern jar......
....$75–100
BALL IDEAL, C-215, ½ gal., colorless ....$.75–1.25
BALL IDEAL, C-247, qt., colorless...$2–3
BALL IDEA, EDMUND A BALL (IN MEDALLION), C-249, qt., aqua, modern jar
....$35–50
BALL IDEAL PATD JULY 14, 1908, C-225, ½ gal., colorless...........$1.50–2.50
BALL IDEAL PATD JULY 14, 1908, C-225, pt., colorless $1.50–2.50
BALL IDEAL PATD JULY 14, 1908 (ALL ON FRONT), C-226, pt., blue........$3–5
BALL IDEAL, THE FISCHER YEARS, MAN'S BUST, qt., colorless, modern jar......
....$35–50
BALL IMPROVED, DOUBLE HELIX, C-253, pt., aqua $3–4
BALL JAR MASONS PATENT 1858, C-277, ½ gal., aqua $7–9
BALL MASON, C-298, pt., greenish aqua, no crossbar on A...................$6–9
BALL MASON (3-L BALL), C-288, ½ gal., aqua $3–4
BALL MASON (3-L LOOP), C-258, qt., aqua ....$.75–1.35
BALL MASON (3-L LOOP), C-258, ½ gal., aqua $3–5
BALL MASON (3-L LOOP), C-258, pt., aqua.............................$2.50–3.50
BALL MASON (3-L VERSION), C-288, qt., colorless $13–17
BALL MASON, beaded neck, C-287, qt., aqua.................................$3–4
BALL MASON, no crossbar on A in MASON, C-298, qt., aqua............$12–15
BALL MASON, sipper, unthreaded, colorless, metal handle $5–6
BALL MASONS PATENT, beaded neck, C-311, qt., colorless $4–5
BALL (DETACHED LINE) MASONS PATENT 1858, qt., aqua $5–6
BALL (SCRIPT) MASONS PATENT NOV 30TH 1858, qt., aqua.....................$4–6
BALL PERFECT MASON, C-345, qt., aqua $6–8
BALL PERFECT MASON, C-349, qt., olive green............................$30–35
BALL PERFECT MASON, C-354, qt., aqua, square............................$5–6
BALL PERFECT MASON, C-368, pt., aqua, no crossbar on A $3–4
BALL PERFECT MASON, block letters, no slant, qt., aqua $10–14
BALL PERFECT MASON, italic/block letters, C-341, pt., aqua..............$10–13
BALL PERFECT MASON, italic/block letters, C-341, qt., aqua................$6–9
BALL PERFECT MASON, no crossbar on A in MASON, C-368, qt., aqua ...$5–6
BALL PERFECT MASON, round, ribbed, qt., aqua $6–8
BALL SANITARY SURE SEAL, undated base, C-377, qt., aqua $6–8
BALL SPECIAL, C-383, ½ gal., aqua $14–18
BALL SPECIAL MADE IN USA, C-386, qt., colorless, with gripper ribs ....
....$.75–1.35
BALL STANDARD, C-396, qt., colorless $10–14
BALL STANDARD, RG SIMPSON, 1952–1982, qt., colorless, new jar, circa 1982
....$40–50
BALL SURE SEAL, PACKED IN ST JOHNSBURY, VERMONT, C-408, aqua....$20–35

BALL SURE SEAL, PATD JULY 14, 08 (ON BASE), C-407, pt., aqua $20–23

BANNER (ENCIRCLED BY) PATD FEB 9TH, 1864, C-416, qt., aqua $125–160

BEAVER, C-438, midget pt., aqua $30–40

BEAVER, C-438, qt., golden amber, potstone crack $225–290

BEE HIVE, C-448, midget pt., colorless $275–360

BELL-SHAPED WAX SEALER, C-3218, qt., ice blue........................$250–350

BELLE PAT DEC 14TH 1869, C-453, qt., aqua $400–475

BENTON MYERS & CO, CLEVELAND, OHIO (ON BASE), C-464, ½ gal., color-
less $9–12

BEST FRUIT KEEPER, C-475, qt., aqua..$20–30

BEST FRUITKEEPER, PAT MAY 5, 1896 (ON LID), C-475, qt., aqua........$35–40

BLOESER, C-483, qt., aqua..$275–325

BLOESER JAR, C-484, qt., aqua.. $130–160

BLOWN-IN TWO-PIECE MOLD, 5¾", medium blue, OP, folded over lip ....
....$250–350

BOSTWICK PERFECT SEAL (IN SCRIPT), C-503, qt., colorless $40–45

BOYD MASON (MASON IN BANNER OVER FAINT GENUINE), C-508, ½ gal.,
colorless $8–10

BOYD PEPFECT (ERROR JAR), C-518, ½ gal., green..........................$12–15

BOYD PERFECT MASON, C-516, qt., aqua......................................$5–6

BOYD PERFECT MASON, nonslanted letters, qt., greenish aqua..............$6–7

BRAUN SAFETY MASON, C-524, pt., colorless................................$6–8

BRIGHTON, CLAMP PAT MARCH 30TH (ON LID), C-529, pt., colorless, original
clamp $120–145

BRIGHTON, CLAMP PATD MARCH 30TH (ON LID), C-529, qt., colorless, repro
clamp $60–70

BROCKWAY CLEAR VU MASON, C-531, qt., colorless .... $.75–1.25

BROCKWAY SUR-GRIP MASON, C-532, qt., colorless $2.50–3.50

BROCKWAY SUR-GRIP MASON, C-532, pt., colorless $2.50–3.50

BROCKWAY SUR-GRIP MASON, C-532, ½ gal., colorless......................$7–9

BUCK GLASS CO (ON LID), C-1072, qt., colorless............................$4–5

BUCKEYE, C-545, qt., aqua, repro clamp $180–210

C BURNHAM & CO MANUFACTURERS, C-561, qt.......................... $600–700

CALCUTTS PATENT APR 11TH (ON CAP), C-566, qt., colorless.............$30–40

CANADIAN JEWELL MADE IN CANADA, C-1363, pt., colorless $2–3

CANADIAN JEWELL MADE IN CANADA, C-1363, qt., colorless $2–3

CANADIAN KING, C-573, qt., colorless $18–23

CANADIAN MASON JAR MADE IN CANADA, C-574, pt., colorless
.... $.75–1.25

CANTON DOMESTIC FRUIT JAR, C-583, qt., colorless, with original lid ..$70–80

CANTON DOMESTIC FRUIT JAR, C-583, pt., colorless, with original clamp ....
....$130–160

CANTON ELECTRIC FRUIT JAR, C-583, ½ gal., medium cobalt...... $2000–2500

CF SPENCERS IMPROVED JAR, C-2812, qt., aqua $140–180

CF SPENCERS PAT 1868 IMPROVED, C-2812, green, repro metal lid with loops
.... $200–260

CF SPENCERS PATENT ROCHESTER, NY, C-2809, 2 qt., aqua, repro metal lid
.... $90–120

CF SPENCERS PATENT ROCHESTER, NY, C-2809, qt., aqua, repro metal lid .....
.... $90–120

CHAMPION PAT AUG 31, 1869, C-601, qt., no lid, repro clamp.........$100–120

CHAMPION PAT AUG 31ST, 1869, C-601, qt., aqua.................................$80–110

CHAS M HIGGINS & CO, BROOKLYN, NY, 3 oz., colorless, screw cap.....$5–6

CHEF (IN FRAME), BERDAN & CO, C-607, qt., aqua.............................$7–8

CHEF (IN FRAME), TOLEDO, OHIO, C-607, pt., colorless $5–6

CHICAGO FRUIT JAR, C-610, qt., aqua $225–275

CLARKS PEERLESS, C-623, ½ gal., aqua $12–15

CLARKS PEERLESS, C-623, pt., aqua $5–7

CLARKS PEERLESS, C-623, pt., aqua $6–8

CLYDE MASON'S IMPROVED, C-640, qt., colorless...........................$12–15

COHANSEY, C-646, qt., aqua $20–25

COHANSEY GLASS MFG CO MOULD #2 (ON BASE), C-643, pt., amber...$22–26

COHANSEY GLASS MFG CO PAT MCH 20 77 (ON BASE), C-651, qt., aqua, barrel-shaped $100–120

COHANSEY GLASS MFG, C-648, pt., aqua....................................$75–100

COHANSEY, SLUG PLATE ON REVERSE, C-646, ½ pt. $110–130

COHANSEY, SLUG PLATE ON REVERSE, C-646, pt. $35–45

COLUMBIA, C-659, pt., colorless $35–40

COLUMBIA, C-659, qt., aqua $18–24

COMMODORE, C-664, qt., aqua $600–800

COMMON SENSE JAR, C-666, qt., aqua, with original yoke clamp..... $600–700

CONSERVE JAR, C-670, ½ gal., colorless...................................$12–16

CONSERVE JAR, C-670, qt., colorless.......................................$4–5.50

CONSERVE JAR, C-670, pt., colorless.......................................$4–5.50

CONSERVE JAR, C-670, pt., colorless..$5–7

CPU (ON MILK GLASS LID), C-678, qt., colorless...........................$12–16

CROWN, C-705, midget pt., greenish aqua..................................$30–40

CROWN (NO DOT CROWN VARIETY), C-690, qt., aqua $22–26

CROWN (WITH E IN DIAMOND, OVER TORONTO), C-708, pt., colorless... $7–10

CROWN (CROWN) (NO DOT CROWN VARIETY), C-690, qt., aqua $10–14

CROWN (NO DOT CROWN VARIETY), midget, aqua $325–375

CROWN CORDIAL & EXTRACT CO NEW YORK, C-689, ½ gal., aqua, lightning putnam (on base) $9–11

CROWN CROWN (RING CROWN), C-698, ½ gal., aqua.......................$13–17

CROWN CROWN (RING CROWN), C-698, qt., aqua $10–13

CROWN EMBLEM (TALL AND SLIM VERSION), C-700, midget, aqua.......$30–35

CROWN MASON, C-723, pt., colorless..$3–5

CRYSTAL MASON, C-730, pt., colorless.....................................$20–25

CUNNINGHAM & CO PITTSBURGH, PA, C-748, pt., aqua $140–180

CUNNINGHAM & CO, PITTSBURGH (ON BASE), qt., medium sapphire blue, IP $3000–4000

CURTICE & MOORE TRADE MARK BOSTON, C-752, 2 qt., colorless.......$20–25

DAISY FE WARD (IN CIRCLE), C-763, qt., aqua $8–10

DAISY FE WARD & CO, C-762, pt., aqua....................................... $8–10

DAISY FE WARD & CO, C-762, qt., aqua...................................... $8–10

DAISY JAR, C-764, qt., colorless...$140–180

DAISY JAR, C-764, qt., colorless, repro clamp $130–160

DEXTER, C-793, qt., aqua...$35–50

DIAMOND FORM EMBOSSED ON SIDE, C-800, ½ gal., aqua $18–23

DIAMOND FRUIT JAR IMPROVED TRADEMARK, C-797, pt., colorless ..$1.50–2.50

DIAMOND FRUIT JAR IMPROVED TRADEMARK, C-797, qt., colorless ..$1.50–2.50

DIAMOND SYMBOL (ON FRONT), C-800, midget, aqua $50–60

DICTATOR, PATENTED DI HOLCOMB, 1869, qt., aqua $55–75
DODGE SWEENEY & CO CALIFORNIA BUTTER, C-816, qt., blue aqua ..$350–450
DODGE SWEENEY & COS CALIFORNIA BUTTER JAR, C-816, qt., aqua. $300–400
DOOLITTLE (BLOCK LETTERS), C-829, qt., aqua............................$35–40
DOOLITTLE (SCRIPT), C-831, pt., colorless $15–18
DOOLITTLE SELF SEALER, C-833, pt., aqua, with original lid and wire...........
....$300–375
DOUBLE SAFETY, SKO (ON BASE), C-835, pt., colorless.....................$7–10
DOUBLE SAFETY, SKO MONO. (ON BASE), C-835, pt., colorless.............$2–4
DREY IMPROVED EVER SEAL, qt., colorless $5–6
DREY IMPROVED EVER SEAL, C-855, pt., colorless, with glass "ears"...........
....$1.50–2.50
DREY IMPROVED EVER SEAL, C-855, qt., colorless, with glass "ears"...........
....$1.50–2.50
DREY IMPROVED EVER SEAL, PATD (ON NECK), pt., colorless................$6–7
DREY IMPROVED EVERSEAL, C-857, ½ gal., colorless..........................$4–6
DREY IMPROVED EVERSEAL, C-857, qt., colorless .... $.50–1.25
DREY MASON (LONG UNDERLINE), C-860, qt., colorless $5–7
DREY PATD 1920 IMPROVED EVER SEAL, pt., colorless......................$9–12
DREY PATD 1920 IMPROVED EVERSEAL, C-856, pt., colorless, with glass "ears"
.... $8–11
DREY PATD 1920 IMPROVED EVERSEAL, C-856, qt., colorless, with glass "ears"
....$3–5
DREY SQUARE MASON, IN CARPENTER'S SQUARE, C-868, qt., colorless $5–7
DREY (IN SCRIPT) MASON, C-860, qt., colorless .... $.75–1.35
DUNKLEY (ON BASE), C-875, pt., colorless $6–9
E-Z SEAL (NO ATLAS), E-Z SEAL REG. (ON BASE), qt., aqua $13–16
EAGLE, C-894, qt., aqua, original lid and yoke............................$80–110
EAGLE, C-894, 2 qt., aqua, original lid and clamp.......................$110–135
EAGLE MASON (DEBOSSED ON 2 SIDES), qt., colorless, with label, modern
....$2–4
EAGLE PATD DEC 28TH 1858, C-895, qt., aqua $60–75
EC HAZARD & CO, SHREWSBURY, NJ (ON BASE), C-1247, qt., colorless.........
.... $10–12
ECLIPSE, C-906, qt., aqua $80–110
ECONOMY (UNDERLINED) TM, PORTLAND, ORE (ON BASE), C-920, qt., color-
less $1.50–2.50
EGC IMPERIAL, WITH CIRCLE, C-984, qt., aqua $18–21
EGC IMPERIAL, WITHOUT CIRCLE, C-985, qt., aqua $18–21
EHE 7 (ON HEEL), SK & CO (ON BASE), C-936, qt., aqua...................$3–4
ELECTRIC (IN SCRIPT, IN CIRCLE), C-937, pt., aqua $12–16
ELECTRIC FRUIT JAR (AROUND WORLD GLOBE), C-943, qt., aqua, repro clamp
....$110–130
ELECTRIC FRUIT JAR (AROUND WORLD GLOBE), C-943, 2 qt., aqua, repro
clamp $110–130
ELECTRIC FRUIT JAR (AROUND WORLD GLOBE), C-943, pt., aqua, with original
clamp $140–150
EMPIRE (WITH STIPPLED CROSS, IN FRAME), C-947, qt., colorless...........$7–8
EMPIRE (WITHIN STIPPLED CROSS, IN FRAME), C-947, 2 qt., colorless ..$12–15
EMPIRE (IN STIPPLED CROSS), C-947, pt., colorless............................$4–6
EUREKA, C-967, pt., colorless $8–10

EUREKA (IN SCRIPT ON JAR'S SIDE), C-967, 1½ pt., colorless $30-40
EUREKA PATD DEC 27TH 1864, C-970, 1½ qt., aqua, repro closure $60-80
EUREKA PATD DEC 27TH 1864, C-970, qt., aqua, with original tin lid $135-160
EUREKA PATD DEC 27TH 1864, C-970, 2 qt., aqua, repro closure.........$65-80
EUREKA PATD DEC 27TH 1864, C-970, qt., aqua, repro closure $65-80
EXCELSIOR IMPROVED (IN 2 STRAIGHT LINES), C-981, 2 qt., greenish aqua ......
....$35-40
EXCELSIOR, MILK BOTTLE-SHAPED, C-978, qt., aqua $200-240
EXCELSIOR, PATD AUG 3RD 1858 (ON LID), C-980, 2 qt., greenish aqua ....
....$40-50
EXWACO (ON BASE), C-987, pt., emerald green $15-25
EXWACO (ON BASE), TALL SLENDER, C-987, pt., amber....................$25-30
F & S (IN CIRCLE), C-1067, pt., aqua...$18-23
F&J BODINE MANUFACTURERS, PHILA, C-489, qt., aqua, original lid $180-220
F&J BODINE MANUFACTURERS, PHILA, C-489, qt., aqua, with repro lid.........
....$140-160
F&S (IN CIRCLE), C-1067, qt., aqua...$18-20
FAMILY FRUIT JAR, C-997, qt., colorless, with original lid..............$250-325
FARLEY CHICAGO, C-1000, qt., colorless..$1-2
FARLEY, SQUAT, pt., colorless, with metal screw cap $4-5
FARM FAMILY (ON LID), pt., colorless, round.................................. $8-10
FB CO/2 (ON BASE), qt., yellow amber, wax sealer $90-110
FCG CO 1 (ON BASE), C-1011, ½ gal., citron $200-250
FLACCUS BROS MUSTARD FRUIT JAR, C-1034, pt., colorless, no cover, small
crack $70-90
FLACCUS BROS SH FRUIT JAR, C-1035, pt., colorless $80-120
FLACCUS BROS SH FRUIT JAR, C-1036, pt., milk glass....................$125-175
FLACCUS BROS SH FRUIT JAR, C-1037, pt., colorless.........................$30-45
FLACCUS BROS SH FRUIT JAR, C-1037, pt., yellow amber................$250-350
FLACCUS BROS SH FRUIT JAR, C-1037, pt., milk glass....................$140-180
FLACCUS BROS STEERS HEAD FRUIT JAR, pt., colorless $35-40
FLACCUS BROTHERS, C-1039, pt., colorless $30-40
FLACCUS TYPE, VINES AND FANCY DECO, ½ pt., blue milk glass.........$30-35
FLACCUS TYPE, VINES AND FANCY DECO, ½ pt., milk glass............... $13-16
FOSTER SEALFAST, FOSTER (ON BASE), C-2708, ½ pt., colorless $6-8
FRANKLIN FRUIT JAR, C-1056, qt., colorless $50-60
FRESHERATOR (IN RECTANGLE), squat, pt., colorless............................$6-8
FRIDLEY & CORMANS LADIES CHOICE, C-1062, pt., aqua, original iron rim
....$800-1200
FROM YOUR FRIENDS AT BALL JOHN W ERICHSON, pt., colorless.........$15-20
FRUIT COMMONWEALTH JAR, C-668, 1½ qt., colorless..................... $90-100
FRUIT COMMONWEALTH JAR, C-668, qt., colorless $90-100
FRUITKEEPER GCCO, C-1066, 2 qt., green $40-45
FRUITKEEPER GCCO, C-1066, qt., green.......................................$35-40
G & D (ON BASE), TEN-SIDED, 2 oz., colorless.................................$4-6
GAYNER GLASS TOP, C-1073, pt., colorless $7-9
GEM, C-1077, midget, aqua $25-30
GEM (CROSS), C-1083, midget, aqua...$40-45
GEM (IN ARCH), C-1102, midget, aqua $110-135
GEM (ON 1 LINE), C-1090, qt., aqua, one base date $6-8
GEM (ON 1 LINE), C-1092, qt., aqua, with more than one base date........$4-6

GEM (ON 1 LINE), C-1094, qt., aqua, different base dates $6–8
GEM CFJ CO, C-1102, qt., aqua $6–8
GEM, WITH HOURGLASS ON REVERSE, C-1081, qt., aqua $16–22
GEM, WITH HOURGLASS ON REVERSE, C-1081, ½ gal., aqua $16–22
GENUINE MASON, C-1126, pt., aqua..$10–12
GENUINE MASON (MASON IN FLAG), C-1124, qt., apple green $10–13
GEO D BROWN, C-542, ½ gal., colorless, repro clamp $35–40
GEO D BROWN, C-542, pt., colorless, repro clamp $35–40
GEO D BROWN, C-542, qt., colorless, repro clamp $35–40
GILBERTS (STAR), qt., aqua, with rare original lid.........................$250–350
GJ CO, C-1133, pt., aqua with large engraved metal lid.................$30–35
GLASSBORO TRADE MARK IMPROVED, C-1138, pt., aqua.....................$12–16
GLENSHAW G MASON, C-1146, pt., colorless.................................$12–18
GLOBE, C-1147, qt., aqua $11–15
GLOBE, PATENTED MAY 25, 1886 (ON LID), C-1147, qt., aqua $14–17
GLOBE, PATENTED MAY 25, 1886 (ON LID), C-1147, 2 qt., amber........$55–60
GLOBE, PATENTED MAY 25, 1886 (ON LID), C-1147, pt., aqua.........$19–24
GLOBE, PATENTED MAY 25, 1886 (ON LID), C-1147, qt., amber $48–55
GLOBE-SHAPED JAR, pt., colorless, screw cap.................................$4–5
GOLD BRAND PURE LEAF LARD, C-1153, qt., aqua............................$55–65
GOOD HOUSE KEEPERS MASON, C-1166, qt., colorless $6–8
GREAT EASTERN PHILADA WHITEHEAD, C-1175, qt., aqua, with glass stopper
....$1300–1800
GREEN MOUNTAIN, C-1178, pt., light aqua $10–13
GREEN MOUNTAIN CA CO (IN FRAME), C-1178, pt., colorless.............$16–20
GREEN MOUNTAIN C-A-CO (IN FRAME), C-1178, ½ gal., colorless.......$16–24
GREEN MOUNTAIN C-A-CO (IN FRAME), C-1178, pt., colorless..............$8–12
GREEN MOUNTAIN C-A-CO (IN FRAME), C-1178, qt., colorless..............$8–12
GREEN MOUNTAIN C.A.CO (IN CIRCLE), C-1177, qt., aqua $8–12
GREEN MOUNTAIN C.A.CO (IN CIRCLE), C-1177, pt., aqua $8–12
GRIFFENS PATENT OCT 7, 1862, C-1179, ½ gal., aqua......................$80–120
GRISWOLDS PATENT 1862, C-1181, qt., light clambroth with amethyst tint ....
....$1200–1500
H J H CO PATD (ON BASE), FOUR SIDES, ½ pt., colorless, ABM $3–4
HAMILTON, C-1214, qt., colorless $50–60
HANSEES PH PALACE HOME JAR, C-1232, pt., colorless...................$90–110
HARTELL & LETCHWORTH (ON METAL CAP), C-1239, ½ gal., aqua......$35–50
HARTELL-LETCHWORTH PATENT 1866, C-1239, qt., aqua, repro lid $65–80
HARTELL-LETCHWORTH PATENT 1866, C-1239, 2 qt., aqua, repro lid $65–80
HARTELLS GLASS AIR TIGHT COVE (ON LID), C-1237, pt., aqua........$110–130
HARTELLS, C-1238, qt., greenish aqua $40–50
HARVEST MASON, C-1241, qt., colorless...$7–8
HASEROT COMPANY CLEVELAND MASON, C-1244, qt., aqua $7–9
HAZEL (ON METAL LID), C-1253, qt., amber................................$45–60
HAZEL ATLAS EZ SEAL, C-1254, qt., aqua $7–10
HAZEL ATLAS LIGHTNING SEAL, C-1256, pt., aqua..........................$8–10
HAZEL ATLAS LIGHTNING SEAL, C-1256, qt., aqua..........................$8–10
HAZEL HA PRESERVE JAR, C-1259, pt., colorless $4–6
HEINZ, WITH STAR DESIGN INSIDE (ON BASE), oval, ½ pt., colorless ...$12–15
HELMES RAILROAD MILLS, C-1263, pt., amber $18–21
HERO (ABOVE CROSS), C-1268, qt., deep aqua...............................$35–50

HERO (CROSS), C-1269, pt., aqua...$17–20
HERO (CROSS), C-1269, qt., aqua...$25–35
HERO IMPROVED, C-1274, qt., aqua $45–55
HERO IMPROVED, C-1274, 2 qt., aqua...$45–55
HERO, WITH MULTIPLE PATENT DATES (ON BASE), C-1272, qt., aqua ...$45–55
HERO, WITH MULTIPLE PATENT DATES (ON BASE), C-1272, 2 qt., aqua.$45–55
HEROINE, C-1276, qt., aqua $45–55
HILTONS PAT MAR 10TH 1868, C-1284, qt., aqua, repro clamp........ $450–600
HJ HEINZ CO PICKLING & PRESERVE WORKS, C-1262, 6¼″ × 5¼″, stone-
ware..$120–160
HK MULFORD CHEMISTS PHILADELPHIA, C-2316, pt., amber.................$2–3
HOLMEGAARD (ON BASE), qt., colorless, Danish $9–12
HONEST MASON JAR PAT 1858, C-1264, pt., colorless $15–18
HOWE JAR, SCRANTON, PA, C-1304, pt., aqua $80–100
HW PETIT WESTVILLE NJ (ON BASE), C-2477, qt., aqua $6–8
HW PETIT WESTVILLE, NJ (ON BASE), C-2477, 2 qt., aqua $12–15
HW PETTIT SALEM NJ (ON BASE), C-2478, 2 qt., aqua...................... $15–18
HW PETTIT WESTVILLE NJ (ON BASE), C-2477, pt., aqua....................$6–8
IDEAL, C&E CO MONOGRAM, C-1315, qt., light green, no lid $7–9
IMPERIAL PAT APRIL 20TH 1886, C-1325, pt., colorless $120–130
IMPROVED (KEYSTONE), C-1330, ½ gal., aqua $25–35
IMPROVED (KEYSTONE), C-1330, qt., aqua $15–23
IMPROVED (KEYSTONE), C-1330, qt., aqua $20–25
IMPROVED GEM MADE IN CANADA, C-1118, pt., colorless..............$1.50–2.50
IMPROVED GEM MADE IN CANADA, C-1118, qt., colorless..............$1.50–2.50
IMPROVED MASON JAR, C-1336, pt., colorless.................................$4–6
INDEPENDENT JAR, C-1340, midget, colorless.................................$40–50
J F G PRODUCTS, C-1365, pt., colorless, figural globe $4–6
J&B (WITHIN OCTAGON) FRUIT JAR, C-1353, qt., aqua, original lid......$75–95
J&B (WITHIN OCTAGON) FRUIT JAR, C-1353, pt., aqua, repro lid.........$35–40
J&B (WITHIN OCTAGON) FRUIT JAR, C-1353, qt., aqua, repro lid.........$35–40
J&B FRUIT JAR, C-1353, pt., aqua, repro lid....................................$40–50
JC BAKERS PATENT AUG 14 1860, C-194, qt., pale blue green, repro clamp
....$150–200
JD WILLOUGHBY PATD 4, 1859 (ON REPRO STOPPER), qt., aqua $40–50
JD WILLOUGHBY PATENTED JAN 4, 1859, C-3172, qt., aqua............. $140–175
JE TAYLOR & CO PURE FOOD (WITHIN CIRCLE), C-2921, qt., aqua $17–21
JEANNETTE J (IN SQUARE) MASON HOME PACKER, C-1356, qt., colorless ....
....$.50–1.40
JEWELL JAR MADE IN CANADA, C-1360, ½ gal., colorless $8–10
JEWELL JAR MADE IN CANADA, C-1360, qt., colorless $2.50–4.00
JEWELL JAR MADE IN CANADA, C-1360, pt., colorless $4–6
JOHN M MOORE & CO, PATD 1861 (ON FRONT), C-2306, qt., deep aqua, small
mouth $300–350
JOHNSON & JOHNSON, C-1375, qt., amber.......................................$12–15
JOHNSON & JOHNSON NEW BRUNSWICK, NJ, USA, ½ pt., amber $9–12
JOHNSON & JOHNSON NEW YORK, 5½″, cobalt blue, square...............$30–35
JOHNSON & JOHNSON NEW YORK, square, qt., amber......................... $9–11
JOS MIDDLEBY JR INC, C-2271, 2 qt., aqua $15–18
JOSHUA WRIGHT, PHILADA, C-3192, 2 qt., aqua, IP $300–400
KC FINEST QUALITY MASON, C-1386, qt., colorless...............................$5–6

KERR SELF SEALING MASON, 65TH ANNIV., C-1424, qt., colorless with blue streak $30–35
KERR SELF SEALING, C-1415, qt., colorless...$5–6
KERR SS WIDE MOUTH MASON, ½ pt., colorless, new jar, circa 1983 ......$3–4
KERR SS WIDE MOUTH MASON, qt., light green, modern $5–6
KILNER JAR IMPROVED REGD, C-1446, qt., colorless..........................$8–12
KILNER JAR, NO REGD, C-1445, qt., colorless $8–12
KING (ON BANNER BELOW CROWN), C-1453, qt., colorless.................$8–10
KING (ON BANNER BELOW CROWN), C-1453, pt., colorless.................$8–10
KING (ON BANNER BELOW CROWN), C-1453, qt., colorless.................$8–10
KINSELLA 1874 TRUE MASON, C-1460, qt., colorless..........................$5–7
KLINE, C-1462, qt. $18–25
KNOWLTON VACUUM (STAR) FRUIT JAR, C-1471, 2 qt., aqua $30–35
KNOWLTON VACUUM (STAR) FRUIT JAR, C-1471, qt., aqua.................$15–25
L & W's XL, C-1585, qt., aqua...$55–70
L G CO (ON BASE), C-1527, ½ gal., dense golden amber.............. $500–600
LAFAYETTE (IN SCRIPT), C-1492, pt., colorless $100–135
LAFAYETTE (IN SCRIPT), C-1492, qt., colorless $100–135
LAFAYETTE (PROFILE), qt., aqua... $700–800
LAFAYETTE FRUIT JAR, C-1492-1, qt., aqua $500–650
LAMB MASON, C-1495, qt., colorless, with zinc lid....................$1.75–2.50
LAMB MASON, C-1496, pt., colorless...$5–6
LAMB MASON, C-1496, qt., colorless, with zinc lid....................$1.75–2.50
LEADER (IN 2 LINES), C-1508, pt., colorless, repro wire $40–45
LEGRAND IDEAL TRADE, "LIJ" MONO., C-1514, qt., aqua, repro lid .. $80–100
LEIFHEIT CONFITURE, RING OF FRUIT, modern German jar, painted lug-type screw cap.. $9–11
LEOTRIC, C-1515, pt., aqua, smooth lip $6–8
LEOTRIC, C-1515, pt., aqua, ground lip $7–9
LEOTRIC, C-1518, pt., colorless, no base embossing $7–9
LEOTRIC (IN CIRCLE), C-1519, qt., aqua $3–5
LEOTRIC (IN CIRCLE), C-1519, ½ gal., colorless............................. $14–18
LEOTRIC (IN CIRCLE), C-1519, qt., colorless $8–12
LEOTRIC (IN CIRCLE), C-1519, pt., aqua $3–4
LEOTRIC (WITHIN CIRCLE), C-1518, 2 qt., aqua $14–18
LEOTRIC, WITH ERASED TRADE MARK ELECTRIC, C-1520, pt., aqua.........$7–9
LIGHTNING, WITH H OVER ANCHOR, C-84, qt., colorless.....................$3–4

Fruit Jar, Lafayette. PHOTO COURTESY OF SKINNER'S, INC.

LIGHTNING, WITH H OVER ANCHOR, C-84, pt., colorless.................$1–1.50
LIGHTNING, WITH H OVER ANCHOR, C-84, qt., colorless.................$1–1.50
LINDELL GLASS CO (ON BASE), C-1559, qt., amber, wax sealer........ $90–120
LOCKPORT MASON, C-1563, qt., colorless......................................$6–8
LOCKPORT MASON, C-1563, pt., aqua $6–8
LOCKPORT MASON, C-1563, qt., aqua $6–8
LOCKPORT MASON, C-1563, qt., aqua $3–5
LOCKPORT MASON, C-1563, ½ gal., aqua $8–12
LOCKPORT MASON, C-1563, pt., aqua $3–5
LOCKPORT MASON IMPROVED, C-1565, pt., aqua...............................$4–5
LONGLIFE MASON, qt., amber...$12–15
LONGLIFE, OBEAR NESTER (ON BASE), C-1566, pt., colorless $3–4
LUDLOWS PATENT JUNE 28, 1859 (ON LID), C-1597, qt., aqua......... $125–165
LUDLOWS PATENT JUNE 28, 1859, C-1597, ½ gal., aqua $70–100
LUSTRE, RE TONGUE & BROS, C-1608, pt., aqua..............................$6–8
LUSTRE RE TONGUE, FANCY FRAME, C-1604, qt., aqua.......................$6–8
LYNCHBURG STANDARD MASON, C-1645, qt., aqua............................$12–15
LYON & BOSSARDS JAR STROUDSBURG, PA, C-1646, qt., aqua, with original
clamp $410–465
LYON & BOSSARDS JAR STROUDSBURG, PA, C-1646, qt., aqua, with repro clamp
.... $175–275
MAGIC FRUIT JAR, C-1657, ½ gal., aqua....................................$90–110
MANSFIELD IMPROVED MASON, C-1672, qt., colorless.......................$10–12
MARIAN JAR MASONS PATENT 1858, C-1677, pt., aqua.....................$17–22
MARSTONS RESTAURANT BOSTON (WITHIN CIRCLE), colorless $15–20
MASCOT TRADEMARK PATD IMPROVED, C-1863, qt., colorless with tudor rose
lid.. $130–160
MASON (KEYSTONE IN CIRCLE), C-1736, qt., aqua..........................$15–20
MASON (KEYSTONE IN CIRCLE), C-1736, qt., aqua...........................$5–6
MASON FRUIT JAR, C-1719, pt., medium amber $250–325
MASON FRUIT JAR, C-1720, pt., medium amber........................... $300–400
MASON FRUIT JAR (IN 3 LINES), C-1721, pt., colorless...................... $8–12
MASON FRUIT JAR (IN 3 LINES), C-1721, ½ gal., colorless................. $10–15
MASON FRUIT JAR (IN 3 LINES), C-1721, qt., colorless.....................$4–6
MASON FRUIT JAR (IN 3 LINES), C-1721, pt., aqua.........................$8–12
MASON, HG CO, C-1842, midget, aqua $250–325
MASON IMPROVED, C-1744, qt., aqua $2–3
MASON IMPROVED, C-1744, ½ gal., aqua $4–5
MASON JAR OF 1872, C-1804, qt., aqua $25–35
MASON JAR OF 1872, C-1804, 2 qt., aqua..................................$25–35
MASON JAR OF 1872, C-1804, pt., aqua $105–125
MASON JAR, ARCHED DESIGN, C-1797, qt., colorless...................... $9–12
MASON PATENT NOV 30TH 1858 (NO S), C-1845, qt., colorless $6–8
MASON PATENT NOV 30TH 1858 (KEYSTONE IN CIRCLE), C-2040, qt., aqua
....$7–9
MASON VACUUM KNOWLTON PATENT, C-2230, 2 qt., aqua, repro clamp.........
....$40–50
MASON VACUUM KNOWLTON PATENT, C-2230, pt., aqua $110–135
MASON, WITH SHEPHERDS CROOK, C-1687, qt., aqua.......................$4–6
MASON, WITH SHEPHERDS CROOK, C-1687, pt., aqua...................... $12–18
MASON, WITH SHEPHERDS CROOK, C-1687, ½ gal., aqua.................. $12–18

Fruit Jar, beaver and Mason's patent.
PHOTO COURTESY OF DAVID SMITH.

MASON.S 2 PATENT NOV 30TH 1858, C-2121, qt., aqua $6–9
MASONS (CROSS) 1858, qt., amber $100–125
MASONS (CROSS) IMPROVED, C-1778, midget, aqua $15–18
MASONS (KEYSTONE) IMPROVED, C-1791, midget, aqua $30–35
MASONS 1 PATENT NOV 30TH 1858, C-2115, qt., aqua......................$10–14
MASONS 2 PATENT NOV 30TH 1858, C-2118, ½ gal., aqua..................$14–18
MASONS 2 PATENT NOV 30TH 1858, C-2118, qt., aqua......................$10–14
MASONS 2 PATENT NOV 30TH 1858, HC&T (BASE), C-2118, ½ gal., aqua........
....$20–30
MASONS 25 PATENT NOV 30TH 1858, C-2191, qt., aqua.....................$11–14
MASONS 404 PATENT NOV 30TH 1858, C-2219, midget, aqua $125–175
MASONS A PATENT NOV 30TH 1858, C-2069, midget, aqua $200–250
MASONS BGCO IMPROVED, pt., light green.................................$75–90
MASONS C PATENT NOV 30TH 1858, C-2075, qt., aqua $8–12
MASONS-C-PATENT NOV 30TH 1858, C-2075, qt., aqua $10–14
MASONS CFJ CO IMPROVED, C-1766, qt., colorless $6–7
MASONS CFJ CO IMPROVED, CLYDE, NY, C-1767, pt., aqua..................$6–8
MASONS CFJ CO IMPROVED, CLYDE, NY, C-1767, midget, aqua..........$18–24
MASONS CFJ CO PATENT NOV 30TH 1858, C-2001, qt., apple green $14–18
MASONS CFJ IMPROVED, CLYDE, NY, C-1767, pt., colorless $8–10
MASONS CFJ IMPROVED, CLYDE, NY, C-1767, qt., aqua $5–7
MASONS CFJ IMPROVED, CLYDE, NY, C-1767, ½ gal., aqua...............$12–16
MASONS CFJCO PATENT NOV 30TH 1858, C-2001, qt., aqua...................$2–3
MASONS CFJCO PATENT NOV 30TH 1858, C-2001, qt., golden amber.............
....$150–200
MASONS CFJCO PATENT NOV 30TH 1858, C-2001, qt., medium yellow amber
....$175–200
MASONS CFJCO PATENT NOV 30TH 1858, C-2001, ½ gal., aqua.............$3–5
MASONS CFJCO PATENT NOV 30TH 1858, C-2001, midget pt., aqua $12–15
MASONS CROSS, C-2020, ½ gal., amber $110–135
MASONS CROSS, C-2020, qt., amber $80–100
MASONS CROSS PATENT NOV 30TH 1858, C-2020, qt., aqua..............$2–2.50
MASONS CROSS PATENT NOV 30TH 1858, C-2020, pt., aqua....................$3–5
MASONS GC CO PATENT NOV 30TH 1858, C-2015, pt., light green $7–9
MASONS GCCO PATENT NOV 30TH 1858, C-2015, pt., aqua................$14–18
MASONS III PATENT NOV 30 1858, C-2130, midget, aqua $110–140
MASONS III PATENT NOV 30 1858, C-2130, qt., aqua $20–25
MASONS IMPROVED PATD, C-1795, qt., aqua...................................$4–6

MASONS IMPROVED, C-1747, pt., colorless $70–90

MASONS IMPROVED, C-1747, 2 qt., colorless.................................$30–40

MASONS IMPROVED, C-1748, 2 qt., amber $100–125

MASONS IMPROVED, CFJ (ON REVERSE), C-1764, ½ gal., aqua..............$3–5

MASONS IMPROVED, CFJ Co, C-1764, midget, colorless $12–15

MASONS IMPROVED, SHIELD EMBLEM, C-1762, midget, aqua..............$50–60

MASONS IMPROVED, WITH CROSS, C-1780, ½ gal., aqua......................$3–5

MASONS KBGCO PATENT NOV 30 1858, C-2039, pt., colorless...........$15–20

MASONS KBGCO PATENT NOV 30 1858, C-2039, pt., aqua.................$15–20

MASONS KEYSTONE IMPROVED, C-1791, ½ gal., aqua......................$23–27

MASONS KEYSTONE PATENT NOV 30TH 1858, C-2045, ½ gal., medium amber
....$250–375

MASONS KEYSTONE PATENT NOV 30TH 1858, C-2046, pt., aqua $6–7

MASONS LGW IMPROVED, C-1793, qt., colorless $18–23

MASONS LGW IMPROVED, C-1793, qt., colorless $15–18

MASONS N PATENT NOV 30TH 1858, C-2094, qt., aqua $7–9

MASONS PATENT, C-1811, qt., ball blue...$7–9

MASONS (ARCHED) PATENT (STRAIGHT), C-1811, ½ gal., deep greenish aqua
....$7–9

MASONS PATENT 1858, C-1822, qt., colorless $4–5

MASONS PATENT 1858, C-1843, ½ gal., honey amber $110–135

MASONS PATENT 1858, C-1843, qt., yellow amber $75–100

MASONS PATENT NOV 30TH 1858, C-1828, pt., aqua....................... $500–600

MASONS PATENT NOV 30TH 1858, C-1843, ½ gal., greenish aqua............$3–4

MASONS PATENT NOV 30TH 1858, C-1843, ½ gal., aqua.......................$4–5

MASONS PATENT NOV 30TH 1858, C-1843, midget, medium blue ...$1000–1500

MASONS PATENT NOV 30TH 1858, C-1859, qt., colorless, with two reversed Ns
....$13–18

MASONS PATENT NOV 30TH 1858, C-1979, qt., aqua, with heart on base.........
....$50–70

MASONS PATENT NOV 30TH 1858, C-1982, midget, with small star on base,
aqua $50–60

MASONS PATENT NOV 30TH 1858, C-1984, midget, with large star on base,
aqua $50–60

MASONS PATENT NOV 30TH 1858, C-2020, qt., yellow amber $100–150

MASONS PATENT NOV 30TH 1858, C-2020, ½ gal., green with amber striations
.... $350–400

MASONS PATENT NOV 30TH 1858, midget, tudor rose, colorless with disk im-
merser $125–160

MASONS (STAR) PATENT NOV 30 1858, C-2068, 4 gal., aqua, repro jar ..$20–25

MASONS PATENT NOV 30TH 1858, qt., aqua, ball on reverse $6–7

MASONS PATENT NOV 30TH 1858, CLYDE, NY (ON BASE), C-2002, midget,
aqua $80–100

MASONS PATENT NOV 30TH 1858, MOORE BROS GLASS (ON BASE), C-1960, qt.,
aqua $5–7

MASONS PATENT NOV 30TH 1858, PAT NOV 26, 67 (ON BASE), C-1962, qt.,
aqua $5–6

MASONS PATENT NOV 30TH 1858, PORT (ON BASE), C-1965, 2 qt., aqua.........
.... $15–18

MASONS PATENT NOV 30TH 1858, WITH CROSS, C-2019, qt., aqua $5–6

MASONS PATENT NOV 30TH 1858, WITH CROSS, C-2019, qt., colorless $7–8

MASONS PATENT NOV 30TH 1858, WITH MILK GLASS LID EMBOSSED WITH BALL, midget, aqua..$110–130

MASONS PATENT NOV 30TH 1858, WITH REVERSED NS, C-1860, midget, aqua $45–55

MASONS PATENT NOV 30TH 1858, WITH REVERSED 9, C-2159, qt., aqua $15–20

MASONS PATENT NOV 30TH 1858, WITH UNDERLINED 5, C-2141, midget, aqua $25–45

MASONS PATENT NOV 30TH 1858- TUDOR ROSE, C-1944, midget, aqua ..$30–40

MASONS PATENT NOV 30TH 1858-HERO GLASSWORKS, similar to C-2013, 3 gal., aqua $500–700

MASONS SGCO PATENT NOV 30TH 1858, C-2056, ½ gal., aqua $10–12

MASONS SGCO PATENT NOV 30TH 1858, C-2056, pt., aqua................ $10–12

MASONS UNION, WITH SHIELD, C-2229, qt., aqua $90–125

MCMECHENS ALWAYS THE BEST OLD VIRGINIA, C-2403, qt., aqua $50–75

MCMECHENS ALWAYS THE BEST, C-2251, colorless, milk glass lid $90–110

MEDFORD PRESERVED FRUIT BUFFALO NY, C-2259, 2 qt., pale cornflower blue $225–275

MICHIGAN MASON, NO SIDE EMBOSSING, C-2269, pt., colorless.......... $18–22

MICHIGAN MASON, SIDE EMBOSSING, C-2269, pt., aqua, "MGC" on base...... ....$30–40

MILLVILLE, C-2278, pt. $40–50

MILLVILLE ATMOSPHERIC FRUIT JAR, C-2278, ½ gal., aqua.............$25–35

MILLVILLE ATMOSPHERIC FRUIT JAR, C-2278, 1½ qt., aqua $25–30

MILLVILLE ATMOSPHERIC FRUIT JAR, C-2278, qt., aqua, with all original metal $20–25

MILLVILLE ATMOSPHERIC-WHITALLS PATENT, C-2280, square shoulder, qt., aqua $110–125

MILLVILLE ATMOSPHERIC-WHITALLS PATENT, C-2280, square shoulder, pt., aqua $110–140

MILLVILLE ATMOSPHERIC-WHITALLS PATENT, C-2280, square shoulder, 2 qt., aqua $130–160

MISSION MASON, WITH BELL, C-2288, qt., colorless..........................$6–8

MODEL JAR PATD AUG 27, 1867, C-2292, qt., aqua.......................$275–375

MODEL JAR PATD AUG 27, 1867, C-2293, ½ gal., aqua $125–160

MONARCH (IN SHIELD), C-2298, qt., colorless................................ $8–10

MOORES PATENT DEC 3D 1861, C-2304, 1½ qt., aqua $70–85

MOORES PATENT DEC 3D 1861, C-2304, 2 qt., aqua.......................$70–85

MOORES PATENT DEC 3D 1861, C-2304, qt., aqua $70–85

MOORES PATENT DEC 3D 1861, C-2304, pt., aqua $110–135

MOTHERS JAR TRADE MARK RE TONGUE (ON FRONT), C-2312, qt., aqua $25–30

MOTHERS JAR TRADE MARK RE TONGUE (ON FRONT), C-2312, pt., aqua $40–45

MOUNTAIN MASON, C-2313, qt., colorless $25–30

MRS CHAPINS MAYONNAISE, pt., colorless.....................................$3–5

MRS GE HALLER PATD FEB 25, 73 (ON STOPPLE), C-1204, qt., aqua. $125–150

NEW PARAGON, C-2397, qt., aqua.. $120–165

NEW PERFECTION, IGCO, C-2349, 2 qt., colorless...........................$35–45

NEWMANS PURE GOLD BAKING POWDER, C-2342, pt., aqua $30–35

NORTON BROS CHICAGO (ON LID), C-2355, pt., with tin handle $45–55
NORTON BROS CHICAGO (ON LID), C-2355, qt................................$40–50
OC FRUIT BOTTLE, C-2359, qt., aqua $38–50
OLD STYLE MUSTARD, C-2377, pt., colorless, with full label $5–6
P LORILLARDS (ON BASE), C-1593, qt., amber $9–12
PATD AUG 5TH 1862 & FEB 9TH 1864 WW LYMAN, C-1630, pt., aqua, with
original tin lid $70–80
PATD FEB 9TH 1864 WW LYMAN, C-1625, pt., aqua........................ $60–90
PAT JAN 12 1886 (ON LID), C-482, qt., aqua $120–140
PATD MARCH 26TH 1867 1 BB WILCOX, C-3157, 2 qt., aqua...............$45–60
PATENT APPLIED FOR BY LUTZ & SCHRAMM CO (ON HEEL) C-1616, qt., pottery,
sherwood $20–25
PATENT SEPT 18, 1860, C-2403, qt., blue aqua $75–90
PATENTED AUG 8TH 1882 (ON LID), C-2419, pt., aqua, repro wire $75–100
PATENTED AUG 8TH 1882 (ON LID), C-2419, 2 qt., aqua, wide mouth...$40–50
PATENTED AUG 8TH 1882 (ON LID), C-2419, qt., aqua, repro wire $50–60
PATENTED AUG 8TH 1882 (ON LID), C-2419, 1½ pt., aqua, narrow mouth.......
....$45–55
PATENTED JULY 19, 1919 BY JOS H SCHRAMM, C-1617, ten panels, qt., pottery
....$20–25
PATENTED JULY 27TH 1886 (ON BASE), GREEK KEY DESIGN, C-2422, ½ gal.,
emerald green $275–350
PATENTED JUN 9, 03. JUNE 23, 03 (ON BASE), 2½″, colorless...............$2–3
PATENTED OCT 19, 1858 (ON LID), C-1238, qt., black $900–1200
PATENTED OCT 19. 1858 (ON LID), C-1238, qt., deep amethyst $450–600
PEARL, C-2433, qt., aqua $30–40
PEERLESS, C-2438, qt., aqua $60–90
PENN, PHILLIPS & CO PITTS PA, C-2442, qt., aqua wax sealer.........$150–200
PEORIA POTTERY (ON BASE), EIGHT-SIDED, WAXSEALER, qt., brown glaze.......
....$40–60
PERFECT SEAL (IN SCRIPT), C-2449, pt., colorless $8–10
PET, C-2474, qt., aqua, repro wire..................................... $60–80
PET, C-2474, 2 qt., aqua, repro wire $60–80
PETALLIKE FLUTING ON SHOULDER, qt., medium cobalt, IP $800–1200
PETIT, C-2477, pt., cornflower blue.....................................$23–32
PINE P MASON, C-2482, pt., colorless $6–8
PINE P MASON, C-2482, qt., colorless $6–7
PORCELAIN LINED, C-2489, 2 qt., aqua $15–18
PORCELAIN LINED, C-2489, ½ gal., aqua $18–23
PORCELAIN LINED, C-2489, qt., aqua $12–15
PORCELAIN LINED, C-2489, midget, repro zinc lid....................... $60–90
PORCELAIN LINED, PAT NOV 26, 67, C-2489, midget, aqua.............. $90–120
POTTER & BODINES AIR TIGHT, C-2502, 1½ qt., aqua, OP $300–375
POTTER & BODINES AIR TIGHT, C-2502, pt., aqua, OP $600–750
POTTER AND BODINES AIR TIGHT, C-2502, qt., aqua, OP.............. $350–400
PRINCESS (ON SHIELD IN FRAME), C-2533, pt., colorless $18–22
PRINCESS (ON SHIELD IN FRAME), C-2533, qt., colorless $15–20
PROTECTOR (ALL PANELS RECESSED), C-2536, qt., aqua, repro lid $24–26
PROTECTOR (ALL PANELS RECESSED), C-2536, pt., aqua, original tin lid ....
....$120–150
PROTECTOR (ONE PANEL RECESSED), C-2537, qt., aqua, repro clamp $24–28

Fruit Jar, Potter and Bodine wax sealer. PHOTO
COURTESY OF SKINNER'S, INC.

PURITAN TRADEMARK FRUIT JAR, C-2542, pt., aqua, repro metal closure ....
.... $200–250
PURITAN TRADEMARK FRUIT JAR, C-2542, qt., aqua $140–180
PURITY OATS, WITH FLOWER, qt., colorless $12–15
PUTNAM (ON BASE), C-1537, ½ pt., aqua, 4¾" × 2½" $65–80
PUTNAM (ON BASE), C-1542, ½ pt., aqua $6–9
PUTNAM (ON BASE), C-1542, pt., amber $50–60
PUTNAM GLASS WORKS, ZANESVILLE (ON BASE), C-2544, qt., aqua $5–6
QUEEN, C-2549, qt., aqua $15–18
QUEEN, C-2549, ½ gal., aqua $18–22
QUEEN, ENCIRCLED BY PATD 1858, 1868, C-2548, qt. $30–35
QUICK SEAL, C-2568, pt., aqua $5–6
QUICK SEAL (IN CIRCLE), C-2569, pt., aqua $6–7
QUICK SEAL PATD JULY 14, 1908, C-2572, qt., aqua $4–5
QUICK SEAL PATD JULY 14, 1908, C-2572, qt., light aqua $3–4
RAG, C-1135, pt., aqua $50–60
RE TONGUE & BROS CO INC LUSTRE, C-1604, pt., colorless $10–12
RE TONGUE & BROS CO INC LUSTRE, C-1604, qt., colorless $8–10
RED CROWN DRIED BEEF (ON LABEL), 2½ oz., pink $4–5
REG US PAT OFF (ON HEEL), C-1540, ½ pt., aqua $7–10
RESERVOIR TO OPEN ADMIT AIR . . ., C-2599, qt., aqua, original glass stopper
.... $400–525
REX, NO 3 (ON BASE), SIEMENS GLAS (ON LID), qt., colorless $8–10
ROBERT ARTHURS PATENT, C-104, pt., pottery $200–250
ROBERT ARTHURS PATENT, C-104, pt., pottery, lip chip $90–120
ROYAL TRADEMARK FULL MEASURE (ON FRONT), C-2554, qt., amber...$45–60
SAFE SEAL (IN CIRCLE ABOVE DATE), C-2655, qt., aqua $6–7
SAFE SEAL (IN CIRCLE), C-2654, pt., aqua $4–5
SAFETY, C-2659, qt., amber $100–140
SAFETY VALVE, C-2663, ½ pt., colorless $8–10
SAFETY VALVE (ON BASE), C-2663, qt., aqua $6–7
SAFETY VALVE, GREEK KEY DESIGN, C-2664, green..................... $120–160
SAFETY VALVE, GREEK KEY DESIGN, C-2664, aqua......................... $25–30
SAFETY VALVE, GREEK KEY DESIGN, C-2664, colorless.................... $30–35
SAFETY VALVE PATD 1895 HC (OVER TRIANGLE), 7½" × 2⅜", pt., aqua.......
.... $75–95

SAFETY VALVE PATD 1895 HC (OVER TRIANGLE), C-2663, ½ pt., squat, colorless $40–45
SAFETY VALVE PATD 1895 HC (OVER TRIANGLE), C-2663, ½ pt., clear... $8–10
SAFETY VALVE PATD 1895 HC (OVER TRIANGLE), C-2663, ½ pt., aqua ..$20–25
SAFETY VALVE PATD 1895 HC (OVER TRIANGLE), C-2663, pt., cornflower blue $30–35
SAFETY VALVE PATD 1895 HC (OVER TRIANGLE), C-2663, ¼ pt., clear.. $30–35
SAFETY VALVE, WITH GREEK DESIGN, C-2664, emerald green $300–350
SAFETY WIDE MOUTH MASON SALEM, C-2666, qt., aqua....................$12–15
SAMCO SUPER MASON (MASON IN PLATE), qt., colorless $5–7
SANETY WIDE MOUTH MASON SALEM, C-2674, qt., aqua $12–15
SB DEWEY JR NO 65 BUFFALO ST, C-790, qt., aqua.....................$500–700
SCHAFFER JAR ROCHESTER, NY, C-2687, pt., aqua, dated lid, original wires $375–460
SCHRAM AUTO B SEALER, C-2695, pt., colorless.............................. $8–10
SCHUTZ MARKE (ON BASE), KIEFFER (ON LID), qt., colorless $9–12
SCRANTON JAR, C-2702, qt., aqua... $400–550
SEALFAST, FOSTER (ON BASE), qt., colorless $4–5
SECURITY SEAL, C-2736, qt., colorless...$4–5
SECURITY SEAL, C-2736, pt., colorless...$5–6
SELCO SURETY SEAL (IN CIRCLE), C-2737, pt., bluish, patented 1908 ... $12–15
SELCO SURETY SEAL (IN CIRCLE), C-2737, qt., bluish, patented 1908 .... $8–10
SILICON (IN CIRCLE), C-2756, qt., aqua $12–15
SILICON GLASS CO (IN CIRCLE), C-2757, qt., aqua $10–12
SIMPLEX MASON, C-2762, pt., colorless $100–135
SIMPLEX MASON, C-2763, pt., colorless $45–65
SKQ QUEEN, C-2562, ½ pt., sun-colored amethyst............................$8–9
SKQ QUEEN TRADEMARK WIDE MOUTH, ½ pt., colorless..................$14–18
SMALLEY AGS, C-2775, qt., amber...$50–65
SMALLEY FULL MEASURE AGS, C-2775, qt., amber with plain zinc lid .$50–60
SMALLEY FULL MEASURE AGS, C-2775, qt., amber, with engraved zinc lid $60–75
SMALLEY FULL MEASURE AGS, C-2775, pt., aqua...........................$15–18
SMALLEY FULL MEASURE AGS, C-2775, qt., colorless....................... $9–12
SMALLEY FULL MEASURE AGS, C-2775, pt., colorless......................$12–15
SMALLEY JAR, C-2796, qt., aqua, repro metal $280–350
SMALLEYS NU SEAL TM, DOUBLE HELIX, C-2785, pt., colorless $4–5
SPENCER, C-2809, qt.. $80–100
SPRATTS PATENT (OUTER EDGE), PATD 1864 (INNER PORTION), qt., screw-on lid..$350–450
ST LOUIS SYRUP & PRESERVING JAR, C-2872, aqua $13–18
STANDARD (FAINT MASTODON ON BACK), C-2832, qt., aqua..............$15–20
STANDARD (OVER FAINT MASTODON), C-2833, qt., aqua $18–25
STAR, C-2850, qt., aqua..$40–55
STAR, ABOVE STAR EMBLEM, C-2850, 2 qt., aqua $175–225
STAR, WITH CURVED LEG ON R, C-2847, qt., aqua $28–38
STRITTMATERS PURE HONEY, C-2888, pt., bluish............................$45–60
SULZBERGERS PURE HORSE RADISH, C-2892, ½ pt., stoneware............$40–50
SUN, pt. $40–60
SUN (IN CIRCLE IN BASE) TRADEMARK JP BARSTOW, 1½ pt., aqua ... $200–240
SUN (WITHIN CIRCLE AND RADIATING LINES), C-2893, pt., aqua $90–110

SUN (WITHIN CIRCLE WITH RADIATING LINES), C-2893, qt., aqua.......$75–90

SUPERIOR AG CO (IN CIRCLE), C-2904, pt., aqua $15–18

SURE SEAL MADE FOR L BAMBERGER, pt., aqua.............................$10–12

SURE SEAL MADE FOR L BAMBERGER, C-414, qt., blue $10–14

TAGLIATELLE, WITH HERMETIC LID, 12 panels, qt., aqua....................$8–10

THE EMPIRE, C-948, pt., colorless $25–30

THE EMPIRE, PAT FEB 13 1866 (ON BASE), C-949, qt., greenish aqua, repro clamp $70–80

THE GEM (1 LINE), PAT DEC 17, 61 (ON BASE), C-1092, 1½ pt., aqua...........
....$25–30

THE (IN INITIAL STROKE OF) MASON, C-1705, pt., colorless $8–10

THOMPSON, C-2933, qt., aqua, without ceramic lid......................$120–150

TIGHT SEAL (IN CIRCLE), C-2944, pt., aqua, dated on reverse $5–6

TIGHT SEAL (IN CIRCLE ABOVE DATE), C-2945, qt., aqua....................$4–5

TM BANNER WARRANTED (IN CIRCLE), C-420, qt., aqua....................$7–8

TM BANNER WM WARRANTED (IN CIRCLE), C-423, qt., aqua $4–6

TM KEYSTONE REG, C-1431, pt., colorless $5–6

TM LIGHTNING, C-1546, pt., aqua...$4–5

TM LIGHTNING (ON BASE), ½ pt., amber, 1988 reproduction.............$13–16

TM LIGHTNING PUTNAM REG (ON BASE), C-1551, ½ gal., colorless.....$14–16

TRADE MARK ADVANCE, C-30, ½ gal., aqua $200–250

TRADE MARK ELECTRIC, SALEM, NJ (ON BASE), C-939, qt., aqua........ $10–14

TRADE MARK LIGHTNING, C-1546, qt., amber.............................$20–30

TRADE MARK LIGHTNING, C-1546, qt., amber, lip crack...................$12–15

TRADE MARK LIGHTNING, C-1546, ½ gal., amber..........................$45–55

TRADE MARK LIGHTNING (ON BASE), C-1543, qt., aqua.....................$3–4

TRADE MARK LIGHTNING PUTNAM, C-1543, pt., aqua, with all embossing on base $3–5

TRADE MARK LIGHTNING, PUTNAM (ON BASE), C-1546, qt., aqua $7–9

TRADE MARK LIGHTNING, PUTNAM (ON BASE), C-1546, pt., aqua . $1.50–3.00

TRADE MARK LIGHTNING, PUTNAM (ON BASE), C-1546, qt., aqua . $1.50–3.00

TRADE MARK THE DANDY, C-770, qt., yellow amber, patented 1885, glass lid
....$80–120

TRADEMARK ADVANCE, PAT APPLIED FOR, C-30, qt., colorless........ $200–250

TRADEMARK BANNER REGISTERED, C-417, ½ pt., colorless.................$30–40

TRADEMARK BANNER WARRANTED (IN CIRCLE), C-421, qt., blue $5–7

TRADEMARK ELECTRIC, C-938, qt., aqua......................................$8–10

TRADEMARK ELECTRIC, C-938, pt., aqua....................................$12–15

TRADEMARK KEYSTONE REGISTERED, C-1430, qt., colorless $6–8

TRADEMARK KEYSTONE REGISTERED, C-1430, pt., colorless $6–8

TRADEMARK KEYSTONE REGISTERED, C-1431, qt., colorless $6–8

TRADEMARK KEYSTONE REGISTERED, C-1431, pt., colorless $6–8

TRADEMARK LIGHTNING, C-1546, qt., yellow olive $75–95

TRADEMARK LIGHTNING, PUTNAM (ON BASE), C-1546, 2 qt., aqua $9–12

TRADEMARK LIGHTNING, HWP (ON BASE), C-1545, 2 qt., amber $75–90

TRADEMARK LIGHTNING, PUTNAM (ON BASE), C-1546, qt., amber.......$30–35

TRADEMARK LIGHTNING PUTNAM (ON BASE), C-1534, 1½ pt., aqua, 7⅛″ × 3⅛″ $30–35

TRADEMARK LIGHTNING REG US PATENT OFFICE, C-1551, ½ gal., clear, base embossed..$2–3

TRADEMARK LIGHTNING REGISTERED US PATENT, C-1548, 2 qt., aqua ..$12–15

Trademark Lightning Registered US Patent, C-1548, qt., deep cornflower blue................$45–50
Tropical Canners, C-2956, pt., colorless................$4–5
Trues Imperial Brand, C-2966, pt., colorless................ $8–11
Trues Imperial Brand DW True Co (All Above Draped Flags, In Frame), 2 qt., colorless................$25–30
Unembossed, 11″, blue aqua, IP................$150–200
Unembossed, Barrel-Shaped Wax Sealer, pottery, ½ gal., yellow ...$20–22
Unembossed, Bell-Shaped Wax Sealer, C-3218, qt., aqua............ $60–80
Unembossed, Hemingray-Type Jar, qt., cobalt blue, tin screw lid . $300–400
Unembossed, Round, Cork Seat, 9½″, aqua, IP................$50–60
Unembossed, Round, Cork Seat, qt., aqua................ $13–16
Unembossed Wax Sealer, qt., colorless................$6–9
Unembossed Wax Sealer, qt., aqua................$5–6
Unembossed Wax Sealer, C-3222, ½ gal., greenish aqua................$7–8
Unembossed Wax Sealer, C-3222, ½ gal., aqua, lip chip................$2–3
Unembossed Wax Sealer, C-3222, ½ gal., colorless................$5–6
Unembossed With Petallike Decoration Around Neck, C-3227, qt., olive green, IP................ $500–650
Union No 1, C-2979, qt., aqua................ $200–260
Union No 4, Wax Seal Groove With Lugs/Ears, C-2981, qt., aqua, made in three-piece mold................$350–450
Valve Jar Co Philadelphia, C-3014, qt., aqua, original glass lid and clamp................ $200–250
Valve Jar Co Philadelphia Patent March 10th 1868, C-3014, qt., aqua................ $300–350
Valve Jar Philadelphia, C-3012, ½ gal., aqua, repro clamp.......... $75–100
Veteran, With Veterans Bust In Circle In Frame, C-3023, qt., aqua................ $12–15
Victor Patented 1899, C-3026, pt., aqua................$50–60
Victor Patented 1899, C-3026, qt., aqua................$40–45
Victory 1 Patd, C-3031, qt., aqua................$14–20
Victory, Encircled By Dates, C-3029, qt., aqua................ $10–12
Victory, Encircled By Patd 1864 & 1867 On Front, C-3034, Pacific SF Glasswork, qt., aqua................ $150–180
Victory Hom Pak Mason, C-3045, qt., colorless................$5–6
Victory I, Encircled By Patd 1864 Reisd 1867, C-3031, qt., aqua $30–35
Victory (In Shield), Victory Jar (On Lid), C-3038, ½ pt., clear $12–15
Victory (In Shield), Victory Jar (On Lid), C-3038, ¼ pt., clear $25–30
Wales (On Base), C-3047, qt., colorless, with repro lid................ $12–15
Wan Eta Cocoa Boston, C-3050, qt., aqua................$7–8
Wan Eta Cocoa Boston, C-3050, pt., amber................ $9–12
Warsaw Salt Co Choice Table Salt, C-3051, 5¾″, amber............ $60–90
Wears (In Circle), C-3055, pt., bluish................ $12–15
Wears Jar (In Circle), C-3056, pt., colorless................ $9–12
Wears Jar (In Circle), C-3056, qt., colorless................ $9–12
Wears Jar (In Stippled Frame), C-3058, qt., colorless................ $9–12
Wears Jar (In Stippled Oval), C-3060, qt., colorless................$7–9
Wech (In Strawberry), C-3066, pt., colorless................ $8–11
Weir Patd Mar 1st 1892 (On Lid), C-3073, pt., pottery................$20–25
Weir Patd Mar 1st 1892 (On Lid), C-3073, qt., pottery................$18–22

WEIR PATD MARCH 1ST 92, APRIL 16 1901 (ON LID), C-3075, pt., pottery ......
....$25–30
WELLS & PROVOST, SPRATTS PATENT, C-2814, qt., two raised knobs . $350–400
WESTERN PRIDE, C-3085, qt., aqua $150–180
WHITALL TATUM & CO (ON GLASS LID), C-3096, ½ gal., colorless, OP.........
....$20–26
WHITNEY-WHITNEY GLASS WORKS, C-3108, qt., deep aqua $400–525
WIDEMOUTH "FAMOUS" JAR (IN CIRCLE), C-998, pt., aqua $16–23
WILCOX, C-3158, qt. $50–75
WINSLOW IMPROVED VALVE JAR, C-3178, qt., deep aqua, with repro clamp ......
....$280–340
WINSLOW JAR, C-3179, pt., aqua... $120–150
WINSLOW JAR, C-3179, qt., aqua...$60–75
WINSLOW PATENTED 1870 PAT 1873, C-3181, pt., aqua $80–110
WOODBURY, "WGW" MONO., C-3185, 2 qt., aqua $30–35
WOODBURY, "WGW" MONO., C-3185, pt., colorless $30–35
WOODBURY, C-3184, pt., aqua $30–35
WOODBURY, C-3184, 2 qt., aqua $25–28
WOODBURY, C-3184, qt., aqua $25–28
WW LYMAN (BELOW) PATD FEB 9TH, 1864, C-1622, qt., aqua, repro lid ....
....$25–30
SYMANS COPENHAGEN SNUFF, C-3089, qt., amber..........................$60–75

GIN BOTTLES

Gin was invented by a Dutch doctor whose original concoction was first
used as a medicine to promote kidney function. Shortly thereafter, the
distinctive flavoring of gin became popular and distilling became more
widespread.

Case gin bottles are tall square-shaped bottles, so called because they
were often shipped in specially made wooden cases. They were made
both in America and Continental Europe, and it is very difficult to determine where a given bottle was made. Also, because of the standard
shape of these bottles, it is often difficult to determine exactly how old
a given case gin bottle is, as they continued to be made for hundreds of
years.

ACA NOLET SCHIEDAM, 10", olive green $35–40
AM BININGER & CO NY, SUPERIOR LONDON DOCK GIN (ON LABEL), 9¼",
emerald green, IP $1200–1600
ASPARAGUS GIN, THE ROTHENBERG CO, colorless $10–12
AVAN HOBOKEN & CO, ROTTERDAM, dark green............................$25–35
BLANKENHEYM & NOLET, 6½", olive $13–16
BOOTHS HIGH & DRY GIN, 10¼", light blue $4–5
CASE GIN, 9⅝", olive amber, OP..$100–125
CASE GIN, 9⅞", green with yellow tint, OP................................ $90–120

Gin Bottle, case gin. PHOTO COURTESY OF NEIL GROSSMAN.

CASE GIN, 9⅞″, olive amber $80–110
CASE GIN, 13″, olive amber..$200–300
CASE GIN, 13⅞″, olive amber, OP $250–400
CASE GIN, 15½″, olive amber, OP $300–550
CASE GIN, 19⅝″, olive amber, OP $500–1000
CASE GIN BOTTLE WITH LABEL, 9¾″, olive green, OP $125–150
CHARLES LONDON CORDIAL GIN, 8″, medium blue green $70–100
COACHMAN, VAN DUNCKS, 8½″, black glass $50–80
DANIEL VISSER & ZONEN, SCHIEDAM, 9″, olive green....................$35–45
EN COOK & CO DISTILLERS BUFFALO NY, 10″, amber $125–150
GIN, BACK BAR BOTTLE, WITH CAP, 10 RIBS, 11″, golden yellow with silver
letters $90–110
GORDON DRY GIN, LONDON, ENGLAND, 9″, light green.....................$4–6
GORDONS LONDON DRY GIN, 9″, colorless $3–5
HERMAN JANSEN SCHIEDAM, 9½″, olive green $30–40
J FERD: NAGEL, WITH MEDALLION AND BUST, 1873, pale yellow green.$55–65
OLD HOLLAND GIN, GREENE & GLADING, emerald green.................$55–70
ROYAL IMPERIAL GIN LONDON, 9¾″, medium cobalt $200–240
ROYAL IMPERIAL GIN LONDON, square, 9¾″, medium cobalt blue $100–135
THE OLIVE TREE, CASE GIN FORM, 9½″, olive green $150–200
UDOLPHO WOLFES SCHIEDAM AROMATIC SCHNAPPES, 9¾″, olive amber, IP ....
....$40–45
UDOLPHO WOLFES SCHIEDAM SCHNAPPS, 8″, yellow olive $40–55
UDOLPHO WOLFES, AROMATIC SCHNAPES, 9″, green $12–15
W HASKAMP & CO, 9″, olive green $30–40
WA GILBEY SILVER STREAM SCHNAPES, 8″, colorless $5–7

GO-WITHS

Go-withs include a wide range of nonbottle items, such as advertising, drinking glasses, boxes, pitchers, etc. When looking at advertising and bottle-related items, watch for sharpness and clarity of colors, and become familiar with the various types of items and of price ranges. Dosage glasses and shot glasses advertising whiskey and bitters companies are very popular.

ADVERTISING DISPLAY CASE, SANFORD INK, with glass shelves and panel sides, 16⅛"...$350–450

ADVERTISING FIGURE, BIG BILL BEST BITTERS, plaster painted figure, 15¼"....
....$900–1100

ADVERTISING HANDBILL, "ELECTRIC BITTERS," 12" × 9", framed.....$40–60

ADVERTISING HANDBILL, "WHEAT BITTERS," 11¾", framed..............$40–60

ADVERTISING PAPERS, "IMPROVED JAUNDICE BITTERS," 17" H × 7" W.........
.... $60–80

ADVERTISING SIGN, BROWNS IRON BITTERS, paper, with pretty girl in center, 15"... $300–500

ADVERTISING SIGN, CORK DISTILLERIES, 16⅜" × 12½", multicolored ....
....$100–150

ADVERTISING SIGN, CORK DISTILLERIES, TIN, painted in various colors, 17" × 12"...$50–75

ADVERTISING SIGN, "DR HOOFLANDS GERMAN BITTERS," 7¼" × 8¾", paper, brown letters.. $60–80

ADVERTISING SIGN, "DRINK BRAEMS BITTERS," 13½", metal, silver with red and black...$75–90

ADVERTISING SIGN, ST 1860 X PLANTATION BITTERS, with factory, paper, 12" × 9"... $300–400

ADVERTISING SIGN, THE BEST BLOOD PURIFIER, DR JAYNES ALTERATIVE, 12" × 15", on glass $700–1000

ADVERTISING SIGN, TIN, PAINES CELERY COMPOUND, 14" × 10" $300–375

ADVERTISING SIGN, TIN, VERMO STOMACH BITTERS, 7" × 9" $150–175

ADVERTISING STAND, CARTERS INKS, wooden with black and gold letters, 18"..
....$250–350

ADVERTISING STORE BOX, "ELECTRIC BITTERS," 22", paper..............$70–90

ALMANAC, "FARMERS & MECHANICS ALMANAC FOR 1856," good condition ....
....$25–30

ALMANAC, "MORNING, NOON AND NIGHT," DRAKES BITTERS, multicolored cover $30–40

BARREL, DISPENSING, "ALPINE BITTERS," 8½", colorless $90–110

BILLHEAD FOR PUTNAM LIGHTNING FRUIT JARS, dated Sept. 1909 ....$20–25

BOX OF BOTTLES, DR ORDWAYS PAIN DESTROYER, wooden box with 150 bottles
....$350–450

BOX, WOODEN ADVERTISING, BUFFALO MINERAL SPRING WATER, 11" × 22" × 15"...$50–60

BROCHURE, FOUR PAGES FOR ATLAS EZ SEAL JARS, 4½" × 7½" $7–8

CALENDAR, "ATWOODS BITTERS," 14¾", paper, unused $35–45

CALENDAR, "SANBORNS THE REXALL STORE," 14", paper, unused......$15–20

CARDBOARD BOX, DAISY SEALING WAX, red and white........................$3–5

CARDBOARD BOX, SAMCO KLIK SEAL WHITE MASON CAPS....................$4–6

CHECKERBOARD, "MALARION COMPANIES REMEDIES," cardboard, 14⅜" square
....$50–60

CHEST HARNESS, "THE ONLY LUNG PAD . . . CURES," cotton, two chest packs
....$150–200

CLOCK, ADVERTISING, LEWIS RED JACKET BITTERS, eight-sided....... $500–700

COPPER TRADE TOKEN, MAGNETIC POWDER & PILLS FOR INSECT & RATS ....
.... $60–90

CRIBBAGE BOARD, "LASHS BITTERS," 4½″ × 13″, wooden $40–60

CRIBBAGE BOARD, WOODEN, LASHS BITTERS FOR HEADACHE, MALARIA, 13″ × 4½″ $40–50

DIAMOND DYE ADVERTISING DISPLAY BOX, wooden with polychrome painting .
.... $600–800

DISPLAY BOX, "LEES STRENGTHENING PLASTER," 9½″, cardboard..... $60–80

DOSE GLASS, "A LITTLE CUBEN BITTERS PLEASE," 2½″, colorless.....$75–95

DOSE GLASS, "ALTER BISMARK, MAGEN BITTERS," 2¼″, colorless ... $90–120

DOSE GLASS, "DAM-I-ANA," 3¼″, colorless $60–90

DOSE GLASS, "DEVIL STOMACH BITTERS," 2⅞″, colorless $80–120

DOSE GLASS, "DR CAPIAS HERB BITTERS," 3³/₁₆″, colorless $60–90

DOSE GLASS, "DR CAPIAS HERB BITTERS," 2⅛″, colorless $175–200

DOSE GLASS, "DR HACKERS SPECIFIC BITTERS," 2⅝″, colorless.........$50–65

DOSE GLASS, "DR HARTERS," 3″, colorless..................................$25–30

DOSE GLASS, "DR HARTERS," 3″, colorless..................................$70–90

DOSE GLASS, "DR PETZOLDS GERMAN BITTERS," 3⁵/₁₆″, colorless.......$30–45

DOSE GLASS, "DR PETZOLDS GERMAN BITTERS, BALT," 2″, colorless . $60–80

DOSE GLASS, "DRINK REX KIDNEY & LIVER BITTERS," 2¼″, colorless ....
....$110–140

DOSE GLASS, "ENJOY LIFE BISMARCK BITTERS," 2¼″, colorless...... $125–160

DOSE GLASS, "HOPKINS UNION BITTERS," 2¼″, colorless $60–80

DOSE GLASS, "HOPKINS UNION BITTERS," 2¼″, colorless with gold rim........
.... $75–100

DOSE GLASS, "KAPUZINGER KLOSTER BITTERS," 3″, colorless........ $135–160

DOSE GLASS, "LEKKO STOMACH BITTERS," 2¼″, colorless $140–165

DOSE GLASS, "PADRES WINE BITTERS TONIC," 1¾″, colorless $30–40

DOSE GLASS, "POLO CLUB BITTERS," 3⅛″, colorless.................... $80–100

DOSE GLASS, "QUININE BITTERS," 3¹/₁₆″, colorless $110–140

DOSE GLASS, "RAMSEYS TRINIDAD AROMATIC BITTERS," 2¾″, colorless........
.... $80–100

DOSE GLASS, "RAMSEYS TRINIDAD AROMATIC BITTERS," 2¾″, colorless........
....$75–90

DOSE GLASS, "ROOSTER BITTERS," 2¼″, colorless $190–220

DOSE GLASS, "ROYAL PEPSIN STOMACH BITTERS," 2″, colorless.....$190–220

DOSE GLASS, "TRY GREENHUTS BITTERS," 2¼″, colorless............$110–140

DOSE GLASS, "UNION BITTERS," 2⅝″, colorless $60–90

DOSE GLASS, "ZALUDOCNE KORKE VINO," 2¼″, colorless $70–90

DOSE GLASS, "ZIEN BROS FAMOUS STOMACH BITTERS," 2¼″, colorless.........
.... $130–160

ENCASED POSTAGE STAMP, AYERS SARSAPARILLA TO PURIFY THE BLOOD ....
.... $125–175

ENCASED POSTAGE STAMP, ST DRAKES PLANTATION BITTERS, metal frame ....
.... $150–200

ENCASED POSTAGE STAMP, TAKE AYERS PILLS, metal frame............. $125–175

FLY TRAP, free-blown, bulbous body, 7½″, colorless.......................$70–90

FUNNEL, "DR VAN DYKES BITTERS," 7½″, copper..........................$70–90

GAME, ADVERTISING, "CLOVER BITTERS," cardboard box with glass cover......
....$50–70

GLASS HOUSE NOTES, REDFORD GLASS CO, four of varying denomination, all unused and uncut $75–90

GLASSHOUSE SCRIPT, $1 FROM THE MANUAL LABOR BANKING HOUSE, DATED 1837 .... $100–125

GLASSHOUSE SCRIPT, $1 FROM THE VERMONT GLASS FACTORY, DATED 1814 .... $70–100

GLASSHOUSE SCRIPT, $5 FROM THE MANUAL LABOR BANKING HOUSE, DATED 1837 ....$70–75

HAT, blown three-mold, GIII-23, 2¼″, cobalt blue, OP................. $600–800

ICE CHIPPING TOOL, "LASHS BITTERS," 8½″, cast iron $40–60

INSULATOR, hollow-blown, with "patent" backwards, 5½″, olive amber........ .... $500–600

LITHOGRAPH, MELLINS FOOD FOR THE BABY, 13″ × 17″, two baby girls....... .... $125–175

LITHOGRAPH, MERCHANTS GARGLING OIL, 14″ × 12″, two women in Victorian dress $350–500

MIRROR, "J WALKER . . . VINEGAR BITTERS," copper, 1½″ $15–20

MIRROR, OR PAPERWEIGHT, "STANDARD BOTTLING CO," 3″, colorless .$50–70

MIRROR, "USE JOHN ROOTS BITTERS," 6⅛″, red background $250–350

MUG, FLACCUS BROS, stoneware with cobalt blue glaze, 4¼″ $125–150

MUG, "HARTMANS BITTERS," 4⅜″, milk glass $30–40

PACKING BOX, DAVIDS ELECTRO CHEMICAL WRITING FLUID, wooden, black letters, 12″ × 6″ $75–100

PACKING BOX, DR RUSSELLS HEPATIC BITTERS, wooden, 6″ × 7″ × 7″........ .... $100–135

PAPER PACKAGE, EDDYS LAMP BLACK, 8¾″ × 4″ $20–30

PAPERWEIGHT, "LITTHAUER STOMACH BITTERS," 4″ × 2½″, colorless $45–60

PITCHER, ADVERTISING "DR HARTERS LITTLE LIVER PILLS", 13″, silver plate $250–400

PITCHER, DEWEYS MANILA BITTERS, ceramic, 10″, pewter rim, flower bouquet $800–1200

PITCHER, "DR VAN DYKES HOLLAND BITTERS," 13⅝″, metal........ $250–300

PITCHER, WITH "JOHN HEER CO, NUKIND COCKTAIL BITTERS," metal, 8½″ $200–250

PLAYING CARDS, BEENET CELEBRATED KIDNEY & LIVER LAXATIVE...$125–150

PLAYING CARDS, "DR VAN DYKES HOLLAND BITTERS," full set $100–125

POSTCARD, GLASS FACTORY, MANNINGTON, W VA, 1908 ....$3–5

PRINTING PLATE PICTURING EIGHT PITTSBURGH FLAKES, 5″ × 3″ $40–50

PRINTING PLATE, "HEALTH WITH METZGERS CATARRAH CURE," copper, 4¼″ × 5¼″ $12–16

ROLLING PIN, dark olive amber with white specks, 13¼″ $70–85

SALT AND PEPPER SET, BALL PERFECT MASON, colorless with zinc lids .$50–70

SCRABBLE GAME LETTERS, ALL 52, "DR WALKERS CAL. BITTERS" $90–120

SHOT GLASS, ARONSONS, SEATTLE, WASH, 2¼″, colorless, gold rim $15–20

SHOT GLASS, ASTOR WINE CO, 2⅛″, colorless................................$15–20

SHOT GLASS, BOURBON (IN FANCY LETTERS), 2¼″, colorless............ $10–15

SHOT GLASS, CARROLL RYE TOASTS, 2⅛″, colorless $25–35

SHOT GLASS, COMPLIMENTS OF BOONE SPRING DISTILERY, 2⅝″, colorless, gold rim $30–40

SHOT GLASS, CYRUS NOBLE OLD GOODS, 2¼″, colorless $15–18

SHOT GLASS, CYRUS NOBLE, PURE OLD HONEST, 2⅛″, colorless $25–35

SHOT GLASS, EL RAY WHISKEY, 2⅛, colorless...................................$18–20

SHOT GLASS, ERIE CLUB WHISKEY, 2¼″, colorless...........................$15–18

SHOT GLASS, GOLD SEAL LIQUOR CO, 2¼″, colorless $18–22

SHOT GLASS, GREAT SCHILLER WHISKEY, 3⅜″, amethyst $30–40

SHOT GLASS, GREEN MOUNTAIN RYE & BOURBON, 2¼″, colorless $20–22

SHOT GLASS, HAYNER, 2½″, colorless..$10–12

SHOT GLASS, INDEPENDENT DISTILLING, 2¼″, colorless $18–20

SHOT GLASS, JH CUTTER, 2⅜″, colorless......................................$20–25

SHOT GLASS, KENTUCKY BOURBON, 2⅛″, colorless...........................$40–45

SHOT GLASS, KRUG BROS CO, 2½″, colorless, with gold rim..............$40–50

SHOT GLASS, MANHATTAN CLUB BOURBON, 2¼″, colorless..............$40–45

SHOT GLASS, MARTELLS WINES, LIQUOR 3″, colorless $12–15

SHOT GLASS, MORVILLE WHISKEY, 2⅛″, colorless............................$35–45

SHOT GLASS, OLD JUDGE WHISKEY, 2⅛″, colorless $20–25

SHOT GLASS, PACIFIC COAST WINE & LIQUOR, 2⅛″, colorless............$15–20

SHOT GLASS, RED TOP RYE, 2″, colorless......................................$18–23

SHOT GLASS, SONOMA WINE CO, 2⅛″, colorless $25–30

SIGN, "1830 DR SIEGERTS ANGOSTURA BITTERS," 13¾″, with bottle ....
....$400–450

SIGN, "IT'S EAGLE ANGOSTURA BARK BITTERS," 12″, with bottle and bar-
tender $750–850

SIGN, METAL, "DRINK BRAEMS BITTERS," 13½″, with bottle $35–45

SIGN, PAPER, "ANDREWS STOMACH BITTERS," 17½″ × 7¾″, in bold print ....
....$50–70

SIGN, PAPER, "BROWNS IRON BITTERS," 12″, with standing girl $225–300

SIGN, PAPER, "DR FORRESTS SHAMROCK BITTERS," 10″ × 8½″, with three-
leaf clover, framed $100–150

SIGN, PAPER, "DR HENRY BAXTERS . . . BITTERS," 11¼″ × 9½″ $110–130

SIGN, REVERSE PAINTED, "ANTI-CHOLERICAL . . . STOMACH BITTERS," 16″ ×
6″ $225–275

SIGN, WOODEN, "LASHS BITTERS," 20″, with woman and horse, faded ....
.... $80–100

SOCK DARNER, colorless body with multicolored splashes, 6¾″ $100–120

STANDARD LIQUOR CO, 2⅜″, colorless...$15–20

STONEWARE MUG, BERGDOLLS BEER, PHILA, PA, with fancy logo $65–75

SULFIDE DECANTER STOPPER, with Napoleon's bust, colorless, 1¾″, base chips
....$50–75

THERMOMETER, "ABBOTTS BITTERS," round with standing man $110–150

THERMOMETER, "CUBAN BITTERS," 24″ H, working condition....... $200–250

TOBACCO POUCH, ". . . BROWNS IRON BITTERS . . .", 5″, leather $30–45

TRADE TOKEN, ". . . FRENCH COGNAC BITTERS," 1″, copper $15–20

TRADE TOKEN, WARRICK & STANGER, WINDOW GLASS WORKS, brass .. $75–100

TRAY, "KAISER WILHELM MAGEN BITTERS," 13½″ × 10¼″, with picture of
bottle...$180–220

TRAY, "ROYAL PEPSIN BITTERS," stamped metal, 12″ $100–150

TRAY, "SANBORNS KIDNEY BITTERS," circular, 12″ $175–225

TRAY, "TRY KALAMAZOO CELERY PEPSIN BITTERS," 16½″, with monk draining
keg $500–600

WITCH BALLS, PAIR, aqua with white loopings, 6¾″, free-blown..... $400–500

WOODEN BOX, "ABBOTTS BITTERS," 9¾″ H × 18″ L × 12½″ W $50–70

WOODEN BOX, "ATWOODS VEGETABLE JAUNDICE BITTERS," 13½" H × 17¼" L.. $60–80
WOODEN BOX, "CINCHONINE STOMACH BITTERS," 11½" H × 14½ L × 13¼ W $100–120
WOODEN BOX, "DR HARTERS WILD CHERRY BITTERS," 9¼" H × 17" L....... .... $125–175
WOODEN BOX, "HARDYS JAUNDICE BITTERS," 11" H × 12" L...........$60–70
WOODEN BOX, "DR HOSTETTERS STOMACH BITTERS," 11" H × 16½" L $125–175
WOODEN BOX, "ELECTRIC BITTERS," 10" H × 20¼" L................$125–150
WOODEN BOX, "LASHS KIDNEY & LIVER BITTERS," 12¼" H × 14¼" L $125–160
WOODEN BOX, "LASHS TONIC BITTERS," 10¼" H × 13" L $30–45
WOODEN BOX, "LUTZ GERMAN STOMACH BITTERS," 9¼" H × 14" L × 11¾" W $60–80
WOODEN BOX, "MARKS KIDNEY & LIVER BITTERS," 10" H × 13¼" L $120–150
WOODEN BOX, "PAINES CELERY COMPOUND," 11" H × 13¾" L $30–45

HOUSEHOLD BOTTLES

This category covers the various utility bottles with contents such as ammonia, blacking (which is actually a shoe polish), and various other oils and liniments for lubrication. Blacking bottles are very popular and are commanding higher and higher prices.

AA COOLEY, HARTFORD, CONN, BLACKING BOTTLE, 4⅝", olive green, OP $60–80
AMERICAN BLUING CO, BUFFALO, NY, 5¼", colorless $3–4
AMMONIA . . . SF GASLIGHT CO, 9⅛", amber $100–120
AMMONIA . . . SF GASLIGHT CO, 9⅛", yellow amber $50–70
AMMONIA . . . SF GASLIGHT CO, 7⅞", deep aqua $40–50
AMMONIA . . . SF GASLIGHT CO, 9", citron $150–225
AMMONIA . . . SF GASLIGHT CO, 9", aqua $75–90
ANTHONY FLINT VARNISH FOR NEGATIVES, 5½", colorless, cylinder $4–6
BENGAL BLUING, 5¾", aqua..$2–3
BF STINSON & CO, BUFFALO, NY, 4½", colorless ....$.50–1.00
BLACK CAT STOVE ENAMEL, 6", colorless..................................$2–3
BLACKING BOTTLE, 4⅝", deep yellow amber, square, OP $45–60
BLACKING BOTTLE, 4⅞", olive amber, square, OP $70–100
BLOWN CYLINDER, 6¼", olive amber, OP, heavy-collared lip $70–90
BOOT, SARATOGA DRESSING, 4¼", aqua $30–45
CARBONA, 5", aqua..$2–3
COCOA NUT OIL, C TOPPAN, 5⅞", aqua, violin shape, OP.............$100–120
COSMOLINE REGISTERED, GLOBE, 3", colorless $1–2
CURTIS & BROWN CO MFG, NY, 3", colorless................................$1–2

DUTCHERS DEAD SHOT FOR BED BUGS, 4⅞″, aqua, with label, OP $60–80

EASTMAN KODAK CHEMICALS, 5¼″, amber $5–8

EASTMAN KODAK, ROCHESTER, NY, 3″, amber $3–4

ECLIPSE FRENCH STAIN GLOSS, 4½″, apple green $3–5

ELECTRICAL BICYCLE LUBRICATING OIL, 4¼″, colorless, oval..........$175–200

FRENCH GLOSS, 4″, colorless $1–2

FS PEASE SEWING MACHINE OIL, 5⅜″, light cornflower blue, OP... $300–500

FURST-McNESS CO, FREEPORT, ILL, 8⅜″, colorless............................$1–2

GREEVER-LOLSPEICH MFG CO, 4½″, colorless ....$.25–.50

HERCULES DISINFECTANT, 6″, amber...$3–4

HOME RELIEF CO, JAMESTOWN, NY, 4½″, aqua................................$2–3

HUTCHINS & MASON KEENE NH WATERPROOF BLACKING, 5⅝″, olive amber, OP, square $1500–2000

KEASBEY & MATTISON CO, 5¼″, light blue......................................$4–5

LAKE SHORE SEED CO, 5½″, aqua..$.50–1.00

LIQUID STOVE POLISH, 6¼″, colorless $1–2

LIQUOZONE-MFG, 6″, amber...$3–4

MELVIN & BADGER CO, BOSTON, 2¾″, colorless.........................$.50–1.00

NATIONAL CASKET CO, colorless, embossed eagle and capitol $18–23

NONTOXO CHEMICAL CO, 2¾″, amber...$1–2

OSBORNS LIQUID POLISH, 3¾″, olive yellow, OP $350–450

PATENT GUTTA PERCHA OIL BLACKING, 5½″, yellow amber, OP . $1500–2000

PATENT OIL BLACKING GUTTA PERCHA FORBES & CO, 5¼″, olive amber, OP, rectangular $1500–2500

PRICES PATENT CANDLE COMPANY LIMITED, 7⅛″, cobalt, OP $125–175

PRICES PATENT CANDLE COMPANY LIMITED, 7⅛″, cobalt................ $75–100

PROF CALLANS WORLD RENOWNED, 4″, aqua $2–3

RACE & SHELDON BOOT POLISH, eight-sided, green, OP............... $200–300

SARATOGA DRESSING, 4½″, aqua, shoe figural $30–40

SHULIFE-FOR SHOES, 3¾″, olive green $4–5

SIMONS-BINGHAMTON, NY, 7″, light green...................................$4–5

SPAULDINGS GLUE, aqua, OP... $13–17

SPECIAL BATTERY OIL, THOMAS EDISON, 4½″, colorless $3–4

SPERM SEWING MACHINE OIL, 4¾″, colorless $2–3

STANDARDISED DISINFECTANT CO, 4¼″, light amber..........................$1–2

TRIUMP SUPERIOR CLOCK OIL, 3½″, colorless $2–3

UPTONS REFINED LIQUID GLUE, C-1753, 2⅞″, aqua, OP, 12-sided......$40–60

USA HOSP. DEPT., 9¼″, yellow olive...................................... $250–300

UTILITY BOTTLE, 11¹/₁₆″ H, 1¾″ lip opening, green, square, OP $225–280

UTILITY BOTTLE, 9⅝″, greenish aqua, square, straight-sided, OP $350–450

INK BOTTLES

Ink bottles and inkwells were among the earliest-produced bottles in America, certainly going back to at least the 18th century. The early ink bottles were generally small in size, as the cost of the ink used to fill them was quite expensive. Usually the black ink was the least costly, whereas blues, greens, and reds were indeed extravagant.

Up until the mid-19th century, ink was made and sold mainly by chemists and apothecary shops. Most of these early bottles were unembossed and would carry only a label mentioning the type of ink and the manufacturer. Molded ink bottles appeared in the United States probably around 1815, with blown three-mold ink bottles becoming very popular through the 1840s. Around this time, also, appeared one of the most commonly found shapes in ink bottles—the umbrella type. This is a multisided conical form of bottle, which is readily found both pontiled and with smooth bases.

Beginning around the mid-19th century, ink bottle manufacturers began to use more unusual colors and employ various unusual shapes, such as figurals of all sorts. One of the more highly collected type of ink bottle is the so-called tea kettle type, in which the neck extends upward at an angle from the base. These were made in an incredible assortment of shapes and colors, and it is very difficult to determine the origin of a given ink bottle since they were made in England, France, and the United States.

Collectors should also become familiar with some of the deceptive reproductions on the market, such as some of the free-blown funnel-type inkwells. The reader is referred to *Ink Bottles and Inkwells* by William E. Covill, Jr., which the letter "C" refers to below.

ALLINGS HIGH SCHOOL INK, C-581, 1⅞″, aqua $125–175
ALLINGS PATD APL 25 1871, C-704, 1⅞″, medium blue green $50–60
AUTOMATIC CONSTANT INKWELL, 3⅜″, colorless........................ $100–130
BARREL-SHAPED INK BOTTLE, C-672, 3″ × 2½″, colorless............. $80–100
BENJAMIN FRANKLIN HEAD FIGURAL, C-1291, 2¾″ × 4″, aqua $275–350
BERTINGUIOT, C-575, 2″ × 2⅜″, olive green, OP......................$150–200
BERTINGUIOT, C-575, 2″ × 2⅜″, olive amber, OP......................$150–180
BERTINGUOIT, C-575, 1¾″ × 2⅜″, black, OP $200–225
BERTINGUOIT, C-576, 2¼″ × 2½″, black $75–90
BLACKWOOD & CO/PATENT/LONDON, offset dome, 2″ × 1¾″, aqua....$30–50
BLOWN INKWELL, C-1035, 1⅞″, medium sapphire blue, OP........... $180–210

Ink Bottle, blown ink. PHOTO COURTESY OF NEIL GROSSMAN.

BLOWN INKWELL, C-1045, 2½″ × 2¾″, aqua, OP......................$160–225
BLOWN THREE-MOLD, C-1175, 1¾″ × 2¼″, olive amber, OP $90–120
BLOWN THREE-MOLD, C-1175, 1¾″ × 2¼″, olive green, OP $140–200
BLOWN THREE-MOLD, C-1182, 1½″, olive amber, OP......................$80–110
BLOWN THREE-MOLD, C-1182, 1½″ × 2¼″, olive green, OP $100–130
BLOWN THREE-MOLD, C-1182, 1½″, olive green, OP, small chip $90–120
BLOWN THREE-MOLD, C-1185, 1⅝″, olive green, OP..................... $90–120
BLOWN THREE-MOLD, C-1188, 1¾″ × 2⅝″, medium olive yellow, OP ....
....$250–325
BLOWN THREE-MOLD, C-1188, 1⅝″ × 1⅞″, olive amber, large crack, OP .....
....$45–55
BLOWN THREE-MOLD, C-1188, 2″ × 2½″, olive amber, OP...........$150–190
BLOWN THREE-MOLD, C-1194, 1½″ × 2¼″, olive amber, OP $110–135
BLOWN THREE-MOLD, C-1196, 1¹³⁄₁₆″, yellow amber, OP.............$150–200
BLOWN THREE-MOLD, C-1196, 1⅞″, olive amber, OP................... $125–175
BLOWN THREE-MOLD, C-1196, 1½″ × 2¼″, deep amber, OP, lip chips........
....$60–75
BLOWN THREE-MOLD, C-1200, 2″ × 2⅝″, olive yellow, OP..........$150–200
BLOWN THREE-MOLD, C-1200, 2″ × 2⅝″, deep olive green, OP $140–190
BLOWN THREE-MOLD, C-1218, 1⅞″ × 2¹⁄₁₆″, pale blue, OP....... $4000–6000
BLOWN THREE-MOLD, C-1221, 1⅜″, golden amber, OP $150–175
BLOWN THREE-MOLD, C-1221, 1½″ × 2¼″, yellow amber, OP...... $130–190
BLOWN THREE-MOLD, C-1221, 1¼″ × 2¼″, olive amber, OP $135–160
BLOWN THREE-MOLD, C-1221, 1½″ × 2¼″, olive amber, OP, lip chip.........
....$35–45
BLOWN THREE-MOLD, C-1221, 1⅜″, olive amber, OP................... $135–165
BLOWN THREE-MOLD, C-1299, 2″ × 2½″, deep olive green, OP $140–180
BLOWN THREE-MOLD, GII-18, 1½″ × 2¼″, yellow olive, OP $140–180
BLOWN THREE-MOLD, GII-2, 1⅞″, olive green, OP $130–155
BLOWN THREE-MOLD, GIII-29, 1½″, olive amber, OP................... $120–150
BLOWN THREE-MOLD INK, C-1182, 1⁹⁄₁₆″, yellow amber, OP $90–120
BLOWN THREE-MOLD INKWELL, C-1182, 1½″ × 2½″, dark amber, OP.........
....$130–150
BLOWN THREE-MOLD INKWELL, C-1194, 1¾″ × 2¼″, olive amber, OP........
....$100–135
BLOWN THREE-MOLD INKWELL, C-1194, 1¾″ × 2¼″, yellow olive, OP, lip
chip..$60–75
BLOWN THREE-MOLD, GI-7, C-1173, deep violet........................ $350–400
BOOT FIGURAL INKWELL, C-1516, 2⅞″ × 3″, turquoise blue.......... $125–185
BUFFALO SHAPE, metal, 2¾″ × 4½″ $80–100

Ink Bottle, blown three-mold. **PHOTO COURTESY**
OF SKINNER'S, INC.

BULLDOG REVOLVING INK STAND, two milk glass bulldog bottles, 4⅜ " ....
.... $400–500
BULLDOG WITH NAPKIN, metal, 3½ " × 5½ " $60–80
BUTLER CIN, square, C-473, 2³/₁₆ ", aqua, OP $70–90
BUTLERS INK CINCINNATI, 12-sided, 3 ", aqua, OP $135–185
BUTLERS INK, CINCINNATI, 12-sided, C-519, 2¾ " × 2 ", aqua, OP .. $125–175
BUTLERS INK CINCINNATI, MASTER INK, 6⅛ ", aqua, OP $200–260
C CHANDLER & CO, COTTAGE INK, 2⅝ ", greenish aqua $125–165
CABIN INK BOTTLE, C-680, 2⅜ ", colorless, small repaired base hole .. $60–80
CABIN INK, patent applied on side panel, 2¾ " × 1¾ " × 2 ", golden amber...
....$1500–2500
CABIN-SHAPED, 4⅝ ", opaque white $150–250
CABIN-SHAPED, C-680, 2½ ", colorless $400–600
CABIN-SHAPED INK BOTTLE, C-677, 3⅛ " × 2½ ", colorless $350–400
CAMEL SHAPE, metal, 4½ " × 8 ", reddish brown with red/green $70–90
CARTER-CARTER, CATHEDRAL MASTER, C-819, 9¾ ", cobalt blue.................
....$50–75
CARTER-CARTER, CATHEDRAL MASTER INK, C-820, 7⅞ ", cobalt, ABM, 100%
label and pour spout $110–135
CARTER-CARTER, CATHEDRAL MASTER INK, C-820, 6¼ ", cobalt, 50% label....
....$160–200
CARTER-CARTER, CATHEDRAL MASTER INK, C-820, ABM, 9¾ ", cobalt, 80%
label and pour spout $80–100
CARTER, CATHEDRAL MASTER INK, C-819, 9¾ ", cobalt blue, lip flake ..$50–60
CARTERS (ON BASE), six-sided, C-555, 2¾ ", cobalt blue $80–100
CARTERS BLAK WRITING FLUID, with label, C-822, 9¼ ", yellow amber ....
....$150–200
CARTERS INK (ON LABEL), eight-sided, C-555, 2⅞ " × 3 ", sapphire blue,
ABM $125–150
CARTERS INK CO, stoneware jug, gal., brown and white $150–175
CARTERS INK, STONEWARE MASTER INK, 27 ", gray...................... $400–500
CARTERS, MA & PA CARTER, porcelain, C-1619, 3¾ ", multicolored figurals....
.... $75–100
CAST IRON INKSTAND, with colorless inkwell, 60% label $60–90
CAST IRON REVOLVING INKSTAND, with a milk glass snail inkwell $80–110
CAST IRON REVOLVING INKSTAND, with a colorless snail inkwell $80–120
CAST IRON REVOLVING INKSTAND, with one cobalt and one white snail ......
....$225–275
CAST IRON REVOLVING INKSTAND, with three colorless glass snail inkwells ......
....$190–225
CAT IN A SHOE, handcarved, wooden, 3⅞ " × 5¾ " $110–150
CENTENNIAL EXHIBITION HALL, C-695, 4½ ", colorless with original metal
cap.. $200–350
CHINA INKWELL, with red, green, and blue floral design, 3⅛ " $50–75
CONE INK, C-23, 2⅜ ", light blue green, OP $20–25
CONICAL INK, C-18, 2¼ ", deep olive amber, OP $100–130
COTTAGE INK, C-693, 2⅛ ", aqua $250–350
COTTAGE-SHAPED INK BOTTLE, cross-hatched roof, 2½ ", aqua $40–60
COTTAGE-SHAPED, PATD MAR 14 1871 (ON BASE), C-685, aqua........$225–275
COVERED INKWELL, free-blown, similar to C-1064, 2 " × 2½ ", cobalt, OP ....
....$200–275

Ink Bottle, offset dome. PHOTO
COURTESY OF NEIL GROSSMAN.

CUT GLASS INKWELL, six straight-cut facets, C-1407, 2⅜″, turquoise blue, cover $125–200
CUT GLASS INKWELL, DOUBLE SET, C-1399, 2¼″, sapphire blue, glass covers $150–200
CUT INK BOTTLE, similar to C-1407, 2″, canary yellow, hinged cover ..$75–95
DAVIDS & BLACK, NEW YORK, cylinder, C-753, 5⅛″, bright emerald green, OP..$120–150
DAVIDS, offset dome, C-616, 1⅞″, medium amber $300–350
DOGS HEAD SHAPE, metal, 4″ × 6″..$70–90
DOMED INK BOTTLE, BEEHIVE FORM, C-649, 1″ × 2¼″, aqua $100–150
DRAPERS IMPROVED PATENT (ON COVER), C-1414, 3″ × 4″, colorless ....
....$100–150
DRSM TWO-PIECE FOUNTAIN INKWELL, 3⅝″, colorless $90–110
DUNBARS BLACK INK (ON LABEL), 6¾″, aqua, OP $50–65
E WATER TROY NY, C-207, 2½″, aqua, OP..................................$325–390
E WATERS, ribbed rectangular, "A" on back, 3¼″, aqua, OP........ $200–225
E WATERS, TROY, NEW YORK, C-207, 2⅜″, aqua, OP, base chip, haze..........
.... $110–150
E WATERS TROY, NEW YORK, MASTER INK, C-774, 8¼″, aqua, OP...$750–950
E WATERS TROY NY, cylinder, C-207, 2⅞″, aqua, OP.................. $350–500
E WATERS/TROY NY, cylinder, C-207, 2¼″ × 1⅜″, aqua, OP, ⅛″ spider crack $150–250
E WATERS TROY NY, MASTER INK, C-773, 5¼″, aqua, OP $450–600
EAGLES HEAD SHAPE, metal, 2¾″, gray...................................... $80–100
EELLS WRITING FLUID, MANSFIELD (ON LABEL), similar to C-982, pottery, 4⅜″ $50–60
ESTES NY INK, C-117, 4⅛″, aqua, OP, eight-sided $500–750
FARLEYS INK, C-526, 1¾″, olive amber, OP, ⅜″ spider crack $120–160
FARLEYS INK, eight-sided, C-528, 3½″, olive amber, OP, major lip repair......
....$100–140
FARLEYS INK, eight-sided, C-526, 1¾″, deep yellow amber, OP $400–500
FARLEYS INK, eight-sided, C-526, 1⅞″ × 1⅞″, amber, OP $300–350
FARLEYS INK, eight-sided, C-527, 2½″, olive amber, OP $750–950
FARLEYS INK, octagon with label, 2¾″, colorless........................ $500–700
FINE BLACK INK MADE & SOLD BY JL THOMPSON, TROY, NY, 5¾″, yellow amber, OP $2300–2800

FREE-BLOWN, bulbous, similar to C-1032, 2⅛″ × 3¼″, light olive amber, OP, lip chip $400–600

FREE-BLOWN, flattened cone, C-1062, 1¼″, aqua, OP, no cover $50–70

FREE-BLOWN, footed, C-1045, 2½″ × 3⅛″, aqua, OP $70–100

FROG SHAPE, metal, 4¼″ × 4½″ $40–60

FUNNEL INKWELL, C-1343, 2⅛″, cobalt blue, OP $55–75

FUNNEL INKWELL, C-1343, 1⅞″, olive amber, OP $60–80

G & RS AMERICAN WRITING FLUID, C-10, 2⅝″, aqua, OP $250–325

G & RS AMERICAN WRITING FLUID, C-10, 2⅝″, aqua, OP $400–500

GEO MCKILLIPS, TORY, CON. 1842 FAIRFAX HS, 1¼″ × 4½″, stoneware $600–900

GIRL PLAYING WITH CAT FIGURAL, porcelain, 5¼″ × 5¼″, multicolored...... .... $100–150

GOVERNMENT WB TODDS WRITING INK, C-329, 3⅛″, blue green $50–65

H & T RED INK, CONE INK, 2½″, aqua, OP $125–175

HAND ON BOX FIGURAL, ceramic, 3″ × 4¼″, multicolored glazes ... $80–120

HARRISONS COLUMBIAN INK, 12-sided, 5½″, aqua, OP, two 1″ pontil cracks, stain $50–70

HARRISONS COLUMBIAN INK, eight-sided, 2″, aqua, OP....................$60–75

HARRISONS COLUMBIAN INK, eight-sided, C-536, 3¾″, aqua, OP....... $60–90

HARRISONS COLUMBIAN INK, C-194, 1⅞″, cobalt blue, OP, cylinder $300–400

HARRISONS COLUMBIAN INK, C-195, 4⅛″, sapphire blue, OP, chip repair $200–300

HARRISONS COLUMBIAN INK, C-529, 1½″, cobalt blue, OP, eight-sided......... .... $3500–4500

HARRISONS COLUMBIAN INK, C-530, 1⅝″ × 1⅞″, medium green, OP.......... ....$1000–1500

HARRISONS COLUMBIAN INK, C-531, 1⅞″, aqua, OP $70–95

HARRISONS COLUMBIAN INK, C-534, 2½″, aqua, OP, eight-sided........$70–95

HARRISONS COLUMBIAN INK, C-536, 3¾″, aqua, OP, eight-sided, lip chips $40–60

HARRISONS COLUMBIAN INK, C-538, 4½″, aqua, OP, 12-sided $60–90

HARRISONS COLUMBIAN INK, C-760, 5¾″, aqua, OP, 12-sided........ $130–180

HARRISONS COLUMBIAN INK, C-764, 5⅞″, cobalt blue, OP, cylinder $750–1000

HARRISONS COLUMBIAN INK, C-765, 7″, sapphire blue, IP, two lip chips $280–360

Ink Bottle, Harrison's gallon. PHOTO COURTESY OF SKINNER'S, INC.

HARRISONS COLUMBIAN INK, CYLINDER, C-195, 4¼″, sapphire blue, OP........
.... $400–500
HARRISONS COLUMBIAN INK, eight-sided, C-530, 1⅝″, aqua, OP....... $60–80
HARRISONS COLUMBIAN INK, 12-sided, C-760, 5⅞″, aqua, OP, portion of lip
was ground... $90–120
HARRISONS COLUMBIAN INK, 12-sided, C-762, 11⅛″, aqua, OP..... $800–1000
HARRISONS COLUMBIAN INK, eight-sided, C-530, 2″ × 4¼″, aqua, OP.........
.... $60–80
HARRISONS COLUMBIAN INK, C-534, eight-sided, aqua, OP, 2″ × ½″, light
inner stain...$65–85
HARRISONS COLUMBIAN INK, OFFSET DOME, C-624, 1¾″ H, aqua, OP, lip
chip..$75–90
HARRISONS COLUMBIAN INK, CYLINDER, C-194, 2″ × 2⅛″, deep sapphire,
OP, neck crack... $80–120
HARRISONS COLUMBIAN INK, CYLINDER, C-764, 5¾″, light green....$150–190
HARRISONS COLUMBIAN INK, MASTER, 12-sided, C-761, 7½″, aqua, IP, lip
chip... $150–175
HARRISONS COLUMBIAN INK, MASTER, C-761, 7½″, aqua, OP, two lip chips...
....$75–90
HARRISONS COLUMBIAN INK, MASTER, C-763, 11¼″, cobalt blue, IP ....
.... $14,000–18,000
HAUTHAWAYS LYNN FURNISHING INK (ON LABEL), 9″, bright green, OP........
....$65–80
HILLS PENNSYLVANIA WRITING INK (ON LABEL), 4⅛″, aqua, OP........$75–85
HOUSE-SHAPED INK, similar to C-694 but larger size, 6½″ × 5″ × 3″, aqua
.... $600–700
HOVER PHILA, C-118, 2¼″, light green, OP $400–500
HOVER PHILA, 12-sided, C-119, 1⅞″, medium emerald green......... $240–300
HOVER PHILA, umbrella, C-118, 2¼″ × 2⅛″, light green, OP.........$175–210
HOVER, PHILA, MASTER INK, cylinder, 9¼″, medium green, IP $140–180
HOVERS INK (ON LABEL), round, 2½″, olive yellow, OP, lip roughness
....$50–60
INK FOR BOOT AND SHOEMAKERS (ON LABEL), 7½″, olive green...... $80–120
INK SANDER, 3″, emerald green, pewter cap...................................$20–30
J & IEM, offset dome, C-628, 1⅝″, yellow amber........................ $140–180
J & IEM, offset dome, C-632, 1⅞″, aqua...................................... $60–90
J & IEM, TURTLE INK, labeled, C-627, 1¾″ × 2¼″, golden amber. $125–150
J RAYNALD, globe-shaped, 2¼″, aqua $500–750
J RAYNALD, globe-shaped, 2¼″, colorless $500–800
JA WILLIAMSON CHEMIST, MASTER INK, 9⅝″, blue green.............. $100–140
JACOBS & BROWN HAMILTON O, 12-sided, 2½″, pale green, OP $350–450
JAMES S MASON & CO, umbrella, 2½″, aqua, OP.........................$125–150
JK PALMER/CHEMIST/BOSTON, MASTER INK, C-770, 9¼″, deep olive amber,
OP $300–400
JONES EMPIRE MASTER INK, similar to C-769, 12-sided, deep green, IP ....
.... $1300–1800
JOSIAH JOHNSONS JAPAN WRITING FLUID, C-1242, pottery, 2½″ $125–175
JS DUNHAM, C-116, 2⅝″, aqua, OP, eight-sided $90–120
JS DUNHAM, eight-sided, 2⅜″, medium green, OP $500–700
JS DUNHAM, eight-sided, C-116, 2¾″, emerald green, OP $1500–2000
JS MASON PHILADA, cylindrical, 4½″ × 1½″, greenish aqua, OP ... $100–150

JS MASON PHILADELPHIA, 4³⁄₈″, aqua, OP, light haze.................... $80–100
L BUTLER, eight-sided, 1¾″, deep aqua, OP..............................$250–350
L POINGELET, 1⅞″, black amber, OP, eight-sided $1200–1500
LABELED UMBRELLA, FARLEYS EXTRA FINE BLACK INK, C-131, eight-sided, 2½″, deep gold amber, OP $140–180
LABELED UMBRELLA INK, "NATIONAL WRITING FLUID," 2½″ × 2¼″, aqua, OP...$50–60
LAUGHLINS AND BUSHFIELD, eight-sided, 2⅞″, aqua.................... $80–100
LEVESONS INKS ST LOUIS, cottage-shaped, 2½″, amber $175–225
LION SHAPE, metal, 4½″ × 10³⁄₈″ $60–75
LIONS HEAD, pottery bottle, C-1590, 1⅞″, brown Rockingham glaze............
.... $200–250
LIONS HEAD SHAPE, metal, 3½″, brown, red, and white paint $45–60
LOCOMOTIVE FIGURAL, PAT OCT 1874, C-715, 2″ × 2⅛″, aqua $750–900
LOCOMOTIVE INK, C-715, 1½″, aqua, wheel chips, stain.............. $300–350
MA & PA CARTER INK SET WITH ADV. BLOTTER, C-1619, "Made in Germany" on base $175–225
MASTER INK, cylinder with pour spout, 7⅝″, red amber, three-piece mold .....
....$50–70
MASTER INK BOTTLE, tapered cylinder, C-933, 5¼″, sapphire blue, OP, pour spout $125–175
MAYNARD & NOYES INK (ON LABEL), cylinder with spout, 8″, olive amber ....
.... $80–100
MELLON-SHAPED, straight ribs, C-1130, 2⅛″ × 2⅞″, olive amber, OP, ground lip... $1500–2000
NA DEPOSE PARIS, rectangular, 2½″, deep cobalt........................... $60–80
NE PLUS ULTRA FLUID, cottage form, C-689, 2⅝″, deep aqua........ $140–185
OPDYKE BROS INK, barrel, C-664, 2½″, aqua..............................$125–150
PAT OCT 17 1865 (ON BASE), barrel, C-669, 2⅛″, aqua, labeled....... $80–120
PATD MAR 14 1871 (ON BASE), cottage shape, C-685, 2½″, aqua $350–450
PATTERSONS EXCELSIOR INK, eight-sided, 2½″, aqua, OP.............. $350–400
PERINE GUYOT, flattened cylinder, 2″ × 2³⁄₈″, olive green, OP........ $80–100
PERINE GUYOT, flattened cylinder, 2″ × 2³⁄₈″, cornflower blue, OP $500–700
PERRY & CO, stoneware inkwell, 3⅝″...$75–90
PETROLEUM WRITING FLUID, PB & CO, C-665, 2⅝″, aqua $120–150
PITKIN TYPE, C-1156, 1⅞″ × 2½″, olive amber, OP, lip bruise $110–140
PITKIN TYPE, 36 swirled ribs, C-1142, 1⅞″, olive yellow, OP, disc crack.......
.... $140–180
PITKIN-TYPE INK BOTTLE, C-1122, 1½″ × 2¼″, dark green, OP ... $700–900
PITKIN-TYPE INKWELL, C-1139, 1³⁄₈″ × 2″, yellow olive, OP, base flake.......
.... $550–700
PITKIN-TYPE INKWELL, C-1139, 1½″ × 2⅛″, golden amber, OP, base crack..
.... $300–400
PITKIN-TYPE INKWELL, C-1147, 2¼″ × 1½″, olive green, OP....... $600–800
PITKIN TYPE INKWELL, 36 swirled ribs, C-1152, 1⅝″, olive green, OP, chips..
....$70–90
PITKIN-TYPE INKWELL, broken swirl, C-1142, 1⅝″ × 2½″, olive green, OP, big chip $90–135
PITKIN-TYPE INKWELL, square, C-1117, 1³⁄₈″ × 1¾″, medium olive green, OP, crack $500–700

PITKIN-TYPE INKWELL, square, 36 swirled ribs, C-1119, 1⅜″, yellow olive, OP
.... $2300–2600

PORCELAIN INKWELL, with painted red, blue, and gold bird and flower deco-
rations $50–75

PRESSED GLASS INKWELL, square, diamond pattern, 1¾″, deep cobalt, metal
cover $100–200

RB SNOW ST LOUIS, 12-sided, 1⅞″, aqua, OP...........................$350–450

RECLINING MAN, pottery, C-1597, 3¾″, brownish glaze $140–180

RECLINING WOMAN, pottery bottle, C-1598, 3⅝″, multicolored brown glaze...
.... $100–125

REDWARE INKWELL, 1¼″ × 2¼″, coggle design on edge...............$125–165

RF, flattened cylinder, C-203, 2″ × 2⅜″, olive amber, OP $500–700

RF, flattened cylinder, C-203, 2⅛″ × 2⅜″, puce, OP $300–400

RF, flattened cylinder, C-203, 2″ × 2⅜″, black, OP.................... $190–230

RIBBED, 12 ribs, covered, C-1066, 2⅛″, deep cobalt blue, OP $190–220

RIBBED, 16 vertical ribs, straight-sided, 1⅝″, aqua, OP.....................$50–70

RINGED INKWELL, similar to C-1169, 1½″ × 2½″, deep olive, OP . $200–300

S FINE BLK INK, C-193, 3″, green, OP $150–225

S. FINE/BLK INK, cylinder, C-192, 3⅛″ × 1⁹⁄₁₆″, olive amber, OP . $750–900

SF CAL INK CO, C-691, 2¼″ × 2″ × 2″, golden amber, cabin-shaped ....
.... $2000–3000

SHAWS INKS ARE THE BEST, octagonal, aqua $20–25

SHEPARD & ALLENS WRITING FLUID (ON LABEL), 6⅜″, deep gold amber ......
.... $75–100

SI COMP, barrel-shaped, C-666, 2″, aqua $90–120

SI COMP, cottage-shaped, C-683, 2⅝″, milk glass $250–350

SLEEPING BOY, ceramic, C-1597, 4″ × 5½″ $200–225

SM BIXBY & CO NY, domed ink, C-590, nine-sided, 1⅞″ × 2¾″, aqua ......
.... $60–85

SNAIL FIGURAL, C-1293, 1⅝″ × 2⅝″, colorless...........................$275–350

SNAKE ON NEST WITH EGGS FIGURAL, ceramic, 2⅝″ × 3¼″, multicolored ...
.... $35–50

SO DUNBAR/TAUNTON, UMBRELLA, C-115, 2⅜″ × 2⅛″, aqua, OP.... $60–90

SO DUNBAR TAUNTON MASS, C-520, 2⅛″, aqua, OP, 12-sided $125–165

SOAPSTONE INKWELL, square, 2⅛″, four quill holes $20–30

SQUARE GREEN INKWELL, with clear applied feet on each corner, silver cap, 2¾″
....$110–140

STAGS HEAD INKWELL, cast iron with clear inkwell, 5½″ $125–145

STEEL PEN INK (ON LABEL), umbrella, eight-sided, 2½″, bluish green, OP ....
.... $90–120

STRIPED GLASS, colorless with white and pink bands swirled, C-1381, 2⅛″ ×
2¾″ $1500–2000

STRIPED GLASS, colorless with white, blue, and amethyst swirled bands, 2¼″ ×
4″, no cap $500–750

TEAKETTLE, C-1235, 2″, citron, no closure............................... $450–600

TEAKETTLE, C-1237, 2⅜″, opaque white, metal cap $350–450

TEAKETTLE, C-1237, 2⅜″, bright apple green, no cap.................$700–1000

TEAKETTLE, C-1257, 2″, cobalt, with cap................................... $400–550

TEAKETTLE, C-1257, 2″ × 3¾″, amethyst, lip chip and crack $90–120

TEAKETTLE, C-1262, 2″, canary, no closure...............................$575–700

TEAKETTLE, C-1266, 2″, deep sapphire, with metal cap................ $400–550

TEAKETTLE, C-1269, 2½″, sapphire blue................................... $500–700

TEAKETTLE, eight-sided with petaled top, C-1269, 2⅛″, light golden amber, no cap...$350–450

TEAKETTLE, barrel shape, C-1285, 2⅛″, cornflower blue, no closure ....
.... $500–700

TEAKETTLE, barrel shape, C-1285, 2⅛″, light blue teal, original cap.............
.... $800–1200

TEAKETTLE, barrel shape, C-1285, 2⅛″, cobalt blue, original cap .$1000–1500

TEAKETTLE, C-1255, raised dome, eight-sided, 2⅛″, cobalt blue $350–400

TEAKETTLE, C-1255, eight-sided, 2″, bright green, 1½″ neck crack ..$110–135

TEAKETTLE, double font, C-1275, 4½″, colorless........................ $400–500

TEAKETTLE, snail type, C-1293, 1⅝″, colorless............................$350–450

TEAKETTLE INK, C-1233, 2″, fiery opal with painted decoration $300–400

TEAKETTLE INK, C-1245, 2″, medium sapphire blue $260–310

TEAKETTLE INK, C-1245, 2″, emerald green............................. $400–500

TEAKETTLE INK, C-1257, 2″, cobalt blue.................................$350–450

TEAKETTLE INK, C-1258, 2″, sapphire blue...............................$400–450

TEAKETTLE INK, C-1261, 2″, amethyst.....................................$350–450

TEAKETTLE INK, eight-sided, C-1248, 1³/₁₆″ colorless, sides are cut and polished $200–300

TEAKETTLE INKWELL, C-1253, 2¼″, colorless with red, blue, and gilt...........
.... $300–350

TEAKETTLE INKWELL, C-1266, 1⅞″, emerald green, two flakes at top ....
....$250–350

TEAKETTLE INKWELL, eight-sided with painted floral decoration, 2⅜″, cobalt
.... $350–400

TEAKETTLE INKWELL, eight-sided, C-1254, 2″, cobalt, with metal cap...........
....$325–400

TEAKETTLE INKWELL, eight-sided, C-1257, 2″, light blue $200–275

TEAKETTLE INKWELL, eight-sided, C-1257, 2″, light amethyst, with metal cap
.... $200–260

TEAKETTLE INKWELL, eight-sided, C-1261, 2″, deep sapphire blue, no cap .....
....$200–275

TEAKETTLE INKWELL, barrel shape with metal cap, C-1286, 2¼″, cobalt ....
.... $750–1000

TEAKETTLE INKWELL, fluted eight-sided, C-1257, 2⅛″, sapphire blue, with metal cap...$250–350

Ink Bottle, teakettle, barrel-shaped.
PHOTO COURTESY OF NEIL GROSSMAN.

Teakettle Inkwell, tapered, eight-sided, C-1268, 2½″, deep yellow green $250–300

Teakettle, Pat July 13th 1880 (On Base), C-1282, 2″, aqua $150–200

Teakettle, Pottery, "Compliments Of The Letort Hotel," 2⅝″ $200–250

Thaddeus Davids & Co Steel Pen Ink (On Label), 6″, C-750, blue green $70–90

Tiffany-Type Inkwell, purple with iridescent blues and pinks, 2¼″ × 3¾″, brass cover $250–350

Tin Ink Sander, similar to C-1730, 2¾″ $25–35

Tin Toleware Ink, eight-sided, 1⅞″, red with gold decoration..........$75–90

Tippecanoe Extract Hard Cider, barrel, C-667, 2″, colorless, two lip chips $175–225

Tippecanoe Extract-Hard Cider, barrel, C-667, 2″ × 2⅛″, colorless $300–375

Titcomb, eight-sided, 2½″, aqua, OP $350–450

Titcombs Ink Cin, 12-sided, 2¾″, aqua, OP $350–425

Triumph-Patent, pottery, 3″, brown and blue glaze $100–130

Turtle-Shaped Inkwell, C-1288, 1⅞″ × 3¾″, colorless $150–250

Twelve-Sided Ink, C-546, 1¹¹⁄₁₆″, light yellow green.................... $90–120

Twelve-Sided Master Ink, fluted shoulder, C-781, dark olive green, IP $3500–4500

Umbrella, 2¾″, peacock blue, eight-sided $750–1000

Umbrella, eight-sided, light green, OP $50–65

Umbrella, 2⅜″, cherry red puce, OP, eight-sided.................... $800–1200

Umbrella, 2¾″, medium green, OP, eight-sided........................ $500–700

Umbrella, 2¾″, deep olive green, OP, eight-sided $300–500

Umbrella, 2⅝″, apricot/copper, OP, eight-sided...................... $750–1000

Umbrella, C-127, eight-sided, cobalt blue, OP...........................$350–450

Umbrella, 12-sided, C-149, 2″, medium puce, OP $250–350

Umbrella, eight-sided, 2½″ × 2⅜″, light green, OP....................$75–95

Umbrella, eight-sided, 2½″ × 2¼″, reddish amber, OP $90–120

Umbrella, eight-sided, C-127, 2¼″, citron, OP $200–300

Umbrella, eight-sided, C-145, 2½″ × 2¼″, orange amber, OP..... $150–175

Umbrella, eight-sided, C-145, 2½″, dark olive amber, OP $90–120

Umbrella Ink, eight-sided, light blue green, OP $55–65

Umbrella Ink, C-137, 2⅝″, orange amber, OP $100–140

Ink Bottle, umbrella type, eight-sided.
PHOTO COURTESY OF NEIL GROSSMAN.

UMBRELLA INK, C-143, 2½", medium amber, OP........................ $120–150
UMBRELLA INK, C-167, 2½", deep cobalt, OP $400–500
UMBRELLA INK, eight-sided, C-180, 2¾", deep cobalt blue $250–350
UMBRELLA INK, 12-sided, C-149, 2⅛" × 1⅞", medium blue green, OP ....
.... $125–150
UMBRELLA INK, eight-sided, 2⅜" × 2⅛", olive green, OP............ $100–140
UMBRELLA INK, eight-sided, C-127, 2½", medium cobalt, OP $450–600
UMBRELLA INK, eight-sided, C-129, 2" × 2¼", blue green, OP......... $50–60
UMBRELLA INK, eight-sided, C-141, 2½", deep olive amber............ $120–150
UMBRELLA INK, eight-sided, C-141, 2⅜", deep olive green $110–140
UMBRELLA INK, eight-sided, C-143, 2½", medium emerald green, OP ....
.... $80–100
UMBRELLA INK, eight-sided, C-143, 2¼", blue green, OP................. $40–50
UMBRELLA INK, eight-sided, C-145, 2¼" × 2¼", deep amber, OP, lip flake..
.... $45–60
UMBRELLA INK, eight-sided, C-179, 2¾" × 2½", deep sapphire blue, OP .....
.... $350–475
UMBRELLA INK, S11 (ON BASE), eight-sided, 2⅜", medium blue green, OP ....
.... $60–80
WADES UNCHANGEABLE BLUE WRITING FLUID (ON LABEL), 12-sided, amber,
OP, 2½" $50–75
WARRENS CONGRESS INK, C-542, 2⅞", aqua, OP, eight-sided $130–190
WARRENS CONGRESS INK, C-542, 2⅞", deep olive yellow, OP, eight-sided .....
.... $800–1100
WE BONNEY, barrel-shaped, C-653, 2⅝", aqua, OP..................... $300–375
WE BONNEY, barrel-shaped, C-655, 2½", aqua.......................... $60–90
WE BONNEY, barrel, C-353, 2⅝", aqua with label....................... $80–110
WE BONNEY, barrel, C-657, 2½", aqua $60–90
WHEELBARROW REVOLVING INKWELL, C-1455, with milk glass snail-type bottle,
3" $250–325
WILLISTONS SUPERIOR INDELIBLE INK, C-488, 2⅜", aqua, OP $250–350
WOODEN INKWELL, five quill holes, C-1662, with two colorless glass inkwells,
gold paint $90–130
WOODS BLACK INK PORTLAND, C-12, 2½", aqua, OP $125–175

LABEL-UNDER-GLASS BOTTLES

Label-under-glass bottles are those which have a thin piece of glass covering the labeled area. This type of bottle was popular in the late 19th and early 20th centuries and is a very collectible area with rapidly increasing prices. Look for the colorful and unusual labels, and check to see if the glass strip covering the label is in good condition.

ADAM WAGNER BAY RUM, barber bottle, 8", colorless................... $250–300
AF PETERSON BAY RUM, barber bottle, 9½", colorless................. $250–300

AMERICAN EAGLE, FLAGS, CANNONS, on flask, 5⅛″, colorless $275–350

A MERRY CHRISTMAS AND HAPPY NEW YEAR, on oval flask with old soldier, 6″, colorless...$550–650

A MERRY CHRISTMAS AND HAPPY NEW YEAR, with Santa's face, flask, 6″, colorless, metal cap $1300–2000

BAY RUM, barber bottle, 10¼″, milk glass...............................$250–300

BAY RUM, with girl's bust, barber bottle, 10⅛″, blue milk glass...... $700–850

BAY RUM, with happy standing girl, 10″, opaque white.................$300–400

BUXTON, pressed inkstand, 2″ × 3⅜″, clear $150–200

CHILDRENS THROAT & CHEST PASTILLES, jar with glass cover, 9½″, colorless .
....$125–150

COCA-COLA, syrup bottle with metal cap, 11½″, colorless.............$350–450

COGNAC, on bar bottle, 12¼″, amber....................................$125–175

COUPLE DANCING WITH VICTORIAN DRESS, 5½″, colorless.............$150–200

CS FAY, barber bottle, 6⅜″, milk glass, OP $125–150

CUPR. SULP./AMM., APOTHECARY JAR, 5¼″, cobalt blue, red and gold label...
....$125–150

EAU DE COLOGNE, with girl, 6¾″, colorless $200–300

GENERAL FITZHUGH LEE, flask, 5⅛″, colorless $250–300

GIRL READING A BOOK, on straight-sided flask, 5⅞″, colorless $500–700

GRAND ARMY ENCAMPMENT 1895, on flask, 6¼″, colorless, oval $350–450

GRAND ARMY ENCAMPMENT 1895, on flask, 7½″, colorless, straight-sided......
....$175–200

HAIR TONIC, barber bottle, 10¼″, milk glass $250–300

HANLENS SHERRY, on back bar bottle, 11″, colorless $650–800

HICKS CAPUDINE LIQUID FOR HEADACHES, 8½″, amber, stopper $400–500

HOLL. GIN, with girls bust, wickered bottle, 11⅞″, amber............. $100–140

JV RICE TONIC, with girl's face, barber bottle, 8⅛″, colorless........ $400–500

KDX FOR DANDRUFF, barber bottle, 7¾″, colorless $100–140

KUMMEL, bar bottle, 11¾″, colorless...................................$125–150

LIGHTNERS HELIOTROPE PERFUMES, 6¼″, milk glass, stopper $200–250

LIGHTNERS MAID OF THE MIST PERFUMES, 6½″, milk glass, stopper............
....$200–250

LINCOLN, GARFIELD & MCKINLEY, on white porcelain flask, 6″ $150–250

LOCOMOTIVE, flask, ½ pt., colorless with multicolored label $400–475

LT RICHMOND P HOBSON, flask, ½ pt., colorless $200–240

LUTZS GERMAN STOMACH BITTERS, L-134L, 7¾″, amber $800–900

MAMMOTH CAVE WHISKEY, pinch bottle, 6¼″, colorless $350–400

MERRY CHRISTMAS AND HAPPY NEW YEAR, on oval flask with elf's figure, colorless $600–775

MERRY CHRISTMAS, HAPPY NEW YEAR, on round flask, with bird, 4⅞″, colorless $400–500

MRS VALENTINE, cylinder, 6″, colorless.................................. $300–400

MS TIERNEY, with eagle and flags on flask, 5¼″, colorless, 2″ cover glass crack $250–300

OLD SCENTER PURE RYE, with dog, back bar bottle, 11¼″, colorless ....
....$2500–3500

ORANGE BITTERS, decanter, 6⅞″, colorless...............................$60–70

PAUL JONES, pinch bottle, 6¼″, colorless $100–125

PEACH PULPY, J HUNGERFORD SMITH CO, 11″, colorless................$100–140

POINTER, with pointing dog, back bar bottle, handled, 9¾", colorless...........
....$450–550
PORT, with reclining woman, on back bar bottle, 11", colorless, 2" crack in
cover $500–650
PORT, with reclining woman, on back bar bottle, 11", colorless $1300–1650
R FINCH TONIC, with girl's face, barber bottle, 8⅛", colorless $250–300
ROSEWOOD DANDRUFF CURE, with woman's bust, barber bottle, 7⅝", colorless
.... $200–225
S WHISKEY, bar bottle, 12¼", amber.. $125–175
SMILING GIRL, with hat on round flask, 5", colorless.................$1500–1800
SMILING GIRL'S BUST, on handled oval flask, 6", colorless................$75–85
SMILING GIRL'S BUST, on round flask, 5", colorless $1200–1500
STANDING GIRL, on oval flask, 6", colorless............................$450–550
STANDING GIRL, on pocket flask, 5¾", colorless $500–700
STANDING WOMAN IN COSTUME, on straight-sided flask, 5¾", colorless.........
....$250–350
STANDING WOMAN IN FULL DRESS, oval flask, 5¾", colorless, screw cap.......
.... $400–600
STANDING WOMAN IN THEATRICAL COSTUME, flask, 5¾", metal cap, colorless
.... $300–500
STROYMERS GRAPE PUNCH, 12", colorless, with metal cap.............. $140–180
33RD NATIONAL ENCAMPMENT, 1899, on flask with flag and eagle, 5⅛", color-
less $250–350
TOILET WATER, with woman's face with hat, 9½", opaque white $500–600
US WARSHIP MAINE, flask, 6", colorless................................... $100–125
WHISKEY, on bar bottle, 11⅞", amber.. $100–150

MEDICINE AND CURES BOTTLES

Medicine bottles comprise one of the largest areas of bottle collecting,
and this area encompasses bottles such as ointments, cures, liniments,
panaceas, balsams, remedies, and all sorts of drug bottles. Though medicine bottles were certainly among the products of the earliest American
glasshouses, it was not until the late 18th century that the embossed
medicine bottle appeared. Turlingtons Balsam, originally imported from
England, was probably one of the first embossed medicines produced in
America. Even with the production of this bottle around the year 1800,
the vast majority of medicine bottles were unembossed and carried only
a paper label until about 1840/1850. Many of these early unembossed
pontiled medicines, usually in shades of dark greens and ambers, can
still be found at reasonable prices. The embossed medicines of the 1830s
and 1840s are fairly common in clear and aqua, whereas the embossed
greens, ambers, and blues often fetch sums in the thousands of dollars.

Starting around the middle of the 19th century and up until the Pure Food and Drug Act of 1906, an amazing assortment of so-called patent medicine bottles were produced which purported to heal any number of maladies, ranging from the common cold to cancer.

When buying and collecting medicine bottles, look for original labels and boxes, and watch for those early unusually embossed bottles. Those which are embossed "Shaker" or "Indian" are usually quite collectible and oftentimes quite valuable. The reader is referred to *Great American Pontiled Medicines* by Frederick Nielsen, which the letter "N" refers to below.

A TEXAS WONDER, HALLS GREAT DISCOVERY, 3½″, colorless................$4–6
A TRASKS MAGNETIC OINTMENT, 2¼″, aqua $2–3
A TRASKS MAGNETIC OINTMENT, 3¼″, aqua $4–7
A TRASKS MAGNETIC OINTMENT, 2½″, aqua $4–7
A TRASKS MAGNETIC OINTMENT, 3¼″, aqua $3–4
AB HOLMES, PHARMACIST, 4″, colorless..$1–2
ABBOTT AIKAL CO, CHICAGO, 2⅝″, colorless $4–7
ABBOTT AIKLORD CO, CHICAGO, 2⅝″, colorless.................................$6–9
ABL MYERS AM/ROCK ROSE/NEW HAVEN, 9½″, emerald green, IP. $550–700
ABL MYERS ROCK ROSE NEW HAVEN, N-465, 9⅜″, deep emerald, IP, exterior wear...$450–650
ABNER ROYCE CO, 5½″, colorless $3–5
ABSORBINE, SPRINGFIELD, MA, 7½″, amber $5–7
AGUA PERUBINAT CONDAL, 10½″, colorless, labeled..........................$6–9
ALEXANDERS SILAMEAU, 6¹/₁₆″, light blue, OP $300–400
ALEXANDERS SILAMEAU, 6¼″, sapphire blue, OP $350–500
ALLENBURYS CASTOR OIL, 7″, amber $5–8
ALLENS ESSENCE OF JAMAICA GINGER, 5½″, aqua $6–9
ALLENS NERVE & BONE LINIMENT, 3⅞″, aqua $6–9
ALLE-RHUME REMEDY CO, 7¾″, colorless, ABM $5–8
ALTERNATIVE SYRUP, PIKE & OSGOOD, 8¾″, olive amber, OP $1200–1800
ALVATUNDER, THE HISEY DENTAL MFG, 3¾″, colorless $2–3
AMERICAN COMPOUND COVENTRY AUBURN, NY, N-7, 7″, aqua, OP....$50–75
AMERICAN COUGH DROPS, 5¼″, colorless, OP.............................$140–180
AMERICAN EAGLE LINIMENT, N-8, 5¼″, aqua, OP, six-sided..........$100–150
AMERICAN EXPECTORANT, N-9, 6″, aqua, OP, eight-sided................$80–120
AMERICAN RHEUMATIC BALSAM, N-14, 6⅛″, deep aqua, OP $300–500
ANDERSONS DERMADOE, 4¼″, aqua, OP $40–50
ANDERSONS DERMADOR, 5¾″, aqua $3–5
ANDERSONS DERMANDOR, 4¼″, aqua $2–4
ANODYNE FOR INFANTS, DR GROVES, 5¾″, colorless $5–7
ARMOURS VIGORALS, CHICAGO, amber, squat body $4–5
ARNICA & OIL LINIMENT, 6½″, aqua $4–5
ARTHURS RENOVATING SYRUP A & A, N-23-A, 7⅝″, medium blue green, IP..
....$700–1000
AS HINDS PORTLAND, ME, 5½″, colorless $4–6
ASTYPTODYAE CHEMICAL CO, 4½″, colorless....................................$4–5
ATHIEUS COUGH SYRUP...$3–5
ATLANTA CHEMICAL CO, 8½″, amber $6–8
ATLAS MEDICINE CO, HENDERSON, NC, 9¼″, amber $10–15

AYERS AGUE CURE LOWELL 7", aqua, OP $125–175
AYERS AGUE CURE, LOWELL, MA, 5¾", aqua............................... $9–14
AYERS CHERRY PECTORAL, aqua, OP $20–25
AYERS CHERRY PECTORAL, LOWELL, 5½", aqua $6–9
AYERS, LOWELL, MASS, USA, 8½" $4–6
AYERS PILLS, square, 2⅜", colorless.................................$1–3
AYERS PILLS, LOWELL, MA, rectangle, 2", aqua $6–8
B DENTON AUBURN NY, 6½", aqua, OP $75–100
B DENTON HEALING BALSAM, eight-sided, 4¼", aqua, OP $35–50
B DENTONS HEALING SYRUP, N-174, 3¾", aqua, OP, eight-sided.......$80–110
B FOSGATES ANODYNE, 4½", aqua $6–8
B FOSCATES ANODYNE CORDIAL, cylinder, 4¾", aqua, OP $12–15
BACHS AMERICAN COMPOUND AUBURN NY, N-23, 7¼", aqua, OP..... $60–90
BAKERS CELERY KOLA, 10", amber.................................$40–50
BALLARD SNOW LINIMENT CO, 4½", colorless.........................$5–8
BALSAM OF WILD CHERRY & TAR, N-38, 7⅜", aqua, OP................$50–75
BALSAM VEGETABLE PULMONARY, 5", aqua $7–9
BARCLAYS AMERICAN BALSAM, N-37, 5¾", aqua, OP $35–45
BARKER MOORE & MEIN, DRUGGIST, 5¼", aqua $4–6
BARKER MOORE & MEIN MEDICINE CO, 6", aqua $1–2
BARKER MOORE & MEIN MEDICINE CO, 6⅜", aqua $4–6
BARKER MORE & MAIN MED CO, PHILA, 8", colorless $2–4
BARNES & PARKE, NY, BALSAM OF WILD CHERRY & TAR, 7½", aqua.. $12–18
BARRLLS COLD CURE, 7", aqua $75–95
BARRYS TRICOPHEROUS FOR THE SKIN, 5¼", aqua, OP $9–12
BARTOW DRUG CO, 3½", colorless $3–5
BATCHELORS, 3", colorless $3–5
BAUMGARDNERS BRAZILIAN PECTORAL, 3¾", aqua, OP $125–150
BAYER ASPIRIN, running up and down as cross sign, 2½", colorless, ABM, screw cap...$3–4
BBB PHILA & ST LOUIS, aqua $20–27
BBB, ATLANTA, GA, 3¾", amber.................................. $9–12
BEARS OIL, N-44, 2¾", aqua, OP $150–200
BEE-DEE LINIMENT, CHATTANOOGA, TN, 5½", colorless.....................$5–7
BEEKMANS PULMONIC SYRUP NEW YORK, N-45, 7⅜", olive green, OP, eight-sided $2000–3000
BEGGS CHERRY COUGH SYRUP, 5¾", aqua, rectangular $3–5
BEGGS DIARRHOEA BALSAM, 5½", aqua $7–10
BELL ANS, 3¾", amber, ABM $1–2
BENNETTS MAGIC CURE, 5¼", deep cobalt $350–450
BENNETTS PHARMACY, ST PETERSBURG, FLA, colorless........................$3–5
BERLIN SERIES, 9⅛", aqua, OP $25–30
BERRY BROS, 11¼", aqua $6–9
BG NOBLE AB MOORE ROSE HAIR GLOSS, 7", aqua, OP................$250–350
BIGELOWS ALTERATIVE CW BLEECKER, 5¾", aqua, OP $60–90
BILLINGS RHEUMATIC LINIMENT, 6", aqua, OP........................... $150–170
BLODGETTS PERSIAN BALM, N-55, 4⅞", aqua, OP $110–135
BLOWN MEDICINE, rectangular with beveled edges, 5⅞", citron, OP, 1½" wide mouth $125–150
BLOWN MEDICINE, rectangular with beveled edges, 6½", olive amber, ⅜" crack $90–110

BLUD LIFE, colorless, ABM $2–3
BM&EA WHITLOCK & 7 CO OWNERS NY, 9⅛", greenish aqua, IP..$190–240
BOERICKE & RUNYON COMPANY, 7¾", colorless................................$2–3
BON OPTO FOR THE EYES, 3¼", colorless $3–4
BONHEUR CO, NARCELLUS, NY, 8¼", colorless $1–2
BONPLANDS FEVER & AGUA REMEDY, 5¼", aqua, OP, label in Spanish ....
....$30–40
BOWERS INFANT CORDIAL, aqua, OP...$30–35
BRADFIELD REGL CO, MOTHERS FRIEND, 6¾", aqua............................$3–5
BRAGGS ARCTIC LINIMENT, N-63, 4", aqua, OP $130–150
BRANDRIFFS VEGETABLE ANTIDOTE FOR AQUE, aqua.......................$25–35
BRANDRIFFS VEGETABLE ANTIDOTE, PIQUA, OH, 8", aqua $7–10
BRANTS INDIAN BALSAM, N-67, 7⅜", aqua, OP, eight-sided $100–150
BRANTS INDIAN PULMONARY BALSAM, eight-sided, 6⅞", aqua, OP $40–60
BRANTS INDIAN PULMONARY BALSAM, N-68, 7", aqua, OP, eight-sided ....
....$50–70
BRANTS INDIAN PULMONARY BALSAM, N-68, 6⅞", colorless, OP, eight-sided
....$300–450
BRANTS INDIAN PULMONARY DRUGGIST, NY, aqua, OP.....................$50–65
BRANTS PURIFYING EXTRACT, 10", aqua, OP $90–110
BREINIG, FRONEFIELD & CO CATTLE LINIMENT, 6¼", aqua, IP........ $90–120
BRIDGES LUNG TONIC, aqua $15–18
BRISTOL MYERS CO, 7¾", amber $2–4
BROMO CAFFEINE, 3¼", cobalt blue...$4–5
BROMO SELTZER, 6", cobalt...$4–6
BROMO SELTZER, 2½", cobalt $2–3
BROMO SELTZER, cylinder, 4", cobalt...$3–4
BROOKS DRUG CO, 8", colorless, labeled..$3–4
BROWN FORMAN CO, 4½", colorless $2–3
BROWN HOUSEHOLD PANACEA & FAMILY LINIMENT, 5⅛", aqua.............$5–8
BROWNS INSTANT RELIEF FOR PAIN, 5¼", aqua.................................$4–6
BUCHANS HUNGARIAN BALSAM OF LIFE, 5¾", aqua, OP $60–70
BUCHANS TONIC MIXTURE, 6⅜", aqua, OP $50–70
BUMSTEADS WORM SYRUP, PHILADA, 4½", aqua $10–12
BURKE & JAMES, 6¼", colorless $3–4
BURLINGTON DRUG CO, BURLINGTON, VT, 5½", colorless, label...........$7–9
BURNETT, 6¾", colorless $3–4
BURNETT, BOSTON, 4¼", colorless $5–7
BURNHAMS BEEF WINE & IRON, 9½", aqua $7–10
BW HAIR & SON ASTHMA CURE LONDON, 5", aqua........................$25–30
BY THE KINGS ROYAL PATENT, TURLINGTON, N-643, 2½", aqua, OP...........
.... $125–175
C BRINCKERHOFFS HEALTH RESTOR., N-75, 7¼", olive yellow, OP ..$350–450
C BRINCKERHOFFS HEALTH RESTORATIVE, N-75, 7½", olive green, OP..........
....$300–375
C HEIMSTREET & CO, eight-sided, 7", cobalt blue $30–35
C HEIMSTREET & CO TROY NY, eight-sided, 7", medium cobalt, OP.............
....$150–200
C MATHEWSONS REMEDY, 6⅞", aqua, OP $70–90
C&R CANADAIGUA NY RINGBONE & SPAVIN, 6½", aqua, OP $250–280
CA NEWMAN DRUGGIST, aqua, OP..$12–15

Medicine, C. Heimstreet & Co. PHOTO COURTESY OF
NEIL GROSSMAN.

CALDWELLS SYRUP PEPSIN, 3″, aqua, rectangle $3–5
CALIFORNIA FIG SYRUP CO, 7″, colorless $4–6
CALIFORNIA FIG SYRUP, WHEELING, W VA, 6″, colorless, ABM $3–4
CALVERTS DERBY CURE FOR INFLUEN, 5½″, aqua...........................$28–35
CAMPBELL VV, 5⅛″, colorless...$3–4
CANTRELLS AGUE MIXTURE, 6″, aqua, OP $50–75
CAPUDINE CHEMICAL CO, RALEIGH, NC, 7½″, amber, ABM $2–4
CARBONA (ON BASE), 5½″, aqua...$2–3
CARBONA & CARBONA PRODUCTS CO, 5⅛″, aqua, 12 panels $6–9
CARLSBAD AH (ON BOTTOM), 4″, colorless..................................$4–5
CARTERS EXTRACT OF SMARTWEED, 5⅜″, aqua, OP $75–100
CARTERS EXTRACT SMART WEED, 5″, aqua $4–6
CARTERS SPANISH MIXTURE, N-108, 8⅛″, olive amber, IP $200–250
CARTERS SPANISH MIXTURE, N-108, 8⅛″, olive green, OP, labeled ..$225–275
CARTERS SPANISH MIXTURE, N-108, 7¾″, yellow amber, IP........... $125–175
CAUVINS SYRUP FOR BABIES $20–25
CELERY COMPOUND, WITH CELERY STALK, 10″, yellow amber $50–70
CELERY COMPOUND, WITH CELERY STALK, 9⅞″, amber, base chip $25–30
CELRO KOLA, PORTLAND, OREGON, amber, square $60–65
CG CLARK CO NEW HAVEN CT, 12 panels, 5½″, aqua $3–5
CG CLARK CO RESTORATIVE, 7¾″, aqua....................................$4–6
CH PHILLIPA, NY, 9¼″, amber..$3–5
CH WEIGLES, embossed on side panels, colorless $6–9
CHAMBERLAINS COLIC, CHOLERA & DIARRHEA REMEDY, 4½″, aqua $8–12
CHAMBERLAINS COUGH REMEDY, 6″, colorless................................$2–3
CHAMBERLAINS COUGH REMEDY, 7″, colorless................................$6–9
CHAMBERLAINS MEDICINE CO, DES MOINES, IOWA, 5¾″, colorless $4–6
CHAPMANS GENUINE BOSTON, 8″, olive green, OP $1400–1800
CHAPMANS GENUINE ESSENCE, 8¼″, bright olive amber, OP $1500–1800
CHAPMANS GENUINE NO SALEM ST, BOSTON, 8¼″, light olive amber, OP .....
....$1000–1500
CHAS D COOPER PHARMACIST, WALDEN, NY, 4½″, colorless...............$3–6
CHAS E. LATHROP PHARMACIST, OMAHA 5¾″, colorless $5–7
CHATTANOOGA MEDICINE CO, 8⅜″, light green, screw top $5–6
CHATTANOOGA MEDICINE CO, WOMANS TONIC, 8½″, aqua...................$6–8
CHEMISTS RUSHTON CLARK & CO, 10″, aqua, OP...........................$20–30
CHLORIDE CALCIUM ST CATHARINES CANADA, 5¾″, deep aqua, OP.. $150–210

CIRCASSIAN LYMPH T & S, 6⅝″, aqua, OP $90–120
CITRATE OF MAGNESIA, 6¾″, colorless, OP $130–160
CITRATE OF MAGNESIA, 6¾″, colorless with olive tint, OP $75–100
CITRATE OF MAGNESIA, blob top, 8¼″, colorless $8–10
CITY DRUG COMPANY, ANACONDA, MT, 4¼″, colorless $3–4
CITY DRUG COMPANY, MERIDIAN, TEXAS, 3¼″ $2–3
CK DONNELL MD, LEWISTON, ME, 6¼″, colorless $4–5
CLARKES LINCOLN WORLD FAMED BLOOD MIX., 7¼″, grayish blue $28–32
CLARKS INFALLIBLE WORM SYRUP, PHILA, aqua, OP $40–50
CLARKS SYRUP, 9¾″, medium green, lip chip $50–70
CLEMENS INDIAN TONIC, N-127, 5⅜″, aqua, OP, 95% label $250–350
CLEMENS INDIAN TONIC, N-127, 5½″, aqua, OP, labeled $300–400
CLEWLEYS MIRACULOUS CURE FOR RHEUMATISM, 6⅛″, aqua $30–45
CLOUDS CORDIAL, 10¾″, yellow $110–140
CO MICHAELIS APOTHECARY, Charleston, SC, aqua, ... $4–6
COD LIVER OIL, 9¾″, aqua $4–6
COD LIVER OIL, with fish in center, 6″, amber, ABM, square $3–4
COD LIVER OIL, with fish in center, 9″, amber, ABM, square $3–4
COD LIVER OIL, HW & CO, NEW YORK, N-131, 10¼″, aqua, OP $120–150
COFFEENS LINIMENT NO 2, N-132, 4⅛″, aqua, OP $40–50
COLTS FOOT EXPECTORANT, 6″, colorless $3–4
COMBAULTS CAUSTIC BALSAM, 6¼″, aqua, screw top $3–4
COMPOUND ELIXIR, 8¾″, aqua $5–7
COMPOUND ELIXIR OF PHOSPHATE & CALISAYA, square, aqua $10–13
COMPOUND EXTRACT OF HOPS & BONESET, 4⅝″, aqua, OP $50–70
COMPOUND EXTRACT OF HOPS & BONESET, N-134, 6″, aqua, OP, neck crack .
.... $25–28
COMPOUND EXTRACT PINE SPLINTERS, ATLANTA, GA, Jacobs Pharmacy, 7½″,
colorless $5–8
COMSTOCK MORSES ROOT PILLS, amber, ... $9–12
CONNELLS BRAHMINICAL MOONPLANT, 8¼″, yellow amber $90–120
CONSTITUTIONAL BEVERAGE, 10¼″, amber $40–65
CONSTOCK & CO INDIAN VEGETABLE ELIXIR, N-136, 4¼″, aqua, op . $125–175
CONVERSE CO, COLUMBUS, OHIO, eight-sided, 6″, colorless $2–3
CORBINS SUMMER COMPLAINT TINCTURE, 4″, aqua, OP, labeled $150–225
CRAIG KIDNEY CURE COMPANY, 9½″, amber $125–175
CRAIGS KIDNEY & LIVER CURE, 9½″, amber $80–120
CRAIGS KIDNEY & LIVER CURE, 9⅝″, amber $80–120
CRUMPTONS STRAWBERRY BALSAM, N-146, 5″, aqua, OP $175–225
CS THUBER ARNOLDS VITAL FLUID, 7″, aqua, OP $110–130
CULLENS REMEDIES ROWAND & WALTON, 5⅞″, aqua, OP $75–100
CUMMINGS VEGETINE, 10″, aqua $9–12
CW ATWELL, PORTLAND, ME, 8″, aqua $5–7
CW SNOW & CO DRUGGISTS, 6⅜″, cobalt blue $70–100
CW SNOW & CO DRUGGISTS, SYRACUSE, 8¼″, cobalt blue $150–200
D ZEUBLINS SAFE & QUICK CURE, 3½″, aqua, OP $200–250
D ZEUBLINS SAFE & QUICK CURE, 3½″, aqua, OP $225–300
DAVIS & MILLERS AMERICAN WORM SYRUP, N-163, 4⅛″, aqua, OP, six-sided
.... $125–165
DAVIS BOTANIC CHOLAGOGUE BUFFALO, 6⅛″, aqua, OP $300–375
DAVIS VEGETABLE PAIN KILLER, 5¾″, aqua $2–3

DEL DR RABELL EMULSION, 9½″, aqua $3–5
DIAPHORTIC COMPOUND, HA TUCKER, MD, 5½″, aqua $6–8
DICKIES ICELAND BALM FOR COUGHS, 5⅞″, aqua, OP $45–65
DILLS BALM OF LIFE, 6″, aqua $3–4
DOCT CURTIS INHALING HYGEAN VAPOR, N-147, 7½″, clear, OP....... $60–90
DOCT CURTIS SHERRY SYRUP, N-149, 7⅜″, colorless, OP $40–55
DOCT FOWLERS ANTI ERICHOLIC, N-231, 6″, aqua, OP $75–100
DOCT HARRISONS CHALYBEATE TONIC, 9⅛″, blue green $75–90
DOCT MARSHALLS AROMATIC CATARRH, 3⅜″, aqua, OP $45–65
DOCTOR EW VONDERSMITH INDIAN COUGH BALM, N-660, 8¼″, aqua, OP, nine-
sided $900–1200
DOCTOR FRANKS TURKEY FEBRIFUGE, 5⅛″, aqua, OP..................$250–350
DOCTOR FRANKS TURKEY FEBRIFUGE, 5⅛″, aqua, OP...................$250–325
DOCTOR P HALLS COUGH REMEDY, N-270, 4¾″, ice blue aqua, OP.....$70–95
DOCTOR THOMAS VICKERS EMBROCATION, OHIO, 4⅜″, aqua, OP $50–70
DONALD KENNEDY & CO, ROXBURY, MA, labeled, 6½″, aqua $4–5
DONNAUDS GOUT REMEDY, 6″, aqua, IP $45–65
DONNELLS RHEUMATIC LINIMENT, 7¼″, aqua...............................$6–9
DOWIE, MOISE & DAVIS WHOLESALE DRUGGIST, 7″, amber $5–7
DPS CO, 3½″, amber...$2–3
DR A BOCHIES GERMAN SYRUP, 6¾″, aqua, square..........................$4–6
DR A FOWLER SYRACUSE, 4⅜″, aqua, OP $30–37
DR A ROES COUGH SYRUP, 4⅞″, aqua, OP $45–65
DR A ROGERS LIVERWORT TAR & CAN, N-528, 7½″, aqua, OP $70–90
DR ADOLF HOMMELS HAEMATOGEN, aqua $12–15
DR ADOLF HOMMELS HAEMATOGEN, 6¾″, light green..........................$3–5
DR ALEXANDER LUNG HEALER, 6½″, aqua, rectangular $7–10
DR ATHERTONS WILD CHERRY SYRUP, N-25, 5¼″, aqua, OP $100–135
DR AW COLEMANS ANTI DYSPECTIC, C-194, 9¼″, deep rich green, IP ....
.... $3000–4000
DR BAKERS PAIN PANACEA, N-34, 5″, light blue green, OP $40–50
DR BELLS PINE TAR HONEY, 5½″, aqua $8–12
DR BIRMINGHAMS ANTI BILIOUS, 8½″, emerald green $250–350
DR BOSANKOS PILE REMEDY, PHILA, PA, 2½″, aqua $5–7
DR BROWDERS COMPOUND SYRUP, N-80, 6⅞″, aqua, OP..................$50–80
DR BROWNS RUTERBA, 8″, amber $12–14
DR BULLOCKS NEPHRETICURN, PROVIDENCE, RI, 7″, aqua $12–15
DR BULLS HERBS & IRON, patent date on base, 9½″, aqua $15–20
DR C GRATTANS DIPTHERIA REMEDY, 7″, aqua $25–35
DR CALDWELLS LAXATIVE SENNA, 7″, colorless, rectangular................$3–4
DR CARTERS COMPOUND, 5⅛″, aqua, OP $40–60
DR CAVANAUGHS PILE SALVE, N-109, 2⅜″, aqua, OP $75–100
DR CF BROWN YOUNG AMERICAN LINIMENT, 4″, aqua $5–7
DR CLARK N YORK, 9⅛″, deep green, IP................................ $800–1000
DR CONVERS INVIGORATING CORDIAL, N-138, 6⅛″, aqua, OP $75–100
DR CRAIGS COUGH & CONSUMPTION CURE, 8″, orange amber $500–700
DR CUMMINGS VEGETINE, aqua..$12–15
DR D JANES CARMENATIVE, PHILA, 5″, aqua................................$3–4
DR D JAYNE SALEM, NJ, aqua, OP....................................... $200–250
DR D JAYNES ALTERATIVE, aqua, OP $20–25
DR D JAYNES ALTERATIVE, PHILA, 5″, aqua...............................$2–4

Dr D Jaynes Carminative Balsam, 5″, aqua $5–7

Dr D Jaynes Carminative Balsam, Phila, aqua, OP $25–30

Dr D Jaynes Expectorant, 6½″, colorless $2–3

Dr D Jaynes Life Preservative, N-338, 5⅝″, aqua, OP............. $500–700

Dr D Jaynes Tonicvermifuce, oval, 4¾″, aqua, OP..........................$7–9

Dr Daniels Cough, Cold & Fever Drops, 4½″, colorless $7–10

Dr Davis's Depurative, 9⅞″, medium green, IP $600–900

Dr Davis's Depurative Phila, N-165, 9½″, deep blue green, IP $1300–1700

Dr Doyen Staphylase Du, 8″, colorless $4–5

Dr DP Brown Buffalo NY, 12-sided, 1³/₁₆″ × 2¼″, olive amber . $500–700

Dr Drakes Group Remedy, 6¼″, colorless.....................................$4–6

Dr EE Dixon, 6½″, colorless..$3–4

Dr Evans Comomile Pills, 3¾″, aqua, OP $15–18

Dr Fahrneys Uterine, 8½″, colorless $12–15

Dr Fausts German Aromatic Wine, 11″, orange amber $150–250

Dr Foords Pectoral Syrup, N-224, 5⅝″, aqua, OP....................$80–100

Dr Foords Tonic & Anodyne Cordial, 5¾″, aqua, ...$45–60

Dr Foords Tonic Cordial Cazenovi A, NY, N-225, 4¼″, aqua, OP $50–70

Dr Forshas Alterative Balm, N-227, 5¼″, aqua, OP..................$50–70

Dr Fragas Cuban Vermifuge, eight panels, 3¾″, aqua $7–9

Dr Franks Turkey Ferbifuge, 5⅛″, aqua, OP $400–525

Dr Friends Cough Balsam, 6⅛″, aqua, OP $50–75

Dr G Goulds Pin Worm Syrup, 5″, aqua, OP...............................$40–60

Dr Gordaks Iceland Jelly, 6¾″, aqua, OP $100–130

Dr GW Denig Chillicothe O, 6″, deep aqua, OP $150–200

Dr H Moyeys Lemon Elixir Herb Compound (On Label), 7¼″, aqua.$6–8

Dr H Swaynes Compound Syrup Of Wild Cherry, 5⅞″, aqua, OP $80–100

Dr H Van Vlecks Family Medicines, N-563, 6½″, aqua, IP .. $125–175

Dr H Vanvlecks Family Medicine, 8″, cornflower blue, OP $600–900

Dr HA Inghams Nervine Pain Extractor, aqua, OP, with two labels.........
....$30–35

Dr HA Inghams Vegetable Pain Extract, 4½″, aqua......................$5–8

Dr Hams Aromatic Invigorating Spirit, 8⅜″, aqua, IP $70–90

Dr Harters Iron Tonic, amber, full label $25–30

Dr Harters Iron Tonic, aqua $15–18

Dr Hartshorns Medicine, 6⅛″, olive amber, OP..................... $600–800

Dr HB Myers Dandelion Wild Cherry, 9½″, aqua, OP............ $300–400

Dr HB Skinner Boston, 6″, olive amber, OP, major lip repair........$90–110

Dr Hersheys Worm Syrup, 5½″, aqua, OP $60–90

Dr HF Peerys Dead Shot Vermifuce, 4″, amber...........................$5–6

Dr Hills Pain Killer Farmer NY, 5¼″, aqua, OP.....................$150–225

Dr Hookers Cough & Croup Syrup, N-303, 5½″, aqua, OP...........$70–90

Dr HW Jackson Druggist Vegetable Home Syrup, 5¾″, olive green, OP ..
....$700–900

Dr HW Jackson Druggist Vegetable Home Syrup, 4½″, olive green, OP ..
....$1000–1500

Dr J M'Clintocks Family Medicines, 4⅝″, colorless, OP, with label ....
....$70–90

Dr J Pettits Canker Balm, 3¼″, colorless, flask-shaped................. $7–10

Dr J Simms & Sons Unequaled Cough Syrup, N-580, 5½″, aqua, OP ....
....$150–200

DR J SUMNERS INFALLIBLE CURE FOR THE HERNIA, 4⅝", aqua, OP ....
.... $750–1000
DR J WEBSTERS CEREVISIA, 7¼", emerald green, OP, labeled $800–1100
DR J WEBSTERS CEREVISIA ANGLICAN A DUPLEX, 7⅛", bright medium green,
OP $800–1200
DR JA KINNEYS COMPOUND VEGITABLE SYRUP, 9", aqua, OP, rectangular......
....$500–750
DR JA SHERMANS RUPTURE CURATIVE COMPOUND, 8¼", cobalt blue............
.... $800–1100
DR JAMES CHERRY TAR SYRUP, 5¾", aqua $5–7
DR JAMES M'CLINTOCK FAMILY MEDICINES, 8½", colorless, OP $45–65
DR JAMES RAINEY VITALITY TABLETS, 3¼", amber.............................$4–5
DR JAMES WORM SYRUP, 5½", aqua $5–7
DR JB LYNAR & SON, LOGANSPORT, IND, 6", colorless $5–8
DR JB LYNAR & SON, LOGANSPORT, IND (ON SEAL) 6", colorless $9–12
DR JE PLOUFS RHEUMATISM CURE, 6⅛", colorless, label............... $90–125
DR JF CHURCHELLS SPECIFIC REMEDY, 7¾", medium emerald green ....
.... $300–350
DR JF CHURCHILLS SPECIFIC REMEDY, N-122, 6⅞", aqua, OP $100–130
DR JN KEELERS VEGETABLE PANACEA, 7", aqua, OP $120–140
DR JOHNSONS HORSE REMEDIES, 6¾", aqua $7–10
DR JONES AUSTRALIAN OIL, 5", amber.. $8–10
DR JONES RED CLOVER TONIC, 8¾", amber, labeled..................... $100–135
DR JR MILLERS BALM, 4¾", colorless...$5–6
DR JS WOODS ELIXIR ALBANY NY, 8¾", emerald green, IP........$1000–1500
DR JS WOODS ELIXIR ALBANY NY, N-700, 9", aqua, IP $400–500
DR JUGS MEDICINE FOR LUNGS, LIVER & BLOOD, 6¼", brown jug......$30–45
DR JW BULLS VEGETABLE BABY SYRUP, round, ¼", aqua $4–6
DR KAYS LUNG BALM, 7¾", aqua, rectangular...................................$6–8
DR KEELEYS DOUBLE CHLORIDE OF GOLD CURE FOR OPIUM HABIT, 5¾", col-
orless, labeled $450–550
DR KELLINGERS MAGIC FLUID, 4⅞", aqua, OP $120–145
DR KENNEDYS, 9", aqua $3–5
DR KENNEDYS FAVORITE REMEDY, 7", colorless $3–4
DR KENNEDYS MEDICAL DISCOVERY, ROXBURY, MASS, aqua.............. $18–24
DR KENNEDYS RHEUMATIC LINIMENT, aqua $8–10
DR KEYSERS PECTORAL SYRUP, 5½", aqua, OP $225–300
DR KIERSTEDS JULEP FOR DIARRHOEA, 4", aqua, OP $60–80
DR KIESOWS ESSENCE OF LIFE, 5", colorless................................$4–6
DR KILMERS, 7¼", colorless, ABM $2–3
DR KILMERS INDIAN COUGH REMEDY CONSUMPTION OIL, NY, aqua......$20–22
DR KILMERS OCEAN WEED HEART REMEDY, aqua...........................$20–25
DR KILMERS SWAMP ROOT KIDNEY CURE, 8¼", aqua $7–10
DR KILMERS SWAMP ROOT KIDNEY LIVER & BLADDER CURE, 8", aqua .. $8–10
DR KILMERS SWAMP ROOT KIDNEY LIVER & BLADDER CURE, 7", aqua $6–8
DR KILMERS SWAMP ROOT KIDNEY LIVER & BLADDER REMEDY, 7", aqua, rec-
tangular.. $8–10
DR KILMERS SWAMP ROOT KIDNEY REMEDY, sample, 4¼", aqua...........$7–9
DR KILMERS SWAMP ROOT, KIDNEY REMEDY, 4¼", aqua, sample $9–12
DR KILMERS U & O ANOINTMENT, 1¾", aqua...............................$3–5
DR KINGS GROUPS COUGH SYRUP, aqua, OP...................................$60–70

Grouping of label-under-glass bottles, including drug, whiskey, wine, and hair tonic. PHOTO COURTESY OF GLASS WORKS AUCTIONS.

Assortment of Pitkin-type flasks. PHOTO COURTESY OF GLASS WORKS AUCTIONS.

Elvis '55 #2, Garnier trout, Beam telephone, and House of Koshu lion man, 1969. PHOTO COURTESY OF DAVID SMITH.

Collection of barber bottles, including Mary Gregory type at right.
PHOTO COURTESY OF GLASS WORKS AUCTIONS.

Sunburst flasks in a wide range of colors. PHOTO COURTESY OF GLASS
WORKS AUCTIONS.

Rare colored bitters bottles, Zingari, Brown's Indian Herb, Woodgate Plantation, Kelley's Old Cabin, Fish, Highland. PHOTO COURTESY OF GLASS WORKS AUCTIONS.

Poison bottles grouping. PHOTO COURTESY OF GLASS WORKS AUCTIONS.

Ezra Brooks quail, Beam blue hen club bottle, Hoffman eagle with music box, and Lionstone western bluebirds. PHOTO COURTESY OF DAVID SMITH.

Colorful collection of Beam cars, red '53 Convention Corvette, turquoise '57 Chevy, black '78 Corvette Pace car, and yellow '68 Pa. Camaro. PHOTO COURTESY OF DAVID SMITH.

Scroll flask grouping. PHOTO COURTESY OF GLASS WORKS AUCTIONS.

Dr. Brown's Indian herb bitters bottles in rare colors. PHOTO
COURTESY OF GLASS WORKS AUCTIONS.

Poison skull, eagle–Willington flask, pattern-molded jug, Royal Italian bitters, S Fine ink, Kimball's Jaundice bitters. PHOTO COURTESY OF SKINNER'S, INC.

A nice assortment of bottles. Note the reproduction EG Booz aqua cabin bottle at right. PHOTO COURTESY OF SKINNER'S, INC.

Concentric ring eagle flask, stocking darner whimsey, Phelp's Arcanum, ribbed tumbler, cathedral pickle, Suffolk pig bitters, blown three-mold decanter, F. Sherwood soda, eagle-sunburst flask. PHOTO COURTESY OF SKINNER'S, INC.

Dr Kings New Discovery For Coughs & Colds, 6¾", colorless $4–5
Dr Kings New Discovery, Chicago, 4¼", colorless $1–2
Dr Kings New Discovery, Chicago, Ill, 4½", aqua $4–5
Dr Kings New Life Pills, 2½", colorless...............................$3–4
Dr Kings Pills, labeled $6–9
Dr Koch Vegetable Tea Co, 9", colorless...............................$4–6
Dr Lindseys Blood Searcher, 8½", colorless $15–22
Dr Linicks Malt Extract, 6", colorless $4–7
Dr LR Parks Egyptian Anodyne, 5⅛", deep aqua, OP $100–140
Dr LR Stafford Olive Tar, 6", colorless $5–6
Dr M Bowmans Healing Balsam, 6½", colorless..........................$4–7
Dr MA Simmons Liver Medicine, aqua...................................$15–20
Dr MA Simmons Liver Medicine, St Louis, 5¾", aqua...................$6–9
Dr Manns Celebrated Ague Balsam, N-414, 6¾", deep aqua, IP.$160–200
Dr Manns Celebrated Ague Balsam, N-414, 6¾", aqua, IP $100–125
Dr Markleys Family Medicines, N-415, 7⅛", aqua, OP.............$80–120
Dr McMunns Elixir Of Opium, aqua, OP...............................$30–40
Dr MG Kerr & Bertolet Compound, 4¾", aqua, OP $60–80
Dr Miles Remedy For The Heart, 8¼", aqua..............................$6–9
Dr Miles Restorative Nervine, 9", aqua, ABM...........................$1–2
Dr Miles Restorative Nervine, 8¼", colorless..........................$1–2
Dr Miles Restorative Tonic, aqua $12–15
Dr Mitchells Ipecac Syrup, N-447, 4⅝", aqua, OP $50–75
Dr Mitchells Ipeccsy Syrup, Perry, NY, aqua, OP.....................$70–80
Dr MM Fenners Peoples Remedies, 6", colorless $5–7
Dr Nywalls Family Medicine, 7½", amber..............................$12–15
Dr O Phelps Brown, 2¾", aqua $2–3
Dr Oreste/Sinanides/Medicinal, coffin shape with glass top, 4½", milk glass.. $450–600
Dr Parks Indian Liniment, 5⅜", colorless $6–9
Dr Perkins Syrup Albany, N-489, 9⅜", rich blue green, IP........ $600–900
Dr Peter Fahrneys & Sons, Chicago, 9", colorless $2–3
Dr Peters Kuriko, 8¾", aqua $4–6
Dr Peters Kuriko, square, 9", colorless...............................$5–7
Dr Pierces Favorite Prescription, 8¼", aqua.......................... $8–10
Dr Pierces Medical Discovery, labeled $13–16
Dr Pinkhams Emmemagogue, N-496, 6⅞", aqua, OP $45–65
Dr Pinkhams Emmenagogue, 5⅞", deep aqua, OP $70–90
Dr Porters, NY, aqua, OP..$12–16
Dr R Goodales American Catarrh Remedy, N-251, 6", aqua, OP ...$70–90
Dr R Sappington Flaxseed Syrup, 7½", aqua.......................... $8–12
Dr Roback Swedish Remedy, N-521 var., 6¼", aqua, OP..........$150–200
Dr Roback Swedish Remedy, N-521, 4½", aqua, OP, eight-sided.... $90–120
Dr Robbs Hippodrome Liniment, N-523, 5¼", aqua, OP $75–100
Dr Roses Antidispeptic Vermifuge Philada, aqua, OP $70–90
Dr Roses For The Lung & Throat Disease, N-533, 5⅜", aqua, OP $60–80
Dr S Fellers Eclectic Liniment, N-212, 4¼", aqua, OP............ $130–150
Dr S Fellers Lung Balsam, N-213, 6½", deep aqua, IP $150–225
Dr S Fitch, 707 Bway, NY, rectangle, 4¾", aqua, OP lip flake $15–20
Dr S Hardys Womans Friend, aqua....................................$20–25
Dr S Pitchers Castoria, 6", aqua $5–7

Dr SA Tuttles Boston Mass, 12 panels, 6¼", aqua $5–7
Dr SA Weavers Canker & Salt Rheum Syrup, N-674, 9⅜", aqua, OP ......
....$65–85
Dr SA Weavers Cankers & Salt Syrup, 7¾", aqua.....................$20–25
Dr Sages Catarrah Remedy..$15–20
Dr Sanfords Invigorator Or Liver Remedy, 7⅝", aqua, OP $75–90
Dr Sanfords Liver Invigorator, aqua...................................$35–45
Dr SBH & Co, PR (On Base), cylinder, 9", colorless.....................$7–10
Dr Schencks Pine Tar For Throat And Lungs, 6⅛", aqua, rectangular ....
....$8–12
Dr Schultz, 6½", aqua $3–4
Dr Seth Arnolds Balsam..$4–6
Dr Seth Arnolds Balsam, Gilman Bros, Boston, 3¾", amethyst $6–9
Dr Seth Arnolds Balsam, Gilman Bros, Boston, 7", aqua...........$10–15
Dr Seth Arnolds Cough Killer, 5½", aqua..............................$4–5
Dr Shoops Family Medicines, 6½", aqua $3–4
Dr Shoops Family Medicines, Racine, Wis, 5½", aqua..................$5–8
Dr Shoops Family Medicines, Racine, Wis, 7", aqua $6–9
Dr Simmons Squaw Vine Wine Compound, 8½", aqua $8–11
Dr Smiths Columbo Tonic, 9⅜", amber...............................$35–44
Dr Southworths Blood & Kidney Remedy, aqua $20–25
Dr SS Fitch, NY, 5", aqua, OP..$20–24
Dr SS Fitch 707 Bway NY, aqua $20–30
Dr Steph Jewetts Celebrated, N-347, 5¼", aqua, OP.................$60–85
Dr Stones Oxford Drops For Cough, N-608, 5", aqua, OP........ $150–175
Dr Sykes Specific Blood Medicine, 6½", colorless.....................$4–6
Dr Tafts Asthmalene NY, 3½", aqua $4–6
Dr Taylors Chronothermal Balsam, N-623, 6⅞", aqua, OP $80–100
Dr Taylors Chronothermal Balsam, N-623, 7⅞", colorlesss, OP. $80–120
Dr Taylors Chronothermal Balsam, N-623-A, 6¾", aqua, OP $60–80
Dr Thachers Liver & Blood Syrup, 7¼", amber, rectangular............$5–7
Dr Thachers Liver & Blood Syrup, sample, 3½", amber, rectangular .$6–9
Dr Thachers Vegetable Syrup, 7", colorless...........................$6–8
Dr Thachers Worm Syrup, 4¼", aqua, square...........................$6–8
Dr Throops Syrup Of Blood Root, 6½", aqua, OP.................. $250–300
Dr Tichenors Antiseptic, 3¾", aqua....................................$4–5
Dr Tobias New York, 4¼", aqua..$4–5
Dr Tobias Venetian Horse Liniment, 6¼", aqua.......................$5–8
Dr Tobias Venetian Horse Lini., N-634-M, 8", aqua, OP..............$70–90
Dr Trues Elixir, 5½", colorless..$4–6
Dr Trues Elixir Established 1851, 7¾", colorless, ABM..................$4–5
Dr Trues Elixir Established 1851, 5½", colorless, ABM..................$2–4
Dr Trues Elixir Worm Expeller, aqua.................................$14–18
Dr Tutts Asparagine, New York, 10¼", aqua $10–14
Dr TW Graydon Diseases Of The Lungs, 5⅞", light amber $7–10
Dr Von Werts Balsam, Watertown, NY, 6", aqua, rectangular $5–7
Dr WB Caldwells Syrup Pepsin, 7¼", colorless $5–6
Dr WB Farrells Arabian Liniment, N-209, 7½", deep aqua, OP. $100–130
Dr WB Farrells Arabian Liniment, N-209, 7½", aqua, IP $150–200
Dr Weavers Canker Cure, 5¼", aqua, OP............................ $300–400
Dr WH Alexanders Wonderful Healing Oil, aqua, labeled.............$6–9

Dr Whites Dandelion Alterative, 9¼", deep aqua $50–70
Dr Williams Anti Dyspeptic Elixir, 6⅜", aqua, OP $75–100
Dr Wilson Horse Ointment, 4¼", emerald green, OP $2000–2500
Dr Wistars Balsam Of Wild Cherry, 6¼", deep aqua, IP.............$45–65
Dr WJ Haas's Expectorant, N-266, 5¼", aqua, OP..................$120–160
Dr WM Korong Hair Coloring Mfr Chemist, 4½", colorless......... $8–11
Drs EE & JA Greene, New York & Boston, 7½", aqua...................$5–7
Druggists Lindsey Ruffin & Co, 6¼", colorless $4–5
Dunbar & Cos Wormwood Cordial, 9⅜", aqua, IP $150–250
Durfee Mfg Co, Grand Rapids, Mich, 7¼", colorless....................$1–3
Durnos The Mountain Indian Liniment, N-183, 5⅞", aqua, OP $75–95
Duttons Vegetable Discovery, 6", aqua $7–9
Dyers Healing Embrocation, N-185, 6⅛", aqua, OP...................$40–50
E Bloch & Co, WB (On Base), 3½", colorless $3–5
EA Buckhouts Dutch Liniment, N-85, 4¾", ice blue, OP......... $300–400
EA Buckhouts Dutch Liniment, N-85, 4⅞", aqua, OP.............$250–350
Ebenezer A Pearls Tincture Of Life, 7¾", aqua $7–10
Eddy & Eddy, 5", colorless $2–3
Edw S Burnham Aopthecary, Charleston, SC, 4¼", aqua $5–7
Ehrlicher Bros Pharmacists, 4¼", colorless...............................$5–7
Eilimans Royal Embrocation For Horses, 7", light aqua $4–5
Elixir Alimentare Ducro A Paris, 8¼", light green $4–6
Elixir Babek For Malaria Chills, aqua................................... $9–12
Ellimans Embrocation, yellowish aqua $20–25
Ellimans Royal Embrocation For Horses, 7", aqua $3–4
Elys Cream Balm, Hay Fever Catarrah, 2⅝", amber $12–15
Empire State Drug Co, 6½", colorless $2–3
Egyptian Chemical Co, Boston, Mass, 7½", colorless, ABM, screw cap ...
....$1–2
ES Skinners Liniment, 6⅞", aqua, OP...................................$175–225
Evans Chemical Co, 6¼", colorless $3–4
Ever Ready Drug Co, Hollywood, 5¾", amber $55–65
Extract Valerian Shaker Fluid, N-570, 3⅞", aqua, OP, label....$100–150
F Browns Essence Of Jamaica Ginger, 5½", aqua $5–6
Farrells Arabian Liniment, aqua, OP $40–50
Fathers Johns Medicine, 9", amber, wide mouth......................$5–8
Fathers Johns Medicine, Lowell 7¼", dark amber $3–5
Fellows & Co Chemists, St John, NB, 8", aqua $9–12
Fellows & Co Chemists, St John, NB, 8", aqua, ABM $6–8
Fellows Syrup Of Hyphosphites, labeled $13–16
Ferrol The Iron Oil Food, Cod Liver Oil, 9¼", amber $9–12
Fetridge & Co Balm Of Thousand Flowers, 5", aqua, OP $35–50
Flaggs Good Samaritans, N-219, 3¾", aqua, OP, five-sided $50–75
Flaggs Good Samaritans Relief, 3⅞", pale cornflower blue, OP, five-sided
....$110–150
Fletchers Castoria, 6", aqua $4–5
Fletchers Castoria, 6", colorless with bluish tint..........................$4–6
Foley & Co, 2½", colorless, sample...$1–2
Foleys & Co, Chicago, USA, 5¼", colorless $1–2
Foleys Cream, Foley & Co, Chicago, USA, 4¼", colorless..............$3–5
Foleys Honey & Tar, 5¼", aqua...$2–4

FOLEYS KIDNEY PILLS, FOLEY & CO, CHICAGO, 2½″, colorless $4-5
FOLGERS OLOSAONEAN, aqua, OP $40-50
FOLGERS OLOSAONIAN NEW YORK, 6⅛″, aqua, OP $20-25
FONTAINES CREAM OF WILD FLOWERS, 4⅞″, aqua, OP $400-500
FOSTERS MOUNTAIN COMPOUND, N-230, 6¼″, aqua, OP $90-125
FOUGERAS COMPOUND IONISED COD LIVER OIL, three-sided, colorless $3-5
FRANK HE EGGLESTON PHARM, LARAMIE, WY, colorless...................$5-7
FRANK WHITMORE PRESCRIPTION DRUGGIST, CONNEAUT, OHIO, colorless .$8-9
FRANKLIN HOWES MEDICAL DISCOVERY, aqua................................. $15-18
FRED KW HALE NATURES HERBAL REMEDIES, aqua $9-12
FREDERICK STEARNS & CO, DETROIT, 4″, amber $2-4
FREYS VERMIFUGE BALTIMORE, square, 4½″, aqua, OP, lip chips......... $7-11
FRIENDS RHEUMATIC DISPELLER, 6⅝″, aqua, OP...................... $400-500
FRIXIE HAIR OIL, HOWARD DRUGS & MEDICINE CO, 2¼″, colorless $3-4
FROG POND CHILL & FEVER TONIC, 6⅞″, deep cobalt, ABM.............$50-75
FROM THE LABORATORY OF GW MERCHANT, 5½″, medium blue green, IP ....
....$120-150
FROM THE LABORATORY OF GW MERCHANT, 5½″, emerald green, OP...........
....$200-250
FROM THE LABORATORY OF GW MERCHANT, 5⅝″, ice blue, OP $250-350
FROM THE LABORATORY OF GW MERCHANT, 5¾″, deep emerald green.........
.... $60-90
FROM THE LABORATORY OF GW MERCHANT, 5½″, aqua, OP $150-200
FROM THE LABORATORY OF GW MERCHANT, 5½″, blue green, OP ..$170-200
FROM THE LABORATORY OF GW MERCHANT, 5½″, medium yellow green ......
....$120-150
FRYS GREAT RHEUMATIC CURE, 8⅝″, colorless with labels and box .. $120-150
FULTONS RADICAL REMEDY, 8¾″, amber.................................... $350-400
FURST MCNESS CO, FREEPORT, ILL, 8¼″, aqua...............................$2-3
G FACCELLA (ON BASE), 6″, aqua $2-3
GARDNERS LINIMENT, N-239, 3⅞″, aqua, OP.................................$50-70
GENESSEE LINIMENT, N-241, 5¼″, aqua, OP $50-60
GENUINE ESSENCE, N-242, 4⅝″, medium-yellow olive, OP........... $500-700
GENUINE FLUID EXTRACTS, HT HELMBOLD, 7¼″, aqua $5-8
GEO W LAIRD & CO/ OLEO-CHYLE, 9⅞″, electric blue.................. $75-100
GEORGE COSTER MOBILE, with black label, 5⅞″, aqua, OP........... $250-300
GERMAN FIR COUGH CURE, 6⅜″, aqua, labeled and original box........$65-80
GERMAN MAGNETIC LINIMENT, N-243, 5″, aqua, OP $60-80
GF HEDRICH APOTHECARY, CHARLESTON, SC, 4⅜″, colorless................$4-6
GH HOLTZMAN, PHARMACIST, 5½″, colorless $3-4
GIBBS BONE LINIMENT, six-sided, 6½″, olive green, OP $400-500
GIBBS BONE LINIMENT, N-245, 6¼″, olive amber, OP, six-sided $300-500
GIBBS BONE LINIMENT, N-245, 6¼″, medium olive green, OP........ $400-525
GIBSONS SYRUP, 9¾″, medium green $140-175
GINSENG PANACEA, N-247, 4⅜″, aqua, OP....................................$70-95
GLASER, KOHN & CO MFG CHEMISTS, 4¼″, colorless.......................$1-2
GLOVERS IMPERIAL MEDICINE, screw top, amber..............................$1-2
GLYCO-THYMOLINE, 2½″, colorless $1-2
GOFFS INDIAN VEGETABLE COUGH SYRUP, aqua ,.........................$25-35
GOLDEN EYE LOTION, LEONARDIS, TAMPA, FLA, 4½″, aqua $6-9
GOLDEN EYE LOTION, LEONARDIS, TAMPA, FLA, 4½″, aqua, ABM.........$3-5

GOLDEN EYE LOTION, LEONARDIS, NEW YORK, 4½", aqua.................$6–9
GOMBAULTS JE CAUSTIC BALSAM, 6½", aqua $3–4
GPR, 6¼", colorless $3–4
GRAFFENBERG CHILDRENS PANACEA, 4¼", aqua, OP $80–95
GRANDJEANS/NEW YORK, pyramid shape, 11¼", aqua, OP $100–160
GRANULAR CITRATE OF MAGNESIA, 6", cobalt............................$30–35
GRAYS CELEBRATED SPARKLING SPRAY, colorless, blob top...................$6–9
GRAYS SYRUP OF RED SPRUCE GUM, 5½", aqua, ABM $2–3
GREAT ENGLISH SWEENY SPECIFIC, 6", aqua $4–5
GREAT WESTERN LINIMENT, N-261, 4¼", aqua, OP $120–140
GREENS TONIC MIXTURE OR FEVER AGUE, 6", aqua, OP $100–125
GREGORYS INSTANT CURE, 6⅜", blue aqua, OP...........................$600–800
GROBERS BOTANIC DYSPEPSIA SYRUP....................................$15–20
GW MERCHANT CARBONIC MINERAL WATER LOCKPORT, 6½", deep green......
....$2500–3500
GW MERCHANT CHEMIST LOCKPORT NY, 5⅝", emerald green, OP $40–60
GW MERCHANT CHEMIST LOCKPORT NY, 7⅜", emerald green $125–170
GW MERCHANT CHEMIST LOCKPORT NY, 7", emerald green, IP $150–200
GW MERCHANT LOCKPORT NY, 5", blue green, OP, flake on lip......$80–100
GW MERCHANT LOCKPORT NY, 5", aqua, OP............................$75–100
GW MERCHANT LOCKPORT NY, 5⅛", medium blue green, OP $250–300
GW STONES COUGH ELIXIR, N-607, 6⅜", aqua, OP $60–75
H LAKES INDIAN SPECIFIC, N-369, 8⅛", aqua, OP $150–225
H.G. & CO, PHILA, cylinder, 3⅞", colorless $8–10
HADLOCKS VEGETABLE SYRUP, 8⅛", aqua, OP, six-sided $350–500
HALLER PROPRIETARY CO, BLAIR, NEB, 7½", colorless $5–6
HALLER PROPRIETARY CO, BLAIR, NEB, 7¼", colorless $4–6
HALLS BALSAM FOR THE LUNGS, 7¼", aqua $4–6
HALLS CATARRAH CURE, 4½", aqua..$3–4
HAMPTONS V TINCTURE MORTIMER, N-277, 6¼", medium yellow amber, OP
.... $400–600
HAMPTONS V TINCTURE MORTIMER, N-277, 6¼", red amber, OP $375–500
HAMPTONS V TINCTURE MORTIMER, N-277, 6⅜", bright olive green, OP.......
.... $1500–2000
HAMPTOMS V TINCTURE MORTIMER, N-277, 6⅜", deep olive amber, OP
.... $600–800
HANCE BROTHERS & WHITE, PHILA, 7", amber $7–9

Medicine, GW Merchant. PHOTO COURTESY OF NEIL
GROSSMAN.

HAND MED CO, PHILA, 5¼", aqua..$4–5
HANDYSIDES CONSUMPTION CURE, 7¼", deep aqua........................$35–45
HARDYS ELIXIR PREPARED BY MCKINSTRY, HUDSON, NY, aqua...........$14–18
HASKINS NERVINE, BINGHAMTON, NY, 8¼", aqua...............................$3–5
HC FARRELLS ARABIAN LINIMENT, PEORIA, N-208, 4⅞", aqua, OP.....$65–80
HEALY & BIGELOW INDIAN SAGWA..$15–20
HEALY & BIGELOW KICKAPOO OIL..$12–15
HECEMAN & CO CHEMISTS NEW YORK, 10½", aqua $6–8
HENRY K WAMPOLE & CO, 4¾", colorless......................................$2–4
HENRY WAMPOLE & CO, PHILA, 8¼", colorless................................$2–3
HENRYS THREE CHLORIDES, 7¼", amber.......................................$3–4
HERB MED CO, WESTON, W VA, 9½", aqua......................................$6–8
HERBINE, ST LOUIS, 6¾", colorless, rectangular $3–4
HF CLARK PHARMACIST, CARBONDALE, 5", colorless $5–7
HHH MEDICINE, CELEBRATED, DDT 1869, aqua................................$6–9
HICKS CAPUDINE, amber, varying sizes..$3–6
HILLSIDE CHEM CO (ON BOTTOM), 7½", amber................................$2–3
HIMALAYA THE KOLA COMPOUND NATURES, 7¼", yellow amber.........$35–45
HIT, ELMIRA, NY, 5½", colorless, rectangular................................$2–3
HK MULFORD CO CHEMIST, PHILA, 5½", amber................................$3–4
HOBO MED CO, BEAUMONT, TEXAS, 8⅛", colorless, screw top...............$2–3
HOFFMANS ANODYNE, labeled, 5", colorless...................................$3–4
HOFFS GERMAN LINIMENT, 12 panels, 5¾", aqua.............................$5–8
HOLLAND DRUG CO, PRESCRIPTIONS A SPECIALTY, 4¾", colorless...........$3–4
HOLLAND HAARLEM OIL, 3½", colorless..$3–4
HOLLIS BALM OF AMERICA, 5", aqua..$5–8
HOLTONS ELECTRIC OIL, 3¼", colorless..$3–5
HOODS TOOTH POWDER, CI HOOD & CO, 3½", colorless $5–7
HOOFS LINIMENT, GOODRICH DRUG CO, 12 panels, 7", aqua, ABM........$3–5
HOP TONIC, 9¾", amber..$60–75
HOPES MAGNETIC OIL, 2⅞", aqua, OP...$75–90
HOUCKS PATENT PANACEA, 6½", aqua, OP $90–120
HOUSES INDIAN TONIC, 5⅜", deep blue aqua, OP $600–800
HOWARDS VEGETABLE CANCER & CANKER SYRUP, 7¼", yellow amber, OP .....
....$1100–1400
HOWLANDS COUGH REMEDY, N-312, 4⅞", aqua, OP....................$100–135
HOWLANDS READY REMEDY, N-312, 4⅞", aqua, OP $130–160
HOWS IMPROVED LINIMENT, 5⅝", aqua, OP $150–200
HUMPHREYS HOMEOPATHIC, 3½", colorless $4–6
HUMPHREYS MARVEL OF HEALING, 5½", colorless $4–6
HUMPHREYS MARVEL WITCHHAZEL, 5½", colorless, ABM....................$3–4
HUNTERS PUL. BALSAM OR COUGH SYRUP, N-319, 5⅞", aqua, OP $60–90
HUNTSA LINIMENT, N-317, 4¾", aqua, OP....................................$40–60
HURDS COUGH BALSAM, 4½, aqua, OP, 95% original label.................$70–90
HUSBANDS CALCINED MAGNESIA, 4¼", colorless...............................$3–4
HUSBANDS CALCINED MAGNESIA, PHILA, 4¼", aqua...........................$5–8
HUXLEY-GLYCERO PHOSPH CO SYRUP, 5¾", amber $3–5
HYATTS INFALLIBLE LIFE BALSAM, deep aqua $120–150
HYATTS INFALLIBLE LIFE BALSAM, NY, aqua................................$17–22
I COVERTS BALSAM OF LIFE, N-142, 5⅞", medium olive amber, OP $400–550
I NEWTONS PANACEA PURIFIER, 7⅜" × 3⁷⁄₁₆", olive amber, OP ...$1000–1500

IMPERIAL HAIR REGENERATOR, NEW YORK, 4½", light green $6–9
INDIAN VEGETABLE BALSAM PHILADA, 4⅜", aqua, OP $70–90
INDIANS PANACEA, 9", olive green, OP $2800–3500
IODINE, 2¼", amber..$1–2
J DENTONS HEALING BALSAM, N-174, 4¼", aqua, OP, eight-sided $75–100
J STARKWEATHERS HEPATIC ELIXIR, N-600, 6⅜", aqua, OP, six-sided . $60–90
JA RICHARDSON APOTHECARY, PHILA, 7", colorless $6–9
JACKSONS ANTIZYME OR FEVER CURE, 4¼", aqua $15–20
JACOBS CHOLERA & DYSENTARY CORDIAL, aqua, OP $80–90
JACOBS CHOLERA & DYSENTARY, N-327, 6⅞", aqua, OP, base crack... $75–110
JAMAICA GINGER, 5¾", colorless, label................................$3–4
JAMES S ROBINSON, MEMPHIS, TN, 7", colorless $3–5
JAYNES & CO, BOSTON, 9½", amber, screw top $2–3
JB WHEATLEYS COMPOUND SYRUP, 6¼", deep aqua, IP.......................$125
JC MAGUIRE CHEMISTS & DRUGGISTS, 7¾", cobalt $35–45
JD GALLUPS GOUT & RHEUMATIC, 4¾", aqua, OP $250–300
JELLY OF POMEGANATE BY DR GORDAK, 6¾", aqua, OP $75–90
JELLY OF POMEGANATE, N-256, 6¾", greenish aqua, OP $100–140
JENKS VEGETABLE EXTRACT, N-345, 4", aqua, OP $60–75
JEWETTS LINIMENT FOR HEAD ACHE, 2¼", aqua, OP $45–65
JEWETTS NERVE LINIMENT, 3", aqua, OP $45–65
JEWETTS STIMULATING LINIMENT, N-348, 2⅞", aqua, OP.................$45–65
JF HART & CO LIMITED TORONTO, 7⅞", cobalt blue $175–225
JGS R NICHOLS & CO, CHEMISTS, 9½", aqua, IP............................$50–60
JH FISHERS WILDFIRE RHEUMATIC LINIMENT, N-217, 5⅞", ice blue aqua, OP .
....$150–240
JJ HUNTS MODERN REMEDY, N-318, 6½", aqua, OP $125–175
JL CURTIS SYRUP OF SASSAFRAS, N-150, 4⅝", aqua, OP $75–100
JL LEAVITT BOSTON, CYLINDER, 8⅜", olive amber, IP $90–120
JNO T BARBEE & CO, 6", colorless..$4–5
JNO WYETH & BRO HYPOPHOSPHITES, 8¾", medium cobalt..............$40–47
JOE EVAN APOTHECARY, WESTCHESTER, PA, 5", colorless.....................$5–7
JOHN G BAKER CO COD LIVER OIL, 9", aqua, labeled and with contents........
....$110–140
JOHN J TUFTS APOTHECARY, PLYMOUTH, NH, 16¾", colorless $4–6
JOHN M WINSLOW ROCHESTER NY, N-693, 5⅞", aqua, OP $90–130

*Left, Medicine, Indian Sagwa. Right,
Medicine, Jacob's cordial.* PHOTOS
COURTESY OF NEIL GROSSMAN.

JOHN P LEE, 4½", colorless $3–4
JOHN WYETH & BRO, PAT MAY 16TH 1899, 6½", cobalt...................$12–18
JOHN WYETH & BRO, PAT MAY 16TH 1899, 3½", cobalt.................... $8–11
JOHN WYETH & BRO TAKE NEXT DOSE AT, WITH DOSE CAP, 5¾", cobalt,
ABM $8–12
JOHN WYETH & BRO TAKE NEXT DOSE AT, WITH DOSE CAP, 5¾", cobalt......
....$15–25
JOHN WYETH & BROTHER LIQUID MALT EXTRACT, 9", amber............. $8–10
JOHNSON & JOHNSON OIL (LABEL), 5", aqua......................................$4–5
JOHNSONS AMERICAN ANODYNE LINIMENT, 4½", aqua, OP............... $14–17
JOHNSONS AMERICAN ANODYNE LINIMENT, 4¼", aqua.......................$6–8
JOHNSONS CHILL & FEVER TONIC, aqua..$12–15
JR BURDSALLS ARNICA LINIMENT, N-92, 5⅜", aqua, OP.................$40–55
JR SPALDINGS ROSEMARY & CASTOR OIL, N-594, 4⅞", aqua, OP $40–50
JS FANCHER GRECIAN DROPS, 7½", aqua, OP $110–130
JW KELLY & CO, 6", colorless..$2–3
JW KELLY PATENT PORTABLE SODA WATER, 5⅛", aqua, OP $60–90
KA KONKA, THE GREAT INDIAN REMEDY...$12–14
KEASBEY & MATTISON CO CHEMISTS, AMBLER, PA, 5", light blue $5–6
KEASBEY & MATTISON PHILADELPHIA, 6", cobalt blue.......................$7–9
KEELEY REMEDY NEUROTENE, 5⅝", colorless....................................$5–7
KEMPS BALSAM, 2⅞", aqua, flask-shaped $7–10
KEMPS BALSAM FOR THROAT & LUNGS, 5¼", aqua $3–5
KEMPS BALSAM FOR THROAT & LUNGS, 5½", colorless $4–6
KEMPS BALSAM FOR THROAT & LUNGS, 8", light blue green $15–19
KEMPS BALSAM FOR THROAT & LUNGS, LEROY, NY, 5¾", aqua $6–8
KENDALLS SPAVIN CURE, 5½", amber $6–8
KENDALLS SPAVIN TREATMENT, 5¼", aqua..$3–5
KENEDYS FAVORITE REMEDY, labeled.. $14–17
KENNEDYS MEDICAL DISCOVERY, 6", colorless..................................$3–4
KEYSTONE DRUG CO, SO BOSTON, VA, 9", colorless $6–8
KICKAPOO SAGE HAIR TONIC, 4½", cobalt blue.............................. $80–120
KLINKERS HAIR TONIC, CLEVELAND, 6", colorless $7–10
KNAPPS EXTRACT OF ROOTS, NY, 5½", aqua $7–9
KOLA CARDINETTE, aqua..$12–15
KUTNOWS POWDER, 4¾", aqua..$4–5
L PIERRE VALIG, NY, LA, GOUTLE, 6", amber...................................$4–5
LA PAGES ANODYNE OIL BUFFALO NY, 4¼", aqua, OP $90–135
LACTOPEPTINE, 4", colorless...$3–4
LAINE CHEM CO, 6½", amber $3–4
LANGENBACHS DYSENTARY CURE, aqua, labeled..............................$20–25
LANGLEY & MICHAELS, SAN FRANCISCO, 6¼", aqua $4–6
LANGLEYS RED BOTTLE ELIXIR, N-370, 5", aqua, OP..................... $80–100
LANMAN & KEMP COD LIVER OIL, 10½", aqua..................................$6–9
LAUGHLINS & BUSHFIELD DRUGGISTS, 8⅞", aqua $90–120
LAXACURE, SOMETHING NEW UNDER THE SUN, with label and box...... $10–15
LE JUNG, 11", amber...$2–3
LEDIARDS MORNING CALL, 9¾", olive green $50–75
LEDIARDS MORNING CALL, 10", emerald green $300–450
LEGRANDS ARABIAN CATARRH REMEDY, NEW YORK, 9", aqua, oval $26–32
LEHMANS NERVE & BONE LINIMENT, 4½", aqua, OP $125–150

LENNON, 3″, aqua $4–5
LEONARDIS BLOOD ELIXIR, TAMPA, FLA, 8¼″, amber $15–20
LEONARDIS WORM SYRUP, 5″, aqua...$5–8
LEWIS & FLETCHERS NEW VEGETABLE COMPOUND, N-381, 7¾″, aqua, IP......
....$400–500
LIE BIG COS COCA BEEF TONIC, aqua $12–15
LIFE TRADE MARK PLANT, 8½″, amber $60–85
LIGHTNING HOT DROPS NO RELIEF NO PAY, 5″, aqua $7–9
LILLY SYRUP, J FISH ROCHESTER, 5⅝″, aqua, OP............................$25–50
LINDSEYS BLOOD SEARCHER, 8⅜″, aqua,................................... $60–80
LINIMENT OR OIL OF LIFE, 16 oz., 10½″, colorless $8–11
LIQUID FRANCONIA, OF WOODWARD, 4¼″, colorless............................$4–5
LIQUID OPODELDOC, 4½″, aqua $5–8
LIQUID OPODELDOC $6–8
LIQUID OZONE CO, 8″, amber...$5–7
LIQUIZONE, 8″, amber $3–4
LIQUOZONE, 5½″, amber...$5–7
LISTERINE, colorless, varying sizes...$3–4
LISTERINE, colorless, varying sizes, ABM...$1–2
LISTERINE, LAMBERT PHARMACAL CO, cylinder, 3″, colorless $2–3
LISTERINE, LAMBERT PHARMACAL CO, cylinder, 5½″, colorless.............$2–3
LISTERINE, LAMBERT PHARMACAL CO, cylinder, 6¾″, colorless.............$2–4
LITCHFIELDS DIPTHERIA VANQUISHER, aqua................................. $12–15
LITTLE GIANT SURE DEATH TO ALL BUGS, 8½″, aqua $7–10
LIVE & LET LIVE CUT RATE DRUG CO, 3½″, colorless $4–5
LM GREEN PROP., WOODBURY NJ, 5″, colorless $3–4
LM GREEN WOODBURY, NJ, 4¼″, colorless $3–4
LOCKYEERS SULPHUR HAIR RESTORER, 7½″, green aqua, oval............$25–35
LOG CABIN COUGH & CONSUMPTION REMEDY, amber $115–130
LOG CABIN EXTRACT, amber $120–150
LOG CABIN HOPS & BUCHC REMEDY, 10″, yellow amber................$180–220
LOG CABIN HOPS AND BUCHU REMEDY, 10″, amber......................$150–200
LONGLEYS PANACEA, 7⅜″, aqua, OP... $100/120
LONGS VEGETABLE PAIN CURE $10–12
LOPERS PANACEA PHILA, 8⅜″, aqua, OP.................................... $80–120
LORDS OPODELDOC, WITH MAN THROWING AWAY HIS CRUTCHES, 5″, aqua....
....$20–30

Medicine, liquid Opodeldoc, flaring lip. PHOTO COURTESY OF
NEIL GROSSMAN.

LOUDEN & COS CHEROKEE LINIMENT, N-396, 5⅜″, aqua, OP $160–190
LOUDEN & COS CURE FOR PILES, 6¾″, aqua, OP....................... $200–300
LOUDEN & COS INDIAN EXPECTORANT, N-399, 7½″, aqua, OP $80–120
LOUDEN & COS INDIAN EXPECTORANT, N-399, 7¼″, colorless, OP $50–70
LOUIS DAUDELIN CO, 8¾″, colorless..$3–4
LQC WISHARTS PINE TREE CORDIAL, 7½″, olive yellow, IP, lip bruise..........
.... $400–600
LUFKIN ECZEMA REMEDY, 7″, colorless, label $5–8
LUYTIES, 6½″, amber...$2–3
LYDIA PINKHAMS MEDICINE, 14½ oz., 8″ oval, aqua....................$4–6
LYDIA PINKHAMS MEDICINE, 14½ oz., 8″ oval, colorless....................$3–5
LYONS LAXATIVE SYRUP, 6¼″, colorless..$3–5
M'LEANS STRENGTHENING CORDIAL, 9″, deep aqua, IP $50–70
MACARTHURS GENUINE YANKEE LINIMENT, N-410, 7¼″, aqua, OP .$350–450
MACASSAR OIL, RECTANGULAR, 3½″, aqua, OP $9–12
MAGNETIC AETHER BY HALSTED & CO, N-273, 4¼″, aqua, OP, nine-sided....
....$60–75
MAIN LINE DRUG STORE, 5¼″, colorless $5–7
MALAKOFF LINDENTHAL BROS NY, triangular, 10″, amber, labeled . $250–300
MARIA H MELLEN COUGH SYRUP, 5½″, aqua, OP $300–375
MARTHA WASHINGTON HAIR RESTORER (ON LABEL), 7″, colorless, full label
and contents $125–150
MB ROBERTS VEGETABLE EMBROCATION, blue green, OP................. $80–100
MB ROBERTS VEGETABLE EMBROCATION, N-524, 5½″, emerald green, OP......
....$100–160
MB ROBERTS VEGETABLE EMBROCATION, N-524-A, 5⅛″, light blue green, OP
....$40–55
MB ROBERTS VEGETABLE EMBROCATION, N-524-B, 5½″, medium emerald green,
OP..$150–200
MCDONALDS ANNIHILATOR, 7⅝″, aqua, OP................................$125–160
MCKESSON & ROBBINS, NY (ON BASE), cylinder, 6¼″, amber..............$4–6
MCNEAL & LIBBY, CHICAGO, square, milk glass $30–40
MD FLINTS WILD CHERRY COMPOUND, eight-sided, 10⅛″, yellow amber.......
....$180–225
MEAD & CARRINGTONS FEVER & AGUE CURE, 6½″, aqua, OP....... $225–300
MEDICO MALT, SYRACUSE, NY, 7¾″, amber....................................$6–7
MENDENHALLS COUGH REMEDY, 4⅜″, aqua, OP $75–100
MES E KIDDER DYSENTARY CORDIAL, aqua, OP............................$60–75
MEXICAN MUSTANG LINIMENT, 7⅜″, deep aqua, IP.....................$125–175
MEXICAN MUSTANG LINIMENT, LYON MFG CO, 7¾″, aqua $7–10
MEYER DILLON DRUG CO, OMAHA, 3¾″, colorless $4–6
MILLARD HOTEL MERRITTS PHARMACY, 6¾″, colorless....................$7–9
MINIARDS LINIMENT, 5⅛″, colorless...$5–6
MITCHELLS EYE SALVE, cobalt blue..$6–8
MITCHELLS EYE SALVE, square, 1⅞″, aqua, OP...............................$50–70
MIXERS CANCER & SCROFULA SYRUP, aqua....................................$14–18
MM FENNER MD, ESTABLISHED 1872, 5¾″, aqua.............................$3–5
MOORES REVEALED REMEDY, 8¾″, amber.....................................$7–10
MOORES REVEALED REMEDY, 9″, amber $40–50
MORLEY BROS (ON LABEL), 7″, aqua $4–5
MORSES CELEBRATED SYRUP, 9½″, medium green, OP................. $400–500

MORTON & CO, 5½″, colorless $4–5
MOSES HOTCHKISS SPECIFIC FOR INFLAMMATION, 2½″, aqua................$2–4
MOSES INDIAN ROOT PILLS, 2½″, amber.. $9–12
MOTHERS FRIEND, 7″, aqua..$4–6
MOTHERS RELIEF, 8″, aqua, OP $125–175
MOXIE NERVE FOOD, 10½″, aqua...$3–5
MOXIE NERVE FOOD, 10″, green $7–10
MOYER BROS WHOLESALE DRUGGISTS, 8¾″, colorless $3–4
MOYERS OIL OF GLADNESS, 5⅝″, aqua...$6–8
MRS DINMORES COUGH & CROUP BALSAM, 6″, aqua............................$7–9
MRS E KIDDERS DYSENTARY CORDIAL, 6½″, aqua, OP.....................$75–85
MRS KIDDER DYSENTARY CORDIAL, 7½″, light olive amber, OP, 3″ crack......
....$150–190
MRS WINSLOWS SOOTHING SYRUP, 5¼″, aqua, OP........................... $14–18
MRS WINSLOWS SOOTHING SYRUP, cylinder, 5″, aqua, OP, light inner stain ....
....$5–6
MUNYONS GERMICIDE SOLUTION, 3¼″, green..................................$4–5
MUNYONS HOMEOPATHIC, 3¼″, colorless...$1–2
MURINE EYE REMEDY, CHICAGO, USA, 3½″, colorless $1–2
MURINE FOR YOUR EYES, cylinder, 4⅛″, colorless, ground top $3–5
MURPHY BROS, 4⅞″, aqua..$4–5
NANKINS SPECIFIC, BORDENTOWN, NY, 6½″, aqua $9–12
NATHAN JARVIS ORRIS TOOTH WASH, N-332, 4⅞″, aqua, OP $160–190
NATIONAL REMEDY CO, 5½″, aqua $2–3
NELLIS RHEUMATIC CURE JP NELLIS, 8¾″, amber........................ $200–300
NELSONS CHILL CURE, NATCHEZ, MI, 6″, colorless...........................$15–22
NERVE & BONE LINIMENT, 4¼″, aqua $4–7
NK BROWNS AROMATIC ESSENCE, 4½″, aqua.....................................$5–8
NYALS EMULSION OF COD LIVER OIL, 9″, amber................................$5–7
NYALS LINIMENT, amber $4–5
OAKLAND CHEMICAL CO, 4¾″, amber...$3–5
OAKLAND CHEMICAL CO, 5¼″, amber...$3–4
OD CHEMICAL CO, NY, 6¼″, amber $4–6
OLDRIDGE BALM OF COLUMBIA FOR RESTORING HAIR, 6¼″, aqua.......$40–55
OLDRIDGES BALM OF COLUMBIA, 5¼″, aqua, OP $40–55
OMEGA CHEMICAL CO, with embossed tree, 5¾″, colorless $3–5
OMEGA OIL ITS GREEN, 4½″, light green $12–15
OMEGA OIL ITS GREEN, 6″, colorless, ABM, screw top.......................$5–7
OMEGA OIL ITS GREEN, 6″, colorless $5–7
OMEGA OIL ITS GREEN, 4½″, colorless $5–7
OO WOODMAN NEW ORLEANS, 5⅛″, aqua, OP $150–225
OPODELDOC LIQUID, cylinder, 4½″, aqua, OP, two lip chips $4–6
ORIGINAL DR CRAIGS KIDNEY CURE, 9½″, amber....................... $200–300
ORIGINAL KIDNEY & LIVER CURE, 9¾″, medium amber............... $300–500
OSGOOD INDIA CHOLAGOUE NEW YORK, aqua, OP............................$30–40
OTIS CLAPP & SONS MALT & COD LIVER OIL COMPOUND, 7¼″, amber...$5–8
OWL DRUG CO, jar with owl on mortar, 3¼″ diam. $60–80
OWL DRUG CO, with owl on mortar, rectangle, 4⅛″, milk glass.........$35–45
OWL DRUG CO, owl on mortar, 5″, milk glass................................$40–50
OWL DRUG CO, owl on mortar, 6¼″, cobalt blue $70–90
OWL DRUG CO, square, 8½″, amber...$45–55

OWL DRUG CO SAN FRANCISCO, owl on mortar, 9⅝″, bright green $55–70
OXIEN PILLS, THE GIANT OXIEN, 2″, colorless $3–4
OZOMULSION, 8¾″, amber $5–8
PAIN EXPELLER, FA RICHTER & CO, NEW YORK, 5″, aqua, rectangular ...$6–9
PAINES CELERY COMPOUND, labeled $10–12
PAINES CELERY COMPOUND, amber $5–6
PAINES CELERY COMPOUND, 10″, aqua $7–9
PAINES CELERY COMPOUND, square, 9½″, amber $8–10
PAINES VEGETABLE PAIN CURER, 5⅜″, aqua, OP $80–120
PALACE DRUG STORE, 4½″, colorless $4–6
PALACE DRUG STORE, 6″, colorless $4–6
PALMETTO PHARMACY, CHARLESTON, SC, aqua $4–6
PALMOLIVE SHAMPOO, BJ JOHNSON, 7¼″, colorless, ABM, rectangular ...$4–6
PALMOLIVE SHAMPOO, BJ JOHNSON, ten panels, 4″, aqua, ABM $5–7
PANOPEPTON, 7¾″, amber $3–5
PARDEES RHEUMATIC REMEDY, labeled, 8½″, aqua $8–12
PARKE DAVIS & CO (ON LABEL), 3½″, black $5–6
PARKE DAVIS & CO (ON LABEL), 5½″, amber $3–4
PARKERS GINGER TONIC, aqua $8–10
PARKERS HAIR BALSAM, NEW YORK, 6½″, amber, rectangular $6–9
PARKS KIDNEY & LIVER CURE, 9⅜″, aqua $100–150
PARTENOPEA CHEMICAL HOUSE, ALLENTOWN, PA, citron $20–30
PARVINS TONIC MIXTURE CINCINNATI, 6″, aqua, OP.....................$125–160
PAWNEE INDIAN TA-HA, PRICE 25 C, 8½″, aqua $20–27
PB WAIT & CO STANLEYS CELERY MALT, 8¼″, yellow amber $75–100
PD & CO (ON BASE), 3¼″, amber $2–3
PEASES EYE WATER, NEWMAN, GA, 4¼″, aqua.................................$4–5
PEOPLES CURE-NOT A PATENT MEDICINE, 7⅞″, deep aqua $125–175
PEOPLES MAGNETIC LINIMENT, 6½″, aqua, OP $80–130
PEPTENZYME, 2½″, cobalt blue $10–13
PEPTO MANGAN, six panels, 7″, aqua...$3–5
PEPTO MANGAN GUDE, six panels, 7″, aqua $5–8
PEPTONOIDS THE ARLINGTON CHEMIST, YONKERS, NY, 6″, amber $5–6
PERRINES APPLE GINGER, 10″, golden amber...................................$70–90
PERRINES GINGER DEPOT No 37, 10″, medium amber...................$100–150
PERRYS HUNGARIAN BALM FOR THE HAIR, 5¾″, aqua, OP, rectangular ....
....$35–50
PERUVIAN SYRUP, 9⅜″, aqua, OP..$50–65
PETER MOLLERS PURE COD LIVER OIL, labeled, 5¾″, colorless.............$2–3
PETER MOLLERS PURE COD LIVER OIL, labeled, 5¾″, colorless.............$3–5
PETETS AMERICAN COUGH CURE, 7″, aqua $6–9
PETETS AMERICAN COUGH CURE, 7″, aqua $6–9
PHELPS ARCANUM WORCESTER MASS, 8¾″, olive amber, OP $600–800
PHELPS ARCANUM WORCESTER MASS, 8¾″, olive green, OP $750–950
PHELPS ARCANUM WORCHESTER MASS, N-493, 8½″, olive amber, OP, polished base chip $500–650
PHILLIPS MILK OF MAGNESIA, 6¾″, blue..$3–4
PISO COMPANY, 5″, emerald green..$5–7
PISO COMPANY, 5½″, colorless $4–5
PISOS CURE FOR CONSUMPTION, 5″, aqua.......................................$4–5
PISOS HAZELTINE & CO, WARREN, PA, 6″, amber...............................$3–4

PL Abbey Co, 8¾", colorless..$8–12
Pohls Drug Store, Tremont, Neb, 6¼", colorless $7–8
Polar Star Cough Cure, 5½", aqua...$5–7
Ponds Extract Catarrh Remedy, 5½", cobalt $140–175
Ponds Extract, 5½", aqua $4–6
Porters Cure Of Pain, Bundysburg, O', 5¼", aqua, OP............ $135–165
Porters Pain King, 6½", colorless $4–6
Potters Catholicon Phila, 7½", aqua, OP.............................$250–350
Potters Liniment External Remedy, N-502, 5½", aqua, OP $125–175
Powells American Liniment, 3¾", aqua, OP $50–70
Prepared By HH Reynolds Batavia, 5¼", olive green, OP.........$800–1100
Prepared By Willaim Coe, Worcester, Mass, 7¼", olive amber, OP........
.... $600–800
Prestons Ver Purifying Catholic, N-504, 9⅝", aqua, OP $35–45
Primleys Iron & Wahoo Tonic, 9½", dark amber $50–60
Prof JR Tilton Great Hair Producer, 6⅞", medium sapphire blue ....
.... $100–120
Prof WH Peeks Remedy, amber...$12–15
Prof WH Peeks Remedy, NY, 8", amber...................................... $7–10
Pure Extract Of Marl With Firwem (On Label), 7½", colorless ..$20–30
Pure Family Nectar, 8⅞", colorless, OP $60–90
Pure & Genuine Four Fold Liniment, 5¼", colorless....................$4–5
Pynchon, Boston, aqua, OP...$12–15
Querus Cod Liver Oil Jelly, 5½", aqua, OP, wide mouth $80–120
Races Indian Blood Renovator, aqua $25–35
Radway & Cos-Circassian Balm, 4¾", aqua, OP $45–65
Ramons Quality Medicine, jar form, 7½", colorless................... $80–120
Ramsons Nerve & Bone Oil, Brown Mfg., 5¾", aqua, rectangle $9–10
Ransom & Stephens Dandelion Panacea, N-512, 8¾", aqua, OP . $140–180
Ransoms Hive Syrup & Tolu, Buffalo, NY, 4½", aqua, square $6–9
Rawleigh, 6¼", colorless, ABM $1–2
Rawleigh, 6", amber, ABM $1–2
RC & A- New York (On Shoulder), 8½", cobalt blue............... $200–300
RE Stieraux Pills, 1¾", colorless..$4–5
RE Woodwards Vegetable Tincture, N-704, 5⅞", aqua, OP $125–150
Reakirts Medicated Breast Julap, 5⅛", aqua, OP.................... $125–165
Rectangular, unembossed, with beveled edges, 7¼", olive green . $200–250
Red Balsam, Taunton, Mass, 12-sided, 4¼", colorless, screw top $2–3
Red Cross Family Liniment, 5½", colorless $2–3
Red Heart Mfg & Med Co, Camden, NJ, 8", colorless....................$3–5
Reed & Carnrick, NY, 4¾", amber...$4–6
Reed & Carnrick Peptenzyme, 4½", cobalt blue.........................$8–12
Reed & Carnrick Pharmacists, New York, 7½", amber $5–8
Reed, Carnrick & Andrus Chemists, 8⅞", cobalt $225–275
Reed, Cutler & Co Vegetable Pulmonary Balsam, 7⅛", aqua, OP ....
....$70–90
Rees Remedy For Piles, 7⅛", aqua, OP $200–260
Renes Magic Oil, labeled $13–16
Resinal Balto MD Chemical Co, 3¼", milk glass..........................$3–4
Restorff & Bettman, six panels, 4¼", aqua $3–5
Rev Gates Magamoose, Philada, aqua $8–11

Rev W Clarks European Cough Remedy, N-124, 7⅝″, aqua, OP.$150–200
Rheumatic Syrup 1882 RS Co, 9¾″, amber $75–95
Rhodes Fever & Ague Cure, 8⅜″, deep aqua, OP $80–120
Rhodes Fever & Ague Cure, N-516, 8¼″, aqua, OP, labeled $80–110
Riccardi Ideal Tonic Blood Purifier, amber.............................. $8–12
Richards Lees Patent And Family Medicines, 5⅛″, aqua, OP....$200–275
Ridakoff Cures Coughs, 5″, aqua...$30–40
Ridgeways Acme Liniment, 7½″, amber $10–15
Risley & Co NY Orange Tonica, 10½″, amber $175–225
Risleys Extract Buchu New York, 7¼″, aqua, OP......................$50–75
River Swamp Chill & Fever Cure, Augusta, GA, 6¼″, golden amber ......
....$450–650
RN Searles Athlophoros, 6¾″, aqua, rectangular $6–9
Robert Gibson & Son Lozenge Makers, 13″, colorless................$25–40
Robinsons American Horse Liniment, 6″, aqua, OP $100–125
Robt E Sellers Vermifuge, cylinder, 4⅜″, aqua, OP...................... $13
Rodericks Wild Cherry Balsam, 3¼″, colorless........................... $8–12
Roderics Wild Cherry Cough Balsam, 5½″, amber, ABM...............$3–5
Roderics Wild Cherry Cough Balsam, 5½″, colorless, ABM............$3–5
Roessmer Pharmacy, Phila, 5½″, colorless $5–7
Rohrers Expectoral Wild Cherry Tonic, with full label, 10½″, amber, IP
.... $350–400
Rohrers Wild Cherry Tonic Expectoral, 10½″, golden amber, IP...........
.... $125–165
Rohrers Wild Cherry Tonic Expectoral, 10½″, bright yellow with olive
tint... $350–400
Root Juice Med Co, 9″, aqua...$3–5
Root Juice Med. Co, Fort Wayne, 8¼″, colorless $3–5
Royal Foot Wash, Eaton Drug Co, Atlanta, GA,...................... $8–12
Royal Gall Remedy, 7½″, dark amber, ABM $4–6
Royces Universal Relief, Wales, Mass, aqua, OP $80–90
RRR Radway & Co, 6⅜″, aqua, rectangular $5–7
RRR Radway & Co, NY, rectangle, 6¼″, aqua............................$5–8
Rubifoam For The Teeth, 4″, colorless.....................................$4–6
Rubifoam For The Teeth, Put Up By EW Hoyt & Co, 4″, colorless...$6–9
Rushs Buchu And Iron, aqua $12–15
Rushs Remedy, AHF Monthly, 6″, aqua $9–12
Rustins Oil For Rheumatism, 5″, aqua, OP $60–75
RV Pierce, MD, Prescribed By, 7″, aqua...................................$3–5
S & D 100, 2½″, colorless..$2–3
Salvation Oil, AC Meyer & Co, Baltimore, MD, 2¼″, aqua $5–6
Salvation Oil, AC Meyer & Co, Trade Mark, 6¾″, aqua $6–8
Sammys Medicine Reaches Through The Entire System, 7″, light blue ....
.... $10–15
San Cura Ointment, 2½″, colorless $2–3
Sandersons Blood Renovator, 8½″, aqua, OP $350–450
Sanfords Extract Of Hamamelis, 9⅜″, cobalt blue $90–120
Sanfords Radical Cure, 7⅝″, cobalt blue, lip flake......................$25–35
Sanfords Radical Cure, 7½″, cobalt blue..................................$30–40
Sanitol For The Teeth, 4″, milk glass $7–10
Sanitol For The Teeth, 4½″, colorless.......................................$6–8

SARGENT & CO AMERICAN CANCHALOG., N-546, 7½", aqua, OP, labeled......
....$175–240
SASSAFRAS EYE LOTION, MAUGH CHUNK, PA, 6", cobalt blue, with eye cup...
....$20–30
SAVE THE BABY, labeled...$10–12
SAVE THE HORSE REMEDY, labeled $13–16
SC DISPENSARY, WITH PALM TREE, aqua....................................$20–30
SC WELLS & CO, LEROY, NY, 5¼", aqua $1–2
SCHNECKS PULMONIC SYRUP, PHILA, 5¾", aqua..............................$6–7
SCHENCKS SEAWEED TONIC, aqua...$24–28
SCHMIDT PHARMACIST, OMAHA 7¼", colorless...............................$5–6
SCOTT & STEWART UNITED STATES SYRUP, N-557, 9¼", aqua, OP .. $350–400
SCOTTS EMULSION COD LIVER OIL, 9", aqua $1–2
SCOTTS EMULSION COD LIVER OIL, LIME & SODA, 7½", aqua...............$2–3
SCOTTS EMULSION, COD LIVER OIL, WITH LIME SODA, aqua, various sizes......
....$4–7
SHAKER BRAND ED PETTENGILL & CO, 5¼", yellow..................$400–500
SHAKER CHERRY PECTORAL SYRUP, N-569, 5½", aqua, OP $225–275
SHAKER SYRUP D MILLER & CO, 7³⁄₁₆", aqua, OP $400–450
SHECUTS SOUTHERN BALM FOR COUGHS, N-574, 6", aqua, OP $125–175
SHILOHS CURE, CONSUMPTION CURE, 5½", aqua $8–11
SHORT STOP FOR COUGHS, HM O'NEIL, NY, 4", aqua, square...........$4–6
SILVER PINE HEALING OIL, 8⅛", aqua $15–19
SILVER PINE HEALING OIL, MINN., 6", colorless.......................$10–12
SIMMONS LIVER REGULATOR, 7", aqua.....................................$15–18
SIMMONS LIVER REGULATOR, 9", aqua.....................................$8–12
SIROP DELACOPHOSPHATE DE CHAUX, 7", aqua..............................$5–6
SKERRETTS OIL B WHEELER, N-586, 9", rich emerald green, OP ... $800–1200
SKERRETTS OIL B WHEELER, N-586, 6¼", emerald green, OP $400–500
SL GREEN DRUGGIST CAMDEN ARK, 3", amber...............................$3–4
SLOANS LINIMENT KILLS PAIN, 5", light blue $5–6
SLOANS LINIMENT, 7", colorless $3–4
SLOANS LINIMENT, #17 (ON BASE), 4¾", colorless.......................$1–2
SLOANS LINIMENT, DR ES SLOAN, 5", colorless $5–8
SLOCOMS COLTS FOOT EXPECTORANT, 3", colorless.........................$2–4
SLOCUMS COLTSFOOT EXPECTORANT, 2¼", aqua..............................$5–8
SM KIER PETROLEUM PITTSBURGH, 6½", aqua, OP...........................$25–30
SMITHS ANODYNE COUGH DROPS, N-588, 5⅞", aqua, OP................ $60–90
SMITHS CURATIVE CLEANSING COMPOUND, 4⅞", aqua, OP, label $400–450
SMITHS GREEN MOUNTAIN RENOVATOR, 7", honey amber, IP .. $500–650
SMITHS GREEN MOUNTAIN RENOVATOR, 7¾", aqua, smooth base, oval shape ..
....$60–85
SMITHS GREEN MOUNTAIN RENOVATOR, 7", olive amber, OP $600–800
SO DUNBAR, TAUNTON, MA, 6", aqua......................................$4–6
SOLOMONS BROS, BRANCH DRUG STORES, BULL ST, 7", aqua $4–6
SOZONDONT, 2½", colorless $3–4
SPARKLENE, 5", amber..$3–5
SPARKS PERFECT HEALTH FOR KIDNEY & LIVER DISEASES, 4", aqua........$7–9
SPARKS PERFECT HEALTH FOR KIDNEY & LIVER, 9⅜", yellow amber $100–135
SPERRYS RHEUMATIC & NERVE LINIMENT, 4⅝", aqua, OP $60–90
SPITH SAN FRANCISCO PHARMACY, 5¼", aqua...............................$6–9

SPOHNS DISTEMPER CURE, 5″, colorless...$7–9
ST JAKOBS OIL, BALTIMORE, MD, 6¼″, aqua $5–6
STEELMAN & ARCHER, PHILA, 6½″, aqua $1–2
STEELMAN & ARCHER, PHILA, PA, 5½″, colorless.........................$2–3
STEIN & CO APOTHECARIER, JERSEY CITY, 5⅜″, colorless...................$4–5
STEPHEN SWEETS INFALLABLE LINI., N-620, 5⅛″, aqua, OP $40–50
STEPHENS CELEBRATED TURKISH KALI, 5″, deep aqua, OP............ $200–250
STEWART D HOWES ARABIAN TONIC, aqua $15–22
SULTAN DRUG CO, ST LOUIS & LONDON, 7¼″, amber $5–6
SW BRISTOLS NERVE & BONE LINIMENT, 5⅛″, aqua, OP $150–200
SWAIMS PANACEA, 8″, olive green..$75–85
SWAIMS PANACEA GENUINE PHILA., N-610, 7¾″, aqua, OP $250–350
SWAIMS PANACEA PHILADA, N-612, 7⅞″, olive green, OP $175–225
SWAIMS PANACEA, PHILADA, aqua $30–35
SWAIMS VERMIFUGE DYSENTARY CHOL., aqua, OP $35–45
SWAMP CHILL & FEVER TONIC, colorless......................................$6–8
SWAYNES BOWEL CORDIAL, N-616, 5⅛″, aqua, OP $60–80
SWEETS BLACK OIL ROCHESTER NY, 6⅛″, emerald green, OP $700–1000
SWEETS BLK OIL ROCHESTER NY, 6⅛″, medium blue green, OP $600–900
SWIFTS SYPHILITIC SPECIFIC, 8⅞″, cobalt blue.......................... $300–400
SYRUP OF HYPOPHOSPHITES, 7¼″, aqua $2–4
TARRANT & CO, 5¼″, colorless $3–5
TAYLORS CELEBRATED OIL, 6⅛″, aqua...$5–8
TAYLORS DRUG STORE, 4″, colorless..$4–6
TAYLORS INDIAN OINTMENT, six-sided, 3″, aqua, OP................ $180–220
TAYLORS OPOCURA, 3″, aqua, OP.. $60–90
TAYLORS OPOCURA, 3″, aqua, OP.. $60–90
TB SMITH KIDNEY TONIC, CYNTHIANA, KY, 10½″, aqua.................. $10–15
TE JENKINS & CO PAROQUET WATER, 8½″, deep yellow green, IP...............
....$1300–1600
TEABERRY FOR THE TEETH & BREATH, 3½″, colorless $6–9
TELLSSIER PREVOST A PARIS, 7¼″, deep emerald green $40–50
TELSSIER PREVOST A PARIS, 7⅛″, colorless, OP $12–15
THE CRAIG KIDNEY CURE COMPANY, 9½″, amber..........................$110–140
THOMAS ELECTRIC OIL, 4¼″, colorless $4–6
THOMAS ELECTRIC OIL, 4¼″, colorless $6–9
THOMPSONS DANDELION & CELERY TONIC, 9¾″, amber....................$15–20
THOMPSONS DRUG STORE, THE MARKET, 5⅝″, colorless.....................$4–6
THOMPSONS HERBAL COMPOUND, 6¾″, aqua, labeled $7–9
THORNS COMPOUND SYRUP OF COD LIVER OIL, 7¼″, aqua, OP, eight-sided ...
.... $300–400
THORNS HOP & BURDOCK TONIC, 6⅜″, yellow...............................$30–45
TILDEN, 7½″, amber $3–4
TILDEN & CO, NEW LEBANON, NY, 6¾″, olive amber, IP.............$375–450
TILDEN & CO, square, 7″, amber... $60–80
TOMS RUSSIAN LINIMENT, N-657, 5⅛″, aqua, OP.........................$160–190
TONSILENE FOR SORE THROAT, 5½″, colorless $3–4
TRUE DAFFYS ELIXIR, 3¾″, light yellow green, OP $200–240
TRUE DAFFYS ELIXIR, 4⅞″, light yellow green, OP $275–375
TUCKER PHARMACAL, BROOKLAND, NY, 5″, colorless $2–3
TURF OIL DOVE & CO, N-646, 5⅛″, aqua, OP, three-sided........... $200–300

Turf Oil Dove & Co Richmond, VA, N-646, 4½", aqua, OP $125–175
Turkish Liniment, 4¾", aqua...$4–6
Turners Balsam, N-647, 4⅞", aqua, OP, eight-sided....................$50–70
Tuttles Elixir Co, Boston Mass, 12-sided, 6¼", colorless $6–7
TW Steellings Rheumatic Liniment, N-604, 5⅛", aqua, OP.........$70–85
University Free Medicine, N-650 var., 4¾", aqua, OP, labeled ... $125–175
US Marine Hospital Service, 5½", colorless................................ $9–12
USA Hosp Dept, 7¼", medium blue $150–200
USA Hosp Dept, 7½", aqua, 2⅛" mouth opening $60–75
USA Hosp Dept, 7", medium olive green, with stopper $500–750
USA Hosp Dept, 9½", clear yellow $400–600
USA Hosp Dept, 9⅜", yellow amber.. $90–120
USA Hosp Dept, 7½", colorless, lip chip $50–75
USA Hosp Dept, 7½", aqua...$100–150
USA Hosp Dept, 7½", aqua, wide mouth $100–150
USA Hosp Dept, 9¼", medium olive green...............................$150–250
USA Hosp Dept, 9⅛", aqua, qt...$200–275
USA Hosp Dept, 9¼", medium olive amber $250–325
USA Hosp Dept, 9⅝", yellow olive $200–275
USA Hosp Dept, 9¼", medium apricot yellow $200–250
USA Hosp Dept, 9", deep blue... $800–1200
USA Hosp Dept, 9¼", medium lemon yellow $750–950
USA Hosp Dept, 7½", colorless...$110–135
USA Hosp Dept, with period after A and T, 9⅜", emerald green.. $800–1200
USA Hosp Dept, SDS (On Base), 9½", apricot yellow $300–500
USA Hosp Dept, SDS (On Base), 9¼", deep red puce.................$500–750
USA Hosp Dept, SDS (On Base), 9¼", medium apricot yellow..... $400–525
V Roussin, Druggist, Muskegon, MI, 7¼", colorless $4–6
Valentine Hassmers Lung & Cough Syrup, 11¾", amber $125–150
Vaughns Vegetable Lithontriptic Mixture, 8", aqua, OP $120–140
Vaughns Vegetable Lithontriptic Mixture, 6⅛", medium emerald green
....$225–275
Vaughns Vegetable Lithontriptic Mixture, 6", aqua $90–125
Vaughns Vegetable Lithontriptic Mixture, 8", deep blue aqua $200–300
Vaughns Vegetable Lithontriptic Mixture, Buffalo, 8⅛", deep aqua, IP
....$180–240
Vaughns Vegetable Lithontriptic Mixture, 6¼", aqua, OP, bruise ....
....$80–120
Vegetable & Hemlock Oil Medical Co, 5", colorless $3–4
Vegetable Pulmonary Balsam, aqua...$5–8
Vermont Liniment, N-657, 5⅛", aqua, OP................................$160–190
Vernal Palemttona/Vernal Remedy Co, 9", aqua, square.............$12–15
W & H Walker, Chemists, 5¾", colorless...................................$2–3
Wards Liniment, aqua.. $8–11
Warners Safe Cure (Around Neck), 9½", amber.......................$110–140
Warners Safe Cure, London, 7¼", golden amber $70–100
Warners Safe Cure, London, Toronto, oval, 11", amber $200–250
Warners Safe Cure London, Toronto, Rochester, 11", amber ..$275–350
Warners Safe Diabetes Cure, Melbourne, 9½", amber............$100–120
Warners Safe Remedies Co, amber, labeled, ABM $90–110
Warranted Pure Cod Liver Oil, 10⅜", aqua, OP $70–90

WAYNES DIURETIC ELIXIR, FE SUIRE & CO, 8″, amber $10–15
WB SLOAN INSTANT RELIEF CHICAGO, 4¾″, aqua, OP................. $200–300
WC SWEET HCR&L ROCHESTER NY, 6″, aqua, OP $15–25
WE BROWN, DRUGGIST, MANCHESTER, IA, colorless...........................$4–5
WE HAGAN & CO TROY NY, eight-sided, 6¾″, cobalt blue...............$50–75
WEBS CATHARTIC A NO. 1 TONIC, 9½″, amber..............................$50–65
WEES'S CRINALGIA NEW YORK, 6″, aqua, OP $120–150
WEISS PHARMACY, PHILA, 6½″, colorless, embossed eagle $8–12
WELLINGS COMPOUND ARNICA LINI., N-677, 5½″, aqua, OP $90–120
WESTLAKES VEGETABLE OINTMENT, 3″, aqua...................................$3–4
WESTLAKES VEGETABLE OINTMENT, 2⅞″, light cornflower blue, OP $50–65
WH BONE CO CC LINIMENT, 6½″, aqua $4–6
WH BULL MEDICINE CO, 9½″, amber..$4–6
WH BULLS MEDICINE BOTTLE, patent date on base, 5¼″, colorless $3–5
WH HARRIS HAIR RESTORATIVE, 7¼″, aqua $60–90
WILFORD HALL LABORATORIES, PORT CHESTER, NY, ½ pt., amber...... $12–15
WINANS BROTHERS INDIAN CURE & BLOOD PURIFIER, 9¼″, aqua, labeled in
box $325–400
WINANTS INDIAN LINIMENT, N-690, 5″, aqua, OP.......................$125–150
WINSTANDLY & NEWKIRKS MAGIC LINIMENT, 3⅞″, aqua, OP $35–45
WINSTANDLY & NEWKIRKS MAGIC LIN., 3⅞″, aqua, OP..................$90–110
WISHARTS PINE TREE CORDIAL, 9¾″, colorless $50–75
WM JAY BARKER, HIRSUTUS, NEW YORK, 5¼″, aqua, ABM, pewter stopper ...
....$5–7
WM JAY BARKER, HIRSUTUS, NEW YORK, 6⅝″, colorless, ABM, pewter
stopper...$5–7
WM R WARNER & CO, PHILA, 4″, cobalt $4–6
WOODWARD CHEMIST-NOTTINGHAM, 6″, light blue...........................$4–6
WR WATSON CH TOWN, PEI, 7″, aqua, OP $80–120
WRIGHTS INSTANT RELIEF, 5″, colorless.....................................$6–8

MILK BOTTLES

Milk bottles comprise an area of collecting which has grown dramatically
in recent years. Milk bottles were originally made in the United States
starting in the 1870s, but most of the collectible bottles found are from
the 1920–1950 period. Up until about 1920, many of the milk bottles
had tin-cap-type closures. Around this time, bottles with crown-type tops
and those with paper caps became more and more popular. Up until the
1920s, most of the bottles used had embossed names on them. Around
this time, pyroglazed bottles became popular. Pyroglazed bottles had
paint or enamel-like decorations and writing on them, in various colors
and scripts. The earliest milk bottles were generally cylindrical in form,

with square milk bottles not coming into common usage until the 1930s. Throughout the history of the milk bottle, the vast majority of the bottles were of colorless glass; however, at least 20 dairies used a green milk bottle and amber milk bottles were even more common. Also, in 1950, Anchor Hocking Glass Company manufactured an experimental ruby red milk bottle for Borden's. These bottles were never used and are extremely rare.

Two of the more collectible types of milk bottles are baby-face-type bottles and Cop-the-Cream-type bottles. The baby-face bottles had an embossed baby's face on the upper part of the neck, and are available in both cylindrical and square shapes. The Cop-the-Cream bottles, which enjoyed great popularity in the late 1930s and 1940s, have a policeman's head and cap embossed into the neck of the bottle. Both these types of bottles, along with the early tin tops, are quite rare and command rising prices.

When collecting milk bottles, watch for unusual pyroglaze designs and colors. On embossed milk bottles, be watchful for embossed standing animals or any unusual embossed figure. Since milk bottles were meant to be used over and over, often the bottles are found with considerable wear—called case wear—which resulted from the bottles being transported about in wooden and metal cases. Watch for case wear when determining values on milk bottles. It is recommended that collectors purchase *Udderly Delightful* by John Tutton.

BABY-FACE MILK BOTTLES

BEECH GROVE DAIRY, UTICA, NY, qt., pyroglazed............................$48–60
BEECH GROVE DAIRY, UTICA, NY, square, qt., pyroglazed.................$34–39
BLAIS FOR MOTHERS WHO CARE, with orange pyro, qt., round, with baby drinking milk $65–85
BROOKFIELD, qt., embossed $35–48
BROOKFIELD, ½ pt., embossed only, no pyro. $30–40
BROOKFIELD BABY TOP (AROUND SHOULDER), square, qt., double baby face ....
....$30–45
BROOKFIELD DAIRY HELLERTOWN, PA, embossed, round, ½ pt. $20–27
BROOKFIELD DAIRY, HELLERTOWN, PA, square, qt., pyroglazed $37–42
CHRIS P KELLER, OWATONNA, MINN, square, qt., pyroglazed.............$35–44
CLOVERLEAF DAIRY, QUINCY, MASS, qt., embossed..........................$35–46
COOPER DAIRY, ELMER, NJ, pt., embossed....................................$30–36
CUMMINGS DAIRY, ARLINGTON, MASS, square, qt., pyroglazed $30–39
DAIRYLEE MILK, YOU CAN WHIP THE CREAM, red and yellow pyro., qt., square, double baby face $50–70
DRESSER HILL FARMS, CHARLTON, MASS, qt., pyroglazed.................$55–65
ERDMAN & SONS, LYKENS, PA, pt., pyroglazed..............................$34–43

FAIRVIEW DAIRY CO, LOCKHAVEN, PA, ½ pt., embossed....................$30–42
FAIRVIEW DAIRY, WALLINGFORD, square, qt., pyroglazed....................$32–37
FLANDERS DAIRY, qt., pyroglazed $45–56
GOLD CREST FARMS, APOLLO, PA, qt., embossed $30–37
GOLDEN DAWN DAIRY, WESTFIELD, NJ, square, qt., pyroglazed $36–43
GOOD RICH DAIRY PRODUCTS, MT CARMEL, PA, pt., embossed $31–38
GOOD RICH DAIRY PRODUCTS, MT CARMEL, PA, ½ pt., embossed.......$30–37
GRAND VIEW DAIRY, CANFIELD, OHIO, square, qt., pyroglazed $34–40
GRAYCE FARMS DAIRY, SCRANTON, PA, square, qt., pyroglazed...........$32–39
GREENLEAF DAIRY, PETERSBURG, VA, square, green pyro., qt., with maple
leaf $40–60
GUIMOND FARMS, FALL RIVER, MASS, qt., pyroglazed $53–61
HARSHBARGER MILK, PA, pt., pyroglazed $34–45
HIDDEN ACRES FARMS, WASHINGTON, NJ, white pyro., qt., square, with four-
leaf clover, clear $30–40
HILLSIDE DAIRY, MIDDLETOWN, CONN, square, qt., pyroglazed...........$35–42
HYPOINT DAIRY, WILMINGTON, DE, qt., pyroglazed $55–68
JJ BROWN DAIRY, TROY, NY, qt., pyroglazed $45–55
LANG BROS DAIRY, square, qt., pyroglazed....................................$34–42
MIRROR LAKE FARM, HERKIMER, NY, qt., pyroglazed $53–59
MURPHYS DAIRY, NEEDHAM, MASS, ½ pt., embossed $30–37
NELSONS DAIRY, square, qt., pyroglazed..$30–36
NORTH HAMPTON DAIRY, NORTH HAMPTON, MASS, qt., embossed.......$32–40
ORCHARD FARM DAIRY, AA APPROVED AYRSHIRE MILK, red pyro, square, qt. ...
....$45–65
PARKDALE DAIRY, WASHINGTON, NJ, qt., pyroglazed.......................$50–60
PECORAS FOR MOTHERS WHO CARE, orange pyro., with baby on top of world,
pt., round $50–70
PECORAS FOR MOTHERS WHO CARE, red and black pyro., with picture of cow
and calf, qt., square...$70–90
PURITY MILK CO, square, qt., pyroglazed $33–40
PURITY MILK CO, LEWISTON, PA, qt., pyroglazed $52–59
RESORVOIR FARM DAIRY, WOONSOCKET, RI, square, qt., pyroglazed......$38–45
RINEHART SUNNY BRAE FARM, qt., pyroglazed..............................$52–65
SACO DAIRY, SACO, MAINE, pt., embossed $35–48
SAWYERS FARM, GILFORD, NH, qt., pyroglazed..............................$55–69
SHAWS DAIRY, BRATTLEBORO, VT, square, qt., pyroglazed.................$40–44
STUDEYS DAIRY, RACINE, WISC, qt., pyroglazed.............................$55–70
SUNCREST FARMS, PROVIDENCE, RI, qt., pyroglazed $50–59
SUNSHINE DAIRY, FRAMINGHAM, MASS, square, qt., pyroglazed $35–40
SUNSHINE DAIRY, ORANGE PYRO, qt., colorless, square......................$40–50
SUPERIOR DAIRY, MILLVILLE, NJ, qt., embossed $40–48
SWEET CLOVER DAIRY, ROOSEVELT, LI, ½ pt., pyroglazed $35–45
UNEMBOSSED, DOUBLE BABY FACE, no pyro., qt., colorless, square......$20–30
UNITED FARMS, ALBANY, NY, qt., pyroglazed................................$53–62
UPTON FARMS, BRIDGEWATER, MASS, pt., black pyro.......................$35–50
VOEGELS PASTEURIZED, IT WHIPS, black pyro., qt., square $40–50
WAITS DAIRY, BELVIDERE, ILL, qt., embossed $38–47
WHITCOMBS FARM, LITTLETON, MASS, qt., pyroglazed......................$55–65
WHITES FARM DAIRY, QUALITY PRODUCTS, square, qt., red and yellow pyro.
....$40–50

COP-THE-CREAM MILK BOTTLES

ARISTOCRAT DAIRY, BALTIMORE, MD, square, qt., pyroglazed.............$60–75
BELMONT DAIRY, WARREN, OHIO, qt., embossed.........................$80–100
BENTLEYS DAIRY, FALL RIVER, MASS, qt., pyroglazed $90–125
BLUE BELL DAIRY, IRVINGTON, NJ, pt..$60–70
BROGANS DAIRY, N BENTON, OHIO, qt., embossed $75–95
CEDAR GROVE DAIRY, HOPE, IND, qt., pyroglazed $80–110
CUPPS DAIRY, WILLIAMSPORT, PA, qt., pyroglazed $90–125
FOUNTIAIN HEAD DAIRY, HAGERSTOWN, MD, qt., pyroglazed...........$80–120
GLENSIDE DAIRY, DEEPWATER, NJ, pt. $60–80
GREEN ACRES FARMS, SCOTTDALE, PA, qt., embossed...................$75–100
GREENLEAF DAIRY, PETERSBURG, PA, square, qt., pyroglazed.............$60–85
GREENWOOD DAIRY, WORCESTER, MASS, qt., pyroglazed $90–120
HILLSIDE DAIRY, MIDDLETOWN, CONN, ½ pt. $60–70
HILLSIDE DAIRY, MIDDLETOWN, CONN, square, qt., embossed.............$45–65
HILLSIDE DAIRY, MIDDLETOWN, CONN, square, qt., pyroglazed...........$60–85
LIBERTY DAIRY, HURON, MICH, qt., pyroglazed............................$90–130
MARTINS DAIRY, LANCASTER, PA, square, qt., pyroglazed $65–80
NICKS DAIRY PRODUCTS, OLD FORGE, PA, pt...............................$62–75
PARAMOUNT, WILKES BARRE, PA, ½ pt. $50–68
RANDLE MILK, ENDICOTT, NY, qt., pyroglazed $80–110
ROYAL FARM DAIRY, qt., embossed...$70–95
STATE ROAD DAIRY, ELDORADO, ILL, qt., pyroglazed....................$80–115
SWEETS DAIRY, FREDONIA, NY, qt., pyroglazed............................$90–125
WAKEFIELD DAIRY, WASHINGTON, DC, square, qt., embossed.............$45–65
WEST END DAIRY, JEANNETTE, PA, qt., pyroglazed $90–120

OTHER MILK BOTTLES

ADLAM GLASS PAIL (ON TIN LID), pail shape, with tin bail, qt., colorless.......
....$250–350
AG SMALLEY (ON BASE AND TOP), with side embossing, ½ pt., clear, tin handle
and top...$350–450
AG SMALLEY (ON BASE AND CAP), no embossing on sides, colorless, with tin
handle and cap, qt. $60–90
AG SMALLEY (ON BASE AND CAP), with embossing on sides, qt., colorless, tin
handle and cap $125–150
ALEX BOLIN & SON, BRADFORD, PA, round, pt., embossed, with original cap .
....$6–7
ALLVINES MILK (IN SCRIPT), KANSAS CITY, KAN, qt., round, black pyro., with
picture of full cow...$20–25
ALTA CREST FARMS, qt., colorless with blue pyro. $60–80
ALTA CREST FARMS, qt., green..$650–800
ANDERSONS CREAMERY, 7 oz., embossed $3–4
ARMOUR CREAMERS, LOUISVILLE, KY, cream jar, embossed.................$3–5
ASSOCIATE DAIRIES, TOPEKA, KANSAS (ON BASE), round, qt., embossed, state
capitol and state...$20–25
AUSABLE DAIRY CORPORATION, AUSABLE FORKS, NY, round, pt., embossed....
....$5–6

BANCROFT, MADISON, WIS, square, qt., red pyro., stubby.....................$4–6

BIG ELM DAIRY COMPANY, qt., green... $200–300

BIG ELM DAIRY COMPANY, qt., green...$150–200

BILLINGS DAIRY, creamer, round, green pyro. $7–9

BORDENS, experimental bottle, qt., ruby red $800–1200

BOWMAN DAIRY COMPANY, CHICAGO, IL, round, pt., embossed $5–6

BRIGHTON PLACE DAIRY, qt., green $250–350

CALHOUN COUNTY CREAMERY, BIRMINGHAM, ALA, qt., embossed.......$12–15

CARNATION (EMBOSSED ON SHOULDERS), square, qt.........................$12–15

CARNATION (EMBOSSED ON SHOULDERS), square, qt., vertical embossing reads "Please Return"...$12–15

CERAMIC CREAMER, round, with double spout, 1 oz., white $3–4.50

CERAMIC CREAMER, round, with spout, ¾ oz., brownish waist ring, rest is beige and white..$5–7

CHIPOLA DAIRY, MARIANNA, FLA, round, qt., red pyro., stubby $5–7

CITY DAIRY CO, STATESBORO, GA, 7 oz., embossed, round, quilted pattern ....
....$4–5

CLINTON MILK CO, qt., light smoky beige...................................$15–20

CLOVERDALE FARMS, BINGHAMTON, NY, qt., amber $35–50

CMDA, CHILLICOTHE, O, round, qt., embossed............................... $9–11

COBLE (IN OBLONG SHIELD), DANDA PROCESS, GENERAL MILLS LABS, qt., square, amber $7–9

COLONIAL DAIRY INC MILK, ALBANY, GA, round, qt., embossed $4–6

COUNTRY FRESH FLAVOR OF WINNISQUAM FARMS, square, gal., amber, white pyro. $10–13.50

CRATE, aluminum, 15″ × 12″ × 10″, Crescent Dairy, Moultrie, GA .. $10–15

CRATE, wood and galvanized steel, 12″ × 6″ × 15″, Crescent Dairy..$20–35

CRESCENT CREAMERY, TECUMSEH, NM, round, qt., red pyro. with nursery rhyme..$20–25

CRESCENT PASTEURIZED MILK & CREAM, creamer, round, ¾ oz., yellow pyro.
....$7–9

DELUXE CREAM SEPERATOR, square, qt., colorless with red pyroglaze............
....$300–450

DESERET LDS CHURCH WELFARE PLAN, SALT LAKE CITY, with pictures of bee hives, red pyro., qt., square $18–22

DIXIE DAIRIES, MACON, GA, round, qt., embossed $4–5

DOC STORK SAYS BABIES DO BETTER ON OUR MILK, round, orange pyro., qt., Hazard, KY $17–21

DRINK VALLOTTONS MILK, ITS BETTER, VALDOSTA, GA, round, qt., picture of doctor, case wear $6–7

DRINK VALLOTTONS MILK, ITS BETTER, VALDOSTA, GA, round, qt., picture of doctor, pyro.. $8–11

EF MAYER, qt., amber $40–60

ELMHURST CREAM CO, ½ pt., light smoky beige...........................$12–15

ESTES PARK CREAMERY, ESTES PARK, COLO, round, qt., red pyro., with boy climbing stairs.. $7–10

FAIRFAX FARMS DAIRY, WASHINGTON, DC, NW, round, qt., 4620 First St.......
....$7–10

FERG CO-34 (ON BASE), qt., amber..$30–35

FIKES DAIRY FARM, MEYERSDALE, PA, round, qt., slug plate embossed, straight-sided body $25–35

FLORIDA STORE BOTTLE, "3c" around shoulder, round, qt., embossed, large map of Florida $8–10

FLORIDA UNIVERSAL STORE BOTTLE, round, pt., embossed, "5c deposit" on shoulder $4–5

FRANKLIN DAIRY, TUPPERLAKE, NY, round, qt., red pyro. $6–7

GABEL-RIDSON FAMOUS JERSEY CREAMERY CO, MILK AND ICE CREAM, pt., embossed $5–6

GALENA DAIRY, GALENA, ILLINOIS, round, pt., slug plate embossing, neck grips $7–9

GASCOYNE DAIRY, LOCKPORT, NY, square, qt., orange pyro., crackle finish, screw top $4–6

GEORGE SIGNOR, KEESEVILLE, NY (ON BOTTOM), round, pt., embossed $4–5

GOODRICH PASTEURIZED DAIRY PRODUCTS, square, qt., chocolate pyro., picture of bottle $4–6

GRANDMA WHEATONS MILKMAID, SOUTH JERSEYS BEST, 18 oz., modern bottle $4–5

GREENLEAF DAIRY, COP THE CREAM, square, qt., green pyro., Petersburg, VA $20–30

HILLCREST FARM DAIRY, TICONDEROGA, NY, square, qt., orange pyro. $5–6

HILTON HARTS DAIRY, FT MYERS, FLA, round, qt., embossed $12–14

HOLLYWOOD WESTERN DAIRY CO . . . , round, qt., embossed $15–20

HOLTS JAR CREAM WHIPS, fruit jar-shape with "Sanety Mason" on back, ½ gal., aqua $200–250

HOOVER MILK CO, PERFECTLY PASTEURIZED MILK, round, qt., New Bethlehem, PA, embossed $7–9

HORLICKS MALTED MILK, RACINE, WISC, round jar, 10 oz., screw cap, stain $3–4

HURSTS DAIRY, EW HURST, MANASSAS, VA, round, qt., embossed $8–10

INDIAN HEAD FARM, FRAMINGHAM, MASS, pt., colorless with embossed Indian head $90–110

JOLLY DAIRY ICE CREAM CO, TIFTON, GA, round, qt., embossed stubby .. $4–5

KEATING, YANKTON, SD, with large shield and crown, qt., red pyro., baby holding milk bottle $18–23

KENT DAIRY, creamer, round, ¾ oz., red pyro. $7–9

LANGS CREAMERY, qt., amber $40–50

LANGS CREAMERY, BUFFALO, NEW YORK, qt., green $250–350

LEHIGH VALLEY COOPERATIVE FARMERS, creamer, round, ¾ oz., green pyro. $7–9

LIBERTY DAIRY PRODUCTS CO, CHICAGO, ILL, qt., round, Statue of Liberty embossed $10–12

LOUX DAIRY, CARTHAPE, MO, round, qt., orange and blue pyro., with farm scene $9–12

MARGROVE INC CREAM CRAFT PRODUCTS, NEWARK, NY, square, qt., red pyro. $4–6

MAYER CHINA, EST 1881, CURTIS 18, creamer, ceramic, ¾ oz., round, with saucer $6–8

MEADOW BROOK PRODUCTS, GREEN RIVER, WYO, round, qt., deep red pyro., two cows, barn, silo, cloud $18–22

MECHANICSBURG CREAMERY, round, pt., embossed, probably Ohio $4–5

MILTS (IN SCRIPT), creamer, round, ¾ oz., red pyro. $7–9

MOJONNIER (IN SCRIPT ON SHIELD), 8 oz., with rubber stopper.............$3–4
NL MARTIN, square tin top, qt., colorless.................................$350–450
MOBHILL MILK I X L, COLO. SPRINGS, COLO, round, qt., green pyro. . $12–15
NORTH SHORE DAIRY CO, CHICAGO, ILL, round, pt., embossed.............$4–6
OLD HOME MILK CO, RENO, NEVADA, round, ½ pt., orange pyro., with cow...
.... $8–10
ORI SMIDER CHOICE DAIRY PRODUCT, CRESCO, MICHIGAN, orange pyro., with
girl and boy.. $12–14
PENN CROSS MILLS, CRESSEN, PA, round, pt., embossed................... $8–10
PENN SUPREME ICE CREAM, PENN DAIRIES, square, qt., orange pyro., Quaker's
head $4–5
PHELPS DAIRY, J WAYCROSS, GA, round, qt., orange pyro. $6–8
PLATTSBURG DAIRY, PLATTSBURG, NY, round, qt., red pyro..................$6–8
POLLY MEADOWS, with girl's head, creamer, round, blue pyro. $8–10
PROPERTY OF IMDOD OF DAYTON OHIO, EMBOSSED, qt., with black pyro., 3¢
store bottle, etc. $12–15
PURE MILK, jar with tin screw-on cap, qt., colorless................... $750–1000
PURITAN MILK, PASTEURIZED . . ., round, qt., red pyro., with housewife and
food $20–25
QUALITY DAIRY, NONE BETTER, creamer, round, red pyro. $6–8
ROSEDALE DAIRY, LARAMIE, WYO, round, qt., green pyro.................. $12–14
ROTHERMELS (ON SIDE), MINERSVILLE, PA (ON BASE), round, qt., embossed
cream separator $60–90
SANCKENS DAIRIES, AUGUSTA, GA, round, pt., embossed.....................$4–5
SANITARY DAIRY, creamer, square, ¾ oz., orange pyro. $7–9
SERVE CREAM TOP DAIRY ICE CREAM, CREAM TOP, square, qt., with green and
orange pyro. $15–20
SOLOMONS DAIRY, MILK & ICE CREAM, QUNICY, FLA, square, qt., black pyro.,
eye looking at bottle $5–7
SOUTHERN MAID INC, BRISTOL, VA, round, pt., embossed...................$6–8
SPRINGDALE DAIRY CO, JAMESTOWN, NY, round, pt., dotted diamond design on
bottle $18–24
STORE 5¢ BOTTLE (IN SQUARE), 24 vertical ribs, pt., embossed.............$6–7
SUNNY DALE DAIRY, UNION CITY, IND, round, qt., pyro. $8–10

Milk Bottles, colored. PHOTO COURTESY OF SKINNER'S, INC.

Left, Milk Bottle, pyroglazed. Right, Milk Bottles, with tin tops and one baby face. PHOTOS COURTESY OF SKINNER'S, INC.

SUPERIOR DAIRY, PUEBLO, COLO, round, qt., orange pyro., picture of man and cow's head $12–15
THATCHERS, WITH MAN MILKING COW, qt., colorless, no closure ... $200–350
TUSCAN DAIRY, creamer, round, ¾ oz., red pyro. $7–9
UNITED STATES DAIRY SYSTEM INC, round, pt., embossed, "United Store" on shoulder $4.50–5.50
UPTOWN DAIRY, CHARLES CITY, IA, square base and round top, creamtop, orange pyro. $20–25
VCS VISIT YOUR CANTEEN FOR QUALITY, round, white pyro., cottage cheese jar...$14–18
VICTORY BOTTLE, BIRMINGHAM, ALA, round, qt., embossed "a war bottle," case wear...$12–15
VICTORY BOTTLE, BIRMINGHAM, ALA, round, qt., embossed "a war bottle" $20–25
WEBER DAIRY CO, JOLIET, ILLINOIS, ¼ pt., round, slug plate embossed $14–18
WECKERLE, qt., green $140–180
WELLS DAIRY COOPERATIVE, COLUMBUS, GA, round, qt., embossed stubby ....
....$3–4
WHITEMAN (ON BASE), dome-type tip top, qt., colorless $250–350
WILLOW SPRINGS FARM, THIENSVILLE, WIS, round, pt., embossed, vertical grip bars..$7–8

MINERAL WATER BOTTLES

For thousands of years, man has believed in the medicinal properties of natural mineral waters. Mineral springs in America were discovered as early as the 17th century, and in the mid-18th century bottled spring water was being sold in the Boston area. By the early 19th century, the spring waters of the Balston and Saratoga spas began a popularity which extended through the 19th and into the 20th century.

It is unknown what types of bottles were used to sell mineral water in the early days, but it was probably some type of free-blown globular bottles. Starting around the 1830s, bottles with the embossed spring names began to appear, and the demand was so great that several glass-houses were started in the Saratoga area with the main purpose being to supply the mineral water companies with enough bottles to sell their product. Many other glasshouses from states such as Pennsylvania and Connecticut also supplied bottles for these mineral water companies.

Many shapes and sizes of bottles were made, with an assortment of colors, and a great deal of interest is directed towards those which have the name of the glasshouse on the bottle, as well as those with embossed eagles and multisided bottles. The reader is referred to *Collectors Guide to Saratoga-Type Mineral Water Bottles* by Donald Tucker.

ADIRONDACK SPRING WHITEHALL NY, N-2B, 7⅞″, emerald green, base chips
....$50–70
ADIRONDACK SPRING WHITEHALL NY, N-2B, pt., emerald green...... $90–120
AKESION SPRING, pt., golden amber, small base chips $90–120
ALBURGH A SPRING VT, V-1, 9½″, yellow amber........................ $175–225
ALBURGH A SPRINGS VT, V-1, qt., yellow amber $40–50
ALPENA MAGNETIC SPRING CO, M-3, qt., amber $300–400
ARTESIAN SPRING CO, S-6, pt., olive green $120–150
ARTESIAN WATER LOUISVILLE KY, pt., deep amber, IP, 12-paneled base ....
.... $400–500
AVON SPRING WATER, N-3, qt., deep olive green.......................... $400–600
AVON SPRING WATER, N-3, qt., aqua $300–400
AVON SPRING WATER CH NOWLEN, N-4, pt., emerald green $150–190
BOLEN WAACK & CO NEW YORK, M-8, ½ pt., green $100–130
BOWMANS VEGETABLE COMPOUND, 7½″, deep aqua, OP $225–260
BUFFALO LITHIA WATER, 9½″, bright green............................... $150–180
BUFFUMS SARSAPARILLA & LEMON MINERAL WATER, ½ pt., IP, sapphire blue
.... $200–300
BUFFUMSA SARSAPARILLA & LEMON, ten-sided, cobalt blue, IP $600–800
BURR & WATER CELEBRATED MINERAL WATERS, sapphire blue, IP....$250–350
BURR & WATERS BOTTLERS, eight-sided, sapphire blue, IP...........$1200–1600
BYRON ACID SPRING WATER, N-5, qt., deep emerald green, IP $1500–2500
CARPENTER & COBB KNICKERBOCKER SODA WATER, ten-sided, medium blue
green, IP $100–135
CARPENTER & COBB KNICKERBOCKER SODA WATER, ten-sided, sapphire blue,
IP, shoulder crack $150–200
CHALYBEATE WATER OF THE AMERICAN SPA, pt., medium emerald green ....
.... $900–1200
CHAMPLAIN SPRING ALKALINE, V-5, qt., green $130–170
CHERRY VALLEY PHOSPHATE WATER, N-8, qt., orange amber, cracked ..$25–35
CLARK & WHITE C NEW YORK, C-11-C, qt., olive green.................$30–40
CLARK & WHITE C NEW YORK, C-11-C, qt., olive amber $30–40
CLARKE & CO NEW YORK, C-8A-1, qt., olive green.......................$110–140

Left, Mineral Water, Clarke & White.
Right, Mineral Water, Congress
Spring Co., sloping shoulder.

PHOTOS COURTESY OF NEIL GROSSMAN.

CLARKE & WHITE, S-C10C2, pt., yellow olive, OP.........................$110–140
CLARKE & WHITE C NEW YORK, C-11B variant 2, pt., olive green.......$70–90
CONGRESS & EMPIRE CO E SARATOGA, E-9-1, qt., emerald green, small lip chip..$25–35
CONGRESS & EMPIRE, HOTCHKISS SONS CW, S-14C, ½ pt., olive green..........
....$275–350
CONGRESS & EMPIRE SPRING CO, HOTCHKISS SONS, S-C15, pt., light olive yellow $140–160
CONGRESS & EMPIRE SPRING CO, HOTCHKISS & CO, qt., emerald green ....
.... $60–80
CONGRESS & EMPIRE SPRING CO, S-14, ½ pt., olive green.............$225–275
CONGRESS & EMPIRE SPRING CO, T-C-14A2, qt., medium yellow green, ⅛″ potstone crack..$50–80
CONGRESS & EMPIRE SPRING CO C SARATOGA, C-19, qt., emerald green........
....$15–25
CONGRESS & EMPIRE SPRING CO C, C-19-A, pt., emerald green..........$40–50
CONGRESS & EMPIRE SPRING CO C, C-19-B, pt., emerald green, lip chip........
.... $15–18
CONGRESS SPRING CO C SARATOGA NY, C-21, qt., emerald green $15–25
DARIEN MINERAL SPRINGS, N-11, pt., medium blue green $400–500
DEEP ROCK SPRING OSWEGO NY, N-13, pt., blue green.................$300–375
DEEP ROCK SPRING OSWEGO NY, N-13, 7¾″, medium blue green .. $200–250
DEEP ROCK SPRING/OSWEGO NY, qt., emerald green $250–300
DEEP ROCK SPRING OSWEGO NY D, pt., aqua.............................. $200–250
DEEP ROCK SPRING TRADE MARK, N-15-A, qt., aqua $90–130
DEEP ROCK SPRING TRADE MARK, N-15A, 7⅞″, aqua $100–150
DL ORMSBY NEW YORK UNION GLASS WORKS, deep cobalt blue, IP .. $140–180
DR BROWN B, medium emerald green, IP $90–125
DR CRONK & GIBBONS IMPROVED MINERAL WATER, cobalt blue, IP, lip chips
....$150–250
DR WIEBERS EUROPEAN MINERAL WATER, 6¾″, medium blue green.. $90–120
E DUFFY NO 44 FILBERTS DYOTTVILLE, deep green, IP $100–150
E MCINTIRE MINERAL WATER, ½ pt., bright green, OP, lip chip......$250–350
EUREKA SPRING CO, S-20, pt., emerald green $400–550
EUREKA SPRING CO SARATOGA, NY, torpedo, 8⅞″, aqua.............. $200–230
EUROPEAN MINERAL WATERS, BROOKLYN, LI, pt., olive green.........$300–375
EXCELSIOR SPRING SARATOGA NY, S-21, qt., emerald green............$175–200

EXCELSIOR SPRING SARATOGA NY, S-26, qt., emerald green............. $80–100
F GLEASON SARSAPARILLA & LEMON, ten-sided, sapphire blue, IP, lip repair...
.... $300–400
F&L SCHAUM BALTIMORE GLASS WORKS, 7⅛″, deep olive green, IP. $400–475
FARGO MINERAL SPRINGS CO, ASHTABULA, OHIO, puce, crown top...... $24–27
GARDNER & LANDON SHARON SULPHUR WATER, qt., olive green, cylinder......
.... $600–900
GETTYSBURG KATALYSINE WATER, M-18, qt., emerald green............... $20–30
GETTYSBURG KATALYSINE WATER, M-18, qt., green $40–50
GEYSER SPRING SARATOGA SPRINGS, S-29B, pt., aqua.................... $90–120
GEYSER SPRING SARATOGA SPRINGS, S-29B, pt., aqua...................... $30–35
GKW (MONO.), WHITNEY GLASSWORKS (ON BASE), M-19, qt., deep blue aqua
.... $60–90
GKW (MONO.), WHITNEY GLASSWORKS (ON BASE), M-19, pt., emerald green .
.... $60–75
GKW (MONO.), WHITNEY GLASSWORKS (ON BASE), M-19, qt., citron............
.... $150–200
GKW (MONO.), WHITNEY GLASSWORKS (ON BASE), M-19, qt., emerald green .
.... $80–95
GLEASON & COLE PITTSBG, ten-sided, deep cobalt blue, IP............ $500–650
GLEASON MINERAL WATER, ten pin, ½ pt., sapphire blue............ $1300–1600
GLEASONS MINERAL WATER ROCHESTER, NY, ten pin, cobalt blue.... $450–650
GRANITE STATE SPRING WATER, 8¾″, colorless, crown top.................. $4–6
GW WESTON & CO SARATOGA NY, E-2-III, qt., olive green $180–220
H HEBER BROOKVILLE MINERAL WATER, ten-sided, aqua.............. $200–240
H KNEBELS MINERAL WATER 458 4TH ST NY, eight-sided, cobalt blue, IP......
.... $150–250
HARRISON VALLEY MINERAL WATER CO, 7 oz., aqua.......................... $5–8
HATHORN SPRING SARATOGA NY, S-33, qt., black amber.................. $35–40
HATHORN SPRING SARATOGA NY, S-33, pt., black amber $15–20
HATHORN SPRING SARATOGA NY, S-33, qt., black amber, lip chip....... $14–18
HATHORN SPRING SARATOGA NY, S-34, qt., amber.......................... $15–20
HIGHROCK CONGRESS SPRING, S-36-1, qt., amber $130–170
HIGHROCK CONGRESS SPRING, S-36-1, pt., amber $190–250
HIGHROCK CONGRESS SPRING 1767, S-36-1, qt., deep olive amber...... $90–120
HIGHROCK CONGRESS SPRING 1767, S36 Type 1, pt., amber $200–300
HOPKINS CHALYBEATE BALTIMORE, M-25, pt., bright yellow green, IP...........
.... $80–100
HOPKINS CHALYBEATE BALTIMORE, M-25, pt., deep olive green, IP $40–55
HOPKINS CHALYBEATE BALTIMORE, M-25, pt., yellow green, IP, pontil crack
.... $75–100
HOWELL & SMITH BUFFALO, medium green, IP, rough lip............... $80–120
HOWELL & SMITH BUFFALO, medium green, IP, stain $100–140
HOWELL & SMITH BUFFALO, cobalt blue, smooth base $90–120
HOWELL & SMITH BUFFALO, sapphire blue, IP, small lip bruise $140–180
J LAKE SCHENECTADY NY, ten pin, cobalt blue, IP, lip bruise......... $150–200
JAS MCDONOUGH GENEVA NY, cobalt blue, IP............................. $240–280
JJ SCHURR SUPERIOR MINERAL WATER, emerald green, IP............. $200–225
JOHN CLARKE, C-3 SIZE B, qt., olive amber................................ $70–90
JOHN H GARDNER & SON SHARON SPRINGS, NY, N-32, pt., blue green $75–90
JOHN H GARDNER & SONS, N-32, pt., blue green......................... $125–150

Jones Patent Mineral Water, 6¾", aqua, IP $1500–2500
JR Donaldson Newark NJ, cobalt blue, IP.............................. $300–425
Kissingen Water Thd The Spa Phil, M-53, pt., yellow olive $160–190
Kissingen Water Thd The Spa Phil, M-53, pt., orange amber........$90–110
Knicker Bocker Soda Water 18SS52, deep teal blue, IP $350–450
Knowlton, DA, Saratoga, NY, qt., medium apricot olive $275–375
Kohl & Beans Mineral Waters, medium blue green, IP $125–150
Lamppins Mineral Water Utica, medium emerald green, IP $100–150
Lynch & Clark New York, C-2B, pt., amber, OP $300–375
Lunch & Clarke, C2B1, pt., deep yellow olive $140–180
Lynch & Clarke New York, C-1-A, qt., olive amber, OP...........$200–300
Lynch & Clarke New York, C-2B, pt., olive amber....................$200–225
M Altenbaugh Mineral Water, ten-sided, 8", deep aqua, IP $375–450
Magnetic Spring Henniker NH, V-10, 9¼", amber, ⅛" lip chip.. $175–200
Magnetic Spring Henniker NH, V-10, qt., amber....................$350–400
Massena Spring Water, N-22, qt., medium teal blue $120–150
Massena Spring Water, N-22, qt., orange amber......................$120–150
Middletown Healing Springs, V-12, qt., amber..........................$30–40
Middletown Healing Springs Grays & Clark, V-12-3, qt., blue green......
.... $130–160
Middletown Healing Springs Grays & Clark, V-12-1, qt., amber .$90–110
Middletown Mineral Spring Co Natures Remedy, V-15, qt., green.........
.... $130–165
Middletown Mineral Spring Co, V-15, qt., emerald green $150–200
Missisquoi A Springs, qt., yellow olive, lip flake.........................$175–225
Missisquoi A Springs, 9½", medium forest green $125–175
Missisquoi A Springs, V-16, qt., olive green...............................$25–30
Missisquoi A Springs, V-16, 9⅝", medium green $40–60
Missisquoi A Springs, V-16, qt., emerald green...........................$30–44
Missisquoi A Springs, V-16, qt., olive green...............................$50–75
Missisquoi A Springs (Squaw), V-17a, qt., olive green $175–225
Missisquoi A Springs, with squaw, V-17-B, qt., medium olive green............
....$350–450
MJ Siebert Pottsville-Superior, ½ pt., cobalt blue, IP $750–950
Moses, Poland Spring Water, 11", colorless, pontil scar $60–80
Moses, Poland Spring Water, 11", green with flaring lip............$150–200
Moses, Poland Spring Water, 11", honey amber $400–550
Mt Clemens Mineral Spring Co, pt., golden yellow..................$475–600
Mt Crawford Hartford CT, ½ pt., cobalt blue, IP $250–300
Mt Crawford Springfield-Union Glass Works, ½ pt., cobalt blue, IP......
....$250–300
Oak Orchard Acid Springs GW Merchant, N-24, qt., blue green, large lip
chip...$30–40
Oak Orchard Acid Springs GW Merchant, N-24, qt., deep yellow green ...
....$125–150
Oak Orchard Acid Springs, Hitchins (On Base), N-25-2, qt., yellow amber
streaks $150–200
Oak Orchard Acid Springs, Hitchins (On Base), N-25-1, qt., yellow green
.... $250–300
Oak Orchard Acid Springs, Hitchins (On Base), N-25-2, qt., medium am-
ber, chip...$70–90

OAK ORCHARD ACID SPRINGS, HITCHINS (ON BASE), N-25-1, qt., deep blue green $150–175

OAK ORCHARD ACID SPRINGS, HITCHINS (ON BASE), N-25-2, qt., amber $75–95

OAK ORCHARD ACID SPRINGS, HITCHINS (ON BASE), N-25-2, qt., yellow olive $150–200

OAK ORCHARD ACID SPRINGS, HITCHINS (ON BASE), N-25-2, qt., yellow green $250–325

OAK ORCHARD ACID SPRINGS, HITCHINS (ON BASE), N-25-2, qt., black amber. $125–150

OAK ORCHARD ACID SPRINGS, HUTCHINS (ON BASE), N-25-1, qt., emerald green $250–350

OAK ORCHARD ACID SPRINGS, N-23, 8¾ ", medium blue green........$250–350

OAK ORCHARD ACID SPRINGS, N-23, qt., deep blue green, ½ " base crack $75–90

OAK ORCHARD ACID SPRINGS, N-23, qt., deep blue green..............$300–375

OAK ORCHARD ACID SPRINGS, N-24, qt., blue green $50–70

OAK ORCHARD, GW MERCHANT, N-24, 9 ", emerald green............... $60–80

OAK ORCHARD HW BOSTWICK, N-25 Type 2 base, 8⅞ ", yellow amber.......... ....$110–135

OAK ORCHARD HW BOSTWICK, N-25 Type 2 base, 8¾ ", golden amber.......... .... $125–175

OAK ORCHARD HW BOSTWICK, N-25 Type 1 base, 9½ ", medium amber........ ....$110–135

OSWEGO DEEP ROCK MINERAL WATER, N-18, qt., deep aqua........... $125–175

PACIFIC CONGRESS WATER, aqua, embossed deer............................$30–40

PAVILION & UNITED STATES SPRING, S-45B, pt., emerald green....... $250–300

POLAND SPRING WATER, Moses figural, 11¼ ", aqua $50–60

POLAND WATER, Moses figural, 10¾ ", amber $450–525

QUAKER SPRINGS LW MEADER & CO, S-43, pt., emerald green $500–750

RAPPS, IMPROVED PATENT, 6½ ", green, OP $250–375

RICHFIELD SPRINGS SULPHUR WATER, N-28, pt., emerald green...... $300–400

S SMITH AUBURN NY 1856 KRS WATER, ten-sided, sapphire blue, IP.. $90–130

S SMITH AUBURN NY 1857, ten-sided, sapphire blue, IP, few small chips....... .... $100–150

S SMITH AUBURN NY 1857, ten-sided, cobalt blue, IP...................$350–475

SARATOGA RED SPRING, S-47B, pt., emerald green, original contents....$70–90

SARATOGA SELTZER WATER, 7½ ", blue green $90–135

SARATOGA SPRING, S-52-B, 7½ ", amber $150–175

SARATOGA VICHY WATER, S-560, qt., red amber $250–350

SARATOGA VICHY WATER, S-560B, pt., yellow amber $150–170

SARATOGA VICHY WATER SARATOGA NY, S-60, qt., amber.............$250–350

SEYMORE, WEBB & CO BUFFALO NY, sapphire blue, IP $550–750

SEYMOUR & CO BUFFALO NY, cobalt blue, IP..............................$100–150

SS SMITH AUBURN NY, cobalt blue, lip chip, rounded base form $75–100

ST CATHARINES MINERAL WATER, 11 ", olive amber.......................$90–120

ST REGIS WATER MASSENA SPRINGS, N-21, qt., medium teal blue green $150–180

ST REGIS WATER MASSENA SPRINGS, N-21B, pt., light greenish aqua .$160–200

STAR SPRING CO SARATOGA NY, S-54, pt., olive amber $90–110

STAR SPRING CO SARATOGA NY, S-54, pt., amber, lip chip................$30–35

Mineral Water, Superior Mineral Water, eight-sided base edge. PHOTO COURTESY OF NEIL GROSSMAN.

STAR SPRING CO SARATOGA NY, S-54, pt., amber $50–60
STIRLINGS MAGNETIC MINERAL SPRINGS, M-49, qt., orange amber $80–90
SUPERIOR SODA WATER, with eagle and shield, 7¾″, medium olive green, IP $1200–1800
SUPERIOR SODA WATER, with eagle and shield, 7¾″, deep blue, IP ....
.... $1200–1800
SYRACUSE SPRINGS D EXCELSIOR AJ DELATOUR, ½ pt., citron $300–400
SYRACUSE SPRINGS EXCELSIOR, N-33, pt., yellow amber $125–150
THE SPA PHILA THD CONGRESS WATER, M-52, 7½″, yellow amber .. $100–130
TWITCHELL SUPERIOR MINERAL WATER, blue green, IP $40–50
TWITCHELL T PHILADA, bluish green, IP $25–30
VERMONT SPRING SAXE & CO SHELDON, VT, V-21-1, qt., emerald green .. $60/75
VICHY WATER PATTERSON & BRAZEAU, NY, M-36, 7⅞″, olive yellow ....
.... $200–225
WASHINGTON LITHIA WELL, S-62, pt., aqua $125–175
WASHINGTON SPRING BALLSTON SPA, S-61, pt., emerald green $375–450
WM A CARPENTERS MINERAL WATER, eight-sided, medium green, IP ....
.... $450–525
WM W LAPPEUS PREMIUM SODA OR MINERAL WATERS, 7″, blue, IP, ten-sided
.... $500–800

NAILSEA-TYPE BOTTLES

Nailsea-type bottles are bottles which have white or colored loopings. These were popular throughout the 19th century and are named for the Nailsea district in England where many of them were made. These bottles were also produced in the United States but it is difficult to tell which bottles are American and which are English or European. Look for unusual looping colors other than the more ordinary white and pink.

BAR BOTTLE, colorless with white loopings, 12⅝″, OP $140–175

Nailsea type, looped flask. PHOTO COURTESY OF
NEIL GROSSMAN.

BELLOWS BOTTLE, colorless cased opaque white with red and blue loopings, 7″,
OP $110–135
BELLOWS BOTTLE, colorless with pink and white stripes, 10½″, OP... $90–120
BELLOWS BOTTLE, footed, colorless with white loopings, 11⅝″, OP... $90–150
BOOT-SHAPED BOTTLE, colorless with white loopings, 8¾″, OP $100–130
COBALT BLUE WITH WHITE SPIRALS, 6″, OP.............................. $75–100
FLASK, colorless body with white loopings, 8″, pontil scar...............$75–115
FLASK, teardrop shape, 7½″, cranberry, OP $70–90
FLASK, teardrop shape, milk glass with rose-colored spots, 6⅝″, OP .. $60–80
FLASK, teardrop shape, vertical ribs, 7¾″, cobalt blue, OP..............$110–140
GEMEL, colorless with amethyst and white loopings, 9¾″, OP.......... $90–120
POWDER HORN, colorless with white loopings, 13½″, OP............... $75–100
POWDER HORN, colorless with white loopings, 10″, OP, ½″ chip...... $80–100
POWDER HORN, footed, colorless with cobalt blue loopings, 11⅜″, OP ....
.... $200–250
POWDER HORN, footed, colorless with white loopings, 12″, OP $200–225
POWDER HORN WHIMSEY, colorless with white and red loopings, OP . $125–175

PATTERN-MOLDED BOTTLES, INCLUDING MIDWESTERN AND STIEGEL-TYPE BOTTLES

Pattern-molded bottles cover a wide area and include those bottles which
are blown into ribbed and pattern molds. Also included are the so-called
Midwestern type, such as the globular bottles and chestnut flasks. Among
the rarest and most desirable of pattern-molded bottles are the Stiegel
type, many of which were made at the Stiegel Glass Manufactory in

Manheim, Pennsylvania, in the late 18th century. However, it is usually very difficult to put a definite attribution on pattern-molded bottles, since many factories in the United States used similar molds, as did English and European glasshouses. As to the Stiegel-type bottles, to date there are only two varieties which can be positively associated with the Stiegel Glass Manufactory—specifically the diamond daisy and the daisy and hexagon designs, which have yet to be associated with any glass factory other than Stiegel's.

Collectors should be aware of several fakes and reproduction pattern-molded bottles, some of which are very well done. As pattern-molded bottles account for some of the most expensive items to be found, collectors should familiarize themselves with the products of the Clevenger Glassworks and those pieces blown by Emil Larsen, as well as some of the reproductions made in Colonial Williamsburg and for the Metropolitan Museum of Art. The reader is referred to *American Bottles and Flasks and Their Ancestry* by McKearin and Wilson.

BEEHIVE BOTTLE, 16 swirled ribs, 8¾", aqua, OP $65–85
BEEHIVE BOTTLE, 16 vertical ribs, 8⅜", light yellow green, OP, base crack....
.... $125–175
BEEHIVE BOTTLE, 16 vertical ribs, 8¾", light green, OP $100–125
BEEHIVE BOTTLE, 24 swirled ribs, 8¼", bluish aqua, OP, applied neck spiral .
.... $600–800
BEEHIVE BOTTLE, 26 vertical ribs, 9⅞", golden amber, OP......... $1400–1800
BEEHIVE BOTTLE, 31 vertical ribs, 9", medium green, OP...........$1800–2200
BEEHIVE BOTTLE, unpatterned, 7¼", greenish aqua, OP, exterior wear $150–175
CHESTNUT, 22 straight ribs, ½ pt., aqua, OP...............................$125–150
CHESTNUT FLASK, ten-diamond pattern, 5¾", medium golden amber, OP ......
.... $2400–3000
CHESTNUT FLASK, 14 ribs swirled to the left, 6¼", tobacco yellow amber, pontil.. $200–300
CHESTNUT FLASK, 16 expanded-diamond pattern, 6", colorless, OP, lip chip...
....$25–30
CHESTNUT FLASK, 16 vertical ribs, 6½", light/medium green, OP, highpoint wear..$325–400
CHESTNUT FLASK, 16 vertical ribs, 5⅞", deep amethyst, OP.......... $250–300
CHESTNUT FLASK, 18 swirled ribs, 6½", yellow amber, OP............$275–375
CHESTNUT FLASK, 18 swirled ribs, 6¼", light green, OP.............$175–200
CHESTNUT FLASK, 18 swirled ribs, 6⅞", light green, OP...............$100–125
CHESTNUT FLASK, 18 swirled ribs, 4⅜", colorless, OP...................$110–140
CHESTNUT FLASK, 20 vertical ribs, 6", light green aqua, OP $90–100
CHESTNUT FLASK, 24 broken-rib pattern, 4⅝", red amber, OP....... $400–500
CHESTNUT FLASK, 24 broken ribs, 6⅝", aqua, OP.......................$250–350
CHESTNUT FLASK, 24-rib broken-swirl pattern, 5¼", red amber, OP.............
.... $1100–1400
CHESTNUT FLASK, 24-rib broken swirl, 5¼", red amber, OP $1100–1400
CHESTNUT FLASK, 24 swirled ribs, 5½", red amber, OP $250–300

CHESTNUT FLASK, 24 swirled ribs, 4⅝", amber, OP $200–250

CHESTNUT FLASK, 24 swirled ribs, 5", medium golden amber, OP.... $75–100

CHESTNUT FLASK, 24 swirled ribs, 5½", light golden amber, OP.... $200–225

CHESTNUT FLASK, 24 vertical ribs, 4¾", golden amber, OP $225–250

CHESTNUT FLASK, 24 vertical ribs, 5¼", yellow with olive tones, OP ....
.... $700–900

CHESTNUT FLASK, 24 vertical ribs, 4¾", yellow amber, OP, lip rough ....
....$180–220

CHESTNUT FLASK, 24 vertical ribs, 8", golden amber, OP.............$800–1100

CHESTNUT FLASK, 24 vertical ribs, 7½", light green, OP $100–125

CHESTNUT FLASK, 24 vertical ribs, 5⅛", dark red amber, OP $250–300

CHESTNUT FLASK, 24 vertical ribs, 4⅜", medium citron, OP, ground lip ....
....$20–30

CHESTNUT FLASK, 32 vertical ribs, 3⅝", colorless, OP, lip chip.........$70–90

CHESTNUT FLASK, swirled 16 ribs, 6¾", greenish aqua, OP $70–90

CHESTNUT FLASK, unpatterned, 6⅞", medium yellow amber, OP $90–120

CHESTNUT FLASK, unpatterned, 5⅛", yellow with olive tones, OP ...$200–275

CLUB BOTTLE, 16 vertical ribs, 8", aqua, OP, light inner stain $125–140

CLUB BOTTLE, 24 broken ribs, 7¾", light cornflower blue, OP $200–250

CLUB BOTTLE, 24 broken ribs, 7⅞", medium yellow green, OP, two spider
cracks $350–450

CLUB BOTTLE, 24 swirled ribs, flattened, 9", light green, OP $350–450

CLUB BOTTLE, 24 swirled ribs, 7½", aqua, OP.........................$100–125

CLUB BOTTLE, 24 vertical ribs, 7½", aqua, OP............................$100–135

CLUB BOTTLE, flattened, 16 swirled ribs, 9", light green, OP $350–450

COLOGNE, six-sided with ovals pattern, BK-3112, 5½", apple green . $500–700

COLOGNE, hexagonal star and punty pattern, 7", canary, with stopper $150–200

CRUET, 14 ribs, blown handle, 8", colorless, OP, blown stopper...... $125–150

DECANTER, pillar-molded, eight ribs, 9½", colorless $125–150

FLASK, ten-diamond pattern, 5", dark golden amber, OP $1400–1700

FLASK, ten-diamond pattern, 4⅞", medium golden amber, OP $200–225

FLASK, ten-diamond pattern, H97-4, 4¾", yellow amber, OP......... $400–600

FLASK, ten-diamond pattern, 5⅜", dark red amber, OP $2000–2500

FLASK, 13-rib mold, black glass with white spots, 4¾", OP........... $250–300

FLASK, 14 vertical ribs, shuttle-shaped, 6½", light green, OP $80–120

FLASK, 15-diamond mold, ½ pt., deep green aqua, OP $350–450

FLASK, 16 swirled ribs, 6½", bright yellow green, OP $300–400

FLASK, 18 vertical heavy ribs, two-piece mold, pt., clear green, OP .. $125–150

FLASK, 20-diamond pattern, similar to H349, 4¼", aqua, OP $150–250

FLASK, 20 swirled ribs, flattened oval shape, 4", cobalt, OP, flaring lip ....
.... $200–300

FLASK, 24 swirled ribs, 6¼", greenish aqua, OP $90–120

FLASK, 24 vertical ribs, 6½", deep golden amber, OP................... $125–160

FLASK, 24 vertical ribs, 6⅜", golden amber, OP $300–400

FLASK, 16 swirled ribs, flattened pear shape, 4⅞", aqua, OP $110–150

FLASK, diamond pattern, 6", pale green, OP $60–75

FLASK OR NURSER, 12-diamond pattern, 7½", greenish aqua, OP........$50–75

FLASK OR NURSER, 16 vertical ribs, 6¼", pale green, OP $50–75

FLASK OR NURSER, teardrop shape, diamond pattern, 8", pale green, OP ....
.... $60–90

FLASK, POCKET, free-blown, 4¾", golden amber, OP $90–120

Left, Pattern Molded, globular bottle with rolled lip. Right, Pattern Molded, globular bottle reproduction with flaring lip. PHOTOS COURTESY OF NEIL GROSSMAN.

FLASK, SWIRLED, 32 ribs, 5⅞", green aqua, OP $80–110
GLOBULAR, 16 swirled ribs, 7¾", aqua, OP, potstone crock $80–100
GLOBULAR, miniature, 32 swirled ribs, 5½", pale aqua, OP $300–350
GLOBULAR BOTTLE, 18 vertical ribs, 8", greenish aqua, OP $110–130
GLOBULAR BOTTLE, 18 vertical ribs, 7", aqua, OP $200–225
GLOBULAR BOTTLE, 24 swirled ribs, 8¾", red amber, OP $450–600
GLOBULAR BOTTLE, 24 swirled ribs, 7⅝", light green, OP, 11" base crack ....
....$40–60
GLOBULAR BOTTLE, 24 swirled ribs, 7⅝", medium citron, OP $2500–3000
GLOBULAR BOTTLE, 24 swirled ribs, 7", smoky amber, OP $750–950
GLOBULAR BOTTLE, 24 swirled ribs, 7⅝", bluish aqua, OP, light inner stain...
.... $250–300
GLOBULAR BOTTLE, 24 swirled ribs, 7¾", medium golden amber, OP...........
.... $450–600
GLOBULAR BOTTLE, 24 swirled ribs, 8" × 6", golden amber, OP, light inner
stain $300–400
GLOBULAR BOTTLE, 24 swirled ribs, 7⅞", medium amber, OP, burst bubble on
rib $325–375
GLOBULAR BOTTLE, 24 swirled ribs, 8¾", medium amber, OP........ $350–450
GLOBULAR BOTTLE, 24 swirled ribs, 9½", aqua, OP $400–475
GLOBULAR BOTTLE, 24 swirled ribs, 8⅞", greenish aqua, OP $325–375
GLOBULAR BOTTLE, 24 swirled ribs, 9⅛", aqua, OP, bruise and large crack ...
....$20–30
GLOBULAR BOTTLE, 24 swirled ribs, 7½", aqua, OP $100–125
GLOBULAR BOTTLE, 24 swirled ribs, 7⅞", red amber, OP, shoulder star crack
.... $140–180
GLOBULAR BOTTLE, 24 swirled ribs, 7¾", medium yellow amber, OP...........
....$375–425
GLOBULAR BOTTLE, 24 swirled ribs, 7⅞", bright yellow amber, OP .$350–450
GLOBULAR BOTTLE, 24 swirled ribs, 7⅛", yellow amber, OP..........$375–425
GLOBULAR BOTTLE, 24 swirled ribs, 7⅝", medium yellow amber, OP...........
....$350–450
GLOBULAR BOTTLE, 24 swirled ribs, 8¼", bright olive yellow, OP ....
....$1800–2300
GLOBULAR BOTTLE, 24 swirled ribs, 9¼", amber, OP $450–525
GLOBULAR BOTTLE, 24 vertical ribs, 7⅞", yellow amber, OP $2500–3000

GLOBULAR BOTTLE, 24 vertical ribs, 7¾", aqua, OP $250–350
GLOBULAR BOTTLE, 25 vertical ribs, 7⅝", medium yellow green, OP, side spider crack $125–175
GLOBULAR BOTTLE, 31 vertical ribs, 7½", greenish aqua, OP $125–150
GLOBULAR BOTTLE, unpatterned, 8¼", medium red amber, OP.......$175–200
GLOBULAR BOTTLE, unpatterned, 9", bluish aqua, OP $120–140
GLOBULAR BOTTLE, unpatterned, 9⅛", medium amber, OP............$175–200
GLOBULAR HANDLED JUG, 24 swirled ribs, 6¼", red amber, OP, sharp impression...$10,000–15,000
HANDLED CHESTNUT BOTTLE, 24 swirled ribs, 8⅝", medium amber, OP.......
.... $400–500
PILLAR-MOLDED BAR BOTTLE, eight ribs, 12", deep blue gray, OP, large donut lip... $1500–2000
PINCH BOTTLE, 24 ribs swirled to the left, 9½", smoky sapphire blue, pontil scar $400–550
PINCH BOTTLE, 24 swirled ribs, 9¾", cobalt blue, OP $350–450
PINCH BOTTLE, ribbed, half-post, 8½", sapphire blue, OP $400–550
POCKET BOTTLE, 12 expanded diamond pattern, light medium green, OP, chip.
.... $130–170
POCKET BOTTLE, 16 vertical ribs, 7⅞", medium amethyst, OP, lip chip ....
.... $125–150
POCKET BOTTLE, 24 vertical ribs, 6", medium yellow green, OP $100–125
PUMPKIN FLASK, 20 vertical ribs, pt., deep olive green, OP, crudely applied lip...$350–450
RIBBED GLOBULAR HANDLED JUG, footed, 4½", aqua, OP $700–900
RIBBED HANDLED JUG, footed, 16 ribs, 5⅜", aqua, OP, haze, handle crack ....
.... $175–225
RIBBED TOILET WATER BOTTLE, 16 vertical ribs, 6", amethyst, OP, with stopper... $1500–2000

Left, Pattern Molded, rare, vertically ribbed, globular bottle (left), club bottle (right), and ten-diamond patterned flask (right front). PHOTO COURTESY OF GLASS WORKS AUCTION. *Right, Pattern Molded, swirled, ribbed, toilet water bottle, ca. 1830.* PHOTO COURTESY OF NEIL GROSSMAN.

STIEGEL TYPE, 20 diamond/cells over flutes, 5½", deep amethyst, OP...........
.... $3000–4000
STIEGEL TYPE, 12-diamond ogival pattern, 5½", deep amethyst, OP ....
.... $3500–4500
STIEGEL TYPE, daisy and hexagon pattern, 6", colorless with purple tint, OP...
.... $600–900
STIEGEL TYPE, diamond daisy, 5½", medium red amethyst, OP....$3000–3750
SWIRLED-RIB CHESTNUT, 24 ribs, 2⅞", aqua, OP........................ $125–175
SWIRLED-RIB FLASK, 24 ribs, similar to H97-7, 4⅝", golden amber, OP........
.... $120–150
SWIRLED-RIB TOILET WATER BOTTLE, 16 ribs, 5¾", deep amethyst, OP, flared
lip...$1500–1800
SWIRLED-RIBBING CHESTNUT, 24 ribs, 5¼", red amber, OP........... $125–150
TOILET WATER BOTTLE, GI-9, 6", colorless, OP, with stopper.......... $90–120

PICKLE BOTTLES

Pickle bottles are among the most beautifully designed and largest in
size of all bottles. Pickle bottles, which ordinarily have wide mouths,
are usually square, but cylindrical and 6- and 8-sided examples can also
be found. One of the most popular types of pickle bottles is the cathedral
or gothic style, which often has fancy gothiclike window panels on the
sides. Pickle bottles ordinarily come in aqua glass, and the collector
should be on the lookout for the more unusual-colored and pontiled examples. The reader is referred to *Ketchup, Pickles and Sauces* by Betty
Zumwalt, which the letter "Z" refers to below, with specific page.
"HM" refers to *American Bottles and Flasks and Their Ancestry* by
McKearin and Wilson.

ATMORES-ATMORES, Z32 right, square, 11⅜", aqua $125–150
ATMORES-ATMORES, Z32 right, square, 11¼", light green............... $125–175
CATHEDRAL, "EHVN/NY" on side, six-sided, 9", deep aqua, IP $150–200
CATHEDRAL, 12 panels with petal design on shoulder and base edge, HM73-7,
11", aqua, IP... $200–250
CATHEDRAL, six-sided, Z455, 13", aqua.................................... $125–175
CATHEDRAL, square with diamond lattice in three panels, 11⅜", aqua............
....$150–200
CATHEDRAL, square with large star on panels, 8⅞", deep aqua, IP, light wear
....$350–450
CATHEDRAL, square with lattice design, HM74-8, 6⅜", aqua, OP $75–125
CATHEDRAL, square with leaf-bead design on panels, HM74-10, 13¾", aqua,
label $60–80
CATHEDRAL, square, Z456, 11⅞", medium emerald green, IP $400–500
CATHEDRAL, square, HM74-11, 11¼", aqua, light stain $75–125

Pickle, cathedral or gothic. PHOTO COURTESY OF NEIL
GROSSMAN.

CATHEDRAL, square, with chain decor on panel edges, 9″, aqua, IP.. $175–225
CATHEDRAL, square, with diamond lattice on three panels, 8¾″, greenish aqua,
light haze.. $125–175
CATHEDRAL, square, with fleur-de-lis-like design in panels, 11¾″, light green,
light wear $350–400
CATHEDRAL, square, Z PG 454 upper left, "X" design on upper halves of pan-
els, 8½″, light green $150–200
CATHEDRAL, square, Z PG 456 upper left, chain decor on panel edges, 11¾″,
deep aqua $150–200
CATHEDRAL, square, Z PG 456 upper right, with chain decor on panel edges,
11⅝″, green.. $175–225
CATHEDRAL, square, Z PG 456 upper right, chain decor on panel edges, 11½″,
IP, light green...$450–550
CATHEDRAL, square, Z PG 457 upper left, 11″, aqua $100–150
CATHEDRAL, Z PG 436, "W. T. & CO" (on base), six-sided, 13⅜″, golden
amber, inner stain $700–900
CATHEDRAL, Z PG 453 upper left, square, 8¾″, aqua......................$30–50
CATHEDRAL, Z PG 455 lower left, scroll-like design on panel bottoms, 11″,
aqua $300–350
CATHEDRAL, Z PG 455 top center, six-sided, 13⅛″, light yellow green..........
....$300–450
CATHEDRAL, Z PG 455 top center, six-sided, 13⅛″, deep aqua, small panel
chip...$150–200
CATHEDRAL, Z PG 456 top center, square, 13¾″, light green......... $250–300
CATHEDRAL, Z PG 456 upper center, square, 11½″, aqua, IP......... $300–400
CATHEDRAL, Z PG 456 upper center, square, 14½″, medium emerald green, IP,
small crack.. $800–1000
CATHEDRAL, Z PG 457 lower center, square, "X" cross pattern, 14″, greenish
aqua $250–300
CATHEDRAL, Z PG 457 lower center, square, "X" pattern on sides, 13¾″,
aqua $300–400
CATHEDRAL, Z PG 457 upper left, square, 8⅝″ aqua, light stain...... $100–125
CATHEDRAL, Z PG 455 top center, six-sided, 11⅜″, bright yellow with amber
tone $1800–2200
CATHEDRAL, PICKLE, 9¼″, aqua $60–75
CATHEDRAL, PICKLE, six-sided, H73-10, 13⅛″, aqua $125–175

CATHEDRAL, PICKLE, square, Z541, 11¾", light green................... $300–400
DAYTON PRENTISS/&/BORDEN/NEW YORK, Z113 left, 7", aqua, OP ... $175–200
EHVB/NY, cathedral, Z411, six-sided, 9", aqua, IP, light inner haze............
.... $150–175
EHVB/NY, cathedral, lattice on sides, six-sided, 11⅝", green/aqua, IP, ⅛"
crack $250–350
ESPY PHIL, round, Z434 top right, 9½", aqua, OP $40–60
ET COWDREY & CO/BOSTON, round, Z91, 6½", amber....................$40–60
GOOFUS PICKLE, 15", bright apple green.......................................$50–60
GP SANBORN & SON/UNION BRAND/BOSTON PICKLES, Z359, 5", aqua .$50–60
GP SANBORN & SON/UNION BRAND/BOSTON PICKLES, Z359, 5", yellow am-
ber..$110–140
GP SANBORN & SON/UNION BRAND/BOSTON PICKLES, Z359, 8", yellow am-
ber.. $110–150
HEINZ NOBLE & CO/PITTSBURGH, PA, square, Z204, 7⅞", deep aqua .$60–70
I.R., PICKLE, Z346, 6½", aqua, IP $75–100
J MCCOLLICK & CO NEW YORK, circular, 11½", blue aqua, IP...... $750–1000
J MCCOLLICK/& CO/NEW YORK, Z289, square, 8½", deep green aqua, IP,
chip..$150–200
JM CLARK & CO-LOUISVILLE, KY, Z83 left, 8½", yellow amber....... $60–90
JM CLARK & CO-LOUISVILLE, KY, Z83, 5¼", yellow amber.............$40–60
JM CLARK & CO-LOUISVILLE, KY, Z83 left, 6⅞", yellow amber........$40–60
MB ESPY, square, similar to Z433 bottom, but no "PHILA" at base edge, 8⅞",
aqua, IP $100–125
MB ESPY/PHILADA, square, Z433 bottom, 11¼", medium teal blue .$200–275
MILWAUKEE PICKLE CO/WAUWATOSA, WIS, round, 12⅝", orange amber.........
.... $200–250
MILWAUKEE PICKLE CO/WAUWATOSA, WIS, round, 9⅝", yellow amber, ⅛" lip
chip.. $100–125
OCTOFOIL BODY, H73-2, 8", olive amber $375–425
PD CODE & CO/SF, round, Z86, 11⅜", deep olive yellow $300–400
PICKLE, corsetted waist, square, Z PG 454 lower right, 7¼", aqua, OP.........
....$50–75
PICKLE, round, Z PG 451 upper center, 10⅛", ice blue, IP $150–200
PICKLE, square, label on one side, "Gerkins From WK Lewis," 12", light
green...$50–75
PICKLE, square, plain panels, 13¾", brilliant yellow olive............. $250–300
QUATROFOIL, H73-2, 7⅞", bright green....................................$225–275
R&F ATMORE, square, Z32 left, 11½", aqua $125–150
SANBORN, PARKER & CO/UNION BRAND/BOSTON, pickles, Z359, 8⅛", yellow
olive.. $250–300
SEVERANCE & TAPPEN, round, Z370, 7½", yellow amber $50–60
SJG (ON SIDE), cathedral, Z PG 162, 9⅛", aqua, OP.................. $200–250
SKILTON FOOTE & CO's/BUNKER HILL PICKLES, Z376-3, 11¼", medium am-
ber.. $400–500
SKILTON FOOTE & CO's/BUNKER HILL PICKLES, Z376-3, 11¼", light yellow
green $400–500
SKILTON FOOTE & CO's/BUNKER HILL PICKLES, Z378, 7⅞", olive yellow ......
.... $125–150
SKILTON FOOTE & CO/BUNKER HILL PICKLES, round, Z378, 5⅜", aqua ....
.... $14–16

SKILTON FOOTE & COS/BUNKER HILL PICKLES, square, Z377, 6¾", yellow amber $50–70

SKILTON FOOTE & COS/BUNKER HILL PICKLES, square, Z377, 6¾", amber, 50% label $60–80

SOL WANGENHEIM & CO/SAN FRAN, Z416, 11¼", aqua $30–50

TB SMITH & CO-PHILADA, round, Z385 left, 10⅝", aqua, OP, tiny lip bruise $40–60

TB SMITH & CO/PHILADA, cathedral, Z385 top right, 8⅞", emerald blue green, OP.. $600–800

TB SMITH & CO/PHILADA, square, Z385 center, 9¼", aqua, OP, base chip $225–275

TB SMITH & CO/PHILADA, Z385 lower right, 11⅛", aqua, IP, with a few polished chips $125–175

TRADE MARK/C.P. CO, square, Z108, 9", aqua............................ $60–80

TRADE MARK/C.P. CO, square, Z108, 11", aqua........................... $60–90

W NUMSEN & SON-BALTIMORE, round, Z320, 10⅜", aqua, OP $300–400

W NUMSEN & SON-BALTIMORE, round, Z320, 9", pale yellowish green, OP.... ....$250–300

W.M.&P./NY, round, Z428-4, 10¼", aqua $40–60

W.M.&P./NY, square, Z430 lower left, 7⅜", yellowish green, OP . $300–400

WD SMITH/NY, pickle, square, Z386, 8⅝", deep aqua, IP $350–450

WD SMITH/NY, square, 8⅝", aqua, IP $275–350

WDS/NY, pickle, Z-386, 7¾", aqua, OP.......................................$100–130

WDS/NY, pickle, square, 7¾", aqua, OP $125–150

WELLS & MILLER/NY, square, Z428-1, 6⅜", medium emerald green, IP....... ....$250–350

WELLS-MILLER &-PROVOST, square, Z428-2, 11½", aqua, IP $225–275

WENDELL & ESPY, round, Z434 top left, 9½", aqua, OP $75–90

WILLIAM UNDERWOOD & COMPANY/128 OZ. round, 12½", aqua, IP .. $90–120

WILLIAM-UNDERWOOD-& COMPANY-BOSTON/32 OZ. Z408, square, 9¾", aqua, light stain.. $60–90

WK LEWIS & CO-BOSTON, Z277, 10¼", bright green, IP, ⅝" lip crack $120–150

WM UNDERWOOD & CO, BOSTON, cathedral, square, 11½", medium emerald, IP..$500–750

WM UNDERWOOD/& CO-BOSTON, Z407 left, 11⅜", aqua, OP......... $225–300

WM UNDERWOOD-CO BOSTON/32 OZ., round, Z408 upper right, 8¼", medium emerald green $70–90

WM UNDERWOOD-CO BOSTON/32 OZ., round, Z408, 8⅜", medium emerald green, OP $200–250

PITKIN-TYPE BOTTLES AND FLASKS

Pitkin-type bottles and flasks are so named because for years it was believed that they were made exclusively at the Pitkin Glassworks of Manchester, Connecticut. All Pitkin items were made by the half-post method, in which the second gather or dip of glass extended only to the lower neck of the bottle, leaving a noticeable edge around the lower neck or shoulder. Ironically, there is currently no proof that Pitkin-type flasks were ever made at the Pitkin Glassworks, though there is substantial evidence of this type of bottle being made in many other glasshouses. These include the Keene Marlborough Street Glassworks in Keene, New Hampshire; Coventry Glassworks in Coventry, Connecticut; numerous Midwestern glasshouses; at least one New Jersey glasshouse; and several other New England glassworks.

The Pitkin-type flasks and ink bottles are relatively common, whereas bottles, jugs, and jars are extremely rare. Also, it must be noted that the half-post method of blowing glass which was used for the Pitkin-type bottles originated in Germany, and Pitkin-type flasks from that area have shown up in the United States. As to attribution of Pitkin items, the New England Pitkins are more apt to have 32 or 36 ribs and are generally of a dark or olive green shading, along with having the elongated type of form; the Midwestern Pitkins are generally found in a wide range of colors and rib count, and are usually more oval-shaped. The German Pitkin flasks are usually of a heavier straight-ribbed variety, as opposed to the swirled or broken-ribbed pattern which is generally found in the American items; they are often found in unusual colors such as dark blue.

The collector should be aware that there are a few reproduction Pitkins on the market, the most common one being a swirl-ribbed variety which has mold seams on the side of the bottle; on genuine Pitkins, there would never be mold seams evident. Interested collectors should read *American Bottles and Flasks and Their Ancestry* by McKearin and Wilson for a much greater detailing of Pitkin-type products.

BROKEN SWIRL, pt., medium green, OP $325–375
BROKEN SWIRL, 16 ribs, pt., deep forest green, OP.......................$350–425
BROKEN SWIRL, 32 ribs, pt., apple green, OP, strong impression..................
....$1200–1500
BROKEN SWIRL, 32 ribs, pt., aqua/light green, OP........................$350–450
BROKEN SWIRL, 36 ribs swirled to the left, 6″, medium amber, OP ....
....$1000–1500

Left, Pitkin Bottle, Midwestern, oval form. Center, Pitkin Bottle, New England. Right, Pitkin Bottle, vertically ribbed, possibly European. PHOTOS COURTESY OF NEIL GROSSMAN.

BROKEN SWIRL, 36 ribs, 7″, olive amber, OP $450–500
BROKEN SWIRL PATTERN, 16 ribs, 5½″, medium olive green, OP $200–250
BROKEN SWIRL PATTERN, 16 ribs, 6⅝″, medium olive green, OP $225–260
BROKEN SWIRL PATTERN, 24 ribs, 6⅝″, medium olive green, OP.... $400–500
BROKEN SWIRL PATTERN, 24 ribs, 6⅞″, olive green, OP, 3/16″ lip chip ....
....$110–130
BROKEN SWIRL PATTERN, 24 ribs, 7⅛″, bright olive yellow, OP...... $500–600
BROKEN SWIRL PATTERN, 30 ribs, 5¾″, olive yellow, OP...............$475–550
BROKEN SWIRL PATTERN, 30 ribs, 6¾″, olive yellow, OP...............$350–450
BROKEN SWIRL PATTERN, 31 ribs, 6″, olive green, OP, rare applied lip..........
....$1300–1600
BROKEN SWIRL PATTERN, 32 ribs, 6¾″, medium greenish aqua, OP, light haze
....$200–240
BROKEN SWIRL PATTERN, 32 ribs, 6¼″, bright medium olive yellow, OP........
.... $500–700
BROKEN SWIRL PATTERN, 32 ribs, 6½″, medium yellow green, OP...$275–350
BROKEN SWIRL PATTERN, 32 ribs, 6¾″, dark sage green, OP $350–450
BROKEN SWIRL PATTERN, 32 ribs, 6¾″, light green, OP $325–425
BROKEN SWIRL PATTERN, 36 ribs, 4⅞″, olive yellow, OP, neck crack ..$30–45
BROKEN SWIRL PATTERN, 36 ribs, 6⅞″, deep olive green, OP $275–350
BROKEN SWIRL PATTERN, 36 ribs, 6¼″, olive green, OP, 3/8″ lower star crack.
....$40–50
BROKEN SWIRL RIBBING, 31 ribs, 6¾″, yellow olive, OP, small lip chip ....
.... $300–400
SWIRL PATTERN, 36 ribs, 5¼″, medium yellow with olive tone, OP ..$260–320
SWIRLED RIB PATTERN, 36 ribs, 5½″, olive yellow, OP, large base chip.........
....$40–50
VERTICAL RIBBING, 18 ribs, 5⅜, deep cobalt, OP $1200–1700
VERTICALLY RIBBED, 12 ribs, 6⅛″, colorless, OP, neck crack $15–25
VERTICALLY RIBBED, 28 ribs, 7¾″, olive amber, OP $400–500
VERTICALLY RIBBED, 36 ribs, 4⅞″, medium olive yellow, OP $500–700
VERTICALLY RIBBED, 36 ribs, 5½″, olive amber, OP, potstone crack.$150–225

POISON BOTTLES

Poisons of various sorts have been used for thousands of years. The first poison bottles used in America may have been flasks blown in the half-post method and pattern molded in a diamond or hobnail pattern.

Because there has always been a need to identify poison containers as such, many of the poison containers from the 19th century clearly had "poison" embossed on the bottle. It soon became evident, however, that it was necessary to have a distinctive form of bottle, one with which someone who could not read or who inadvertently grabbed the bottle at night would know that it was of a toxic nature. Thus, a wide variety of bottle shapes were employed for poison, such as skulls, coffins, bottles with a diamond- or lattice-type pattern, and multisided bottles with very prominent vertical or horizontal ribbing. Also, it was first felt that dark colors such as blues and browns were more identifiable, but at some point in the 1930s it was determined that the strange shapes and colors might actually be attracting the attention of children, and that more attention should be given to finding safer closures on bottles.

When handling poison bottles extreme caution must be used, since it is quite common to find poison bottles complete with original contents. When purchasing poison bottles, try to determine if the original poison bottle came with a ground glass stopper, which can easily be determined by looking for a frosted area on the inside of the neck where the stopper was ground to form an airtight seal. If the glass stopper is missing, it can have a dramatic effect on the value of the bottle. Also, be on the lookout for unusual-size poison bottles and any of the unusual figurals such as the skull, leg bone, or coffin. The reader is referred to *Collectors Guide to Poison Bottles* by Roger Durflinger, which the letter "D" refers to below.

BLOWN FLASK SHAPE WITH HOBNAILS, half-post, 4½″, colorless, OP $125–150
CARBOLIC ACID POISON (ON LABEL), lattice design, 4⅜″, clear..........$45–55
CERAMIC SKELETON FIGURAL BOTTLE, 8″, brown and white glaze.... $125–150
COFFIN-SHAPE, WITH "NORWICH 16A" (ON BASE), with four pointed diamonds, D-2, 7⅜″, cobalt.. $900–1200
COFFIN-SHAPED WITH "POISON," D-2, 3⅜″, amber $250–300
COW-SHEAF OF WHEAT, flask, 4⅞″, aqua, OP............................$125–150
DUTCHERS DEAD SHOT FOR BED BUGS, 4⅞″, aqua, OP, with label $50–70
FIGURAL CERAMIC SKULL, atop books, 1⅞″, painted.......................$25–35
HORIZONTAL RIBS, DIAMOND-SHAPED "POISON," D-67, 5″, bright green....... ....$65–85
LATTICE AND DIAMOND PATTERN WITH GLASS STOPPER, D-41, 3¾″, cobalt blue...$60–75
MELVIN & BADGER APOTHECARIES, 5″, cobalt, horizontal lines..........$25–35

MELVIN & BADGER APOTHECARIES, 6¾″, cobalt, horizontal lines........$65–80

NOT TO BE TAKEN, six-sided, D-53, with stopper, 6⅛″, cobalt blue $30–35

OWL DRUG CO, with one winged owl on mortar, D-22, 7¾″, cobalt blue
.... $400–500

OWL DRUG CO-EMBOSSED OWL, two-sided, 3¼″, amber $40–50

OWL DRUG CO-POISON, with owl on mortar, three-sided, D-22, 6″, cobalt
blue... $135–175

POISON, vertically with skull and crossbones, D-3, 2¾″, cobalt blue, ABM ....
....$75–90

POISON, with skull and crossbones, D-7, ABM, 3¼″, cobalt blue........$50–70

POISON, coffin-shaped, with label, ABM, 3½″, cobalt blue................$75–90

POISON, with full label, three-sided, D-24, 10⅛″, golden amber $300–400

POISON, with skull and crossbones and stars, lattice, D-68, 4⅝″, amber, labels,
round... $600–750

POISON, eight-sided, metal screw cap, D-66, 2¾″, cobalt blue $125–150

POISON-16 OZ-USE WITH CAUTION, D-61, 8⅞″, cobalt blue..............$90–110

POISON-16 OZ-USE WITH CAUTION, D-61, 8¾″, cobalt blue..............$80–110

POISON-BOWMANS DRUG STORES, D-78, 7½″, cobalt blue $450–600

POISON-EMBOSSED OWL-"OWL DRUG CO," D-22, 2⅞″, cobalt blue, three-
sided $125–150

POISON-EMBOSSED OWL-"OWL DRUG CO," D-22, 3⅝″, cobalt blue, three-
sided $125–150

POISON-EMBOSSED OWL-"OWL DRUG CO," D-22, 9⅜″, cobalt blue, three-
sided $550–700

POISON-EMBOSSED OWL-"OWL DRUG CO," D-22, 4¾″, cobalt blue, three-
sided $150–200

POISON-EMBOSSED OWL-"OWL DRUG CO," D-22, 4¹⁵/₁₆″, cobalt blue, three-
sided $140–180

POISON-EMBOSSED OWL-"OWL DRUG CO," D-22, 7¾″, cobalt blue, three-
sided $350–450

POISON-JNO WYETH & BRO, rectangle, D-36, 2⅝″, cobalt blue $50–70

POISON-"OWL DRUG CO," with owl embossed on same panel, three-sided, 6³/₁₆″,
cobalt blue $50–70

POISON, "PAT APPD FOR NB & CO" (ON BASE), D-63, 3⅝″, yellow amber
.... $375–450

POISON-POISON, D-42, 3⅜″, yellow amber $40–60

POISON-POISON, triangular, 2¾″, amber, labeled $40–45

Poison, two large. PHOTO COURTESY OF
SKINNER'S, INC.

POISON-POISON, square with horizontal lines, D-42, 3⅛", cobalt blue, ABM... .... $10–15

POISON-POISON, square, D-11, 4⅜", amber $40–50

POISON-POISON, three-sided, D-33, 5¼", cobalt blue $120–150

POISON-POISON-NORWICH/4A, coffin-shaped, D-2, 4¹⁵/₁₆", amber...$1200–1500

POISON/SKULL AND CROSSBONES, D-68, 4⅝", yellow amber $750–850

POISON-SKULL AND CROSSBONES/"DP", D-4, 3", cobalt blue..... $1600–2000

POISON/TINCT/IODINE, with skull and crossbones, D-6, ABM, 2⅝", amber $20–30

QUILTED DIAMOND DESIGN, HB Co (ON BASE), D-41, 3¾", cobalt blue, original stopper $65–75

QUILTED DIAMOND PATTERN, with glass stopper, D-41, 4¾", cobalt, stopper, chip... $60–75

QUILTED DIAMOND PATTERN, D-41, 11¼", cobalt blue, no stopper .. $600–750

QUILTED DIAMOND PATTERN, D-41, 9¼", cobalt blue, original stopper.......... .... $500–800

QUILTED DIAMOND PATTERN, D-41, 5½", cobalt blue, stopper missing .$40–55

QUILTED DIAMOND PATTERN, D-41, 7¼", cobalt blue, stopper missing .$50–60

QUILTED DIAMOND PATTERN, D-41, 4¼", moss green, stopper missing.......... .... $375–475

QUILTED DIAMOND PATTERN, D-41, 11¼", cobalt blue, original stopper......... .... $700–1200

QUILTED DIAMOND PATTERN, with label, D-41, 7½", cobalt blue, stopper missing... $75–100

QUILTED DIAMOND PATTERN, EMBOSSED BASE READS "USPHS," 6¼", cobalt, with stopper... $250–350

QUILTED DIAMOND PATTERN, HB Co (ON BASE), D-41, 7", cobalt blue, original stopper.. $120–150

QUILTED DIAMOND PATTERN, HB Co (ON BASE), D-41, 5½", cobalt blue, original stopper $100–150

QUILTED DIAMOND PATTERN, WT & Co (ON BASE), D-41, 7¼", cobalt blue, original stopper $200–300

QUILTED DIAMOND PATTERN, WT & Co (ON BASE), D-41, 5⅜", cobalt blue, original stopper $75–125

QUILTED DIAMOND PATTERN, WT & Co (ON BASE), D-41, 6¾", cobalt blue, original stopper $200–300

QUILTED SIDES, oval, with label panel, 3", amber $5–7

Poison, skull, cobalt blue. PHOTO COURTESY OF SKINNER'S, INC.

SKELETON FIGURAL, CERAMIC, D-70, 5¾", brown and white glaze...$150–200

SKULL AND CROSSBONES, "PD & CO" (ON BASE), D-5, 2⅜", amber...........
....$550–750

SKULL FIGURAL, D-1, 4⅛", cobalt blue, ¼" lip roughness $1200–1400

SKULL FIGURAL, D-1, 4¼", cobalt blue $2000–3000

SKULL FIGURAL, "POISON" (ON FACE), 1984 PATD (ON BASE), D-1, 3½", blue, nose repair $800–1000

SKULL FIGURAL, CERAMIC, 5½" × 7¼" $400–500

TRIANGULAR WITH "POISON," D-24, 10⅜", amber......................$200–275

TRILOIDS-POISON, three-sided, D-18, 3¼", cobalt blue, ABM.............$12–15

USAGE EXTREME-NOT TO BE TAKEN, "RIGO"(ON BASE), D-57a, 5", cobalt blue...$40–60

VAPO CRESOLENE, square, 4", colorless $3–5

VERTICALLY RIBBED, rectangular, D-27, 3¹/₁₆", cobalt blue, ABM $4–6

VERTICALLY RIBBED, six-sided, 5¼", green $5–7

VERTICAL RIBS WITH "POISON" AT A DIAGONAL, 13⅞", olive green, with stopper... $200–230

POTTERY BOTTLES

Pottery bottles often are found in figural form and were popular in the 18th and 19th centuries. Collectors should be on the lookout for specific potters' marks such as those used in the Bennington Potteries in the 19th century, as well as the Anna Pottery of Anna, Illinois. The latter produced, among other items, the so-called Railroad Pig Bottles which have a railroad map incised in blue over the body of the pig. The reader is referred to *Decorated Stoneware Pottery of North America* by Donald Blake Webster.

Pottery, Bennington-type book. PHOTO COURTESY OF NEIL GROSSMAN.

BOOK FIGURAL, BENNINGTON BATTLE, 10½″, brown, tan, cream, and green glazes $800–1200
BOOK FIGURAL, BENNINGTON BATTLE, 11″ × 8″ × 3¹/₁₆″ $800–1200
BOOK FIGURAL, DEPARTED SPIRITS, 5¾″, brown and orange glazes ..$250–350
BOOK FIGURAL, UNEMBOSSED, 5¾″, brown, cream, and yellow glazes ....
.... $300–400
BOOK FIGURAL, UNEMBOSSED, 10¾″, brown and cream glazes $300–350
BOOT-SHAPED BOTTLE, 6¼″, light brown glaze with white buttons $70–90
CANTEEN-SHAPED FLASK WITH MAN, BARREL, AND CHILDREN, 8″, mottled brown glaze... $60–90
COACHMAN FIGURAL, 10½″, tan and brown glaze, boot chip...........$225–275
CROCK, ADVERTISING HJ HEINZ CO, 5⅜″, unhandled.................. $250–400
DOUBLE EAGLE FLASK, pt., tan and brown $300–500
FLASK, WITH EAGLE AND MORNING GLORY, pt., brown and tan glazes ....
....$300–375
INK, JOSIAH JONSON JAPAN WRITING FLUID, C-1242, 2½″ $125–175
JC STEVENS WINE & SPIRIT MERCHANT, 8¼″, tan and brown glaze. $400–600
JUG, ADVERTISING BELLS SARSAPARILLA, 7¼″, handled................ $200–250
JUG, ADVERTISING DAVIS ASHLEYS HONEY BALSAM, 11½″ $150–250
MAN WITH LARGE FLOPPY HAT WITH PIPE, 8⅛″, white clay with bluish glaze
....$300–375
MASONIC-EAGLE FLASK, GIV-24, pt., redware $450–650
MERMAID, 8″, brown glaze.. $100–150
MERMAID BOTTLE, 7¾″, brown glaze...$70–90
PIG FIGURAL, BIELERS RONNY CLUB, 9½″, brown and tan glaze......$350–450
PIG FIGURAL, EMBOSSED "WHISKEY 1875" AND "PUT YOUR MOUTH TO MY," 9″, beige glaze.. $1400–1800
POWDER FLASK WITH DOG WITH BIRD IN MOUTH, 9¾″, brown and tan glaze
....$250–350
QUEEN VICTORIA FIGURAL, 7⅞″, tan and brown, an early English piece ....
....$250–350
SCEPTER FIGURAL, STEPHEN GREEN IMPERIAL POTTERIES, 11″, tan and brown
....$350–450
VICTORIAN WOMAN FIGURAL, with fan and umbrella, 7⅞″, cream with brown and blue $900–1200
WOMENS BUST FIGURAL, with angels on lower half, 8¼″ $40–60

Pottery, Anna-type pig. PHOTO COURTESY OF NEIL GROSSMAN.

Left, Reproduction, EG Booz cabin with bevel at roof edges that extends below the first row of shingles. Right, Reproduction, eagle–cornucopia. PHOTOS COURTESY OF NEIL GROSSMAN.

REPRODUCTION BOTTLES

Though many bottle collectors shudder when they hear the word reproduction, the collecting of reproduction bottles is attracting more and more people every year. Most interest in reproduction bottles centers around the products made by the Clevenger Glass Works of New Jersey, whose operations began in the 1930s, as well as the handcrafts of Emil Larsen, who operated around the same time period. Interested readers should review the chapter titled "Fakes, Reproductions, and Repairs" to become more comfortable with some of the signs of the reproduction pieces. The reader is referred to *American Bottles and Flasks and Their Ancestry* by McKearin and Wilson, pgs. 678–708.

EG BOOZS OLD CABIN WHISKEY, 7⅝″, greenish aqua $60–90
FLASK, 12-diamond pattern, 4¾″, amethyst, OP, possibly Emil Larson..........
.... $130–160

Left, Reproduction, eagle-grapes, with pebbly surface. Center, Reproduction, Jenny Lind. Right, Reproduction, Simon's Centennial Bitters, with pebbly surface. PHOTOS COURTESY OF NEIL GROSSMAN.

FLASK, ribbed and swirled, possibly Emil Larson, 4¾″, amethyst, OP ....
.... $110–150
FLASK, swirled ribbing, 6″, amethyst, OP...................................$250–325
FLASK, swirled ribs, possibly Emil Larson, 6″, amethyst, OP..........$125–150
FLASK, with two strips of rigaree, 5½″, amethyst with green rigaree, OP ....
....$150–200
JENNY LIND-GLASS FACTORY, GI-107a, calabash, emerald green, OP $15–20

SARSAPARILLA BOTTLES

Sarsaparilla originally gained its popularity in the 17th century as a blood purifier, and for many years it was believed to be a cure for syphilis. In the United States, interest in sarsaparilla began in the 1820s when the drink was being advertised as helping with the ''perspiratory functions of the skin and imparting tone and vigor to debilitated constitutions.'' As the century went on, the boasted curative powers of sarsaparilla were elevated to the point of quackery. Doctor Townsend's sarsaparilla, one of the more popular brands among bottle collectors, was touted as being a ''wonder and blessing of the new age/the most extraordinary medicine in the world.'' Generally, sarsaparilla bottles are of aqua or green coloration, but a few rare examples in blues and other colors exist. The reader is referred to *American Sarsaparilla Bottles* by John DeGrafft.

ADAMS & CARROLL SOLE AGENTS, D-1, 9⅝″, aqua...................... $75–100
AH BULL EXTRACT OF SARSAPARILLA, D-28, 7″, aqua, OP, lip chip....$20–26
AH BULL EXTRACT OF SARSAPARILLA, D-28, 6⅞″, aqua, OP $75–90
ALLEN SARSAPARILLA CO, D-7, 9½″, aqua $50–75
ALLENS SARSAPARILLA, D-8, 8¼″, aqua............................$25–45
AYERS CONCENTRATED COMPOUND EXT, D-9, 7¾″, aqua, OP............$35–50
BELLS SARSAPARILLA, AM ROBINSON, D-18, 9¼″, aqua, with full label ....
....$70–90
BF WILLIAMS SYRUP OF SARSAPARILLA, D-223, 9½″, aqua, IP.....$1000–1500
BRISTOLS EXTRACT OF SARSAPARILLA, D-22, 5¾″, deep aqua, OP..... $75–100
BRISTOLS EXTRACT OF SARSAPARILLA, 5½″, aqua, OP $65–75
BRISTOLS EXTRACT OF SARSAPARILLA, BUFFALO, D-22-2, 5½″, aqua, OP.......
....$75–95
BRISTOLS EXTRACT OF SARSAPARILLA, BUFFALO, D-22, 5½″, aqua, OP ....
....$40–55
BRISTOLS GENUINE, D-23, aqua $55–75
BRISTOLS GENUINE SARSAPARILLA, JDG-23, 11″, aqua $20–30
BRISTOLS GENUINE SARSAPARILLA, D-23, 10⅜″, aqua, IP $400–500
BRISTOLS SARSAPARILLA, D-22-2, 5½″, aqua, OP $45–55
BROWNS SARSAPARILLA, D-24, 9¼″, aqua...................................$15–25

BURR & WATERS SARSAPARILLA, D-32 var, 10½″, light brown pottery ....
.... $225–300
CD COS SARSAPARILLA RESOLVENT, D-40, 8½″, amber....................$45–60
CHARLES JOLY PHILADELPHIA, D-114, 10″, amber, crown top $35–50
CHARLES JOLY PHILADELPHIA, D-114, 9¾″, yellow, stain $25–30
CORWITZ SARSAPARILLA, D-47, 9½″, aqua....................................$55–75
CROWELL, CRANE & BRIGHAM YELLOW DOCK, D-51, 9¼″, aqua, OP ....
.... $200–300
DALTONS SARSAPARILLA & NERVE TONIC, 9½″, aqua, in box $50–75
DALTONS SARSAPARILLA & NERVE TONIC, 9½″, aqua $18–24
DEWITTS SARSAPARILLA, CHICAGO, D-61, 9″, aqua........................$35–45
DR AP SAWYERS ECLIPSE SARSAPARILLA, D-63, 9″, aqua.................$60–75
DR AS HOPKINS COMPOUND EXT, D-103, 9″, aqua $75–100
DR BAILEYS ELLIOT BROS & CO BRISBANE, aqua.........................$100–150
DR BELDINGS WILD CHERRY SARSA, D-16, 9″, aqua $50–70
DR BLACKWELLS SARSAPARILLA, D-21-1, 9¾″, aqua, IP $225–275
DR CRONKS SARSAPARILLA BEER, 12-sided, D-50, 10″, gray pottery... $80–120
DR CRONKS SARSAPARILLA BEER, eight-sided, D-50-4, gray pottery... $125–160
DR CRONKS, WS SHERMAN, eight-sided, brownish pottery.............$150–200
DR CUMMINGS CO EXT OF SARSA, D-53, 7½″, aqua $75–100
DR CUMMINGS COMPOUND EXTRACT, D-52, 7″, aqua, OP, small spider crack
....$150–200
DR ER PALMERS COMPOUND EXTRACT, D-161, 9¼″, aqua.............$375–475
DR GUYSOTTS, D-90-1, aqua $75–100
DR GUYSOTTS, B & P NEW YORK, D-90-6, 8¾″, aqua, rectangular .. $125–160
DR GUYSOTTS COMPOUND EXTRACT, D-90, 9½″, olive amber, OP, 3″ shoulder
crack $60–90
DR GUYSOTTS COMPOUND EXTRACT, D-90, 9¼″, deep olive amber, OP ....
....$1300–1800
DR GUYSOTTS COMPOUND EXTRACT, D-90-9, 9⅜″, aqua, OP $150–250
DR GUYSOTTS YELLOW DOCK, deep aqua, IP $75–95

Sarsaparilla, Old Dr. Townsend's. PHOTO COURTESY
OF NEIL GROSSMAN.

DR GUYSOTTS YELLOW DOCK, D-90, 9″, aqua $20–30
DR GUYSOTTS YELLOW DOCK, D-90, 10″, deep aqua, IP $150–200
DR GUYSOTTS YELLOW DOCK, oval, D-90, 10⅛″, deep blue aqua, IP...........
....$250–350
DR IRA BAKERS, D-11, aqua, stained...$80–100
DR IRA BAKERS, D-11, colorless $100–150
DR J ROSES SARSAPARILLA, JDG-182, 9⅜″, aqua, IP $200–260
DR JARMANS, D-113, aqua...$45–55
DR MILES WINE OF SARSAPARILLA, D-151, 9″, aqua.....................$55–75
DR MORLEYS SARSAPARILLA & 100 POTASS, D-155, 9½″, aqua $70–105
DR MYERS VEGETABLE EXTRACT, D-158, 9⅞″, aqua, OP.............. $225–300
DR POPES SARSAPARILLA (ON LABEL), D-PL-71, 6½″, aqua, OP........$30–45
DR RUSSELLS BALSAM OF HOREHOUND, D-185, 9⅜″, aqua, OP $150–250
DR STOCKERS SARSAPARILLA, 9½″, pale green aqua, OP...............$400–600
DR THOMSONS SARSAPARILLA, D-204, 9″, aqua $50–75
DR TOWNSENDS, JDG-206, 9½″, olive amber, OP $150–200
DR TOWNSENDS SARSAPARILLA, 9⅝″, green with yellow tint, IP $130–170
DR TOWNSENDS SARSAPARILLA, D-206, 9⅝″, yellow, OP............$1750–2250
DR TOWNSENDS SARSAPARILLA, D-206, 9⅝″, olive green, OP $80–120
DR TOWNSENDS SARSAPARILLA, D-206, 9⅜″, deep green with a hint of yellow,
IP $140–180
DR TOWNSENDS SARSAPARILLA, D-206, 9¾″, medium blue green, IP $140–180
DR TOWNSENDS SARSAPARILLA, D-206, 9½″, olive amber, OP $80–120
DR TOWNSENDS SARSAPARILLA, D-206, 9½″, medium olive green, OP ....
.... $90–120
DR TOWNSENDS SARSAPARILLA ALBANY, D-206, 9⅜″, olive green, OP ....
.... $100–130
DR TOWNSENDS SARSAPARILLA ALBANY, D-206, 9½″, olive amber, OP..........
.... $100–130
DR TOWNSENDS SARSAPARILLA IIII, D-206, 9½″, deep amber, OP... $300–400
DR TUTTS, NEW YORK, D-209-2, 7½″, amber $75–95
DR WEBSTERS SARSAPARILLA, D-213, 5¾″, aqua, OP.................... $110–150
DR WILCOX'S COMPOUND EXTRACT OF, D-221-1, 9⅜″, deep blue green, IP,
backwards "S" $600–800
DR WINSLOWS SARSAPARILLA, D-225, 8⅞″, aqua...........................$70–95
DR WOODWORTHS, BIRMINGHAM, CT, D-229, 9¾″, aqua, OP.........$100–150
DR WYNKOOPS KATHARISMICHONDURAS, D-232, 10⅛″, cobalt blue, OP.........
....$1400–1900
EDWIN N JOY CO SAN FRANCISCO, D-115, 8¾″ aqua $30–45
EMERSONS 50¢ SARSAPARILLA, D-66, 9½″, aqua............................$45–65
FOLEYS SARSAPARILLA, D-72, 9″, amber $30–45
GOLD METAL SARSAPARILLA, D-81, 9″, amber $65–90
GOOCHS EXTRACT OF SARSAPARILLA, D-82, 9¼″, colorless, label $40–45
GRAEFENBERG CO, SARSAPARILLA COMPOUND, D-84, 7″, aqua, OP $70–90
GRIFFITHS SARSAPARILLA, aqua $100–150
HALLS, D-92-2, aqua $75–100
HALLS SARSAPARILLA, JR GATES & CO, D-92, 9″, aqua....................$45–70
HAMBOLTS (ON LABEL), D-PL-38, aqua, OP $60–90
ID BULLS EXT OF SARSAPARILLA, D-29, 6¾″, aqua, OP...................$40–55
INDIAN SARSAPARILLA, JJ MACK & CO, D-110, 9″, aqua, double-collared lip
....$150–225

J CALEGARIS COMPOUND EXTRACT, D-36, 7″, aqua $85–110
J&T HAWKS MASURYS SARSAPARILLA, D-142-2, 11¼″, aqua $250–325
JA TARRANT, DRUGGIST, NY, aqua, OP, labeled...........................$70–100
JOHN BULL EXTRACT OF SARSAPARILLA, D-30, 8¾″, light green.......$90–135
JOHN BULLS, D-30-9, 9″, cornflower blue, IP...............................$475–550
JOHN BULLS EXTRACT OF SARSAPARI, 8¾″, aqua.............................$30–40
JOYS VEGETABLE SARSAPARILLA, D-115-var, 8¾″, amber, labeled $70–90
KELLEY & CO SARSAPARILLA, D-117, 7¾″, aqua, OP.....................$80–120
KENNEDYS SARSAPARILLA, D-119, 9⅝″, amber.............................$50–75
KENNEDYS SARSAPARILLA, D-119, 9½″, amber, labeled $120–160
KENNEDYS SARSAPARILLA, D-119-var, 9½″, aqua, double-collared lip $130–180
LANGLEYS, D-126-2, green $450–650
LANGLEYS, D-126-2, aqua..$200–300
LEONS SARSAPARILLA, D-128, 9″, aqua....................................$70–90
LEVINGS & CO, D-129, 7¾″, blue green $250–325
LOG CABIN SARSAPARILLA, D-138, 9″, amber............................$100–150
MANNERS DOUBLE EXTRACT, D-140, 7¾″, aqua............................$70–90
MASURYS, JT HAWKS, ROCHESTER, NY, D-143-2, 11¼″, aqua........ $200–250
MASURYS SARSAPARILLA CATHARTIC, D-143, 6½″, aqua, OP..........$125–160
MASURYS SARSAPARILLA COMPOUND, 11⅜″, aqua $350–400
MASURYS SARSAPARILLA COMPOUND, D-143-1, 8¼″, aqua, OP....... $200–250
MCLEANS SARSAPARILLA, D-148, 9¼″, light green......................$75–95
MYERS, D-158, aqua, IP $300–400
MYERS VEGETABLE EXTRACT, D-158, 8⅛″, aqua, lip chip $80–110
OLD DR J TOWNSENDS SARSAPARILLA, D-206-3, 9¾″, blue green, IP............
....$150–180
OLD TOWNSENDS SARSAPARILLA, NEW YORK, D-206-3, 9½″, emerald green,
IP $180–250
PRIMLEYS SARSAPARILLA, D-172-2, 9½″, aqua, "Sherman Primley" on side
....$50–65
RADWAYS SARSAPARILLIAN RESOLVENT, D-176, 7½″, aqua.................$15–25
RIKERS, D-180, colorless, slight purple..$60–80
RUSHS SARSAPARILLA, NEW YORK, D-184, 8¾″, aqua $35–50
SANDS GENUINE, D-188-1, aqua...$75–100
SANDS GENUINE SARSAPARILLA, D-188, aqua, OP $90–130
SANDS GENUINE SARSAPARILLA, NEW YORK, 10″, aqua, rectangle $100–130
SANDS SARSAPARILLA, D-187, 6″, aqua, OP $35–50
SANDS SARSAPARILLA, NEW YORK, aqua, OP $30
SHAKER (WITH LABEL), D-123, aqua $75–100
SKODAS DISCOVERY, BELFAST, ME, D-196, 9″, amber $75–95
STEVENS SARSAPARILLA, D-198, 8¼″, aqua $30–45
TURNERS SARSAPARILLA BUFFALO NY, D-208, 12″, deep aqua........ $300–400
TURNERS SARSAPARILLA BUFFALO NY, D-208, 12½″, aqua..............$300–375
WALKERS, D-211, aqua..$135–175
WESTS SARSAPARILLA, D-215, 8¾″, aqua $70–95
WETHERELLS SARSAPARILLA, D-216, 9⅜″, aqua $75–105
WG KIDDER COMP TINCT SARSAPARILLA, D-121, 7¾″, aqua $90–130
WHIPPLES SARSAPARILLA, D-217, 9⅛″, aqua................................$70–95
WS GREEN COMPOUND SARSAPARILLA BEER, D-88, pt., reddish brown pottery
....$225–300
YAGERS SARSAPARILLA, D-233, 8¾″, amber.................................$50–70

SCENT AND SMELLING BOTTLES

Scent and smelling bottles were important luxuries of Colonial America, made to help those of a feminine persuasion deal with some of the disagreeable aspects of colonial life. With tight corsets and mammoth hoop skirts and garments the fashion rage of the day, smelling bottles were necessary to help women overcome the fainting and dizzy spells which often accompanied such tight and cumbersome clothing. Scent bottles, which were often filled with aromatic scents, were used to help the fairer sex overcome odiferous nuances associated with such things as the lack of bathing and sanitary facilities, and animals. Scent and smelling bottles were generally very small in size, and were often made in beautiful shapes and colors. The reader is referred to *American Bottles and Flasks and Their Ancestry* by McKearin and Wilson, pgs. 378–408, which the letter "H" refers to below.

ACORN-SHAPED, 2¾″, turquoise, with metal cap and chain.............. $90–125
BLOWN, HOURGLASS SHAPE, in cobalt with clear rigaree, 2¾″, OP.. $500–600
CONCENTRIC RING PATTERN ON OVAL, 2″, sapphire blue, OP $150–175
CONCENTRIC RING PATTERN, H105-13, 2⅜″, cobalt blue, OP......... $400–600
FLATTENED CHESTNUT, colorless with red and blue loopings, 2½″, OP ....
.... $175–225
HEART-SHAPED, H104-8, 2¼″, colorless $125–200
HEXAGONAL, with wide ogival panels, 2⅝″, black, metal cap $70–90
HEXAGONAL, with wide ogival panels, 2⅝″, fiery opal, metal cap $40–60
PRINCE OF WALES FEATHERS SCENT, raised feather pattern, 2¼″, deep blue,
OP..$110–140
RIBBED, 16 ribs slightly swirled, 3″, cobalt blue, OP $100–150
RIBBED, 18 swirled ribs, 2⅞″, colorless, OP $90–125
RIBBED, 20 swirled ribs, 2¾″, cobalt blue, OP $125–175
RIBBED, 20 swirled ribs, 3⅛″, pale green, OP............................ $100–145
RIBBED, 20 vertical ribs, 3⅛″, cobalt blue, OP........................... $90–130
RIBBED, 24 swirled ribs, pinched center, 3¾″, colorless, OP $100–150
RIBBED, 24 vertical ribs, 2⅞″, light green, OP $130–180
RIBBED, 26 swirled ribs, 3¼″, colorless, OP $90–120
RIBBED SCENT, 12 swirled ribs, 3⅛″, sapphire blue, OP................$150–200
RIBBED SCENT BOTTLE, 16 swirled ribs, 2⅞″, amethyst, OP...........$150–200
SALEM WITCH 1692 LUSCOMBS WITCH LIQUID, 3⅛″, teal blue, with glass
stopper.. $125–175
SEAHORSE, colorless with white loopings, 2⅜″, OP...................... $100–150
SEAHORSE, see H102, nos. 6–14, colorless with colorless rigaree, 2½″, OP ....
.... $60–90
SEAHORSE SCENT, 30-rib swirled mold, colorless with colorless rigaree, 3″,
OP..$110–140
SEAHORSE SCENT, cobalt with white loopings and white rigaree, 1⅝″, OP ......
.... $400–500
SEAHORSE SCENT, colorless with black and white loopings, 2¼″, OP $175–225
SEAHORSE SCENT, colorless with colorless rigaree, 2½″, OP.............$60–65

Scent/Smelling, two seahorse-shaped.
PHOTO COURTESY OF SKINNER'S, INC.

SEAHORSE SCENT, colorless with white loopings, 2½", OP $300–350
SEAHORSE SCENT, cobalt blue with colorless rigaree, 2½", OP $300–400
SEAHORSE SCENT, light teal green with white loopings, colorless rigaree, 2¼", OP $250–350
SEAHORSE SCENT, pale blue, white, and amethyst loopings, colorless rigaree, 2½", OP $250–350
SEAHORSE SCENT, white with yellow amethyst and blue loopings, OP, clear rigaree, with stopper $550–700
SUNBURST, ten rays and dots, 2⅝", colorless, OP $200–275
SUNBURST, 12 rays, nine beads, similar to H105-4, 2¾", colorless, OP $60–90
SUNBURST, circular, corrugated rim, H105-8, 1⅝", deep cobalt, OP $400–600
SUNBURST, flattened ellipse, 2⅝", amethyst, OP........................$250–375
SUNBURST, oval, 1⅞", colorless, OP $150–250
SUNBURST, shield-shaped, 2¹⁵⁄₁₆", amethyst, OP......................... $400–600
SUNBURST, shield type, 2⅞", deep cobalt, OP .... $300–$450
SUNBURST, shield type, 2¾", colorless, OP...............................$180–250
SUNBURST, starburst shape, 2¾", cobalt blue, metal cap................$250–350
SUNBURST SCENT, H105-4, 2¾", colorless with amethystine tint, OP. $180–220
TAPERED CYLINDER WITH HOBNAIL-LIKE PATTERN, 2⅞", cobalt, metal cap $140–200
TAPERED FORM WITH RIGAREE, close to H102-1, 3⅝", colorless, OP . $90–150
VERTICALLY RIBBED, 26 ribs, 1⅞", teal blue $60–80
WAISTED OCTAGONAL, H106-9, 2½", sapphire blue, metal cap $40–60
WAISTED OCTAGONAL, H106-9, 2½", fiery opal, metal cap................$50–70

SEAL BOTTLES

Seal bottles are those which have an applied glass seal on the shoulder or side of the bottle. The seal itself was a molten blob of glass placed on the side of the finished bottle; it was then stamped with a metal dye upon which some pertinent information had been engraved.

Early seal bottles, which were ordinarily used by nobility and wealthy people, carried with them great prestige and were usually symbols of rank, position, and wealth. The seals often contained a date, name, initials, coat of arms or other symbol of significance. In the 17th and 18th centuries, the use of seals became widespread among tavern owners. It is unclear when the first seal bottles were manufactured in the United States, but it is possible that some may have been made in New Jersey around 1750.

Seal bottles are valuable not only because of their beauty and rarity, but because of their historical significance as well. Bottle researchers have been able to very specifically identify bottle forms and changes in forms which corresponded with the dates on the seals. Seals are found on a wide variety of bottles ranging from the early shaft-and-globe-type wine bottles through the squat wine bottles, case gin bottles, and handled chestnut bottles of the mid-19th century, and even thereafter.

Collectors should be aware that the date on a sealed bottle may not always correspond with the year of manufacture, though a thorough understanding of the evolution of wine bottle form should help to confirm the age of a given bottle. Interested collectors are well-advised to read *Understanding Antique Wine Bottles* by Roger Dunbrell, as well as *American Bottles and Flasks and Their Ancestry* by McKearin and Wilson which the letter "H" refers to below.

A.B. (ON SEAL), shaft and globe, 6″ H × 2½″ base, olive green, OP $6000–8000

A.S./C.R., (ON SEAL), straight-sided cylinder, 11½″, olive green, three-piece mold, OP..$60–85

AM FILLMORE 1740, octagonal bottle, 9¾″, olive green, OP, ⅜″ spider crack $4500–5500

B GRIEVE 1727, mallet bottle, 5¾″, olive green, OP................. $2000–2300

BENJ FREDENHAM MARZARION 1717, onion form, 7″, olive green, OP........... .... $3500–4000

BENJN & HANNAH EDWARDS 1714, onion form, 7¼″ × 5¾″, deep olive green, OP..$1600–2200

Seal, a late 18th-century bottle. PHOTO COURTESY OF SKINNER'S, INC.

BOAR BENEATH CROWN, straight-sided form, 11¼″, olive green, OP .. $90–120

BRANDY 1815, cylinder, 12½″ × 4¼″, olive green, OP $200–250

COMET (IMPRESSED ON SEAL), 12½″, olive green, smooth base $90–100

CROWN & BULL (ON SEAL), onion with flat sides, 8¾″, olive amber, OP, crack $800–1000

DRAGON WITH WREATH (ON SEAL), metal form, 7½″, olive green, OP, crack $700–900

E GREENE 1805 (ON SEAL), 10″, olive green, OP $400–500

E HERBERT 1721, mallet, 7½″ × 5¾″, black, OP $1200–1600

EMMAN COLL, nearly straight-sided, 15½″, olive amber, OP $110–150

FLEUR-DE-LIS ON CHEVERON WITH SCROLLS, onion, 6¼″, olive green, OP.... .... $1000–1200

FORTUNE SEQUATTIR, 9″, olive green, OP $200–300

I ALSOP 1763, 12″, deep olive green, OP................................. $600–800

I BURTON NC, mallet seal bottle, 7¾″, medium olive green, OP, neck crack $500–700

I FEATHERS, 1789 (ON SEAL), 10⅝″, deep olive green, OP.............$190–230

I WATSON BILTONPARK ESQR, nearly straight-sided, 9⅜″ × 4½″, green, OP $200–250

I WATSON ESQ BILTONPARK, 9″, olive amber, OP $250–350

I.C. (ON SEAL), onion-form bottle, 6⅞″, olive green, OP, small stone crack $900–1200

IC 1731, mallet seal bottle, D plate 25, 7½″, olive green, OP $2000–2500

ICC (ON SEAL), long-necked seal bottle, 10″, olive green, OP $200–300

JAMES OAKES BURY 1771, straight-sided, 10¾″, olive green, OP $200–250

JAS OAKES BURY 1793, 9¾″, olive green, OP $250–350

JN BATHE 1799, cylinder, 9″ × 4¼″, black, OP $500–600

JNO FURSE 1823, WITH RICKETTS & CO GLASSWORKS (ON BASE), 10¼″, olive amber $140–180

JOHN WILSON 1741, mallet seal bottle, 8⅛″, olive green, OP.......$1200–1400

JOHN WINN JR (ON SEAL), three-piece mold, 8½″, olive green, OP. $250–300

JOS RISDON 1818, straight-sided bottle, 9¾″, olive green, OP..........$160–200

L FULL 1733, mallet seal bottle, 6⅛″, olive green, OP, 2″ lip crack $600–800

L FULL 1733, onion/mallet, 6½″ × 4¼″, olive green, OP, 2″ crack.......... .... $800–950

LS 1723 (ON SEAL), onion with flat sides, D plate 19, 6½″, olive green, OP $3500–4000

MARCELIN/DAVID, cylinder, jar form, 9½″, aqua, OP $200–250

MR 1729, mallet bottle, 7⅜″, olive green, OP, ⅝″ spider crack $700–900

MR JAS WILSON KIRKLAND 1770, almost straight-sided, long neck, 11⅞″, green, OP..$350–450

P BAFTARD 1725, bladder shape, 7¼″ × 5¼″ × 4″, olive green, OP $1300–1600

P BAFTARD 1726 (ON SEAL), bladder shape, 7¼″, olive green, OP, ½″ lip edge chip.. $2000–2500

P GREGORY BIDDEFORD 1771, cylinder, 9¾″ × 4¼″, black, OP..... $400–600

PF HERRING (ON RIBBON SEAL), 8⅜″, amber $70–90

POPES MITRE ABOVE "WB," onion bottle, 4¾″ H × 3⅝″ base, olive green, OP, chip.. $800–1000

PWA, 1799 (ON SEAL), 10½″, olive green, OP............................ $300–400

RHC 1815, straight-sided bottle, 10⅜″, olive green, OP $160–190

RHC 1816, 10¾″, olive amber, OP $150–200

RSL 1723, mallet seal bottle, 9¼″, olive green, OP $1000–1400

SHOOTING STAR (ON SEAL), cylinder, 13″, olive green $90–120

SIR W STRICKLAND BAR BOYNTON (ON SEAL), 10½″, olive amber, OP..........
.... $150–200

T 1770, seal bottle, nearly straight-sided, 11¼″, olive amber, OP.... $650–800

TC PEARSALL (ON SEAL), 10½″, olive green $400–450

THREE BIRDS IN CHEVRON BELOW ARM WITH DAGGER, onion, 5¹¹⁄₁₆″, olive
green, OP $1300–1600

THREE LIONS ON A SHIELD (ON SEAL), onion bottle, 5⅜″ × 4¼″, olive green,
OP $3500–4000

THREE STARS ON A CHEVRON, bladder form, 7⅞″, olive green, OP..............
.... $800–1200

THS SMITH KINGSWAY 1735, mallet seal bottle, 7¼″, olive green, OP...........
.... $1500–2000

TW 1757, mallet seal bottle, 8⅞″, olive green, OP $450–600

W LUDLOW (ON SEAL), form similar to H52-9, 12½″ × 5⅞″, dark olive green,
OP $400–550

WB 1765, squat seal bottle, 9″, olive green, OP $500–600

SNUFF BOTTLES

Snuff was introduced into Europe in the 16th century. It was a tobacco preparation which had been treated with a mixture of common salt and aromatic substances for scent and flavor such as cinnamon, nutmeg, and lavender. Snuff, which was generally inhaled via a powder form, was originally more popular than smoking tobacco and was used in both a recreational and sinus-clearing capacity. In the mid-18th century, snuff began to be advertised as a cure for headaches, catarrh, and other disorders.

Exactly when the first snuff bottles were blown in America is unclear, but it is certain that bottles were used in the 18th century, many of which were doubtless imported from England and Europe. Most of the 18th- and early 19th-century snuff bottles were unembossed and generally straight-sided, either square or rectangular with beveled edges which were blown in clay molds. The bottles were made with both narrow and wide mouths.

Early embossed snuff bottles are very rare and the first one made in America was blown in the 1820s. In the 19th century, snuff began to appear in rectangular and cylindrical aqua and colorless bottles, occasionally embossed with the maker's name or labeled. The reader is referred to *American Bottles and Flasks and Their Ancestry* by McKearin and Wilson, pgs. 259–262.

BLOWN, cylinder, flaring lip, 5¾″, 2⅝″ mouth, olive amber, OP $225–275
BLOWN, rectangular with beveled edges, 5⅝″, deep olive amber, OP, crude $200–250
CYLINDRICAL, 3½″, olive amber, OP, light inner stain $175–190
DOCT MARSHALLS SNUFF, 3¼″, aqua, OP, labeled $50–75
E ROOME TROY NEW YORK, 4½″, olive green, OP $150–175
E ROOME TROY NEW YORK, 4½″, olive amber, OP, original label $150–200
E ROOME TROY NEW YORK, 4¼″, pale bluish green, OP $500–700
E ROOME/TROY/NEW YORK, labeled, 4¼″, olive amber, OP $150–200
JJ MAPES No 61 FRONT ST N YORK, rectangle with beveled edges, 4⅜″, red amber, OP $600–900
JJ MAPES No 61 FRONT ST N YORK, rectangle, 4⅝″, olive amber, OP $600–850
LEVI GARRETT & SONS, labeled square with chamfered corners, 4⅜″, amber, OP... $180–220
OTTO LANDSBERG & CO, CELEBRATED SNUFF, 5″, cobalt $18–25
RECTANGULAR, with beveled edges, 5¼″, olive amber, OP, two shoulder bruises $70–90
RECTANGULAR, with beveled edges, 4½″, olive amber, OP, sheared lip $45–60
RECTANGULAR, with beveled edges, 6¼″, olive amber, lip chip, wear ..$30–40
RECTANGULAR, with beveled edges, 4½″, olive green, OP $60–70
RECTANGULAR, with beveled edges, 6⅝″, olive yellow, OP $600–800
SQUARE, 4¾″, olive amber, OP, crude, flaring lip $400–500
SQUARE BOTTLE, blown, unembossed, 6″ × 3″, emerald green, OP.$275–350
SQUARE SNUFF BOTTLE, 4″, yellow amber, OP $125–175
TRUE CEPHALIC SNUFF BY THE KINGS PATENT, 3¾″, aqua, OP....... $150–190
TRUE CEPHALICK SNUFF BY THE KINGS PATENT, 3½″, deep aqua, OP $150–200
WYMANS COPENHAGEN SNUFF, C-3089, qt., amber $60–75

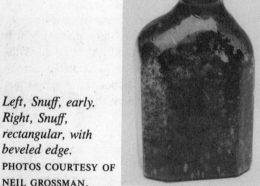

Left, Snuff, early. Right, Snuff, rectangular, with beveled edge.
PHOTOS COURTESY OF NEIL GROSSMAN.

SODA BOTTLES

It was the popularity of mineral water which eventually led to the invention of soda. Basically, soda was artificially carbonated water, and it was being made in America in the first quarter of the 19th century. Then, in the 1830s, an English immigrant named John Matthews introduced the use of marble chips, which were broken down to form carbonic acid, into making soda water. In fact, by purchasing all the scrap marble which had been left over from the building of St. Patrick's Cathedral in New York City, Mr. Matthews had enough marble to make 25 million gallons of soda water! In the 1830s, various flavors also began to be added to the soda water.

As to the forms used for these early soda bottles, they were often similar to the types used for mineral waters. Because carbonated water was being used, however, a sturdier vessel had to be invented, which soon led to the use of the thick-walled blob top-type of soda bottle, which continued to be used into the 20th century. Also, because of the dangers of the corks popping out from the high pressure, several innovative solutions were developed, such as the Hutchinson-type wire stoppers, lightning-type wire stoppers, Cod stopper bottles, and the so-called "torpedo"-style bottles which lay on their sides, thus allowing the soda to keep the cork moist and prevent the cork from drying and popping out of the bottle. The reader is referred to *American Bottles and Flasks and Their Ancestry* by McKearin and Wilson, pgs. 233–244.

A M'FARLAND PHILADA REGISTERED, teal blue, IP $80–120
A SCHROTH SCH.LL HAVEN SUPERIOR MINERAL WATER UNION GLASS WORKS, 7³⁄₈″, blue, IP $350–450
A URMAN, KERSEY, PA, Hutchinson stopper, greenish aqua $9–12
AC BOTTLING CO, ARKANSAS CITY, KS, crown top, 6½ oz., colorless $3–5
ACME SODA WATER, PITTSBURGH, aqua $18–20
AERATED SODA WATER, cobalt blue, IP $90–120
AF DIETZ, KNOWERVUILLE, ALBANY CO NY, green, Hutchinson type, embossed cow... $20–30
ALBERT KING, CLARIDGE, PA, colorless, Hutchinson $25–35
AM FARLAND PHILADA, deep teal blue, IP $50–60
ARCHDEACON'S/MINERAL WATERS/PATTERSON, 1850, 7¼″, emerald green, IP, lip bruise $250–300
ARIZONA BOTTLING WORKS, PHOENIX, green, Hutchinson type $60–80
ARROWS, COCA-COLA BOTTLE, CINCINNATI, OHIO $45–50
ASHLAND BOTTLING WORKS, ASHLAND, WI, green, Hutchinson type....$25–35
ATLANTA CONSOLIDATED BOTTLING CO, green, Hutchinson type $10–12
AW SCHRADER, SCRANTON, PA, 6½″, aqua, Hutchinson $20–30
B&G SAN FRANCISCO-SUPERIOR MINERAL WATER, 7″ sapphire blue, IP, tiny base flake... $250–350

BACONS SODA WORKS, SONORA, CA, green, Hutchinson type..............$20–25
BALDY & BOWLES ACME, SHELTON, CT, colorless, Hutchinson...........$18–22
BALTIMORE LOOP, MISSOULA BOTTLING WORKS, MT, clear, Hutchinson type
....$25–30
BELFASR GINGER ALE CO, SAN FRAN, green, Hutchinson type............$35–40
BENNETTSVILLE BOTTLING WORKS, SC, colorless, Hutchinson $30–40
BLOUNT SPRINGS NATURAL SULPHUR WATER, cobalt blue.................$50–70
BOYD & BEARD/MINERAL WATER-B/ BOTTLE/, never sold, 7″, yellow green, IP,
neck flake.. $100–150
BOYD & BEARD/MINERAL WATER/B- PATENT, 6½″, yellowish green, IP.........
....$150–200
BOYD-BALT, ten-pin shape, 8½″ smooth base, applied lip, deep olive green,
base flake.. $500–600
BRUMMEL & BYRNE RICHMOND, VA, 8″, medium green, IP, ⅜″ lip chip......
....$35–45
BRUNSWICK COCA-COLA BOTTLING CO, BRUNSWICK, GA, Hutchinson ....
.... $400–500
BUCKLEY & WOODLIEF, 1000 CARONDELET STR, green, Hutchinson type ....
....$20–25
BUFFUM & CO PITTSBURGH SARSA. & MINERAL WATER, cobalt blue, ten-pin
shape..$1200–1500
BUFFUMS SARSAPARILLA & LEMON MINERAL WATER, ten-sided, cobalt blue, IP
.... $350–500
C ABEL & CO ST LOUIS, MISSOURI, 12-sided, ½ pt., pale blue green, IP, lip
bruise $40–55
C ABEL & CO ST. LOUIS MO SODA WATER, 12-sided, ½ pt., light blue green,
IP.. $125–175
C. CLEMINSHAW/SODA &/MINERAL WATER/TROY, NY, 6⅞″, sapphire blue, IP
....$150–200
C MATCHIN DANVILLE/UNION GLASS WORKS, 7″, cobalt blue, IP ... $750–900
C WHITTEMORE NEW YORK, blue aqua, IP $40–60
CALUMET BOTTLING WORK, M COHS PROP., green, Hutchinson type $10–14
CAMER & JACKY, PHILLIPSBURG, MT, aqua, Hutchinson type $25–30
CANTRELL & COCHRANE, 9½″, aqua, rounded bottom........................$7–9
CANTRELL COCHRANE, blue aqua, crown top $2–3
CARPENTER & COBB KNICKERBOCKER, ten-sided, light blue green, IP, potstone
bruise $160–220
CARPENTER & COBB KNICKERBOCKER SODA WATER, SARATOGA SPRINGS, 7⅝″
ten-sided, IP.. $700–900
CARPENTER & COBB KNICKERBOCKER SODA WATER SARATOGA SPRINGS, 7¼″
ten-sided, light green, OP... $125–175
CC KNICKER BOCKER SODA WATER, ten-sided, 7¼″ cobalt blue, IP. $200–300
CC SODA, COCA-COLA BOTTLING CO, WINFIELD, KS, 6½ fl oz., clear, crown
top $7–9
CD EGERT & CO, ALBANY, NEW YORK, 7″, reddish puce $250–325
CHANNEMANN & CO, ST LOUIS, MO, blob top, clear, light stain............$6–9
CHAPMANS SODA, round bottom, 8″, OP, rolled lip, aqua, cleaned.. $300–400
CHAS CABLE & SON-PO'KEEPSIE PREMIUM SARSAPARILLA, 7″, medium green,
IP.. $450–600
CIRCLE ARROW ABM 1912, JACKSON, TN, Coca-Cola bottle...........$100–150
CITY BOTTLING CO, NEW ORLEANS, LA, green, Hutchinson type $18–22

CITY STEAM BOTTLING WORKS, HANOVER YORK COUNTY, PA, colorless, Hutchinson..$25–35

CL KORNAHRENS, CHARLESTON, SC, green, Hutchinson type.............$20–30

CLARK & CO, pt., olive amber..$60–75

CLARKE & WHITE, pt., olive amber, OP................................... $90–100

CLARK & WHITE, C, NEW YORK, qt., olive green $20–30

CLARKE & WHITE C NEW YORK (WITH BACKWARD W), qt., olive green ....
....$175–250

CLARKSVILLE BOTTLING WORKS, CLARKSVILLE, TEXAS, aqua, Hutchinson.......
....$15–20

CLAUSS BROTHERS, ELIZABETH, NJ, Hutchinson stopper, aqua............. $7–10

CLICQUOT CLUB, aqua, crown top..$1–2

CLOVERDALE SPRING CO, green, crown top, four- or eight-leaf clover on base
....$2–3

CM EVANS, APOLLO ITHIA SPRINGS, SMITHVILLE, MO, green, Hutchinson type $20–30

CO JOHNSON & CO, TRENTON, NJ, green, Hutchinson type................$20–22

COCA-COLA (IN MIDDLE OF BOTTLE), HUNTSVILLE, ALA, light honey amber
....$40–50

COCA-COLA (IN MIDDLE OF BOTTLE), HUNTSVILLE, ALA, light honey amber, 6½ oz...$40–50

COCA-COLA (IN MIDDLE OF BOTTLE), HUNTSVILLE, ALA, dark amber ..$40–50

COCA-COLA (IN MIDDLE OF BOTTLE), HUNTSVILLE, ALA, light honey amber, 7 oz...$40–50

COCA-COLA (SCRIPT, FRONT BASE), JACKSON (ON REAR BASE), dark amber.....
....$55–70

COCA-COLA (SCRIPT, FRONT BASE), JACKSON (ON REAR BASE), light amber.....
....$55–70

COCA-COLA AND ARROWS (ON SHOULDERS), MEMPHIS, TN..............$30–35

COCA-COLA (AT BASE), CINCINNATI, OH.......................................$35–42

COCA-COLA BIRMINGHAM BOTTLING CO, Hutchinson $400–500

COCA-COLA BOTTLING CO (ON FRONT), NO 02, NO COCA-COLA (ON SHOULDER), COLUMBUS, OH 35–45

COCA-COLA BOTTLING CO, ANNISTON, ALA, colorless $14–17

COCA-COLA BOTTLING CO, BUFFALO, NY, colorless $7–10

COCA-COLA BOTTLING CO, WINONA, MINN, green, seltzer bottle $125–150

COCA-COLA BOTTLING CORP, ROCHESTER, NY, eight panels, colorless, 30 oz.,
....$75–100

COCA-COLA BOTTLING CORP, ROCHESTER, NY, eight panels, colorless, 6½ oz.
....$30–40

COCA-COLA BOTTLING WORKS, ROCHESTER, NY, colorless $8–10

COCA-COLA BOTTLING WORKS, ROCHESTER, NY, pt., colorless........ $100–140

COCA-COLA CROWN CARBONATING CO, HAMLET, NC, aqua...............$20–30

COCA-COLA (ON BASE), REGISTERED AND PHILA, PA (ON BACK SIDE) .$30–35

COCA-COLA (ON BASE), REGISTERED AND SCRANTON, PA (ON BACK SIDE).....
....$40–50

COCA-COLA (ON SHOULDERS), COCA COLA BOTTLING, COLUMBUS, OH, 6½ oz...$40–45

COCA-COLA (ON SHOULDERS), INDIANA, PA (ON BASE)....................$70–90

COCA-COLA (ON SHOULDERS), PITTSBURG, PA (ON FRONT BASE), 6½ oz. ......
....$40–44

COCA-COLA (ON SHOULDERS), PITTSBURGH, PA (ON FRONT BASE) $30–35
COCA-COLA TRADEMARK REGISTERED (IN SCRIPT), all embossing on shoulders
....$35–40
COCA-COLA WILSON GOLDSBORO, NC, colorless $18–22
COCA-COLA (IN SCRIPT AT BASE), HUNTSVILLE, ALA 60–80
COCA-COLA (IN SCRIPT), KNOXVILLE, TN, aqua $55–70
COCA-COLA (IN SCRIPT, FRONT BASE), CHATTANOOGA, TN (ON BASE), light
amber $40–48
COCA-COLA (IN SCRIPT, FRONT BASE), JOHNSON CITY (ON REAR BASE) ....
.... $60–80
COCA-COLA (ON FRONT, REAR SHOULDER), CHATTANOOGA, TN (ON FRONT
BASE), ARROW $60–90
COCA-COLA (ON SHOULDERS AND FRONT BASE), KNOXVILLE, TN, WITH AR-
ROWS $35–45
COCA-COLA, BIRMINGHAM, ALA, colorless, straight-sided, label $90–100
COCA-COLA, BOTTLING WORKS (SCRIPT), 30 oz., aqua $125–165
COCA-COLA, BOTTLING WORKS (SCRIPT), 7 oz., colorless $30–40
COCA-COLA, CAMPELLSVILLE, KY, amber, paper label $90–100
COCA-COLA, CINCINNATI, OHIO, WITH ARROW, amber $20–30
COCA-COLA, CLEVELAND, OHIO, yellow amber $17–23
COCA-COLA, CLEVELAND, OHIO, dark amber $18–22
COCA-COLA (IN SCRIPT ON SHOULDER AND BOTTOM WITH ARROW), HOLLY
SPRINGS, MS $50–60
COCA-COLA, JACKSON, TENN, ARROWS, amber $80–95
COCA-COLA, JOHNSON CITY, TENN, amber..................................$40–50
COCA-COLA, KNOXVILLE, TN..$35–40
COCA-COLA, LARGE ARROW, KNOXVILLE, TENN, amber,...................$35–45
COCA-COLA, LEXINGTON, KY, amber, ...$50–60
COCA-COLA, LOUISVILLE, KY, ARROWS, amber,............................$50–65
COCA-COLA, MIDDLESBORO, KY, amber....................................... $80–100
COCA-COLA (ON BASE), RICHMOND (ON BACK BASE), registered on front, am-
ber..$40–45
COCA-COLA, PENSACOLA, FLA, colorless, straight-sided $80–100

Soda, Codd type. PHOTO COURTESY OF NEIL GROSSMAN.

Coca-Cola, Roxboro, NC, colorless, straight-sided, label...............$90–110
Coca-Cola, Toledo, Ohio, colorless $20–30
Coca-Cola, Toledo, Ohio, amber $20–30
Coca-Cola, Tupelo, Mississippi, amber, worn $150–200
Coca-Cola, Whitesburg, KY, amber $125–175
Coca-Cola, Williamsport, PA, 7 oz., amber $40–50
Coca-Cola, Wilmington, NC (All In Script On Base) $45–55
Coca-Cola, Winchester, KY, amber $100–140
Concord Bottling Co, Concord, NH, green, Hutchinson type, labeled ......
....$45–60
Congress & Empire, C, plain back, pt., olive green $55–65
Cowan Bros, Jamestown, NY, Hutchinson stopper, colorless..............$9–12
Crystal Palace Premium Soda Water, 7¼″ emerald green, IP, lip bruise
....$350–450
Crystal Palace Premium Soda Water, 7¼″, deep blue green, IP, bruises on face...$450–500
DA Knowlton, high-shouldered type, qt. $30–45
Dan McPolin, Park City Bottling Works, UT, green, Hutchinson type, base bruise $30–40
Dan McPolin, Park City Utah, purple, Hutchinson type................$50–60
Dearborn 83 Third Avenue Superior Plain Soda, aqua, ten-pin $50–70
Delaney & Young, Eureka, CA, clear, crown top..........................$3–4
Diamond Bottling Works, Miami, OK, green, Hutchinson type $30–40
Dixon & Carson 41 Walker St NY, emerald green $75–110
Donat & Motis, Chicago, Ill, green, Hutchinson type...................$12–15
DR Brown, cylindrical, ½ pt., green, IP $150–200
DR Brown New York B, medium emerald green, IP $175–225
Dyottville Glass Works/Philada, three-mold, qt., olive amber, IP, small lip chip, wear...$125–175
E Bigelow/& Co/Springfield Mass-Soda Water, 7⅜″, sapphire blue, IP, lip flake...$125–175
E Bigelow/Springfield/Mass-Porter & Ale, 6¼″, medium green, IP ....
....$80–120
E Carrolls Soda & Sarsaparilla Depot, 7″, aqua $200–250
E Smith Elmira, NY, ½ pt., cobalt blue, IP $300–400
E.S.&H.-Superior/Soda Water/Union Gls Works, 7½″, emerald green, IP
....$100–150
Eagle NY-Union Glass Works, Phila, 7¼″ medium cobalt blue, IP ....
....$500–700
Empire Spring Co E, qt., blue green $30–40
EW&Co, with eagle and shield, aqua...$30–42
Excelsior Soda Works Co Ltd Hilo, aqua, Hutchinson..................$25–30
Excelsior Water, eight-sided, 7¼″, teal, IP, small lip flake $125–175
F Fladung, Reading, O, green, Hutchinson type $20–25
F Hearle, East London, 8″, aqua, "torpedo" Cod $10–15
F Scrader/Phila XXX/Scranton, PA, 6⅛″, medium blue green, IP, inner lip bruise $60–90
Fabrica, Los Angeles, green, Hutchinson type $20–30
FC Banker, Fulton Chain, NY, colorless, Hutchinson $15–17
FX Spitznagel, Buffalo, NY, Hutchinson stopper, greenish aqua $9–12
G Ebberwein, Savannah GA, aqua, Hutchinson type......................$20–25

G Krieger, Buffalo, NY, Hutchinson stopper, greenish aqua $9–12

Galena Bottling Works, Galena, Kan, aqua, Hutchinson $12–15

Gardner & Co, ten-sided, cobalt blue $140–170

GB Selmer/California/Pop Beer-1872, 10½″, dark olive amber, light wear
.... $75–100

Genuine Belfast Ginger Ale GD Dows, aqua, round bottom $15–20

Geo Eagle, with embossed ribs, 6⅞″ medium green $500–650

Geo F Hewett Co, 1894, Worcester, MA, 11″, colorless, Hutchinson $20–30

Geo Gemenoen/Savannah/Geo, with eagle and flags, 7¼″, emerald green, IP,
light wear $200–275

Geo Jones, Fonda, NY, colorless, Hutchinson $12–14

Geo Schroeder, East St Louis, aqua, Hutchinson type $14–17

Geo Upp, Jr-York, PA, ten-pin shape, aqua 8½″, smooth base, minor wear
.... $350–450

Gettysburgh Katalysine Water, qt., light olive green $40–45

Geyser Soda, El Billings, Sac City, aqua, Hutchinson type $20–22

Geyser Spouting Spring, pt., aqua $40–45

Gibson & Co Mineral Water, ten-sided, light green, IP $600–850

Glazer Beverages-Seattle, USA, with seltzer siphon, 13″, canary ... $50–60

Gleason & Cole Pittsb.g, ten-sided, cobalt blue, IP $200–300

Gold Metals, Belfast 1895, 9″, colorless $6–8

GS Cushing Lowell Patent Pentucket Spring, emerald green, IP $75–100

H Denhalter & Son, Salt Lake City, UT, green, Hutchinson type, top bro-
ken off $5–7

H Schramm, Fullersburg, Ill, green, Hutchinson type, stain $7–8

H Schramm, Fullersburg, Ill, green, Hutchinson type $12–14

H Stater, Berlin, WI, green, Hutchinson type $25–35

H/Harris & Sons/Albany/Mineral Water, 7½″, pale aqua, IP $225–275

Hagertys/Glass Works/NY (On Base), 6⅜″, aqua $50–75

Haight & O'Brien, St Louis, MO, blob top, aqua, OP $12–14

Hamaku Soda Works Honokaa, colorless $15–20

Hamilton Glas Works NY, light green, IP $15–25

Hathorn Spring Saratoga, NY, qt., deep yellow olive $55–65

Hathorn Spring Saratoga, NY, qt., emerald green $40–50

Hathorn Spring Saratoga, NY, qt., black $70–75

Hayes Bros, Chicago, Ill, colorless, Hutchinson $10–13

Hennessy & Nolan, aqua, Hutchinson type $16–20

Henry Kaltenmeier, Clifton, SI, light green, Hutchinson type $20–24

Henry Roll, Blue Island, Ill, colorless, Hutchinson $18–23

Hollister & Co, Honolulu, aqua, Hutchinson $20–25

Home Bottling Co, Tulsa, OK, 7¾″, with swastika-type emblem $20–30

Hope Seltz & Mineral Water Manu, New Orlean, LA, green, Hutchinson
type $16–22

Houppert & Smyly, Birmingham, Ala, clear, Hutchinson type $12–16

Hudor Water Co, Buffalo, NY, lightning stopper, 14½″, blob top, color-
less $9–11

Huntington Coca-Cola Company, Huntington, WV, amber $30–40

HW Darling & Son, Newport, VT, blue aqua, Hutchinson $17–22

Hygeia Bottling Works, Pensacola, Fla, green, Hutchinson $18–20

ISP Lititz Springs Beverage Co, colorless, ten-pin shape $7–10

J & Dearborn/NY, H-241, 7¼″, cobalt blue, IP $400–500

J CARINS & BLOCK & CO ST LOUIS, MO, aqua, OP, blob top............. $10–13
J LAKE SCHENECTADY NY, cobalt blue, IP................................. $240–300
J LAKE SCHENECTADY, NY, ten-pin shape, 8″, cobalt blue $300–450
J LAKE, SCHENECTADY, NY, ten-pin shape 7⅝″, sapphire blue, IP, inner lip chip... $200–250
J OGDEN PITTSBURGH, emerald green, IP..................................$150–200
J SCHWEINHART PITTSBURGH PA, cobalt blue..................................$50–70
J SIMONDS/BOSTON/MINERAL WATER, 7⅛″, green, IP, small lip chip . $75–125
J ZERBE/DUNCANSVILLE, 7½″ cobalt blue, IP, ¼″ base chip......... $200–250
J&A DEARBORN MINERAL WATERS NEW YORK, eight-sided 6⅞″, medium teal blue, IP, small chip $150–200
J&A DEARBORN NEW YORK MINERAL WATERS, UNION GLASS WORKS, 8″, sapphire blue, IP..$200–275
JA LOMAX 14 & 16 CHARLES PLACE, cobalt blue........................... $90–120
JA LOMAX 14.16 & 18 CHARLES PLACE, cobalt blue........................$50–60
JA LOMAX/14 & 15/CHARLES PLACE/CHICAGO, 6⅞″, sapphire blue, exterior stain $60–90
JACKSONS NAPA SODA SPRINGS, aqua, Hutchinson type.....................$18–25
JAMES MEACHER, NEW BRUNSWICK, NJ, green, Hutchinson type $18–23
JD KANE, PHILADA, deep teal blue $30–40
JJ SPRENGER, ATLANTA, GA, aqua, Hutchinson type......................... $8–12
JJ SPRENGER, ATLANTA, GA, green, Hutchinson type, repaired lip..........$3–4
JOHN GRAF, MILWAUKEE, WI, green, Hutchinson type $18–20
JOHN MYNDERSE, SCHENECTADY, NY, clear, Hutchinson type............. $9–12
JOHNSTON & CO PHILADA, emerald green, IP $80–120
JT BROWN CHEMIST BOSTON-DOUBLE SODA WATER, 8⅞″, torpedo, deep aqua, potstone crack... $60–90
JT BROWN CHEMIST BOSTON-DOUBLE SODA WATER, torpedo, 9″, smooth base, minor wear.. $300–400
JW GARRISON BULLET STREET LOUISVILLE, aqua, IP, stain................$35–45
JW HARRIS SODA, NEW HAVEN, CONN, eight-sided, 7⅝″, sapphire blue, IP, few lip/rib chips.. $250–300
KEENEN MFG CO, BUTTE, MT, olive green, Hutchinson type $20–25
KNAPP ROOT BEER, labeled.. $15–18
L BEARD/MINERAL WATER-UNION GLASS WORKS/PHILA, 6⅞″, yellow green, IP... $125–175
L STEINBERGER, JERSEY CITY, NJ, Hutchinson stopper, aqua $9–12
LA LUZ MALAGARA HERMANOS LEON, GTO, green, Hutchinson type...$25–35
LA SIBERIA, FABRICA DE GASEOSAS, green, Hutchinson type $20–30
LAHANINA ICE CO, LTD, aqua, Hutchinson....................................$15–20
LANCASTER GLASS WORKS NY, sapphire blue, IP $75–100
LANCASTER GLASS WORKS NY, medium emerald green, IP $35–45
LANCASTER GLASS WORKS, medium cobalt blue, IP $125–175
LANCASTER X GLASS WORKS NY XX, sapphire blue, IP, small lip bruise........
....$35–44
LANCASTER X GLASS WORKS NY, 7″, teal blue, IP $150–175
LANCASTER X GLASS WORKS NY XX, sapphire blue, IP, inner lip bruise........
....$30–35
LANCASTER XXX GLASSWORKS NY, medium green, IP, chips $35–45
LANCASTER/GLASS WORKS/NY, 6″, medium sapphire blue, IP......... $150–175
LAVA HOT SPRINGS BOTTLING WORKS, IDAHO, 7½ oz., colorless $3–4

LEALAND ICE & COLD STORAGE CO, LELAND, MS, green, Hutchinson type.....
.... $14–18
LUKE BEARD, emerald green, ten-pin, OP $40–55
M MCCORMACKS CELEBRATED GINGER ALE, medium cobalt blue, round bottom $150–200
MANANTIAL DE AGUAS MINERALES, MEXICO, green, Hutchinson type ..$30–40
MANSFIELD BOTTLING CO, MANSFIELD, AR, green, Hutchinson type .. $60–80
MASSENA SPRING WATER, qt., blue $125–150
MASSENA SPRING WATER, qt., amber $175–190
ME SCOTT BOSTON MINERAL WATER, medium green, IP.............. $100–130
MERRITT & CO, HELENA, MT, aqua green, Hutchinson type.............. $8–12
METCALF & SONS BOTTLING WORKS, SALT LAKE, UT, colorless, Hutchinson type $20–30
MISSION DRY SPARKLING (ON BASE), black, crown top $4–5
MISSISQUOI A SPRING, qt., emerald green $75–90
MISSISQUOI A SPRING, with squaw and papoose, qt., yellow green..... $90–125
MO BENNETT, CHEYENNE, WY, green, Hutchinson type $15–18
MONROE BOTTLING WORKS, MONROE, LA, green, Hutchinson type......$20–25
MT CRAWFORD HARTFORD, CT UNION GLASS WORKS, cobalt blue, IP..... $250–350
MT CRAWFORD HARTFORD, CT-UNION GLASS WORKS, 7½", cobalt blue, IP, base flake...$225–275
MT CRAWFORD SPRINGFIELD, ten-sided base, ½ pt., deep sapphire blue, IP ....
.... $180–230
MT GROVE BOTTLING WORKS, GUS TRENKEL, MO, aqua, Hutchinson type......
.... $18–22
MT PLEASANT BOTTLING WORKS, MT PLEASANT, IA, green, Hutchinson type
.... $10–12
N DENHALTER & SON, SALT LAKE CITY, UT, green, Hutchinson type ..$70–85
NEW SOUTH BOTTLING WORKS, NEW ORLEANS, LA, green, Hutchinson type
.... $18–22
NEWTON & CO BOTTLERS NEW YORK PREMIUM N, green, IP $175–250
NEWTON & OLIVER BOTTLING WORKS, MANSFIELD, MO, colorless, Hutchinson type $25–30
NEWTON/BOTTLER-BROADWAY/316/NEW YORK, 7⅛", cobalt blue, IP, ⅛" potstone crack.. $600–750
OAK ORCHARD ACID SPRINGS, qt., yellow amber.......................... $90–120
OAK ORCHARD ACID SPRINGS, qt., green $55–70
OGDEN & GIBSON PITTSBURGH, deep aqua, IP $125–165
OGDEN BOTTLING WORKS, OGDEN, UTAH, purple, Hutchinson type, embossed eagle $40–50
OMAHA BOTTLING CO, OMAHA, NE, green, Hutchinson type $9–12
OWEN CASEY EAGLE SODA WORKS SAC CITY, deep sapphire blue $40–55
PACIFIC BOTTLING WORKS, TACOMA, WA, green, Hutchinson type $20–22
PARK CITY BOTTLING CO, CAPA CITY, UTAH, 7 oz., colorless...............$3–4
PAT WHALENS BOTTLING WORKS, HOXIE, AR, green, Hutchinson type ..$50–65
PATTERSON ICE MFG & SUPPLY CO, PATTERSON, LA, light green, Hutchinson type $18–23
PAUL VANDNEBERG, ROSELAND, ILL, aqua, Hutchinson type...............$18–22
PENNO'S/MINERAL-WATER/PROVIDENCE/RI, 7½", yellowish green, IP, lip bruise..$100–150
PEPSI COLA ESCAMBIA BOTTLING CO, PENSACOLA, FLA, Hutchinson. $400–500

PEPSI COLA JESSUPS BOTTLING WKS, CHARLOTTESVILLE, NC, aqua......$35–40
PEPSI COLA, BIRMINGHAM, ALA, dark amber $20–30
PEPSI COLA, KNOXVILLE, TENN, aqua...$13–17
PEPSI COLA, NEW BERN, NC, amber $25–35
PHILADA GLASS WORKS/BURGIN & SONS, 7¼", medium emerald green, IP, light wear...$60–75
PJ SERWAZI, MANAYUNK, PA, colorless, Hutchinson.......................$18–24
PRATT BROS, PIPESTONE, MN, green, Hutchinson type $14–18
PRIDE BOTTLING CO, CHICAGO, ILL, light aqua, Hutchinson type, deer embossed $18–25
PRIESTS NATURAL SODA, aqua, Hutchinson type.............................$18–24
PROPERTY OF COCA-COLA BOTTLING WORKS, JONESBORO, AR, all embossing on front.. $200–300
QUALITY BEVERAGES, PERRYTON, TEXAS, green, crown top................ $8–10
QUEEN CITY WATER CO, lightning stopper, 13½", aqua, blob top $6–8
R.C. & T. NEW YORK, cylindrical, ½ pt., puce, IP $1800–2200
RAMON SANTAELLA, OAXACA, MEX, green, Hutchinson type $25–35
RENFRO MANUFACTURING CO, ATLANTA, GA, green, Hutchinson type..$20–24
ROCKY MOUNTAIN BOTTLING CO, BUTTE, MT, green, Hutchinson type, stain $8–10
ROCKY MOUNTAIN BOTTLING CO, BUTTE, MT, green, Hutchinson type $14–18
RODGER & WELLER SCHENECTADY NY, light blue green, IP............. $90–120
RODGER & WELLER SCHENECTADY NY, aqua, IP $120–150
ROSS'S, BELFAST, 9", aqua, round bottom....................................$6–8
S & J MARLOR PROV RI, blue green, IP, ½" lip crack $50–75
S PREMIUM MINERAL WATERS, eight-sided, 7⅝", deep green, IP $175–225
S SMITH AUBURN NY 1857, ten-sided, cobalt blue, IP.................. $400–500
S SMITH, AUBURN NY, ten-pin form, 8⅜", cobalt, smooth base, light wear $500–650
S SMITH/KNICKERBOCKER/MINERAL & SODA/WATERS/NEW YORK, 6¾", green, IP, light wear..$170–200
S SMITH KR S WATER 1856 AUBURN NY, ten-sided, 7⅜", medium sapphire blue, IP...$150–250
S&P SAUGERTUS SUPERIOR MINERAL WATER UNION GLASS WORKS, 7⅝", teal, IP, lip crack $150–200
SARATOGA A SPRING CO, pt., bright yellow green $140–180
SARATOGA HIGHROCK, pt., deep emerald green...........................$240–280
SARATOGA RED SPRING, pt., emerald green $40–50
SARATOGA RED SPRING, CONGRESS, qt., blue green....................$110–130
SARATOGA (STAR) SPRING, qt., yellow amber............................... $80–100
SARATOGA (STAR) SPRING, qt., yellow amber, base bruise.................$60–70
SARATOGA (STAR) SPRING, qt., yellow amber, burst bubble $50–60
SARATOGA (STAR) SPRINGS, qt., deep olive green.........................$110–130
SARATOGA VICHY SPOUTING SPRING, pt., aqua $75–85
SCHULTZ & WALKER, NY, SCHWALBACH, amber.......................... $85–105
SCHWARZENBACH BREWING CO, Hutchinson stopper, colorless $8–10
SEITZ & BRO EASTON PA, eight-sided, cobalt blue, IP $90–120
SHAW & CO, PORT ELIZABETH, 7½", aqua, Cod bottle......................$6–8
SK MAURER TAYLORSVILLE, PA, medium blue green.......................$50–65
SOUTHERN BOTTLING CO, ATLANTA, GA, colorless, Hutchinson, lip chips, stain $6–9

Soda, torpedo-shaped. PHOTO COURTESY OF NEIL GROSSMAN.

SOUTHERN BOTTLING CO, ATLANTA, GA, colorless, Hutchinson.......... $10–14
SOUTHERN BOTTLING CO TERRELL TEX, 6⅜″, aqua, Hutchinson stopper........
....$60–75
SOUTHWICK & TUPPER, NEW YORK, ten-sided, 7½″, cobalt blue, IP . $275–350
SS KNICKER BOCKER SODA WATER, ten-sided, 7½″, cobalt blue, IP .. $150–200
ST JOSEPH BOTTLING CO, ST JOSEPH, MO, green, Hutchinson type $23–28
STANDARD BOTTLING CO, SPRINGFIELD, MO, aqua, Hutchinson type $25–30
SUMTER BOTTLING WORKS, SUMTER, SC, purple, Hutchinson type $30–40
SUPERIOR SODA WATER, with eagle on shield, ½ pt., deep blue, IP .. $500–600
SUPERIOR SODA WATER, with eagle and flags, olive amber, IP........ $900–1200
SWEENY & CHERRY/33 NORFOLK ST/NEW YORK, 7¼″, cobalt blue ... $125–150
SYRACUSE SPRINGS, EXCELSIOR, pt., deep red amber.........................$70–90
TASSIE & CO BROOKLYN, eight-sided, deep emerald green, IP $1500–2000
TEMMETT & SONS, OGDEN, UTAH, green, Hutchinson type $20–30
THE SARATOGA SPOUTING SPRINGS, qt., aqua..................................$40–50
THE SPA PHILA, THD, CONGRESS WATER, pt., yellow amber........... $150–175
TRADEMARK COCA-COLA BOTTLING WORKS AND CLARKSBURG, W VA (ON
FRONT), 6½ oz...$70–90
TUPPER & BEEBE NEW YORK, ten-sided, light blue green, IP...........$160–220
TW GILLETT, NEW HAVEN, eight-sided, 7⅝″, medium cobalt blue, IP, ⅜″ base
chip..$250–350
TWEDDLE'S/CELEBRATED/SODA OR MINERAL/WATERS, 7¾″, medium blue, IP
....$150–250
TWEDDLES CELEBRATED SODA OR MINERAL WATER, emerald green, IP ....
....$110–150
TWEDDLES CELEBRATED SODA OR MINERAL WATERS, emerald green, IP.........
....$90–120
TWIN CITY BOTTLING WORKS, TEXARKANA, AR, aqua, Hutchinson type.........
....$10–12
TWIN CITY BOTTLING WORKS, TEXARKANA, AR, aqua, Hutchinson type.........
....$15–18
UNION GLASS WORKS/H KNEBEL-NEW YORK, 7⅜″, deep aqua, exterior wear
....$60–90
UNION LAVA WORKS/CONSHOHOCKEN/PATD 1852, 7¼″ cobalt blue, IP, ¼″ lip
bruise.. $300–400
VARTRAY, BUFFALO, NY, 6 oz., crown top, colorless...........................$2–3
VERMONT SPRINGS SAXE & CO, SHELDON, VT, qt., bright emerald green.......
....$90–120

Vess Dry Registered, 6½ oz., green $2–3
Vincent Hathaway & Co Boston Ginger Ale, aqua, round bottom..$20–30
Vinita Bottling Works, Vinita, IT, green, Hutchinson type...........$20–25
W Eagle New York, Union Glass Works, Phila, 7¼″ sapphire blue, IP,
light wear $200–250
W Eagles Superior Soda, cylinder, ½ pt., deep sapphire blue, IP . $250–300
W Heiss Jrs Superior-Eagle, H-69, ½ pt., deep sapphire, IP $1500–2000
W Riddle Philada, green, IP $20–30
W Ryer, ½ pt., deep sapphire blue, IP, lip bruise $70–90
Wailua Soda Works Ltd, aqua...$20–25
Waimea Water Co Ltd, aqua, Hutchinson $20–25
Waldron Bottling Works, Waldron, AR, colorless, Hutchinson $18–25
Waldron Bottling Works, Waldron, Ark, colorless, Hutchinson $15–20
Waring Webster & Co, eight-sided, deep cobalt blue, IP $450–550
Warsaw Bottling Works, 9″, green, Hutchinson.........................$15–20
Washington Lithia Well, pt., aqua.......................................$275–325
WH Cawley Co DBW, Dover NJ, green, Hutchinson type...............$20–30
Wm A Carpenters Mineral Water Hudson, NY, 7″, eight-sided, yellow
green, IP, few small chips $375–475
Wm Eagle New York Premium Soda Water, ½ pt., sapphire blue, IP ....
....$150–250
Wm Eagle New York Premium Soda Water, eight-sided, 7¼″, cobalt blue,
IP, light wear..$150–200
Wm P Davis & Co Excelsior Mineral Water Brooklyn, 7½″, IP, cobalt
....$125–175
Wm Russell Balt, torpedo shape, medium green......................$800–1200
Wm W Lappeus Premium Soda, ten-sided, cobalt blue, IP $350–500
Yuncker Bottling Co, Tacoma, WA, green, Hutchinson type..........$20–23

TARGET BALLS

Target balls are small round bottles which were used much as clay pi-
geons are used today for target practice. Target balls were filled with
smoke, confetti, silk ribbon or feathers to clearly mark when they were
shot in midair. Although the bottles were introduced to America in the
1850s, they did not gain wide popularity until the 1860s and 1870s when
Buffalo Bill Cody and Annie Oakley used them in their Wild West shooting shows. In the early days, the target balls were thrown by hand into
the air, but in the 1880s a mechanical device was invented to throw the
balls. By 1900, target balls had all but become obsolete, due to the
invention of the clay pigeon. They are rare today since they were made
to be broken, and they come in a variety of colors. Target balls have also
become extremely collectible and costly in recent years.

Target Ball, Bogardus. PHOTO COURTESY OF
SKINNER'S, INC.

BOGARDUS, QUILTED, 2½", light yellow olive..............................$280–320
BOGARDUS, QUILTED, 2½", cobalt blue $450–600
BOGARDUS, QUILTED, 2½", amber $100–150
BOGARDUS, QUILTED, 2½", deep yellow olive $325–425
BOGARDUS, QUILTED, 2½", medium olive green...................... $300–500
BOGARDUS, QUILTED, 2½", olive amber................................. $300–500
C NEWMAN, amber, 2½" $700–900
HOCKEY PATENT, 2½", light green $500–800
IRA PAINES FILLED BALL, 2½", yellow amber........................... $200–250
L JONES GUNMAKER BLACKBURN, 2¾", light cobalt blue $200–300
L JONES GUNMAKER BLACKBURN, 2¾", aqua $250–350
NB GLASS WORKS PERTH, 2½", cornflower blue......................... $75–100
NB GLASS WORKS, PERTH, 2½", cobalt blue, ⅛" stress crack......... $75–100
NB GLASS WORKS, PERTH, 2½", cobalt blue, backward "SS" variant ....
.... $100–150
NB GLASS WORKS, PERTH, 2⅞", aqua...................................... $75–100
QUILTED PATTERN, MAN SHOOTING GUN, colorless $100–150
QUILTED PATTERN, MAN SHOOTING GUN, amethyst $150–250
QUILTED PATTERN, MAN SHOOTING GUN, light sapphire blue $450–550
QUILTED PATTERN, MAN SHOOTING GUN, Seven-Up green $150–250
STAR DESIGN, 2½", amber $600–900
TARGET BALL THROWER, all metal, 14" H × 19½" L × 11¾" W... $500–800
UNEMBOSSED, 2½", medium amber $40–55
UNEMBOSSED, 2½", yellow amber $40–60
UNEMBOSSED, square pattern with central band, 2¾", medium cobalt blue......
.... $100–125
WW GREENER ST MARYS WORKS, 2½", cornflower blue.................. $60–90
WW GREENER ST MARYS WORKS, 2½", amethyst $125–175

WARNER BOTTLES

The H.H. Warner Company of Rochester, New York, produced over 20
different varieties of proprietary medicines beginning in 1879. Warner,

who previously had been a safe salesman, sold a variety of remedies developed by a Doctor Craig, one of which had allegedly ridded Warner of Bright's disease. Warner's products were extensively sold and well marketed, and branch offices were opened in London, Melbourne, Frankfurt, Prague, and other foreign cities. Warner bottles are frequently found with their original colorful labels and boxes. Additionally, Warner Almanacs were issued during the 1880s which are also popular with collectors.

LOG CABIN COUGH & CONSUMPTION REMEDY, 9¼″, amber $125–175
LOG CABIN COUGH & CONSUMPTION REMEDY, 6⅞″, amber $100–120
LOG CABIN EXTRACT ROCHESTER NY, 8¼″, amber...................... $80–100
LOG CABIN HOPS & BUCHC REMEDY, 10″, amber $200–250
LOG CABIN SARSAPARILLA ROCHESTER NY, 9″, amber................. $125–150
LOG CABIN SCALPINE ROCHESTER NY, 8¾″, amber $300–360
TIPPECANOE, canoe-shaped, 8¾″, amber................................... $75–100
TIPPECANOE, canoe-shaped, 9″, yellow amber, labeled.................$250–350
WARNERS SAFE BITTERS, 9½″, amber......................................$500–750
WARNERS SAFE CURE, 9⅝″, amber.. $125–175
WARNERS SAFE CURE (ON SHOULDER), 9½″, golden amber, oval shape ....
.... $125–175
WARNERS SAFE DIABETES CURE, 9½″, amber $90–130
WARNERS SAFE KIDNEY & LIVER CURE, A&DHC (ON BASE), 9½″, amber.....
....$75–95
WARNERS SAFE KIDNEY & LIVER CURE, 9⅜″, amber.................... $125–175
WARNERS SAFE KIDNEY & LIVER CURE, LEFT-HAND SAFE, 9½″, amber ....
.... $100–130
WARNERS SAFE NERVINE, A&DHC (ON BASE), 9½″, yellow, light stain.........
.... $180–140
WARNERS SAFE NERVINE, A&DHC (ON BASE), 7½″, amber........... $125–175
WARNERS SAFE NERVINE, A&DHC (ON BASE), 9¾″, amber, stain ... $100–135
WARNERS SAFE NERVINE, 7⅜″, medium amber.............................$25–30
WARNERS SAFE NERVINE, 9¾″, amber...$30–40
WARNERS SAFE NERVINE, 7¼″, amber, small lip bruise...................$30–40
WARNERS SAFE RHEUMATIC CURE, 9½″, amber $50–70

Warner's, Kidney & Liver Cure. PHOTO COURTESY OF NEIL GROSSMAN.

WARNERS SAFE TONIC, 7½″, amber $400–550
WARNERS SAFE TONIC, 9½″, amber $225–275
WARNERS SAFE TONIC BITTERS, 7⅜″, deep amber $300–400

WHIMSEYS

Whimseys are decorative nonfunctional items often fashioned by glass blowers for their friends and families as gifts. In addition, mass quantities of whimseys were imported from England and elsewhere, such as glass rolling pins and bellows bottles.

Collectors should be ever vigilant for any free-hand pieces that have been made out of ordinary bottles, such as the glass mug listed below which was made from a Harrison's ink bottle. Also watch for bottles which have been converted into handled jugs, as well as bottles that were formed into fruit jars or snuff jars and any bottles or containers which have any applied figures or handles.

BELLOWS BOTTLE, footed with rigaree, 16½″, red body, clear foot, rigaree chips $90–120
CANE, colorless with red, white, and blue spirals, 41″ $125–175
CANNON-SHAPED POWDER HORN, 14″, OP, colorless with blue and red looping $150–175
HAT MADE FROM PINT-SIZE BALL FRUIT JAR, 3¾″, aqua, OP $450–500
HAT, MINIATURE, 1½″, cobalt blue, OP $125–175
HAT, MRS M GARDNERS INDIAN BALSAM, 1⅛″ × 2⅜″, aqua, OP... $700–900
MINIATURE BELLOWS, colorless cased red with opaque white stripes, 4″, OP $120–140
MUG, MADE FROM HARRISONS INK BOTTLE, 2¹/₁₆″, cobalt blue, OP ....
.... $5000–7500

Whimsey, blown three-mold, possibly a candlestick.
PHOTO COURTESY OF DAVE SMITH.

Left, Whimsey, rolling pin. Right, Whimsey, witch balls. PHOTOS
COURTESY OF SKINNER'S, INC.

PIPE, free-blown, 17″, yellow olive, OP $125–160
PIPE, opaque white with pink loopings, 13½″ $250–325
ROLLING PIN, 12¾″, cobalt blue, OP $90–125
ROLLING PIN, 14″, amethyst $90–110
ROLLING PIN, free-blown, 14½″, greenish aqua, OP $50–65
ROLLING PIN, aqua with opaque white loopings, 16¾″ $125–175
ROLLING PIN, dark olive amber with white specks, 14″, OP $100–140
TURTLE DOORSTOP, 6¾″ × 4¾″, amber...................................$150–250
TURTLE DOORSTOP, aqua with cobalt shell, 7½″, solid glass $400–500
WITCH BALL, 5¾″, deep amethyst..$100–200
WITCH BALL, colorless with white loopings, 6½″ $150–200
WITCH BALL, white milk glass with orange and brown loopings, 5″ ..$250–375
WITCH BALLS, PAIR, opaque white with pink loopings, 3″ $400–500

WHISKEY BOTTLES

Man has enjoyed alcoholic beverages for thousands of years, and whiskey
is a relative newcomer to the spirits field. Embossed whiskey bottles
became widely available in the 19th century and come in a wide variety
of shapes, sizes, and colors.

A COLBURN CO, 4⅞″, amethyst, picnic flask................................$30–40
A MCGINNIS COMPANY BALTIMORE, MD, 3¾″, colorless, square $6–9
A MERRY CHRISTMAS, NAPPY NEW YEAR, pt., smoky aqua.............$110–140
ADAMS HOUSE EUROPEAN PLAN, G HALL (ON LABEL), 3⅝″, colorless flask ...
....$20–30
ADOLPH HARRIS & CO, SAN FRAN, 10⅛″, light amber....................$14–18
AMBROSIAL/BM&EAW & CO, handled chestnut, 9″, amber, OP.......$90–140
ARGONAUT, E MARTIN & CO, SAN FRAN, 11″, amber.....................$20–30
BAILEYS WHISKEY, HUEY & CHRIST, 9¾″, colorless $7–9
BALDWINS CELEBRATED WINES & BRANDIES, qt., colorless $20–30

BARNER & KEHLENBECK, SAN FRAN, 12″, light amber......................$20–30
BEISER & FISHER NY, pig figural, 9¼″, golden amber.................$400–500
BELLMORE WHISKEY, qt., colorless, with full labels $25–30
BENNETT & CARROLL, PITTS, PA, 8¼″, golden amber, IP.............$250–275
BERTIN & LEPORI, B-33...$12–16
BILLIE TAYLOR WHISKEY, 9½″, amber, squatty $40–45
BLACK CAT RARE & OLD WHISKEY, bar bottle, qt., colorless $1500–2000
BM&EAW AMBROSIAL, handled, 8⅞″, golden amber, OP $75–100
BORGFELDT-PROPPE CO, SAN FRAN., 9½″, light amber....................$20–22
BROOKVILLE DISTILLING CO, qt., colorless.................................. $7–10
BRUNSING, TOLLE & POSTEL, SAN FRAN, 11⅛″, amber $20–30
BUCHANANS EXTRACT OF CORN SUGAR, cannon, 9″, amber.......... $800–1000
BULL DURHAM WHISKEY, qt., golden amber $800–950
BURBANK BOND WHISKEY, pt., amber, rectangular............................$3–5
CALIFORNIA WINE CO, TS MITCHELL AGENT (ON BASE), amber.........$15–20
CARROL RYE, ½ pt., amber..$10–12
CARTAN, MCCARTHY & CO, SAN FRAN, 11½″, light amber $10–15
CASPERS WHISKEY, 11⅞″, cobalt blue, lip chip, light stain............. $200–250
CASPERS WHISKEY, 11⅞″, cobalt blue $250–350
CERRUTI MERCANTILE CO INC, SF, CAL 11⅜″, amber $18–22
CHESTNUT GROVE C WHARTON, 9½″, amber $250–325
CHESTNUT GROVE WHISKEY, flattened handled jug, 9″, golden amber, OP......
....$50–70
CHESTNUT GROVE WHISKEY CW, handled chestnut, 8⅞″, amber, OP ....
....$220–225
CHESTNUT GROVE WHISKEY CW, handled chestnut, 8¾″, amber, OP $90–120
COCA MUSCATEL, 9½″, amber $5–6
CR GIBSON, SALAMANCA, NY, 8½″, colorless..................................$4–6
CROWN DISTILLERIES COMPANY, 11″, light amber $14–18
CROWN DISTILLERIES COMPANY, 4⅜″, amber, squatty, inner screw threads.....
....$30–40
CROWN DISTILLERIES COMPANY, 9¾″, amber $20–30
CROWN DISTILLERIES COMPANY, 5¼″, light amber, inside screw threads...... $25–30
CUNNINGHAMS & IHMSEN PITTS PA (ON BASE), 10″, yellow amber.....$20–25
CUNNINGHAMS & IHMSEN, PITTS, PA (ON BASE), 9″, yellow amber $35–50
DAVY CROCKETT PURE OLD BOURBON, 11⅞″, amber $30–40
DAVY CROCKETT PURE OLD BOURBON, 12″, amber $25–35
DR ABERNATHYS, B-3...$12–15
DR ABERNATHYS GREEN GINGER BRANDY, 11″, amber $30–40
DR BELLS PEPTENIZED PORT, amber, bell-shaped..........................$130–160
DR MCCABE ST LOUIS MO MEDICATED BRANDY, 11″, amber $175–250
DR MCMUMMS ELIXIR OF OPIUM, aqua, OP $18–24
DRINK WHILE IT LASTS FROM THE HOGS. . . . , 6¾″, colorless, pig-shaped ...
....$160–190
DRY GIN, enameled bar bottle, 10¾″, colorless...............................$15–25
DUFFY CRESCENT SALOON, figural pig, 7¾″, colorless.................. $400–550
DUFFY MALT WHISKEY CO, 10½″, amber.. $7–10
DUFFY MALT WHISKEY COMPANY, 4″, amber $20–30
DUFFYS MALT WHISKEY 1860 BOSTON, handled decanter, 9⅝″, colorless ....
....$120–150
DUNBAR & CO WORM WOOD CORDIAL, deep aqua $350–475

E COMMINS & CO, SAN FRAN, 12″, dark amber, four-piece mold......$75–100
E&B BEVAN PITTSTON PA IXL VALLEY WHISKEY, 7″, black, IP ...$1200–1500
EA FARGO WHOLESALE LIQUORS, SAN FRAN, 11¾″, medium amber.....$18–22
EAGLE NEST WW NIECE, REDONDO, CAL, ½ pt., colorless................. $8–11
EDWARD OULLAHAN, pocket flask, ½ pt., colorless..........................$40–60
EE HALL ESTABLISHED 1842, 11⅜″, dark amber...............................$25–35
EG BOOZS OLD CABIN WHISKEY, CABIN, GVII-3, qt., deep gold amber, base bruise and crack $240–280
EGG NOG PATENTED 1859, PUT UP BY AMERICAN DESICC, 9″, yellow amber
....$300–375
EH TAYLOR & SONS, FRANKFORT, KY, 5¾″, amethyst......................$18–22
ELLENVILLE GLASS WORKS (ON BASE), cylinder, 11⅛″, olive green $30–40
EMBOSSED SAFE IN CIRCLE, ½ pt., amber $60–75
EXTRA BOURBON OF THE EXCELSIOR, 10″, aqua.............................$55–70
F CHEVALIER CO CASTLE WHISKEY, SAN FRAN, 11″, medium amber $20–30
F CHEVALIER CO OLD CASTLE, SAN FRAN, 11⅛″, amber, inside screw threads
....$25–30
F CHEVALIER CO OLD, SAN FRAN, 11¼″, amber, inside screw threads..$25–30
F CHEVALIER CO WHISKEY MERCHANTS, 1898, 9⅝″, amber, rectangle .$30–35
F CHEVALIER CO WHISKEY MERCHANTS, SAN FRAN, 11½″, amber $40–50
F CHEVALIER CO WHISKEY MERCHANTS, ½ pt., amber $10–12
F ZIMMERMAN & CO MAIL ORDER HOUSE, PORTLAND, 12¼″, light amber .....
....$14–18
FLASK, unembossed with basket-weave pattern, 9¼″, colorless..............$2–4
FLASK, unembossed, 6¼″, aqua...$2–3
FLASK, unembossed, 8″, light green $2–4
FLASK, unembossed, 7½″, honey amber $3–4
FOREST LAWN JVH, bulbous, 7½″, deep yellow olive, IP $90–120
FOUR ROSES, white enameling, 3″, colorless, bulb-shaped decanter......$40–50
FRED RASCHEN, SACRAMENTO, CAL, 11¾″, amber $12–18
FULL QUART, DONNELLY RYE, 10¼″, amber....................................$10–15
FW ECKEL, NIAGARA FALLS, NY, 9¾″, colorless $4–5
G ROTTANZI LIQUOR DEALER, 6½″, colorless...................................$55–75
GEO S LADD, B-395..$15–20
GEO S LADD & CO WHOLESALE LIQUOR, STOCKTON, 11⅛″, medium amber....
....$15–25
GEO WISSEMANN, SACRAMENTO, CAL, 10¾″, amber, inside screw threads ......
....$20–30
GEO ZANTZINGER (ON SHOULDER), 11⅝″, olive amber, OP $125–175
GH MOORE OLD BOURBON & RYE, 12″, amber................................$25–35
GINTER CO IMPORTERS, 10⅛″, yellow green....................................$50–75
GLEN GARRY BLENDED SCOTCH WHISKEY, stoneware.........................$20–25
GOLDEN AGE RYE, on bar bottle, 10¾″, colorless with gilt decoration..$40–50
GOOD NIGHT, with man's face, flask, 4″, fiery opal, with screw cap $60–75
GPR WHISKEY, 6¼″, colorless...$1–2
GR GIBSON, SALAMANCA, NY, 10¼″, amber.....................................$5–6
GREAT SEAL, THE STYRON BEGGS CO, NEWARK, OHIO, 5″, amethyst ... $14–16
GREETING THEODORE NETTER, 6″, cobalt blue.............................$150–200
GREETINGS THEODORE NETTER, barrel, 6″ × 2¼″, cobalt blue....... $125–175
GUCKENHEIMER RYE, on bar bottle, 10¾″, colorless with gilt decoration........
....$40–60

H L Rye Bourbon, 10⅞″, dark amber..$20–25
H Pharazyn, Indian warrior shape, 12¼″, yellow amber............. $450–600
HA Graefs Son Canteen, NY, flask, 6½″, deep gold amber....... $300–400
Halls, Luhrs & Co, Sacramento, 11⅞″, amber..........................$18–23
Hall, Luhrs & Co, Sacramento, 12″, dark amethyst...................$14–18
Handled Whiskey, free-blown bulbous body, 6¼″, OP, puce.........$110–130
Hanely, B-305 ....$10–12
Hanley Mercantile Co, San Fran, 10½″, amber.......................$14–18
Hanover Rye, back bar bottle, qt., colorless............................ $300–400
Harmony Club J Grossman Sons, ½ pt., amber.........................$12–15
Hawkins Rye, Full Quart, 10½″, aqua.................................$10–14
Hayner Distilling Co, 9½″, colorless, pt. $18–24
Hayner Distilling Co, Dayton, Ohio, 11½″, sun-colored $8–12
Hayner Whiskey, Distillery Troy Ohio, 11½″, colorless.................$4–5
Henry Campe & Co, San Fran., 10¾″, aqua $14–18
Henry Chapman & Co Sole Agents Montreal, 5¾″, yellow amber, 70%
label.. $125–175
Here Is To You Merry Christmas, flask, 4⅜″, gold paint on milk glass......
....$75–85
HF&B, NY, melon-shaped, 9½″, deep red amber $80–110
Hildebrandt Posner, B-330...$12–15
Hildebrandt, Posner & Co, SF Cal, 9¾″, amber, squatty............$25–28
Hildebrandt, Posner & Co, SF Cal, 11½″, light amber...............$18–22
Hildebrandt, Posner & Co, SF, 6½″, colorless, picnic flask $30–40
Hollywood Whiskey, 11″, amber $10–12
Hollywood Whiskey, amber...$12–15
IW Harper Whiskey, 2⅞″, colorless, bulb-shaped decanter.............$30–40
Ixl Valley Whiskey, E&B Bavan, with stars embossed, 7″, dark amber, IP
.... $900–1200
Jesse Moore, B-487...$12–15
Jesse Moore & Co, Louisville, KY, 11¾″, amber, blob top $30–35
Jesse Moore-Hunt Co, Trade Mark, 11⅝″, amber $10–15
JFT & Co Philad, handled and ribbed, 7″, golden amber, OP $140–180
JFT & Co Philad, ribbed, bulbous, handled jug, 7¼″, golden amber, OP.....
.... $300–350
JFT & Co, Philada, handled jug, bulbous, 7⅛″, light gold amber . $300–400
JH Cutter Old Bourbon, Bottled By Hotaling, 11¾″, amber......$20–30
JH Cutter Old Bourbon, E Martin & Co., 11¾″, medium amber ..$75–95
JH Cutter Old Bourbon, Hotaling & Co, Sole Agents, 11¾″, amber.....
....$40–50
JH Duker & Bro Quincy Ill, pumpkinseed flask, 6″, colorless........$35–45
JM Roney Wholesale Liquors, Santa Rosa, 6½″, colorless...........$20–25
JN Kline & Cos Aromatic Digestive Cordial, sapphire blue, labeled ....
....$225–275
JN Kline & Cos Aromatic Digestive Cordial, 5½″, amber teardrop-shaped
flask $100–150
Jno F Horne Knoxville, Tenn, qt., amber $40–60
John Bull Figural, 11⅜″, golden amber $200–250
John W Gryan, ½ pt., amber..$30–40
Jos Melczer & Co, Los Angeles, ½ pt., colorless, screw cap............$6–8

Jos Myers Son & Co Philadelphia, cylinder, qt., deep golden yellow, labeled $75–90
JT Gayen Altona, cannon figural, 13¾″, medium red amber $700–1000
Kelloggs Nelson County Extra Kentucky Bourbon, 11¾″, light amber
....$18–22
Klein, Cuccenheim & Co, ½ pt., colorless $12–15
Lachman & Jacobi, San Francisco, New York, 11¼″, amber.........$23–28
Lady's Leg, UM (On Base), 10″, amber, three-piece mold $50–60
Lady's Leg, Unembossed, 12″, green...$50–65
Lake Keuka Vintage Co, Bath, NY, 11½″, colorless.......................$3–5
Lancaster Glass Works Lancaster NY (On Base), barrel, olive yellow .....
....$250–350
Lancaster Glass Works Lancaster NY (On Base), barrel, orange amber
....$160–230
Lancaster Glass Works, Lancaster, NY, barrel-shaped, 9⅝″, medium
copper..$150–200
Landregan & White Wholesale Liquor, ½ pt., colorless, flask $15–22
Langert Wine Co, Spokane, Wash, 11¾″, colorless.....................$20–30
Larrys Whiskey, WL & Co, 11⅛″, amber...................................$25–35
Levaggi Co, San Francisco, 11⅛″, amber..................................$20–22
Leventhal Bros, San Francisco, ½ pt., amber, screw cap $6–8
Louis Tanssig, B-680 ....$2–3
Louis Taussig & Co, San Fran., 12″, colorless............................$35–45
Louis Weber Louisville KY (On Shoulder), 10″, honey amber ... $180–250
M Cronan & Co, Sacramento, Cal, 11⅞″, amber........................ $14–18
M Saltzman & Co, Purity Above All, spiral ridgy neck, qt., amber . $9–12
M Saltzman & Co, Purity Above All, spiral ridgy neck, qt., light
amethyst $10–12
Man And Dog At Lamppost, pt., colorless, pumpkinseed flask......$200–275
Manhattan Club Pure Rye Whiskey, qt., amber..........................$30–40
McDonald & Kohn, B-449 .... $10–12
McLeod & Hatje, B-452.. $9–11
McLeod & Hatje, Wine & Liquor, 11⅝″, dark amber...................$14–18
Meyerfeld, Mitchell & Co, Days Of 49, 10¾″, colorless.............$20–30
MF Biern, Magnolia Hotel, Phila, 6⅞″, medium golden amber, teardrop
form...$300–450
Millers Extra, E Martin & Co Old Bourbon, 7¼″, amber flask............
....$100–135
Mint Exchange Liquors, 5¼″, colorless, picnic flask $60–75
Mist Of The Morning, barrel shape, 10″, amber.........................$120–150
MJH & Co (On Base), 11¾″, amber, blob top $15–20
Mohawk Whiskey Pure Rye, medium honey amber, Indian figural ....
....$1000–1500
Mohawk Whiskey Pure Rye, Indian figural, 12½″, golden amber ....
....$1900–2400
New England Glass Co (On Base), H45-8, 8½″, olive green, OP $200–260
NM Uri & Co, Louisville, KY, 3½″, amber, rectangle................... $14–18
NM Uri & Co. Louisville, KY, amber, rectangular....................... $10–13
Occidental Oakland, Cal, Frank Pereira, ½ pt., colorless............ $8–11
OK Old Bourbon Castle Whiskey, blob top, 12″, medium amber .$250–325

OLD BELLE OF ANDERSON SOUR MASH, 8″, milk glass $40–60
OLD BUSHMILLS DISTILLER LIMITED, 10″, light green $10–14
OLD CONTINENTAL WHISKEY, 9¼″, deep yellow amber $650–800
OLD FITZGERALD HANDMADE POTSTILL, 4¼″, colorless $14–16
OLD GILT EDGE WHISKEY, 11½″, medium amber............................$18–22
OLD GOVERNMENT WHISKEY, 10⅞″, light amber............................$20–30
OLD NICK NEGRITA, 5¼″, honey amber $6–8
OLD PEPPER WHISKEY, 4¾″, light amber, squat $35–45
OLD PRENTICE WHISKEY, enameled on bar bottle, 11¼″, colorless.......$50–60
OLD QUAKER, 9½″, colorless, with original label $60–90
OLD VELVET BRANDY, vertical ribs, applied medallion, 9¾″, golden amber,
OP.. $400–600
OREGON IMPORTING CO, PORTLAND, OR, 11½″, dark amber $25–35
P CLAUDIUS & CO DISTILLERS, SAN FRAN, 10¾″, amber, inside screw threads
....$20–30
P CLAUDIUS & CO, SAN FRAN, 11″, amber, inside screw threads $20–30
PA CRANE WHOLESALE LIQUORS, ½ pt., colorless...........................$20–30
PAUL FRIEDMAN, PF, SAN FRAN, 11″, amber.................................$15–18
PAUL JONES (WHITE ENAMELING), 3″, colorless, bulb-shaped decanter .$35–45
PAUL JONES BOURBON, Louisville seal....................................... $10–12
PEPPER DISTILLERY SOUR MASH, 11¾″, light amber.....................$120–140
PF HERRING (ON RIBBON SEAL), 8⅜″, amber...........................$75–90
PH HANRAHAN, OAKLAND, CAL, 11⅜″, amber $30–35
PHOENIX BOURBON, NABER, ALFS & BRUNE, 11¾″, medium amber, small
bird...$75–90
PHOENIX BOURBON, NABER, ALFS & BRUNE, 11¾″, medium amber, large bird
....$125–150
PHOENIX OLD BOURBON, 6⅜″, amber $125–165
PHOENIX OLD TRADE MARK BOURBON, 6½″, light amber $75–100
PICNIC, pumpkinseed flask, 6″, yellow green............................$175–225
POTTER & BODINE (ON BASE), cylinder, 11¼″, olive amber...............$60–85
PROMOTION WINE & LIQUOR CO, 11¾″, light amber $20–30
QUAKER MAID WHISKEY, 4⅝″, amethyst $14–18
QUEEN OF NELSON, 3½″, colorless, bulb-shaped decanter $30–40
RB CUTTER PURE BOURBON, handled, 8½″, deep red amber, OP ... $200–225
RB CUTTER/LOUISVILLE, KY, handled jug, 8½″, amber, OP $120–150
RB CUTTERS PURE BOURBON, handled, 8⅛″, red amber, OP, handle crack ....
....$70–90
RG CO, PHILADA, 4⅞″, colorless, squatty $18–23
RIDGEWAY STRAIGHT CORN WHISKEY, stoneware, miniature...............$45–55
RIP VAN WINKLE PURE RYE SF EAGAN WHISKY, pt., amber flask $75–100
RIP VAN WINKLE PURE SF EAGAN RYE WHISKY, qt., amber flask $120–145
ROSENBAUM BROS OLD KENTUCKY WHISKIES, ceramic pig, 6⅞″ L .. $300–400
ROSENBAUM BROS OLD KENTUCKY WHISKIES, pottery pig, 7¼″ $400–450
ROTH & CO, FULL QUART, SAN FRAN, 11⅞″, amber $14–18
ROTH & CO, SAN FRANCISCO, 11⅝″, amber.................................$12–15
ROTHENBERG CO WHOLESALE LIQUORS, rectangle, 10⅛″, amber.........$15–20
ROTHENBERG CO, ROSEMOND A, 11¼″, amber, square.....................$20–30
RUSCONI FISHER, B-609 .... $10–12
RYE, bar bottle, triangular, with colorless cut glass stopper, 9½″, red ..$40–45
RYE (IN SILVER OVERLAY), bar bottle, straight-sided, 11½″, amber.... $75–100

S Tobias & Son Phila (On Base), 9½″, black, IP........................$110–140
Saratoga Liquor, Seattle, Wash, ½ pt., colorless $7–11
SB Rothenberg & Co Old Judge Kentucky Bourbon, 11½″, red amber
....$100–130
Schiele Old 91 Whiskey, 4¼″, colorless $15–25
Shea Bocqueraz, B-633 ....$10–12
Shea-Bocqueraz Co, San Francisco, 11⅞″, light amber $30–40
Siebe Bros & Plagemann, San Fran, 11⅛″, amber $10–12
Simmonds Nabob, 10½″, amber, blob top...................................$50–65
Slaters Premium Bourbon, 11¾″, amber.....................................$15–20
Slaters Premium Bourbon, 11⅞″, golden amber.........................$50–60
Smokine, cabin figural, 6⅞″, amber..$150–225
Sonn Bros, NY Distilleries, 8″, colorless, metal screw top..............$4–5
Spring Hill Bourbon, 11″, purple...$80–100
Spruance, Stanley & Co, San Fran, 11¾″, medium amber............$30–35
SSPB (On Base), strap flask, pt., deep yellow green........................$12–15
Star Whiskey, handled jug, 8¼″, deep golden amber............ $260–300
Star Whiskey, handled conical jug, 8¼″, golden amber......... $200–250
Star Whiskey New York WB Crowell, Jr, 8″, yellow amber, OP, handled
....$500–625
Star Whiskey New York WB Crowell, Jr, 8⅛″, medium amber, OP........
....$300–400
Strap Flask, unembossed, ½ pt., pale yellow citron $20–30
Stricklands, 7″, golden amber, pocket flask..............................$150–200
Sunflower Pennsylvania Rye, 10⅜″, amber...............................$30–35
Sutterhome Wine & Dist Co, 11″, light amber $30–40
Tavern McCoy Bros, Los Angeles, Cal, ½ pt., colorless................ $9–11
Taylor & Williams, Distillers, Louisville, KY, 3¼″, colorless flask.......
....$10–14
Theo Gier Co, Oakland, Cal, rectangle, 10⅛″, amber................... $15–17
TJ Flack & Sons Premium Baltimore, 7¼″, amber.................. $225–300
Tom Gin, enameled bar bottle, 10¾″, colorless............................$15–25
Turner Brothers New York, barrel, 9⅞″, copper, lip chip........... $70–100
Turner Brothers New York, barrel, 9⅞″, medium olive green, lip chip .....
....$350–450
Turner Brothers New York, barrel, 10¼″, medium amber $75–100
Turner Brothers New York, barrel, 10¼″, yellow amber $60–90

Whiskey, Turner Brothers, barrel. PHOTO COURTESY OF NEIL GROSSMAN.

TURNER BROTHERS, barrel-shaped, 9⅞″, yellow amber, lip rough, light stain $90-120
TURNER BROTHERS, square, 10″, olive amber.....................................$60-75
TURNER BROTHERS NEW YORK, BUFFALO, barrel, 10¼″, olive amber, lip chip $80-110
UDOLPHO WOLFES AROMATIC SCHNAPPS, 8½″, pale grassy green........$25-30
UDOLPHO WOLFES AROMATIC SCHNAPPS, 9½″, almost yellow $24-28
UDOLPHO WOLFES AROMATIC SCHNAPPS, 8½″, light olive yellow $20-24
UDOLPHO WOLFES AROMATIC SCHNAPPS, 9½″, honey amber..............$20-25
UDOLPHO WOLFES AROMATIC SCHNAPPS, with 85% label, 8⅛″, olive green, IP $100-150
UNEMBOSSED, strap-sided flask, pt., milk glass, smooth base.............$70-90
UNION BOTTLE, flask, pt., colorless $50-70
UNION PACIFIC TEA CO NY, 4½″, colorless flask $100-135
VAN DUNCKS GENEVER, COACHMAN, 9½″, amber.........................$100-150
VERTICALLY RIBBED FLASK, 20 ribs, pt., medium olive green, OP $125-175
W FRANK & SONS PITTSBURGH, PA, flask, pt., amber, inner screw threads..... .... $100-125
W GILMORE & SONS PAVILION NY, 10¼″, medium olive green $15-20
W GILMORE & SONS PAVILION NY, 10¼″, blue green.....................$20-30
WALTER MOISE & CO, pt., amber $12-15
WARRANTED FLASK, 9½″, colorless $1-2
WB HOUCHIN, NELSON CO KY, 11⅛″, dark amethyst.....................$35-40
WE TRUST GAR, IN BLUE SLIP, ceramic pig, 7″ $200-250
WEEKS & POTTER, fifth, with inside screw thread, amber $15-20
WEIL BROS, B-718 ....$6-8
WH JONES & CO, ESTABLISHED 1851, 9⅝″, colorless, with walking bear........ .... $20-30
WHARTONS WHISKEY, pocket flask, 5½″, cobalt blue $140-160
WHARTONS WHISKEY 1850 CHESTNUT GROVE, 5⅝″, aqua, teardrop shape $500-650
WHARTONS WHISKEY 1850 CHESTNUT GROVE, handled, 10″, yellow amber with label.. $200-250
WHARTONS WHISKEY 1850 CHESTNUT GROVE, handled, 10″, amber ..$250-325
WHARTONS WHISKEY 1850 CHESTNUT GROVE, 5¼″, golden amber, teardrop shape.. $250-350
WHYTE & MACKEY, 9¾″, colorless...$5-6
WILMERDING-LOEWE CO, KELLOGGS, 11¾″, amber $14-18
WINEDALE CO, OAKLAND, CAL, 11⅛″, amber................................$14-16
WISHARTS PINE TREE CORDIAL, teal blue $70-100
WJ VAN SCHUYVER & CO, FULL QUART, 10¼″, amber, rectangle $10-12
WJ VAN SCHUYVER, PORTLAND, OREGON, 11¼″, amber...................$14-18
WM HOELSCHER & CO, SAN FRANCISCO, 10½″, amber......................$14-18
WM JACKSON & CO DISTILLERS, 7″, olive green, teardrop shape $175-250
WM WATSON CO, OAKLAND, CAL, 9½″, amber, square.....................$30-40
WM WATSON CO, OAKLAND, CAL, 11½″, amber..............................$18-22
WOLF, WREDEN & CO, SAN FRANCISCO, 12″, amber.....................$90-120
WORMSER BROS SAN FRANCISCO, barrel, yellow amber................... $450-600
WORMSER BROS SAN FRANCISCO, barrel, 9½″, olive yellow............ $400-500
WP MARTIN 312 MARKET ST NEWARK NJ, 5½″, colorless, pumpkinseed flask $60-90

NEW BOTTLES

AVON BOTTLES

Avon has been calling for more than 50 years, and the call from collectors for imaginative, decorative toiletries and cosmetic bottles has brought a stampede upon the antique shops. As the modern leader in the nonliquor bottle field, Avon's vast range of bottles offers almost unlimited opportunities for the collector. Since none of their figurals are extremely rare, a complete collection of them is possible, though it would contain hundreds of specimens.

Today, the Avon figurals—shaped as animals, people, cars, and numerous other objects—are the most popular of the company's bottles, but not always the most valuable. Some of the early nonfigurals of the pre–World War II era sell for high prices because of their scarcity. Since there were virtually no Avon collectors in those days, very few specimens were preserved.

Avon collecting has become such a science that all of its bottles, and even the boxes that they came in, have been carefully catalogued. In fact, everything relating to Avon is now regarded as collectible, including brochures, magazines ads, and anything bearing the Avon name. Of course, the older material is more sought after than items of recent vintage.

Avon bottles are readily obtainable through specialized dealers and numerous other sources. Since some people who sell the Avons are unaware of their value, the collector can often find bargain prices at garage sales or flea markets.

Although it seems that every possible subject has been exhausted, Avon continues to bring out original bottles in a variety in sizes, colors, and decorative designs. The new figurals in its line are issued in limited editions, with editions being rather large in order to accommodate the collector as well as the general public. Collectors of new Avons should purchase the new issues as soon as they reach the market since they often sell out quickly. When an Avon product has sold out, its price begins rising and can double in less than a year depending on its popularity. Even though this does not always happen, the original retail price will be lower than can be expected later on in the collectors' market.

Although Avon is the oldest toiletry company issuing decorative bottles, collecting interest in its products did not become widespread until stimulated by the 1965 release of an after-shave lotion in a stein decanter and a men's cologne in an amber boot. The interest created by those toiletries led many people to investigate the earlier Avon products, partly for collecting and partly for use as decorations. At that time they could be purchased inexpensively from secondhand shops and thrift bazaars. Unfortunately, by then many of the older ones had perished and were just not to be found.

By the late sixties, Avons were plentiful in antique shops with prices on the rise. Some collecting clubs were established. The early seventies saw further increases in collecting activity. The company, well aware of what was happening, expanded its line of figurals to meet public demand.

Many collectors doubt that modern Avon figurals can ever become really valuable because of the large quantities made. But with natural loss, passage of time, and increasing collector demand, Avon figurals may well reach respectable prices in five or ten years, making the 1984 prices look like great bargains.

Just as with many other collectibles, the Avons that prove least popular when issued sometimes end up being the scarcest and costliest. This is why collectors automatically buy each one as they come out.

Avon began as the California Perfume Company, founded by D.H. McConnell, a door-to-door salesman who gave away perfume samples to prevent doors from being slammed in his face. Eventually he started selling perfume and abandoned bookselling. Although it was located in New York, the name "Avon" was initially used in 1929 in conjunction with the California Perfume Company or C.P.C. After 1939 it was known exclusively as Avon. The C.P.C. bottles are naturally very desirable, having been used in relatively small quantities and not having been well preserved. These bottles are impossible to date accurately because many designs were used with various preparations. In most cases, sales do not occur frequently enough to establish firm price levels. Therefore, the prices listed in this book should be regarded only as being approximate.

There are numerous possible approaches to Avon collecting. The most popular is to amass as many figurals as one's budget, time, and energy (not to mention luck) allow. They can also be collected by subject matter, or according to the type of product they originally contained—such as perfume or after shave. Another favorite specialty is Avons with figural stoppers.

ABRAHAM LINCOLN, WILD COUNTRY AFTER SHAVE, 1970–72 ....$2.25–3.25
AFTER SHAVE ON TAP, WILD COUNTRY, 1974–75 ....$2.50–3.25
AMERICAN BELLE, SONNET COLOGNE, 1976–78 ....$4.75–5.50
AMERICAN EAGLE, WINDJAMMER AFTER SHAVE, 1971–72 ....$3–3.50
AMERICAN SCHOONER, OLAND AFTER SHAVE, 1972–73 ....$3.50–4.50
ANGLER, WINDJAMMER AFTER SHAVE, 1970............................$4.50–5.75
APOTHECARY, BREATH FRESH, 1973 ....$4–5
APOTHECARY, LEMON VELVET MOIST. LOTION, 1973–76...............$3.50–4.75

APOTHECARY, SPICY AFTER SHAVE, 1973–74 ....$4–5
ARISTOCRAT KITTENS SOAP, 1971 ....$4.75–5.75
ARMOIRE DECANTER, CHARISMA BATH OIL, 1972–75 ....$4–5
ARMOIRE DECANTER, ELUSIVE BATH OIL, 1972–75 ....$4–5
ARMOIRE DECANTER, FIELDS AND FLOWERS BATH OIL, 1972–75 ....$3.50–4.50
AUTO, BIG MACK TRUCK, WINDJAMMER AFTER SHAVE, 1973–75 ....$5–5.75
AUTO, CORD, 1937 MODEL, WILD COUNTRY AFTER SHAVE, 1974–75 ....
....$6.25–7.25
AUTO, COUNTRY VENDOR, WILD COUNTRY AFTER SHAVE, 1973.....$6.50–7.50
AUTO, DUSENBERG, SILVER, WILD COUNTRY AFTER SHAVE, 1970–72 ....
....$7.50–8.75
AUTO, DUNE BUGGY, SPORTS RALLY BRACING LOTION, 1971–73 ... $4.50–5.00
AUTO, ELECTRIC CHARGER, AVON LEATHER COLOGNE, 1970–72.....$5.75–6.50
AUTO, ELECTRIC CHARGER, SPICY AFTER SHAVE, 1970–72............$4.75–5.75
AUTO, HAYES APPERSON, 1902 MODEL, AVON BLEND 7 AFTER SHAVE, 1973–74
....$5.75–4.50
AUTO, MAXWELL 23, DEEP WOODS AFTER SHAVE, 1972–74..........$4.50–5.50
AUTO, MG, 1936, WILD COUNTRY AFTER SHAVE, 1974–75...........$3.75–4.50
AUTO, MODEL A, WILD COUNTRY AFTER SHAVE, 1972–74 ....$3.50–4.25
AUTO, RED DEPOT WAGON, OLAND AFTER SHAVE, 1972–73..........$5.75–6.75
AUTO, ROLLS ROYCE, DEEP WOODS AFTER SHAVE, 1972–75.........$6–7.50
AUTO, STANLEY STEAMER, WINDJAMMER AFTER SHAVE, 1971–72....$5.25–6.25
AUTO, STATION WAGON, TAI WINDS AFTER SHAVE, 1971–73..........$6.50–7.75
AUTO, STERLING 6, SPICY AFTER SHAVE, 1968–70.....................$5.50–6.75
AUTO, STERLING SIX II, WILD COUNTRY AFTER SHAVE, 1973–74....$3.75–4.50
AUTO, STUTZ BEARCAT, 1914 MODEL, AVON BLEND 7 AFTER SHAVE, 1974–77..
....$4.75–5.50
AUTO, TOURING T, TRIBUTE AFTER SHAVE, 1969–70....................$5.50–6.25
AUTO, VOLKSWAGEN, RED, OLAND AFTER SHAVE, 1972 ....$4.75–5.75
AVON BABY SOAP, 1969–75 .... $1.00–1.35
AVON OPEN, WILD COUNTRY AFTER SHAVE, 1972–75................. $5.00–6.25
AVON OPEN, WINDJAMMER AFTER SHAVE, 1969–70.....................$5.25–6.25
AVONSHIRE BLUE SOAPS, 1971–74 ....$4–4.50
BABY GRAND PIANO, PERFUME GLACE, 1971–72 ....$7–9
BATH URN, LEMON VELVET BATH OIL, 1971–73............................$4–4.50
BEAUTIFUL AWAKENING, ROSES ROSES, 1973–74 ....$4.75–5.50
BENJAMIN FRANKLIN, WILD COUNTRY AFTER SHAVE, 1974–76 ......$3.50–3.75
BIG BERRY STRAWBERRY, BATH FOAM, 1973–74..............................$2–2.50
BIG GAME RHINO, TAI WINDS AFTER SHAVE, 1972–73.................$3.75–4.25
BIRD HOUSE POWDER BUBBLE BATH, 1969................................$6.50–7.75
BIRD OF PARADISE COLOGNE DECANTER, SKIN SO SOFT BATH OIL, 1972–74....
....$3.50–4.25
BLACKSMITHS ANVIL, DEEP WOODS AFTER SHAVE, 1972–73..........$3.75–4.75
BLOODHOUND PIPE, DEEP WOODS AFTER SHAVE, 1976 .... $5.00–6.00
BLUE MOO SOAP ON A ROPE, 1972.......................................$4.50–6.00
BON BON BLACK, FIELD & FLOWERS COLOGNE, 1973..................$4.75–5.75
BON BON WHITE, OCCUR COLOGNE, 1972–73 ....$4.75–5.50
BON BON WHITE, TOPAZE COLOGNE, 1972–73 ....$4.50–5.75
BOOT GOLD TOP, AVON LEATHER AFTER SHAVE, 1966–71............ $2.50–3.00
BUFFALO NICKLE, LIQUID HAIR LOTION, 1971–72 ....$3.50–4.50
BULLDOG PIPE, OLAND AFTER SHAVE, 1972–73........................$3.50–4.50

BUNNY PUFF & TALC, HER PRETTINESS PERFUME TALC, 1969–72 ......$3–3.50
BUTTERCUP CANDLESTICK, SONNET COLOGNE, 1974 ....$7–8
BUTTERCUP SALT SHAKER, SONNET COLOGNE, 1974 ....$2.00–2.50
BUTTERFLY, OCCUR COLOGNE, 1972–73 ....$4–4.50
BUTTERFLY, SOMEWHERE COLOGNE, 1972–73............................$4–4.50
BUTTERFLY, UNFORGETTABLE COLOGNE, 1972–73.......................$3.75–4.75
BUTTERFLY, UNFORGETTABLE COLOGNE, 1974–76.....................$1.25–2.00
CAMPER, DEEP WOODS AFTER SHAVE, 1972–74 ....$5.75–7.00
CANADA GOOSE, DEEP WOODS COLOGNE, 1973–74 ....$4–4.50
CANDLESTICK COLOGNE, ELUSIVE, 1970–71 ....$5.25–5.75
CANDLESTICK COLOGNE, MOONWIND, 1972–75............................$3.50–4.50
CANDLESTICK COLOGNE, ROSES WIND, 1972–75..........................$3.50–4.50
CAPITAL DECANTER, TRIBUTE AFTER SHAVE, 1970–71 ....$4.00–4.75
CASEYS LANTERN, ISLAND LIME AFTER SHAVE, 1966–67 ....$30–40
CATCH A FISH, FIELD FLOWERS COLOGNE, 1976–78 ....$6–7
CHIMNEY LAMP, MOONWIND, 1973–74.....................................$4.25–5.50
CHRISTMAS ORNAMENT, GREEN OR RED, 1970–71 ....$1.25–1.75
CHRISTMAS ORNAMENT, ORANGE, BUBBLE BATH, 1970–71 ....$2.25–2.75
CLASSIC BEAUTY, FIELD FLOWERS BODY LOTION, 1972–76....................$2–3
CLASSIC DECANTER, SKIN SO SOFT BATH OIL, 1969–70 ....$4.00–5.50
CLASSIC LION, DEEP WOODS AFTER SHAVE, 1973–75 ....$4–5
CLEAN SHOT, 1970–72...$4.50–5.00
CLUB BOTTLE, 1906 AVON LADY, 1977.......................................$25–28
CLUB BOTTLE, 1ST ANNUAL, 1972 ....$150–200
CLUB BOTTLE, 2ND ANNUAL, 1973 ....$45–60
CLUB BOTTLE, 5TH ANNUAL, 1976 ....$25–30
CLUB BOTTLE, BUD HASTIN, 1974 ....$70–95
CLUB BOTTLE, CPC FACTORY, 1974...$30–40
COCKATOO POWDER, FLORAL MEDLEY, 1972–73.........................$5.25–5.75
COLLECTOR'S PIPE, WINDJAMMER AFTER SHAVE, 1973–74 ....$2.75–3.25
COLOGNE CLASSIC, UNFORGETTABLE, 1967–68 ....$3–4
COLOGNE MIST, SOMEWHERE, 1966–67 ....$.50–.75
COLOGNE ROYAL, FIELD FLOWERS, 1972–74 ....$2.00–2.50
COLOGNE, ROSES, ROSES, 1972–74 ....$2.75–3.50
COMPOTE DECANTER, MOONWIND, 1972–75 ....$4–5
CORNUCOPIA, SKIN SO SOFT, 1971–76......................................$4.75–5.75
COUNTRY KITCHEN, MOISTURE HAND LOTION, 1973–75...............$3.50–4.75
COUNTRY STORE COFFEE MILL, FIELD FLOWERS, 1972–74............$2.50–2.75
COURTING CARRIAGE, FLOWER TALK COLOGNE, 1973–74 ....$3.50–4.25
COVERED WAGON, WILD COUNTRY AFTER SHAVE, 1970–71 ....$4.25–5.00
CREAMERY DECANTER, ROSES ROSES BODY LOTION, 1973–75........$3.25–4.00
CRYSTALLINE COLOGNE, SOMEWHERE, 1970–71 ....$5–6
DOLPHIN SOAP DISH AND HOSTESS SOAPS, 1970–71 ....$8.25–9.50
DUTCH GIRL FIGURINE, SOMEWHERE, 1973–74................................$8–10
DUTCH TREAT DEMI CUP, HAWAIIAN WHITE GINGER, 1971...........$4.50–5.25
EIGHT BALL DECANTER, SPICY AFTER SHAVE, 1973 ....$2.75–3.50
ELECTRIC GUITAR, WILD COUNTRY AFTER SHAVE, 1974–75...........$3.75–4.25
ELIZABETHAN FASHION FIGURE, FIELD FLOWERS COLOGNE, 1972........$13–16
EMERALD BUD VASE, OCCURI COLOGNE, 1971 ....$2.25–3.25
EMOLLIENT FRESHNER, MOONWIND, 1972–74...........................$1.50–2.25
ENCHANTED FROG CREAM SACHET, SONNET, 1973–76 ....$3–3.25

English Provincial, 1972–74, any series .... $.75–1.00
Excalibur Cologne, Excalibur, 1969–73 .... $2.50–3.25
Fashion Boot, Moonwind Cologne, 1972–76 .... $5.75–6.50
Fashion Boot, Sonnet Cologne, 1972–76 .... $5.50–6.25
Fashion Figurine, Bird Of Paradise, 1971–72 .... $9–11.25
Fashion Figurine, Brocade, 1971–72 .... $8.50–11.00
Fashion Figurine, Field Flowers, 1971–72 .... $9–11
Fashion Figurine, Roaring 20s, Unforgettable, 1972–74 .... $7.50–9.50
First Class Male, Wild Country After Shave, 1970–71 .... $3.00–3.50
First Down, Soap On A Rope, 1970–71 .... $6.75–8.00
First Down, Wild Country After Shave, 1970 .... $3–3.25
First Volunteer, Tai Winds Cologne, 1971–72 .... $6.00–7.00
Floral Duet Hawaiian White Ginger, 1972–73 .... $3.25–4.00
Flower Basket Soap Dish And Hostess Soaps, 1972–74 .... $6–6.75
Flower Maiden, Cotillion, 1973–74 .... $5–6.50
Fragrance & Frills, Soap, 1972–75 .... $6.50–7.75
French Telephone, Moonwind Foaming Bath Oil, 1971 .... $20–24
Garden Girl, Sweet Honesty Cologne, 1978–79 .... $3–3.50
Garnet Bud Vase, To A Wild Rose Cologne, 1973–76 .... $3.50–4.50
Gavel, Island Lime After Shave, 1967–68 .... $7–7.50
George Washington, Spicy After Shave, 1970–72 .... $2–2.50
George Washington, Tribute After Shave, 1970–72 .... $2–2.50
Gift Cologne, Topaze, 1969 .... $3.25–3.75
Gift Of The Sea, Soaps And Baskets, 1987 .... $3.25–3.50
Grade Avon Hostess Soap, 1971–72 .... $6.00–7.25
Grecian Pitcher, Skin So Soft Bath Oil, 1972–76 .... $3.25–4.25
Hearth Lamp, Roses, Roses, 1973–76 .... $6–7.50
Hobnail Bud Vase, Roses Cologne, 1973–74 .... $4–5
Hobnail Decanter, Moonwind Bath Oil, 1972–74 .... $4.75–5.75
Honeysuckle Floral Duet Set, 1972–73 .... $3.00–4.00
Indian Chieftan, Protein Hair Lotion, 1972–75 .... $2.00–2.50
Indian Head Penny, Bravo After Shave, 1970–72 .... $4–4.25
Inkwell, Windjammer After Shave, 1969–70 .... $5.50–7.00
Iron Horse Shaving Mug, Avon Blend 7 After Shave, 1974–76 .... $3–3.50
King, Tai Winds After Shave, 1972–73 .... $4.50–5.75
Kitten Petite, Moonwind Cologne, 1973–74 .... $3–3.25
Koffee Klatch, Honeysuckle Foam Bath Oil, 1971–74 .... $4.50–5.75
Koffee Klatch, Lilac Foaming Bath Oil, 1971–74 .... $4.50–5.50
Leisure Hours, Charisma Bath Oil, 1970–72 .... $4.50–5.50
Leisure Hours, Regence Bath Oil, 1970–72 .... $5–5.75
Liberty Bell, Tribute After Shave, 1971–72 .... $4.25–5.50
Liberty Dollar, Oland After Shave, 1970–72 .... $4.25–5.25
Lip Pop Colas, Cherry, 1973–74 .... $1.00–1.50
Lip Pop Colas, Cola, 1973–74 .... $1.00–1.50
Lip Pop Colas, Strawberry, 1973–74 .... $1.00–1.50
Little Girl Blue, Brocade, 1972–73 .... $7–8
Little Girl Blue, Cotillion, 1972–73 .... $6.75–8.00
Long Drive, Electric Pre-Shave, 1973–75 .... $2.75–3.25
Looking Glass, Brocade Cologne, 1970–72 .... $6.75–7.75
Looking Glass, Elusive Cologne, 1970–72 .... $6.75–8.00
Looking Glass, Regence Cologne, 1970–72 .... $6.75–8.00

Love Bird Perfume, Elusive, 1969–70.................................$5.50–6.50
Lovely Touch Decanter, Rich Moisture Body Lotion, 1971........$1–1.50
Mandolin, Perfume Glace, 1971–72 ....$8–9.25
Mighty Mitt Soap On A Rope, 1969–72 ....$6.75–8.00
Ming Cat, Bird Of Paradise Cologne, 1971............................$5–6.25
Mini Bike, Sure Winner Bracing Lotion, 1972–73 ....$3–4.25
Moonwind Perfumed Soaps, 1972–73...............................$5.25–6.25
Nile Blue Bath Urn, Skin So Soft Bath Oil, 1972–74............$2.75–3.50
Nile Blue Bath Urn, Skin So Soft, 1972–74................................$4–6
Old Faithful, Wild Country After Shave, 1972–73 ....$4.25–5.50
Opening Play, Dull Golden, Spicy After Shave, 1968–69 ....$8–9.50
Opening Play, Shiny Golden, Spicy After Shave, 1968–69.......... $14–17
Oriental Egg Peach Orchard, Moonwind Perfume, 1974–75 . $6.25–7.00
Oriental Figurine, Pomander, 1972.....................................$6–7.50
Owl Fancy, Roses, Roses, 1974–76 ....$3–4
Owl Soap Dish And Soaps, 1970–71.................................$8.00–10.00
Parlor Lamp Set, Moonwind Cologne And Talc, 1971–72 ....$6–7.25
Partridge & Pear Gift Soaps, 1974–75 ....$7–9
Partridge, Occur, 1973–75...$4.25–4.75
Peanuts Gang Soaps, 1970–72..$8–9
Peek-A-Boo Soap On A Rope, 1970....................................$6.75–8.00
Peggy Pelican Soap On A Rope, 1972–73 .... $5.00–6.25
Pennsylvania Dutch Cologne, Patchwork, 1973–74 ....$4.75–5.50
Pennsylvania Dutch Sachet, Sonnet, 1973–75......................$4.75–5.50
Period Piece, Moonwind, 1972–73.......................................$4–4.50
Piano Decanter, Tai Winds After Shave, 1972 .... $3.25–4.00
Picture Frame, Elusive, 1970–71...................................... $10–11
Picture Frame, Regence, 1970–71...................................... $10–11
Pineapple, Moisturized Hand Lotion, 1973–74 .... $2.25–3.00
Pineapple Petite, Roses, Roses Cologne, 1972–74 ....$2.25–3.25
Pipe, Full, Decanter, Brown, Spicy After Shave, 1971–72 .....$2.75–3.25
Pipe, Full, Decanter, Green, Spicy After Shave, 1972–74 .....$2.75–3.25
Pitcher And Bowl, Delft Blue, 1972–74....................................$8–9
Pony Decanter, Short, Wild Country After Shave, 1968–69..$3.50–4.75
Pony Express, Avon Leather After Shave, 1971–72................$3.50–3.75
Precious Owl, Charisma, 1972–74 ....$2.50–3.00
Precious Owl, Field Flowers, 1972–74.................................$2.50–3.25
President Lincoln, Tai Winds After Shave, 1973.......................$6–7.25
President Washington, Deep Woods After Shave, 1974–76.....$3.50–4.25
Purse Petite, Field Flowers Cologne, 1971 ....$3.50–4.50
Queen Of Scots, Sweet Honesty Cologne, 1973–76............. $3.00–3.25
Queen, Tai Winds After Shave, 1973–74.............................. $4.00–4.25
Rainbow Trout, Deep Woods After Shave, 1973–74.......................$3–4
Regal Peacock, Sonnet Cologne, 1973–74...........................$5.25–6.25
Remember When School Desk, Cotillion Cologne, 1972–74...$4.50–5.25
Rook, Spicy After Shave, 1973–74....................................$3.75–4.50
Royal Coach, Bird Of Paradise Bath Oil, 1972–73 ....$4.75–5.50
Royal Swan, Bird Of Paradise, 1971–72 ....$4.75–5.50
Royal Apple, Bird Of Paradise Cologne, 1972–73 ....$2.75–3.50
Scent Of Roses Decanter, Cologne Jelly, 1972–73 .... $2.00–2.50
Scent With Love, Elusive Perfume, 1971–72 ....$8.50–9.75

SCENT WITH LOVE, FIELD FLOWERS PERFUME, 1971–72 .... $8.50–10.00
SCENT WITH LOVE, MOONWIND PERFUME, 1971–72 .... $8.50–10.00
SEA HORSE MINIATURE, HERE'S MY HEART COLOGNE, 1973–76 ..... $3.25–3.75
SEA MAIDEN, SKIN SO SOFT BATH OIL, 1971–72 .... $4.25–5.25
SEA SPRITE, ELUSIVE, 1973–76 .... $4–5
SEA TREASURE, FIELD FLOWERS, 1971–72 .... $6–7.50
SEA TROPHY, WINDJAMMER AFTER SHAVE, 1972 .... $4.50–5.50
SECRETAIRE, MOONWIND FOAMING BATH OIL, 1972–75 .... $5.50–6.75
SHAMPOO SHOWER SOAP, FOR MEN, 1972–73 .... $5–6.50
SIDE-WHEELER, TRIBUTE AFTER SHAVE, 1970–71 .... $4–4.50
SIDE-WHEELER, WILD COUNTRY AFTER SHAVE, 1971–72 .... $3–3.75
SITTING PRETTY, COTILLION COLOGNE, 1971–73 .... $4.50–5.75
SKIN SO SOFT SOFTENER, DELFT BLUE, 1972–74 .... $5–5.50
SLIPPER SOAP AND PERFUME CHARISMA, 1970–71 .... $7.00–8.25
SMALL WORLD PERFUME GLACE, SMALL WORLD, 1971–72 .... $3–4
SMART MOVE, OLAND COLOGNE, 1973–74 .... $2.75–3.25
SNAIL PERFUME, BROCADE, 1968–69 .... $8–10
SNOOPY SOAP DISH REFILLS, 1968–76 .... $2.75–3.25
SNOOPYS BUBBLE TUB, 1971–72 .... $3.50–4.00
SNOOPYS SURPRISE, SPORTS RALLY BRACING LOTION, 1969–71 .... $3–4
SNOWBIRD, SONNET CREAM SACHET, 1973–74 .... $3–3.75
SOAP BOAT, FLOATING DISH AND SOAP, 1973–74 .... $3.50–4.00
SOAP FOR ALL SEASONS, 1973 .... $5.50–6.75
SONG BIRD, COTILLION COLOGNE, 1971–72 .... $4.00–4.75
SONG BIRD, UNFORGETTABLE COLOGNE, 1971–72 .... $3.50–4.50
SPIRIT OF ST LOUIS, EXCALIBUR AFTER SHAVE, 1970–72 .... $6.00–7.50
SPRING TULIPS SOAPS, 1970–73 .... $7.50–9.00
STAGE COACH, WILD COUNTRY AFTER SHAVE, 1970–77 .... $4.75–5.50
STRAWBERRIES & CREAM, BATH FOAM, 1970 .... $3.25–3.75
STRAWBERRY BATH FOAM, BATH FOAM, 1971–72 .... $3.25–4.00
STRAWBERRY BATH GELEE, BATH GELEE, 1971–72 .... $4–4.75
SUPER CYCLE, ISLAND LIME AFTER SHAVE, 1971–73 .... $5.25–5.75
SUPER CYCLE, WILD COUNTRY AFTER SHAVE, 1971–72 .... $4.75–5.50
SURE WINNER SHOWER SOAP, 1972–73 .... $4.50–6.00
SWAN LAKE, BIRD OF PARADISE, 1972–76 .... $4–4.50
SWEET SHOPPE PIN CUSHION, MOONWIND, 1972–74 .... $5.50–6.50
SWINGER GOLF BAG, WILD COUNTRY AFTER SHAVE, 1969–71 .... $5–6
TEE OFF, ELECTRIC PRE-SHAVE, 1973–75 .... $2–2.50
TEE OFF, HAIR LOTION, 1973–75 .... $2.50–3.75
TEN POINT BUCK, WILD COUNTRY AFTER SHAVE, 1973–74 ...... $5–6.25
THOMAS JEFFERSON, WILD COUNTRY AFTER SHAVE, 1977–78 ...... $4–4.75
TIFFANY LAMP, SONNET, 1972–74 .... $7–9
TOWN PUMP, WINDJAMMER AFTER SHAVE, 1968–69 .... $4–4.50
TREASURE TURTLE, FIELD FLOWERS COLOGNE, 1971–73 .... $4.25–4.75
TUB RACERS, THREE CARS, 1969 .... $7–9
TWENTY-DOLLAR GOLD PIECE, WINDJAMMER AFTER SHAVE, 1971–72 ....
.... $4.25–5.25
UNCLE SAM PIPE, DEEP WOODS AFTER SHAVE, 1975–76 .... $4–4.75
VENETIAN PITCHER COL MIST, PATCHWORK, 1973–75 .... $4–5
VICTORIAN FASHION FIGURINE, FIELD FLOWERS COLOGNE, 1973–74 ..... $22–27
VICTORIAN PITCHER, SKIN SO SOFT BATH OIL, 1971–72 .... $7–8.25

VICTORIAN WASHSTAND, CHARISMA FOAM BATH OIL, 1973–74 ...... $5.00–6.25
VICTORIANA PITCHER AND BOWL, FIELD FLOWERS BATH OIL, 1971–72 ....
.... $8.75–10.00
VICTORIANA POWDER SACHET, FIELD FLOWERS, 1971–72 ....$6–7.50
VICTORIANA PITCHER AND BOWL, SKIN SO SOFT, 1971–72.......... $8.50–10.00
WESTERN BOOT, WILD COUNTRY AFTER SHAVE, 1973–75 .... $2.50–3.00
WISE CHOICE, EXCALIBUR AFTER SHAVE, 1969–70.....................$4.00–4.75

BALLANTINE BOTTLES

Ballantine figural bottles are made to contain Ballantine imported Scotch
whiskey. These ceramic bottles are brightly colored, generally reading
"Blended Scotch Whiskey, 14 Years Old." When the bottle represents
an animal or human figure, the head is the cap. Most of the Ballantine
figurals are on sporting themes, such as Fisherman, Duck, and Golf Bag.
Also collectible are the older Ballantine bottles which are nonfigurals but
are often very decorative, such as a three-inch pottery jug in which the
company's product was marketed around 1930.

DUCK...$7–9
FISHERMAN.. $8–10
GOLF BAG $7–9
MALLARD DUCK $5–7
OLD CROW CHESSMAN $7–8
SCOTTISH KNIGHT... $9–11
SEATED FISHERMAN $10–12
SILVER KNIGHT.. $12–15
ZEBRA.. $12–15

BARSOTTINI BOTTLES

The Barsottini bottle manufacturers from Italy, unlike other foreign companies, do not use American or nongeographic themes for the avid U.S.
market. Barsottini bottles mostly represent European subjects, such as
architectural bottles of the Arc de Triomphe, the Eiffel Tower, and the
Florentine Steeple. Subjects from European history included an antique
Florentine cannon from the early days of gunpowder. Most Barsottini
bottles are large ceramics, often in gray and white to represent the brick-

work of buildings. Prices vary depending on quantities imported to this country and the extent of their distribution.

ALPINE PIPE, ceramic, 10″	$7–11
ANTIQUE AUTOMOBILE, ceramic, coupe	$5–8
ANTIQUE AUTOMOBILE, open car	$5–8
CLOCK, with cherub	$30–40
CLOWNS, ceramic, 12″ each	$8–11
EIFFEL TOWER, gray and white, 15″	$7–11
FLORENTINE CANNON, 15″ L	$13–19
FLORENTINE STEEPLE, gray and white	$8–11
MONASTERY CASK, ceramic, 12″	$13–19
PARIS ARC DE TRIOMPHE, 7½″	$9–12
PISA'S LEANING TOWER, gray and white	$9–12
ROMAN COLISEUM, ceramic	$6–9
TIVOLI CLOCK, ceramic, 15″	$12–15

JIM BEAM BOTTLES
AUTOMOBILES AND TRANSPORTATION SERIES

CHEVROLET

1957 CONVERTIBLE, black, new	$85–95
1957 CONVERTIBLE, red, new	$75–85
1957, black	$70–80
1957, dark blue, PA	$70–80
1957, red	$80–90
1957, sierra gold	$140–160
1957, turquoise	$50–70
1957, yellow hot rod	$65–75
CAMARO 1969, blue	$55–65
CAMARO 1969, burgundy	$120–140
CAMARO 1969, green,	$100–120
CAMARO 1969, orange	$55–65
CAMARO 1969, pace car	$60–70
CAMARO 1969, silver	$120–140
CAMARO 1969, yellow, PA	$55–65
CORVETTE 1986, pace car, yellow, new	$60–85
CORVETTE 1984, black	$70–80
CORVETTE 1984, bronze	$100–120
CORVETTE 1984, gold	$100–120

CORVETTE 1984, red	$55–65
CORVETTE 1984, white	$55–65
CORVETTE 1978, black	$140–170
CORVETTE 1978, pace car	$135–160
CORVETTE 1978, red	$50–60
CORVETTE 1978, white	$40–50
CORVETTE 1978, yellow	$40–50
CORVETTE 1963, black, PA	$75–85
CORVETTE 1963, blue, NY	$90–100
CORVETTE 1963, red	$60–70
CORVETTE 1963, silver	$50–60
CORVETTE 1955, black, new	$110–140
CORVETTE 1955, copper, new	$90–100
CORVETTE 1955, red, new	$110–140
CORVETTE 1954, blue, new	$90–100
CORVETTE 1953, white, new	$100–120

DUSENBURG

CONVERTIBLE, cream	$130–140
CONVERTIBLE, dark blue	$120–130
CONVERTIBLE light blue	$80–100
CONVERTIBLE COUPE, gray	$160–180

FORD

INTERNATIONAL DELIVERY WAGON, black	$80–90
INTERNATIONAL DELIVERY WAGON, green	$80–90
FIRE CHIEF 1928	$120–130
FIRE CHIEF 1934	$60–70
FIRE PUMPER TRUCK 1935	$45–60
MODEL A, ANGELOS LIQUOR	$180–200
MODEL A, PARKWOOD SUPPLY	$140–170
MODEL A 1903, black	$35–45
MODEL A 1903, red	$35–45
MODEL A 1928	$60–80
MODEL A FIRE TRUCK 1930	$130–170
MODEL T 1913, black	$30–40
MODEL T 1913, green	$30–40
MUSTANG 1964, black	$100–125
MUSTANG 1964, red	$35–45
MUSTANG 1964, white	$25–35
PADDY WAGON 1930	$100–120
PHAETON 1929	$40–50
PICKUP TRUCK 1935	$20–30
POLICE CAR 1929, blue	$75–85
POLICE CAR 1929, yellow	$350–450
POLICE PATROL CAR 1934	$60–70
POLICE TOW TRUCK 1935	$20–30
ROADSTER 1934, cream, PA, new	$80–90
THUNDERBIRD 1956, black	$60–70

THUNDERBIRD 1956, blue, PA $70–80
THUNDERBIRD 1956, gray $50–60
THUNDERBIRD 1956, green $60–70
THUNDERBIRD 1956, yellow $50–60
WOODIE WAGON 1929 ....$50–60

MERCEDES
1974, blue $30–40
1974, gold $60–80
1974, green $30–40
1974, mocha $30–40
1974, red $30–40
1974, sand beige, PA $30–40
1974, silver, Australia $140–160
1974, white $35–45

TRAINS
BAGGAGE CAR $40–60
BOX CAR, brown $50–60
BOX CAR, yellow $40–50
BUMPER $5–8
CABOOSE, gray $45–55
CABOOSE, red $50–60
CABOOSE, yellow $40–50
CASEY JONES WITH TENDER $65–80
CASEY JONES CABOOSE $40–55
CASEY JONES ACCESSORY SET $50–60
COAL TENDER, no bottle $20–30
COMBINATION CAR $55–65
DINING CAR $75–90
FLAT CAR $20–30
GENERAL LOCOMOTIVE $60–70
GRANT LOCOMOTIVE $50–65
LOG CAR $40–55
LUMBER CAR $12–18
OBSERVATION CAR $15–23
PASSENGER CAR $45–53
TANK CAR $15–20
TRACK $4–6
TURNER LOCOMOTIVE $80–100
WATERTOWER $20–30
WOOD TENDER $40–45
WOOD TENDER, no bottle $20–25

OTHER
AMBULANCE $18–22
ARMY JEEP $18–20
BASS BOAT $12–18
CABLE CAR $25–35

CIRCUS WAGON	$20–30
ERNIE'S FLOWER CART	$20–30
GOLF CART	$20–30
HC COVERED WAGON 1929	$10–20
JEWEL TEA	$70–80
MACK FIRE TRUCK 1917	$120–135
MISSISSIPPI PUMPER FIRETRUCK 1867	$115–140
OLDSMOBILE 1903	$25–35
OLSONITE EAGLE RACER	$40–55
POLICE PATROL CAR 1934, yellow	$110–140
SPACE SHUTTLE	$20–30
STUTZ 1914, gray	$40–50
STUTZ 1914, yellow	$40–50
THOMAS FLYER 1909, blue	$60–70
THOMAS FLYER 1909, ivory	$60–70
VENDOME WAGON	$60–70
VOLKSWAGON, blue	$40–50
VOLKSWAGON, red	$40–50

OTHER SERIES

The Executive series, which consists of 22K-gold decorated bottles, was issued to mark the corporation's 160th anniversary which distinguished the Beam Distilling Co. as one of the oldest American business enterprises.

In the same year, Beam started its Regal China series, one of the most popular series of Beam bottles. The Regal China bottles, issued annually at intervals, honor significant people, places or events, concentrating on subjects based on Americana and the contemporary scene. The sport figurals, a frequent subject for Beam Regal Chinas, are handsome, striking, and very decorative. The first Regal China bottle, the Ivory Ashtray, still sells in a modest price range.

The following year, in 1956, the Beam Political Figures series started off with the traditional elephant and donkey, representing the Republican and Democratic parties, and has been issued with variations every four years for the presidential election.

Customer Specialties, bottles made on commission for customers who are usually liquor dealers or distributors, had its inception with a bottle created for Foremost Liquor Stores of Chicago.

In 1958 and 1959, the State series commemorated the admittance of Alaska and Hawaii into the Union during the 1950s. The Beam Distilling Co. continues to issue bottles in honor of other states with the intention of making bottles for each of the 50 states.

Over 500 types of Beam bottles have been issued since 1953. Beam's ceramic bottles, produced by the Wheaton Glass Co. of Millville, New

Jersey, are considerably more popular than the glass bottles, probably because of their pleasing coloration.

Note: In the following listings, it should be noted that similar grouped items are arranged chronologically by *date*.

AC SPARK PLUG (1977), replica of a spark plug in white, green, and gold.......
....$22–26
AIDA (1978), figurine of character from the opera of the same name. Woman is dressed in blue and yellow with black cone-shaped hat. The first in the Opera series, this bottle comes with a music box which plays a selection from the *Egyptian March*. Bottle and base make up two-piece set................. $140–160
AHEPA 50TH ANNIVERSARY (1972), this striking Regal China bottle was designed in honor of AHEPA'S (American Hellenic Education Progressive Association) 50th anniversary. The Order's anniversary logo is reproduced on the front. Current officers listed on the back. The "Greek Key" design appears on both the bottle and the stopper, which is a hollow vase. The bottle's neck is a traditional Greek column. 12″ $4–6
AKRON RUBBER CAPITAL (1973), a unique Regal China creation honoring Akron, Ohio, the rubber producing capital of the world. This creation is in the shape of an automobile tire and features a mag wheel. In the center of the wheel is the inscription Rubber Capital Jim Beam Bottle Club $15–20
ALASKA (1958), star-shaped bottle in turquoise blue and gold. Symbols of Alaskan industry in corners of star, gold "49" in center. Regal China, 9½″ ....
....$55–60
ALASKA (1964-65), re-issued as above..$40–50
ALASKA PURCHASE (1966), blue and gold bottle with star-shaped stopper. Mt. McKinley pictured with state flag on top. Regal China, 10″ $4–6
AMERICAN SAMOA (1973), the enchantment of one of America's outside territorial possessions is captured in this genuine Regal China bottle. The seal of Samoa signifies friendship, the whip and staff signify authority and power held by the great chiefs..$5–7
AMERICAN VETERANS $4–7
ANTIQUE CLOCK $35–45
ANTIOCH (1967), the Regal China Company is located in Antioch, Illinois. This decanter commemorates the Diamond Jubilee of Regal. Large Indian head ("Sequoit") on one side. Blue and gold diamond on reverse. Regal China, 10″ ......
....$5–7
  With arrow package $6–8
ANTIQUE COFFEE GRINDER (1979), replica of a box coffee mill used in the mid-19th century. Brown with black top and crank which moves, gold lettering......
.... $10–12
ANTIQUE GLOBE (1980), represents the Martin Behaim globe of 1492. The globe is blue and rotates on the wooden cradle stand $7–11
ANTIQUE TELEPHONE 1897 (1978), gold base with black speaker and ear phone. Replica of an 1897 desk phone. The second in the series of antique telephones
....$50–60
ANTIQUE TRADER (1968), the widely read *Antique Trader* weekly newspaper forms this bottle with the front page clearly shown in black and red, alongside the *1968 National Directory of Antique Dealers*. Both are on a black base. Regal China, 10½″ $4–6

APPALOOSA (1974), the appaloosa was the favorite horse of the Old West and is shown on this bottle trotting along above an embossed horseshoe marked "Appaloosa." His body is brown and white while his tail and mane are black. The stopper is formed by his head. Regal China, 10" $12–15
ARIZONA (1968), embossed scene of canyon, river, and cactus in blue, yellow, and brown, "The Grand Canyon State, Arizona" in gold. Map embossed on stopper. Reverse has scenes of Arizona life. Regal China, 12" $4–6
ARMADILLO $8–12
ARMANETTI AWARD WINNER (1969), a pale blue bottle in the shape of the number 1, to honor Armanetti, Inc. of Chicago as "Liquor Retailer of the Year" in 1969. In shield, gold and blue lettering proclaims "Armanetti Liquors 1969 Award Winner." Heavily embossed gold scrolls decorate the bottle $6–8
ARMANETTI SHOPPER (1971), the front of the bottle has a man pushing a shopping cart and the slogan "It's Fun to Shop Armanetti—Self Service Liquor Store." On the back of the bottle, there is an embossed view of the store with other Illinois locations of Armanetti stores. 11¾" $6–8
ARMANETTI VASE (1968), yellow-toned decanter embossed with many flowers and a large letter A for Armanetti $5–7
BACCHUS (1970), this bottle was issued by the Armanetti Liquor Stores of Chicago, Illinois. The body of the bottle is made of a circular medallion showing Bacchus. The medallion is topped by grapes. The stopper is circular and bears the symbol of Armanetti Liquors. Regal China, 11¾" $6–9
BARNEY'S SLOT MACHINE (1978), replica of the world's largest slot machine which is located in Barney's Casino on the South Shore at Lake Tahoe, Nevada. Red with small black stopper at the top $14–16
BARRY BERISH (1985), Executive series $110–140
BARRY BERISH (1986), Executive series, bowl $110–140
BARTENDER'S GUILD (1973), a commemorative Regal China bottle honoring the International Bartenders' Association on the first International Cocktail Competition in the United States $4–7
BASEBALL (1969), this baseball-shaped bottle was issued to commemorate the 100th anniversary of the professional sport. "Professional Baseball's 100th Anniversary—1869–1969" is gold and black on the front. Decal of player in action on top. Reverse has history of growth of baseball $18–20
BEAM POT (1980), shaped like a New England bean pot, a colonial scene is depicted on the front. On the back, there is a large map of the New England states. The stopper is a large gold dome. This is the club bottle for the New England Beam Bottle and Specialties Club $12–15

Jim Beam, bass boat.
PHOTO COURTESY OF DAVE SMITH.

BEAVER VALLEY CLUB (1977), figurine of a beaver sitting on a stump wearing blue pants, white shirt, red jacket, black bow, and hat. The beaver is saluting. A club bottle to honor the Beaver Valley Jim Beam Club of Rochester.... $8–12

BELL SCOTCH (1970), tan center, gold base, brown top with coat of arms of Arthur Bell & Sons on front. Bottle is in the shape of a large handbell. Regal China, 10½″ $4–7

BEVERAGE ASSOCIATION, NLBA $4–7

THE BIG APPLE (1979), apple-shaped bottle with embossed Statue of Liberty on the front with New York City in the background and the lettering "The Big Apple" over the top... $8–12

BING'S 31ST CLAM BAKE BOTTLE (1972), an inspired Regal China bottle heavily decorated in gold. The front features a three-dimensional reproduction of the famous Pebble Beach, California, wind-swept tree overlooking the Pacific Ocean. The back commemorates the 31st Bing Crosby National Pro-Am Golf Tournament at the world famous Pebble Beach course, January 1972. The stopper is the official seal of the tourney. 10¾″ $25–30

BING CROSBY NATIONAL PRO-AM (1970) $4–7

BING CROSBY NATIONAL PRO-AM (1971) $4–7

BING CROSBY NATIONAL PRO-AM (1972) $15–25

BING CROSBY NATIONAL PRO-AM (1973), the fourth in its series honoring the Bing Crosby Golf Tournament, genuine Regal China bottle in luxurious fired 22K gold with a white stopper, featuring replicas of the famous Crosby hat, pipe, and golf club $18–23

BING CROSBY NATIONAL PRO-AM (1974) $15–25

BING CROSBY NATIONAL PRO-AM (1975) $45–65

BING CROSBY 36TH (1976), same as the Floro de Oro except for the medallion below the neck. Urn-shaped bottle with pastel wide band and flowers around the middle. Remainder of bottle is shiny gold with fluting and designs.......$15–25

BING CROSBY NATIONAL PRO-AM (1977) $12–18

BING CROSBY NATIONAL PRO-AM (1978) $12–18

BLACK KATZ (1968), same kitty, different color: black cat, green eyes, red tongue, white base. Both Katz are Regal China, 14½″ $7–12

BLUE CHERUB EXECUTIVE (1960), blue and white decanter with heavily embossed figures of cherubs with bow and arrow gold details. Scrolls and chain holding Beam label around neck. Regal China, 12½″ $70–90

BLUE DAISY (1967), also known as Zimmerman Blue Daisy. Light blue with embossed daisies and leaves around bottle. Background resembles flower basket... $10–12

BLUE GILL, FISH... $12–16

BLUE GOOSE ORDER..$4–7

BLUE JAY (1969), tones of sky blue on the bird's body with black and white markings. Black claws grip "oak tree stump" with acorns and leaves embossed..$4–7

BLUE GOOSE (1979), replica of a blue goose with its characteristic grayish-blue coloring. Authenticated by Dr. Lester Fisher, director of Lincoln Park Zoological Gardens in Chicago $7–9

BLUE HEN CLUB.. $12–15

BLUE SLOT MACHINE (1967) $10–12

BOBBY UNSER OLSONITE EAGLE (1975), replica of the racing car used by Bobby Unser. White with black accessories and colored decals $40–50

BOB DEVANEY $8–12

BOB HOPE DESERT CLASSIC (1973), the first genuine Regal China bottle created in honor of the Bob Hope Desert Classic, an annual charity fund-raising golf tournament. A profile of Bob Hope is shown on the front side, with a golf ball and tee perched at the tip of his nose $8–9

BOB HOPE DESERT CLASSIC (1974), this Regal China creation honors the famous Bob Hope Desert Classic. Bob Hope silhouette and the sport of golf is a color feature of the bottle $8–12

BOHEMIAN GIRL (1974), this bottle was issued for the Bohemian Cafe in Omaha, Nebraska, to honor the Czech and Slovak immigrants in the United States. She is wearing a white skirt decorated with flowers; also a white skirt and blue vest. Her white cap is the stopper. Regal China, 14¼ " $10–15

BONDED GOLD $4–7

BONDED MYSTIC (1979), urn-shaped bottle with fluting on sides and lid. Small scroll handles, open work handle on lid. Burgundy-colored $4–7

BONDED SILVER $4–7

BOOT HILL (See Dodge City)

BORIS GODINOV, WITH BASE (1978), 2nd in the Opera series $350–450

BOURBON BARREL $18–24

BOWLING PROPRIETORS $4–7

BOYS TOWN OF ITALY (1973), a handsome genuine Regal China bottle created in honor of the Boys Town of Italy. This home for Italian orphans began after World War II. The bottle features a map of Italy, showing the various provinces of that country $7–10

BOWL (1986), Executive series $20–30

BROADMOOR HOTEL (1968), to celebrate the 50th anniversary of this famous hotel in Colorado Springs, Colorado, Beam issued this bottle replica complete with details of windows, doors, roof tiles, and tower capped with a "roof" stopper. The base bears the legend "1918—The Broadmoor—1968" in white ovals on a black background $4–7

BUFFALO BILL (1971), the front of this bottle shows a bust of Buffalo Bill with his name above. The back illustrates his adventures as an Indian fighter and Pony Express rider. The stopper is a small figure of a buffalo. The bottle is beige and gold. Regal China, 10½ " $4–7

BULL DOG (1979), bull dog with yellow infantry helmet with "Devil Dogs" embossed on front. Real leather collar with metal studding around his neck. The mascot of the United States Marine Corps, this bottle honors their 204th anniversary $15–18

CABLE CAR (1968), a gray-green bottle in the form of a San Francisco cable car, complete with doors, windows, and wheels. A gold label with "Van Ness Ave., California & Market Streets" in black on one end, "Powell & Mason Streets" on the side. The stopper is the front light. Regal China, 4½ " H, 7 " L $4–6

CABOOSE (1980), red caboose with black trim. Sign on side reads "New Jersey Central." Has movable wheels and gold lanterns on each side $50–60

CALIFORNIA MISSION (1970), this bottle was issued for the Jim Beam Bottle Club of Southern California in honor of the 200th anniversary of the California Missions. A priest is shown leaning with one hand on his staff and the other around an Indian boy. Above them is a doorway and the steeple of the mission. The stopper is the very top of the mission. Regal China, 14 " $10–15

CALIFORNIA RETAIL LIQUOR DEALERS ASSOCIATION (1973), made of genuine Regal China, this bottle was designed to commemorate the 20th anniversary of the California Retail Liquor Dealers Association. The bottle depicts the emblem of the association showing a liquor store superimposed on the state of California $6–9

CAL-NEVA (1969), this is a standard square bottle, green-toned with "Reno 100 Years" deeply embossed and "Cal-Neva, Casino—Hotel, Reno—Lake Tahoe" in the oval-shaped emblem. Regal China, 9½ " $5–7

CAMELLIA CITY CLUB (1979), replica of the cupola of the State Capitol building in Sacramento surrounded with camellias, since the capitol is known as "The Camellia Capitol of the World"..$18–23

CAMEO BLUE (1965), also known as the Shepherd Bottle. Scenes of shepherd and dog in white on the sky blue square-shaped bottle. White glass stopper, 12¾ " $4–6

CANNON (1970), this bottle was issued to commemorate the 175th anniversary of the Jim Beam Co. The bottle is octagonal with the muzzle of the cannon at a 45-degree angle with the base. The stopper is the end of the muzzle. Some of these bottles have a small chain shown on the cannon and some do not. Those without the chain are harder to find and more valuable. 8 " ....

    Chain..$2–4

    No chain $9–13

CANTEEN (1979), replica of the exact canteen used by the armed forces with simulated canvas covering which has snap flaps and chained cap........... $8–12

CAPTAIN AND MATE (1980), a sea-faring captain with blue jacket, white cap, and yellow duffel bag over his shoulder. The captain has his other arm around the shoulder of a small boy dressed in a red jacket and blue pants. He holds a toy boat $10–12

CARDINAL (KENTUCKY CARDINAL) (1968), a bright red bird with a black mask, tail, and markings, perched on a dark tree-stump-shaded base.............$40–50

CARMEN (1978), figurine of Carmen from the character in the opera of the same name. The third issue in the Opera series, it is a woman dressed in Spanish clothes of white, blue, gold, and red. She wears a small black cone-shaped hat. Music box plays *Habanera*, which is from the opera. Part of three-piece set which includes base and paperweight.. $140–180

CAROLIER BULL (1984), Executive series......................................$18–23

CATFISH..$16–24

CATHEDRAL RADIO (1979), replica of one of the earlier dome-shaped radios. Brown with gold trim and a large domed-shaped lid......................... $12–15

CATS (1967), trio of cats—Siamese, Burmese, and Tabby. Colors are gray with blue eyes, dark brown and white with yellow eyes, and white and tan with blue eyes. Regal China, 11½ " H, each..$6–9

CEDARS OF LEBANON (1971), this bottle shows a green tree rising above a background of a gray- and gold-colored building. This bottle was issued in honor of the Jerry Lewis Muscular Dystrophy Telethon held in 1971. Near the base of the bottle, the words "Tall Cedars of Lebanon" appear. The stopper is the upper half of the tree. Regal China, 9¾ " $5–7

CHARISMA (1970), Executive series...$4–7

CHARLIE MCCARTHY (1976), replica of Edgar Bergen's puppet from the 1930s. A black ribbon is attached to his monocle $20–30

CHERRY HILLS COUNTRY CLUB (1973), a very handsome genuine Regal China bottle, commemorating the 50th anniversary of the famous Cherry Hills Country Club. Located in Denver, Colorado, Cherry Hills has hosted some of the top professional golf tournaments. The front of the bottle illustrates the many activities available at Cherry Hills, while the name of the club circles the bottom in luxurious 22K gold $4–7

CHEYENNE, WYOMING (1977), circular decanter in shape of a wheel. Spokes separate scenes of Cheyenne history. Regal China $4–6

CHICAGO CUBS, Sports series...$30–40

CHICAGO SHOW BOTTLE (1977), stopper is a gold loving cup standing on a black pedestal. Commemorates the 6th Annual Chicago Jim Beam Bottle Show $10–14

CHRISTMAS TREE...$150–200

CHURCHILL DOWNS—PINK ROSES (1969), same as below, pink embossed roses $5–7

CHURCHILL DOWNS—RED ROSES (1969), "Churchill Downs—Home of the 95th Kentucky Derby" is embossed in gold on the front, around the main paddock building. The shell-shaped bottle comes with red roses framing the scene. Reverse: "Aristedes," first Derby winner in 1875, on a decal. Regal China, 10¾" $9–12

CIRCUS WAGON (1979), replica of a circus wagon from the late 19th century. Blue with gold embossing, white wheels, which are movable, with red trim $24–26

CIVIL WAR NORTH (1961), blue and gray bottle depicting Civil War battle scenes. Stopper has Lee's face on one side, Grant's on the other. Regal China, 10¾" (when sold as a pair)..$10–15

CIVIL WAR SOUTH (1961), one side portrays the meeting of Lee and Jackson at Chancellorsville. On the other side a meeting of southern Generals. Regal China, 10¾" (when sold as a pair)...$25–35

CLEAR CRYSTAL BOURBON (1967), patterned embossed with "swirl" stopper. Starburst design on base of the bottle. Clear glass, 11½" $5–7

CLEAR CRYSTAL SCOTCH (1966), the original patterned embossed bottle. Glass stopper ("Doorknob"). Bottom is unpatterned and has number and date of issue, 11½" $9–12

CLEAR CRYSTAL VODKA (1967), same as above $5–8

CLEOPATRA RUST (1962), same as Cleopatra Yellow. Scene with Mark Antony and Cleopatra in white on rust-red background...................................$3–5

CLEOPATRA YELLOW (1962), black and purple, two-handled, amphora decanter. Yellow figures of Mark Antony in armor and Cleopatra beside the Nile. Pyramid and sphinx background. Egyptian border design circles bottle, white stopper. Rarer than Cleopatra Rust. Glass, 13¼" $8–12

CLINT EASTWOOD (1973), a handsome genuine Regal China bottle, commemorating the Clint Eastwood Invitational Celebrity Tennis Tournament held in Pebble Beach. The bottle features two tennis rackets across the front while the stopper features an exact likeness of Clint Eastwood. Two ribbons adorn the front of the bottle: one with stars on a field of blue, the other in red with the name of the tournament emblazoned in 22K gold $14–17

COCKTAIL SHAKER (1953), glass, Fancy Diz. Bottle, 9¼" $2–5

COFFEE GRINDER $8–12

COFFEE WARMERS (1954), four types are known in red, black, gold, and white

necks; plastic cord over cork. The Corning Glass Co. made the Pyrex bottles.
Round stoppers are made of wood. Pyrex glass, 9 " $7–12
COFFEE WARMERS (1956), two types with metal necks and handles: black and
gold stripes on one, gold neck with black handle on the other. White star design
on sides of Pyrex glass on both. Round black plastic tops. Some have holder-
type candle warmers. Pyrex glass, 10 " $2–5
COHO SALMON (1976), gray with black speckles. Official seal of the National
Fresh Water Fishing Hall of Fame is on the back $10–13
COLIN MEAD $180–210
COLBALT (1981), Executive series... $18–23
COLLECTOR'S EDITION (1966), set of six, glass, famous paintings: *The Blue Boy,
On the Terrace, Mardi Gras, Austide Bruant, The Artist Before His Easel,* and
Laughing Cavalier, each..$2–5
COLLECTORS EDITION VOLUME II (1967), a set of six flask-type bottles painted
gold with pictures from the Renaissance period: *George Gisze, Soldier and Girl,
Night Watch, The Jester, Nurse and Child,* and *Man on Horse,* each $2–5
COLLECTORS EDITION VOLUME III (1968), a set of eight bottles covered with a
blue velvet finish and picturing a famous American painting on each: *On the
Trail, Indian Maiden, Buffalo, Whistler's Mother, American Gothic, The Ken-
tuckian, The Scout,* and *Hauling in the Gill Net,* each..........................$2–5
COLLECTORS EDITION VOLUME IV (1969), a set of eight bottles with a brown
leatherlike finish and setting on an angle. Each has a picture of a painting by a
famous French artist. They are *Balcony, The Judge, Fruit Basket, Boy with Cherries, Emile Zola, The Guitarist Zouave,* and *Sunflowers,* each................$2–5
COLLECTORS EDITION VOLUME V (1970), a set of six bottles finished in a gold-
flecked red paint with more French paintings featured. These include *Au Cafe,
Old Peasant, Boaring Party, Gare Saint Lazare, The Jewish Bride,* and *Titus at
Writing Desk,* each $2–5
COLLECTORS EDITION VOLUME VI (1971), this set of three bottles look like green
picture frames around three more art masterpieces. They are *Charles I* by Van
Dyck, *The Merry Lute Player* and *Boy Holding Flute* by Frans Hals, each .$2–5
COLLECTORS EDITION VOLUME VII (1972), this set of three bottles is three
different-colored, framed oval pictures of famous European paintings. These are
The Bag Piper, Prince Baltasor, and *Maidservant Pouring Milk,* each $2–5
COLLECTORS EDITION VOLUME VIII (1973), this selection of three bottles fea-
tures contemporary American artist Edward H. Weiss' portraits of *Ludwig Van
Beethoven, Wolfgang Mozart,* and *Frederic Francis Chopin,* each $2–5

Jim Beam, collector series. PHOTO COURTESY OF
DAVE SMITH.

COLLECTORS EDITION VOLUME IX (1974), this set of three bottles has a wood-tone finish and features scenes of bird life designed and painted by James Lockhart, one of the finest wildlife artists in America today. The birds include the *Cardinal, Ring-Neck Pheasant*, and the *Woodcock*, each $3–6

COLLECTORS EDITION VOLUME X (1975), a set of three different-colored bottles featuring diamond-shaped pictures of the *Sailfish, Rainbow Trout*, and *Large-mouth Bass* as painted by the esteemed naturalist Jim Lockhart, each.......$3–6

COLLECTORS EDITION VOLUME XI (1976), each of this set of three bottles features one of three reproductions of Jim Lockhart's paintings of the *Chipmunk, Bighorn Sheep*, and *Pronghorn Antelope*, each $3–6

COLLECTORS EDITION VOLUME XII (1977), a set of four bottles of painted glass, each painted a different color and having a different reproduction of James Lockhart's on the front. Each picture is framed with a gold border. *German Short-haired Pointer* is black with gold matting and black stopper, *Labrador Retriever* is dark purple...$3–6

COLLECTORS EDITION VOLUME XIV (1978), a set of four flask-type bottles. Glass made to appear like brown leather with framed wildlife scenes on the front which are reproductions of paintings by James Lockhart. Each picture has embossed details. The names and themes of the bottles are: *Raccoon, Mule Deer, Red Fox*, and *Cottontail Rabbit*, each...$3–6

COLLECTORS EDITION VOLUME XV (1979), a set of three flasks, each with a different reproduction of Frederic Remington's paintings titled: *The Cowboy 1902, The Indian Trapper 1902*, and *Lieutenant S.C. Robertson 1890*, each.......$2–5

COLLECTORS EDITION VOLUME XVI (1980), set of three flasks, each depicting scenes of ducks in flight on the front with an oval background and a bamboo-style frame. Large domed lids. *The Mallard, The Redhead, The Canvasback*. Artwork by James Lockhart, one of the best-known wildlife artists in America, each $3–6

COLLECTORS EDITION VOLUME XVII (1981), three flask bottles with ball-type lids featuring three more paintings by Jim Lockhart. These triangular pictures are of the *Great Elk, Pintail Duck*, and the *Horned Owl* (also known as the car owl), each...$3–6

COLORADO (1959), light turquoise showing pioneers crossing the rugged mountains with snow-capped peaks in background. "Colorado" and "1859–1959" in gold. Bottle has a leather thong. Regal China, 10¾"....................$20–25

COLORADO CENTENNIAL (1976), replica of Pike's Peak with a miner and his mule in front with the word "Colorado" above the base $8–12

COLORADO SPRINGS $4–7

COMPUTER, DEMOCRAT (1984) $12–18

COMPUTER, REPUBLICAN (1984) $12–18

CONVENTION BOTTLE (1971), created to commemorate the occasion of the first national convention of the National Association of Jim Beam Bottle and Specialty Clubs hosted by the Rocky Mountain Club, Denver, Colorado, June 1971. 11" $5–7

CONVENTION NUMBER 2 (1972), this beautiful Regal China creation honors the second annual convention of the National Association of Jim Beam Bottle and Specialty Clubs, held June 19–25 in Anaheim, California. Stopper features the national symbol of the Beam Bottle Club. 10" $20–30

CONVENTION NUMBER 3—DETROIT (1973), round blue bottle designed like the world with a green U.S. outstanding and a large numeral 3. The stopper is a bust of a golden fox. Commemorates the third annual convention of Beam Bottle

Collectors held in Detroit. 14″ $10–12

CONVENTION NUMBER 4—PENNSYLVANIA (1974), a black and gold Amish wagon commemorating the annual convention of the Jim Beam Bottle Clubs held in Lancaster, Pennsylvania. On the back is listed in gold all the member clubs. A green fox is in the driver's seat. 7½″ $80–100

CONVENTION NUMBER 5—SACRAMENTO (1975), the famous gold pan frames an embossed scene of Sutter's Fort in Sacramento, California. Gold nuggets gleam in the miner's pan and in the transparent stopper of the bottle. On the back: "Hosted by Camellia City Jim Beam Bottle Club 1975." 10¾″ $5–7

CONVENTION NUMBER 6—HARTFORD (1976), Charter Oak and gold lettering on the front. A map of the United States is on the back. Commemorates the annual convention of the Jim Beam Bottle Club held in Hartford, Connecticut.....$5–7

CONVENTION NUMBER 7—LOUISVILLE (1978) $5–7

CONVENTION NUMBER 8—CHICAGO (1978), embossed scene with the Sears Tower, Hancock Building, Marina City, and Water Tower with Lake Michigan at the base. Commemorates the eighth Beam convention held in Chicago $8–12

CONVENTION NUMBER 9—HOUSTON (1979), the mascot of the Beam clubs, a gray poodle named Tiffany, sits on the side of a space capsule. Commemorates the ninth Beam convention, which was held in Houston......................$20–30

  Cowboy, beige..$35–45
  Cowboy, in color..$35–45

CONVENTION NUMBER 10—NORFOLK (1980), the sailing ship *USS Beam* passing between the spokes of ship's helm, with a gold flag atop the mast. The *USS Beam* is located at the Norfolk Naval Base where the tenth convention was held $18–22

  Waterman, pewter..$35–45
  Waterman, yellow..$35–45

CONVENTION NUMBER 11—LAS VEGAS (1981), a Las Vegas dealer fox stands behind a barrel marked "Jim Beam Since 1795" dealing poker to two players while the chips are stacked by their hands. On the dealer's back is the logo of the International Association of Jim Beam Bottle and Specialty Clubs, 10″ $20–22

  Showgirl, blonde $45–55
  Showgirl, brunette $45–55

CONVENTION NUMBER 12—NEW ORLEANS (1982), an unusual bottle that represents a Mardi Gras float with Rex, the King of the Mardi Gras, waving to the crowd. This is a green bottle, embellished with gold and "1982 Mardi Gras Rex" on the front. The bottle is open through the center around Rex. 9¼″ $30–35

  Buccaneer, gold $35–45
  Buccaneer, in color $35–45

CONVENTION NUMBER 13—ST. LOUIS (1983), Stein.........................$55–70

  Gibson girl, blue $65–80
  Gibson girl, yellow $65–80

CONVENTION NUMBER 14—FLORIDA, KING NEPTUNE (1984) $15–20

  Mermaid, blonde..$35–45
  Mermaid, brunette..$35–45

CONVENTION NUMBER 15—LAS VEGAS (1985) $40–50

CONVENTION NUMBER 16—PILGRIM WOMAN, BOSTON (1986) $35–45

  Minuteman, color.. $85–105
  Minuteman, pewter $85–105

CONVENTION NUMBER 17—LOUISVILLE (1987) $55–75
  Kentucky Colonel, blue.. $85–105
  Kentucky Colonel, gray.. $85–105
CONVENTION NUMBER 18—BUCKY BEAVER (1988) $30–40
  Portland rose, red...$30–40
  Portland rose, yellow...$30–40
CONVENTION NUMBER 19—KANSAS CITY (1989) $40–50
COWBOY (1979), either antique tan or multicolored. Cowboy leaning on a fence with one hand on his belt buckle and the other holding a rifle. His cowboy hat is the stopper. Awarded to collectors who attended the 1979 convention for the International Association of Beam Clubs....................................$35–50
CPO OPEN $4–7
CRAPPIE (1979), figure of a silver- and black-speckled crappie commemorates the National Fresh Water Fishing Hall of Fame...............................$10–14
DARK EYES BROWN JUG (1978), beige, both flecked with color; the brown jug has red flecks, the beige jug has brown flecks. Regular jug shape with small handle at neck with black stopper $4–6
D-DAY $12–18
DELAWARE BLUE HEN BOTTLE (1972), this diamond-shaped bottle, fashioned of genuine handcrafted Regal China, commemorates the state of Delaware, "the first state of the Union." The front of the bottle depicts the act of ratification of the Federal Constitution on December 7, 1787. The back shows the Delaware State House, a state map, and the famous Twin Bridges $4–7
DELCO FREEDOM BATTERY (1978), replica of a Delco battery. Entire plastic top is removable $18–22
DELFT BLUE (1963), "Windmill Bottles"; a reverse has scene of embossed Dutch windmills on gray-white bottle. Dutch fishing boats under sail on front in "Delft" in dark blue handle and stopper, 13 " $3–5
DELFT ROSE (1963), rarer than Delft Blue; same as above; sailing scene in pale blue and pink. Windmill scene embossed on reverse. Glass, 13 " $4–6
DEL WEBB MINT (1970), a large gold "400" and "Del Webb's Las Vegas" embossed under crossed checkered flags. Stopper is gold dune buggy. Checkered flags on edge of bottle. "Mint" on front for the Vegas Hotel that originally had the bottle. Regal China, china or metal stopper, 13 " ....
  Metal stopper $10–12
  China stopper...$50–60
DEVIL DOG...$15–25
DIAL TELEPHONE (1980), black reproduction of a 1919 desk model telephone with a movable dial. The fourth in a series of Beam telephone designs ..$40–50
DODGE CITY (1972), this bottle was issued to honor the centennial of Dodge City. The bottle is roughly triangular and depicts the city as it must have looked a century ago. Above the town, the famous cemetery Boot Hill appears. A circular plaque on the bottle acknowledges the centennial. The stopper is a six-pointed sheriff's badge. Regal China, 10 " $5–6
DOE (1963), pure white neck markings, natural brown body. "Rocky" base. Regal China, 13½ " $10–12
DOE—RE-ISSUED (1967), as above $10–12
DOG (1959), long-eared Setter dog, soft brown eyes, black and white coat. Regal China, 15¼ " $20–25

DON GIOVANNI (1980), figurine of Don Giovanni from the Mozart opera of the same name. The fifth in the Operatic series, this bottle has a music box which plays the duet *La ci darem la mano* $140–180

DONKEY AND ELEPHANT ASHTRAYS (1956), they were made to be used as either ashtrays with coasters or book ends. The stylized elephant and donkey heads are in lustrous gray china. The Beam label fits the round coaster section of the bottle. Regal China, 10″, pair $12–16

DONKEY AND ELEPHANT CAMPAIGNERS (1960), elephant is dressed in a brown coat and blue vest with a gold chain. He carries a placard stating "Republicans—1960" and the state where the bottle is sold. Donkey is dressed in black coat, tan vest, and gray pants. His placard reads "Democrats—1960" and state where sold. Regal China, 12″, pair $12–16

DONKEY AND ELEPHANT BOXERS (1964), the G.O.P. elephant has blue trunks with red stripes, white shirt, and black top hat with stars on the band. His gloves are brown. The donkey has red trunks with a blue stripe, black shoes, and top hat. The hat band is white with red and blue stars, pair...................... $14–18

DONKEY AND ELEPHANT CLOWNS (1968), both are dressed in polka dot clown costumes. Elephant has red ruffles and cuffs with blue dots. Donkey has blue with red dots. Yellow styrofoam straw hat and clown shoes on both elephant and donkey. Their heads are the stoppers. Regal China, 12″, pair................$4–7

DONKEY AND ELEPHANT FOOTBALL ELECTION BOTTLES (1972), "Pick the winning team." The Democratic donkey and the G.O.P. elephant are depicted in football costumes atop genuine Regal China footballs in this 1972 version of Beam's famous election bottle series. Each is 9½″, pair $6–9

DONKEY NEW YORK CITY (1976), donkey wearing blue coat and black patriot hat stands inside broken drum decorated with stars, banner, and plaque in red, white, and blue. Commemorates the National Democratic Convention in New York City $10–12

DUCK (1957), green-headed mallard, bright yellow bill, brown breast, black wings. Regal China, 14¼″ $15–20

DUCKS AND GEESE (1955), a scene of wild ducks and geese flying up from marshes in white is featured on this clear glass decanter. A round tall bottle with a large base and slender tapering neck. Tall gold stopper sits in a flared top, 13½″ $5–8

DUCKS UNLIMITED MALLARD (1974)..$40–50

DUCKS UNLIMITED WOOD DUCK (1975), wood duck nestled against a tree stump with Ducks Unlimited logo on front, 9″ $45–50

DUCKS UNLIMITED 40TH MALLARD HEN (1977), white bottle with base designed to appear as if it is floating in water; also has a brown mallard hen sitting on it. The number "40" in green is on the front, plaques on the base and at the neck of the bottle..$40–50

DUCKS UNLIMITED MALLARD (1978), head of a mallard duck on a semicircular-shaped bottle with a medallion-type stopper. Ducks Unlimited is a conservation organization, 9¼″ $35–45

DUCKS UNLIMITED CANVASBACK DRAKE (1979), replica of a canvasback drake preparing to take off in flight with his wings spread. Light gray with black and burgundy coloring on wings and neck. 8″....................................$30–40

DUCKS UNLIMITED BLUE-WINGED TEAL (1980), two ducks made of bisque, dark brown coloring with blue markings. The sixth in a series, 9½″ $40–45

Ducks Unlimited Green-Winged Teal (1981) $35–45
Ducks Unlimited Wood Ducks (1982).......................................$35–45
Ducks Unlimited American Widg Pr (1983)..............................$35–45
Ducks Unlimited Mallard (1984)..$55–75
Ducks Unlimited Pintail Pr (1985)...$30–40
Ducks Unlimited Redhead (1986) $15–25
Ducks Unlimited Blue Bill (1987) $40–60
Ducks Unlimited Black Duck (1989)......................................$50–60

Eagle (1966), white head, golden beak, deep rich brown plumage, yellow claws on "tree trunk" base. Regal China, 12½" $10–13

Eldorado (1978), gray-blue or beige, teardrop-shaped bottle on pedestal stand, dome-shaped stopper, mottled, 13″ $7–9

Election, Democrat (1988)..$30–40

Election, Republican (1988)..$30–40

Elephant And Donkey Supermen (1980), set of two. Representing the Democratic and Republican political parties, the elephant and the donkey are both dressed as Superman in yellow and gray outfits. Each carries the world on his shoulders $10–14

Elephant Kansas City (1976), elephant standing inside broken drum decorated in red, white, and blue with stars; banner, coat, and black patriot hat stands inside broken drum decorated with stars, banner, and plaque in red, white, and blue. Commemorates the National Democratic Convention in New York City $8–10

Elks..$4–7

Elks National Foundation... $8–12

Emerald Crystal Bourbon (1968), emerald green bottle, patterned embossed glass. Flat stopper, "swirl" embossed. Green glass, 11½″ $3–5

Emmett Kelly (1973), a delightful genuine Regal China creation. An exact likeness of the original Emmett Kelly, as sad-faced Willie the Clown, who has captivated and won the hearts of millions from the Big Top of television, 14″ $18–22

Emmett Kelly, Native Son..$50–60

Ernie's Flower Cart (1976), replica of an old-fashioned flower cart used in San Francisco. Wooden cart with movable wheels. In honor of Ernie's Wines and Liquors of northern California $24–28

Evergreen, club bottle $7–10

Jim Beam, Executive series, 1969, urn. PHOTO COURTESY OF DAVE SMITH.

EXPO 74 (1974), this bottle was issued on the occasion of the World's Fair held at Spokane, Washington, in 1974. A very unusual bottle; six-sided panels form the bottle's sides. The top of the bottle is a clock tower. The stopper is the roof of the tower. Regal China, 7¼″ $5–7

FALSTAFF (1979), replica of Sir John Falstaff with blue and yellow outfit holding a gold goblet. Second in the Australian Opera series. Music box which plays *Va, vecchio, John*. Limited edition of 1000 bottles, comes with base $150–160

FANTASIA BOTTLE (1971), this tall, delicately handcrafted Regal China decanter is embellished with 22K gold and comes packaged in a handsome midnight blue and gold presentation case lined with red velvet. 16¼″ $5–6

FATHERS DAY CARD $15–25

FEMALE CARDINAL (1973), the body of the bird is mostly brown with a red beak and some red on the tail feathers. The stopper is the upper part of the bird. Regal China, 13½″ $8–12

FIESTA BOWL, glass $8–12

FIESTA BOWL (1973), the second bottle created for the Fiesta Bowl. This bottle is made of genuine Regal China, featuring a football player on the front side, 13¼″ $9–11

FIGARO (1977), figurine of the character Figaro from the opera *Barber of Seville*. Spanish costume in beige, rose, and yellow. Holds a brown guitar on the ground in front of him. Music box plays an aria from the opera $140–170

FIGHTING BULL $12–18

FIJI ISLANDS $4–6

FIRST NATIONAL BANK OF CHICAGO (1964), *Note*: Beware of reproductions. Issued to commemorate the 100th anniversary of the First National Bank of Chicago. About 130 were issued: 117 were given as mementoes to the bank directors, none for public distribution. This is the most valuable Beam bottle known. Sky blue color, circular shape, gold embossed design around banner lettered ''The First National Bank of Chicago.'' Center oval was ornate bank logo ''1st,'' and ''100th Anniversary'' in gold. Gold embossed ''1st'' on stopper. Bottom marked ''Creation of James B. Beam Distilling Co.—Genuine Regal China.'' Reverse: Round paper label inscribed ''Beam Congratulates the First National Bank of Chicago—100th Anniversary. 100 Years of Successful Banking'' $1900–2400

FISH (1957), sky blue sailfish, pink underside, black dorsal fin and side markings on ''ocean waves'' base. Regal China, 14″ $15–18

Jim Beam, fire truck.
PHOTO COURTESY OF DAVE SMITH.

FISH HALL OF FAME..$25–35

FIVE SEASONS (1980), the club bottle for the Five Seasons Club of Cedar Rapids honors their home state, Iowa. The bottle is shaped like Iowa with a large ear of corn. The top of the corn is the lid $10–12

FLEET RESERVE ASSOCIATION (1974), this bottle was issued by the Fleet Reserve Association to honor the Career Sea Service on their 50th anniversary. The bottle is roughly triangular with the words "Loyalty Protection Service" embossed on the front. The stopper is plain. Regal China, 9" $5–7

FLORIDA SHELL (1968), shell-shaped bottles made in two colors—mother-of-pearl and iridescent bronze—for a shimmering luminescent effect. Reverse has map of Florida and "Sea Shell Headquarters of the World." Regal China, 9¾"
....$4–6

FLORO DE ORO (1976), urn-shaped bottle with pastel band around middle and yellow and blue flowers; remainder of the bottle is gold with fluting and designs, gold handle, 12" $10–12

FLOWER BASKET (1962), blue basket filled with embossed pastel flowers and green leaves resting on gold base; gold details and stopper. Regal China, 12¼"
.... $30–35

FOOTBALL HALL OF FAME (1972), this bottle is a reproduction of the striking new Professional Football Hall of Fame Building, executed in genuine Regal China. The stopper is in the shape of half a football, 9¾" $14–18

FOREMOST—BLACK AND GOLD (1956), Pylon-shaped decanter with a deep black body embossed with gold nuggets. The square white stopper doubles as a jigger. This is the first Beam bottle issued for a liquor retailer, Foremost Liquor Store of Chicago; many others have followed. Regal China $225–250

FOREMOST—GRAY AND GOLD (1956), same as above. Tapered decanter with gray body and gold nuggets. Both decanters are 15½" H and are Regal China ....
....$225–250

FOREMOST—SPECKLED BEAUTY (1956), the most valuable of the Foremost bottles. Also known as the Pink Speckled Beauty, was created in the shape of a Chinese vase and spattered in various colors of pink, gold, black, and gray. The spattered colors may vary from bottle to bottle since it was hand-applied. Regal China, 14½" $500–600

Fox (1967), blue coat $65–80

Fox (1971), gold coat $35–48

Fox, green coat $12–18

Fox, white coat $20–30

Fox, on a dolphin $12–15

Fox, Uncle Sam $5–6

Fox, Kansas City, blue, miniature...$20–30

Fox, Red Distillery.. $1100–1300

FRANKLIN MINT $4–7

FRENCH CRADLE TELEPHONE (1979), replica of a French cradle telephone. The third in the Telephone Pioneers of America series, 7¼" $20–22

GALAH BIRD (1979), rose-colored Galah bird which is part of the cockatoo family from South Australia. It has a white plume on its head and touches of gray and white feathers... $14–16

GEM CITY, club bottle $35–45

GEORGE WASHINGTON COMMEMORATIVE PLATE (1976), plate-shaped bottle with a painting of George Washington in the center bordered by a band of gold. The bottle is blue with lettering around the outside rim. Commemorates the U.S. Bicentennial, 9½″ $12–15

GERMAN BOTTLE—WEISBADEN (1973), this bottle, of genuine Regal China, depicts a map of the famous Rhine wine-growing regions of Germany. Special attention is given to the heart of this wine country at Weisbaden, 11″ $4–6

GERMAN STEIN $20–30

GERMANY (1970), this bottle was issued to honor the American Armed Forces in Germany. The body of the bottle is made up of a plaque on both sides showing rustic German scenes. The stopper is plain. Regal China, 10″ $4–6

GLEN CAMPBELL 51ST (1976), guitar-shaped bottle with a bust of Glen Campbell sculptured at top of guitar. Lid is the ends of gold clubs. Honors the 51st Los Angeles Open, a golf tournament held at the Riviera Country Club between February 16–20. 12¾″ $7–10

GOLDEN CHALICE (1961), chalice with gray-blue body, gold accents. Band of embossed pastel flowers on the neck. Gold scrolled neck and base. Regal China, 12¼″ $40–50

GOLDEN GATE (1969), this almond-shaped bottle has "Las Vegas" embossed in bright gold in a banner on the front. Mountains, a helicopter, a golfer, and gambling montage, with "Golden Gate Casino" in gold on a shield are featured. Regal China, 12½″ $40–50

GOLDEN JUBILEE (1977), Executive series $8–12

GOLDEN NUGGET (1969), same as above; "Golden Nugget" in gold on shield in front. Regal China, 12½″ $35–42

GOLDEN ROSE (1978), three versions of this urn-shaped bottle; yellow embossed rose with a blue background framed in gold band, remainder of bottle gold-mottled with two handles. Yellow Rose of Texas version has the name of this bottle beneath the rose, the Harolds Club VIP version has its title lettered under the rose also, 11½″ $15–20

GRAND CANYON (1969), "Grand Canyon National Park 50th Anniversary" in a circle around a scene of the Canyon in black with "1919–1969" in earth-red. A round bottle (same as Arizona) with a "stick up" spout and round stopper embossed with map of Arizona. Regal China, 12½″ $7–9

GRANT LOCOMOTIVE (1979), replica of Grant Locomotive, black engine with gold trim and bells, red wheels that move. 9″ $55–65

GRAY CHERUB (1958), checkered design, bordered with scroll work, accented with 22K gold. Three embossed cherubs on neck. Regal China, 12″ .$240–260

Jim Beam, globe. PHOTO COURTESY OF DAVE SMITH.

GREAT CHICAGO FIRE BOTTLE (1971), this historical decanter was created to commemorate the great Chicago fire of 1871, and to salute Mercy Hospital which rendered service to the fire victims. This first hospital of Chicago was started in 1852 by the Sisters of Mercy. The new Mercy Hospital and Medical Center, opened in 1968, is depicted on the reverse side. The front of the bottle shows towering flames engulfing Chicago's waterfront as it appeared on the evening of October 8, 1871. The look of actual flames has been realistically captured in this Regal China masterpiece, 7½″ $18–22

GREAT DANE (1976), white with black markings and gold collar, 7″ $7–9

GREEN CHINA JUG (1965), deep mottled green china jug, with embossed branches and buds on side. Solid handle. Regal Glass, 12½″ $4–6

HANK WILLIAMS, JR..$40–50

HANNAH DUSTIN (1973), a beautiful Regal China creation designed after the granite monument erected in her memory on Contoocook Island, in the Merrimack River north of Concord. This was where, in 1697, Hannah Dustin, her nurse, and a young boy made their famous frantic escape from Indians, who held them captive for two weeks. 14½″ $10–12

HANSEL AND GRETEL BOTTLE (1971), the forlorn, lost waifs from the Brothers Grimm beloved fable *Hansel and Gretel* are depicted on the front of this charming and beautiful Regal China bottle. Above them, the words, "Germany . . . Land of Hansel and Gretel" stand out in gold. 10¼″ $4–6

HARLEY DAVIDSON 85TH ANNIVERSARY DECANTER $110–150

HARLEY DAVIDSON 85TH ANNIVERSARY STEIN $180–220

HAROLDS CLUB—MAN-IN-A-BARREL (1957), this was the first in a series made for the famous Harolds Club in Reno, Nevada. The man-in-a-barrel was an advertising logo used by the club. In 1957, Jim Beam issued a bottle using the figure of "Percy" in a barrel with "Harolds Club" embossed on the front. "Percy" has a top hat, a monocle, a mustache, a white collar, and a bright red tie and spats. He stands on a base of "Bad News" dice cubes. Regal China, 14″ $380–410

HAROLDS CLUB—SILVER OPAL (1957), issued to commemorate the 25th anniversary of Harolds Club; bright silver color with a snowflake design center and a red label. Glass, 11⅛″ $20–22

HAROLDS CLUB—MAN-IN-A-BARREL-2 (1958), twin brother of Percy No. 1. No mustache, "Harolds Club" inscribed on base of the bottle. Regal China, 14″ $140–160

HAROLDS CLUB—NEVADA (GRAY) (1963), "Harolds Club of Reno" inscribed on base of bottle created for the "Nevada Centennial—1864–1964" as a state bottle. Embossed picture of miner and mule on the "Harolds" side, crossed shovel and pick are on stopper. Embossed lettering on base is gray-toned and not bold. This is a rare and valuable bottle $90–110

HAROLDS CLUB—NEVADA (SILVER) (1964), same as above. Base lettering now reads "Harolds Club Reno." The letters are bolder and are bright silver............$90–110

HAROLDS CLUB—PINWHEEL (1965), a round bottle supporting a design of a spinning pinwheel of gold and blue, with gold dots on the edge. "Harolds Club Reno" embossed in gold in the center, "For Fun" on the stopper. Regal China, 10½″ $40–45

HAROLDS CLUB—BLUE SLOT MACHINE (1967), a blue-toned "One Armed Bandit" with two gold bells showing in the window, and a gold-colored handle; the money slot is the stopper. "Harolds Club Reno" and a large "H" on a pinwheel emblem are on the front. Regal China, 10⅜″ $10–14

HAROLDS CLUB—VIP EXECUTIVE (1967), an Aladdin's lamp-shaped decanter. "Harolds Club Reno" embossed gold label on bottle. Overall gold and green color on bottle. Limited quantity issued. Regal China, 12½" $50–60

HAROLDS CLUB—VIP EXECUTIVE (1968), an overall bubble pattern in cobalt blue with silver trim and handle distinguishes this bottle. "Harolds Club Reno" in silver, on an embossed oval emblem, is in the center of the bottle. Regal China, 12¾" $55–65

HAROLDS CLUB—GRAY SLOT MACHINE (1968), same as "Covered Wagon" but with an overall gray tone. Regal China, 10⅜" $4–6

HAROLDS CLUB—VIP EXECUTIVE (1969), an oval-shaped decanter with an overall motif of roses. "Harolds Club Reno" is embossed in gold on the yellow-toned bottle. The bottle was used as a Christmas gift to the casino's executives. Regal China, 12½" $260–285

HAROLDS CLUB—COVERED WAGON (1969–70), a Conestoga wagon with "Harolds Club" embossed on the side pulled by a galloping ox, driven by a cowboy. The bottle is "arch"-shaped, framing Nevada's mountains and the wagon. Regal China, 10" $4–6

HAROLDS CLUB (1970 ....$40–60

HAROLDS CLUB (1971) $40–60

HAROLDS CLUB (1972) $18–25

HAROLDS CLUB (1973) $18–24

HAROLDS CLUB (1974) $12–16

HAROLDS CLUB (1975) $12–18

HAROLDS CLUB VIP (1976), same as Floro de Oro except for the Harolds Club patch on the base. Urn-shaped bottles with pastel band of blue and yellow flowers around the middle. Remainder of the bottle has very shiny gold with fluting and designs. 12" $18–22

HAROLDS CLUB (1977) $20–30

HAROLDS CLUB (1978) $20–30

HAROLDS CLUB VIP (1979), double-urn-shaped bottle with wide alternating bands of gold and mother-of-pearl with double scroll handles on large screw lid. 11½" $20–30

HAROLDS CLUB (1980) $25–35

HAROLDS CLUB (1982) $110–145

HARP SEAL $12–18

HARRAHS CLUB NEVADA—GRAY (1963), this is the same round bottle used for the Nevada Centennial and Harolds Club with the miner, mule, and lettered "Nevada Centennial." The base has "Harrah's Reno and Lake Tahoe" embossed on the gray-tone base. Regal China, 11½" $500–550

HARRAHS CLUB NEVADA—SILVER (1963), same as above. Nevada Centennial bottle, "Harrah's Reno and Lake Tahoe" embossed on base in silver. Regal China, 11½" $800–1000

HARRY HOFFMAN $4–7

HARVEYS RESORT HOTEL AT LAKE TAHOE, glass, 11½" $6–10

HATFIELD (1973), the character of Hatfield from the famous story of the Hatfield and McCoy feud. Hatfield is shown standing holding a rifle at his side. He is dressed all in black. On the base of the bottle he is referred to as "Devil Anse Hatfield." His hat is the stopper. Regal China, 14" $15–16

HAWAII (1959), tribute to 50th state. Panorama of Hawaiian scenes, palm trees, the blue Pacific, outriggers, and surfboarders. Gold "50" in star. Regal China, 8½" $35–36

HAWAII—RE-ISSUED (1967), as above $40–42

HAWAII (1971) $6–8

HAWAII ALOHA (1971), pear-shaped bottle with picture of Hawaiian king on the front and a scene of mountain and palm tree on reverse. 11" $6–10

HAWAIIAN OPEN BOTTLE (1972), cleverly decorated to simulate a pineapple with the famous "Friendly Skies" logo in gold, this genuine Regal China bottle honors the 1972 Hawaiian Open Golf Tournament. The reverse side commemorates United Air Lines' 25th year (1972) of air service to Hawaii. The stopper is designed to look like pineapple leaves. 10" $6–8

HAWAIIAN OPEN (1973), the second bottle created in honor of the United Hawaiian Open Golf Classic. Of genuine Regal China designed in the shape of a golf ball featuring a pineapple and airplane on front. 11" $7–9

HAWAIIAN OPEN (1974), genuine Regal China bottle commemorating the famous 1974 Hawaiian Open Golf Classic. 15" $5–8

HAWAIIAN OPEN OUTRIGGER (1975), a very unusual bottle. Two native girls are paddling an outrigger canoe on a wave beautifully colored in different shades of blue. The bottle is shaped like the wave. The stopper is the very top of the wave. Regal China, 8½" $9–11

HAWAII PARADISE (1978), commemorates the 200th anniversary of the landing of Captain Cook. Embossed scene of a Hawaiian resort framed by a pink garland of flowers. Black stopper, 8¾" $15–17

HEMISFAIR (1968), the Lone Star of Texas crowns the tall gray and blue "Tower of the Americas." "The Lone Star State" is lettered in gold over a rustic Texas scene. The half map of Texas has "Hemisfair 68—San Antonio." Regal China, 13" $8–10

HERRE BROTHERS $25–35

HOBO, AUSTRALIA $10–14

HOFFMAN (1969), the bottle is in the shape of the Harry Hoffman Liquor Store with the Rocky Mountains in the background. Beam bottles and "Ski Country—USA" are in the windows. Reverse: embossed mountain and ski slopes with skier. Regal China, 9" $4–7

HOLIDAY—CAROLIERS $40–50

HOLIDAY—NUTCRACKER $40–50

HOME BUILDERS (1978), replica of a Rockford Builders bungalow, brown with touches of black. Oval medallion on the roof reads "Your Best Bet—A Home of Your Own." This bottles commemorates the 1979 convention of the Home Builders...$24–28

HONE HEKE.. $200–250

HONGA HIKA (1980), Honga Hika is the most famous warchief of the Ngapuki tribe. This is the first in a series of authentic Maori warrior bottles ...$220–240

HORSE (APPALOOSA).. $8–12

HORSE (BLACK) (1962), black horse with white on blaze nose, white hooves, and black tail. Regal China, 13½" $18–22

HORSE (BLACK)—RE-ISSUED (1967), as above $10–12

HORSE (BROWN) (1962), brown horse with white blaze on nose, black hooves and tail. Regal China, 13½" H $18–22

HORSE (BROWN)—RE-ISSUED (1967), as above $10–12

HORSE (MARE AND FOAL)..$35–46

HORSE (OH KENTUCKY) $70–85

HORSE (PEWTER) $12–17

HORSE (WHITE) (1962), white mustang with white flowing mane and tail. Regal China, 13½" $18–20

HORSE (WHITE)—RE-ISSUED (1967), as in previous entry $12–17
HORSESHOE CLUB (1969), same as Reno and Cal-Neva bottles with "Reno's Horseshoe Club" and a horseshoe in yellow and black on the emblem. 9¼" ...
....$4–6
HULA BOWL (1975), brown football resting on a stand with a red helmet on the top. Medallion-type plaque on the front, football player in the center $8–10
HYATT HOUSE—CHICAGO $7–10
HYATT HOUSE—NEW ORLEANS $8–11
IDAHO (1963), bottle in the shape of Idaho. Skier on slope on one side and farmer on other side. Pick and shovel on stopper. Regal China, 12¼" $30–40
ILLINOIS (1968), the log cabin birthplace of "Abe Lincoln" embossed on front; oak tree and banner with 21 stars (21st state) and "Land of Lincoln." Made to honor the Sesquicentennial 1818–1968 of Illinois, home of the James B. Beam Distilling Co. Regal China, 12¾" $4–6
INDIANAPOLIS SESQUICENTENNIAL $4–6
INDIANAPOLIS 500 .... $9–12
INDIAN CHIEF (1979), seated Indian chief with a peace pipe across his arm. Tan-colored with touches of brown, green, and red $9–12
INTERNATIONAL CHILI SOCIETY (1976), upper body of a chef with recipe of C.V. Wood's World Championship Chili $9–12
ITALIAN MARBLE URN (1985), Executive series $12–17
IVORY ASHTRAY (1955), designed for a dual purpose: as a bottle and as an ash-tray. Bottle lies flat with cigarette grooves and round coaster seat. Ivory color. Regal China, 12¾" $8–10
JACKALOPE (1971), the fabulous Wyoming jackalope, a rare cross between a jackrabbit and antelope. It has the body and ears of the western jackrabbit and the head and antlers of an antelope. Golden brown body on prairie grass base. Regal China, 14" $5–8
JAGUAR $18–23
JEWEL T MAN—50TH ANNIVERSARY $35–45
JOHN HENRY (1972), this bottle commemorates the legendary Steel Drivin' Man. He is black and is shown barechested. In each hand he holds a steel hammer. Embossed on the base is "Big Bend Tunnel West Virginia." Regal China, 12¾"
.... $18–22
JOLIET LEGION BAND (1978), shield-shaped bottle with embossed details resem-bling a coat of arms in blue, green, and gold. Commemorates the 26 national championships won by the band. 12¼" $14–15
KAISER INTERNATIONAL OPEN BOTTLE (1971), this handsome Regal China cre-ation commemorates the fifth Annual Kaiser International Open Golf Tourna-ment played that year at Silverado in California's beautiful Napa Valley. The stopper is a golf ball decorated with the Kaiser International Open logo sus-pended over a red tee. The logo is repeated, in gold against a blue field, in the center of the front panel and is surrounded by a ring of decorated golf balls. Listed on the back are the particulars of the tournament. 11¼" $5–6
KANGAROO (1977), kangaroo with its baby in its pouch on a green pedestal. The head is the stopper. 11¾" $10–14
KANSAS (1960), round yellow-toned bottle shows harvesting of wheat on one side and "Kansas 1861–1961 Centennial" embossed in gold. On the other side, sym-bols of the modern age with aircraft, factories, oil wells, and dairies. Leather thong. Regal China, 11¾" $35–45
KENTUCKY BLACK HEAD—BROWN HEAD (1967), the stopper is a horse's head;

some are made in brown, some black. State map on bottle shows products of Kentucky—tobacco, distilling, farming, coal, oil, and industries. Regal China, 11½″

  Black head.. $12–18
  Brown head...$20–28
  White head $18–23
KENTUCKY DERBY 95TH (1969), pink, red roses...............................$4–7
KENTUCKY DERBY 96TH (1970), double rose................................$15–25
KENTUCKY DERBY 97TH (1971) $4–7
KENTUCKY DERBY 98TH (1972), designed to commemorate the 98th Run for the Roses at Churchill Downs showing Canonero II, 1971 winner, garlanded with the traditional American Beauty roses. The reverse side depicts famous Churchill Downs clubhouse in relief and etched in gold. The stopper is a replica of an American Beauty rose. 11″ $4–6
KENTUCKY DERBY 100TH (1974), this bottle commemorates the 100th anniversary of the running of the Kentucky Derby. The number "100" is embossed very large on the bottle and the interior of the numbers is decorated with pink flowers with green leaves and stems. Also on the front of the bottle are embossings of the first Derby winner, Aristides, and the 100th winner, Cannonade. Both horses' portraits are framed by horseshoes. 7½″ $7–10
KEY WEST (1972), this bottle was issued to honor the 150th anniversary of Key West, Florida. It is roughly triangular with embossed details such as palm trees and surf. Regal China, 9¾″ $5–7
KING KAMEHAMEHA (1972), a replica of the famous King Kamehameha statue, this genuine Regal China bottle has been designed to commemorate the 100th anniversary of King Kamehameha Day. A hero of the Hawaiian people, King Kamehameha is credited for uniting the Hawaiian Islands $8–11
KING KONG (1976), three-quarter body of King Kong. Commemorates Paramount's movie release in December 1976. 9¾″ $8–10
KIWI (1974), the kiwi bird is shown protecting its egg near a tree stump. The kiwi's feathers are brown and the egg is white. The stopper is plain. Regal China, 8½″ $5–8
KOALA BEAR (1973), the koala bear, the native animal of Australia. A genuine Regal China creation. The bottle features two koala bears on a tree stump. The top of the stump is its pourer, with the name Australia across the front of the bottle. 9″ $12–14
LARAMIE (1968), "Centennial Jubilee Laramie Wyo. 1868–1968" embossed around cowboy on bucking bronco. Locomotive of 1860s on reverse. 10½″ .....
....$4–6

Jim Beam, King Kong. PHOTO COURTESY OF DAVE SMITH.

LARGEMOUTH BASS TROPHY BOTTLE (1973), created in honor of the National Fresh Water Fishing Hall of Fame, located in Hayward, Wisconsin, completed in 1974. A genuine Regal China creation designed after the largemouth bass. Its stopper features the official seal of the Hall of Fame........................ $10–14

LAS VEGAS (1969), this bottle was also used for Customer Specials, Casino series. Almond-shaped with gold embossed "Las Vegas" in a banner, scenes of Nevada, and a gambling montage. Reverse: Hoover Dam and Lake Mead. Regal China, 12½" $4–6

LIGHT BULB (1979), regular bottle shape with replica of a light bulb for the stopper, picture of Thomas Edison in an oval, letter of tribute to Edison on the back. 11¼" $14–16

LOMBARD (1969), a pear-shaped decanter, embossed with lilacs and leaves around a circular motto "Village of Lombard, Illinois—1869 Centennial 1969"; lilac-shaped stopper. Reverse has an embossed outline map of Illinois. Colors are lavender and green. 12¼" $4–6

LONDON BRIDGE..$4–7

LOUISVILLE DOWNS RACING DERBY (1978), short oblong-shaped bottle. Scene with horse, buggy, and rider on the front framed by wide white band with gold lettering. Medallion-type stopper, 9½" $4–6

LOUISIANA SUPERDOME... $8–11

LVNH OWL $20–30

MADAME BUTTERFLY (1977), figurine of Madame Butterfly character from the opera of the same name. Female dressed in blue and black kimono holding a realistic fan made of paper and wood. Music box plays *One Fine Day* from the opera; includes base and paperweight, 16½" $340–370

THE MAGPIES (1977), black magpie sitting on tip of a football with the name "The Magpies" on the front, honors an Australian football team. 10½" $18–20

MAINE (1970), a green triangular bottle with the outline of the state on the front and wording "The Pine Tree State." 12" $4–6

MAJESTIC (1966), royal blue decanter with handle, on a base of golden leaves. Gold scrolled stopper and lip. Regal China, 14½".............................$20–24

MALE CARDINAL.. $18–24

MARBLED FANTASY (1965), decanter on a blue marbled base, set in a cup of gold with a heavy gold ring around the center. Gold lip and handle, blue and gold stopper. Regal China, 15" $38–42

MARINA CITY (1962), commemorating modern apartment complex in Chicago. Light blue with "Marina City" in gold on the sides. Regal China, 10¾" $10–15

MARINE CORPS..$25–35

MARK ANTONY (1962), same as Cleo bottles, amphora decanter, two handles, white stopper. Mark Antony alone before Nile scene, white on rust background. Bottle color is black-purple. Glass, 13¼" $18–20

MARTHA WASHINGTON (1976), designed like a collector's plate, with a portrait of Martha Washington encircled by a band of white with the outside rim in light blue and gold embossed lettering. 9½" $5–6

McCOY (1973), the character of McCoy from the famous story of the Hatfield and McCoy feud. McCoy is shown seated holding a rifle. On the base of the bottle he is referred to as "Randolph McCoy." The stopper is his hat. Regal China, 12" $14–17

McSHANE—MOTHER-OF-PEARL (1979), Executive series $85–105

McSHANE—TITANS (1980) $85–105

McShane—Cobalt (1981), Executive series................................ $115–135
McShane—Green Pitcher (1982), Executive series $80–105
McShane—Green Bell (1983), Executive series $80–110
Mephistopheles (1979), part of the Opera series, this figurine depicts Mephistopheles from the opera *Faust*. The music box plays *Soldier's Chorus*, bottle and base make up two-piece set. 14½″ $160–190
Michigan Bottle (1972), the map of the Great Lakes State adorns the front of this striking commemorative Regal China bottle. The state flower and the major cities are shown along with an inset plaque of an antique automobile, one of Michigan's traditional symbols. A capsule description of the state, a drawing of the magnificent Mackinac Bridge, and the state motto of the "Wolverine State" appear on a scroll on the back. The stopper depicts an antique wooden wheel on one side and a modern automobile wheel on the other. 11⅞″ $7–9
Milwaukee Stein..$30–40
Minnesota Viking (1973), a strikingly handsome Regal China creation designed after the famous Viking statue in Alexandria, Minnesota, known as the Largest Viking in the World. The bottle features a helmet as its stopper. The back depicts a replica of the Kensington Runestone. 14″ $9–12
Mint 400 (1970), China stopper $80–105
Mint 400 (1970), the annual Del Webb Mint 400 was commemorated by a striking Regal China sculpture which captured the feeling of the desert, surrounded by mountains, beneath a blue Las Vegas sky. It is the home of one of the racing world's most grueling off-road events. The bottle's most prominent feature is the gold-painted motorcycle racer on the stopper. Black and white checkered flags are crossed on the front above large gold letters. Black and white checks edge the sides. A decal on the reverse details information about the race. 8¼″ $5–6
Mint 400 (1971), same as above $5–6
Mint 400 (1972), this bottle commemorates the fifth annual Greatest Off-Road Race held by Del Webb and Mint 400. A black and white checkered flag has the name in large gold letters across the flag. 11¼″ $5–7
Mint 400 (1973), an all-gold bottle honors the sixth annual Mint 400 Sahara Desert Rally, the world's greatest off-road race. An embossed scene is on the back. 13″ $6–8
Mint 400 (1974), metal stopper $4–7
Mint 400, 7th Annual (1975), the checkerboard finish flag serves as a background for the emblem of the Mint 400 Desert Race. This $100,000-purse event includes both auto and cycle contests and they are shown on the gold-embossed back of the bottle. 8¼″ $5–6
Mint 400 8th Annual (1976), medallion-shaped bottle. White bottle with gold lettering and gold center with black lettering. Commemorates the Mint 400, a road race sponsored by Del Webb's Hotel and Casino in Las Vegas. 10″ $9–12
Mississippi Fire Engine (1978), replica of the 1867 fire engine; red and black with brass simulated fittings. Bells, lanterns, water pump, and engine mountings are authentic. 11¾″ $120–130
Model A Ford 1903 (1978), replica of Henry Ford's Model A Ford in red with black trim or black with red trim. Simulated brass and trim. Stopper at the rear of the car. 8″ $38–42
Model A Ford 1928 (1980), beige Model A with black accessories; authentic details for the headlights, trim, and interior. Stopper underneath the rear trunk and spare tire. 6½″ $65–75

Montana (1963), tribute to gold miners. Names of "Alder Gulch," "Last Chance Gulch, Bannack," and "Montana, 1864 Golden Years Centennial 1964" are embossed on bottle. Regal China, 11½ " $50–60

Monterey Bay Club (1977), based on the bandstand in Watsonville city park, honors the Monterey Bay Beam Bottle and Specialty Club. 7½ " $9–12

Mortimer Snerd (1976), country boy with buck teeth, straw hat, and bow tie; replica of famous character created by Edgar Bergen. 12 " $24–28

Mother-Of-Pearl (1979), double-urn-shaped bottle with wide alternating bands of gold and mother-of-pearl with double scroll handles on large screw lid. Identical to the Harolds Club VIP bottle except no lettering on the front. 11½ " $10–12

Mount St. Helens (1980), depicts the eruption of Mount St. Helens on May 18, 1980. A small vial of ash from the explosion is attached on the back. 9¼ " ... $20–22

Mr. Goodwrench (1978), half-figure of Mr. Goodwrench based on the General Motors advertisement. The figure is the stopper which sits on a rectangular base. Blue and white, 13½ " $24–28

Musicians On A Wine Cask (1964), old-time tavern scene: musicians, guitar, and accordion, embossed on cask-shaped embossed bottle. Wooden barrel effect and wood base. Gray china color. Regal China, 9¾ " $4–6

Muskie (1971), the muskie is the state fish of Wisconsin. The bottle is a figure of the fish, the stopper is the head, the fish rests on a platform of water. Also on the bottle is a plaque indicating the muskie as the Wisconsin state fish. The bottle was issued in honor of the National Fresh Water Fishing Hall of Fame. Regal China, 14½ " $14–18

National Tobacco Festival (1973), Regal China bottle commemorating the 25th anniversary of the National Tobacco Festival. The festival was held in Richmond, Virginia, on October 6–13. On the base of the special bottle, historic data of the growth and development of the tobacco industry is featured. The unique closure is the bust of an American Indian...$7–8

Nebraska (1967), round bottle bears the words, "Where the West Begins" with a picture of a covered wagon drawn by oxen. Regal China, 12¼ " $7–9

Nebraska Football (1972), this strikingly handsome genuine Regal China creation commemorates the University of Nebraska's national championship football team of 1970–71 season. The stopper features an exact likeness of Bob Devaney, the Cornhuskers' head coach. 8¾ " $5–8

Nevada (1963), circular silver and gray bottle, with silver "Nevada," bearing outline of state with embossed mountain peaks, forests, and a factory. Reverse is a miner and donkey. Same bottle used by Harolds Club and Harrah's Regal China. 11½ " $34–38

New Hampshire (1967), blue-tone bottle in the shape of the state. Decal of state motto, seal, flower, and bird. Stopper in the shape of the Old Man of the Mountain. Regal China, 13½ " $4–8

New Hampshire Eagle Bottle (1971), under the New Hampshire banner on this beautiful Regal China bottle, a solid gold eagle against a blue field stands as a proud reminder of the original symbol, a great carved wooden bird, which was placed atop the New Hampshire State House when it was built in 1818. On the back of the bottle, beneath the slogan "Granite State," a decal recounts the history of the first New Hampshire eagle. 12½ " $18–23

New Jersey (1963), gray map of state filled with embossed colorful fruits, vegetables, and flowers, set on pyramid-shaped bottle. "New Jersey—The Garden State, Farm & Industry" in gold. Regal China, 13½ " $40–50

NEW JERSEY YELLOW (1963), same as previous entry, yellow-toned map of New Jersey. 13½″ $40–50

NEW MEXICO BICENTENNIAL (1976), square-shaped bottle with blue center. White lettering and gold eagle embossed on front. The governor's home is on the back. 10½″ $8–12

NEW MEXICO STATEHOOD (1972), commemorating New Mexico's 60 years of statehood, this dramatic genuine Regal China bottle has been designed to represent the historical Indian ceremonial wedding vase which was used through the centuries by the New Mexico Indians in tribal wedding ceremonies. 9½″ .$7–9

NEW YORK WORLD'S FAIR (1964), the emblem of the New York World's Fair of 1964, the Unisphere, forms the shape of this bottle. Blue-tone oceans, gray continents crossed by space flight routes. Emblem embossed in gold "1964 World's Fair—1965." Stopper has Unisphere. Regal China, 11½″ $5–6

NORTH DAKOTA (1964), embossed memorial picture of a pioneer family in "North Dakota—75" embossed in gold in banner. Yellows, greens, and browns. Regal China, 11¾″ $45–55

NORTHERN PIKE (1977), Replica of the Northern Pike. Green and yellow with pointed head. The sixth in a series of bottles designed for the National Fresh Water Fishing Hall of Fame. 9″ $14–18

NUTCRACKER TOY SOLDIER (1978), figurine based on the toy soldier character in the ballet *The Nutcracker Suite*. This is not part of the Opera series. Small man dressed in red and white uniform with blue suspenders and gold trim. The music box plays a selection from *The Parade of the Toy Soldiers*. 12½″ $90–120

OHIO (1966), bottle in shape of state. One side bears state seal, other side has pictures of state industries. Regal China, 10″ $5–6

OHIO STATE FAIR (1973), a handsome bottle made of genuine Regal China, created in honor of the 120th Ohio State Fair. 10¾″ $5–6

OLYMPIAN (1960), green urn decanter. Chariot, horses, and warriors design in white on light blue bottle. White glass stopper, embossed base. Glass, 14″ $2–4

ONE HUNDRED FIRST AIRBORNE DIVISION (1977), honors the division known during World War II as the Screaming Eagles. A gold flying eagle atop a white pedestal. 14″ $8–10

OPALINE CRYSTAL (1969), milk glass bottle; same pattern and embossing, and stopper. Milk glass, 11½″ $4–6

OREGON (1959), green-tone bottle to honor centennial of the state. Depicting famous scenery on both sides. Two beavers on bottle neck. Regal China, 8¾″ $20–25

OREGON LIQUOR COMMISSION $25–35

OSCO DRUGS.. $12–17

PANDA (1980), adult panda on the ground with two cubs climbing the stump of a tree. Authenticated by Dr. Lester Fisher, Director of the Lincoln Park Zoological Gardens in Chicago $20–22

PAUL BUNYAN $4–7

PEARL HARBOR MEMORIAL (1972), honoring the Pearl Harbor Survivors Association, this handsome genuine Regal China bottle is emblazoned with the motto: "Remember Pearl Harbor—Keep America Alert." The stopper features the official seal of the armed services that were present December 7, 1941—the Army, Navy, Marine Corps, and Coast Guard. The stopper is set off by an American eagle. 11½″ $14–18

PEARL HARBOR SURVIVORS ASSOCIATION (1976), medallion-shaped bottle with flying eagle in the center with a blue background and white lettering around the border. On the back, a scene of the island Oahu, with three battleships. 9¾″
....$5–7

PENNSYLVANIA (1967), keystone-shaped bottle in blue tones. Decal of state seal "Historic Pennsylvania—The Keystone State" on front. Reverse: scenes of history and industry. Keystone stopper with gold "1776." Regal China, 11½″ .....
....$4–6

PENNSYLVANIA DUTCH, club bottle.. $8–12

PERMIAN BASIN OIL SHOW (1972), this dramatic genuine Regal China bottle is fashioned after an oil derrick and its attendant buildings. Commemorates the Permian Basin Oil Show in Odessa, Texas, October 18–21, 1972. The building is inscribed: "The E. E. 'Pop' Harrison No. 1 Well." The back of the flag says: "The oil industry provides energy, enterprise, employment for the nation." The stopper is fashioned in the shape of the logo for the Oil Field Workers Show with their motto "Let's Go." 13″ $4–6

PETROLEUM MAN $4–7

PHEASANT (1960), ring-necked pheasant with red-circled eyes, green and blue head, and soft brown plumage perched on a fence base. Regal China, 13″ ......
.... $14–18

PHEASANT (1961), re-issued also: '63, '66, '67, '68. As above............. $8–11

PHI SIGMA KAPPA (CENTENNIAL SERIES) (1973), a Regal China creation commemorating the 100th anniversary of this national fraternity dedicated to the promotion of brotherhood, the stimulation of scholarship, and the development of character. The fraternity insignia is in silver on a magenta background outlined in white and lavender $3–4

PHOENICIAN (1973), an elegantly handcrafted genuine Regal China, heavily embellished with 22K gold and featuring a floral design on the front. Each bottle comes in its own handsome presentation case lined with velvet $6–9

PIED PIPER OF HAMLIN (1974), this charming bottle of genuine Regal China was especially produced for the United States Armed Forces in Europe as a commemorative of the famous German legend, the Pied Piper of Hamlin. 10¼″ ....
....$3–6

PONDEROSA (1969), the home of the Cartwrights of "Bonanza" TV fame. A replica of the Ponderosa Ranch log cabin in brown tones. Reverse: Lake Tahoe. Bottles in green-lined box are worth more. Regal China, 7½″ H, 10″ W .$4–6

Jim Beam, political.
PHOTO COURTESY OF DAVE SMITH.

PONDEROSA RANCH TOURIST (1972), commemorating the one millionth tourist to the Ponderosa Ranch. This horseshoe-shaped bottle of genuine Regal China features the Ponderosa Pine and "P" symbol that has made the ranch famous. The stopper is traditional ten-gal. hat made famous by Dan Blocker. 11 "..... $14–16

PONY EXPRESS (1968), clearly embossed figure of horse and Pony Express rider with "Sacramento, Calif.—October 1861" and "St. Joseph, Mo.—April 1860" and stars around figure. Reverse: map of the Pony Express route. Yellow and brown tones. 11 " $9–12

POODLE—GRAY AND WHITE (1970), both poodles sit up with one paw on a ball. The gray has a green-banded ball embossed "Penny," the white has a blue-banded ball. Black eyes and nose with a gold color on each. Regal China, 12 ", pair $5–6

PORTLAND ROSE FESTIVAL (1972), to commemorate the 64th Portland (Oregon) Rose Festival which began in 1889. The Regal China bottle is encompassed in a garland of red roses which is commemorative of the oldest and largest rose show in America. On the reverse side there is a brief description of the festival with the very poignant line, "For You a Rose in Portland Grows." 10¼ " $5–8

PORTOLA TREK (1969), this gold glass bottle has a painting of the Portola Trek reproduction in full color on the front. This bottle was issued to celebrate the 200th anniversary of San Diego. 11 " $3–6

POULAN CHAIN SAW (1979), replica of the Poulan chain saw with a plastic handle and blade. Green body with silver blade and black trim. 7 " $24–28

POWELL EXPEDITION (1969), gold glass bottle with a full-color painting depicting John Wesley Powell's survey of the Colorado River and his traversing the Grand Canyon. 11 " $3–5

PREAKNESS (1970), this bottle was issued to honor the 100th anniversary of the running of the Preakness. The body of the bottle is made up of a horseshoe surrounding the trophy awarded the Preakness winner, the Woodlawn Vase. In lettering on the horseshoe is "Pimlico Race Course." A wreath of daisies tops the horseshoe. The stopper is plain. Regal China, 11 " $5–6

PREAKNESS PIMLICO (1975) $4–7

PRESIDENTIAL (1968), Executive series $4–7

PRESTIGE (1967), Executive series $4–7

PRETTY PERCH (1980), spiny-finned fish with dark bands, touches of orange on the fins. The eighth in a series, this fish is used as the official seal of the National Fresh Water Fishing Hall of Fame. 9 " $13–16

Jim Beam, Preakness and Las Vegas convention. PHOTO COURTESY OF DAVE SMITH.

PRIMA-DONNA (1969), same as Cal-Neva with Prima-Donna Casino and show girls on the emblem. 9¼ " $4–6

PROFESSIONAL GOLF ASSOCIATION...$4–7

QUEENSLAND (1978), in the shape of the province Queensland, the Sunshine State of Australia. Embossed lettering and details, gold star on the back, medallion-type stopper with "Australia" in center. 8½ " $20–22

RABBIT...$4–7

RAINBOW TROUT (1975), rainbow trout mounted on an oval plaque made to look like wood. Produced for the National Fresh Water Fishing Hall of Fame. Their official seal is on the back. 7½ " $12–15

RALPH CENTENNIAL (1973), made of genuine Regal China, this bottle was designed to commemorate the 100th anniversary of the Ralph Grocery Co. in California. The bottle depicts two sides of a coin struck especially for the occasion and an early version of a Ralph's delivery wagon. 7¾ " $10–14

RALPHS MARKET.. $8–12

RAM (1958), stylized ram in soft tans and browns. Calender mounted on green base and a round thermometer in the curve of the horn (without thermometer, value is less). Regal China, 12½ " $40–55

RAMADA INN (1976), a Ramada Inn attendant is shown as a sentinel at the door to a small narrow building of red, white, and blue. Gold shingles with a black lid on the chimney. 11 " $10–12

RED MILE RACETRACK.. $8–12

REDWOOD (1967), pyramid-shaped bottle, "Coast Redwoods" embossed on front in tones of brown and green. "Redwood Empire of California" lettered below tree. Reverse: scenes of Redwood country. Regal China, 12¾ " $6–8

REFLECTIONS (1975), Executive series $8–12

REGENCY (1972), this elegantly handcrafted Regal China bottle is heavily embellished with fired 22K gold and features a bouquet of tiny flowers about its mid-section. Each bottle comes in its own handsome dark red presentation case lined with velvet $7–9

REIDSVILLE (1973), this bottle was issued to honor the city of Reidsville, North Carolina, on the occasion of its centennial. The bottle is circular with leaves surrounding a central plaque bearing the slogan "Yesterday Today Tomorrow." The bottle is blue and the stopper is circular and bears the date "1973." Regal China, 12 " $5–6

RENEE THE FOX (1974), this interesting Regal China bottle represents the companion for the International Association of Jim Beam Bottle and Specialities Club's mascot. Renee the fox is the life-long companion of Rennie the fox. 12½ " $7–9

RENNIE THE RUNNER (1974), Rennie the fox is shown running in his brown running suit, white running shoes, and black top hat. On a string around his neck is the seal of the International Association of Beam Clubs. 12½ " ... $9–12

RENNIE THE SURFER (1975), Rennie the fox dressed in an old-fashioned bathing suit and a black top hat rides a small surfboard. He holds a bottle of Beam behind him with one hand. 12½ " $9–12

RENO (1968), "100 Years—Reno" embossed over skyline of downtown Reno. "The Biggest Little City in the World" lettered over skyline. Reverse: "Reno 100 Years" and scenes of Reno. Regal China, 9¼ " $4–6

REPUBLIC OF TEXAS (1980), star-shaped bottle with gold spout, handle, and top. White with a red border; symbols of the state are represented on the front. The stopper is a gold star. 12¾ " $12–20

REPUBLICAN CONVENTION (1972), gold, with plate $500–700

REPUBLICAN FOOTBALL (1972), gold $350–450
RICHARD HADLEE $110–135
RICHARDS—NEW MEXICO (1967), created for Richards Distributing Co. of Albuquerque, New Mexico. Lettered "New Mexico" and "Richard Says Discover New Mexico" in blue. Embossed scene of Taos pueblo. Picture of Richard on stopper and front. Regal China, 11″ $8–10
ROBIN (1969), an olive gray bird with a soft red breast, dark-toned head and tail. The robin has a yellow beak and stands on a tree trunk with an embossed branch and leaves. Regal China, 13½″ $5–6
ROCKY MARCIANO (1973), a handsome genuine Regal China bottle in honor of Rocky Marciano, the world's only undefeated boxing champion. The bottle takes the shape of a rock, with a likeness of Rocky Marciano on the front. The back of the bottle features Marciano's complete professional record of 49 fights, all victories (43 knockouts and 6 decisions) $14–16
ROCKY MOUNTAIN, club bottle.. $10–15
ROYAL CRYSTAL (1959), starburst design embossed on both sides on this clear flint glass decanter. Gold label on neck and flat black stopper. Starburst theme appears on label and stopper. Glass, 11½″ $3–6
ROYAL DI MONTE (1957), mottled design, black and white bottle. Handpainted with 22K gold and bordered in gold. Gold and black stopper. Regal China, 15½″ $45–55
ROYAL EMPEROR (1958), made in the shape of a classic Greek urn. Warrior figure with spear, helmet, and fret design in white on purple black glass. White glass stopper. Glass, 14″ $3–6
ROYAL GOLD DIAMOND (1964), diamond-shaped decanter set on a flaring base, all in mottled gold. Gold chain holds label. Regal China, 12″ $30–35
ROYAL GOLD ROUND (1956), mottled with 22K gold, in classic round shape with graceful pouring spout and curved handle. Gold neck chain holds label. Regal China, 12″ $80–90
ROYAL OPAL (1957), a round handled bottle of opal glass. Embossed geometric design on one side. White glass stopper. Bottle made by Wheaton Glass of Millville, New Jersey. Same bottle in silver was used for Harolds Club, 25th anniversary. Glass, 10¾″ $5–7
ROYAL PORCELAIN (1955), gleaming black decanter, tapered with a large flared pouring lip, white stopper, gold cord and tassel. Regal China, 14½″ .$380–420
ROYAL ROSE (1963), decanter, gold embossed with handpainted roses on a background of soft blue; gold spout, stopper, base, and handle. Regal China, 17″
....$30–34
RUBY CRYSTAL (1967), amethyst-colored, patterned embossed bottle. Swirl glass stopper. When bottle is filled with bourbon it's ruby red. Sunburst pattern on bottom. Amethyst glass, 11½″ $6–9
RUIDOSO DOWNS (1968), a round decanter with a unique "horsehead" stopper. Embossed silver horseshoe, branding iron, and cowboy hat; "Ruidoso Downs—New Mexico, World's Richest Horse Race" on front. Reverse: red, white, and blue emblem. The bottle is known in pointed and flat ears. Regal China, 12¾″
    Pointed ears $24–26
    Flat ears $4–6
SAHARA INVITATIONAL BOTTLE (1971), introduced in honor of the Del Webb 1971 Sahara Invitational Pro-Am Golf Tournament. The prominent feature of this Regal China bottle is a large "Del Webb Pro-Am 1971" golf ball atop a red tee on the face. Listed on the back are the winners of this annual contest from 1958–1970. 12″ $6–8

SAM BEAR—DONKEY (1973), Political series............................. $1500–2000
SAMOA $4–7
SAN DIEGO (1968), issued by the Beam Co. for the 200th anniversary of its founding in 1769. Honoring Junipero Serra, Franciscan missionary. "Serra" and "Conquistador" embossed on gold front. Regal China, 10 "..................$4–6
SAN DIEGO—ELEPHANT (1972)..$15–25
SANTA FE (1960), Governor's Palace, blue-toned sky, date 1610–1960 (350th anniversary). Navaho woman with Indian basket on reverse. Gold lettering. Regal China, 10 " $120–140
SCCA, etched..$15–25
SCCA, smooth $12–18
SCREECH OWL (1979), either red or gray shading. Birds are bisque replicas of screech owls, authenticated by Dr. Lester Fisher, director of the Lincoln Zoological Gardens in Chicago. 9¾ " $18–22
SEAFAIR TROPHY RACE (1972), this dramatic genuine Regal China creation commemorates the Seattle Seafair Trophy Race, August 6, 1972, and features an unlimited hydroplane at speed with picturesque Mt. Rainier in the background. 11½ " $5–6
SEATTLE WORLD'S FAIR (1962), the Space Needle, as this bottle is known, is embossed in gold on one side, "Century 21" on the other. Pylon-shaped with color scenes of fruit, airplanes over mountains, salmon, etc. Stopper is the Fair's revolving restaurant. Regal China, 13½ " $10–12
SEOUL—KOREA (1988) $60–75
SHERATON INN $4–6
SHORT DANCING SCOT (1963), a short barrel-shaped bottle with the dancing Scot and music box in the base. Square-shaped stopper; a rare bottle. Glass, 11 " $50–65
SHORT-TIMER (1975), brown army shoes with army helmet sitting on top. Produced for all who have served in the armed forces. 8 "......................$15–20
SHRINERS (1975), embossed camel on front of bottle in blue, green, and brown with bright red blanket flowing from the camel's saddle. A gold scimitar and star centered with a fake ruby is on the back. 10½ " $10–12
SHRINERS—INDIANA $4–7
SHRINERS PYRAMID (1975), this bottle was issued by the El Kahir Temple of Cedar Rapids, Iowa. It is shaped like a pyramid with embossing on the sides of the various insignia of the Shriners. The bottle is white and brown and made to look as if it were made of brick. The stopper is the very top of the pyramid. Regal China, 5 " $10–12
SHRINERS RAJAH (1977), pretzel-shaped bottle with a Shriner's sword in the center. Stopper is red and shaped like a Shriner's cap with a black tassel. 8¾ " $24–28
SHRINERS TEMPLE (1972), this beautiful Regal China bottle features the traditional symbols of Moila Templei, the scimitar, star and crescent, fez, and the pyramid with the stopper as the head of a sphinx. This bottle is unique in that it features three simulated precious stones, two of them in the handle of the sword and the third in the center point of the star. 11½ " $20–25
SHRINERS WESTERN ASSOCIATION $15–25
SIERRA EAGLE $15–22
SIGMA NU FRATERNITY (1977), rectangular bottle with the badge and coat of arms of the Sigma Nu Fraternity embossed on the front. White and gold lettering and designs. Medallion-type stopper... $9–12
SIGMA NU FRATERNITY—KENTUCKY $8–12

Jim Beam, slot machine.
PHOTO COURTESY OF DAVE SMITH.

SIGMA NU FRATERNITY—MICHIGAN...$18-23
SMITHS NORTH SHORE CLUB (1972), commemorating Smith's North Shore Club, at Crystal Bay, Lake Tahoe. This striking genuine Regal China bottle features the anchor, symbol of the club, and is topped by a giant golden golf ball. 12″
....$10-12
SMOKED CRYSTAL (1964), dark green in tone and resembling a genie's magic bottle, this tall bottle has a bulbous embossed base and a slender tapering shape, topped by an embossed glass topper. Glass, 14″ $6-9
SNOW GOOSE (1979), replica of a white goose with black wingtips. Authenticated by Dr. Lester Fisher, director of Lincoln Park Zoological Gardens in Chicago. 11½″ $8-10
SNOWMAN $125-175
SOUTH CAROLINA (1970), the Palmetto State celebrated its tricentennial, 1670-1970. Palmetto trees are embossed on the outline map of the state which is outlined in gold. The South Carolina Dispensary is on the back. 9¼″ $4-6
SOUTH DAKOTA—MOUNT RUSHMORE (1969), the faces of Washington, Jefferson, T. Roosevelt, and Lincoln are shown in relief in white with blue sky and green forest. This landmark is the Mount Rushmore National Memorial. Reverse: scroll with information about Memorial. Regal China, 10½″ $4-6
SOUTH FLORIDA—FOX ON DOLPHIN (1980), a fox dressed in hunting garb rides a dolphin. This bottle was sponsored by the South Florida Beam Bottle and Specialties Club which is located in Miami. 14½″ $14-16
SOVEREIGN (1969), Executive series...................................$4-7
SPENGERS FISH GROTTO (1977), designed as a small boat with the captain at the helm. Brown, yellow, and blue, made in conjunction with Spenger's Fish Grotto Restaurant in Berkeley, California...$18-22
SPORTS CAR CLUB OF AMERICA (1976), six-sided front with a Ridge-Whetworth wire wheel in the center on pedestal foot. Brief history of the club on the back. 11″ $5-7
STATUE OF LIBERTY (1975), figural bottle with gold-embossed Statue of Liberty on the front with light blue background. Green base with plaque. 12½″ . $8-12
STATUE OF LIBERTY (1985) $18-20
ST. BERNARD (1979), replica of a St. Bernard with a small cask of Beam around his neck held by a real leather collar. 6½″ $30-34
ST. LOUIS, club bottle.......................................:.............$10-15

St. Louis Arch (1964), the silhouette of St. Louis with the Mississippi River flowing past. The famous stainless steel arch frames the bottle; "St. Louis, Gateway to the West" and "200 Years" embossed in gold. The ferry boat "Admiral" is on the back. Regal China, 11″ $10–12

St. Louis Arch—Re-issue (1967), same as above........................... $16–18

St. Louis Statue (1972), this handsome Regal China bottle features the famous statue of St. Louis on horseback atop its pedestal base. The entire statue is fired gold. The back bears the inscription, "Greater St. Louis Area Beam and Specialties Club." 13¼″ $8–10

Sturgeon (1980) Exclusive issue for a group that advocates the preservation of sturgeons. Long brown colored fish. 6¼″ $14–17

Stutz Bearcat 1914 (1977), either yellow and black or gray and black. Replica of the 1914 four-cylinder Stutz Bearcat. Authentic details with movable windshield. Stopper is under plastic trunk and spare wheel. 7″ $45–55

Submarine—Diamond Jubilee $35–45

Submarine Redfin (1970), embossed submarine on ocean blue background. "Manitowoc Submarine Memorial Association" in black. Round stopper with map of Wisconsin. Regal China, 11½″ $5–7

Superdome (1975), replica of the Louisiana Superdome which opened in August 1975. White and gold with black lettering around the top. 6½″ $5–8

Swagman (1979), replica of an Australian hobo called a swagman who roamed that country looking for work during the Depression. He wears a grayish outfit with red kerchief around his neck. A brown dog and a sheep are curled around his feet. 14″ $10–12

Sydney Opera House (1977), replica of the building housing the Sydney Opera in Sydney, Australia. Music box is in the base. 8½″ $9–12

Tall Dancing Scot (1964), a small Scotsman encased in a glass bubble in the base dances to the music of the base. A tall pylon-shaped glass bottle with a tall stopper. No dates on these bottles. Glass, 17″ $9–12

Tavern Scene (1959), two "beer stein" tavern scenes are embossed on sides, framed in wide gold band on this round decanter. Regal China, 11½″ ..$45–55

Telephone No. 1 (1975), replica of a 1907 phone of the Magneto wall type which was used from 1890 until the 1930s. 9½″ $25–30

Telephone No. 2 (1976), replica of an 1897 desk set........................$30–40

Telephone No. 3 (1977), replica of a 1920 cradle phone $15–20

Telephone No. 4 (1978), replica of a 1919 dial phone $40–50

Telephone No. 5 (1979), pay phone...$25–35

Telephone No. 6 (1980), battery phone $20–30

Telephone No. 7 (1981), digital dial phone $35–45

Ten-Pin (1980), designed as a bowling pin with two red bands around the shoulder and the neck. Remainder of the pin is white, screw lid. 12″ $8–11

Texas Hemisfair $7–11

Texas Rose (1978), Executive series...$14–18

Thailand (1969), embossed elephant in the jungle and "Thailand—A Nation of Wonders" on the front. Reverse: a map of Thailand and a dancer. Regal China, 12½″ $4–6

Thomas Flyer 1907 (1976), replica of the 1907 Thomas Flyer, 6-70 Model K Flyabout which was a luxury car of its day. Comes in blue or white. Plastic rear trunk covers the lid to the bottle...$60–70

Tiffiny Poodle (1973), genuine Regal China bottle created in honor of Tiffiny, the poodle mascot of the National Association of the Jim Beam Bottle and Specialties Clubs. 8½″ $20–22

TIGER—AUSTRALIAN $14–18

THE TIGERS (1977), tiger head on top of a football which reads "The Tigers." Honors an Australian football team. 7¾" $20–24

TITIAN (1980), urn-shaped bottle, reproduces the designs created by the Venetian artist Titian in his oil paintings. Long fluted neck, with double-scrolled handle. 12½" $9–12

TOBACCO FESTIVAL.. $8–12

TOMBSTONE $4–7

TRAVELODGE BEAR...$4–7

TREASURE CHEST (1979), partially open treasure chest with gold coins, pearls, and jewelry. The lid is a screw top. 6" $8–12

TROUT UNLIMITED (1977), large traditionally shaped bottle with a large yellow trout placed across the front of the bottle at the shoulder. Stopper reads "Limit Your Kill, Don't Kill Your Limit." To honor the Trout Unlimited Conservation Organization. 12" $14–18

TRUTH OR CONSEQUENCES FIESTA (1974), a ruggedly handsome Regal China bottle in honor of Ralph Edward's famous radio and television show and the city of Truth or Consequences, New Mexico. 10" $5–6

TURQUOISE CHINA JUG (1966), alternating bands of scrolled designs spiral up the turquoise decanter. Regal China, 13¼" $4–6

TWIN BRIDGES BOTTLE (1971), designed to commemorate the largest twin bridge complex of its kind in the world. The twin bridges connect Delaware and New Jersey and serve as major links between key East Coast cities. Handsomely accented in gold and bearing the shield of the Twin Bridges Beam Bottle and Specialties Club, this Regal China bottle portrays the twin spans on the front and provides a descriptive story on the back. The stopper is a replica of the bridge toll house. 10½" $40–42

TWIN CHERUBS (1974), Executive series $8–12

TWIN DOVES (1987), Executive series... $18–23

US OPEN (1972), whimsically depicts Uncle Sam's traditional hat holding a full set of golf clubs. This charming Regal China creation honors the US Open Golf Tourney at the famous Pebble Beach course in California. 10½" $9–12

VENDOME DRUMMERS WAGON (1975), replica of a delivery wagon; green and cream wood with yellow wheels, which are plastic. Honored the Vendomes of Beverly Hills, California, a food-chain store which was first established in 1937. 8½" $60–70

VFW BOTTLE (1971), a handsome Regal China creation designed to commemorate the 50th anniversary of the Department of Indiana VFW. This proclamation is made on the neck of the bottle, in a plaque in the shape of the state of Indiana, over a striking reproduction of the medal insignia of the VFW. 9¾" $5–6

VIKING (1973), the Viking is holding a shield and sword and is leaning against a stone. The words "Minnesota, Land of the Vikings" appear on the shield. On the stone is recorded the Viking exploration of 1362. The stopper is his helmet. Regal China, 14" $9–12

VOLKSWAGEN COMMEMORATIVE BOTTLE—TWO COLORS (1977), commemorating the Volkswagen Beetle, the largest-selling single production model vehicle in automotive history. Handcrafted of genuine Regal China, this unique and exciting bottle will long remain a memento for bottle collectors the world over. 14½" $40–50

VONS MARKET...$28–35

WALLEYE PIKE (1977), tall blue bottle with a large figurine of a yellow pike at the base. Designed for the National Fresh Water Fishing Hall of Fame in Hayward, Wisconsin $12–15

WALLEYE PIKE (1987).. $17–23

WASHINGTON (1975), a state series bottle to commemorate the Evergreen State, which was honored with this green bottle featuring an apple and a fir tree in bas relief. 10″ $5–6

WASHINGTON—THE EVERGREEN STATE (1974), the club bottle for the Evergreen State Beam Bottle and Specialties Club is contoured to the shape of the state. The green bottle has evergreen trees embossed on it and a unique stopper with an exact replica of a small evergreen branch in a transparent enclosure. 10″ ....
.... $10–12

WASHINGTON STATE BICENTENNIAL (1976), patriot dressed in black and orange holding drum. Liberty bell and plaque in front of drummer. 10″ $10–12

WATERMAN (1980), in pewter or glazed. Boatman at helm of his boat wearing rain gear. Glazed version in yellow and brown. 13½″ $100–130

WESTERN SHRINE ASSOCIATION (1980), designed to commemorate the Shriners' convention in 1980 which was held in Phoenix, Arizona. Rounded surface with a desert scene; red stopper designed as a fez with a tassel $20–22

WEST VIRGINIA (1963), waterfall scene in blue and green with gold embossed "Blackwater Falls—West Virginia—1863 Centennial 1963" surrounded by scrolled picture frame bottle. Reverse: state bird, red cardinal, and gold "35" in a star. Bear's head and maple leaf on each side of stopper. 10¼″ .. $130–140

WHITE FOX (1969), this bottle was issued for the second anniversary of the Jim Beam Bottles and Specialties Club, Berkeley, California. It shows a standing fox with his arms folded behind him. He is wearing a white jacket and a gold medallion and chain. The medallion displays a happy birthday message to the Berkeley Club. 12½″ $25–30

WISCONSIN MUSKIE BOTTLE (1971), this striking Regal China sculpture pays tribute to the state fish of Wisconsin, as the mighty muskellunge dances on his powerful tail in a burst of gold-flecked blue water. 14″ $15–17

WOODPECKER (1969), bright glazed red head, white breast and markings, black beak, and dark wings and tail. Woody grips a tree trunk base. Regal China, 13½″ $6–8

WYOMING (1965), an embossed bucking bronco with a cowboy hanging on with mountains in the background and "Wyoming—The Equality State" in gold on tones of blue and tan. A rectangle shape of a pyramid, with a gold buffalo on the stopper. Reverse: state bird, flower, and Old Faithful. Regal China, 12″ ....
.... $40–50

YELLOW KATZ (1967), the emblem of the Katz Department Stores (Missouri), a green-eyed meowing cat, is the head (and stopper) of this bottle. The pylon-shaped, orange color body has a curved tail. The Katz commemorates the 50th birthday of the store. 14½″ $15–17

YELLOW ROSE (1978), Executive series $7–10

YELLOWSTONE PARK CENTENNIAL.. $4–7

YOSEMITE (1967), oval-shaped bottle with scenes from the park and trees embossed on the front. "Yosemite California" lettered on front. Gold pine tree on stopper. 11″ $4–6

YUMA RIFLE CLUB $18–23

ZIMMERMAN—ART INSTITUTE $5–8

ZIMMERMAN BELL (1976), bell-shaped bottle in colbalt blue with flowers and foliage embossed in blue and gold. Designed for Zimmerman Liquor Store of Chicago. 12½″ $6–7

ZIMMERMAN BELL (1976), bell-shaped bottle in light blue with lavender lid. Floral and foliage designs embossed on the front. 12½″ $6–7

ZIMMERMAN—BLUE BEAUTY (1969), the name "Zimmerman's Liquors" is embossed in bright gold on a sky blue bottle decorated with flowers and scrolls. Reverse has Chicago skyline embossed on blue-toned bottle. Arrow with "Zimmerman's" points to store. Regal China, 10″ $9–12

ZIMMERMAN—BLUE DAISY $4–6

ZIMMERMAN CHERUBS (1968), winged cherubs and leaves and vines are embossed over the surface of these slender round pink and lavender bottles. They were issued for the Zimmerman Liquor Stores of Chicago. Regal China, 11½″
....$4–6

ZIMMERMAN—CHICAGO..$4–6

ZIMMERMAN—ELDORADO $4–7

ZIMMERMAN—GLASS (1969), a white outline of the Chicago skyline with "Zimmerman's" store on front of this glass bottle. White stopper has Max Zimmerman's portrait. Glass, 11¼″ $7–9

ZIMMERMAN OATMEAL JUG $40–50

ZIMMERMAN—THE PEDDLER BOTTLE (1971), this unusual bottle in genuine Regal China was made in honor of Zimmerman's, the world's largest liquor store in Chicago, Illinois. Max Zimmerman, The Peddler himself, who specializes in personal service and works the counters of the store himself, is famous for his Stetson hat and cowboy boots. He is affectionately known in the trade as Max the Hat. Zimmerman's has always been active in merchandising Beam's collectors' bottles. 12″ $4–6

ZIMMERMAN TWO-HANDLED JUG (1965), shaped and colored like an avocado, this dark green bottle has embossed grapes and grape leaves on the front, and two side handles. Regal China, 10¼″ $45–60

ZIMMERMAN VASE, brown...$6–9

ZIMMERMAN VASE, green..$6–9

ZIMMERMAN—50TH ANNIVERSARY $35–45

BISCHOFF BOTTLES

Founded at Trieste, Italy, in 1777, Bischoff's was issuing decorative figurals in the 18th century long before the establishment of most companies who presently issue figural bottles. The early specimens are extremely rare because of limited production and loss over the years. Since sales do not occur often enough for firm values to be established, they are not included in this listing.

Imported into the United States in 1949, the modern Bischoff's attracted little notice at first due to lack of American interest in bottle collecting at that time. Most sales were made for gift giving. The bottles are produced by the foremost glass, pottery, and porcelain companies in Bohemia, Czechoslovakia, Murano, Italy, Austria, and Germany.

KORD BOHEMIAN DECANTERS

Handblown, handpainted glass bottles were created in Czechoslovakia by the Kord Co., based on a long tradition of Bohemian cut, engraved, etched, and flashed glass. Typical Bohemia themes were used to decorate the decanters. Complete bottles with stoppers and labels are very difficult to find today.

Cut glass and ruby-etched decanters, traditional forms of Bohemian glass, were imported into the United States in the early 1950s. Cut glass specimens are of lead crystal with hand cutting. The ruby-etched decanters are executed in the usual two-layer manner with the exterior ruby glass etched through to show the clear glass beneath. Designs are quite elaborate including leaping deer, castles, scrolls, foliage, wild birds, grapes, and latticework. The overall color can be amber or topaz with ruby the most common.

When the underlayer of glass is opaque, the cut designs show very distinctly. Several of the etched decanters, made in Austria and Germany, should have labels indicating the place of origin. Most Bischoff Kord Bohemian decanters had matching sets of glasses.

The Double Dolphin, Hunter and Lady, and Horse's Head decanters are thick handblown glass made in Czechoslovakia. Not as rare as the ruby-etched decanter since importation continues, they have value only when complete with stoppers.

AMBER FLOWERS (1952), a two-toned glass decanter. Amber flowers, stems, and leaves on a pale amber background. The long tapering neck is etched in panels and circles. The stopper is dark amber and handground to fit. 15½″ $30–40
AMBER LEAVES (1952), multitoned bottle with dark amber leaves and flowers on pale amber etched background. Stopper neck and base are cut in circles and panels. Round bottle with long neck. 13½″ $30–40
ANISETTE (1948–51), clear glass bottle with two handles and a ground glass stopper. Clear glass ribbing on sides of bottle. 11″ $20–30
BOHEMIAN RUBY-ETCHED (1949–51), etched design in typical Bohemian style; castle, birds, deer, and scrolls and curlecues in clear glass, ruby red color flashed on bottle, except for etching and cut neck. Ground glass, etched stoppers on this tall, round, decanter, tapered neck. 15½″ $30–40
CORONET CRYSTAL (1952), a broad band of flowers, leaves, and scrolls circle this multitoned bottle. The designs are cut in dark amber glass revealing the opaque pale amber background. Stopper neck and base are cut in circles and panels. A round tall bottle. 14″ $30–40
CUT GLASS DECANTER (BLACKBERRY) (1951), a geometric design handcut overall on this lead glass decanter. The stopper is cut and ground to fit the bottle. 10½″
....$32–42

CZECH HUNTER (1958), round thick clear glass body with green collar and green buttons and heavy round glass base. The stopper head is of glass with a jaunty green Bohemian hat with feather crowning, pop-eyes, white mustache, and red button nose. 8½" $18–26

CZECH HUNTER'S LADY (1958), "Mae West"-shaped decanter of cracked clear glass. Green collar at neck of bottle with amber glass stopper head. Brown hair, glasses, and yellow earrings make up the lady's head. She's taller than the hunter. 10" $18–26

DANCING—COUNTRY SCENE (1950), clear glass handblown decanter with hand-painted and signed colorful scene of peasant boy and girl doing a country dance beside a tree, Bohemian village background. Spider bold white lines painted on bottle and stopper. 12¼" $25–35

DANCING—PEASANT SCENE (1950), colorful peasants in costume, dancing to music of bagpipes, handpainted and signed. The decanter is of pale amber glass, fine black lines painted on bottle. Stopper is ground to fit and fine-line painted. 12" $25–35

DOUBLE-DOLPHIN (1949–69), fish-shaped twin bottles joined at the bellies. They are made of handblown clear glass and have fins and "fish tail" ground glass stoppers; each has fish eyes and mouth $20–30

FLYING GEESE PITCHER (1952), same as below, but with green glass handle and stopper. This pitcher has a glass base $15–25

FLYING GEESE PITCHER (1957), clear crystal handled pitcher. Handpainted and signed; colorful scene of wild geese flying over Czech marshes. Gold neck, pouring lip, and stopper. 9½" $15–25

HORSE HEAD (1947–69), pale amber-colored bottle in the shape of a horse's head. Embossed details of horse's features are impressed on this handblown bottle. Round pouring spout on top. 8" $15–25

JUNGLE PARROT—AMBER GLASS (1952), same as below, except bottle is flashed a yellow amber color $25–35

JUNGLE PARROT—RUBY GLASS (1952), profusely handetched jungle scene with parrot, monkeys, insects, flowers, leaves, cut through the ruby-flashed body. A tall round decanter with tapering etched neck. 15½" $20–30

OLD COACH BOTTLE (1948), old-time coach and white horses handpainted on a handblown Bohemian glass bottle, pale amber color. Round ground glass stopper. Bottle and stopper are both numbered. 10" $25–35

OLD SLEIGH BOTTLE (1949), handpainted, signed, Czech winter old-time sleigh scene. Driver sits on lead horse and blows trumpet, passengers on top of coach are pouring drinks. Glass decanter has fine white trace lines. Glass stopper is clear and painted. 10" $22–32

WILD GEESE—AMBER GLASS (1952), same as below, except bottle is a flashed yellow amber color. (Matching glasses were made for both the ruby and amber.) $25–35

WILD GEESE—RUBY GLASS (1952), etched design of wild geese rising above the marshes. A tall round decanter with tapering etched neck, and etched hand-ground stopper. Ruby-red color "flashed" on bottle. 15½". (Matching glasses were made for both the ruby and amber.) $25–35

VENETIAN GLASS FIGURALS

Bischoff's Venetian glass figurals are made in limited editions by the Serguso Glass Co. in Murano, Italy, a town historically famous for its artistic glass. The Bischoff figurals, originally containing the firm's liquors, are quite unique in design and color. Chief themes depict natural subjects such as birds, mammals, and fish.

BLACK CAT (1969), glass black cat with curled tail. 12″ L $18–25
DOG—ALABASTER (1969), seated alabaster glass dog. 13″ $35–45
DOG—DACHSHUND (1966), alabaster long dog with brown tones. 19″ L $40–50
DUCK (1964), alabaster glass tinted pink and green, long neck, upraised wings.
11″ L $42–52
FISH—MULTICOLOR (1964), round fat fish, alabaster glass. Green, rose, yellow
.... $18–25
FISH—RUBY (1969), long, flat, ruby glass fish. 12″ L $25–35

CERAMIC DECANTERS AND FIGURALS

Many of the most interesting, attractive, and valuable Bischoff bottles are made of ceramic, stoneware or pottery. They have a "rougher" surface appearance than the glass or porcelain bottles. Values quoted are for complete bottles with handles, spouts, and stoppers in mint condition.

AFRICAN HEAD (1962) $15–18
BELL HOUSE (1960) $30–40
BELL TOWER (1960) $15–30
BOY (CHINESE) FIGURAL (1962) $30–40
BOY (SPANISH) FIGURAL (1961) $25–35
CLOWN WITH BLACK HAIR (1963) $30–40
CLOWN WITH RED HAIR (1963) $15–25
DEER FIGURAL (1969) $20–25
EGYPTIAN DANCING FIGURAL (1961) $12–17
EGYPTIAN PITCHER—2 MUSICIANS (1969) $15–24
EGYPTIAN PITCHER—3 MUSICIANS (1959) $20–28
FLORAL CANTEEN (1969) $18–22
FRUIT CANTEEN (1969) $13–19
GIRL IN CHINESE COSTUME (1962) $30–40
GIRL IN SPANISH COSTUME (1961) $30–40
GREEK VASE DECANTER (1969) $13–19
MASK—GRAY FACE (1963) $16–26
OIL AND VINEGAR CRUETS—BLACK AND WHITE (1959) $18–25
VASE—BLACK AND GOLD (1959) $19–22
WATCHTOWER (1960) $12–16

BORGHINI BOTTLES

Borghini bottles, exported from Pisa, Italy, are ceramics of modernistic style, dealing mostly with historical themes. Their sizes vary more than bottles from other manufacturers. Easily obtainable in the United States, as is often the case with imported bottles, their prices vary greatly in different parts of the country. The lowest values tend to be in areas either closest to the points of distribution or heaviest in retail sale. Most of the recent Borghini bottles are stamped "Borghini Collection Made in Italy."

CATS, black with red ties. 6" $11–15
CATS, black with red ties. 12" $10–13
FEMALE HEAD, ceramic. 9½" $11–15
PENGUIN, black and white. 6" $8–11
PENGUIN (1969), black and white. 12" $12–16

MARIE BRIZARD BOTTLES

The Marie Brizard bottles are ceramics, usually deep brown in color, with distinctive modeling. New editions are issued only occasionally. The Chessman series, which consists of bottles representing figures from the chessboard, are their most popular products. Among the more valuable of the Brizard bottles is a large model of a Parisian kiosk or newsstand, standing 11½" H.

BISHOP, ceramic chessman, dark brown $20–25
CASTLE, ceramic chessman, dark brown $20–25
KIOSK, colorful Parisian signpost. 11½" $7–10
KNIGHT, ceramic chessman, dark brown $20–25
LADY IN ERMINE CAPE, 7" $25–35
PAWN, ceramic chessman, dark brown $20–27

EZRA BROOKS BOTTLES

Ezra Brooks rivals Jim Beam as one of the chief whiskey companies in America manufacturing figural bottles. First issuing figurals in 1964, Brooks started a decade later than Beam, but became competitive because of effective promotion and a heavy production schedule. Due to creative design, imaginative choice of subjects, and an efficient distribution network, the Ezra Brooks bottles are collected throughout the country.

Some of the Brooks figurals deal with traditional themes for bottles such as sports and transportation. But Brooks has designed bottles based on subjects that are both surprising and striking. The very realistic Maine Lobster is among its masterpieces—a bottle that looks good enough to eat. One of the most popular series of their bottles represents various antiques, a subject neglected by most manufacturers. These include an Edison phonograph, a grandfather clock, and a Spanish cannon.

While the number of bottles produced fluctuates each year, Brooks usually adds new editions annually, often highlighting an American historical event or anniversary.

The Ezra Brooks Distilling Co., located in Frankfort, Kentucky, manufactures bottles containing Kentucky bourbon. Before 1968 their most brisk sales occurred around the Christmas/New Year season as the majority were bought for gift giving. When interest grew in the United States for figural bottles, most sales were to collectors.

ALABAMA BICENTENNIAL (1976) $12–14
AMERICAN LEGION (1971), distinguished embossed star emblem born out of WW I struggle. Combination blue and gold. On blue base $20–30
AMERICAN LEGION (1972), Ezra Brooks salutes the American Legion, its Illinois Department, and Land of Lincoln and the city of Chicago, host of the Legion's 54th national convention $45–55
AMERICAN LEGION (1973), Hawaii, our 50th state, hosted the American Legion's 1973 annual convention. It was the largest airlift of a mass group ever to hit the islands. Over 15,000 Legionnaires visited the beautiful city of Honolulu to celebrate the Legion's 54th anniversary $10–12
AMERICAN LEGION (1977), Denver $19–22
AMERICAN LEGION (1973), Miami Beach $8–12
AMVETS (1974), dolphin $8–10
AMVETS (1973), Polish Legion $14–18
ANTIQUE CANNON (1969) $6–9
ANTIQUE PHONOGRAPH (1970), Edison's early contribution to home entertainment. White, black, morning glory horn, red. Richly detailed in 24K gold $8–12
ARIZONA (1969), man with burro in search of Lost Dutchman Mine; golden brown mesa, green cactus, with 22K-gold base; "Arizona" imprinted $4–8
AUBURN 1932 (1978), classic car $18–20
BADGER No. 1 (1973), boxer $9–11
BADGER No. 2 (1974), football $10–14
BADGER No. 3 (1974), hockey $9–12
BALTIMORE ORIOLE WILDLIFE (1979) $20–30
BARE KNUCKLEFIGHTER (1971) $5–7
BASEBALL HALL OF FAME (1973), baseball fans everywhere will enjoy this genuine Heritage China ceramic of a familiar slugger of years gone by $20–22
BASKETBALL PLAYER (1974) $14–16
BEAR (1968) $5–9
BENGAL TIGER WILDLIFE (1979) $20–30
BETSY ROSS (1975) $8–12
BIG BERTHA, Nugget Casino's very own elephant with a raised trunk; gray, red, white, and black; yellow and gold trim. Blanket and stand $10–13

BIG DADDY LOUNGE (1969), salute to South Florida's state liquor chain and Big Daddy Lounges. White, green, red...$4–6
BIGHORN RAM (1973) $14–18
BIRD DOG (1971)... $12–14
BORDERTOWN, Borderline Club where California and Nevada meet for a drink. Brown, red, white. Club building, with vulture on roof stopper, and outhouse $5–10
BOWLER (1973)..$4–6
BOWLING TENPINS (1973), in colonial days, Massachusetts and Connecticut banned bowling at ninepins along with dice and cards. But bowlers avoided the law by simply adding a tenth pin. Thus tenpin bowling was born. Today the sport of bowling is enjoyed by more than 30,000,000 Americans................. $9–12
BRAHMA BULL (1972)... $10–12
BUCKET OF BLOOD (1970), fabled Virginia City, Nevada, saloon. Bucket-shaped bottle. Brown, red with gold lettering on reverse side $5–7
BUCKING BRONCO (1973), Rough Rider $7–9
BUCKY BADGER, football $20–25
BUCKY BADGER (1975), hockey $18–24
BUCKY BADGER (1973), No. 1, boxer............................... $9–12
BUFFALO HUNT (1971) $5–7
BULLDOG (1972), mighty canine mascot and football symbol. Red, white $10–14
BULL MOOSE (1973)... $12–15
BUSY BEAVER, this genuine Heritage China ceramic is a salute to the beaver $4–7
CABIN STILL, hillbilly, papers from company, gallon $20–35
CABLE CAR (1968), San Francisco's great trolley-car ride in bottle form. Made in three different colors: green, gray, and blue, with red, black, and gold trim. Open cable car with passengers clinging to sides $5–6
CALIFORNIA QUAIL (1970), widely admired game bird-shape bottle. Crested head stopper. Unglazed finish. Green, brown, white, black, gray................. $8–10
CANADIAN HONKER (1975)... $9–12
CANADIAN LOON WILDLIFE (1979) $25–35
CARDINAL (1972)..$20–25
CASEY AT BAT (1973) $6–10
CEREMONIAL INDIAN (1970) $15–18
CB CONVOY RADIO (1976) $5–9
CHAROLAIS BEEF (1973), the Charolais have played an important role in raising the standards of quality in today's cattle.. $10–14
CHEYENNE SHOOT-OUT (1970), honoring the Wild West and its Cheyenne Frontier Days. Sheriff and outlaw shoot-out over mirrored bar. Brown tone with multicolors $6–10
CHICAGO FIRE (1974) $20–30
CHICAGO WATER TOWER (1969) $8–12
CHRISTMAS DECANTER (1966) $5–8
CHRISTMAS TREE (1979) $13–17
CHURCHILL (1970), commemorating "Iron Curtain" speech at Westminster College; Churchill at lectern with hand raised in V sign. Fulton, Missouri, gold color...$5–9

CIGAR STORE INDIAN (1968), sidewalk statue in bottle form. The original Wooden Indian first appeared in 1770. Dark tan..$4–6

CLASSIC FIREARMS (1969), embossed gun set consisting of Derringer, Colt 45, Peacemaker, Over and Under Flintlock, Pepper box. Green, blue violet, red.... ....$15–19

CLOWN (1978), Imperial Shrine.. $9–11

CLOWN BUST NO. 1 (1979), Smiley $22–28

CLOWN BUST NO. 2 (1979), cowboy $20–25

CLOWN BUST NO. 3 (1979), Pagliacci $15–22

CLOWN BUST NO. 4, Keystone cop...$30–40

CLOWN BUST NO. 5, Cuddles $20–30

CLOWN BUST NO. 6, tramp...$20–30

CLOWN WITH ACCORDION (1971) $15–18

CLOWN WITH BALLOON (1973) $20–32

CLUB BOTTLE, birthday cake.. $9–12

CLUB BOTTLE, distillery... $9–12

CLUB BOTTLE (1973), the third commemorative Ezra Brooks Collectors Club bottle is created in the shape of America. Each gold star on the new club bottle represents the location of an Ezra Brooks Collectors Club $14–18

CLYDESDALE HORSE (1973), in the early days of distilling, Clydesdales carted the bottles of whiskey from the distillery to towns all across America......... $8–12

COLT PEACEMAKER (1969), flask...$4–8

CONQUISTADORS, tribute to a great drum and bugle corps. Silver-colored trumpet attached to drum..$6–9

CONQUISTADORS DRUM AND BUGLE (1972)....................................$12–15

CORVETTE INDY PACE CAR (1978) $45–55

CORVETTE (1976), 1957 classic...$110–140

COURT JESTER, a common sight in the throne rooms of Europe. Yellow and blue suit, pointed cap $5–7

DAKOTA COWBOY (1975)..$34–44

DAKOTA COWGIRL (1976) $20–26

DAKOTA GRAIN ELEVATOR (1978) $20–30

DAKOTA SHOTGUN EXPRESS (1977) $18–22

DEAD WAGON (1970), to carry gunfight losers to Boot Hill, old-time hearse with tombstones on side. Vulture adornment on stopper. White, with black details... ....$5–7

DELTA BELLE (1969), proud paddlewheel boat on the New Orleans to Louisville passage; steamboat shape with embossed details. White, brown, red with 22K-gold trim $6–7

DEMOCRATIC CONVENTION (1976) $10–16

DERRINGER (1969), flask $5–8

DISTILLERY (1970), club bottle, reproduction of the Ezra Brooks Distillery in Kentucky, complete with smokestack. Beige, black, brown with 22K-gold color $9–11

DUESENBERG, jaunty vintage convertible. Famous SJ model reproduction complete with superchargers and white sidewalls. Blue and gold, or solid gold color...$24–33

ELEPHANT (1973), based on an Asian elephant which has small ears and tusks $7–9

ELK (1973), while the elk herd is still relatively scarce in the United States, the elk name flourishes as a symbol for many worthwhile organizations, especially those whose primary object is the practice of benevolence and charity in its broadest sense. Ezra Brooks salutes these organizations with this genuine Heritage China ceramic bottle $20–28

ENGLISH SETTER—BIRD DOG (1971), happy hunting dog retrieving red pheasant. White-flecked with black, yellow base...$14–17

EQUESTRIENNE (1974) $7–10

ESQUIRE, ceremonial dancer..$10–16

FARTHINGTON BIKE (1972)...$6–8

FIRE ENGINE (1971)...$14–18

FIREMAN (1975)..$18–23

FISHERMAN (1974) $8–12

FLINTLOCK (1969), dueling pistol rich in detail. Japanese version has wooden rack; "Made in Japan" on handle. Heritage China gun has plastic rack, less detail. Gun-metal gray and brown, silver and gold trim. ....

    Japanese...$7–9

    Heritage...$12–16

FLORIDA "GATORS" (1973), tribute to the University of Florida Gators football team $9–11

FOE EAGLE (1978) $15–20

FOE FLYING EAGLE (1979) $20–25

FOE EAGLE (1980) $25–40

FOE EAGLE (1981) $18–28

FOOTBALL PLAYER (1974) $10–14

FORD MUSTANG $20–30

FORD THUNDERBIRD—1956 (1976)..$70–80

FOREMOST ASTRONAUT (1970), tribute to major liquor supermart, Foremost Liquor Store. Smiling "Mr. Bottle-Face" clinging to space rocket on white base $5

FRESNO DECANTER, map of famed California grape center. Stopper and inscription has gold finish. Blue, white $5–12

FRESNO GRAPE WITH GOLD..$48–60

FRESNO GRAPE (1970) $6–11

GAMECOCK (1970), all feathers and fury against rival birds. Red with yellow base $9–13

GO BIG RED No. 1, No. 2, AND No. 3, football-shaped bottle with white bands and laces on base embossed "Go Big Red." Brown, white, gold detail. ....

    No. 1 with football (1972)......................................$20–28

    No. 2 with hat (1971) $18–22

    No. 3 with rooster (1972)..$10–14

GOLDEN ANTIQUE CANNON (1969), symbol of Spanish power. Embossed details on barrel, wheels, and carriage. Dark brown, with lavish 22K-gold trim ...$5–7

GOLDEN EAGLE (1971), rich plumage, sitting on a branch. Gold color... $18–22

GOLDEN GRIZZLY BEAR (1970), a bear-shaped bottle, on haunches. Brown with gold highlights $4–6

GOLDEN HORSESHOE (1970), salute to Reno's Horseshoe Club. Good luck symbol on horseshoe. 24K-gold covered, in a blue base..................................$7–9

GOLDEN ROOSTER No. 1, a replica of the famous solid gold rooster on display

at Nugget Casino in Reno, Nevada. Glowing rooster in 22K gold on black base
....$35–50
GOLD PROSPECTOR (1969), rugged miner with white beard panning for gold.
Black, pink, and gold trim..$5–9
GOLD SEAL (1972) $12–14
GOLD TURKEY $35–45
GO TIGER GO (1973) $10–14
GRANDFATHER CLOCK (1970), brown with gold highlights, embossed detail .....
....$5–7
GRANDFATHER CLOCK (1970)..$12–20
GREATER GREENSBORO OPEN (1972), to commemorate this event, Ezra Brooks
has designed this genuine Heritage Ceramic bottle...........................$16–19
GREATER GREENSBORO OPEN (1972), green and gold........................$15–20
GREATER GREENSBORO OPEN (1973), golfer $17–24
GREATER GREENSBORO OPEN (1974), map $29–36
GREATER GREENSBORO OPEN (1975), cup..$25–30
GREATER GREENSBORO OPEN (1977), club and ball $20–25
GREAT STONE FACE—OLD MAN OF THE MOUNTAIN (1970), famous profile found
in mountain of New Hampshire. Stopper has seal of New Hampshire.... $10–14
GREAT WHITE SHARK (1977) $8–14
HAMBLETONIAN (1971), harness racer honors the NY town and race track that
sired harness racing and trotting; horse pulling driver and sulky. Green, brown,
white, yellow, blue; gold base.. $13–16
HAPPY GOOSE (1975)..$12–15
HAROLDS CLUB DICE (1968), Lucky 7 dice combination topped with H-cube
stopper, on round white base. Red and white with gold trim................. $8–12
HEREFORD (1971) $12–15
HEREFORD (1972), brown, white face $12–15
HISTORICAL FLASK (1970), eagle, blue..$3–5
HISTORICAL FLASK (1970), flagship, purple $3–5
HISTORICAL FLASK (1970), Liberty, amber..$3–5
HISTORICAL FLASK (1970), *Old Ironsides*, green.............................$3–5
HISTORICAL FLASK (1970), set of four...$3–5
HOLLYWOOD COPS (1972) $12–18
HOPI INDIAN (1970), "Kachina Doll." Creative tribe doing ritual song and dance.
White, red ornamental trim..$15–20
HOPI KACHINA (1973), genuine Heritage China ceramic reproduction of a Hum-
mingbird kachina doll...$50–75
IDAHO—SKI THE POTATO (1973), Ezra Brooks salutes the beautiful state of Idaho,
its ski resorts, and famous Idaho potatoes, with this genuine Heritage China
ceramic bottle $8–10
INDIANAPOLIS 500, sleek, dual-exhaust racer. White, blue, black, silver trim ...
....$30–35
INDIAN CEREMONIAL, colorful tribal dancer from New Mexico reservation. Mul-
ticolored, gold trim...$13–18
INDIAN HUNTER (1970), traditional buffalo hunt. Indian on horseback shooting
buffalo with bow and arrow. White horse, brown buffalo, yellow base... $12–15
IOWA FARMER (1977) $55–65
IOWA GRAIN ELEVATOR (1978)...$25–34

IRON HORSE LOCOMOTIVE, replica of old-time locomotive, complete with funnel, cow-catcher, and oil-burning headlamp. Black and red with 22K-gold trim $8–14

JACK O' DIAMONDS (1969), the symbol of good luck, a bottle in the shape of the "Jack" right off the card. A royal flush decorates the front. White, red, blue, and black $4–6

JAY HAWK (1969), funny bird with a large head perched on a "tree trunk" base. Symbol of Kansas during and after Civil War. Yellow, red, blue, and brown $6–8

JESTER (1971) $6–8

JUG, OLD-TIME, 1.75 Liter $9–13

KACHINA DOLL NO. 1 (1971) $80–100

KACHINA DOLL NO. 2 (1973), hummingbird $10–60

KACHINA DOLL NO. 3 (1974) $50–60

KACHINA DOLL NO. 4 (1975) $20–25

KACHINA DOLL NO. 5 (1976) $30–40

KACHINA DOLL NO. 6 (1977), white buffalo $25–35

KACHINA DOLL NO. 7 (1978), mud head $35–45

KACHINA DOLL NO. 8 (1979) $50–60

KANSAS JAYHAWK (1969) $4–7

KATZ CATS (1969), seal point and blue point. Siamese cats are symbolic of Katz Drug Co. of Kansas City, Kansas. Gray and blue, tan and brown $8–12

KATZ CATS PHILHARMONIC (1970), commemorating its 27th annual Star Night, devoted to classical and pop music. Black tuxedo, brown face, pair $6–10

KEYSTONE COP (1980) $32–40

KEYSTONE COPS (1971) $25–35

KILLER WHALE (1972) $15–20

KING OF CLUBS (1969), figure of card symbol. Sword and orb symbolize wisdom and justice. Royal flush in clubs in front. Yellow, red, blue, black, and white with gold trim $4–6

KING SALMON (1971), bottle in shape of leaping salmon, natural red $18–24

LIBERTY BELL (1970), replica of the famous bell complete with wooden support. Dark copper color, embossed details $5–6

LINCOLN CONTINENTAL MARK I (1941) $20–25

LION ON THE ROCK (1971) $5–7

LIQUOR SQUARE (1972) $5–7

LITTLE GIANT (1971), replica of the first horse-drawn steam engine to arrive at the Chicago fire in 1871. Red, black with gold trim $11–16

MAINE LIGHTHOUSE (1971) $18–24

MAINE LOBSTER (1970), bottle in lobster shape, complete with claws. Pinkish-red color. Bottle is sold only in Maine $15–18

MAN-O-WAR (1969), Big Red captured just about every major horseracing prize in turfdom. Replica of famous horse in brown and green, 22K-gold base. Embossed "Man-O-War" $10–16

M & M BROWN JUG (1975) $15–20

MAP (1972), USA club bottle $7–9

MASONIC FEZ (1976) $12–15

MAX (1976), The Hat, Zimmerman $20–25

MILITARY TANK (1971) $15–22

MINNESOTA HOCKEY PLAYER (1975) $18–22

MINUTEMAN (1975) $10–15

MISSOURI MULE (1972), brown $7–9

Moose (1973) $20–28
Motorcycle, motorcycle rider and machine. Rider dressed in blue pants, red
jacket, with stars and stripes helmet. Black motorcycle with red tank on silver
base $10–14
Mountaineer (1971), figure dressed in buckskin, holding rifle. "Mountaineers
Are Always Free" embossed on base. Bottle is handtrimmed in platinum. One
of the most valuable Ezra Brooks figural bottles............................$40–55
Mr. Foremost (1969), an authentic reproduction of the famous bottle-shaped
symbol of Foremost Liquor stores, Mr. Foremost, known for good wines and
spirits. Red, white, and black $7–10
Mr. Maine Potato (1973), from early beginnings the people of Maine have built the
small potato into a giant industry. Today potatoes are the number one agricultural crop
in the state. Over 36 billion pounds are grown every year........................ $6–10
Mr. Merchant (1970), Jumping Man; whimsical, checkered-vest caricature of
amiable shopkeeper, leaping into the air, arms outstretched. Yellow, black ......
....$6–10
Mule $8–12
Mustang Indy Pace Car (1979) $20–30
Nebraska—Go Big Red! (1972), genuine Heritage China reproduction of a game
ball and fan, trimmed in genuine 24K gold....................................$12–15
New Hampshire State House (1970), 150-year-old State House. Embossed
doors, windows, steps. Eagle-topped stopper. Gray building with gold ... $9–13
North Carolina Bicentennial (1975) $8–12
Nugget Classic, replica of golf pin presented to golf tournament participants.
Finished in 22K gold.. $7–12
Oil Gusher, bottle in shape of oil-drilling rig. All silver, jet-black stopper in
shape of gushing oil..$6–8
Old Capital (1971), bottle in shape of Iowa's seat of government when the corn
state was still frontier territory. Embossed windows, doors, pillars. "Old Capital
Iowa 1840–1857" on base. Reddish color with gold dome stopper........$30–40
Old EZ No. 1 (1977), barn owl..$25–35
Old EZ No. 2 (1978), eagle owl...$40–55
Old EZ No. 3 (1979), show owl $20–35
Old Man Of The Mountain (1970) $10–14
Old Water Tower (1969), famous landmark. Survived the Chicago fire of 1871.
Embossed details, towers, doors, stones, windows. Gray and brown gold base
....$12–16
Oliver Hardy Bust..$12–18
Ontario 500 (1970), California 500 is a speedway classic with an "Indy"-style
racing oval. Red, white, blue, and black with silver trim $18–22
Overland Express (1969), brown stagecoach bottle.........................$17–20
Over-Under Flintlock (1969), flask $6–9
Panda—Giant (1972), giant panda ceramic bottle...........................$12–17
Penguin (1972), Ezra Brooks salutes the penguin with a genuine Heritage China
ceramic figural bottle $8–10
Penny Farthington High-Wheeler (1973), Ezra Brooks salutes the millions
of cyclists everywhere and the new cycling boom with this genuine Heritage
China ceramic of the Penny Farthington bicycle............................. $9–12
Pepperbox (1969), flask...$4–6
Phoenix Bird (1971), famous mythical bird reborn from its own ashes honoring
Arizona. Blue bird with outstretched wings arising from gold flames $20–26

PHOENIX JAYCEES (1973), Ezra Brooks is proud to honor the Phoenix Jaycees and the Rodeo of Rodeos with this Heritage China reproduction of a silver saddle $10–14
PHONOGRAPH $15–20
PIANO (1970), an old-time piano player and his upright piano. Player wears blue pants, striped shirt, red bow tie, black derby, and yellow vest. Piano is brown in gold trim $12–13
PIRATE (1971), a swashbuckling sailor with beard, eye patch, and hook hand who flew the Jolly Roger (skull and crossbones) o'er the 7 Seas. Black hat, jacket, boots, yellow striped shirt, pistol, sword, and treasure chest on gold base........ $6–10
POLISH LEGION AMERICAN VETS (1978) $18–26
PORTLAND HEAD LIGHTHOUSE (1971), it has guided ships safely into Maine Harbor since 1791. White, red trim, gold light stopper. "Maine" embossed on rock base $18–24
POT-BELLIED STOVE (1968), old-time, round coal-burning stove with ornate legs and fire in the grate. Black and red $5–6
QUEEN OF HEARTS (1969), playing card symbol with royal flush in hearts on front of bottle $4–6
RACCOON WILDLIFE (1978) $30–40
RAM (1973) $13–18
RAZORBACK HOG (1969), bright red hog with white tusks and hooves running on green grass... $12–18
RAZORBACK HOG (1979)... $20–30
RED FOX (1979), wildlife.. $30–40
RENO ARCH (1968), honoring the Biggest Little City in the World, Reno, Nevada. Arch shape with "Reno" embossed on yellow. Front of bottle multicolor decal of dice, rabbit's foot, roulette wheel, slot machine, etc. White and yellow, purple stopper.. $4–8
SAILFISH (1971), leaping deep-water sailfish with a swordlike nose and large spread fin. Blue-green luminous tones on green waves base.................. $7–11
SALMON (1971), Washington King $20–26
SAN FRANCISCO CABLE CAR (1968).. $4–8
SAN FRANCISCO CABLE CAR (1968).. $5–8
SEA CAPTAIN (1971), salty old seadog, white hair and beard, in blue captain's jacket with gold buttons and sleeve stripes, white cap, gold band. Holding pipe, on wooden stanchion base... $10–14
SEALION—GOLD (1972), Ezra Brooks commemorates the state of California and its world-famous marine showmen with the California Sealion ceramic bottle, handdetailed in 24K gold.. $11–14
SENATOR (1971), cigar-chomping, whistle-stopping state senator, stumping on a platform of pure nostalgia. Black western hat and swallow-tail coat, red vest, string tie, gold, black, red, white.. $13–16
SENATORS OF THE US (1972), Ezra Brooks honors the senators of the United States of America with this genuine Heritage ceramic old-time courtly senator..
.... $10–13
SETTER (1974) $10–15
SHRINE KING TUT GUARD (1979).. $16–24
1804 SILVER DOLLAR (1970), commemorates the famous and very valuable 1804 silver dollar. Embossed replica of the Liberty Head dollar. Platinum-covered round dollar-shaped bottle on black or white base................................ $5–8
SILVER SADDLE (1973) $22–25

SILVER SPUR BOOT (1971), cowboy-boot-shaped bottle with silver spur buckled on. "Silver Spur—Carson City Nevada" embossed on side of boot. Brown boot with platinum trim... $7–11

SIMBA (1971), beautifully detailed lion is reddish-brown color. Head of lion is stopper. Rock base is dark gray.. $9–12

SKI BOOT (1972), Ezra Brooks salutes the exciting sport of skiing with this genuine Heritage ceramic ski boot $5–7

SLOT MACHINE (1971), a tribute to the slots of Las Vegas, Nevada. A replica of the original nickel Liberty Bell slot machine invented by Charles Fey in 1895. The original is in Reno's Liberty Belle Saloon. Top window shows two horseshoes and a bell; bottom panel shows prizes. Gray body with gold trim. $18–24

SNOWMOBILES (1972), a tribute to the chief means of transportation in Alaska and Canada $8–11

SOUTH DAKOTA AIR NATIONAL GUARD (1976)................................$18–22

SPIRIT OF '76 (1974) $5–7

SPIRIT OF ST. LOUIS (1977), 50th anniversary $6–11

SPRINT CAR RACER, a decanter replica of the race car sponsored by Ezra Brooks. Supercharged racer with black Firestone racing tires, and silver and blue trim. Goggled driver in white and red jumpsuit at wheel. Cream-colored car with silver and blue trim $30–40

STAGECOACH (1969).. $10–12

STAN LAUREL BUST (1976) $10–16

STOCK MARKET TICKER (1970), a unique replica of a ticker-tape machine. Gold-colored mechanism with white market tape under plastic dome. Black base with embossed plaque "Stock Market Quotations" $8–11

STONEWALL JACKSON (1974) $22–28

STRONGMAN (1974) $8–12

STURGEON (1975) $20–28

JOHN L. SULLIVAN (1970), the great John L., last of the bare knuckle fighters, in fighting stance. Mustached with red tights, gold belt cord, white gym shirt. John stands on a gold base..$15–20

SYRACUSE—NEW YORK (1973), Ezra Brooks salutes the great city of Syracuse, its past and its present $11–16

TANK PATTON (1972), reproduction of a U.S. Army tank. Turret top with cannon is the stopper. Embossed details on tracks, tools, etc. Camouflage green and brown $16–20

TECUMSEH (1969), the figurehead of the *U.S.S. Delaware*, this decanter is an embossed replica of the statue at the United States Naval Academy in Annapolis, MD. Feathers in quiver-form stopper. Gold figure on brown wood base....$5–6

TELEPHONE (1971), a replica of the old-time upright handset telephone, 24K-gold body, mouth piece, and base trim; black receiver, wires, base, and head. Mouthpiece and head form the stopper $16–19

TENNIS PLAYER (1972), Ezra Brooks salutes tennis lovers everywhere with this genuine Heritage China ceramic tennis player bottle.......................... $8–12

TERRAPIN (1974), Maryland $14–16

TEXAS LONGHORN (1971), realistic longhorn on tall green Texas grass base. Longhorn head is stopper. Reddish-brown body, white horns and mask, gold-trimmed base $18–22

TICKER TAPE (1970) $8–12

TIGER ON STADIUM (1973), to commemorate college teams who have chosen the tiger as their mascot.. $12–17

TOM TURKEY, replica of the American white feathered turkey. Tail spread, red head and wattles, yellow feet and beak. On a brown tree trunk base $18–24

TONOPAH (1972).. $12–15

TOTEM POLE (1972), Ezra Brooks commemorates the totem art of the American Indian with this genuine Heritage China reproduction of an ornate, intricately designed Indian totem pole $10–14

TOTEM POLE (1973), the Indians of North America have a proud history and in many instances that history is beautifully portrayed in totem pole art. It is a truly remarkable art form that will enrich the world for generations to come. Ezra Brooks commemorates the totem pole art of the North American Indian with this genuine Heritage China reproduction of an ornate, intricately designed Indian totem pole $12–18

TRACTOR (1971), a model of the 1917 Fordson made by Henry Ford. Embossed details of engine and hood seat and steering wheel. Red tractor wheels, gray body with silver trim.. $9–11

TRAIL-BIKE RIDER (1972), Ezra Brooks salutes the trail-bike riders of America with this genuine Heritage China ceramic bottle............................. $10–12

TROJAN HORSE (1974)... $15–18

TROJANS—USC FOOTBALL (1973), a tribute to the Trojans who have given U.S.C. seven Pacific-Eight Conference titles, six Rose Bowl teams, 23 All-Americans, two Heisman Trophy winners (Mike Garrett and O.J. Simpson), three undefeated seasons, and three national championships $10–14

TROUT & FLY (1970), the rainbow trout leaping and fighting the McGinty Fly. A luminescent replica of this angler's dream on a blue water base, complete with scales, fins, and flashing tail.. $7–11

TRUCKIN' & VANNIN' (1977) $7–12

VERMONT SKIER (1972) $10–12

VFW—VETERANS OF FOREIGN WARS (1973), Ezra Brooks salutes the Veterans of Foreign Wars of the United States and the 1.8 million fighting men of five wars who wear the Cross of Malta $6–10

VIRGINIA—RED CARDINAL (1973), a glorious bird, the cardinal represents this illustrious state $15–20

WALGREEN DRUGS (1974) $16–24

WEIRTON STEEL (1973) $15–18

WESTERN RODEOS (1973), Ezra Brooks salutes the rodeo, from its early pioneers to its professional circuit riders, with this genuine Heritage China bottle.........
.... $17–23

WEST VIRGINIA—MOUNTAINEER (1971)..$65–75

WEST VIRGINIA—MOUNTAIN LADY (1972) $14–20

WHALE (1972)... $14–20

WHEAT SHOCKER (1971), the mascot of the Kansas football team in a fighting pose. Wheat yellow figure with black turtleneck sweater; "Wheat Shocker" embossed in yellow on front. Wheat stalk tops are the stopper, wheat plants are the base $5–7

WHISKEY FLASKS (1970), reproductions of collectible American patriotic whiskey flasks of the 1800s: *Old Ironsides*, Miss Liberty, American Eagle, Civil War Commemorative. Embossed designs in gold on blue, amber, green, and red....
.... $12–14

WHITETAIL DEER (1947) $18–24

WHITE TURKEY (1971) $20–25

WICHITA $4–8

WICHITA CENTENNIAL (1970), replica of Wichita's center of culture and commerce, Century II, the round building with the square base. Blue roof with gold airliner atop symbol of "Air Capital of the World." Blue, brown, black, and gold $4–6
WINSTON CHURCHILL (1969) $6–10
ZIMMERMAN'S HAT (1968), a salute to "Zimmerman's—World's Largest Liquor Store." A replica of the store, embossed windows, doors, and roof. The Zimmerman Hat caps the store and is the bottle stopper. Red, white, brown, and gold $5–6

J.W. DANT BOTTLES

The bottles of J.W. Dant Distilling Co. from Louisville, Kentucky, are not as numerous as those of Ezra Brooks and Jim Beam, the other major Kentucky distilleries, but their following is strong. Introduced in 1968, the Dant figurals carry American themes, including patriotic events, folklore, and animal species such as the mountain quail, woodcock, and prairie chicken. Dant's preoccupation with American history originates from the period of its establishment in 1863 during the Civil War.

Most Dant bottles are conventionally shaped with historical scenes in full color. The back of all rectangular bottles carries an embossed American eagle and shield with stars. Several of the Boston Tea Party bottles have an error: the eagle's head faces his left side instead of his right.

All Dant bottles are limited editions and the company assures customers that the molds will not be reused.

ALAMO...$4–6
AMERICAN LEGION...$3–7
ATLANTIC CITY $4–6
BOBWHITE...$6–8
BOEING 747 ....$5–8
BOSTON TEA PARTY, eagle to left $4–6
BOSTON TEA PARTY, eagle to right...$9–12
BOURBON $3–5
PAUL BUNYAN $5–7
CALIFORNIA QUAIL $7–9
CHUKAR PARTRIDGE..$7–9
CLEAR TIP PINCH $7–9
CONSTITUTION AND GUERRIERE $5–7
DUEL BETWEEN BURR AND HAMILTON $8–10
EAGLE...$6–9
FORT SILL CENTENNIAL (1969) $7–11
PATRICK HENRY $4–7
INDIANAPOLIS 500 ....$7–11

GARNIER BOTTLES

The prestigious figural bottles of the Garnier firm are among the oldest ones issued continuously since 1899 by a spirits company. But during the American Prohibition and World War II, which eliminated the majority of the Garnier market, production ceased temporarily. Garnet et Cie, a French firm founded in 1858, is recognized as the pioneer of the modern "collector" bottle for liquor. Of course, figural and other decorative bottles for liquor existed before the Garnier products but these were not issued in the form of a series which encouraged the building up of a collection. Garnier actually had a line of figural bottles 50 years before Jim Beam. Some antique historians claim to have found a relationship between Garnier bottles and the later Hummel porcelain figurines, believing that the former inspired the latter. The two companies' figurals are similar.

The older Garniers, produced prior to World War II, are scarce and valuable. They are not listed because their price levels are difficult to establish. Some of the better known "old Garniers" are the Cat (1930), Clown (1910), Country Jug (1937), Greyhound (1930), Penguin (1930), and Marquise (1931). Garnier released its new figurals gradually with only 52 available within a 31-year span. But since 1930, new figurals have been produced more frequently.

ALADDIN'S LAMP (1963), silver. 6½" $38–48
ALFA ROMEO 1913 (1970), red body, yellow seats, black trim. 4" × 10½" .....
.... $19–27
ALFA ROMEO 1929 (1969), pale blue body, red seat, black trim. 4" × 10½" ...
.... $19–27

ALFA ROMEO RACER (1969), maroon body, black tires and trim. 4″ × 10″ .....
....$19–27
ANTIQUE COACH (1970), multicolor pastel tones. 8″ × 12″ $25–30
APOLLO (1969), yellow quarter-moon, blue clouds, silver Apollo spaceship.
13½″ $17–22
AZTEC VASE (1965), stone tan, multicolor Aztec design. 11¾″ $15–20
BABY FOOT—SOCCER SHOE (1963) ....
 Black with white trim. 3¾″ × 8½″ $10–20
 1962 soccer shoe, large $7–11
BABY TRIO (1963), clear glass, gold base. 6¼″ $7–10
BACCUS FIGURAL (1967), purple, brown, flesh tones. 13″ $20–25
BAHAMAS, black policeman, white jacket and hat, black pants, red stripe, gold
details...$15–24
BALTIMORE ORIOLE (1970), multicolor, green, yellow, blue. Approx. 11″
....$10–16
BANDIT FIGURAL (1958), pin-ball shape, multicolor, 11½″ $10–14
BEDROOM CANDLESTICK (1967), white with handpainted flowers. 11½″ .$20–25
BELLOWS (1969), gold and red. 4″ × 14½″ $14–21
BIRD ASHTRAY (1958), clear glass, gold stopper. 3″..........................$3–4
BLUEBIRD (1970), two blue birds, multicolor green, brown, and yellow. Approx.
11″ $12–18
BOUQUET (1966), white basket, multicolor flowers. 10¾″ $15–25
BULL (AND MATADOR) ANIMAL FIGURAL (1963), a rocking bottle, bronze and
gold. 12½″ × 12½″ $17–23
BURMESE MAN VASE (1965), stone gray, multicolor Eastern design. 12″ ....
....$15–25
CANADA, Mountie in red jacket, black jodphurs, brown boots.............$11–14
CANDLESTICK (1955), yellow candle, brown holder with gold ring. 10¾″ ....
....$25–35
CANDLESTICK GLASS (1965), ornate leaves and fluting. 10″ $15–25
CANNON (1964), with wheels and carriage, mottled yellow-brown. 7½″ × 13½″
....$48–58
CARDINAL STATE BIRD—ILLINOIS (1969), bright red bird, green and brown tree.
11½″ $12–15
CAT—BLACK (1962), black cat with green eyes. 11½″ $15–25
CAT—GRAY (1962), grayish-white cat with yellow eyes. 11½″ $15–25
CHALET (1955), white, red, green and blue. 9″ $40–50
CHIMNEY (1956), red bricks and fire, white mantel with picture. 9¾″ ..$55–65
CHINESE DOG (1965), Foo dogs, carved, embossed, ivory white on dark blue
base. 11″ $15–25
CHINESE STATUETTE—MAN (1970), yellow robe, dark skin, blue base. 12″ .....
....$15–25
CHINESE STATUETTE—WOMAN (1970), ebony skin tones, lavender robe, blue
base. 12″..$15–25
CHRISTMAS TREE (1956), dark green tree, gold decorated, white candles, red
flame. 11½″ $58–68
CITROEN, 1922 (1970), yellow body, black trim wheels. 4″ × 10½″ $20–30
CLASSIC ASHTRAY (1958), clear glass, round with pouring spout. 2½″ $5–8
CLOCK (1958), clear glass, round on black base. Working clock in center. 9″ ..
....$20–30
CLOWN HOLDING TUBA (1955), green clown with gold trim. 12¾″ $15–25

COFFEE MILL (1966), white with blue flowers $20–30

COLUMBINE FIGURAL (1968), female partner to harlequin, green and blue, black hair and mask. 13″...$20–30
  Harlequin $30–40

DRUNKARD—DRUNK ON LAMPOST, figure in top hat and tails holding "wavy" lampost; black, red, blue, and white. 14¾″ $15–20

DUCKLING FIGURAL (1956), yellow duckling, white basket and red flowers, pink hat $18–26

DUO (1954), two clear glass bottles stacked, two pouring spouts. 7¼″ ..$12–18

EGG FIGURAL (1956), white egg-shape house; pink, red, green. 8¾″....$68–78

EIFFEL TOWER (1951), ivory with yellow tones ....
  13½″ $15–25
  12½″ $14–20

ELEPHANT FIGURAL (1961), black with ivory white tusks. 6¾″ $20–30

EMPIRE VASE (1962), green and white, gold design and trim. 11½″ $10–18

FIAT 500, 1913 (1970), yellow body, red hub caps, black trim. 4″ × 10¾″ ....
....$20–30

FIAT NEUVO, 1913 (1970), open top, blue body and hub caps, yellow and black trim. 4″ × 10¾″ $20–30

FLASK GARNIER (1958), clear glass, embossed cherries. 3″ $9–12

FLYING HORSE PEGASUS (1958), black horse, gold mane and tail, red "marble" candle holder. 12″ $50–60

FORD, 1913 (1970), green open body and wheels, black trim. 4″ × 10¾″ ......
....$20–30

FOUNTAIN (1964), brown with gold lion head spout and embossing. 12½″ ......
....$24–34

GIRAFFE (1961), yellow marble, modern animal figure. 18″ $20–35

GOLDFINCH (1970), yellow bird, black wings and tail, green and brown leaves and limbs. 12″ $12–16

GOOSE (1955), white with gold decoration, modern swirl-shaped goose. 9¼″ ...
....$14–24

GRENADIER (1949), light blue soldier with sword in uniform of 1880s (faceless figure). 13¾″ $55–65

HARLEQUIN STANDING (1968), columbine's mate, brown costume, blue cape, black cap and shoes. 13¼″ $13–19

HARLEQUIN WITH MANDOLIN (1958), seated comedy figure, mandolin and mask, white with multicolored circles, black buttons and shoes. 14½″ $30–40

HORSE PISTOL (1964), embossed brown antique pistol, gold details. 18″ $15–25

HUNTING VASE (1964), tan and gold with embossed hunting scene. 12¼″ ....
....$25–35

HUSSAR (1949), French Cavalry soldier of 1800s holding sword, maroon color. 13¾″ $25–33

INDIA, turbaned figure, white jacket, blue kilts, red sash $10–14

INDIAN (1958), Big Chief with headdress, bowling-pin shape, bright Indian design colors. 11¾″ $15–20

JOCKEY (1961), bronzed gold horse and jockey rocking bottle. 12½″ × 12″ ....
....$25–35

LANCER (1949), light green soldier holding drum. 13″......................$15–22

LOCOMOTIVE (1969), tan, old-fashioned locomotive. 9″ $15–25

LOG—ROUND (1958), brown and tan log shape, silver handle and spout. 10″ ...
....$20–30

LONDON—BOBBY, dark blue uniform, silver helmet shield.................\$12–18
LOON (1970), sitting bird; white, brown, tan, blue base. 11″..............\$10–18
MAHARAJAH (1958), white and gold Indian ruler with turban. 11¾″.....\$68–78
M.G. 1933 (1970), green body, orange trim, white wheels. 4″ × 11″..\$15–25
MOCKINGBIRD (1970), black and white bird on tree stump. 11″............\$8–14
MONTMARTRE JUG (1960), colorful Parisian Bohemian scene, green. 11″........
....\$12–18
MONUMENTS (1966), a cluster of Parisian monuments; Eiffel Tower spout, mul-
ticolor. 13″..\$15–25
NAPOLEON ON HORSEBACK (1969), rearing white horse, Napoleon in red cloak,
black hat, and uniform. 12″..\$20–30
NATURE GIRL (1959), native girl under palm tree, black with bronze. 13″.......
....\$10–14
NEW YORK POLICEMAN, dark blue uniform with gold shield and buttons.........
....\$9–13
PACKARD, 1930 (1970), orange body, cream roof and wheels, black trim. 4″ ×
10″...\$20–30
PAINTING (1961), multicolor painting of girl in tan wood frame. 12″....\$25–35
PARIS, French policeman in black, white gloves, hat, and garness........\$10–15
PARIS TAXI (1960), old-time cab; yellow body, red windows and headlights, black
wire frame. 9″ × 10½″...\$20–30
PARTRIDGE (1961), multicolor game bird, on leaf base. 10″.................\$25–35
PHEASANT (1969), multicolor game bird on rocking tree-trunk base. 12″........
....\$25–30
PIGEON—CLEAR GLASS (1958), bird-shape bottle, gold stopper. 8″......\$10–14
PONY (1961), modern-shaped horse, wood grain tan. 8¾″.................\$25–35
POODLE (1954), begging poodles in white or black with red trim. 8½″.\$12–15
RENAULT, 1911 (1969), green body and hood, red hubs, black trim. 4″ × 10¾″.......
....\$20–30
ROAD RUNNER (1969), multicolor bird, green cactus pouring spout. 12″........\$10–15
ROBIN (1970), multicolor bird on tree stump with leaves. 12″.............\$10–14
ROCKET (1958), rocket-shape bottle, wire holder, yellow nose. 10¾″...\$11–14
ROLLS ROYCE 1908 (1970), open touring car in yellow, red seats and hubs, black
trim. 4″ × 10½″...\$20–30
ROOSTER (1952), crowing rooster with handle, black or maroon with gold trim.
12″...\$15–25
SAINT TROPEZ JUG (1961), colorful French Riviera scene, tan jug, black handle
....\$20–30
SCARECROW (1960), yellow straw body and hat, green jacket, red stripe face and
tie, bird on shoulder. 12″...\$25–35
SHERIFF (1958), two guns, badge and cowboy hat, pin-ball shape, white and
gold. 12″...\$15–25
SNAIL (1950), white and brown with spiral shell. 6½″ × 10″............\$58–68
SOCCER SHOE (1962), black shoe, white laces. 10″ L.......................\$30–40
S.S. FRANCE—LARGE (1962), commemorative model of ocean liner, black hull,
blue-green decks, red and black stacks, with gold labels. 5″ × 19″...\$80–130
S.S. FRANCE—SMALL (1962), same as above. 4½″ × 14″................\$50–60
S.S. QUEEN MARY (1970), black hull, green-blue decks, blue water, three red
and black stacks. 4″ × 16″...\$24–32
STANLEY STEAMER 1907 (1970), open blue car, yellow and black trim. 4″ ×
10½″...\$20–30

TEAPOT (1961), yellow and black striped body, black handle and spout. 8½″
....$15–25
TEAPOT, 1935...$20–30
TROUT (1967), gray-blue speckled leaping trout, water base. 11″ $17–22
VALLEY QUAIL (1969), black-marked bird on wood base. 11″ $8–12
VIOLIN (1966), white violin, handpainted flowers and details. 14″ $30–36
WATCH—ANTIQUE (1966), antique pocket watch, tan and gold. 10″ $20–30
WATERING CAN (1958), handpainted design, handle and pouring spout. 7″......
.... $12–18
WATER PITCHER (1965), glass body, silver base, handle, and top. 14″ ... $12–18
YOUNG DEER VASE (1964), embossed figures, tan color. 12″ $25–35

HOFFMAN BOTTLES

The Hoffman bottles are limited edition ceramics. Each issue is restricted in the number of bottles made and when this designated number is reached the mold is destroyed to prevent reproductions in the future. Consequently, the "out of production" designs quickly become collectors' items achieving high prices on the market. Hoffmans have sometimes been called the Hummels of the bottle world because they often depict figures in European dress at various kinds of occupations. These include a shoemaker, a doctor, and a bartender. However, the firm also focused upon American themes, such as its 1976 centennial bottles with Pioneer of 1876 and Hippie of 1976.

OCCUPATION SERIES

MR. BARTENDER WITH MUSIC BOX, *He's a Jolly Good Fellow*............$25–30
MR. CHARMER WITH MUSIC BOX, *Glow Little Glow Worm*................ $10–13
MR. DANCER WITH MUSIC BOX, *The Irish Washerwoman*.................$18–22
MR. DOCTOR WITH MUSIC BOX, *As Long as He Needs Me*................$20–25

Hoffman, Mr. Lucky. PHOTO COURTESY OF DAVE SMITH.

Mr. Fiddler With Music Box, *Hearts and Flowers* $20–22
Mr. Guitarist With Music Box, *Johnny Guitar* $20–22
Mr. Harpist With Music Box, *Do-Re-Mi*.................................... $10–15
Mr. Lucky With Music Box, *When Irish Eyes Are Smiling* $14–18
Mrs. Lucky With Music Box, *The Kerry Dancer* $12–15
Mr. Policeman With Music Box, *Don't Blame Me* $30–35
Mr. Sandman With Music Box, *Mr. Sandman* $10–20
Mr. Saxophonist With Music Box, *Tiger Rag* $15–20
Mr. Shoe Cobbler With Music Box, *Danny Boy* $15–20

BICENTENNIAL SERIES, 4/5-QT. SIZE

Betsy Ross With Music Box, *Star Spangled Banner* $30–40
Generation Gap, depicting "100 Years of Progress," 2-oz. size $30–38
Majestic Eagle With Music Box, *America the Beautiful* $60–80

C. M. RUSSELL SERIES, 4/5-QT. SIZE

Buffalo Man... $18–23
Flathead Squaw $15–18
Last Of Five Thousand $14–18
Red River Breed $23–28
The Scout.. $30–40
The Stage Drive $20–30
Trapper $20–30

JAPANESE BOTTLES

Bottlemaking in Japan is an ancient art. Although the collectible bottles presently produced in Japan are mainly for exportation, they still reflect native designing in their characteristic shapes and handsome enameling. Japanese bottles are increasing in numbers on the American market but prices remain modest. Japan produces figural bottles also. The popular Kamotsuru bottles picture characters from Japanese mythology.

Daughter $12–18
Faithful Retainer.. $25–35
Golden Pagoda $12–18
"Kiku" Geisha, blue. 13¼" $20–30
Maiden $12–18
Noh Mask $12–18
Okame Mask.. $50–70
Playboy.. $14–24
Princess $14–24
Red Lion Man $40–60

SAKE GOD, colorful robe, porcelain. 10″ $20–30
SAKE GOD, white, bone china. 10″ $12–15
WHITE LION MAN $35–50
WHITE PAGODA $15–20
"YURI" GEISHA, pink, red sash. 13¼″ $35–45

HOUSE OF KOSHU

ANGEL, with book. 7 oz. $5–8
ANGEL, sitting on a barrel. 17 oz. $5–8
BEETHOVEN BUST, 7 oz. $5–8
CENTURIAN BUST, 7 oz. $5–8
CHILDREN, 7 oz. $6–10
DECLARATION OF INDEPENDENCE $4–6
GEISHA, blue $40–45
GEISHA, cherry blossom $30–35
GEISHA, lily $25–35
GEISHA, violet $30–40
GEISHA, wisteria $30–40
GEISHA, lavender, with fan $45–50
GEISHA, reclining $60–70
GEISHA, sitting $45–50
LIONMAN, red $40–45
LIONMAN, white $80–95
PAGODA, green $25–30
PAGODA, white $20–25
PAGODA, gold $15–20
SAILOR, with a pipe $6–9

KAMOTSURU BOTTLES

DAOKOKU, god of wealth $9–13
EBISU, god of fishermen $10–15
GODDESS OF ART $8–12
HOTEI, god of wealth $7–10

KENTUCKY GENTLEMEN BOTTLES

Kentucky Gentlemen, another Kentucky whiskey distiller, issues figural bottles. Their figurals are released less frequently than those of Beam or Brooks. To date, they have concentrated on ceramics, picturing costumes worn at various times in American history, especially from the Civil War

period. Large-sized, more than a foot high, they are impressively modeled and colored. Each stands on a rectangular base, the front of which
reads ''Kentucky Gentlemen.''

CONFEDERATE INFANTRY, in gray uniform, with sword. 13½″ $10–14
FRONTIERSMAN (1969), coonskin cap, fringed buckskin, powder horn, and long
rifle, tan. 14″ $12–15
PINK LADY (1969), long bustle skirt, feathered hat, parasol, pink. 13¾″ ....
....$20–32
KENTUCKY GENTLEMEN (1969), figural bottle; frock coat, top hat, and cane;
''Old Colonel,'' gray ceramic. 14″ $12–15
REVOLUTIONARY WAR OFFICER, in dress uniform and boots, holding sword.
14″ $12–16
UNION ARMY SERGEANT, in dress blue uniform, with sword. 14″ $9–13

LIONSTONE BOTTLES

Lionstone Distillery, a relative newcomer into the ranks of figural bottle
makers, has already garnered a substantial reputation. Their bottles stress
realism in design with a great variety of subjects. Lionstone combines
the better elements of classical porcelain-making with the traditional art
of bottle manufacturing in their creations. Prices of the more popular
issues have increased rapidly. Lionstone produced the most ambitious of
all collector bottles in terms of components and detail. Their Shoot-out
at O.K. Corral, based upon an authentic incident in Old West history,
consists of three bottles with nine human figures and two horses.

Lionstone issues all their bottles in series form, including the Oriental
Worker series, Dog series, Sports series, Circus series, and Bicentennial
series, with new ones added periodically. The most popular with collectors
are the Western Figurals, a lengthy series depicting various characters from
western American history such as Jesse James, Sod Buster, Mountain Man,
Highway Robber, and Gentleman Gambler. Lionstone's Annie Oakley bottle comes complete with guns and sharpshooter medals.

Since prices of Lionstones on the collector market continue to be firm,
buyers should investigate the possibility of spirits dealers still having
some old unsold stock on hand.

BAR SCENE NO. 1.. $125–140
BARTENDER $18–22
BELLY ROBBER $12–16
BLACKSMITH $20–30
MOLLY BROWN.. $18–25

Buffalo Hunter	$25–35
Calamity Jane	$18–23
Camp Cook	$13–17
Camp Follower	$9–12
Canadian Goose	$45–55
Casual Indian	$8–12
Cavalry Scout	$8–12
Cherry Valley Club	$50–60
Chinese Laundryman	$12–15
Annie Christmas	$10–15
Circuit Judge	$8–12
Corvette, 1.75 liters	60–72
Country Doctor	$12–18
Cowboy	$8–10
Frontiersman	$14–16
Gambels Quail	$8–12
Gentleman Gambler	$25–35
God Of Love	$17–22
God Of War	$17–22
Gold Panner	$25–35
Highway Robber	$15–20
Jesse James	$18–23
Johnny Lightning	$50–65
Judge Roy Bean	$20–30
Lonely Luke	$45–60
Lucky Buck	$18–24
Mallard Duck	$35–45
Miniatures—Western (Six)	$85–110
Mint Bar, with frame	$700–900
Mint Bar, with nude and frame	$1000–1250
Mountain Man	$15–20
Annie Oakley	$14–16
Pintail Duck	$40–55
Proud Indian	$10–14
Railroad Engineer	$15–18
Renegade Trader	$15–18
Riverboat Captain	$10–15
Roadrunner	$28–36
Saturday Night Bath	$60–70
Sheepherder	$25–35
Sheriff	$10–12
Sod Buster	$13–16
Squawman	$20–30
Stagecoach Driver	$45–60
STP Turbocar	$40–50
STP Tubocar, with gold and platinum, pair	$150–185
Telegrapher	$15–20
Tinker	$25–30
Tribal Chief	$25–30
Al Unser No. 1	15–20
Wells Fargo Man	$8–12
Woodhawk	$15–17

BICENTENNIAL SERIES

FIREFIGHTERS No. 1 (old item) $110–120
MAIL CARRIER..$23–29
MOLLY PITCHER...$10–12
PAUL REVERE $10–12
BETSY ROSS $15–25
SONS OF FREEDOM $25–34
GEORGE WASHINGTON $15–25
WINTER AT VALLEY FORGE $16–20

BICENTENNIAL WESTERNS

BARBER $30–40
FIREFIGHTER No. 3..$60–70
INDIAN WEAVER..$20–24
PHOTOGRAPHER...$34–40
RAINMAKER $22–28
SATURDAY NIGHT BATH..$50–65
TRAPPER $30–36

BIRD SERIES (1972–74)

BLUEBIRD—EASTERN...$18–24
BLUEBIRD—WISCONSIN $20–30
BLUEJAY $20–25
PEREGRINE FALCON...$15–18
MEADOWLARK $15–20
MOURNING DOVES $50–70
SWALLOW..$15–18

CIRCUS SERIES (MINIATURES)

THE BAKER..$10–15
BURMESE LADY...$10–15
FAT LADY...$10–15
FIRE-EATER $10–15
GIANT WITH MIDGET $10–15
GIRAFFE-NECKED LADY..$10–14
SNAKE CHARMER..$10–15
STRONG MAN $10–15
SWORD SWALLOWER $10–15
TATTOOED LADY $10–15

DOG SERIES (MINIATURES)

BOXER..$10–15
COCKER SPANIEL...$9–12
COLLIE...$10–15

POINTER $10–15
POODLE $10–15

EUROPEAN WORKER SERIES

THE COBBLER $20–35
THE HORSESHOER $20–35
THE POTTER $20–35
THE SILVERSMITH $25–35
THE WATCHMAKER $20–35
THE WOODWORKER $20–35

ORIENTAL WORKER SERIES

BASKET WEAVER $25–35
EGG MERCHANT $25–35
GARDNER $25–35
SCULPTOR $25–35
TEA VENDOR $25–35
TIMEKEEPER $25–35

SPORTS SERIES

BASEBALL $22–30
BASKETBALL $22–30
BOXING $22–30
FOOTBALL $22–30
HOCKEY $22–30

TROPICAL BIRD SERIES (MINIATURES)

BLUE-CROWNED CHLOROPHONIA $12–16
EMERALD TOUCANET $12–16
NORTHERN ROYAL FLYCATCHER $12–16
PAINTED BUNTING $12–16
SCARLET MACAW $12–16
YELLOW-HEADED AMAZON $12–16

OTHER LIONSTONE BOTTLES

BUCCANEER $25–35
COWGIRL $45–55
DANCEHALL GIRL $50–55
FALCON $15–25
FIREFIGHTER No. 2 .... $80–120
FIREFIGHTER No. 4, emblem $25–35

FIREFIGHTER NO. 5, 60th anniversary $22–27
FIREFIGHTER NO. 6, fire hydrant $40–45
FIREFIGHTER NO. 6, in gold or silver $250–350
FIREFIGHTER NO. 7, helmet $60–90
FIREFIGHTER NO. 8, fire alarm box $45–60
FIREFIGHTER NO. 8, in gold or silver $90–120
FIREFIGHTER NO. 9, extinguisher $55–60
FIREFIGHTER NO. 10, trumpet.. $55–60
FIREFIGHTER NO. 10, gold $200–260
FIREFIGHTER NO. 10, silver $125–175
INDIAN MOTHER AND PAPOOSE $50–65
THE PERFESSER.. $40–45
ROSES ON PARADE $60–80
SCREECH OWLS.. $50–65
UNSER-OLSONITE EAGLE $35–45

OTHER MINIATURES

BARTENDER $12–15
CLIFF SWALLOW MINIATURE.. $9–12
DANCEHALL GIRL MINIATURE.. $15–22
FIREFIGHTER EMBLEM... $24–31
FIREFIGHTER ENGINE NO. 8 .... $24–31
FIREFIGHTER ENGINE NO. 10 .... $24–31
HORSESHOE MINIATURE... $14–20
KENTUCKY DERBY RACE HORSE, Cannanade.................................. $33–43
LUCKY BUCK $10–12
RAINMAKER $10–14
SAHARA INVITATIONAL NO. 1.. $33–43
SAHARA INVITATIONAL NO. 2.. $33–43
SHEEPHERDER $12–15
SHOOT-OUT AT OK CORRAL, set of three $250–300
WOODPECKER $10–15

LUXARDO BOTTLES

Made in Torreglia, Italy, the Girolamo Luxardo bottles boast a long and distinctive history. Imported into the United States in 1930, the bottles gradually acquired an impressive following among American collectors. Chiefly a manufacturer of wine, Luxardo also sells liquors.

The Luxardo line, extremely well modeled and meticulously colored, captures the spirit of Renaissance glass. Varying hues of color are blended on most specimens which radiate brilliantly when light shines through the bottles. The effective coloring techniques of the Luxardo bottles compare to those of ancient Egypt where color was the most important consideration. While Egyptian bottles were often colored garishly, the Luxardos carefully balance splashiness and restraint—the dominant colors never obscure the pastel shades.

Many of Luxardo's bottles, both glass and majolica, are figural. Natural history subjects as well as classical themes predominate. Most of the majolica decanters can be reused as vases, jars, lamp bases or ashtrays.

The firm maintains a regular schedule for its bottle production. Between three to six new designs are chosen each January for that year's production. The most popular, such as the Cellini bottle introduced in the early 1950s, continue to be used. Occasionally a design is discontinued after just one year. The Chess Set, produced in 1959, was discontinued because of manufacturing difficulty.

Unfortunately, the names and dates of production of the earlier Luxardo decanters are mostly unknown, due to many owners removing the paper identification labels.

The rare Zara decanters, made before World War II, are expected to increase further in value and scarcity. The First Born of the Murano Venetion glass, if ever located, will command a very strong price. Eventually, all the Naponelli "signed" decanters should rise markedly in value because of the small quantities issued.

Although the knowledgeable dealers are aware of the Luxardo prices, remarkable bargains are sometimes obtainable by shopping at garage sales, thrift stores, and charity outlets.

Specimens in mint condition with the original manufacturer's label always command the highest sums. All prices listed are for empty bottles in fine to mint condition.

If current or recent Luxardo bottles are not available at your local spirits dealer, the dealer can order them from the American distributor, Hans Schonewalk, American Beverage Brokers, 420 Market Street, San Francisco, California 94111.

ALABASTER FISH FIGURAL (1960–68) $30–40
ALABASTER GOOSE FIGURAL (1960–68), green and white, wings, etc $25–35
AMPULLA FLASK (1958–59)...$20–30
APOTHECARY JAR (1960), handpainted multicolor, green and black.......$20–30
ASSYRIAN ASHTRAY DECANTER (1961), gray, tan, and black................$15–25
AUTUMN LEAVES DECANTER (1952), handpainted, two handles............$35–45
AUTUMN WINE PITCHER (1958), handpainted country scene, handled pitcher
....$30–40
BABYLON DECANTER (1960), dark green and gold $16–23
BIZANTINA (1959), gold embossed design, white body $28–38
BLUE AND GOLD AMPHORA (1968), blue and gold with pastoral scene in white oval..$20–30
BLUE FIAMMETTA OR VERMILLIAN (1957), decanter $20–27

BROCCA PITCHER (1958), white background pitcher with handle, multicolor flowers, green leaves $28–37

BUDDHA GODDESS FIGURAL (1961) ....
  Goddess head in green-gray stone $14–19
  Miniature $11–16

BURMA ASHTRAY SPECIALTY (1960), embossed white dancing figure, dark green background $20–25

BURMA PITCHER SPECIALTY (1960), green and gold, white embossed dancing figure.. $14–19

CALYPSO GIRL FIGURAL (1962), black West Indian girl, flower headdress in bright color...$20–25

CANDLESTICK ALABASTER (1961)...$30–35

CELLINI VASE (1958–68), glass and silver decanter, fancy.................. $14–19

CELLINI VASE (1957), glass and silver handled decanter, fancy, with serpent handle.. $14–19

CERAMIC BARREL (1968), barrel shape, barrel color, painted flowers, embossed scroll with cameo head on decorative stand.................................... $14–19

CHERRY BASKET FIGURAL (1960), white basket, red cherries............... $14–19

CLASSICAL FRAGMENT SPECIALTY (1961), embossed classic Roman female figure and vase $25–33

COCKTAIL SHAKER (1957), glass and silver decanter, silver-plated top ... $14–19

COFFEE CARAFE SPECIALTY (1962), old-time coffee pot, with handle and spout, white with blue flowers... $14–19

CURVA VASO VASE (1961), green, green and white, ruby red...............$22–29

DERUTA AMPHORA (1956), colorful floral design on white, two-handled decanter $11–16

DERUTA CAMEO AMPHORA (1959), colorful floral scrolls and cameo head on eggshell white, two-handled vase $25–35

DERUTA PITCHER (1953), multicolor flowers on base perugia, white single-handled pitcher.. $11–16

DIANA DECANTER (1956), white figure of Diana with deer on black, single-handled decanter $11–16

DOGAL SILVER AND GREEN DECANTER (1952–56), handpainted gondola $14–19

DOGAL SILVER RUBY (1952–56), handpainted gondola, silver band neck $14–18

DOGAL SILVER RUBY DECANTER (1956), handpainted Venetian scene and flowers $17–22

DOGAL SILVER SMOKE DECANTER (1952–55), handpainted gondola....... $14–19

DOGAL SILVER SMOKE DECANTER (1953–54), handpainted gondola....... $11–16

DOGAL SILVER SMOKE DECANTER (1956), handpainted silver clouds and gondola... $11–16

DOGAL SILVER SMOKE DECANTER (1956), handpainted gondola, buildings, flowers, neck bands $14–18

DOLPHIN FIGURAL (1959), yellow, green, blue $42–57

"DOUGHNUT" BOTTLE (1960), CLOCK BOTTLE (1959), cherry Este working clock in doughnut-shaped bottle...$15–20

DRAGON AMPHORA (1953), two-handled white decanter with colorful dragon and flowers $10–15

DRAGON PITCHER (1958), one handle, white pitcher, color dragon, and scroll work.. $14–18

DUCK-GREEN GLASS FIGURAL (1960), green and amber duck, clear glass base $35–45

EAGLE (1970) $45–55

EGYPTIAN SPECIALTY (1960), two-handled amphora, Egyptian design on tan and gold background $14–19

ETRUSCAN DECANTER (1959), single-handled black Greek design on tan background $14–19

    Except A, earthen brown $13–18

EUGANEAN BRONZE (1952–55) $14–19

EUGANEAN COPPERED (1952–55), Majolica................................ $13–18

FAENZA DECANTER (1952–56), colorful country scene on white single-handled decanter $21–28

FIGHTING COCKS (1962), combination decanter and ashtray, black and red fighting birds.. $14–19

FISH—GREEN AND GOLD GLASS FIGURAL (1960), green, silver, and gold, clear glass base $30–40

FISH—RUBY MURANO GLASS FIGURAL (1961), ruby-red tones of glass...$30–40

FLORENTINE MAJOLICA (1956), round-handled decanter, painted pitcher, yellow, dragon, blue wings $20–30

GAMBIA (1961), black princess, kneeling holding tray, gold trim. 10¾" .. $8–12

GOLDEN FAKIR, seated snake charmer, with flute and snakes, ...

    1961, gold $26–37

    1960, black and gray $26–37

GONDOLA (1959), highly glazed abstract gondola and gondolier in black, orange, and yellow; stopper on upper prow. 12¾" $21–27

GONDOLA (1960), same as 1959, stopper moved from prow to stern $14–19

GRAPES, PEAR FIGURAL..$24–34

MAYAN (1960), a Mayan temple god head mask; brown, yellow, black, white. 11" $15–25

MOSAIC ASHTRAY (1959), combination decanter ashtray; mosaic pattern of rearing horse ....

    Black, yellow, green. 11½" $15–25

    Black, green; miniature. 6" $10–14

NUBIAN, kneeling black figure, gold dress and headdress

    9½" $14–19

    As above, miniature. 4¾" $6–10

OPAL MAJOLICA (1957), two gold handles, translucent opal top, pink base; also used as lamp base. 10" $14–19

PENGUIN MURANO GLASS FIGURAL (1968), black and white penguin, crystal base $25–30

PHEASANT MURANO GLASS FIGURAL (1960), red and clear glass on a crystal base $35–45

PHEASANT RED AND GOLD FIGURAL (1960), red and gold glass bird on crystal base $40–60

PRIMAVERA AMPHORA (1958), two-handled vase shape, with floral design in yellow, green, and blue. 9¾" $14–19

PUPPY CUCCIOLO GLASS FIGURAL (1961), amber and green glass $26–37

PUPPY MURANO GLASS FIGURAL (1960), amber glass, crystal base $26–37

SILVER BLUE DECANTER (1952–55), handpainted silver flowers and leaves.......
....$22–28

SILVER BROWN DECANTER (1952–55), handpainted silver flowers and leaves.....
....$26–37

SIR LANCELOT (1962), figure of English knight in full armor with embossed shield, tan-gray with gold. 12" $14–19

SPRINGBOX AMPHORA (1952), vase with handle; leaping African deer with floral and lattice background; black, brown. 9¾" $14–19
SQUIRREL GLASS FIGURAL (1968), amethyst-colored squirrel on crystal base..... ....$40–50
SUDAN (1960), two-handled classic vase, incised figures, African motif in browns, blue, yellow, and gray. 13½" $14–19
TORRE ROSA (1962), rose-tinted tower of fruit. 10¼" $16–24
TORRE TINTA (1962), multicolor tower of fruit, natural shades............. $18–22
TOWER OF FRUIT (1968), various fruits in natural colors. 22¼" $16–24
TOWER OF FRUIT MAJOLICAS TORRE BIANCA (1962), white and gray tower of fruit. 10¼" $16–24

McCORMICK BOTTLES

The McCormick bottles are made for retailing McCormick Irish Whiskey. There are four different series: Cars, Famous Americans, Frontiersmen Decanters, and Gunfighters. The category for cars includes various forms of transportation. The lengthiest series has been the Famous American, encompassing celebrities from Colonial times to the 20th century. Released in limited numbers, the prices on all of the McCormicks are automatically higher than most figurals.

BARREL SERIES

BARREL (1958), with stand and shot glasses $25–30
BARREL (1968), with stand and plain hoops $14–18
BARREL (1968), with stand and gold hoops $18–26

BIRD SERIES

BLUE JAY (1971) $20–25
CANADIAN GOOSE, miniature $18–25
GAMBEL'S QUAIL (1982) $45–55
RING NECK PHEASANT (1982) $45–55
WOOD DUCK (1980) 30–35

CAR SERIES

PACKARD (1937) $25–35
THE PONY EXPRESS...$20–25
THE SAND BUGGY COMMEMORATIVE DECANTER $35–50

CONFEDERATE SERIES

JEB STUART $25–35
JEFFERSON DAVIS..$25–30
ROBERT E. LEE...$25–35
STONEWALL JACKSON $25–35

COUNTRY AND WESTERN SERIES

HANK WILLIAMS, SR. (1980) $50–55
HANK WILLIAMS, JR. (1980)...$70–80
TOM T. HALL (1980) $32–42

ELVIS PRESLEY SERIES

ELVIS '55 (1979) $40–50
ELVIS '55, mini $25–35
ELVIS '55 (1980), mini..$20–30
ELVIS '68 (1980) $40–50
ELVIS '68 (1981), mini..$25–35
ELVIS '77 (1978) $65–80
ELVIS '77 (1979), mini..$32–40
ELVIS BUST (1978)..$24–35
ELVIS DESIGNER I, music box plays *Are You Lonesome Tonight?* $85–100
ELVIS DESIGNER II, music box plays *It's Now or Never*...................$140–160
ELVIS GOLD (1979) $180–220
ELVIS KARATE $100–130
ELVIS SERGEANT $190–210
ELVIS SILVER (1980)..$120–135

FAMOUS AMERICAN
PORTRAIT SERIES

ABE LINCOLN, with law book in hand $35–45
ALEXANDER GRAHAM BELL, with apron...$10–15
CAPTAIN JOHN SMITH $12–20
CHARLES LINDBERGH $24–28
ELEANOR ROOSEVELT...$12–20
GEORGE WASHINGTON CARVER $28–40
HENRY FORD...$20–25
LEWIS MERIWETHER...$16–20
POCAHONTAS...$30–42
ROBERT E. PERRY...$26–35
THOMAS EDISON...$33–44
ULYSSES S. GRANT, with coffee pot and cup....................................$15–25
WILLIAM CLARK $14–18

FOOTBALL MASCOTS

ALABAMA BAMAS	$26–34
ARIZONA SUN DEVILS	$39–48
ARIZONA WILDCATS	$21–27
ARKANSAS HOGS (1972)	$42–48
AUBURN WAR EAGLES	$16–24
BAYLOR BEARS (1972)	$24–30
CALIFORNIA BEARS	$20–25
DRAKE BULLDOGS (1974), blue helmet and jersey	$14–19
GEORGIA BULLDOGS, black helmet and red jersey	$12–19
GEORGIA TECH YELLOWJACKETS	$15–25
HOUSTON COUGARS (1972)	$20–30
INDIANA HOOSIERS (1974)	$14–24
IOWA CYCLONES (1974)	$45–55
IOWA HAWKEYES (1974)	$60–70
IOWA PURPLE PANTHERS	$32–42
LOUISIANA STATE TIGERS (1974)	$14–19
MICHIGAN STATE SPARTANS	$15–20
MICHIGAN WOLVERINES (1974)	$15–25
MINNESOTA GOPHERS (1974)	$8–12
MISSISSIPPI REBELS (1974)	$8–12
MISSISSIPPI STATE BULLDOGS (1974), red helmet and jersey	$12–18
NEBRASKA CORNHUSKERS (1974)	$12–18
NEBRASKA FOOTBALL PLAYER	$35–45
NEBRASKA, Johnny Rogers, No. 1	$230–260
NEW MEXICO LOBO	$32–40
OKLAHOMA SOONERS WAGON (1974)	$20–28
OKLAHOMA SOUTHER COWBOY (1974)	$14–18
OREGON BEAVERS (1974)	$10–18
OREGON DUCKS (1974)	$12–18
PURDUE BOILERMAKER (1974)	$15–25
RICE OWLS (1972)	$20–30
SMU MUSTANGS (1972)	$17–24
TCU HORNED FROGS (1972)	$25–30
TENNESSEE VOLUNTEERS (1974)	$8–12
TEXAS A & M AGGIES (1972)	$22–30
TEXAS TECH RAIDERS (1972)	$20–26
TEXAS HORNS (1972)	$23–33
WASHINGTON COUGARS (1974)	$20–25
WASHINGTON HUSKIES (1974)	$15–25
WISCONSIN BADGERS (1974)	$15–25

FRONTIERSMEN COMMEMORATIVE DECANTERS, 1972

DANIEL BOONE	$15–22
DAVY CROCKETT	$17–25
JIM BOWIE	$12–15
KIT CARSON	$14–18

GENERAL

A & P Wagon $50–56
Airplane (1969), Spirit of St. Louis $60–80
American Bald Eagle (1982) $30–40
American Legion Cincinnati (1986) $25–35
Buffalo Bill (1979) $70–80
Cable Car $25–30
Car (1980), Packard 1937, black or cream; first in a series of classic cars, rolling
wheels, and vinyl seats $30–40
Chair, Queen Anne $20–30
Ciao Baby (1978) $20–25
Clock (1971), cuckoo $25–35
De Witt Clinton Engine (1970) $40–50
French Telephone (1969) $20–28
Globe (1971), Angelica $25–32
Henry Ford (1977) $20–24
Hutchinson Kansas Centennial (1972) $15–25
Jester (1972) $20–28
Jimmy Durante (1981), with music box, plays *Inka Dinka Do* $31–40
Joplin Miner (1972) $15–25
JR Ewing (1980), with music box, plays theme song from "Dallas" $22–27
JR Ewing, gold-colored $50–55
Julia Bulette (1974) $140–160
Lamp, hurricane $13–18
Largemouth Bass (1982) $20–28
Lobsterman (1979) $20–30
Louis Armstrong $60–70
Mark Twain (1977) $18–22
Mark Twain, mini $13–18
McCormick Centennial (1956) $80–120
Mikado (1980) $60–80
Missouri Sesquicentennial China (1970) $5–7
Missouri Sesquicentennial Glass (1971) $3–7
Ozark Ike (1979) $22–27
Paul Bunyan (1979) $25–30
Pioneer Theatre (1972) $8–12
Pony Express (1978) $20–25
Renault Racer (1969) $40–50
Sam Houston (1977) $22–28
Stephen F. Austin (1977) $14–18
Telephone Operator $45–55
Thelma Lu (1982) $25–35
US Marshal (1979) $25–35
Will Rogers (1977) $18–22
Yacht Americana (1971) $30–38

GUNFIGHTER SERIES

Bat Masterson $20–30

BILLY THE KID $25-30
BLACK BART $26-35
CALAMITY JANE $25-30
DOC HOLIDAY $25-35
JESSE JAMES..$20-30
WILD BILL HICKOK $21-30
WYATT EARP..$21-30

JUG SERIES

BOURBON JUG $62-70
GIN JUG $6-10
OLD HOLIDAY BOURBON (1956), embossed lettering in various sizes $6-18
PLATTE VALLEY (1953), traditional jug shape with two small handles from shoulders to neck..$3-6
PLATTE VALLEY, ½ pt. $3-4
VODKA JUG...$6-10

KING ARTHUR SERIES

KING ARTHUR ON THRONE...$30-40
MERLIN THE WIZARD WITH HIS WISE OLD MAGICAL ROBE (c. 1979)....$25-35
QUEEN GUINEVERE, THE GEM OF ROYAL COURT $12-18
SIR LANCELOT OF THE LAKE IN ARMOR, A KNIGHT OF ROUNDTABLE... $12-18

THE LITERARY SERIES

HUCK FINN (1980), sits fishing, leaning on a tree trunk, and smoking a pipe
....$20-25
TOM SAWYER (1980), stands in front of a fence scratching his head $22-26

MINIATURES

CHARLES LINDBERGH MINIATURE (1978).......................................$10-14
CONFEDERATES MINIATURE SET (FOUR) (1978) $40-50
HENRY FORD MINIATURE (1978)..$10-14
MARK TWAIN MINIATURE (1978) $12-18
MINIATURE GUNFIGHTERS (EIGHT) (1977).....................................$110-140
MINIATURE NOBLE (1978)..$14-20
MINIATURE SPIRIT OF '76 (1977)...$15-25
PATRIOT MINIATURE SET (EIGHT) (1976) $250-350
PONY EXPRESS MINIATURE (1980)..$15-18
WILL ROGERS MINIATURE (1978) $12-16

THE PATRIOTS

BENJAMIN FRANKLIN (1975) $13-17
BETSY ROSS (1975)..$20-25

GEORGE WASHINGTON (1975)..$20–27
JOHN HANCOCK (1975)..$14–18
JOHN PAUL JONES (1975) $15–20
PATRICK HENRY (1975)..$14–18
PATRICK HENRY, miniature $12–15
PAUL REVERE (1975) $20–25
SPIRIT OF '76 (1976) $50–60
THOMAS JEFFERSON (1975) $14–18

PIRATES SERIES

PIRATE, No. 1 (1972) $10–12
PIRATE, No. 2 (1972) $10–12
PIRATE, No. 3 (1972) $8–12
PIRATE, No. 4 (1972) $8–12
PIRATE, No. 5 (1972) $8–12
PIRATE, No. 6 (1972) $8–12
PIRATE, No. 7 (1972) $8–12
PIRATE, No. 8 (1972) $8–12
PIRATE, No. 9 (1972) $8–12
PIRATE, No. 10 (1972) $20–28
PIRATE, No. 11 (1972) $20–28
PIRATE, No. 12 (1972) $20–28

RURAL AMERICANA SERIES

WOMAN FEEDING CHICKENS (1980), young woman with white bonnet and apron
tossing feed; two chickens at her feet..$25–35
WOMAN WASHING CLOTHES (1980), sitting on a low table.................$30–40

SHRINE SERIES

CIRCUS...$20–35
DUNE BUGGY (1976) $25–35
IMPERIAL COUNCIL $20–25
JESTER (MIRTH KING) (1972) $30–40
THE NOBLE (1976) $25–32

SPORTS SERIES

AIR RACE PROPELLER (1971) $15–20
AIR RACE PYLON (1970)..$10–15
JOHNNY RODGERS No. 1 (1972)...$160–195
JOHNNY RODGERS No. 2 (1973)...$70–85
KC CHIEFS (1969) $18–25
KC ROYALS (1971) $10–15
MUHAMMUD ALI (1980) $20–30
NEBRASKA FOOTBALL PLAYER (1972) $35–45
SKIBOB (1971) $10–11

TRAIN SERIES

JUPITER ENGINE (1969)..$20–25
MAIL CAR (1970) $25–28
PASSENGER CAR (1970) $35–45
WOOD TENDER (1969)..$14–18

DESTROYED BOTTLES

FAMOUS AMERICANS (c. 1976)
FRONTIERSMEN SERIES (c. 1975)
GUNFIGHTER SERIES (c. 1972)
PATRIOT DECANTERS (c. 1976)

OLD BLUE RIBBON (OBR) BOTTLES

Old Blue Ribbon (OBR) bottles are made to contain the company's liquors. With a relatively late start in issuing figural bottles, this firm has released a large number in recent years. The OBR bottles with historical themes are distinctive for their realism, such as the Jupiter '60 series depicting various railroad cars from the 19th century. OBR is the only bottle maker with a Hockey series; each bottle in this group relates to a different professional hockey team. The company also issues a Transportation series, which includes such diverse representations as a hot-air balloon and a 5th Avenue New York bus.

AIR RACE DECANTER (PYLON) $18–26
BLUE BIRD $14–19
CABOOSE MKT...$20–30
EASTERN KENTUCKY UNIVERSITY...$15–21
JUPITER '60 MAIL CAR $13–17
JUPITER '60 PASSENGER CAR..$16–23
JUPITER '60 WOOD TENDER..$13–17
JUPITER '60 LOCOMOTIVE $15–22
KC ROYALS...$19–26
PIERCE ARROW $13–15
SANTA MARIA COLUMBUS SHIP $15–20
TITANIC OCEAN LINER...$35–45

TRANSPORTATION SERIES

BALLOON $9–12
5TH AVE BUS $14–21
PRAIRIE SCHOONER $10–11
RIVER QUEEN $10–15
RIVER QUEEN, gold $20–25

HOCKEY SERIES

BOSTON BRUINS $14–18
CHICAGO BLACK HAWKS $14–18
DETROIT RED WINGS $14–18
MINNESOTA NORTH STARS $14–18
NEW YORK RANGERS $14–18
ST. LOUIS BLUES $14–18

OLD COMMONWEALTH BOTTLES

The brand name Old Commonwealth is produced by J.P. Van Winkle and Son. Opening in 1974, it was one of the newer companies involved in producing collector decanters with high-quality whiskey. The company presently bottles its products at the Hoffman Distilling Co., located in Lawrenceburg, Kentucky. Their ceramic decanters are manufactured in the Orient, but they brew their own 80-proof Kentucky bourbon whiskey, which is distributed nationally.

Their decanters are easily identified because the titles of most pieces appear on front plaques. The first Old Commonwealth mini piece was made in 1980 when a small version of Coal Miner No. 1 was offered. Today, the majority of the decanters are produced in regular and miniature sizes.

ALABAMA CRIMSON TIDE (1981), University of Alabama symbol; front of elephant thrusting through a large red "A," elephant's foot propped on top of a football, "Crimson Tide" printed on the front $23–30
BULLDOGS (1982), the mascot of the Georgia Bulldogs; front portion of a bulldog stands in the center of a large "G" with one front paw propped on a football $20–30
CHIEF ILLINI NO. 1 (1979), the mascot for the University of Illionois; warrior stands with arms up and spread wide, dressed in beige buckskin and ceremonial warbonnet $70–85

CHIEF ILLINI NO. 2 (1981), the mascot of the University of Illinois; warrior running with arms flung back to the sides, dressed in beige buckskins and orange feathered headdress; a large letter "I" in orange and blue stands behind him $55-65

CHIEF ILLINI NO. 3 (1979)..$65-75

COAL MINER NO. 1 (1975), man stands holding shovel in one hand and other hand on jacket; bucket of coal at his feet $80-100
   Mini (1980) $20-30

COAL MINER NO. 2 (1976), man stands with pick in one hand and a lantern in the other; wears blue mining outfit with red kerchief; plaque reads "Old Time Coal Miner"...$20-30
   Mini (1982) $19-23

COAL MINER NO. 3 (1977), miner kneels on one leg, holding a shovel in one hand and coal in the other hand; bucket of coal at his feet $28-36
   Mini (1981)..$20-25

COAL MINER—LUNCH TIME NO. 4 (1980), miner sits eating lunch, red apple in one hand; wears blue overalls and red miner's hat $33-43
   Mini $15-20

COTTONTAIL (1981), jumping rabbit lands on front feet with hind feet extended in the air; short stump $25-35

ELUSIVE LEPRECHAUN (1980), leprechaun sits on top of a pot of gold with arms wrapped around bent knees; wears dark green hat and boots, and red jacket $24-30

FISHERMAN, "A KEEPER" (1980), old man sits holding fish in both hands, his pole tucked in one arm; fishing tackle sits on the ground...................$20-30

GOLDEN RETRIEVER (1979), dog sits with game lying between front feet........ ....$30-40

KENTUCKY THOROUGHBREDS (1976), red mare and colt with dark manes and tails, prancing on blue grass..$30-40

KENTUCKY WILDCAT $32-42

LSU TIGER (1979), the mascot for Louisiana State University; ferocious tiger stands with front legs resting on stone structure, a football under one paw, "LSU" in yellow on structure $45-55

LUMBERJACK...$15-25

MISSOURI TIGER...$35-45

OLD RIP VAN WINKLE NO. 1 (1974), old man sits on stump with legs crossed and musket held across his lap; wears green hat and jacket, and red pants....... ....$40-50

OLD RIP VAN WINKLE NO. 2 (1975), old man sprawled with his back resting against a stump, sleeping, musket held between crossed hand.............$35-45

OLD RIP VAN WINKLE NO. 3 (1977), old man stands stroking his long white beard, musket propped on ground, held in crook of arm; wears tattered clothes $30-40

POINTING SETTER DECANTER (1965), dog on point; brown, tan, and white; glass. 12″ $16-23

QUAIL ON THE WING DECANTER (1968), round glass bottle, three-color design. 12″ $7-12

REBEL YELL RIDER (c. 1970), figurine, Confederate cavalryman bottle in six colors, sold only in the South. 9¾″ $23-32

RIP VAN WINKLE FIGURINE (1970), famous Catskill character with blunderbuss and elf, multicolor. 9¼″ $32–40
SONGS OF IRELAND (1972), porcelain...$15–20
SONS OF ERIN (1969), porcelain $6–9
SOUTH CAROLINA TRICENTENNIAL (1970)......................................$12–19
TENNESSEE WALKING HORSE (1977), black prancing horse, red and yellow bridle, stands on aqua green grass...$24–35
USC TROJAN (1980), the mascot for the University of Southern California; a warrior stands at base of pillar with sword, shield, and Trojan helmet ...$45–55
   Mini $11–16
WELLER MASTERPIECE (1963), white porcelain apothecary bottle, rebus design, gold bands. 10⅝″ $26–35
WESTERN BOOT DECANTER (1982), replica of a brown leather boot with exact shading. 10½″ $20–25
   Mini. 4″ $8–12
WESTERN LOGGER (1980), man stands on log, holding a logger's tool in one hand and an axe in the other hand $25–34
WILDCATS (1982), the mascot for Kansas State; front portion of figure thrusts through a large letter ''K'' with front paw propped on a football $40–46
WINGS ACROSS THE CONTINENT (1972), porcelain, duck finial............$16–23
YANKEE DOODLE, Yankee figure wearing blue pants, white shirt, yellow vest, and black hat rides brown pony, on large stand with brick fence, plaque on front with part of the song, music box plays *Yankee Doodle*. 11″ $25–32

MODERN FIREFIGHTERS SERIES

Note: The following are listed consecutively by number.

MODERN HERO NO. 1 (1982), stands clutching an axe and oxygen mask, wears black firefighting outfit with yellow stripes, number ''1'' on helmet. 12″ $25–35
   Mini $8–12
THE NOZZLEMAN NO. 2 (1982), firefighter kneels on rubble of bricks, holding fire hose; wears oxygen mask over face and yellow tank on his back; number ''2'' on helmet. 9½″ $30–40
   Mini. 5″ $17–24
ON CALL NO. 3 (1982), pair of black firefighting boots with yellow toes, red helmet rests on top of boots, number ''3'' on helmet. 8½″ $45–55
   Mini $15–24
FALLEN COMRADE NO. 4 (1982), pair of firefighters with one unconscious on his back, the other kneels next to him while placing an oxygen mask over the victim's face; kneeling firefighter wears helmet with the number ''4.'' 7″ $30–40
   Mini. 3½″ $17–25

WATERFOWLER SERIES

Note: The following are listed consecutively by number.

WATERFOWLER NO. 1 (1979), hunter with shotgun slung under one arm and two ducks held in the other hand, wears beige hunter's jacket and hat........$40–50
HERE THEY COME NO. 2 (1980), hunter kneels in front on log, aiming his shotgun; black hunting dog sits at his side..$32–42

GOOD BOY NO. 3 (1981), hunter kneels beside tree stump with shotgun in one hand and the other hand cradling a retrieved duck hanging from the mouth of a black bird dog $32–42

OLD FITZGERALD BOTTLES

Old Fitzgerald bottles are made by the Old Fitzgerald Distilling Co. to contain their whiskey and bourbon. Old Fitzgeralds are sometimes called Old Cabin Still bottles after one of the brand names under which they are sold. The company issues both decanter-style and figural bottles. The decanters are ceramics in various styles and colors. Its figurals portray many different Irish and American subjects. New figurals are added to the line irregularly. The number of bottles issued by this firm is small.

AMERICAS CUP COMMEMORATIVE (1970) $15–22
BLARNEY CASTLE (1970), porcelain $12–19
BROWSING DEER DECANTER (1967), deer and woods scene; brown, tan, and white; amber stopper..$15–22
CALIFORNIA BICENTENNIAL (1970) $15–22
CANDLELITE DECANTER (1955), removable gold candle holder mounted on flint glass, pair $9–12
COLONIAL DECANTER (1969), glass $4–7
CROWN DECANTER $5–9
GOLD COASTER DECANTER (1954), flint glass decanter, gold metal coaster.......
....$10–15
"GOLDEN BOUGH" DECANTER (1971), glass $4–9
GOLD WEB DECANTER (1953), flint glass, gold web and frame fused onto decanter $10–16
HILLBILLY (1969), same bottle as 1954 Hillbilly; more detail and color. 11½"
....$13–18
HILLBILLY BOTTLE (1954), pt., hillbilly on barrel with rifle; in brown, tan, black, and green. 9⅛" $13–18
HILLBILLY BOTTLE (1954), qt., same as above. 11⅜" $13–18
HILLBILLY BOTTLE (1954), gal., same as above, very rare $60–85
JEWEL DECANTER (1951–52), flint glass, beveled neck $9–15
LEAPING TROUT DECANTER (1969) $11–16
LEPRECHAUN BOTTLE (1968), porcelain bottle; gold band, green shamrocks, Irish verse. 10⅛" $25–32
LSU ALUMNI DECANTER (1970) $25–32
MAN O'WAR DECANTER (1969), glass $5–9
MEMPHIS COMMEMORATIVE (1969), porcelain $8–12
NEBRASKA (1971) $27–32
NEBRASKA (1972) $18–25
OHIO STATE CENTENNIAL (1970) $12–18

Old Fitzgerald, Rip Van Winkle. PHOTO COURTESY
OF DAVE SMITH.

OLD CABIN STILL DECANTER (1958), gold letters "Old Cabin Still" infused on
flint glass bottle; solid faceted stopper..$16–23
PILGRIM LANDING COMMEMORATIVE (1970) $14–24

SKI COUNTRY BOTTLES

Ski Country produces limited edition bottles in two sizes—regular and
miniature. The company offers many different bottle series including
Indians, owls, game birds, and Christmas and customer specialties. The
bottles manufactured by Ski Country are exquisitely detailed and highly
sought after by collectors.

ANIMALS

BADGER FAMILY...$35–45
 Mini $16–24

Ski Country, fox on a log. PHOTO COURTESY OF
DAVE SMITH.

Bobcat Family	$45–60
Mini	$16–25
Coyote Family	$37–48
Mini	$17–23
Kangaroo	$22–32
Mini	$18–28
Koala	$20–28
Raccoon	$36–45
Mini	$25–30
Skunk Family	$40–50
Mini	$22–26
Snow Leopard	$36–43
Mini	$30–35

BIRDS

Blackbird	$34–40
Mini	$29–30
Black Swan	$30–35
Mini	$18–24
Blue Jay	$50–60
Mini	$42–49
Cardinal	$55–70
Mini	$35–45
Condor	$45–55
Mini	$25–30
Gamecocks	$120–130
Mini	$40–46
Gila Woodpecker	$55–65
Mini	$26–32
Peace Dove	$50–60
Mini	$20–26
Peacock	$80–100
Mini	$45–60
Penguin Family	$45–55
Mini	$21–27
Wood Duck	$175–200
Mini	$125–150

CHRISTMAS

Bob Cratchit	$40–50
Mini	$25–30
Mrs. Cratchit	40–50
Mini	$25–30
Scrooge	$40–50
Mini	$15–20

Ski Country, Ring Master,
P.T. Barnum. PHOTO COURTESY OF
DAVE SMITH.

CIRCUS

CLOWN	$44–52
Mini	$27–33
ELEPHANT ON DRUM	$35–45
Mini	$35–45
JENNY LIND, blue dress	$55–75
Mini	$48–60
LION ON DRUM	$31–36
Mini	$23–28
PALOMINO HORSE	$40–48
Mini	$30–40
P.T. BARNUM	$32–40
Mini	$20–25
RINGMASTER	$20–25
Mini	$15–18
TIGER ON BALL	$35–44
Mini	$31–37
TOM THUMB	$20–25
Mini	$16–21

CUSTOMER SPECIALTIES

AHRENS-FOX FIRE ENGINE	$140–180
BONNIE AND CLYDE, pair	$60–70
Mini, pair	$55–62
CAVEMAN	$16–23
Mini	$18–22
MILL RIVER COUNTRY CLUB	$38–47
OLYMPIC SKIER, gold	$85–110
OLYMPIC SKIER, red	$23–30
Mini, red	$30–35
OLYMPIC SKIER, blue	$25–32
Mini, blue	$35–40
POLITICAL DONKEY AND ELEPHANT	$50–60

DOMESTIC ANIMALS

BASSET HOUND $45–55
   Mini $26–32
HOLSTEIN COW..$45–60

EAGLES, FALCONS, AND HAWKS

BIRTH OF FREEDOM $85–95
   Mini $65–75
EAGLE ON THE WATER $90–110
   Mini $38–45
EASTER SEALS EAGLE $48–60
   Mini $22–29
FALCON GALLON $350–425
GYRFALCON $54–60
   Mini $27–34
HARPY EAGLE $85–105
   Mini $80–95
MOUNTAIN EAGLE $130–150
   Mini $100–120
OSPREY HAWK..$140–160
   Mini $100–120
PEREGRINE FALCON..$75–85
   Mini $18–25
PRAIRIE FALCON...$65–80
   Mini $35–48
RED SHOULDER HAWK $60–70
   Mini $34–40
REDTAIL HAWK..$75–95
   Mini $33–40
WHITE FALCON $68–75
   Mini $30–40

FISH

MUSKELLUNGE $30–37
   Mini $17–21
RAINBOW TROUT $40–50
   Mini $24–30
SALMON..$30–35
   Mini $18–22
TROUT, mini, brown..$27–32

GAME BIRDS

BANDED MALLARD...$50–60

Ski Country, trout. PHOTO COURTESY OF
DAVE SMITH.

CHUKAR PARTRIDGE $33–40
  Mini $16–21
KING EIDER DUCK $50–60
MALLARD (1973) $50–60
PHEASANT, standing, mini $52–62
PHEASANT, golden $40–45
  Mini $24–30
PHEASANT IN THE CORN $50–60
  Mini $30–39
PHEASANTS FIGHTING $70–80
  Mini $35–45
PHEASANTS FIGHTING, ½ gal. $145–165
PINTAIL $76–85
PRAIRIE CHICKEN $55–65
RUFFED GROUSE $40–50
  Mini $22–28
TURKEY $80–100
  Mini $100–120

GRAND SLAM

DESERT SHEEP $75–90
  Mini $25–30
MOUNTAIN SHEEP $50–60
  Mini $24–30
STONE SHEEP $50–65
  Mini $27–34

HORNED AND ANTLERED ANIMALS

ANTELOPE $45–60
BIG-HORN RAM $65–75
  Mini $25–31
MOUNTAIN GOAT $30–45
  Mini $38–48
MOUNTAIN GOAT, gal. $525–600

White Tail Deer $30–95
  Mini $34–40

INDIANS

Ceremonial Antelope Dancer..$52–62
  Mini $36–45
Ceremonial Buffalo Dancer $150–185
  Mini $32–38
Ceremonial Deer Dancer $85–100
  Mini $40–48
Ceremonial Eagle Dancer..$185–205
  Mini $24–34
Ceremonial Falcon Dancer $85–100
  Mini $35–45
Ceremonial Wolf Dancer..$50–60
  Mini $32–40
Chief No. 1 ....$105–125
  Mini $14–20
Chief No. 2 ....$105–125
  Mini $14–20
Cigar Store Indian $32–40
Dancers Of The Southwest, set $250–300
  Mini $140–175

OWLS

Barn Owl $48–55
  Mini $20–24
Great Gray Owl $48–55
  Mini $20–25
Horned Owl..$60–70
  Mini $70–80
Horned Owl, gal. $700–800
Saw Whet Owl $40–45
  Mini $20–25
Screech Owl Family $80–90
  Mini $68–75
Spectacled Owl $70–85
  Mini $58–68

RODEO

Barrel Racer $58–68
  Mini $20–26
Bull Rider..$42–49
  Mini $22–28
Wyoming Bronco $48–66
  Mini $25–35

APPENDIXES

APPENDIX A: TRADEMARKS

FOREIGN

A in a circle: Alembic Glass Industries, Bangalore, India.

A (big) in center of italic GM: Australian Glass Mfg. Co., Kilkenny, So. Australia.

A.B.C.: Albion Bottle Co. Ltd., Oldbury, Nr. Birmingham, England.

A G B Co: Albion Glass Bottle Co., England; trademark is found under Lea & Perrins, circa 1880–1900.

A.G.W.: Alloa Glass Limited, Alloa, Scotland.

AVH-A.: Van Hoboken & Co., Rotterdam, The Netherlands, 1800–1898.

B & Co. L: Bagley & Co., Ltd., est. 1832, still operating (England).

Beaver: Beaver Flint Glass Co., Toronto, Ontario, Canada, circa 1897–1920.

Bottle in frame: Veb Glasvoerk Drebkau Drebkau, N.L. Germany.

Crown with figure of a crown: Excelsior Glass Co., St. Johns, Quebec, and later Diamond Glass Co., Montreal, Quebec, Canada, circa 1879–1913.

Crown with three dots: Crown Glass, Waterloo, N.S. Wales.

CS & Co.: Cannington, Shaw & Co., St. Helens, England, circa 1872–1916.

D in center of a diamond: Dominion Glass Co., Montreal, Quebec, Canada.

D.B.: In a book frame, Dale Brown & Co., Ltd., Mesborough, Yorks, England.

Excelsior: Excelsior Glass Co., St. John, Quebec, Canada, 1878–1883.

Fish: Veb Glasvoerk Stralau, Berlin.

Hamilton: Hamilton Glass Works, Hamilton, Ontario, Canada, 1865–1872.

Hat: Brougba, Bulgaria.

HH: Werk Hermannshutte, Czechoslovakia.

Hunyadi Janos: Andreas Saxlehner, Buda-Pesth, Austria-Hungary, circa 1863–1900.

IYGE all in a circle: The Irish Glass Bottle, Ltd., Dublin.

KH: Kastrupog Holmeqaads, Copenhagen.

L. on a bell: Lambert S.A., Belgium.

LIP: Lea & Perrins, London, England, 1880–1900.

LS in a circle: Lax & Shaw, Ltd., Leeds, York, England.

M in a circle: Cristales Mexicanos, Monterey, Mexico.

N in a diamond: Tippon Glass Co., Ltd., Tokyo, Japan.

NAGC: North American Glass Co., Montreal, Quebec, Canada, 1883–1890.

PG: Verreries De Puy De Dome, S.A. Paris.

R: Louis Freres & Co., France, circa 1870–1890.

S in a circle: Vetreria Savonese. A. Voglienzone, S.A. Milano, Italy.

S.A.V.A. all in a circle: Asmara, Ethiopia.

S & M: Sykes & Macvey, Castleford, England, 1860–1888.

T in a circle: Tokyo Seibin Co., Ltd., Tokyo, Japan.

vFo: Vidreria Ind. Figuerras Oliveiras, Brazil.

VT: Ve-Tri S.p.a., Vetrerie Triventa, Vicenza, Italy.

VX: Usine de Vauxrot, France.

WECK in a frame: Weck Glaswerk G.mb.H, ofligen, Bonn.

Y in a circle: Etairia Lipasmaton, Athens, Greece.

UNITED STATES

The words and letters in italic are only a representation or brief description of the trademark as it appeared on a bottle. This is followed by the complete name and location of the company and the approximate period of time in which the trademark was in use.

A: John Agnew & Son, Pittsburgh, PA, 1854–1866.

A in a circle: American Glass Works, Richmond, VA, and Paden City, WV, circa 1909–1936.

A in a circle: Armstrong Cork Co., Glass Division, Lancaster, PA, 1938–1968.

A & B together (AB): Adolphus Busch Glass Mfg. Co., Belleville, IL, and St. Louis, MO, circa 1904–1907.

A & Co.: John Agnew & Co., Pittsburgh, PA; Indian Queen, Ear of Corn, and other flasks, circa 1854–1892.

A B Co.: American Bottle Co., Chicago, IL, 1905–1930.

A B G M Co.: Adolphus Busch Glass Mfg. Co., Bellville, IL, and St. Louis, MO, circa 1886–1928.

A C M E: Acme Glass Co., Olean, NY, circa 1920–1930.

A & D H C: A. & D.H. Chambers, Pittsburgh, PA; Union flasks, circa 1842–1886.

AGEE and Agee in script: Hazel Atlas Glass Co., Wheeling, WV, circa 1921–1925.

A.G.W. Co.: American Glass Works, Ltd., 1880–1905.

AGW: American Glass Works, circa 1880.

Anchor figure with H in center: Anchor Hocking Glass Corp., Lancaster, OH, circa 1955.

A.R.S.: A.R. Samuels Glass Co., Philadelphia, PA, circa 1855–1872.

A S F W W Va.: A.S. Frank Glass Co., Wellsburg, WV, circa 1859.

ATLAS: Atlas Glass Co., Washington, PA, and later Hazel Atlas Glass Co., 1896–1965.

AVH: A. Van Hoboken & Co., Rotterdam, The Netherlands, 1800–1898.

Ball and Ball in script: Ball Bros. Glass Mfg. Co., Muncie, IN, and later Ball Corp., 1887–1973.

Bernardin in script: W.J. Latchford Glass Co., Los Angeles, CA, circa 1932–1938.

The Best: Gillender & Sons, Philadelphia, PA, circa 1867–1870.

B F B Co.: Bell Fruit Bottle Co., Fairmount, IN, circa 1910.

B.G. Co.: Belleville Glass Co., IL, circa 1882.

Bishop's: Bishop & Co., San Diego and Los Angeles, CA, 1890–1920.

B K: Benedict Kimber, Bridgeport and Brownsville, PA, circa 1822–1840.

Boyds in script: Illinois Glass Co., Alton, IL, circa 1900–1930.

Brelle (in script) Jar: Brelle Fruit Jar Mfg. Co., San Jose, CA, circa 1912–1916.

Brilliantine: Jefferis Glass Co., Fairton, NJ, and Rochester, PA, circa 1900–1905.

C in a circle: Chattanooga Bottle & Glass Co. and later Chattanooga Glass Co., since 1927.

C in a square: Crystal Glass Co., Los Angeles, CA, circa 1921–1929.

C in a star: Star City Glass Co., Star City, WV, since 1949.

Canton Domestic Fruit Jar: Canton Glass Co., Canton, OH, circa 1890–1904.

C & Co. or C Co.: Cunninghams & Co., Pittsburgh, PA, 1880–1907.

CCCo: C. Conrad & Co. (Beer), 1878–1883.

C C Co.: Carl Conrad & Co., St. Louis, MO, 1876–1883.

C C G Co.: Cream City Glass Co., Milwaukee, WI, 1888–1893.

C.F.C.A.: California Fruit Canners Association, Sacramento, CA, circa 1899–1916.

C G M Co.: Campbell Glass Mfg. Co., West Berkeley, CA, 1885.

C G W: Campbell Glass Works, West Berkeley, CA, 1884–1885.

C & H: Coffin & Hay, Winslow, NJ, circa 1838–1842.

C L G Co.: Carr-Lowrey Glass Co., Baltimore, MD, circa 1889–1920.

Clyde, N.Y.: Clyde Glass Works, Clyde, NY, circa 1870–1882.

The Clyde in script: Clyde Glass Works, Clyde, NY, circa 1895.

C. Milw: Chase Valley Glass Co., Milwaukee, WI, circa 1880.

Cohansey: Cohansey Glass Mfg. Co., Philadelphia, PA, 1870–1900.

CS & Co.: Cannington, Shaw & Co., St. Helens, England, circa 1872–1916.

C.V. Co. No. 1 & No. 2: Milwaukee, WI, 1880–1881.

DB: Du Bois Brewing Co., Pittsburgh, PA, circa 1918.

Dexter: Franklin Flint Glass Works, Philadelphia, PA, circa 1861–1880.

Diamond (plain): Diamond Glass Co., since 1924.

The Dictator: William McCully & Co., Pittsburgh, PA, circa 1855–1869.

Dictator: Same as above, only circa 1869–1885.

D & O: Cumberland Glass Mfg. Co., Bridgeton, NJ, circa 1890–1900.

D O C: D.O. Cunningham Glass Co., Pittsburgh, PA, circa 1883–1937.

D S G Co.: De Steiger Glass Co., LaSalle, IL, circa 1867–1896.

Duffield: Duffield, Parke & Co., Detroit, MI, 1866–1875.

Dyottsville: Dyottsville Glass Works, Philadelphia, PA, 1833–1923.

Economy (in script) Trade Mark: Kerr Glass Mfg. Co., Portland, OR, 1903–1912.

Electric Trade Mark in script: Gayner Glass Works, Salem, NJ, circa 1910.

Electric Trade Mark: Same as above, only circa 1900–1910.

Erd & Co., E R Durkee: E.R. Durkee & Co., New York, NY, post-1874.

E R Durkee & Co: Same as above, only circa 1850–1860.

Eureka 17: Eureka Jar Co., Dunbar, WV, circa 1864.

Eureka in script: Same as above, only circa 1900–1910.

Everlasting (in script) Jar: Illinois Pacific Glass Co., San Francisco, CA, circa 1904.

Excelsior: Excelsior Glass Co., St. John, Quebec, Canada, 1878–1883.

F inside of a jar outline: C. L. Flaccus Glass Co., Pittsburgh, PA, circa 1900–1928.

F & A: Fahnstock & Albree, Pittsburgh, PA, 1860–1862.

FL or FL & Co.: Frederick Lorenz & Co., Pittsburgh, PA, circa 1819–1841.

G E M: Hero Glass Works, Philadelphia, PA, circa 1884–1909.

G & H: Gray & Hemingray, Cincinnati, OH, circa 1848–1864.

Gilberds: Gilberds Butter Tub Co., Jamestown, NY, circa 1883–1890.

Greenfield: Greenfield Fruit Jar & Bottle Co., Greenfield, IN, circa 1888–1912.

H (with varying numbers): Holt Glass Works, West Berkeley, CA, circa 1893–1906.

Hamilton: Hamilton Glass Works, Hamilton, Ontario, Canada, 1865–1872.

Hazel: Hazel Glass Co., Wellsburg, WV, 1886–1902.

Heinz & Noble: Same as above, only circa 1869–1872.

Helme: Geo. W. Helme Co., Jersey City, NJ, circa 1870–1895.

Hemingray: Hemingray Brothers & Co. and later Hemingray Glass Co., Covington, KY, since 1864.

F. & J. Heinz: Same as above, only circa 1876–1888.

H.J. Heinz: H.J. Heinz Co., Pittsburgh, PA, circa 1860–1869.

H.J. Heinz Co.: Same as above, only since 1888.

HS in a circle: Twitchell & Schoolcraft, Keene, NH, 1815–1816.

Hunyadi Janos: Andreas Saxlehner, Buda-Pesth, Austria-Hungary, circa 1863–1900.

I G: Illinois Glass, F inside of a jar outline, C.L. Flaccus, Pittsburgh, PA, circa 1900–1928.

I G: Illinois Glass Co., Alton, IL, before 1890.

I G Co.: Ihmsen Glass Co., Pittsburgh, PA, circa 1870–1898.

I.G. Co.: Same as above, only circa 1895.

I.G. Co. (monogram): Illinois Glass Co. on fruit jar, 1914.

IG Co in a diamond: Same as above, only circa 1900–1916.

Ill. Glass Co.: 1916–1929.

Improved G E M: Hero Glass Works, Philadelphia, PA, circa 1868.

I.P.G. (in diamond): Illinois Pacific Glass Corp., San Francisco, CA, 1925–1930.

I P G: Same as above, only 1902–1932.

JAF & Co., Pioneer and Folger: J.A. Folger & Co., San Francisco, CA, since 1850.

J D 26 S: John Duncan & Sons, New York, NY, circa 1880–1900.

J R: Stourbridge Flint Glass Works, Pittsburgh, PA, circa 1823–1828.

JSB (monogram): Joseph Schlitz Brewing Co., Milwaukee, WI, circa 1900.

J T: Mantua Glass Works and later Mantua Glass Co., Mantua, OH, circa 1824.

J T & Co.: Brownsville Glass Works, Brownsville, PA, circa 1824–1828.

Kensington Glass Works: Kensington Glass Works, Philadelphia, PA, circa 1822–1932.

Kerr in script: Kerr Glass Mfg. Co. and later Alexander H. Kerr Glass Co., Portland, OR; Sand Spring, OK; Chicago, IL; Los Angeles, CA, since 1912.

K H & G: Kearns, Herdman & Gorsuch, Zanesville, OH, 1876–1884.

K & M: Knoz & McKee, Wheeling, WV, 1824–1829.

K Y G W and KYGW Co: Kentucky Glass Works Co., Louisville, KY, 1849–1855.

Lamb: Lamb Glass Co., Mt. Vernon, OH, 1855–1964.

L G Co: Louisville Glass Works, Louisville, KY, circa 1880.

Lightning: Henry W. Putnam, Bennington, VT, 1875–1890.

L I P: Lea & Perrins, London, England, 1880–1900.

L K Y G W: Louisville Kentucky Glass Works, Louisville, KY, circa 1873–1890.

L & W: Lorenz & Wightman, PA, 1862–1871.

"Mascot," "Mason," and M F G Co: Mason Fruit Jar Co., Philadelphia, PA, all circa 1885–1900.

Mastadon: Thomas A. Evans Mastadon Works and later Wm. McCully & Co., Pittsburgh, PA 1855–1887.

MG (slant letters): Maywood Glass, Maywood, CA, 1930–1950.

M.G. CO.: Missouri Glass Co., 1900.

M.G. Co: Modes Glass Co., IN, 1895–1904.

M. G. W.: Middletown Glass Co., NY, circa 1889.

Moore Bros.: Moore Bros., Clayton, NJ, 1864–1880.

N B B G Co: North Baltimore Bottle Glass Co., North Baltimore, OH, 1885–1930.

O: Owen Bottle Co.

O-D-1 0 & diamond & I: Owens Ill. Pacific Coast Co., CA, 1932–1943. Mark of Owen-Ill. Glass Co. merger in 1930.

P G W: Pacific Glass Works, San Francisco, CA, 1862–1876.

Premium: Premium Glass Co., Coffeyville, KS, circa 1908–1914.

Putnam Glass Works in a circle: Putnam Flint Glass Works, Putnam, OH, circa 1852–1871.

P & W: Perry & Wood and later Perry & Wheeler, Keene, NH, circa 1822–1830.

Queen (in script) Trade Mark (all in a shield): Smalley, Kivlan & Onthank, Boston, MA, 1906–1919.

R: Louis Freres & Co., France, circa 1870–1890.

R & C Co: Roth & Co., San Francisco, CA, 1879–1888.

Rau's: Fairmount Glass Works, Fairmount, IN, circa 1898–1908.

Red with a key through it: Safe Glass Co., Upland, IN, circa 1892–1898.

R G Co: Renton Glass Co., Renton, WA, 1911.

Root: Root Glass Co., Terre Haute, IN, 1901–1932.

S in a side of a star: Southern Glass Co., LA, 1920–1929.

S.B. & G. Co.: Streator Bottle & Glass Co., IL, 1881–1905.

S & C: Stebbins & Chamberlain or Coventry Glass Works, Coventry, CT, circa 1825–1830.

S F G W: San Francisco Glass Works, San Francisco, CA, 1869–1876.

S & M: Sykes & Macvey, Castleford, England, 1860–1888.

S.F. & P.G.W.: John Wieland's extra pale Cac. Bottling Works S.F., CA.

Squibb: E.R. Squibb, M.D., Brooklyn, NY, 1858–1895.

Standard (in script) Mason: Standard Corp. Glass Co. and later Standard Glass Co., Marion, IN, circa 1894–1932.

Star Glass Co.: Star Glass Co., New Albany, IN, circa 1860–1900.

Swayzee: Swayzee Glass Co., Swayzee, IN, 1894–1906.

T C W: T.C. Wheaton Co., Millville, NJ, since 1888.

T S: Coventry Glass Works, Coventry, CT, 1820–1824.

W & CO: Thomas Wightman & Co., Pottsburgh, PA, circa 1880–1889.

W C G Co: West Coast Glass Co., Los Angeles, CA, 1908–1930.

WF & S MILW: William Franzen & Son, Milwaukee, WI, 1900–1929.

W G W: Woodbury Glass Works, Woodbury, NJ, 1882–1900.

W T & Co: Whitall-Tatum & Co., Millville, NJ, 1857–1935.

APPENDIX B: BOTTLE CLUBS

UNITED STATES

ALABAMA

Alabama Bottle Collectors Society—2768 Hanover Circle, Birmingham, AL 35205, (205) 933-7902.

Azalea City Beamers Bottle & Spec. Club—100 Bienville Avenue, Mobile, AL 36606, (205) 473-4251.

Bama Beamers Bottle & Spec. Club—Rt. 1, P.O. Box 72, Sheffield, AL 35660, (205) 383-6884.

Choctaw Jim Beam Bottle & Spec. Club—218 S. Hamburg Street, Butler, AL 36904, (205) 459-3140.

Heart of Dixie Beam Bottle & Spec. Club—2136 Rexford Road, Montgomery, AL 36116.

Mobile Bottle Collectors Club—7927 Historic Mobile Parkway, Theodore, AL 36582, (205) 653-0713.

Mobile Bottle Collectors Club—Rt. 4, P.O. Box 28, Theodore, AL 36582.

Montgomery, Alabama, Bottle Club—1940A Norman Bridge Court, Montgomery, AL 36104.

Montgomery Bottle & Insulator Club—2021 Merrily Drive, Montgomery, AL 36111, (205) 288-7937.

North Alabama Bottle & Glass Club—P.O. Box 109, Decatur, AL 35601.

Tuscaloosa Antique Bottle Club—1617 11th Street, Tuscaloosa, AL 35401.

Southern Beamers Bottle & Spec. Club—1400 Greenbrier Road, Apt. G-3, Anniston, AL 36201, (205) 831-5151.

Vulcan Beamers Bottle & Spec. Club—5817 Avenue Q, Birmingham, AL 35228, (205) 831-5151.

ALASKA

Alaska Bottle Club (formerly The Anchorage Beam Club)—8510 E. 10th, Anchorage, AK 99504.

ARIZONA

Avon Collectors Club—P.O. Box 1406, Mesa, AZ 86201.

Fort Smith Area Bottle Collectors Association—4618 S. "Q," Fort Smith, AZ 72901.

Kachina Ezra Brooks Bottle Club—3818 W. Cactus Wren Drive, Phoenix, AZ 85021.

Pick & Shovel A.B.C. of Arizona, Inc.—P.O. Box 7020, Phoenix, AZ 85011. Meets 8:00 P.M. first Wednesday at 531 E. Bethany Home Road., Phoenix (Stuckey Ins. Agency). Newsletter: *The Blister*. Club formed 1969, has 40 family members.

Southern AZ Historical Collector's Association, Ltd.—6211 Piedra Seca, Tucson, AZ 85718.

Tri-City Jim Beam Bottle Club—2701 E. Utopia Road, Sp. #91, Phoenix, AZ 85024, (602) 867-1375.

Valley of the Sun Bottle & Specialty Club—212 E. Minton, Tempe, AZ 85281.

White Mountain Antique Bottle Collectors Association—P.O. Box 503, Eager, AZ 85925.

Wildcat Country Beam Bottle & Spec. Club—2601 S. Blackmoon Drive, Tucson, AZ 85730, (602) 298-5943.

ARKANSAS

Fort Smith Area Bottle Collectors Assn.—2201 S. 73rd Street, Ft. Smith, AR 72903.

Hempsted County Bottle Club—710 S. Hervey, Hope, AR 71801.

Little Rock Antique Bottle Collectors Club—12 Martin Drive, North Little Rock, AR 72118, (501) 753-2623.

Madison County Bottle Collectors Club—Rt. 2, Box 304, Huntsville, AR 72740.

Razorback Jim Beam Bottle & Spec. Club—2609 S. Taylor, Little Rock, AR 72204, (501) 664-1335.

Southwest Arkansas Bottle Club—Star Route, Delight, AR 71940.

CALIFORNIA

A.B.C. of Orange County—P.O. Box 10424, Santa Ana, CA 92711. Meets first Monday at 7:30 P.M., Willard Jr. High School, Santa Ana. Newsletter: *The Bottle Bulletin*. Club formed 1968, has 60 members.

Amethyst Bottle Club—3245 Military Avenue, Los Angeles, CA 90034.

Antique Bottle Club Association of Fresno—P.O. Box 1932, Fresno, CA 93718.

Antique Bottle Collectors of Orange County—223 E. Ponona, Santa Ana, CA 92707.

A, OK Beamers—7650 Balboa Boulevard, Van Nuys, CA 91406, (213) 787-2674.

Argonaut Jim Beam Bottle Club—8253 Citadel Way, Sacramento, CA 95826, (916) 383-0206.

Avon Bottle & Specialties Collectors—Southern California Division, 9233 Mills Avenue, Montclair, CA 91763.

Bay Area Vagabonds Jim Beam Club—224 Castleton Way, San Bruno, CA 94066, (415) 355-4356.

Beach Cities Beamers—3111 Highland Avenue, Manhattan Beach, CA 90266.

Beam Bottle Club of Southern California—3221 N. Jackson, Rosemead, CA 91770.

Beaming Beamers Jim Beam Bottle & Spec. Club—3734 Lynhurst Way, North Highlands, CA 95660, (916) 482-0359.

Beam's Orange County Bottle & Spec. Club—1516 E. Harmony Lane, Fullerton, CA 92631, (714) 526-5137.

Bidwell Bottle Club—Box 546, Chico, CA 95926.

Bishop Belles & Beaux Bottle Club—P.O. Box 1475, Bishop, CA 93514.

Blossom Valley Jim Beam Bottle & Spec. Club—431 Grey Ghost Avenue, San Jose, CA 95111, (408) 227-2759.

Bodfish Beamers Jim Beam Bottle Club—19 Dow Drive, P.O. Box 864-A, Bodfish, CA 93205, (714) 379-3280.

California Ski Country Bottle Club—212 South El Molino Street, Alhambra, CA 91801.

Camellia City Jim Beam Bottle Club—3734 Lynhurst Way, North Highlands, CA 95660.

Central Calif. Avon Bottle & Collectible Club—P.O. Box 232, Amador City, CA 95601.

Cherry Valley Beam Bottle & Specialty Club—6851 Hood Drive, Westminster, CA 92683.

Chief Solano Bottle Club—4-D Boynton Avenue, Sulsun, CA 94585.

Curiosity Bottle Association—Box 103, Napa, CA 94558.

Fiesta City Beamers—329 Mountain Drive, Santa Barbara, CA 93103.

First Double Springs Collectors Club—13311 Illinois Street, Westminster, CA 92683.

Five Cities Beamers—756 Mesa View Drive, Sp. 57, Arroyo Grande, CA 93420.

Fresno Raisin Beamers—3850 E. Ashian #A, Fresno, CA 93726, (209) 224-3086.

Glass Belles of San Gabriel—518 W. Neuby Avenue, San Gabriel, CA 91776.

Glasshopper Figural Bottle Association—P.O. Box 6642, Torrance, CA 90504.

Golden Bear Ezra Brooks Bottle Club—8808 Capricorn Way, San Diego, CA 92126.

Golden Bear Jim Beam Bottle & Specialty Club—8808 Capricorn Way, San Diego, CA 92126.

Golden Gate Beam Club—35113 Clover Street, Union City, CA 94587, (415) 487-4479.

Golden Gate Historical Bottle Society—P.O. Box 2129, Alameda, CA 94501.

Greater Cal. Antique Bottle Collectors—P.O. Box 55, Sacramento, CA 95801.

Grizzly Guzzlers Jim Beam Bottle Club—40080 Francis Way, P.O. Box 3725, Big Bear Lake, CA 92351.

High Desert Bottle Hunters—P.O. Box 581, Ridgecrest, CA 93558.

Highland Toasters Beam Bottle & Spec. Club—1570 E. Marshall, San Bernardino, CA 92404, (714) 883-2000.

Hoffman's Mr. Lucky Bottle Club—2104 Rhoda Street, Simi Valley, CA 93065.

Hollywood Stars-Ezra Brooks Bottle Club—2200 N. Beachwood Drive, Hollywood, CA 90028.

Humboldt Antique Bottle Club—P.O. Box 6012, Eureka, CA 95501.

Jewels of Avon—2297 Maple Avenue, Oroville, CA 95965.

Jim Beam Bottle Club—139 Arlington, Berkeley, CA 94707.

Jim Beam Bottle Club of So. Calif.—1114 Coronado Terrrace, Los Angeles, CA 90066.

Juniper Hills Bottle Club—Rt. 1, Box 18, Valyerma, CA 93563.

Kern County Antique Bottle Club—P.O. Box 6724, Bakersfield, CA 93306.

Lilliputian Bottle Club—5119 Lee Street, Torrance, CA 90503.

Lionstone Bottle Collectors of America—P.O. Box 75924, Los Angeles, CA 90075.

Livermore Avon Club—6385 Claremont Avenue, Richmond, CA 94805.

Lodi Jim Beam Bottle Club—429 E. Lodi Avenue, Lodi, CA 95240.

Los Angeles Historical Bottle Club—P.O. Box 60762, Terminal Annex, Los Angeles, CA 90060, (213) 332-6751.

Mission Bells (Beams)—1114 Coronada Terrrace, Los Angeles, CA 90026.

Mission Tesore Jim Beam Bottle & Spec. Club—7701 E. Zayante Road, Felton, CA 95018, (408) 335-4317.

Mission Trails Ezra Brooks Bottles & Specialties Club, Inc.—4923 Bel Canto Drive, San Jose, CA 95124.

Mission Trail Historical Bottle Club—P.O. Box 721, Seaside, CA 93955, (408) 394-3257.

Modesto Beamers—1429 Glenwood Drive, Modesto, CA 95350, (209) 523-3440.

Modesto Old Bottle Club (MOBC)—P.O. Box 1791, Modesto, CA 95354.

Monterey Bay Beam Bottle & Specialty Club—P.O. Box 258, Freedom, CA 95019.

Motherlode Bottle Club—P.O. Box 337, Angels Camp, CA 95222.

M. T. Bottle Club—P.O. Box 608, Solana Beach, CA 92075.

Mt. Bottle Club—422 Orpheus, Encinitas, CA 92024.

Mt. Diablo Bottle Club—4166 Sandra Circle, Pittsburg, CA 94565.

Mt. Diablo Bottle Society—1699 Laguna #110, Concord, CA 94520.

Mt. Whitney Bottle Club—P.O. Box 688, Lone Pine, CA 93545.

Napa-Solano Bottle Club—1409 Delwood, Vallejo, CA 94590.

National Jim Beam Bottle & Spec. Club—5005 Cochrane Avenue, Oakland, CA 94618, (415) 655-5005.

Northern California Jim Beam Bottle & Specialty Club—P.O. Box 186, Montgomery Creek, CA 96065.

Northwestern Bottle Club—P.O. Box 1121, Santa Rosa, CA 95402. Meets 4th Tuesday January, April, June, September, October, Coddingtown Community Meeting Room, Santa Rosa. Newsletter: *The Glassblower.* Club formed 1966, has 29 family members.

Northwestern Bottle Collectors Association—1 Keeler Street, Petaluma, CA 94952.

Ocean Breeze Beamers—4841 Tacayme Drive, Oceanside, CA 92054, (714) 757-9081.

Original Sippin Cousins Ezra Brooks Specialties Club—12206 Malone Street, Los Angeles, CA 90066.

Palomar Jim Beam Club—246 S. Las Posas, P.O. Box 125, San Marcos, CA 92069, (714) 744-2924.

Pebble Beach Jim Beam Bottle Club—419 Alvarado Street, Monterey, CA 93940, (408) 373-5320.

Peninsula Bottle Club—P.O. Box 886, Belmont, CA 94002.

Petaluma Bottle & Antique Club—P.O. Box 1035, Petaluma, CA 94952.

Quail Country Jim Beam Bottle & Spec. Club—625 Pleasant, Coalinga, CA 93210.

Queen Mary Beam & Specialty Club—P.O. Box 2054, Anaheim, CA 92804.

Relic Accumulators—P.O. Box 3513, Eureka, CA 95501.

Santa Barbara Beam Bottle Club—5307 University Drive, Santa Barbara, CA 93111.

Santa Barbara Bottle Club—P.O. Box 30171, Santa Barbara, CA 93105.

San Bernardino County Historical Bottle and Collectible Club—P.O. Box 127, Bloomington, CA 92316. Meets 4th Tuesday, 7:30 P.M., San Bernardino Co. Museum, Redlands, CA, (714) 244-5863. Newsletter: *Bottle Nooz.* Club formed 1967, has 60 members.

San Diego Antique Bottle Club—P.O. Box 536, San Diego, CA 92112.

San Diego Jim Beam Bottle Club—2620 Mission Village Drive, San Diego, CA 92112.

San Francisco Bay Area Miniature Bottle Club—160 Lower Via Casitas #8, Kentfield, CA 94904.

San Joaquin Valley Jim Beam Bottle & Specialties Club—4085 N. Wilson Avenue, Fresno, CA 93704.

San Jose Antique Bottle Collectors' Assn.—P.O. Box 5432, San Jose, CA.

San Luis Obispo Antique Bottle Club—124-21 Street Paso Robles, CA 93446. Meets 3rd Saturday, private homes. Club formed in 1965, has 30 family members.

Santa Maria Beam & Spec. Club—528 E. Harding, Santa Maria, CA 93454, (805) 922-1238.

Sequoia Antique Bottle Society—1900 4th Avenue, Kingsburg, CA 93631.

Shasta Antique Bottle Collectors Association—Rt. 1, Box 3147-A, Anderson, CA 96007.

Sierra Gold Ski Country Bottle Club—5081 Rio Vista Avenue, San Jose, CA 95129.

Ski-Country Bottle Club of Southern California—3148 N. Walnut Grove, Rosemead, CA 91770.

Solar Country Beamers—940 Kelly Drive, Barstow, CA 92311, (714) 256-1485.

South Bay Antique Bottle Club—2589½ Valley Drive, Manhattan Beach, CA 90266.

Southern California Miniature Bottle Club—5626 Corning Avenue, Los Angeles, CA 90056.

Southwestern Wyoming Avon Bottle Club—301 Canyon Highlands Drive, Oroville, CA 95965.

Stockton Historical Bottle Society, Inc.—P.O. Box 8584, Stockton, CA 95204.

Sunnyvale Antique Bottle Collectors Association—613 Torrington, Sunnyvale, CA 94087.

Superior California Bottle Club—P.O. Box 555, Anderson, CA 96007.

Taft Antique Bottle Club—P.O. Box 334, Taft, CA 93268.

Teen Bottle Club—Rt. 1, Box 60-TE, Eureka, CA 95501.

Tehama County Antique Bottle Club—Rt. 1, Box 775, Red Bluff, CA 96080. Meets 7:30 P.M. 1st Wednesday at Lassen View School, (916) 527-1680. Club formed 1960, has 55 family members.

Tinseltown Beam Club—4117 E. Gage Avenue, Bell, CA 90201, (213) 699-8787.

Western World Collectors Assn.—P.O. Box 409, Ontario, CA 91761. Meets every 3rd Wednesday, 7:30 P.M., at Upland Lumber Co., 85 Euclid Avenue, Upland, CA, (714) 984-0614. Club formed in 1971, has 150 family members.

Wildwind Jim Beam Bottle & Specialties Club—905 Eaton Way, Sunnyvale, CA 94087, (408) 739-1558.

World Wide Avon Collectors Club—44021 Seventh Street, E. Lancaster, CA 93534, (805) 948-8849.

COLORADO

Alamosa Bottle Collectors—Rt. 2, Box 170, Alamosa, CO 81101.

Avon Club of Colorado Springs, CO—707 N. Farragut, Colorado Springs, CO 80909.

Colorado Mile-High Ezra Brooks Bottle Club—7401 Decatur Street, Westminster, CO 80030.

Foot-Hills Jim Beam Bottle & Spec. Club—1303 Kilkenny Street, Boulder, CO 80303, (303) 665-3957.

Four Corners Bottle & Glass Club—P.O. Box 45, Cortez, CO 81321.

Horsetooth Antique Bottle Collectors, Inc.—P.O. Box 944, Ft. Collins, CO 80521.

Lionstone Western Figural Club—P.O. Box 2275, Colorado Springs, CO 80901.

Mile-Hi Jim Beam Bottle & Spec. Club—13196 W. Green Mountain Drive, Lakewood, CO 80228, (303) 986-6828.

National Ski Country Bottle Club—1224 Washington Avenue, Golden, CO 80401, (303) 279-3373.

Northeastern Colorado Antique Bottle Club—P.O. Box 634, Ft. Morgan, CO 80701.

Northern Colorado Antique Bottle Club—227 W. Beaver Avenue, Ft. Morgan, CO 80701.

Northern Colorado Beam Bottle & Spec. Club—3272 Gunnison Drive, Ft. Collins, CO 80526, (303) 226-2301.

Ole Foxie Jim Beam Club—P.O. Box 560, Westminster, CO 80020.

Peaks & Plains Antique Bottle Club—P.O. Box 814, Colorado Springs, CO 80901.

Rocky Mountain Jim Beam Bottle & Specialty Club—Alcott Station, P.O. Box 12162, Denver, CO 80212.

Telluride Antique Bottle Collectors—P.O. Box 344, Telluride, CO 8143.

Western Figural & Jim Beam Specialty Club—P.O. Box 4331, Colorado Springs, CO 80930.

Western Slope Bottle Club—607 Belford Avenue, Grand Junction, CO 81501.

CONNECTICUT

Connecticut Specialty Bottle Club, Inc.—P.O. Box 624, Stratford, CT.

The Milk Route—4 Ox Bow Road, Westport, CT 06880.

Somers Antique Bottle Club—Somers, CT 06071, (203) 487-1071.

Southern Connecticut Antique Bottle Collectors Association, Inc.—Ole Severson, 11 Dartmouth Drive, Huntington, CT 06484, (203) 929-5197.

Western Connecticut Jim Beam Bottle & Spec. Club—Rt. 1, Box 442, Old Hawleyville Road, Bethel, CT 06801, (203) 744-6118.

DELAWARE

Blue Hen Jim Beam Bottle & Spec. Club—303 Potomac Drive, Wilmington, DE 19803, (302) 652-6378.

Mason-Dixon Bottle Collectors Association—P.O. Box 505, Lewes, DE 19958.

Tri-State Bottle Collectors and Diggers Club—730 Paper Mill Road, Newark, DE 19711.

FLORIDA

Antique Bottle Collectors Assn. of Florida—5901 S.W. 16th Street, Miami, FL 33144. Meets 2nd Tuesday, 7:30 P.M., at school, (305) 266-4854. Newsletter: *Whittlemark*. Club formed 1965, has 55 members.

Antique Bottle Collectors of Florida, Inc.—2512 Davie Boulevard, Ft. Lauderdale, FL 33312.

Antique Bottle Collectors of North Florida—P.O. Box 14796, Jacksonville, FL 32210.

Bay Area Historical Bottle Collector—P.O. Box 3454, Apollo Beach, FL 33570.

Central Florida Insulator Club—3557 Nicklaus Drive, Titusville, FL 32780, (305) 267-9170.

Central Flordia Jim Beam Bottle Club—1060 W. French Avenue, Orange City, FL 32763, (904) 775-7392.

Crossarms Collectors Club—1756 N.W. 58th Avenue, Lauderhill, FL 33313. Meets every other month, 3rd Wednesday at above address, Newsletter: *Crossarms*. Club formed 1975.

Deep South Jim Beam Bottle & Spec. Club—16100 S.W. 278th Street, Homestead, FL 33031, (305) 248-7301.

Everglades A.B.C.—6981 S.W. 19th Street, Pompano, FL 33068. Club formed 1977, has 44 members.

Everglades Antique Bottle & Collectors Club—400 S. 57 Terrace, Hollywood, FL 33023, (305) 962-3434.

Florida Panhandle Jim Beam Bottle & Spec. Club—706 James Court, Ft. Walton Beach, FL 32548, (904) 862-3469.

Gateway of the Palms Beam Bottle & Spec. Club—6621 Katherine Road, West Palm Beach, FL 33406, (305) 683-3900.

Gold Coast Collectors Club—Joseph I. Frakes, P.O. Box 10183, Wilton Manors, FL 33305.

Halifax Historical Society—224½ S. Beach Street, Daytona Beach, FL 32018.

Harbor City—1232 Causeway, Eau, FL 32935.

Longwood Bottle Club—P.O. Box 437, Longwood, FL 32750.

Mid-State Antique Bottle Collectors—88 Sweetbriar Branch, Longwood, FL 32750, 834-8914.

M. T. Bottle Collectors Assn., Inc.—P.O. Box 581, Deland, FL 32720.

Northwest Florida Regional Bottle Club—P.O. Box 282, Port St. Joe, FL 32456.

Original Florida Keys Collectors Club—P.O. Box 212, Islamorada, FL 33036.

Oviedo Bottling Works—c/o Mike Pierson, 7630 Broken Arrow Tr., Winter Park, FL 32792.

Pensacola Bottle & Relic Collectors Association—1004 Freemont Avenue, Pensacola, FL 32505.

Ridge Area Antique Bottle Collectors—1219 Carlton, Lake Wales, FL 33853.

Sanford Antique A.B.C.—2656 Grandview Avenue, Sanford, FL. Meets 2nd Tuesday, 8:00 P.M., (305) 322-7181. Newsletter: *Probe*. Club formed 1966, has 50 members.

Sarasota-Manatee A.B.C. Assn.—Rt. 1, Box 74-136, Sarasota, FL 33583, (813) 924-5995. Meets 3rd Wednesday, 7:30 P.M., in members' homes. Newsletter: *The Glass Habit*. Club formed 1969, has 20 members.

South Florida Jim Beam Bottle & Specialty Club—7741 N.W. 35th Street, West Hollywood, FL 33024.

Suncoast Antique Bottle Club—P.O. Box 12712, St. Petersburg, FL 33733.

Suncoast Jim Beam Bottle & Spec. Club—P.O. Box 5067, Sarasota, FL 33579.

Tampa Antique Bottle Collectors—P.O. Box 4232, Tampa, FL 33607.

West Coast Florida Ezra Brooks Bottle Club—1360 Harbor Drive, Sarasota, FL 33579.

GEORGIA

Bulldog Double Springs Bottle Collector Club of Augusta, Georgia—1916 Melrose Drive, Augusta, GA 30906.

Coastal Empire Bottle Club—P.O. Box 3714, Station B, Savannah, GA 31404.

The Desoto Trail Bottle Collectors Club—406 Randolph Street, Cuthbert, GA 31740.

Flint Antique Bottle & Coin Club—c/o Cordele-Crisp Co., Recreation Department, 204 2nd Street North, Cordele, GA 31015.

Flint River Jim Beam Bottle Club—Rt. 3, P.O. Box 6, Camilla, GA 31730, (912) 336-7034.

Georgia Bottle Club—2996 Pangborn Road, Decatur, GA 30033.

Georgia-Carolina Empty Bottle Club—P.O. Box 1184, Augusta, GA 30903.

Macon Antique Bottle Club—P.O. Box 5395, Macon, GA 31208. Meets 7:30 P.M., 2nd Monday, Robert Train Recreation Center. Newsletter: *Glass Heart of Georgia*. Club formed 1968, has 20 members.

Macon Antique Bottle Club—c/o 5532 Jane Run Circle, Macon, GA 31206. Meets 7:30 P.M., 2nd Monday, at Robert Train Recreation Center. Newsletter: *Heart of Georgia News*, has 30 members.

The Middle Georgia Antique Bottle Club—2746 Alden Street, Macon, GA 31206.

Peachstate Bottle & Specialty Club—5040 Vallo Vista Court, Atlanta, GA 30342.

Peachtree Jim Beam Bottlers Club—224 Lakeshore Drive, Daluth, GA 30136, (404) 448-9013.

Peanut State Jim Beam Bottle & Spec. Club—767 Timberland Street, Smyrna, GA 30080, (404) 432-8482.

Southeastern Antique Bottle Club—P.O. Box 657, Decatur, GA 30033.

HAWAII

Hauoli Beam Bottle Collectors Club of Hawaii—45-027 Ka-Hanahou Place, Kaneohe, HI 96744.

Hawaii Bottle Collectors Club—6770 Hawaii Kai Drive, Apt. 708, Hawaii Kai, HI 96825.

IDAHO

Buhl Antique Bottle Club—500 12th, N. Buhl, ID 83316.

Eagle Rock Beam & Spec. Club—3665 Upland Avenue, Idaho Falls, ID 83401, (208) 522-7819.

Em Tee Bottle Club—P.O. Box 62, Jerome, ID 83338.

Fabulous Valley Antique Bottle Club—P.O. Box 769, Osburn, ID 83849.

Gem Antique Bottle Collectors Assn., Inc.—P.O. Box 8051, Boise, ID 83707.

Idaho Beam & Spec. Club—2312 Burrell Avenue, Lewiston, ID 83501, (208) 743-5997.

Idaho Bottle Collectors Association—4530 S. 5th Street, Pocatello, ID 83201.

Inland Empire Jim Beam Bottle & Collectors' Club—1117 10th Street, Lewiston, ID 83501.

Rock & Bottle Club—Rt. 1, Fruitland, ID 83619.

Treasure Valley Beam Bottle & Spec. Club—2324 Norcrest Drive, Boise, ID 83705, (208) 343-6207.

ILLINOIS

A.B.C. of Northern Illinois—P.O. Box 23, Ingleside, IL 60041, (815) 338-2567. Meets 1st Wednesday, 8:00 P.M., at Jones Island Meeting House, Grayslake, IL. Newsletter: *Pick & Probe*. Formed 1973, has 29 members.

Alton Area Bottle Club—2448 Alby Street, Alton, IL, (618) 462-4285.

Blackhawk Jim Beam Bottle & Specialties Club—2003 Kishwaukee Street, Rockford, IL 61101.

Central Illinois Jim Beam Bottle & Spec. Club—3725 S. Sand Creek Road, Decatur, IL 62521.

Central & Midwestern States Beam & Specialties Club—44 S. Westmore, Lombard, IL 60148.

Chicago Ezra Brooks Bottle & Specialty Club—3635 W. 82nd Street, Chicago, IL 60652.

Chicago Jim Beam Bottle & Specialty Club—1305 W. Marion Street, Joliet, IL 60436.

Dreamer Beamers—5721 Vial Parkway, LaGrange, IL 60525, (312) 246-4838.

Eagle Jim Beam Bottle & Spec. Club—1015 Hollycrest, P.O. Box 2084 CFS, Champaign, IL 61820, (217) 352-4035.

1st Chicago A.B.C.—P.O. Box A-3382, Chicago, IL 60690. Meets 3rd Friday, 7:00 P.M., at St. Daniels Church, 5400 S. Nashville, Chicago. Newsletter: *Mid-West Bottled News*. Formed 1969, has 50 members.

Heart of Illinois Antique Bottle Club—2010 Bloomington Road, East Peoria, IL 61611.

Illini Jim Beam Bottle & Specialty Club—P.O. Box 13, Champaign, IL 61820.

Illinois Bottle Club—P.O. Box 181, Rushville, IL 62681.

International Association of Jim Beam—4338 Saratoga Avenue, Downers Grove, IL 60515.

Kelly Club—147 North Brainard Avenue, La Grange, IL 60525.

Land of Lincoln Bottle Club—2515 Illinois Circle, Decatur, IL 62526.

Lewis & Clark Jim Beam Bottle & Specialty Club—P.O. Box 451, Wood River, IL 62095.

Lionstone Bottle Collectors of America—P.O. Box 2418, Chicago, IL 60690.

Little Egypt Jim Beam Bottle & Spec. Club—Rt. 2, Flat Rock, IL 62427, (618) 584-3338.

Louis Joliet Bottle Club—12 Kenmore, Joliet, IL 60433.

Metro East Bottle & Jar Association—309 Bellevue Drive, Belleville, IL, (618) 233-8841. Meets 2nd Tuesday at O'Fallon Township Bldg., 801 E. State Street, O'Fallon, IL. Newsletter: *Metro-East Bottle & Jar & Insulator Relater*. Club formed 1971, has 26 members.

Metro East Bottle & Jar Association—1702 North Keesler, Collinsville, IL 62234.

Metro East Bottle & Jar Association—P.O. Box 185, Mascoutah, IL.

National Ezra Brooks Club—645 N. Michigan Avenue, Chicago, IL 69611.

North Shore Jim Beam Bottle & Spec. Club—542 Glendale Road, Glenview, IL 60025.

Pekin Bottle Collectors Assn.—P.O. Box 372, Pekin, IL 61554, (309) 347-4441. Meets 3rd Wednesday, Pekin Chamber of Commerce. Club formed 1970, has 80 members.

Rock River Valley Jim Beam Bottle & Spec. Club—1107 Avenue A., Rock Falls, IL 61071, (815) 625-7075.

Starved Rock Jim Beam Bottle & Spec. Club—P.O. Box 177, Ottawa, IL 61350, (815) 433-3269.

Sweet Corn Capital Bottle Club—1015 W. Orange, Hoopeston, IL 60942.

Tri-County Jim Beam Bottle Club—3702 W. Lancer Road, Peoria, IL 61615, (309) 691-8784.

INDIANA

City of Bridges Jim Beam Bottle & Spec. Club—1017 N. 6th Street, Logansport, IN 46947, (219) 722-3197.

Crossroads of America Jim Beam Bottle Club—114 S. Green Street, Brownsburg, IN 46112, (317) 852-5168.

Fort Wayne Historical Bottle Club—5124 Roberta Drive, Fort Wayne, IN 46306. Meets 2nd Wednesday at library branches. Club formed 1970, has 20 members.

Hoosier Jim Beam Bottle & Specialties Club—P.O. Box 24234, Indianapolis, IN 46224.

Indiana Ezra Brooks Bottle Club—P.O. Box 24344, Indianapolis, IN 46224.

Lafayette Antique Bottle Club—3664 Redondo Drive, Lafayette, IN

47905. Meets 4:00 p.m., 1st Sunday, at Jenks Rest, Columbian Park, Lafayette, IN. Club formed in 1977, has 8 members.

Michiana Jim Beam Bottle & Specialty Club—58955 Locust Road, South Bend, IN 46614.

Mid-West Antique Fruit Jar & Bottle Club—P.O. Box 38, Flat Rock, IN 47234.

The Ohio Valley Antique Bottle and Jar Club—214 John Street, Aurora, IN 47001.

Steel City Ezra Brooks Bottle Club—Rt. 2, Box 32A, Valparaiso, IN 46383.

Three Rivers Jim Beam Bottle & Spec. Club—Rt. 4, Winchester Road, Ft. Wayne, IN 46819, (219) 639-3041.

We Found 'Em Bottle & Insulator Club—P.O. Box 578, Bunker Hill, IN 46914.

IOWA

Five Seasons Beam & Spec. Club of Iowa—609 32nd Street, NE, Cedar Rapids, IA 52402, (319) 365-6089.

Gold Dome Jim Beam Bottle & Spec. Club—2616 Hull, Des Moines, IA 50317, (515) 262-8728.

Hawkeye Jim Beam Bottle Club—658 Kern Street, Waterloo, IA 60703, (319) 233-9168.

Iowa Antique Bottlers—1506 Albia Road, Ottumwa, IA 52501, (319) 377-6041. Meets 4 times a year at various places. Newsletter: *The Iowa Antique Bottlers*. Club formed 1968, has 60 members.

Iowa Great Lakes Jim Beam Bottle & Spec. Club—Green Acres Mobile Park, Lot 88, Estherville, IA 51334, (712) 362-2759.

Larkin Bottle Club—107 W. Grimes, Red Oak, IA 51566.

Midlands Jim Beam Bottle & Spec. Club—Rt. 4, Harlan, IA 51537, (712) 744-3686.

Quad Cities Jim Beam Bottle & Spec. Club—2425 W. 46th Street, Davenport, IA 52806, (319) 391-4319.

Shot Tower Beam Club—284 N. Booth Street, Dubuque, IA 52001, (319) 583-6343.

KANSAS

Air Capital City Jim Beam Bottle & Spec. Club—3256 Euclid, Wichita, KS 67217, (316) 942-3162.

Bud Hastin's National Avon Collector's Club—P.O. Box 12088, Overland Park, KS 66212.

Cherokee Strip Ezra Brooks Bottle & Specialty Club—P.O. Box 631, Arkansas City, KS 67005.

Flint Hills Beam & Specialty Club—201 W. Pine, El Dorado, KS 67042.

Jayhawk Bottle Club—7919 Grant, Overland Park, KS 66212.

Kansas City Antique Bottle Collectors—5528 Aberdeen, Shawnee Mission, KS 66205, (816) 433-1398. Meets 6 P.M., 2nd Sunday, at 1131 E. 77th, Kansas City, MO 64125. Newsletter: *Privy Primer*. Club formed 1974, has 15 family members.

Southeast Kansas Bottle & Relics Club—115 N. Lafayette, Chanute, KS 66720, (316) 431-1643. Meets 7:30 P.M., 1st Wednesday, at First National Bank community room. Newsletter: *S.E. Kantique News*. Club formed 1973, has 40 members.

Walnut Valley Jim Beam Bottle & Spec. Club—P.O. Box 631, Arkansas City, KS 67005, (316) 442-0509.

Wichita Ezra Brooks Bottle & Specialties Club—8045 Peachtree Street, Wichita, KS 67207.

KENTUCKY

Derby City Jim Beam Bottle Club—4105 Spring Hill Road, Louisville, KY 40207.

Gold City Jim Beam Bottle Club—286 Metts Court, Apt. 4, Elizabethtown, KY 42701, (502) 737-9297.

Kentuckiana A.B. & Outhouse Society—5801 River Knolls Drive, Louisville, KY 40222, (502) 425-6995.

Kentucky Bluegrass Ezra Brooks Bottle Club—6202 Tabor Drive, Louisville, KY 40218.

Kentucky Cardinal Beam Bottle Club—428 Templin, Bardstown, KY 41104.

Land by the Lakes Beam Club—Rt. 6, Box 320, Cadiz, KY 42211, (502) 522-8445.

Louisville Bottle Collectors—11819 Garrs Avenue, Anchorage, KY 40223.

Pegasus Jim Beam Bottle & Spec. Club—9405 Cornflower Road, Valley Station, KY 40272, (502) 937-4376.

LOUISIANA

Ark-La-Tex Jim Beam Bottle & Spec. Club—1902 Carol Street, Bossier City, LA 71112, (318) 742-3550.

Bayou Bottle Bugs—216 Dahlia, New Iberia, LA 70560.

"Cajun Country Cousins" Ezra Brooks Bottle & Specialties Club—1000 Chevis Street, Abbeville, LA 70510.

Cenia Bottle Club—c/o Pam Tullos, Rt. 1, Box 463, Dry Prong, LA 71423.

Crescent City Jim Beam Bottle & Spec. Club—733 Wright Avenue, Gretna, LA 70053, (504) 367-2182.

Dixie Diggers Bottle Club—P.O. Box 626, Empire, LA 70050.

Historical Bottle Association of Baton Rouge—1843 Tudor Drive, Baton Rouge, LA 70815.

Ken Tally Jim Beam Bottle Club—110 Ken Tally Estates, Hammond, LA 70401, (504) 345-6186.

New Albany Glass Works Bottle Club—732 N. Clark Boulevard, Parksville, LA 47130.

New Orleans Antique Bottle Club—c/o Ralph J. Luther, Jr., 4336 Palmyra Street, New Orleans, LA 70119. Meets 7:30 P.M., last Friday of the month, at Banks St. Social Club, 423 S. Lopez Street. Newsletter: *Crescent City Comments*. Club formed 1969, has 42 family members.

North East Louisiana A.B.C.—P.O. Box 4192, Monroe, LA 71291, (318) 322-8359. Meets 7:00 P.M., 3rd Thursday, at Ouachita Valley Library. Newsletter: *Glass Treasures*. Club formed 1972, has 25 family members.

Red Stick Jim Beam Bottle Club—2127 Beaumont, Suite 4, Baton Rouge, LA 70806.

Sanford's Night Owl Beamers—Rt. 2, Box 102, Greenwell Springs, LA 70739, (504) 261-3658.

Shreveport Antique Bottle Club—1157 Arncliffe Drive, Shreveport, LA 71107, 221-0089.

MAINE

Dirigo Bottle Collectors Club—R.F.D. 3, Dexter, ME, (207) 924-3443. Meets 1st Tuesday at Eastern Maine Vocational Tec. Institute, Hogan Road, Bangor, ME. Newsletter: *The Paper Label*. Club formed 1969, has 21 members.

Dover Foxcroft Bottle Club—50 Church Street, Dover Foxcroft, ME 04426.

The Glass Bubble Bottle Club—P.O. Box 91, Cape Neddick, ME 03902.

Jim Beam Collectors Club—10 Lunt Road, Falmouth, ME 04105.

Kennebec Valley Bottle Club—9 Glenwood Street, Augusta, ME 04330.

Mid-Coast Bottle Club—c/o Miriam Winchenbach, Waldoboro, ME 04572.

New England Bottle Club—45 Bolt Hill Road, Eliot, ME 03903.

Paul Bunyan Bottle Club—237 14th Street, Bangor, ME 04401.

Pine Tree Antique Bottle Club—Buxton Road, Saco, ME 04072.

Pine Tree State Beamers—15 Woodside Avenue, Saco, ME 04072, (207) 284-8756.

Tri-County Bottle Collectors Association—R.F.D. 3, Dexter, ME 04930.

Waldo County Bottlenecks Club—Head-of-the-Tide, Belfast, ME 04915.

MARYLAND

Antique Bottle Club of Baltimore—c/o Fred Parks, 10 S. Linwood Avenue, Baltimore, MD 21224, (301) 732-2404. Club meets 2nd Friday of every month at 7:30 P.M. at Ridgely Middle School, corner of Ridgely Road and Charmuth Road, Lutherville, MD. Club formed 1970.

Blue & Gray Ezra Brooks Bottle Club—2106 Sunnybrook Drive, Frederick, MD 21201.

Catoctin Jim Beam Bottle Club—c/o Ron Danner, 1 North Chatham Road, Ellicott City, MD 21063, (301) 465-5773. Club meets 3rd Monday of every month at Ernie's Restaurant in Frederick, MD.

Mason Dixon Bottle Collectors Association—601 Market Street, Denton, MD 21629.

Mid-Atlantic Miniature Whiskey Bottle Club—208 Gloucester Drive, Glen Burnie, MD 21061, (301) 766-8421.

South County Bottle Collector's Club—Bast Lane, Shady Side, MD 20867.

MASSACHUSETTS

Baystate Beamers Bottle & Spec. Club—27 Brookhaven Drive, Ludlow, MA 01056, (413) 589-0446.

Berkshire Antique Bottle Assoc.—R.D. 1, West Stockbridge, MA 01266.

The Cape Cod Antique Bottle Club—c/o Mrs. John Swanson, 262 Setucket Road, Yarmouth, MA 02675.

Merrimack Valley Antique Bottle Club—c/o M. E. Tarleton, Hillside Road, Boxford, MA.

New England Beam & Specialty Club—1104 Northampton Street, Holyoke, MA 01040.

Scituate Bottle Club—54 Cedarwood Road, Scituate, MA 02066.

Yankee Pole Cat Insulator Club—105 Richards Avenue, North Attleboro, MA 02760.

MICHIGAN

Central Michigan Krazy Korkers Bottle Club—Mid-Michigan Community College, Clare Avenue, Harrison, MI 48625.

Chief Pontiac Antique Bottle Club—13880 Neal Road, Davisburg, MI 48019, c/o Larry Blascyk, (313) 634-8469.

Dickinson County Bottle Club—717 Henford Avenue, Iron Mountain, MI 49801.

Flint Antique Bottle Collectors Association—450 Leta Avenue, Flint, MI 48507.

Flint Eagles Ezra Brooks Club—1117 W. Remington Avenue, Flint, MI 48507.

Grand Valley Bottle Club—31 Dickinson S.W., Grand Rapids, MI 49507.

Great Lakes Jim Beam Bottle Club of Michigan—1010 South Harvey, Plymouth, MI 48170, (313) 453-0579.

Great Lakes Miniature Bottle Club—P.O. Box 245, Fairhaven, MI 48023.

Huron Valley Bottle Club—12475 Saline-Milan Road, Milan, MI 48160.

Kalamazoo A.B.C.—628 Mill Street, Kalamazoo, MI 49001, (616) 342-5077. Meets 2nd Monday at 628 Mill Street in Kalamazoo at 7 P.M. Club formed 1979, has 42 members.

Lionstone Collectors Bottle & Specialties Club of Michigan—3089 Grand Blanc Road, Swartz Creek, MI 48473.

Manistee Coin & Bottle Club—207 E. Piney Road, Manistee, MI 49660.

Metro & East Bottle and Jar Assn.—309 Bellevue Park Drive, Fairview Heights, MI.

Metro Detroit Antique Bottle Club—28860 Balmoral Way, Farmington Hills, MI 48018. Meets 3rd Thursday, 7:30 P.M., at Hazel Park Recreation Center. Has 50 family members.

Michigan Bottle Collectors Association—144 W. Clark Street, Jackson, MI 49203.

Michigan's Vehicle City Beam Bottles & Specialties Club—907 Root Street, Flint, MI 48503.

Mid-Michee Pine Beam Club—609 Webb Drive, Bay City, MI 48706.

Northern Michigan Bottle Club—P.O. Box 421, Petoskey, MI 49770.

Old Corkers Bottle Club—Rt. 1, Iron River, MI 49935.

Red Run Jim Beam Bottle & Spec. Club—172 Jones Street, Mt. Clemens, MI 48043, (313) 465-4883.

Traverse Area Bottle & Insulator Club—P.O. Box 205, Acme, MI 49610.

West Michigan Avon Collectors—331 Bellevue S.W., Wyoming, MI 49508.

W.M.R.A.C.C.—331 Bellevue S.W., Grand Rapids, MI 49508.

Wolverine Beam Bottle & Specialty Club of Michigan—36009 Larchwood, Mt. Clemens, MI 48043.

World Wide Avon Bottle Collectors Club—22708 Wick Road, Taylor, MI 48180.

Ye Old Corkers—c/o Janet Gallup, Box 7, Gastr, MI 49927. Meets 7:15 P.M. at Bates Twp. School. Club formed 1968, has 20 members.

MINNESOTA

Arnfalt Collectors Beam Club—New Richard, MN 56072.

Dump Diggers—P.O. Box 24, Dover, MN 55929.

Gopher State Jim Beam Bottle & Spec. Club—1216 Sheridan Avenue N., Minneapolis, MN 55411, (612) 521-4150.

Heartland Jim Beam Bottle & Spec. Club—Box 633, 245 Elm Drive, Foley, MN 56329, (612) 968-6767.

Hey! Rube Jim Beam Bottle Club—1506 6th Avenue N.E., Austin, MN 55912, (507) 433-6939.

Lake Superior Antique Bottle Club—P.O. Box 67, Knife River, MN 55609.

Minnesota's First Antique B.C.—5001 Queen Avenue, N. Minneapolis, MN 55430. Meets 8:00 P.M., 1st Thursday, in members' homes. Newsletter: *Bottle Diggers Dope.* Club formed 1966, has 48 members.

North Star Historical Bottle Association, Inc.—P.O. Box 30343, St. Paul, MN 55175.

Paul Bunyan Jim Beam Bottle & Spec. Club—Rt. 8, Box 656, Bemidji, MN 56601, (218) 751-6635.

Truman, Minnesota Jim Beam Bottle & Spec. Club—Truman, MN 56088, (507) 776-3487.

Viking Jim Beam Bottle & Spec. Club—8224 Oxborough Avenue S., Bloomington, MN 55437, (612) 831-2303.

MISSISSIPPI

Gum Tree Beam Bottle Club—104 Ford Circle, Tupelo, MS 38801.

Magnolia Beam Bottle & Spec. Club—2918 Larchmont, Jackson, MS 39209, (601) 354-1350.

Middle Mississippi Antique Bottle Club—P.O. Box 233, Jackson, MS 39205.

Oxford Antique Bottlers—128 Vivian Street, Oxford, MS 38633.

South Mississippi Antique Bottle Club—203 S. 4th Avenue, Laurel, MS 39440.

South Mississippi Historical Bottle Club—165 Belvedere Drive, Biloxi, MS, 388-6472.

MISSOURI

A.B.C. of Central Missouri—726 W. Monroe, Mexico, MO 65265, (314) 581-1391. Meets 7:30 P.M., 1st Wednesday, at Farm & Home Bldg., E. Broadway, Columbia, MO. Newsletter: *No Deposit No Return.* Club formed in 1974, has 20 family members.

Antique Bottle & Relic Club of Central Missouri—c/o Ann Downing, Rt. 10, Columbia, MO 65210.

Arnold, Missouri Jim Beam Bottle & Spec. Club—1861 Jean Drive, Arnold, MO 63010, (314) 296-0813.

Barnhart, Missouri Jim Beam Bottle & Spec. Club—2150 Cathlin Court, Barnhart, MO 63012.

Bud Hastin's National Avon Club—P.O. Box 9868, Kansas City, MO 64134.

Chesterfield Jim Beam Bottle & Spec. Club—2066 Honey Ridge, Chesterfield, MO 63017.

"Down in the Valle" Jim Beam Bottle Club—528 St. Louis Avenue, Valley Park, MO 63088.

The Federation of Historical Bottle Clubs—10118 Schuessler, St. Louis, MO 63128, (314) 843-7573.

Festus, Missouri Jim Beam Bottle & Spec. Club—Rt. 3, Box 117H, Frederick Road, Festus, MO 63028.

First Capital Jim Beam Bottle & Spec. Club—731 McDonough, St. Charles, MO 63301.

Florissant Valley Jim Beam Bottles & Spec. Club—25 Cortez, Florissant, MO 63031.

Greater Kansas City Jim Beam Bottle & Specialty Club—P.O. Box 6703, Kansas City, MO 64123.

Kansas City Antique Bottle Collectors Association—1131 E. 77 Street, Kansas City, MO 64131.

Maryland Heights Jim Beam Bottle & Spec. Club—2365 Wesford, Maryland Heights, MO 63043.

Mineral Area Bottle Club—Knob Lick, MO 63651.

Missouri Arch Jim Beam Bottle & Spec. Club—2900 N. Lindbergh, St. Ann, MO 63074, (314) 739-0803.

Mound City Jim Beam Decanter Collectors—42 Webster Acres, Webster Groves, MO 63119.

North-East County Jim Beam Bottle & Spec. Club—10150 Baron Drive, St. Louis, MO 63136.

Northwest Missouri Bottle & Relic Club—3006 S. 28th Street, St. Joseph, MO 64503.

Rock Hill Jim Beam Bottle & Spec. Club—9731 Graystone Terrace, St. Louis, MO 63119, (314) 962-8125.

Sho Me Jim Beam Bottle & Spec. Club—Rt. 7, Box 314-D, Springfield, MO 65802, (417) 831-8093.

St. Charles, Mo. Jim Beam Bottle & Spec. Club—122 S. Cardinal, St. Charles, MO 63301.

St. Louis Antique Bottle Collectors Assn.—306 N. Woodlawn Avenue, Kirkwood, MO 63122.

St. Louis Ezra Brooks Ceramics Club—Webster Acres, Webster Groves, MO 63119.

St. Louis Jim Beam Bottle & Spec. Club—2900 Lindbergh, St. Ann, MO 63074, (314) 291-3256.

Troy, Missouri Jim Beam Bottle & Spec. Club—121 E. Pershing, Troy, MO 63379, (314) 528-6287.

Valley Bank Park Jim Beam Bottle & Spec. Club—614 Benton Street, Valley Park, MO 63088.

Walnut Park Jim Beam Bottle & Spec. Club—5458 N. Euclid, St. Louis, MO 63114.

West County Jim Beam Bottle & Spec. Club—11707 Momarte Lane, St. Louis, MO 63141.

MONTANA

Hellgate Antique Bottle Club—P.O. Box 411, Missoula, MT 59801.

NEBRASKA

Cornhusker Jim Beam Bottle & Spec. Club—5204 S. 81st Street, Ralston, NE 68127, (402) 331-4646.

Mini-Seekers—"A" Acres, Rt. 8, Lincoln, NE 68506.

Nebraska Antique Bottle and Collectors Club—P.O. Box 37021, Omaha, NE 68137.

Nebraska Big Red Bottle & Specialty Club—N Street Drive-in, 200 S. 18th Street, Lincoln, NE 68508.

NEVADA

Jim Beam Bottle Club of Las Vegas—212 N. Orland Street, Las Vegas, NV 89107.

Las Vegas Bottle Club—3115 Las Vegas Boulevard N., Space 56, North Las Vegas, NV 89030, (702) 643-1101. Meets 7:30 P.M., 1st Wednesday, at 2832 E. Flamingo Road, Las Vegas. Newsletter: *The Front Line*. Club formed 1976, has 45 members.

Las Vegas Bottle Club—884 Lulu Avenue, Las Vegas, NV 89119.

Lincoln County A.B.C.—P.O. Box 191, Calente, NV 89008, (702) 726-3655. Meets 7:30 P.M., 2nd Tuesday, at Pioche Housing Admin. Bldg. Newsletter: *Bottle Talk*. Club formed 1971, has 30 members.

Nevada Beam Club—P.O. Box 426, Fallon, NV 89406.

Reno/Sparks A.B.C.—P.O. Box 1061, Verdi, NV 89439. Meets 3rd Wednesday at McKinley Park School. Newsletter: *Diggers Dirt*. Club formed 1965, has 30 members.

Southern Nevada Antique Bottle Club—431 N. Spruce Street, Las Vegas, NV 89101.

Virginia & Truckee Jim Beam Bottle & Specialties Club—P.O. Box 1596, Carson City, NV 89701.

Wee Bottle Club International—P.O. Box 1195, Las Vegas, NV 89101.

NEW HAMPSHIRE

Bottlers of New Hampshire—125A Central Street, Farmington, NH 03835.

Granite State Bottle Club—R.F.D. 1, Belmont, NH 03220.

Yankee Bottle Club—P.O. Box 702, Keene, NH 03431.

NEW JERSEY

Antique Bottle Collectors Club of Burlington County—18 Willow Road, Bordentown, NJ 08505.

Artifact Hunters Association, Inc.—c/o 29 Lake Road, Wayne, NJ 07470.

The Jersey Devil Bottle Diggers Club—14 Church Street, Mt. Holly, NJ 08060.

Jersey Jackpot Jim Beam Bottle & Spec. Club—197 Farley Avenue, Fanwood, NJ 07023, (201) 322-7287.

The Jersey Shore Bottle Club—P.O. Box 995, Toms River, NJ 08753.

Jersey Shore Bottle Collectors—Box 95, Toms River, NJ 08753.

Lakeland A.B.C.—18 Alan Lane, Mine Hill, Dover, NJ 07801, (201) 366-7482. Meets 3rd Friday, except July and August, at Roosevelt School on Hillside Avenue, Succasuna, NJ, in the cafeteria. Has 50 members.

Lionstone Collectors Club of Delaware Valley—R.D. 3, Box 93, Sewell, NJ 08080.

Meadowland Beamers—413 24th Street, Union City, NJ 07087, (201) 865-3684.

New Jersey Ezra Brooks Bottle Club—S. Main Street, Cedarville, NJ 08311.

North Jersey Antique Bottle Collectors Assoc.—560 Overlook Drive, Wyckoff, NJ 07481.

South Jersey's Heritage Bottle & Glass Club, Inc.—P.O. Box 122, Glassboro, NJ 08028, (609) 423-5038. Meets 7:30 P.M., 4th Wednesday, September through June, at Owen's III Club House, 70 Sewell Street, Glassboro, NJ. Newsletter. Club formed 1970, has 200 members.

Sussex County Antique Bottle Collectors—Division of Sussex County Historical Society, 82 Main Street, Newton, NJ 07860.

Trenton Jim Beam Bottle Club, Inc.—17 Easy Street, Freehold, NJ 07728.

Twin Bridges Beam Bottle & Specialty Club—P.O. Box 347, Pennsville, NJ 08070.

West Essex Bottle Club—76 Beaufort Avenue, Livingston, NJ 07039.

NEW MEXICO

Cave City Antique Bottle Club—Rt. 1, Box 155, Carlsbad, NM 88220.

Roadrunner Bottle Club of New Mexico—2341 Gay Road S.W., Albuquerque, NM 87105.

NEW YORK

Auburn Bottle Club—297 S. Street Road, Auburn, NY 13021.

Big Apple Beamers Bottle & Spec. Club—2901 Long Branch Road, Oceanside, NY 11572, (516) 678-3414.

Catskill Mountains Jim Beam Bottle Club—Six Gardner Avenue, Middletown, NY 10940.

Chautauqua County Bottle Collectors Club—Morse Motel, Main Street, Sherman, NY 14781.

Eastern Monroe County Bottle Club—c/o Bethlehem Lutheran Church, 1767 Plank Road, Webster, NY 14580.

Empire State Bottle Collectors Association—c/o Donald Tupper, 8780 Oswego Road, Clay, NY 13041.

Empire State Jim Beam Bottle Club—P.O. Box 561, Main Street, Farmingdale, NY 11735.

Finger Lakes Bottle Club Association—P.O. Box 815, Ithaca, NY 14850.

Genessee Valley Bottle Collectors Assn.—P.O. Box 7528, West Ridge Station, Rochester, NY 14610, (716) 872-4015. Meets 7:30 P.M., 3rd Thursday, at Klem Road School, Webster, NY. Newsletter: *Applied Seats*. Club formed 1969, has 155 family members.

Greater Catskill Antique Bottle Club—P.O. Box 411, Liberty, NY.

Hudson River Jim Beam Bottle and Specialties Club—48 College Road, Monsey, NY 10952.

Hudson Valley Bottle Club—c/o Robert Jordy, 255 Fostertown Road, Newburgh, NY 12550.

Long Island Antique Bottle Assoc.—P.O. Box 147, Bayport, NY 11705.

National Bottle Museum—c/o Marilyn Stephenson, Pres., 45 West High Street, Ballston Spa, NY 12020.

Niagara Frontier Beam Bottle & Spec. Club—17 Ravensbrook Court, Getzville, NY 14066, (716) 688-6624.

North Country Bottle Collectors Association—Rt. 1, Canton, NY 13617.

Rensselaer County Antique Bottle Club—P.O. Box 792, Troy, NY 12180.

Rochester New York Bottle Club—7908 West Henrietta Road, Rush, NY 14543.

Southern Tier Bottle & Insulator Collectors Association—47 Dickinson Avenue, Port Dickinson, NY 13901.

Suffolk County Antique Bottle Association of Coney Island, Inc.—P.O. Box 943, Melville, NY 11746.

Tryon Bottle Badgers—P.O. Box 146, Tribes Hill, NY 12177.

Twin Counties Old Bottle Club—Don McBride, Star Route, Box 242, Palenville, NY 12463, (518) 943-5399.

Upper Susquehanna Bottle Club—P.O. Box 183, Milford, NY 13807.

Warwick Valley Bottle Club—Box 393, Warwick, NY 10990.

Western New York B.C.A.—c/o 62 Adams Street, Jamestown, NY 14701, (716) 487-9645. Meets 7:30 P.M., 4th Wednesday, except January, Ell South Campus, Rt. 20, Orchard Park. Newsletter: *Traveler's Companion*. Club formed 1967, has 40 club members.

Western New York Bottle Collectors—87 S. Bristol Avenue, Lockport, NY 14094.

West Valley Bottleique Club—Box 204, Killbuck, NY 14748, (716) 945-5769. Meets 8:00 P.M., 3rd Thursday, at West Valley American Legion, Rt. 240, West Valley, NY. Newsletter: *The Bottleique Banner*. Club formed 1967, has 36 family members.

NORTH CAROLINA

Blue Ridge Bottle and Jar Club—Dogwood Lane, Black Mountain, NC 28711.

Carolina Bottle Club—c/o Industrial Piping Co., Anonwood, Charlotte, NC 28210.

Carolina Jim Beam Bottle Club—1014 N. Main Street, Burlington, NC 27215.

Catawba Valley Jim Beam Bottle & Spec. Club—265 5th Avenue, N.E., Hickory, NC 28601, (704) 322-5268.

Goldsboro Bottle Club—2406 E. Ash Street, Goldsboro, NC 27530.

Greater Greensboro Moose Ezra Brooks Bottle Club—217 S. Elm Street, Greensboro, NC 27401.

Kinston Collectors Club, Inc.—325 E. Lenoir, Kinston, NC 28501.

Pelican Sand Dunners Jim Beam Bottle & Spec. Club—Lot 17-J, Paradise Bay Mobile Home Park, P.O. Box 344, Salter Path, NC 28575, (919) 247-3290.

Tar Heel Jim Beam Bottle & Spec. Club—6615 Wake Forest Road, Fayetteville, NC 28301, (919) 488-4849.

Wilmington Bottle & Artifact Club—183 Arlington Drive, Wilmington, NC 28401, (919) 763-3701. Meets 1st Wednesday, Carolina Savings & Loan board room. Club formed 1977, has 25 members.

Wilson Antique Bottle & Artifact Club—Rt. 5, Box 414, Wilson, NC 27893.

Yadkin Valley Bottle Club—General Delivery, Gold Hill, NC 28071.

OHIO

Beam on the Lake Bottle & Spec. Club—9151 Mentor Avenue, F 15, Mentor, OH 44060, (215) 255-0320.

Buckeye Bottle Club—229 Oakwood Street, Elyria, OH 44035.

Buckeye Bottle Diggers—Rt. 2, P.O. Box 77, Thornville, OH.

Buckeye Jim Beam Bottle Club—1211 Ashland Avenue, Columbus, OH 43212.

Carnation City Jim Beam Bottle Club—135 W. Virginia, Sebring, OH 44672, (216) 938-6817.

Central Ohio Bottle Club—931 Minerva Avenue, Columbus, OH 43229.

Diamond Pin Winners Avon Club—5281 Fredonia Avenue, Dayton, OH 45431.

The Federation of Historical Bottle Clubs—c/o Gary Beatty, Treasurer, 9326 Court Road 3C, Galion, OH 44833.

Findlay Antique Bottle Club—P.O. Box 1329, Findlay, OH 45840, (419) 422-3183. Meets 2nd Sunday at 7:00 P.M. at Findlay College Croy Center, Findlay, OH. Newsletter: *Whittlemarks*. Club formed 1976, has 35 members.

First Capitol B.C.—c/o Maxie Harper, Rt. 1, Box 94, Laurelville, OH 43135.

Gem City Beam Bottle Club—1463 E. Stroop Road, Dayton, OH 45429.

Greater Cleveland Jim Beam Club—5398 W. 147th Street, Brook Park, OH 44142, (216) 267-7665.

Heart of Ohio Bottle Club—P.O. Box 353, New Washington, OH 44854, (419) 492-2829.

Jeep City Beamers—531A Durango, Toledo, OH 43609, (419) 382-2515.

Jefferson County A.B.S.—1223 Oakgrove Avenue, Steubenville, OH 43952.

Lakeshore Beamers—2681 Douglas Road, Ashtabula, OH 44004, (216) 964-3457.

Maple Leaf Beamers—8200 Yorkshire Road, Mentor, OH 44060, (216) 255-9118.

Northern Ohio Jim Bottle Club—43152 Hastings Road, Oberlin, OH 44074, (216) 775-2177.

North Eastern Ohio Bottle Club—P.O. Box 57, Madison, OH 44057, (614) 282-8918.

Northwest Ohio Bottle Club—104 W. Main, Norwalk, OH 44857.

Ohio Bottle Club—c/o Linda Koch, 4248 Reimer Road, Norton, OH 44203.

Ohio Ezra Brooks Bottle Club—8741 Kirtland Chardon Road, Kirtland Hills, OH 44094.

Pioneer Beamers—38912 Butternut Ridge, Elyria, OH 44035, (216) 458-6621.

Queen City Jim Beam Bottle Club—4327 Greenlee Avenue, Cincinnati, OH 45217, (513) 641-3362.

Rubber Capitol Jim Beam Club—151 Stephens Road, Akron, OH 44312.

Sara Lee Bottle Club—27621 Chagrin Boulevard, Cleveland, OH 44122.

Southwestern Ohio Antique Bottle and Jar Club—P.O. Box 53, North Hampton, OH. Meets 1st Sunday at 1:30 P.M. at Meat Cutters Local 430 Hall, 1325 E. 3rd Street, Dayton, OH. Newsletter: *Shards*. Formed 1976, has 29 family members.

Tri-State Historical Bottle Club—817 E. 7th Street, Dewey, OK 74029.

OKLAHOMA

Bar-Dew Antique Bottle Club—817 E. 7th Street, Dewey, OK 74029.

Frontier Jim Beam Bottle & Spec. Club—P.O. Box 52, Meadowbrook Trailer Village, Lot 101, Ponca City, OK 74601, (405) 765-2174.

Green Country Jim Beam Bottle & Spec. Club—Rt. 2, P.O. Box 233, Chouteau, OK 74337, (918) 266-3512.

McDonnel Douglas Antique Club—5752 E. 25th Place, Tulsa, OK 74114.

Ponca City Old Bottle Club—2408 Juanito, Ponca City, OK 74601.

Sooner Jim Beam Bottle & Spec. Club—5913 S.E. 10th, Midwest City, OK 73110, (405) 737-5786.

Southwest Oklahoma Antique Bottle Club—35 S. 49th Street, Lawton, OK 73501.

Tulsa Antique Bottle & Relic Club—P.O. Box 4278, Tulsa, OK 74104.

OREGON

Central Oregon Bottle & Relic Club—671 N.E. Seward, Bend, OR 97701.

Central Oregon Bottle & Relic Club—1545 Kalama Avenue, Redmond, OR 97756.

Central South Oregon Antique Bottle Club—708 S. F. Street, Lakeview, OR 97630.

Emerald Empire Bottle Club—P.O. Box 292, Eugene, OR 97401.

Frontier Collectors—504 N.W. Bailey, Pendleton, OR 97801.

Gold Diggers Antique Bottle Club—1958 S. Stage Road, Medford, OR 97501.

Lewis & Clark Historical Bottle & Collectors Soc.—8018 S.E. Hawthorne Boulevard, Portland, OR.

Lewis & Clark Historical Bottle Society—4828 N.E. 33rd, Portland, OR.

Molalla Bottle Club—Rt. 1, Box 205, Mulino, OR 97042.

Oregon Antique Bottle Club—Rt. 3, Box 23, Molalla, OR 97038.

Oregon Beamer Beam Bottle & Specialties—P.O. Box 7, Sheridan, OR 97378.

Oregon B.C.A.—3661 S.E. Nehalem Street, Portland, OR 97202. Meets 8:00 P.M. every 3rd Saturday, except July and August. Newsletter: *The Bottle Examiner*. Club formed 1966, has 60 family members.

Pioneer Fruit Jar Collectors Association—P.O. Box 175, Grand Ronde, OR 97347.

Siskiyou Antique Bottle Collectors Assn.—P.O. Box 1335, Medford, OR 97501.

PENNSYLVANIA

Anthracite Jim Beam Bottle Club—406 Country Club Apartments, Dallas, PA 18612.

Antique Bottle Club of Burlington County—8445 Walker Street, Philadelphia, PA 19136.

Beaver Valley Jim Beam Club—1335 Indiana Avenue, Monaca, PA 15061.

Bedford County Antique Bottle Club—107 Seifert Street, Bedford, PA 15522.

Camoset Bottle Club—P.O. Box 252, Johnstown, PA 15901.

Christmas Valley Beamers—150 Second Street, Richlandtown, PA 18955, (215) 536-4636.

Classic Glass Bottle Collectors—2, Cogan Station, PA 17728.

Cumberland Valley Jim Beam Club—P.O. Box 132 (219 Adelia Street), Middletown, PA 17057, (717) 944-5376.

Delaware Valley Bottle Club—12 Belmar Road, Hatboro, PA 19040.

Del-Val Bottle Club—Rt. 152 & Hilltown Pike, Hilltown, PA. Mailing address: Duffield's, 12 Belmar Road, Hatboro, PA 19040.

East Coast Double Springs Specialty Bottle Club—P.O. Box 419, Carlisle, PA 17013.

East Coast Ezra Brooks Bottle Club—2815 Fiddler Green, Lancaster, PA 17601.

Endless Mountain Antique Bottle Club—P.O. Box 75, Granville Summit, PA 16926.

Erie Bottle Club—P.O. Box 373, Erie, PA 16512.

Flood City Jim Beam Bottle Club—231 Market Street, Johnston, PA 15901.

Forks of the Delaware Bottle Collectors, Inc.—Box 693, Easton, PA 18042.

Friendly Jim's Beam Club—508 Benjamin Franklin H.W. East, Douglasville, PA 19518.

Indiana Bottle Club—240 Oak Street, Indiana, PA 15701.

Keystone Flyers Jim Beam Bottle Club—288 Hogan Boulevard, Box 42, Lock Haven, PA 17745, (717) 748-6741.

Kiski Mini Beam and Spec. Club—816 Cranberry Drive, Monroeville, PA 15146.

Laurel Valley Bottle Club—618 Monastery Drive, Latrobe, PA 15650, (412) 537-4800. Meets at 8:00 P.M., last Saturday, at Oak Grove Civil Center. Newsletter: *Digger's Delight*. Formed 1975, has 35 members.

Middletown Area B.C.A.—P.O. Box 1, Middletown, PA 17057, (717) 939-0288. Meets 2nd Tuesday, 7:30 P.M., at Middletown Elks Lodge, Emaus Street, Middletown. Club formed 1973, has 54 members.

Pagoda City Beamers—735 Florida Avenue, Riverview Park, Reading, PA 19605, (215) 929-8924.

Penn Beamers' 14th—15 Gregory Place, Richboro, PA 18954.

The Pennsylvania Bottle Collectors Association—825 Robin Road, Lancaster, PA 17601.

Pennsylvania Dutch Jim Beam Bottle Club—812 Pointview Avenue, Ephrate, PA 17522.

Philadelphia Bottle Club—8203 Elberon Avenue, Philadelphia, PA 19111.

Philadelphia Coll. Club—8445 Walker Street, Philadelphia, PA. Meets 1st Monday at 8:00 P.M. at Trevose Savings Bank, L Street and Hunting Park Avenue. Club has 25 members.

Pittsburgh Bottle Club—P.O. Box 401, Ingomar, PA 15127.

Pittsburgh Bottle Club—1528 Railroad Street, Sewickley, PA 15143.

Susquehanna Valley Jim Beam Bottle & Spec. Club—64 E. Park Street, Elizabethtown, PA 17022, (717) 367-4256.

Tri-County Antique Bottle & Treasure Club—R.D. 2, P.O. Box 30, Reynoldsville, PA 15851.

Valley Forge Jim Beam Bottle Club—1219 Ridgeview Drive, Phoenixville, PA 19460, (215) 933-5789.

Washington County Bottle & Insulator Club—R.D. 2, P.O. Box 342, Carmichaels, PA 15320, (412) 966-7996. Meets 7:30 P.M., 1st Tuesday, at Washington County City Building. Newsletter: *Bottle Nut News*. Club has 40 members.

Whitetail Deer Jim Beam Bottle Club—94 Lakepoint Drive, Harrisburg, PA 17111 (717) 561-2517.

RHODE ISLAND

Little Rhody Bottle Club—c/o Ted Baldwin, 3161 West Shore Road, Warwick, RI 02886.

Seaview Jim Beam Bottle & Spec. Club—362 Bayview Avenue, Cranston, RI 02905, (401) 461-4952.

SOUTH CAROLINA

Greer Bottle Collectors Club—P.O. Box 142, Greer, SC 29651.

Lexington County Antique Bottle Club—201 Roberts Street, Lexington, SC 29072.

Palmetto State Beamers—908 Alton Circle, Florence, SC 29501, (803) 669-6515.

Piedmont Bottle Collectors—c/o R.W. Leizear, Rt. 3, Woodruff, SC 29388.

South Carolina Bottle Club—1119 Greenbridge Lane, Columbia, SC 29210. Meets 8:00 P.M., 1st Thursday, at Dewey's Antique. Newsletter: *South Carolina Bottle News*. Club formed 1970, has 35 members.

Union Bottle Club—107 Pineneedle Road, Union, SC 29379.

Upper Piedmont Bottle and Advertising Collectors Club—c/o R.W. Leizear, Rt. 3, Woodruff, SC.

TENNESSEE

Cotton Carnival Beam Club—P.O. Box 17951, Memphis, TN 38117.

Memphis Bottle Collectors Club—232 Tifton Road, Memphis, TN 38111, (901) 272-8998.

Middle Tenn. Bottle Collector's Club—P.O. Box 120083, Nashville, TN 37212, (615) 269-4402. Meets 2nd Tuesday at 7:00 P.M., Donelson Branch Public Library. Newsletter: *Notes From a Bottle Bug*. Club formed March 1969, has 45 members.

Music City Beam Bottle Club—2008 June Drive, Nashville, TN 37214, (615) 883-1893.

TEXAS

Alamo Chapter Antique Bottle Club Association—701 Castano Avenue, San Antonio, TX 78209.

Alamo City Jim Beam Bottle & Spec. Club—5785 FM 1346, P.O. Box 20442, San Antonio, TX 78220.

Austin Bottle & Insulator Collectors Club—1614 Ashberry Drive, Austin, TX 78723.

Cowtown Jim Beam Bottle Club—2608 Roseland, Ft. Worth, TX 76103, (817) 536-4335.

El Paso Insulator Club—Martha Stevens, Chairman, 4556 Bobolink, El Paso, TX 79922.

The Exploration Society—603 9th Street NAS, Corpus Christie, TX 78419, 922-2902.

Foard C. Hobby Club—P.O. Box 625, Crowell, TX 79227.

Fort Concho Bottle Club—1703 W. Avenue, N. San Angelo, TX 76901.

Foursome (Jim Beam)—1208 Azalea Drive, Longview, TX 75601.

Golden Spread Jim Beam Bottle & Spec. Club—1104 S. Maddox, Dumas, TX 79029, (806) 935-3690.

Gulf Coast Beam Club—128 W. Bayshore Drive, Baytown, TX 77520.

Gulf Coast Bottle & Jar Club—P.O. Box 1754, Pasadena, TX 77501, (713) 592-3078. Meets 7:30 P.M., 1st Monday, at 1st Pasadena State Bank, corner of Southmore and Tarter. Newsletter: *Gulf Coast Bottle & Jar Club News*. Club formed 1969, has 55 family members.

Oil Patch Beamers—1300 Fairmont -112, Longview, TX 75604, (214) 758-1905.

Republic of Texas Jim Beam Bottle & Specialty Club—616 Donley Drive, Euless, TX 76039.

San Antonio Antique Bottle Club—c/o 3801 Broadway, Witte Museum-Auditorium, San Antonio, TX 78209.

UTAH

Utah Antique Bottle and Relic Club—1594 W. 500 No., Salt Lake City, UT 84116, (801) 328-4142.

Utah Antique Bottle Club—P.O. Box 15, Ogden, UT 84402.

VIRGINIA

Apple Valley Bottle Collectors Club—P.O. Box 2201, Winchester, VA 22601. Meets 2 P.M., 3rd Sunday, at Gore-Volunteer Fire Hall, U.S. 50. Newsletter: *Bottle Worm*. Club formed 1973, has 36 members.

Bottle Club of the Virginia Peninsula—P.O. Box 5456, Newport News, VA 23605.

Buffalo Beam Bottle Club—P.O. Box 434, Buffalo Junction, VA 24529, (804) 374-2041.

Chesapeake Bay Beam Bottle & Spec. Club—515 Briar Hill Road, Norfolk, VA 23502, (804) 461-3763.

Country Cousins Beam Bottle & Spec. Club—Rt. 2, Box 18C, Dinwiddle, VA 23841, (804) 469-7414.

Dixie Beam Bottle Club—Rt. 4, Box 94-4, Glen Allen, VA 23060.

Hampton Roads Area Bottle Collector's Assn.—Virginia Beach Federal Savings & Loan, 4848 Virginia Beach Boulevard, Virginia Beach, VA.

Merrimac Beam Bottle & Spec. Club—433 Tory Road, Virginia Beach, VA 23462, (804) 497-0969.

Metropolitan Antique Bottle Club—109 Howard Street, Dumfries, VA 22026, 221-8055.

Old Dominion Beam Bottle & Spec. Club—624 Brandy Creek Drive, Mechanicsville, VA 23111, (804) 746-7144.

Potomac Bottle Collectors—6602 Orland Street, Falls Church, VA 22043, (703) 534-7271 or 534-5619. Meets 8:00 P.M., 1st Monday, at Coca-Cola plant, Seminary Road. Club formed 1972, has 156 members.

Richmond Area B.C. Assn.—7 N. 8th Street, Richmond, VA 23219.

Meets 7:30 P.M., 3rd Monday, at Bank of Virginia, 8th and Main. Newsletter: *The Bottle Digger*. Club formed 1970, has 20 members.

Shenandoah Valley Beam Bottle & Spec. Club—11 Bradford Drive, Front Royal, VA 22630, (703) 743-6316.

Tidewater Beam Bottle & Specialty Club—P.O. Box 14012, Norfolk, VA 23518.

Ye Old Bottle Club—General Delivery, Clarksville, VA 23927.

WASHINGTON

Antique Bottle and Glass Collectors—P.O. Box 163, Snohomish, WA 98290.

Apple Capital Beam Bottle & Spec. Club—300 Rock Island Road, E. Wenatchee, WA 98801, (509) 884-6895.

Blue Mountain Jim Beam Bottle & Spec. Club—P.O. Box 147, Russet Road, Walla Walla, WA 99362, (509) 525-1208.

Capitol Collectors & Bottle—P.O. Box 202, Olympia, WA 98507.

Cascade Treasure Club—254 N.E. 45th, Seattle, WA 98105.

Chinook Ezra Brooks Bottle Club—233 Kelso Drive, Kelso, WA 98626.

Evergreen State Beam Bottle & Specialty Club—P.O. Box 99244, Seattle, WA 98199.

Inland Empire Bottle & Collectors Club—7703 E. Trent Avenue, Spokane, WA 99206.

Klickital Bottle Club Association—Goldendale, WA 98620.

Mt. Rainer Ezra Brooks Bottle Club—P.O. Box 1201, Lynwood, WA 98178.

Northwest Jim Beam Bottle Collectors Association—P.O. Box 7401, Spokane, WA 99207.

Northwest Treasure Hunter's Club—E. 107 Astor Drive, Spokane, WA 99208.

Pacific Northwest Avon Bottle Club—25425 68th S. Kent, WA 98031.

Seattle Jim Beam Bottle Collectors Club—8015 15th Avenue, N.W., Seattle, WA 98107.

Skagit Bottle & Glass Collectors—1314 Virginia, Mt. Vernon, WA 98273.

South Whedley Bottle Club—c/o Juanita Clyde, Langley, WA 98260.

Washington Bottle Collectors Association—P.O. Box 80045, Seattle, WA 98108. Meets 5 P.M., 2nd Saturday, at King Co. Recreation Center, 46th and 188th Streets. Newsletter: *Ghost Town Echo*. Club formed 1966, has 30 family members.

WEST VIRGINIA

Blennerhassett Jim Beam Club—Rt. 1, 26 Popular Street, Davisville, WV 26142, (304) 428-3184.

Wild & Wonderful West Virginia Ezra Brooks Bottle & Specialty Club—1924 Pennsylvania Avenue, Weirton, WV 26062.

Wild Wonderful W. VA. Jim Beam Bottle & Spec. Club—3922 Hanlin Way, Weirton, WV 26062, (304) 748-2675.

WISCONSIN

Badger Bottle Diggers—1420 McKinley Road, Eau Claire, WI 54701.

Badger Jim Beam Club of Madison—P.O. Box 5612, Madison, WI 53705.

Belle City Jim Beam Bottle Club—8008 104th Avenue, Kenosha, WI 53140, (414) 694-3341.

Bucken Beamers Bottle Club of Milw. WI.—N. 95th Street, W. 16548 Richmond Drive, Menomonee Falls, WI 53051, (414) 251-1772.

Cameron Bottle Diggers—P.O. Box 276, 314 South 1st Street, Cameron, WI 54822.

Central Wisconsin Bottle Collectors—1608 Main Street, Stevens Point, WI 54481.

Heart of the North Beam Bottle and Bottle Club—1323 Eagle Street, Rhinelander, WI 54501, (715) 362-6045.

Hooten Beamers—2511 Needles Lane, Wisconsin Rapids, WI 54494, (715) 423-7116.

Indianhead Jim Beam Club—5112 Berry Street, Rt. 7, Menomonee, WI 54751, (715) 235-5627.

Lumberjack Beamers—414 N. 5th Avenue, Wausau, WI 54401, (715) 842-3793.

Milwaukee Antique Bottle Club—N. 88 W. 15211 Cleveland Avenue, Menomonee Falls, WI 53051.

Milwaukee Antique Bottle Club, Inc.—2343 Met-To-Wee Lane, Wauwatosa, WI 53226, (414) 257-0156. Meets 7:30 P.M., 1st Wednesday, 8701 W. Chambers Street, Cooper Park. Newsletter: *Cream City Courier*. Club formed 1973, has 57 members.

Milwaukee Jim Beam Bottle and Specialties Club, Ltd.—N. 95th Street W. 16548 Richmond Drive, Menomonee Falls, WI 53051.

Packerland Beam Bottle & Spec. Club—1366 Avondale Drive, Green Bay, WI 54303, (414) 494-4631.

Shot Tower Jim Beam Club—818 Pleasant Street, Mineral Point, WI 53565.

South Central Wisconsin Bottle Club—c/o Dr. T.M. Schwartz, Rt. 1, Arlington, WI 53911.

Sportsman's Jim Beam Bottle Club—6821 Sunset Strip, Wisconsin Rapids, WI 54494, (715) 325-5285.

Sugar River Beamers—Rt. 1, Box 424, Brodhead, WI 53520, (608) 897-2681.

WYOMING

Cheyenne Antique Bottle Club—4417 E. 8th Street, Cheyenne, WY 82001.

Insubott Bottle Club—P.O. Box 34, Lander, WY 82520.

CANADA

St. John B.C.—25 Orange Street, St. John N.B. E2L 1L9, 652-3537. Meets 8 P.M., 1st Monday, at N.B. Museum. Newsletter: *The Historical Flask*. Club formed 1969, has 25 members.

APPENDIX C: BOTTLE DEALERS

UNITED STATES

ALABAMA

BIRMINGHAM—Steve Holland, 1740 Serene Dr., Birmingham, AL 35215, 853-7929. Bottles dug around Alabama.

BIRMINGHAM—Walker's Antique Bottles, 2768 Hanover Circle, Birmingham, AL 35205, (205) 933-7902. Medicines, crown sodas.

FORT PAYNE—Terry & Katie Gillis, 115 Mountain Dr., Fort Payne, AL 35967, (205) 845-4541.

FORT PAYNE—C.B. and Barbara Meares, Rt. 3, Box 161, Ft. Payne, AL, (205) 638-6225.

MOBILE—Bottles and Stuff, Clinton P. King, 4075 Moffatt Rd., Mobile, AL 36618, (205) 344-2959. Pontiled medicines, local bottles, black glass, pottery.

MOBILE—Loretta and Mack Wimmer, 3012 Cedar Cresent Dr., Mobile, AL 36605.

OZARK—Old Time Bottle House and Museum, 306 Parker Hills Dr., Ozark, AL 36360. Old bottles, stone jugs, fruit jars.

SPANISH FORT—Elroy and Latrelle Webb, 203 Spanish Main, Spanish Fort, AL 36527, (205) 626-1067.

THEODORE—Ed's Lapidary Shop, 7927 Historic Mobile Parkway, US Hwy. 90, Theodore, AL 36582, (205) 653-0713. Locally dug bottles.

ARIZONA

PHOENIX—The Brewery, 1605 N. 7th Ave., Phoenix, AZ 85007, (602) 252-1415. Brewery items.

PHOENIX—Tom and Kay Papa, 3821 E. Mercer Lane, Phoenix, AZ 85028, (602) 996-3240.

PINETOP—Ray and Dyla Lawton, Box 374, Pinetop, AZ 85935, (602) 366-4449.

ARKANSAS

ASHDOWN—Buddy's Bottles, 610 Park Ave., Ashdown, AR 71822, (501)

898-5877. Hutchinson sodas, medicines, Arkansas bottles always wanted.

JACKSONVILLE—Charles and Mary Garner, 620 Carpenter Dr., Jacksonville, AR 72076, (501) 982-8381.

RISON—Rufus Buie, P.O. Box 226, Rison, AR 71665, (501) 325-6816.

CALIFORNIA

AROMAS—Bobbie's Country Store, in the Big Red Barn, 1000 El Camino Real, Hwy. 101, P.O. Box 1761, Carmel, CA 93921, (408) 394-3257.

BEVERLY HILLS—Alex Kerr, 9584 Wilshire Blvd., Beverly Hills, CA 90212, (213) 762-6320.

BUENA PARK—Walter Yeargain, 6222 San Lorenzo Dr., Buena Park, CA 90620, (714) 826-5264.

BUTLER—Wayne Hortman, P.O. Box 183, Butler, CA 31006, (912) 862-3699.

CHICO—Randy Taylor, 566 E. 12th St., Chico, CA (916) 342-4928.

CITRUS HEIGHTS—Duke Jones, P.O. Box 642, Citrus Heights, CA 95610, (916) 725-1989. California embossed beers.

CONCORD—Stoney and Myrt Stone, 1925 Natoma Dr., Concord, CA 94519, (415) 685-6326.

CORONA—Russell Brown, P.O. Box 441, Corona, CA 91720, (714) 737-7164.

CYPRESS—Gary and Harriet Miller, 5034 Oxford Dr., Cypress, CA 90630, (714) 828-4778.

FILLMORE—Mike and Joyce Amey, 625 Clay St., Fillmore, CA 93015, (805) 524-3364.

HESPERIA—Gene and Phyllis Kemble, 14733 Poplar St., Hesperia, CA 92345, (714) 244-5863.

HUNTINGTON BEACH—Larry Caddell, 15881 Malm Circle, Huntington Beach, CA 92647, (714) 897-8133.

LOS ALTOS—Louis and Cindy Pellegrini, 1231 Thurston, Los Altos, CA 94022, (415) 965-9060.

MARIETTA—John and Estelle Hewitt, 366 Church St., Marietta, CA 30060, (404) 422-5525.

REDDING—Byrl and Grace Rittenhouse, 3055 Birch Way, Redding, CA 96002, (916) 243-0320.

REDDING—Ralph Hollibaugh, 2087 Gelnyose Dr., Redding, CA 96001, (916) 243-4672.

SACRAMENTO—George and Rose Reidenbach, 2816, -"P" St., Sacramento, CA 95816, (916) 451-0063.

SACTO—Peck and Audie Markota, 4627 Oakhallow Dr., Sacto, CA 95842, (916) 334-3260.

SAN FRANCISCO—Bill Groves, 2620 Sutter St., San Francisco, CA 94115, (415) 922-6248.

SAN JOSE—Terry and Peggy Wright, 6249 Lean Ave., San Jose, CA 95123, (408) 578-5580.

SOLANA BEACH—T.R. Schweighart, 1123 Santa Luisa Dr., Solana Beach, CA 92075.

STOCKTON—Frank and Judy Brockman, 104 W. Park, Stockton, CA 95202, (209) 948-0746.

SUTTER CREEK—The Glass Bottle, now in "Creekside Shops," 22 Main St., Sutter Creek, Hwy. 49. Mailing address: P.O. Box 374, Sutter Creek, CA 95685, (209) 267-0122. Old figural, perfumes, whiskey, milk.

WESTWOOD—Whitman's Bookkeeping Service, 219 Fir St., P.O. Drawer KK, Westwood, CA 96147, (916) 256-3437. Soda.

WINDSOR—Betty and Ernest Zumwalt, 5519 Kay Dr., Windsor, CA 95492, (707) 545-8670.

YREKA—Sleep's Siskiyou Specialties, 217 W. Miner, P.O. Box 689, Yreka, CA 96097.

COLORADO

SNOWMASS VILLAGE—Jim Bishop, Box 5554, Snowmass Village, CO 81615. 923-2348. Miniature liquor.

CONNECTICUT

ASHFORD—Woodlawn Antiques, P.O. Box 277, Mansfield Center, Ashford, CT 06250, (203) 429-2983. Flasks, bitters, inks.

FAIRFIELD—Stephen Link, 953 Post Rd., Fairfield, CT 06430.

HARTFORD—B'Thea's Cellar, 31 Kensington St., Hartford, CT 06112, (203) 249-4686.

LIME ROCK—Mary's Old Bottles, White Hollow Rd., Lakeville, CT 06039, (203) 435-2961. Bottles.

MYSTIC—Bob's Old Bottles, 656 Noank Rd., Rt. 215, Mystic, CT 06355, (203) 536-8542.

NEW HAVEN—Gerald "J." Jaffee and Lori Waldeck, P.O. Box 1741, New Haven, CT 06507, (203) 787-4232. Poisons (bottles), insulators.

NEWTOWN—Time In A Bottle, Gail Quick, Rt. 25, Hawleyville, CT 06440, (203) 426-0031.

NIANTIC—Albert Corey, 153 W. Main St., Niantic, CT 06357, (203) 739-7493. No. Eastern bottles, jars, stoneware.

SAYBROOK—Bill Stankard, 61 Old Post Rd., Saybrook, CT 06475, (203) 388-4235.

WATERTOWN—George E. Johnson, 2339 Litchfield Rd., Watertown, CT 06795, (203) 274-1785.

WOODSTOCK—Norman and Elizabeth Heckler, Woodstock Valley, CT 06282, (203) 974-1634.

FLORIDA

BROOKSVILLE—E.S. and Romie Mackenzie, Box 57, Brooksville, FL 33512, (904) 796-3400.

FORT MEADE—M and S Bottles and Antiques, Marlaine and Steve, 421 Wilson St., Mailing address: Rt. 2, Box 84B3, Fort Meade, FL 33841, 285-9421.

FT. PIERCE—Gore's Shoe Repair, 410 Orange Ave., Ft. Pierce, FL 33450. Old bottles, Florida bottles, black glass.

HOLLISTER—This-N-That Shop (Albert B. Coleman), P.O. Box 185, Hollister, FL 32047, (904) 328-3658.

HOLLYWOOD—Hickory Stick Antiques, 400 So. 57 Terr., Hollywood, FL 33023, 962-3434. Canning jars, black glass, household.

JACKSONVILLE—The Browns, 6512 Mitford Rd., Jacksonville, FL 32210, 771-2091. Sodas, mineral waters, milk, glass, black glass.

KEY LARGO—Dwight Pettit, 33 Sea Side Dr., Key Largo, FL 33037, (305) 852-8338.

NEW PORT RICHEY—Gerae and Lynn McLarty, 6705 Dogwood Ct., New Port Richey, FL 33552, (813) 849-7166.

ORMOND BEACH—Mike Kollar, 50 Sylvania Pl., Ormond Beach, FL 32074.

PALMETTO—Jon Vander Schouw, P.O. Box 1151, Palmetto, FL 33561, (813) 722-1375.

SANFORD—Hidden Bottle Shop, 2656 Grandview, Sanford, FL 32771, 322-7181.

TALLAHASSEE—Harry O. Thomas, 2721 Parson's Rest., Tallahassee, FL 32308, (904) 893-3834.

TITUSVILLE—Insulators–L. L. Linscott, 3557 Nicklaus Dr., Titusville, FL 32780, (305) 267-9170. Fruit jars, porcelain insulators.

GEORGIA

BUTLER—Wayne's Bottles, Box 183, Butler, GA 31006, (912) 862-3699. Odd colors, odd shapes.

DUNWOODY—Carlo and Dot Sellari, Box 888553, Dunwoody, GA 30338, (404) 451-2483.

EATONTON—James T. Hicks, Rt. 4, Box 265, Eatonton, GA 31024, (404) 485-9280.

LAURENCEVILLE—Dave and Tia Janousek, 2293 Mulligan Circle, Laurenceville, GA 30245.

MACON—Schmitt House Bottle Diggers, 5532 Jane Rue Circle, Macon, GA 31206, (912) 781-6130. Indiana, Kentucky bottles.

NEWNAN—Bob and Barbara Simmons, 152 Greenville St., Newnan, GA 30263, (404) 251-2471.

HAWAII

HONOLULU—The Hawaiian Antique Bottle Shop, Kahuku Sugar Mill, P.O. Box 495, Honolulu, HI 96731, (808) 293-5581. Hawaiian soda, whiskey, medicine, milk.

HONOLULU—The Hawaii Bottle Museum, 1044 Kalapaki St., P.O. Box 25153, Honolulu, HI 96825, (808) 395-4671. Hawaiian bottles, Oriental bottles, and pottery.

IDAHO

BUHL—John Cothern, Rt. 1, Buhl, ID 83316, (208) 543-6713.

SILVER CITY—Idaho Hotel, Jordan St., Box 75, Murphy, ID 83650, (208) 495-2520.

ILLINOIS

ADDISON—Ronald Selcke, 4N236 8th Ave., Addison, IL 60101, (312) 543-4848.

ALTON—Sean Mullikin, 5014 Alicia Dr., Alton, IL 62002, (312) 466-7506.

ALTON—Mike Spiiroff, 1229 Alton St., Alton, IL 62002, (618) 462-2283.

BELLEVILLE—Wayne and Jacqueline Brammer, 309 Bellevue Dr., Belleville, IL 62223, (618) 233-8841.

CERRO GORDO—Marvin and Carol Ridgeway, 450 W. Cart, Cerro Gordo, IL 61818, (217) 763-3271.

CHAMPAIGN—Casad's Antiques, 610 South State St., Champaign, IL 61820, (217) 356-8455. Milk bottles.

CHICAGO—Tom and Gladys Bartels, 5315 W. Warwick, Chicago, IL 60641, (312) 725-2433.

CHICAGO—Ernest Brooks, 9023 S. East End, Chicago, IL 60617, (312) 375-9233.

CHICAGO—1st Chicago Bottle Club, P.O. Box A3382, Chicago, IL 60690.

CHICAGO—Fruit Jars, 5003 West Berwyn, Chicago, IL 60630, (312) 777-0443. Fruit jars.

CHICAGO—Joe Healy, 3421 W. 76th St., Chicago, IL 60652.

CHICAGO—William Kiggans, 7747 South Kedzle, Chicago, IL 60652, (312) 925-6148.

CHICAGO—Carl Malik, 8655 S. Keeler, Chicago, IL 60652, (312) 767-8568.

CHICAGO—Jerry and Aryliss McCann, 5003 W. Berwyn, Chicago, IL 60630, (312) 777-0443.

CHICAGO—Louis Metzinger, 4140 N. Mozart, Chicago, IL 60618, (312) 478-9034.

CHICAGO—L.D. and Barbara Robinson, 1933 So. Homan, Chicago, IL 60623, (312) 762-6096.

CHICAGO—Paul R. Welko, 5727 S. Natoma Ave., Chicago, IL 60638, (312) 582-3564. Blob top and Hutchinson sodas.

CHICAGO HTS.—Al and Sue Verley, 486 Longwood Ct., Chicago Hts., IL 60411, (312) 754-4132.

DEERFIELD—Jim Hall, 445 Partridge Lane, Deerfield, IL 60014, (312) 541-5788.

DEERFIELD—John and Claudia Panek, 816 Holmes, Deerfield, IL 60015, (312) 945-5493.

DIETERICH—Ray's and Betty's Antiques, Dieterich, IL 62424, (217) 925-5449. Bitters.

ELMWOOD PARK—Keith and Ellen Leeders, 1728 N. 76th Ave., Elmwood Park, IL 60635, (312) 453-2085.

GODFREY—Jeff Cress, 3403 Morkel Dr., Godfrey, IL 62035, (618) 466-3513.

HICKORY HILLS—Doug and Eileen Wagner, 9225 S. 88th Ave., Hickory Hills, IL 60457, (312) 598-4570.

HILLSBORO—Jim and Penny Lang, 628 Mechanic, Hillsboro, IL 62049, (217) 532-2915.

INGELSIDE—Art and Pat Besinger, 611 Oakwood, Ingelside, IL 60041, (312) 546-2367.

LaGRANGE—John Murray, 301 Hillgrove, LaGrange, IL 60525, (312) 352-2199.

LAKE VILLA—Lloyd Bindscheattle, P.O. Box 11, Lake Villa, IL 60046.

LEMONT—Russ and Lynn Sineni, 1372 Hillcrest Rd., Lemont, IL 60439, (312) 257-2648.

MOKENA—Neal and Marianne Vander Zande, 18830 Sara Rd., Mokena, IL 60448, (312) 479-5566.

MORRISON—Emma's Bottle Shop, Emma Rosenow, Rt. 3, Morrison, IL 61270, (815) 778-4596. Beers, inks, bitters, sodas.

O'FALLON—Tom and Ann Feltman, 425 North Oak St., O'Fallon, IL 62269, (618) 632-3327.

PARK FOREST—Vern and Gloria Nitchie, 300 Indiana St., Park Forest, IL 60466, (312) 748-7198.

PARK RIDGE—Ken's Old Bottles, 119 East Lahon, Park Ridge, IL 60068, (312) 823-1267. Milks, inks, sodas, and whiskeys.

PEKIN—Harry's Bottle Shop, 612 Hillyer St., Pekin, IL 61555, (309) 346-3476. Pottery, beer, sodas, and medicines.

PEKIN—Oertel's Bottle House, Box 682, Pekin, IL 61555, (309) 347-4441. Peoria pottery, embossed picnic beer bottles, fruit jars.

QUINCY—Bob Rhinberger, Rt. 7, Quincy, IL 62301, (217) 223-0191.

RIVERDALE—Bob and Barbara Harms, 14521 Atlantic, Riverdale, IL 60627, (312) 841-4068.

SAUK VILLAGE—Ed McDonald, 3002 23rd St., Sauk Village, IL 60511, (312) 758-0373.

TRENTON—Jon and Char Granada, 631 S. Main, Trenton, IL 62293, (618) 224-7308.

WHEATON—Ben Crane, 1700 Thompson Dr., Wheaton, IL 60187, (312) 665-5662.

WHEATON—Scott Garrow, 2 S. 338 Orchard Rd., Wheaton, IL.

WHEELING—Hall, 940 E. Old Willow Rd., Wheeling, IL 60090, (312) 541-5788. Sodas, inks, medicines, etc.

WHEELING—Steve Miller, 623 Ivy Ct., Wheeling, IL 60090, (312) 398-1445.

WOODSTOCK—Michael Davis, 1652 Tappan, Woodstock, IL 66098, (815) 338-5147.

WOODSTOCK—Mike Henrich, 402 McHenry Ave., Woodstock, IL 60098, (815) 338-5008.

INDIANA

BOGGSTOWN—Ed and Margaret Shaw., Rt. 1, Box 23, Boggstown, IN 46110, (317) 835-7121.

CLINTON—Tony and Dick Stringfellow, 714 Vine, Clinton, IN 47842, (317) 832-2355.

FLORA—Bob and Morris Wise, 409 E. Main, Flora, IN 46929, (219) 967-3713.

FORT WAYNE—Annett's Antiques, 6910 Lincoln Hwy. E., Fort Wayne, IN 46803, (219) 749-2745.

GOSHEN—Gene Rice, 61935 CR37, Rt. 1, Goshen, IN 46526.

GOSHEN—Wayne Wagner, 23558 Creek Park Dr., Goshen, IN 46526.

GREENFIELD—George and Nancy Reilly, Rt. 10, Box 67, Greenfield, IN 46140, (317) 462-2441.

INDIANAPOLIS—John and Dianna Atkins, 3168 Beeler Ave., Indianapolis, IN 46224, (317) 299-2720.

NOBELSVILLE—Rick and Becky Norton, Rt. G, Box 166, Noblesville, IN 46060, (317) 844-1772.

PERU—Herrell's Collectibles, 265 E. Canal St., Peru, IN 46970, 473-7770.

SCOTTSBURG—Fort Harrod Glass Works, 160 N. Gardner St., Scottsburg, IN 47170, (812) 752-5170.

TERRE HAUTE—Harry and Dorothy Frey, 5210 Clinton Rd., Terre Haute, IN 47805, (812) 466-4642.

WESTFIELD—Doug Moore, 9 Northbrook Circle, Westfield, IN 46074, (317) 896-3015.

IOWA

ELKADER—The Bottle Shop, 206 Chestnut, S.E. Mailing address: Box 188, Max Hunt, Elkader, IA 52043, (319) 245-2359. Sarsaparilla and bitters.

STORM LAKE—Ralph and Helen Welch, 804 Colonial Circle, Storm Lake, IA 50588, (712) 732-4124.

KANSAS

HALSTEAD—Doanald Haury, Rt. 2, Halstead, KS 67056, (316) 283-5876.

LAWRENCE—Mike Elwell, Rt. 2, Box 30, Lawrence, KS 66044, (913) 842-2102.

MERRIAM—Dale Young, 9909 West 55th St., Merriam, KS 66203, (913) 677-0175.

PAOLA—Stewart and Sons Old Bottle Shop, 610 E. Kaskaskia, Paola, KS 66071, (913) 294-3434. Drugstore bottles, blob-top beers.

TOPEKA—Joe and Alyce Smith, 4706 West Hills Dr., Topeka, KS 66606, (913) 272-1892.

KENTUCKY

ALEXANDRIA—Michael and Kathy Kolb, 6 S. Jefferson, Alexandria, KY 41001, (606) 635-7121.

JEFFERSONTOWN—Paul Van Vactor, 10004 Cardigan Dr., Jeffersontown, KY 40299.

LOUISVILLE—Gene Blasi, 5801 River Knolls Dr., Louisville, KY 40222, (502) 425-6995.

LOUISVILLE—Jerry and Joyce Phelps, 6013 Innes Trace Rd., Louisville, KY 40222.

LOUISVILLE—Paul and Paulette Van Vactor, 300 Stilz Ave., Louisville, KY 40299, (502) 895-3655.

PADUCAH—Earl and Ruth Cron, 808 N. 25th St., Paducah, KY 42001, (502) 443-5005.

LOUISIANA

BATON ROUGE—Sidney and Eulalle Genius, 1843 Tudor Dr., Baton Rouge, LA 70815, (504) 925-5774.

BATON ROUGE—Bobby and Ellen Kirkpatrick, 7313 Meadowbrook Ave., Baton Rouge, LA 70808.

BATON ROUTE—Sheldon L. Ray, Jr., Summer address: 2316 Amalie, Monroe, LA 71201. Mailing address: P.O. Box 17238, LSU, Baton Rouge, LA 70893, (504) 388-3814.

JENNINGS—Cajun Pop Factory, P.O. Box 1113, Jennings, LA 70546, (318) 824-7078. Hutchinsons, blob-tops, and pontil sodas.

MONROE—Everett L. Smith, 100 Everett Dr., Monroe, LA 71202, 325-3534. Embossed whiskeys.

NATCHITOCHES—Ralph and Cheryl Green, 515 Elizabeth St., Natchitoches, LA 71457.

NEW ORLEANS—Bep's Antiques, 3923 Magazine St., New Orleans, LA 70115, 891-3468. Antique bottles, import bottles.

NEW ORLEANS—Dr. Charles and Jane Aprill, 484 Chestnut, New Orleans, LA 70118, (504) 899-7441.

RUSTON—The Dirty Digger, 1804 Church St., Rushton, LA 71270, (318) 255-6112.

RUSTON—Bob and Vernell Willett, 1804 Church St., Ruston, LA 71270, (318) 255-6112.

MAINE

BETHEL—F. Barrie Freeman, Antiques, Paradise Hill Rd., Bethel, ME 04217, (207) 824-3300.

BRYANT POND—John and Althea Hathaway, Bryant Pond, ME 04219.

EAST WILTON—Don McKeen Bottles, McKeen Way, P.O. Box 5A, E. Wilton, ME 04234.

MILFORD—Spruce's Antiques, Main St., P.O. Box 295, Milford, ME 04461, (207) 827-4756.

SEARSPORT—Morse and Applebee Antiques, US Rt. 1, Box 164, Searsport, ME 04974, (207) 548-6314. Early American glass.

WALDOBORO—Wink's Bottle Shop, Rt. 235, Waldoboro, ME 04572, (207) 832-4603.

WALDOBORO—Daniel R. Winchenbaugh, RFD 4, Box 21, Waldoboro, ME 04572, (207) 832-7702.

MARYLAND

NORTH EAST—Pete's Diggins, Rt. 40 West, RR 3, Box 301, North East, MD 21901, (301) 287-9245.

SUDLERSVILLE—Fran and Bill Lafferty, Box 142, Sudlersville, MD 21668.

MASSACHUSETTS

DUXBURY—Joe and Kathy Wood, 49 Surplus St., Duxbury, MA 02332,(617) 934-2221.

LEVERETT—Metamorphosis, 46 Teewaddle Rd., RFD 3, Leverett, MA 01002. Hairs, medicines.

LITTLETON—The Thrift & Gift Shop, Littleton Common, Box 21, Littleton, MA (617) 486-4464.

MANSFIELD—Shop in my home, 211 East St., Mansfield, MA 02048, (617) 339-6086. Historic flasks.

NORTH EASTON—The Applied Lip Place, 26 Linden St., North Easton, MA 02356, (617) 238-1432. Medicines, whiskeys.

WELLESLEY—Carlyn Ring, 59 Livermore Road, Wellesley, MA 02181, (617) 235-5675.

WEST SPRINGFIELD—Leo A. Bedard, 62 Craig Dr., Apt. 7A, West Springfield, MA 01089. Bitters, whiskeys, medicines.

YARMOUTH—Gloria Swanson Antiques, 262 Setucket Rd., Yarmouth, MA 02675, (617) 398-8848. Inks.

MICHIGAN

ANN ARBOR—John Wolfe, 1622 E. Stadium Blvd., Ann Arbor, MI 48104, (313) 665-6106.

BLOOMFIELD HILLS—Jim and Robin Meehan, 25 Valley Way, Bloomfield Hills, MI 48013, (313) 642-0176.

BUCHANAN—Old Chicago, 316 Ross Dr., Buchanan, MI 49107, (616) 695-5896. Hutchinson sodas, blob beers.

CLARKLAKE—Fred and Shirley Weck, 8274 S. Jackson Rd., Clarklake, MI 49234, (517) 529-9631.

DAVISBURG—Chief Pontiac Antique Bottle Shop, 13880 Neal Rd., Davisburg, MI 48019, (313) 634-8469.

DETROIT—Michael and Christina Garrett, 19400 Stout, Detroit, MI 48219, (313) 534-6067.

DUNDEE—Ray and Hillaine Hoste, 366 Main St., Dundee, MI 48131, (313) 529-2193.

GAINES—E & E Antiques, 9441 Grand Blanc Road, Gaines, MI 48436, (517) 271-9063. Fruit jars, beer bottles, milks.

GRAND RAPIDS—Dewey and Marilyn Heetderks, 21 Michigan N.E., Grand Rapids, MI 49503, (616) 774-9333.

IRON RIVER—Sarge's, 111 E. Hemlock, Iron River, MI 49935, (906) 265-4223. Old mining town bottles, Hutchinsons.

KALAMAZOO—Mark and Marty McNee, 1009 Vassar Dr., Kalamazoo, MI 49001, (616) 343-9393.

KALAMAZOO—Lew and Leon Wisser, 2837 Parchmount, Kalamazoo, MI 49004, (616) 343-7479.

LATHRUP VILLAGE—The Jar Emporium, Ralph Finch, 19420 Saratoga, Lathrup Village, MI 48076, (313) 569-6749. Fruit jars.

MANISTEE—Chris and Becky Batdorff, 516 Maple St., Manistee, MI 49660, (616) 723-7917.

MONROE—Don and Glennie Burkett, 3942 West Dunbar Rd., Monroe, MI 48161, (313) 241-6740.

STAMBAUGH—Copper Corner Rock & Bottle Shop, 4th and Lincoln, Stambaugh, MI 49964, (906) 265-3510. Beer, Hutchs, medicines.

ST. JOSEPH—Anvil Antiques, two blocks So. of exit 27, I-94, 3439 Hollywood Rd., St. Joseph, MI 49085, (616) 429-5132. Bottles, insulators.

STUGIS—John and Kay Petruska, 21960 Marathon Rd., Sturgis, MI 49091, (616) 651-6400.

WUCHANAN—James Clengenpeel, 316 Ross Dr., Wuchanan, MI 49107, (616) 695-5896.

MINNESOTA

EXCELSIOR—Jim Conley, P.O. Box 351, Excelsior, MN 55331, (612) 935-0964.

MINNEAPOLIS—Steve Ketcham, P.O. Box 24114, Minneapolis, MN 55424, (612) 920-4205.

MINNEAPOLIS—Neal and Pat Sorensen, 132 Peninsula Rd., Minneapolis, MN 55441, (612) 545-2698.

RICHFIELD—Ron and Vernie Feldhaus, 6904 Upton Ave., S. Richfield, MN 55423, (612) 866-6013.

ST. PAUL—J & E, 1000 Arcade St., St. Paul, MN 55106, 771-9654.

MISSISSIPPI

BILOXI—Vieux Beloxie Bottlery Factory Restaurant, US 90 E., Biloxi, MS 39530, (601) 374-0688. Mississippi bottles.

COLUMBIA—Robert A. Knight, 516 Dale St., Columbia, MS 39429, (601) 736-4249. Mississippi bottles and jugs.

McCOMB—Robert Smith, 623 Pearl River Ave., McComb, MS 39648, (601) 684-1843.

STARKVILLE—Jerry Drott, 710 Persimmon Dr., P.O. Box 714, Starkville, MS 39759, (601) 323-8796. Liniments, drug stores.

VICKSBURG—Ted and Linda Kost, 107 Columbia Ave., Vicksburg, MS 39180, (601) 638-8780.

MISSOURI

ELSBERRY—Dave Hausgen, Rt. 1, Box 164, Elsberry, MO 63343, (314) 898-2500.

GLENCOE—Sam and Eloise Taylor, 3002 Woodlands Terrace, Glencoe, MO 63038, (314) 273-6244.

HANNIBAL—Bob and Debbi Overfield, 2318 Chestnut St., Hannibal, MO 63401, (314) 248-9521.

INDEPENDENCE—Mike and Carol Robison, 1405 N. River, Independence, MO 64050, (816) 836-2337.

KANSAS CITY—Donald Kimrey, 1023 W. 17th St., Kansas City, MO 64108, (816) 741-2745.

KANSAS CITY—Robert Stevens, 1131 E. 77th, Kansas City, MO 64131, (816) 333-1398.

LINN CREEK—The Bottle House, 1 mile north of Linn Creek on Hwy. 54, Rt. 1, Box 111, Linn Creek, MO 65052, (314) 346-5890.

ST. LOUIS—Gene and Alberta Kelley, 1960 Cherokee, St. Louis, MO 63126, (314) 664-7203.

ST. LOUIS—Jerry Mueller, 4520 Langtree, St. Louis, MO 63128, (314) 843-8357.

ST. LOUIS—Terry and Luann Phillips, 1014 Camelot Gardens, St. Louis, MO 63125, (314) 892-6864.

ST. LOUIS—Hal and Vern Wagner, 10118 Schuessler, St. Louis, MO 63128, (314) 843-7573. Historical flasks, colognes, early glass.

TAYLOR—Barkely Museum, one mile south on U.S. 61 (service road), Taylor, MO (314) 393-2408. 10,000 old bottles for sale, plus thousands of other collector items.

TIPTON—Joseph and Jean Reed, 237 E. Morgan, Tipton, MO 65081, (816) 433-5937.

WESTPHALIA—Randy and Jan Haviland, American Systems Antiques, Westphalia, MO 65085, (314) 455-2525.

NEBRASKA

OMAHA—Born Again Antiques, 1402 Williams St., Omaha, NE 68108, 341-5177.

OMAHA—Karl Person, 10210 "W" St., Omaha, NE 68127, (402) 331-2666.

OMAHA—Fred Williams, 5712 N. 33rd St., Omaha, NE 68111, (402) 453-4317.

NEVADA

FALLON—Don and Opal Wellman, P.O. Box 521, Fallon, NV 89406, (702) 423-3490.
SPARKS—Don and Bonnie McLane, 1846 F. St., Sparks, NV 89431, (702) 359-2171.

NEW HAMPSHIRE

AMHERST—Dave and Carol Waris, Boston Post Rd., Amherst, NH 03031, (603) 882-4409.
DOVER—Bob and Betty Morin, RD 3, Box 280, Dover, NH 03820.
EXETER—Lucille Stanley, 9 Oak St., Exeter, NH 03833, (603) 772-2296.
HAMPSTEAD—Murray's Lakeside Bottle Shop, Benson Shores, P.O. Box 57, Hampstead, NH 03841, (603) 329-6969. All types: pontils, bitters, sarsaparillas, balsams, hairs, labeled, medicines, general line. Open 7 days, mail order too.
MANCHESTER—Jim and Joyce Rogers, Harvey Rd., Rt. 10, Manchester, NH 03103, (603) 623-4101.
TROY—House of Glass, 25 High St., Troy, NH 03465, (603) 242-7947.

NEW JERSEY

BRANCHVILLE—Richard and Lesley Harris, Box 400, Branchville, NJ 07826, (201) 948-3935.
CALIFON—Phil and Flo Alvarez, P.O. Box 107, Califon, NJ 07830, (201) 832-7438.
ENGLEWOOD—Ed and Carole Clemens, 81 Chester Pl., Apt. D-2, Englewood, NJ 07631, (201) 569-4429.
FLEMINGTON—John Orashen, RD 6, Box 345-A, Flemington, NJ 08822, (201) 782-3391.
HOPEWELL—Tom and Marion McCandless, 62 Lafayette St., Hopewell, NJ 08525, (609) 466-0619.
HOWELL—Howell Township, Bruce and Pat Egeland, 3 Rustic Drive, Howell, NJ 07731, (201) 363-0556. Second shop open 7 days a week at shop 106, building 3, Red Bank Antique Center, West Front St. and Bridge Ave., Red Bank, N.J.
MICKLETON—Sam Fuss, Harmony Rd., Mickleton, NJ 08056, (609) 423-5038.

SALEM—Old Bottle Museum, 4 Friendship Dr., Salem, NJ 08079, (609) 935-5631. 10,000 old bottles for sale, plus thousands of other collector items.

NEW MEXICO

ALBUQUERQUE—Irv and Ruth Swalwell, 8826 Fairbanks NE, Albuquerque, NM 87112, (505) 299-2977.

DEMING—Krol's Rock City & Mobile Park, 5 miles east of Deming on State Hwy. 26, Star Rt. 2, Box 15A, Deming, NM 88030. Hutch sodas, inks, Avons.

NEW YORK

AUBURN—Brewster Bottle Shop, 297 South St. Rd., Auburn, NY 13021, (315) 252-3246. Milk bottles.

BALLSTON LAKE—Tom and Alice Moulton, 88 Blue Spruce Lane, RD 5, Ballston Lake, NY 12019.

BINGHAMTON—Jim Chamberlain, RD 8, 607 Nowland Rd., Binghamton, NY 13904, (607) 772-1135.

BINGHAMTON—Jo Ann's Old Bottles, RD 2, Box 638, Port Crane, NY 13833, (607) 648-4605.

BLODGETT MILLS—Edward Pettet, P.O. Box 1, Blodgett Mills, NY 13738, (607) 756-7891. Inks.

BLOOMING GROVE—Old Bottle Shop, Horton Rd., P.O. Box 105, Blooming Grove, NY 10914, (914) 496-6841.

CENTRAL VALLEY—J. J.'s Pontil Place, 1001 Dunderberg Rd., Central Valley, NY, (914) 928-9144.

CLIFTON PARK—John Kovacik, 11 Juniper Dr., Clifton Park, NY 12065, (518) 371-4118.

CLIFTON PARK—Richard Strunk, RD 4, Grooms Rd., Clifton Park, NY 12065. Bottles, flasks, bitters, Saratogas.

CRANBERRY LAKE—The Bottle Shop Antiques, P.O. Box 503, Cranberry Lake, NY, (315) 848-2648.

ELMA—Leonard and Joyce Blake, 1220 Stolle Rd., Elma, NY 14059, (716) 652-7752.

LEROY—Kenneth Cornell, 78 Main, Leroy, NY 14482, (716) 768-8919.

LOCH SHELDRAKE—The Bottle Shop, P.O. Box 24, Loch Sheldrake, NY 12759, (914) 434-4757.

MONTICELLO—Manor House Collectibles, Rt. 42, South Forestburgh, RD 1, Box 67, Monticello, NY 12701, (914) 794-3967. Whiskeys, beers, sodas.

NEW WINDSOR—David Byrd, 43 E. Kenwood Dr., New Windsor, NY
12550, (914) 561-7257.

NEW YORK CITY—Chuck Moore, 3 East 57th St., N.Y.C., NY 10022.

NEW YORK CITY—Bottles Unlimited, 245 East 78th St., N.Y.C., NY
10021, (212) 628-8769. 19th and 18th century.

ROCHESTER—Burton Spiller, 169 Greystone Lane, Apt. 31, Rochester,
NY 14618, (716) 244-2229.

ROCHESTER—Robert Zorn, 23 Knickerbocker Ave., Rochester, NY
14615, (716) 254-7470.

WEBSTER—Dick and Evelyn Bowman, 1253 LaBaron Circle, Webster,
NY 14580, (716) 872-4015.

NORTH CAROLINA

BLOWING ROCK—Vieve and Luke Yarbrough, P.O. Box 1023, Blowing
Rock, NC 28605, (704) 963-4961.

CHARLOTTE—Bob Morgan, P.O. Box 3163, Charlotte, NC 28203, (704)
527-4841.

DURHAM—Clement's Bottles, 5234 Willowhaven Dr., Durham, NC
27712, (919) 383-2493. Commemorative soft drink bottles.

GOLD HILL—Howard Crowe, P.O. Box 133, Gold Hill, NC 28071,
(704) 279-3736.

GOLDSBORO—Vernon Capps, Rt. 5, Box 529, Goldsboro, NC 27530,
(919) 734-8964.

RALEIGH—Rex D. McMillan, 4101 Glen Laurel Dr., Raleigh, NC 27612,
(919) 787-0007. N.C. blobs, saloon bottles, colored drug store.

NORTH DAKOTA

MANDAN—Robert Barr, 102 N. 9th Ave. N.W., Mandan, ND 58554.

OHIO

AKRON—Don and Barb Dzuro, 5113 W. Bath Rd., Akron, OH 44313,
(216) 666-8170.

AKRON—Jim Salzwimmer, 3391 Tisen Rd., Akron, OH 44312, (216)
699-3990.

BEACHWOOD—Allan Hodges, 25125 Shaker Blvd., Beachwood, OH
44122, (216) 464-8381.

BLUFFTON—Schroll's Country Shop, 3 miles east of county line on Co.
Rd. 33, (419) 358-6121.

BYESVILLE—Albert and Sylvia Campbell, RD 1, Box 194, Byesville,
OH 43723, (614) 439-1105.

CINCINNATI—Kenneth and Dudie Roat, 7755 Kennedy Lane, Cincinnati, OH 45242, (513) 791-1168.

CLEVELAND—Joe and Mary Miller, 2590 N. Moreland Blvd., Cleveland, OH 44120, (216) 721-9919.

DAYTON—Don and Paula Spangler, 2554 Loris Dr., Dayton, OH 45449, (513) 435-7155.

DUBLIN—Roy and Barbara Brown, 8649 Dunsinane Dr., Dublin, OH 43017, (614) 889-0818.

FRANKFORT—Roger Durflinger, P.O. Box 2006, Frankfort, OH 45628, (614) 998-4849.

HANNIBAL—Gilbert Nething, P.O. Box 96, Hannibal, OH 43931. Hutchinson sodas.

LANCASTER—R.J. and Freda Brown, 125 S. High St., Lancaster, OH 43130, (614) 687-2899.

LEWISTOWN—Sonny Mallory, P.O. Box 134, Lewistown, OH 43333, (513) 686-2185.

NORTH HAMPTON—John and Margie Bartley; 160 South Main, North Hampton, OH 45319, (513) 964-1080.

POWHATAN POINT—Bob and Dawn Jackson, 107 Pine St., Powhatan Point, OH 43942, (614) 795-5567.

REYNOLDSBURG—Bob and Phyllis Christ, 1218 Creekside Place, Reynoldsburg, OH 43068, (614) 866-2156.

SPRINGFIELD—Ballentine's Bottles, 710 W. First St., Springfield, OH 45504, (513) 399-8359. Antique bottles.

SPRINGFIELD—Larry R. Henschen, 3222 Delrey Rd., Springfield, OH, (513) 399-1891.

STEUBENVILLE—Tom and Deena Caniff, 1223 Oak Grove Ave., Steubenville, OH 43952, (614) 282-8918.

STEUBENVILLE—Bob and Mary Ann Willamagna, 711 Kendall Ave., Steubenville, OH 43952, (614) 282-9029

STOW—Doug and Joann Bedore, 1483 Ritchie Rd., Stow, OH 44224, (216) 688-4934.

TORONTO—Bob Villamagna, 1518 Madison Ave., P.O. Box 56, Toronto, OH 43964, (614) 537-4503. Tri-state area bottles, stoneware.

WARREN—Michael Cetina, 3272 Northwest Blvd. N.W., Warren, OH 44485, (216) 898-1845.

WASHINGTONVILLE—Al and Beth Bignon, 480 High St., Washingtonville, OH 44490, (216), 427-6848.

WAYNESVILLE—The Bottleworks, 70 N. Main St., P.O. Box 446, Waynesville, OH 45068, (513) 897-3861.

WELLINGTON—Elvin and Cherie Moody, Trails End, Wellington, OH 44090, (216) 647-4917.

XENIA—Bill and Wanda Dudley, 393 Franklin Ave., Xenia, OH 45385, (513) 372-8567.

OKLAHOMA

ENID—Ronald and Carol Ashby, 831 E. Pine, Enid, OK 73701. Rare and scarce fruit jars.

OKLAHOMA CITY—Joe and Hazel Nagy, 3540 NW 23, Oklahoma City, OK 73107, (405) 942-0882.

SANDSPRINGS—Larry and Linda Shope, 310 W. 44th, Sandsprings, OK 74063, (918) 363-8481.

OREGON

HILLSBORO—Robert and Marguerite Ornduff, Rt. 4, Box 236-A, Hillsboro, OR 97123, (503) 538-2359.

PORTLAND—Alan Amerman, 2311 S.E. 147th, Portland, OR 97233, (503) 761-1661. Fruit jars.

PORTLAND—The Glass House, 4620 S.E. 104th, Portland, OR 97266, (503) 760-3346. Fruit jars.

PENNSYLVANIA

ALBURTIS—R. S. Riovo, 686 Franklin St., Alburtis, PA 18011, (215) 965-2706. Milk bottles, dairy go-withs.

BRADFORD—Ernest Hurd, 5 High St., Bradford, PA 16701, (814) 362-9915.

BRADFORD—Dick and Patti Mansour, 458 Lambert Dr., Bradford, PA 16701, (814) 368-8820.

CANONSBURG—John and Mary Schultz, RD 1, Box 118, Canonsburg, PA 15317, (412) 745-6632.

COUDERSPORT—The Old Bottle Corner, 508 South Main St., Mailing address: 102 West Maple St., Coudersport, PA 16915, (814) 274-7017. Fruit jars, blob tops.

EAST GREENVILLE—James A. Hagenbach, 102 Jefferson St., East Greenville, PA 18041, (215) 679-5849.

EAST PETERSBURG—Jere and Betty Hambleton, 5940 Main St., East Petersburg, PA 17520, (717) 569-0130.

HATBORO—Al and Maggie Duffield, 12 Belmar Rd., Hatboro, PA 19040, (215) 675-5175. Hutchinsons and inks.

LANCASTER—Barry and Mary Hogan, 3 Lark Lane, Lancaster, PA 17603.

LEVITTOWN—Ed Lasky, 43 Nightingale Ln., Levittown, PA 19054, (215) 945-1555.

MARIENVILLE—Harold Bauer Antique Bottles, 136 Cherry St., Marienville, PA 16239.

McKEES ROCKS—Chuck Henigin, 3024 Pitch Fork Lane, McKees Rocks, PA 15136, (412) 331-6159.

MUNCY—Harold Hill, 161 E. Water St., Muncy, PA 17756, (717) 546-3388.

PIPERSVILLE—Allen Holtz, RD 1, Pipersville, PA 18947, (215) 847-5728.

PITTSBURGH—Carl and Gail Onufer, 210 Newport Rd., Pittsburgh, PA 15221, (412) 371-7725. Milk bottles.

ROULETTE—R.A. and Esther Heimer, P.O. Box 153, Roulette, PA 16746, (814) 544-7713.

STRONGSTOWN—Butch and Gloria Kim, RD 2, Box 35, Strongstown, PA 15957.

RHODE ISLAND

KENYON—Wes and Diane Seemann, Box 49, Kenyon, RI 02836, (203) 599-1626.

SOUTH CAROLINA

EASHEY—Bob Durham, 704 W. Main St., Eashey, SC 29640.

MARION—Tony and Marie Shank, P.O. Box 778, Marion, SC 29571, (803) 423-5803.

TENNESSEE

KNOXVILLE—Ronnie Adams, 7005 Charlotte Dr., Knoxville, TN 37914, (615) 524-8958.

McMINNVILLE—Terry Pennington, 415 N. Spring St., McMinnville, TN 37110. Jack Daniels, amber Coca-Cola.

MEMPHIS—Bluff City Bottlers, 4630 Crystal Springs Dr., Memphis, TN 38123, (901) 353-0541. Common American bottles.

MEMPHIS—Larry and Nancy McCage, 3772 Hanna Dr., Memphis, TN 38128, (901) 388-9329.

MEMPHIS—Tom Phillips, 2088 Fox Run Cove, Memphis, TN 38138, (901) 754-0097.

TEXAS

AMARILLO—Robert Snyder, 4235 W. 13th St., Amarillo, TX 79106.

EULESS—Mack and Alliene Landers, P.O. Box 5, Euless, TX 76039, (817) 267-2710.

HOUSTON—Bennie and Harper Leiper, 2800 W. Dallas, Houston, TX 77019, (713) 526-2101.

PASADENA—Gerald Welch, 4809 Gardenia Trail, Pasadena, TX 77505, (713) 487-3057.

PORT ISABEL—Jimmy and Peggy Galloway, P.O. Drawer A, Port Isabel, TX 78578, (512) 943-2437.

RICHARDSON—Chuck and Reta Bukin, 1325 Cypress Dr., Richardson, TX 75080, (214) 235-4889.

SAN ANTONIO—Sam Greer, 707 Nix Professional Bldg., San Antonio, TX 78205, (512) 227-0253.

VERMONT

BRATTLEBORO—Kit Barry, 88 High St., Brattleboro, VT 05301, (802) 254-2195.

VIRGINIA

ALEXANDRIA—A. E. Steidel, 6167 Cobbs Rd., Alexandria, VA 22310.

ARLINGTON—Dick and Margie Stockton, 2331 N. Tuckahoe St., Arlington, VA 22205, (703) 534-5619.

CHESTERFIELD—Tom Morgan, 3501 Slate Ct., Chesterfield, VA 23832.

FREDERICKSBURG—White's Trading Post, Boutchyards Olde Stable, Falmouth, VA. 1903 Charles St., Fredericksburg, VA 22401, (703) 371-6252. Fruit jars, new and old bottles.

HINTON—Vic and Betty Landis, Rt. 1, Box 8A, Hinton, VA 22801, (703) 867-5959.

HUNTLY—Early American Workshop, Star Route, Huntly, VA 22640, (703) 635-8252. Milk bottles.

MARSHALL—John Tutton, Rt. 1, Box 261, Marshall, VA 22115, (703) 347-0148.

RICHMOND—Lloyd and Carrie Hamish, 2936 Woodworth Rd., Richmond, VA 23234, (804) 275-7106.

RICHMOND—Jim and Connie Mitchell, 5106 Glen Alden Dr., Richmond, VA.

WASHINGTON

BELLEVUE—Don and Dorothy Finch, 13339 Newport Way, Bellevue, WA 98006, (206) 746-5640.

BREMERTON—Ron Flannery, 423 N.E. Conifer Dr., Bremerton, WA 98310, (206) 692-2619.

SEATTLE—John W. Cooper, 605 N.E. 170th St., Seattle, WA 96155, (206) 364-0858.

WISCONSIN

ARLINGTON—Mike and Carole Schwartz, Rt. 1, Arlington, WI 53911, (608) 846-5229.

MEQUON—Jeff Burkhardt, 12637 N. River Forest Cir., Mequon, WI 53092, (414) 243-5643.

MEQUON—Bor Markiewicz, 11715 W. Bonniwell Rd., Mequon, WI 53092, (414) 242-3968.

OSKOSH—Richard Schwab, 65-5 Lareen Rd., Oskosh, WI 54901, (414) 235-9962.

STEVENS POINT—Bill and Kathy Mitchell, 703 Linwood Ave., Stevens Point, WI 55431, (715) 341-1471.

WAUTOMA—George and Ruth Hansen, Rt. 2, Box 26, Wautoma, WI 54962, (414) 787-4893.

FOREIGN

CANADA

BADEN, ONTARIO—John and Sara Moore, Rt. 2, Baden, Ontario.

DOLLARD-DES-ORMEAUX, P.Q.—Richard Davis, 39 Brunswick #115, Dollard-Des-Ormeaux, P.Q., (314) 683-8522.

OTTAWA, ONTARIO—Paul Hanrahan, 292 Byron Ave. #2, Ottawa, Ontario, (613) 929-5675.

CENTRAL AMERICA

BELIZE CITY, BELIZE—Emory King, 9 Regent Street, Belize City, Belize.

BELIZE CITY, BELIZE—Paul Hunt, Managing Director, Fort George Hotel, Belize Hotels Limited, Belize City, Belize.

ENGLAND

TRENT—David Geduhon, Box 85, Cayuga Ind. & Burton-on-Trent, England.

YORKSHIRE—John Morrison, 33 Ash Grove, Leeds G., Yorkshire, England.

GLOSSARY

Amber-colored glass: Nickel was added in glass production to obtain this common bottle color. The theory was that the dark color would prevent the sun from spoiling the contents of the bottle.

Amethyst-colored glass: This is clear glass that has been exposed to the sun or a very bright light for a period of time, and has turned a light purple color. *Note:* Only glass containing manganese will turn purple. This glass has remained in production since 1800.

Applied lip: On older bottles (pre-1880), the neck was applied after removal from the blowpipe; the seams, therefore, ended below the top of the lip. This helps distinguish old bottles from new—if the seam ends below the top of the lip it is usually a handblown applied top; if it runs to the very top of the lip, the bottle was probably machine-made.

Aqua-colored glass: This is the natural color of glass. The shades of aqua depend on the iron oxide contained in the sand used in glass production. This type of glass was produced until the 1930s.

Black glass: Carbon was added in glass production to obtain this dark olive green color. This type of glass was produced between 1700–1880.

Blob seal: A popular way of identifying an unembossed bottle was to apply a molten coin-shaped blob of glass to the shoulder of the bottle, into which a seal with the logo or name of the distiller, date, or product name was impressed.

Blob top: A large thick blob of glass was placed around the lip of soda or mineral water bottles. The wire that held the stopper was seated below the blob and anchored the wire when the stopper was closed, to prevent carbonation from escaping.

Blowpipe: This is a long tube used by the blower to pick up the molten glass which is then either blown in mold or free-blown outside a mold to create unlimited varieties of shapes.

Cobalt-colored glass: This color was used in the days of patented medicines and poisons to distinguish them from the rest of the bottles.

Ground pontil: This is the pontil scar that has been ground off.

Imperfections: Bubbles of all sizes and shapes, bent shapes and necks, imperfect seams, errors in spelling, and embossing increase rather than decrease the value of old bottles, providing these imperfections were formed as a part of the natural production of the bottle. The more imperfections, the greater the value.

Kick-up bottom: An indented bottom of any bottle is known as a "kick-up." This can vary from deep indentations to a very slight impression. Wine bottles as a group are usually indented.

Lady's leg: These were called by the manufacturers "long bulbous neck." The shape of the neck earned this type of bottle its nickname.

Milk glass: Tin is added in glass production to obtain this color, primarily used for cosmetic bottles.

Mold, full-height three-piece: The entire bottle was formed in the mold, and the two seams run the height of the bottle to below the lip on both sides.

Mold, three-piece dip: In this mold the bottom part of the bottle mold was one piece and the top, from the shoulder up, was two separate pieces. Mold seams appear circling the bottle at the shoulder and on each side of the neck. These bottles date from 1806–1889.

Opalization: This is seen on the frosty bottle or variated color bottle that has been buried in the earth in mud or silt, and minerals in these substances have interacted with the glass of the bottle to create these effects. Many collectors place a high value on bottles of this type.

Pontil marks: To remove the newly blown bottle from the blowpipe, an iron rod with a small amount of molten glass was applied to the bottom of the bottle after the neck and lip were finished. A sharp tap removed the bottle from the pontil, leaving a jagged glass scar. This "pontil scar" can be either round, solid or ring-shaped. On better bottles, the jagged edges were ground down. These marks date from 1618–1866; also, some modern handblown bottles have them.

Pumpkinseed: A small round flat flask, often found in the western areas. Generally made of clear glass, the shape resembled nothing more than the seed of the grown pumpkin. These bottles are also known as "Mickies," "saddle flasks," or "two-bit ponies."

Round bottoms: Many soda bottles containing carbonated beverages were made of heavy glass, designed in the shape of a torpedo. This enabled the bottle to lie on its side, keeping the liquid in contact with the cork, and preventing the cork from drying and popping out of the bottle.

Sheared lip: In the early years of bottle making, after the bottle was blown, a pair of scissorlike shears clipped the hot glass from the blowpipe. Frequently no top was applied, and sometimes a slight flange was created. The sheared top is a usual feature of old patriotic flasks. These bottles were produced from 1800–1830.

Snap: A more effective way of detaching the blown bottle from the blowpipe was the "snap." This device, which made its appearance in the 1860s, was used to grip the blown bottle in a spring cradle in which a cup held the bottom of the bottle. The bottles, held in a snap during manufacture, have no pontil scars or marks, but may have grip marks on the side.

Turn-mold bottles: These are bottles which were turned in forming in a mold containing a special solvent. The action of turning and the solvent erased all seams and mold marks, and imparted a higher luster to the finished bottle. As a group, most old wine bottles were made this way.

White mold, or whittle marks: Many molds used in the 1800s and earlier were carved of wood. Bottles formed in these molds have genuine "whittle marks." The same effect was also caused by forming hot glass in cold early morning molds; this combination caused "goose pimples" on the surface of these bottles. As the mold warmed, the later bottles were smooth. "Whittle mold" and "whittle mark" bottles are in demand and command high prices.

BIBLIOGRAPHY

Armans of Newport, *Bottle Sales Catalogs,* 207 High Point Avenue, Portsmouth, RI 02871.

Bangert, Albrecht, *Antiquitaten Glas,* Wilhelm Heyne Verlag Munchen, 1977.

Beck, Doreen, *The Book of Bottle Collecting,* Hamlin Publishing Group, Ltd., 1973.

Creswick, Alice M., *Redbook Number 5: The Collectors Guide to Old Fruit Jars,* 1986.

DeGrafft, John, *American Sarsaparilla Bottles,* 1980.

Dumbrell, Roger, *Understanding Antique Wine Bottles,* Antique Collectors Club, 1983.

Eikelberner, George and Serge Agadjanian, *The Compleat American Glass Candy Containers Handbook,* Adele Bowden, 1986.

Gardner, Paul Vickens, *Glass,* Smithsonian Illustrated Library of Antiques, 1979.

Garths Auctions, Inc., *Bottle Sale Catalogs,* 2690 Stratford Road, Delaware, OH 43015.

Glass Works Auctions, *Bottle Sale Catalogs,* P. O. Box 187, East Greenille, PA 18041.

Harmer Rooke Galleries, *Bottle Sale Catalogs,* 3 East 57th Street, New York, NY 10022.

Heckler, Norman, *Bottle Sale Catalogs,* Bradford Corner Road, Woodstock Valley, CT 06282.

——, *American Bottles in the Charles B. Gardener Collection,* Robert W. Skinner, Inc., 1975.

Holiner, Richard, *Collecting Barber Bottles,* Collector Books.

Hunter, Frederick William, *Stiegel Glass,* Dover Publications, New York, 1950.

Innes, Lowell, *Pittsburgh Glass 1797–1891,* Houghton Mifflin Company, Boston, 1976.

Ketchum, William C. Jr., *A Treasury of American Bottles,* Rutledge Books, 1975.

Klesse, Brigitt and Hans Mayr, *European Glass from 1500 to 1800, the Ernesto Wolf Collection,* Kremayr and Scheriau, 1987.

Knittle, Rhea Mansfield, *Early American Glass,* Garden City Publishing Company, 1948.

Kovill, William E. Jr., *Ink Bottles and Ink Wells*, William L. Sullwold, 1971.

Lee, Ruth Webb, *Antique Fakes and Reproductions*, Ruth Webb Lee, 1950.

McKearin, Helen and George S., *American Glass*, Crown Publishers, New York, 1956.

———, *Two Hundred Years of American Blown Glass*, Crown Publishers, 1950.

McKearin, Helen and Kenneth M. Wilson, *American Bottles and Flasks and Their Ancestry*, Crown Publishers, New York, 1978.

Namiat, Robert, *Barber Bottles with Prices*, Wallace Homestead Book Company, 1977.

Nielsen, Frederick, *Great American Pontiled Medicines*, The Cortech Corporation, Cherry Hill, NJ, 1978.

Northend, Mary Harrod, *American Glass*, Tudor Publishing Company, New York, 1940.

Pepper, Adeline, *The Glass Gaffers of New Jersey*, Charles Scribners Sons, New York, 1971.

Ring, Carlyn, *For Bitters Only*, The Nimrod Press, Inc., 1980.

Schwartz, Marvin D., "American Glass," from the pages of *Antiques* magazine, Volume 1; *Blown and Molded*, Pyne Press, Princeton, 1974.

Skinner's, Inc., *Bottle Sale Catalogs*, Route 117, Bolton, MA 01740.

Sloan, Gene, *Perfume and Scent Bottle Collecting*, Wallace Homestead Book Company, 1986.

Spiegel, Walter Von, *Glas*, Battenberg Verlag, Munchen, 1979.

Spillman, Jane Shadel, *Glass Bottles, Lamps and Other Objects*, Alfred A. Knopf, New York, 1983.

Toulouse, Julian Harrison, *Bottle Makers and Their Marks*, Thomas Nelson Incorporated, 1971.

Tucker, Donald, *Collectors Guide to the Saratoga Type Mineral Water Bottles*, privately printed, 1986.

Tuckhaber, Bernard C., *Saratogas*, Bernard C. Tuckhaber, 1976.

Tutton, John, *Udderly Delightful*, John Tutton, 1989.

Umberger, Joe and Arthur L., *Collectible Character Bottles*, Corker Book Company, Tyler, TX, 1969.

Watson, Richard, *Bitters Bottles*, Thomas Nelson & Sons, 1965.

Webster, Donald Blake, *Decorated Stoneware Pottery of North America*, Charles E. Tuttle Company, Rutland, VT, 1985.

Wilson, Kenneth M., *New England Glass and Glass Making*, Thomas Y. Crowell Company, 1972.

Zumwalt, Betty, *Ketchup, Pickles, Sauces*, Mark West Publishers, 1980.

INDEX